Live Music on Your PC

LIMITED WARRANTY AND DISCLAIMER OF LIABILITY

A-LIST, LLC., INDEPENDENT PUBLISHERS GROUP AND/OR ANYONE WHO HAS BEEN INVOLVED IN THE WRITING, CREATION OR PRODUCTION OF THE ACCOMPANYING CODE ("THE SOFTWARE") OR TEXTUAL MATERIAL IN THE BOOK, CANNOT AND DO NOT WARRANT THE PERFORMANCE OR RESULTS THAT MAY BE OBTAINED BY USING THE CODE OR CONTENTS OF THE BOOK. THE AUTHORS AND PUBLISHERS HAVE USED THEIR BEST EFFORTS TO ENSURE THE ACCURACY AND FUNCTIONALITY OF THE TEXTUAL MATERIAL AND PROGRAMS CONTAINED HEREIN; WE HOWEVER MAKE NO WARRANTY OF ANY KIND, EXPRESSED OR IMPLIED, REGARDING THE PERFORMANCE OF THESE PROGRAMS OR CONTENTS.

THE AUTHORS, THE PUBLISHER, DEVELOPERS OF THIRD PARTY SOFTWARE, AND ANYONE INVOLVED IN THE PRODUCTION AND MANUFACTURING OF THIS WORK SHALL NOT BE LIABLE FOR DAMAGES OF ANY KIND ARISING OUT OF THE USE OF (OR THE INABILITY TO USE) THE PROGRAMS, SOURCE CODE, OR TEXTUAL MATERIAL CONTAINED IN THIS PUBLICATION. THIS INCLUDES, BUT IS NOT LIMITED TO, LOSS OF REVENUE OR PROFIT, OR OTHER INCIDENTAL OR CONSEQUENTIAL DAMAGES ARISING OUT OF THE USE OF THE PRODUCT.

THE USE OF "IMPLIED WARRANTY" AND CERTAIN "EXCLUSIONS" VARY FROM STATE TO STATE, AND MAY NOT APPLY TO THE PURCHASER OF THIS PRODUCT.

Live Music on Your PC

E. Medvedev,
V. Trusova

alist

Copyright (c) 2002 by A-LIST, LLC

All rights reserved.

No part of this publication may be reproduced in any way, stored in a retrieval system of any type, or transmitted by any means or media, electronic or mechanical, including, but not limited to, photocopy, recording, or scanning, *without prior permission in writing* from the publisher.

A-LIST, LLC
295 East Swedesford Rd.
PMB #285
Wayne, PA 19087
702-977-5377 (FAX)
mail@alistpublishing.com
http://www.alistpublishing.com

This book is printed on acid-free paper.

All brand names and product names mentioned in this book are trademarks or service marks of their respective owners. Any omission or misuse (of any kind) of service marks or trademarks should not be regarded as intent to infringe on the property of others. The publisher recognizes and respects all marks used by companies, manufacturers, and developers as a means to distinguish their products.

Live Music on Your PC
By E. Medvedev, V. Trusova

      ISBN: 1-931769-06-0

Printed in the United States of America
02 03 7 6 5 4 3 2 1

A-LIST, LLC titles are distributed by Independent Publishers Group and are available for site license or bulk purchase by institutions, user groups, corporations, etc.

Book Editor: Jessica Mroz

CONTENTS

Foreword _____ 1

Chapter 1: "Live" Music and Non-Verbal Intelligence _____ 5
  The Idea in Music _____ 5
  The Musical Context _____ 6

Chapter 2: Musical Language and Computer Technology _____ 11
    Means of Musical Expression _____ 14
    How to Listen to a Musical Composition _____ 15
    If You've Got the Desire, You'll Find a Way _____ 15

Chapter 3: The Sawpro Program: Live Recording in a Virtual Studio _ 19
  Description of the SAWPro Interface _____ 21
    General Information about the Program _____ 21
    SAWPro Installation _____ 23
    Recommendations for Configuring SAWPro to Work with Your Sound Card _ 23
    Creating a Comfortable User Environment _____ 25
      Creating a Working Screen _____ 25
      Modifying the Working Screen _____ 28
    Custom Configuration Options _____ 29
    The SAWPro File Formats _____ 30
    Setting the Number of Undos _____ 31
    Description of the *MultiTrack View* Window _____ 33
      Normal and Output Tracks _____ 33
      Moving Tracks around the Screen _____ 35
      The *Multitrack* Cursor _____ 36
      The Track. Description of Tracks for Sound Recording and Processing _ 36
      The *Effects Patch Builder* Window _____ 40
      The *REC* Button _____ 45

Contents

Marking off a Clip Fragment in the *MultiTrack View* Window	46
Importing Sound Files to SAWPro	47
The *Open SoundFile* Window	47
Creating a Region in SAWPro	48
Some Suggestions on Importing Sound Files	51
Description of the Virtual Tape Recorder	52
The *Record Remote Transport* Panel	52
Preparing for Recording	53
The *Full Duplex* Mode. The *S-R-P* Button	53
The *Full Duplex* Mode Recording	54
The *Record Panel* (the Second Part of the Virtual Tape Recorder)	57
The *Remote Transport* Window	58
Non-Destructive Audio Editing	60
Copying a Region in the *MultiTrack View* Window	61
Clip Handling Techniques; Toolbars	62
Additional Non-Destructive Editing Tricks	68
Playback of Recorded Material: A Description of the Remote Transport Panel	74
A Brief Description of the *Remote Transport* Panel Buttons	74
Ways of Working with the *Remote Transport* Panel	75
MultiTrack View Hotkeys	76
Some Hotkeys	77
The *Full View* and *SoundFile View* Windows	81
Creating a Region; Problems with the Final Result	82
The Graphical Representation of the Sound File	84
The *SoundFile View* Window	84
Displaying Regions: the *Regions View* Window	85
The Hot Track Clip List: the Sequence View Window	88
Working With Markers: the Markers View Window	89
Saving a Project	91
Recording a Live Performance	93
SAWPro & Computer Configuration: General Advice for Beginners	93
Connecting to the Sound Card; Adjusting the Recording Level	95
The Microphone	95
The Mixer	95
Home Studio Setup	96
Adjusting the Recording Level	97
Adjusting the Volume Level When Recording	98
The Amplitude Peak Limiter	99

The Project Sample Rate and Bit Resolution	101
Mono and Stereo Recording	103
Ways of Recording	103
Overdubbing	103
Punch Mode Recording	107
Recording a Complicated Instrumental or Vocal Part	109
Snapping to the Musical Meter and Tempo	110
Enabling the Tempo Mode	111
The Tempo Mode Options	113
Processing Sound in SAWPro	114
Attaching Sound Processing Program Modules	115
Saw Native Standard Virtual Effects	116
A Brief Description of Built-In SAWPro Effects	116
Interaction between SAWPro and DirectX & VST Virtual Effects	120
Some Distinctions between VST and DirectX Effects	122
About Moving Preset Files	124
Types of VST Effects	126
Additional Settings	126
Destructive Editing	127
Can One Do without Destructive Editing?	127
Destructive Editing Techniques	128
Destructive Editing in the *SoundFile View* Window	129
Intermediate Mixing	132
Mixing Mechanics	133
Mixing Techniques	134
SAWPro Mixing and Mastering	139
Applying the Meter Bridge Program Module to Indicate the Volume Level	140
The *Meter Bridge* Configuration Menu	141
Changing the Look of the *Meter Bridge*	142
The Virtual Mixer	144
Adjusting in the *OFFSET* Mode	147
Examples to Illustrate Using Automation	149
Moving and Copying Volume and Pan Adjustment Curves	151
The Hot Track and Its Connection with the Virtual Mixer	152
The Specifics of Using the POST FADER Button. in the Effects Patch Builder Window	154
The SAWPro Mixing Technique	154
Preparing for Mixing	154

VIII Contents

    Final Mixing — 155
    Some Practical Suggestions — 156
  Mastering in SAWPro — 157
    Attaching the *Comp/Gate/Limiter* Module — 157
    Commercial Virtual Effects — 159

Chapter 4: Cool Edit Pro as a Universal Solution for Home Studios — 161

  A Description of the Cool Edit Pro Interface — 165
    Installing the Software — 165
    Configuring Cool Edit Pro. The *Options* Menu — 167
      The *System* Tab — 168
      Configuring the Multitrack (the *Multitrack* Tab) — 170
    The *Edit Waveform View Editing* Window — 171
      Configuring the Toolbars — 171
      The Number of Toolbar Rows — 172
      Recording — 175
      Audio Processing in Cool Edit Pro — 186
      Description of the *Transform* Menu's Effects — 186
      Effects Based on Transforming the Signal Amplitude — 188
      Effects Based on the Signal's Delay — 203
      Effects that Correct the Frequency Response — 216
      Noise Reduction Effects — 224
      Effects that Change the Duration and Pitch of the Sound — 233
      The *Favorites* Menu — 234
      File Formats of Cool Edit Pro — 237
      The *Edit* Menu — 242
    The *Multitrack View* Window — 246
      The Session as an Analogy to the EDL File of SAWPro — 246
      The *Track Info* Panel — 249
  Recording and Playback in the *Multitrack View* Window — 251
    Using Pop-up Menus — 251
      The Clip Pop-up Menu (*WAVE PROPERTIES*) — 252
      The Track Pop-up Menu (*TRACK PROPERTIES*) — 256
    Snapping to the Musical Measure and Tempo — 258
    The Fragment Recording Mode — 258
      The *Punch In* Mode — 258
    Using the Take History Submenu — 260
    Using the Loop Duplicate Function — 261

Methods of Editing the Audio Material in the Multitrack View Window	262
Graphically Editing the Volume and Panorama	264
Applying the Effects of the Transform Menu	265
Batch Processing in Cool Edit Pro	267
Mixing and Mastering in Cool Edit Pro	271
Background Mixing	271
Using the List of Markers — Cue List	272
Specific Features of Mixing in the 32-bit Format	273
Intermediate Mixing	274
Mixing	276
Mastering	277

Chapter 5: The Samplitude 2496 Application as a High-Quality Virtual Studio _____ 279

The Samplitude 2496 Interface	282
Program Installation	282
The Main Window of the Program	282
Setting up the System Menu	290
Additional Settings	295
Types of Projects in Samplitude 2496	297
The RAM Wave Project	297
The HD Wave Project	299
The Virtual Project	300
Additional Types of Files	301
Areas of Applying RAM Wave and HD Wave Projects	304
The VIP Multitrack. Its Similarity to and Difference from the Multitracks of SAWPro and Cool Edit Pro	305
Similarities to SAWPro and Cool Edit Pro Multitracks	305
The Differences between Samplitude's Multitrack and the Multitracks of SAWPro and Cool Edit Pro	306
Creating a New VIP Project	306
The *Setup for New VIP* Dialog Box	307
Importing MIDI Files	310
Recording and Playback in the VIP Window	311
The Purpose of the *?, M, S, L, V, P,* and *R* Buttons	311
Recording a Wave Project Using the *Record Parameter* Dialog Box	315
How to Record Takes in the *Record Parameter* Dialog Box	320
The *Punch In* Recording Mode	323
Recording in the *Punch In* Mode	323

Contents

- The Playback Modes _____ 329
  - The *Play* Toolbar _____ 329
  - The Range _____ 330
  - Working with Ranges _____ 330
  - The *Play to/from Cut* Playback Modes _____ 332
- Additional Services of Samplitude 2496 _____ 333
  - *Positionbar* _____ 333
  - Additional Buttons of a Virtual Project _____ 337
  - Splitting the Project Window _____ 337
  - The VIP Display Mode _____ 339
  - Pop-up Menu _____ 340
- Sound Processing in Samplitude 2496 _____ 341
  - Non-Destructive Sound Processing _____ 341
    - The Object _____ 341
    - Object Handles _____ 343
    - Object Normalization _____ 346
    - Object Editor _____ 346
    - Using Virtual Effects of DirectX Plug-ins in the Object Editor _____ 355
  - Connecting DirectX Plug-ins to a Track of the Multitrack _____ 359
    - Controlling a Group of Effects on One Track _____ 361
    - The *Samplitude Mixer*, Built-in Effects of Samplitude 2496, and Enabling DirectX Plug-ins _____ 364
    - Some "Tricks" in *Samplitude Mixer* _____ 376
    - Using the *Surround Panning Module* _____ 377
    - Intermediate Mixing Using Track Bouncing _____ 383
  - Destructive Sound Processing _____ 387
    - Destructively Editing the Objects of a VIP Project _____ 387
    - Destructively Editing an HD or RAM Wave Project _____ 391
    - Connecting an External Sound Editor _____ 392
    - Using Plug-ins _____ 393
  - Built-in Virtual Effects of Samplitude 2496 _____ 395
    - The *Normalize* Effect _____ 395
    - The *Switch Channels* Effect _____ 396
    - The *Parametric Equalizer* Effect _____ 397
    - The *Graphic Equalizer* Effect _____ 398
    - The *FFT Analyzer/Filter* Effect _____ 398
    - The *Compressor/Expander/Noise Gate/Limiter* Effect _____ 407
    - The *Multiband Dynamics* Effect _____ 409

The *Room Simulator* Effect	413
The *Echo/Delay/Reverb* Effect	416
The *Convolution* Effect	417
The *Noise Reduction* Effect	418
The *Dehisser* Effect	419
The *Resampling/Time Stretching/Pitch Shifting* Effect	420
The *Multi Band Stereo Enhancer* Effect	422
Editing a Virtual Project	424
VIP Mouse Editing Modes	424
The *Universal* Mode	425
The *Range* Mode	425
The *Object and Curve* Mode	425
The *Draw Volume* Mode	427
The *Draw Panorama* Mode	428
The *Object* Mode	428
The *Curve Move and Grab* Mode	428
The *Mouse Mode Samplitude 4.0* Mode	429
The *Scrubbing Mouse* Mode	429
The *Cut Mouse* Mode	431
The *Zoom Mouse* Mode	432
Moving, Copying, and Splitting Objects	433
Moving Objects	433
Copying Objects	434
Splitting Objects	435
A Virtual Loop Object	435
Using the Markers	436
Creating an AUDIO CD in Samplitude 2496	438
Mixing and Mastering in Samplitude 2496	438
Mixing	438
Mastering	440
Burning an AUDIO CD in Samplitude 2496	446

Chapter 6: The Cubase VST 24 Application and Creating "Live" Midi Sound — 451

The MIDI Interface	455
A MIDI Device	457
Sound Tracks and MIDI Channels	458
The Cubase VST 24 Interface	458
The Main Arrangement Window	458

Contents

Types of Tracks	463
The Basic Components of the Cubase VST 24 Interface	464
The File Formats of Cubase VST 24	471
Song	471
Arrangement	471
Part	472
Drum Map	472
Setup	472
Grooves	472
Cubase VST 24 Editors	473
Key Edit	473
MIDI Controllers	474
Drum Edit	480
Score Edit	483
List Edit	485
Special Messages in Cubase VST 24	491
"Live" MIDI Recording with Cubase VST 24	492
Recording Modes	492
The *Overdub* Mode	492
The *Replace* Mode	493
The *Punch* Mode	494
Cycle Record	495
The *Mix* Mode	495
The *Punch* Mode	496
The *Normal* Mode	496
The *Cycle Functions* Menu	496
Switching between Tracks in the Cycle Record Mode	497
The *Undo* Command	504
The *Inspector* Panel	504
Editing the Arrangement	512
The *Transpose/Velocity* Module	516
Editing Percussion Parts	520
Stage 1	521
Stage 2	523
Stage 3	527
Graphically Editing MIDI Messages	528
Another Technique for "Enlivening" MIDI	533
Step-by-Step Recording	533

Using Plug-ins	534
The Studio Module Plug-in	534
The MIDI Processor Plug-in	538
The Arpeggiator Plug-in	542
The Styletrax Plug-in	545
Quantization in Cubase VST 24	560
Creating a Groove	570
Working with Audio in Cubase VST 24	573
Setting up Cubase VST 24 to Work with Audio	573
Audio Clip Recording	578
Cycle Audio Recording	581
Editing Audio Events in Audio Editor	583
Coordinating Audio and MIDI Tempos	585
The VST Pool Window	587
Sound Processing in Cubase VST 24	589
Inserting Master Effects	594
Using Automation	594

Chapter 7: Using Cubase VST 24 in Combination with Samplitude 2496 — 599

Exporting a Song from Cubase VST 24 to a MIDI File	601
Importing a MIDI File to Samplitude 2496	602
Synchronization of Cubase VST 24 and Samplitude 2496	605

Chapter 8: Mastering in the WaveLab 3.0 Application — 609

Quantization Noise	611
Some Major Points of Analog-to-Digital Sound Conversion	611
Some "Hidden" Features of SAWPro	622
The Master Section in WaveLab	625
The Virtual Effects Necessary for Mastering	631
The ME FreeFilter Intelligent Equalizer	632
The Toolbox of the ME FreeFilter Effect	634
The Learning Section of the ME FreeFilter Effect	636
Improving the Equalizing Quality	639
The Waves C4 Multiband Parametric Processor	642
High-Level Compression (the Downward Compressor)	646
High-Level Expansion (the Upward Expander)	646
Low-Level Compression (the Upward Compressor)	647

      Low-Level Expansion, Noise Gate (the Downward Expander) — 648
    The Hyperprism Harmonic Exciter — 649
    The Hyperprism Bass Maximizer Effect — 651
    The Waves L1—Ultramaximizer+ Effect — 653
    A Chain of Plug-ins for Mastering — 656
Writing the AUDIO CD — 657
The Audio Montage Virtual Editing Environment — 660

Chapter 9: "Tube" Mastering in the T-RackS Application — 665

The Interface of T-RackS (Version 1.1) — 667
The TUBE-COMP Module — 672
The EQUALIZER Module — 673
The MULTIBAND-LIMITER Module — 674
The OUTPUT STAGE Module — 674

Appendix: CD Description — 677

Index — 681

Foreword

There is a common misconception going around that a PC is like a "guillotine" for sound, and that a personal computer is not particularly appropriate for recording music. This idea, though, is from the last century, and no longer applicable to our day and age.

Certain publications devoted to computer music try to push additional equipment (that's supposedly necessary for creating more or less "quality" music on a PC), while sales people try to convince the musician that creating a waveform of acceptable quality just can't be done without buying equipment that often ends up costing as much as the computer itself (or more).

So what is the amateur — for whom music is a hobby — to do when he or she doesn't plan on investing colossal amounts of money in the final product?

We, the authors, are convinced that there is an alternative.

Today, we can boldly say that virtual software for processing sound provides for a relatively high quality musical end product using only the computer. The secret of such quality lies in the fact that the sound processing algorithms in these virtual devices are the same ones used in their "older brothers" — actual hardware devices.

This is all to say that today we are undergoing the process of virtualization of sound processing equipment, which is gradually moving from the material sphere to the virtual one. We are very eager that those of us living in these times — our readers — are able to take full advantage of this tendency as early as possible and with the maximum possible gain.

We are sure that, in order to create music of relatively good quality, you have to:

- Want to write it
- Have a computer with a sound card
- Have the necessary software
- Be able to work with this software

(If you're able to check off the first three points, then this book is for you.)

In this book, we describe the algorithms that provide for a high quality of sound (when used correctly, of course). It is this last phrase that captures the essence of our pages — how to correctly use the software's capabilities to get a real, "life-like" sound.

2 Live Music on Your PC

The popularity of the MP3 format is increasing by leaps and bounds. Among typical users, the common opinion is that the format's capabilities in most cases completely satisfy the listener. Moreover, many think that the quality of MP3 is not much different from the quality of a CD. This is one of the reasons why professional mastering is not quite a reality for amateur computer musicians who, for example, just want to publish their song on the Internet in MP3 format or record them onto audiocassettes.

The topic of mastering with the help of certain software is given a fair amount of space in the book. As a preview, we suppose we could say that the computer is able of imitating even lamp sound.

Note that progress in a virtual studio can be measured by the extent to which the algorithms in it are constantly perfecting themselves both in the quality of the sound that comes out and in their functional capabilities. This is why the material contained in this book is structured to give the reader the ability to master even the later versions of the software that we will cover.

Chapter 1

"Live" Music and Non-Verbal Intelligence

Chapter 1: "Live" Music and Non-Verbal Intelligence

> "The composition, performance, and reception of music should have an idea attached to it, which is exactly what makes them creative, i.e., what makes them fall within the boundaries of art."
>
> *Moris Bonfeld*[1]

The Idea in Music

Having a point is a requirement for creativity, that is, for something to be considered as belonging to the world of art. This axiom is characteristic for all types of human creative activity, including music.

A musical (artistic) composition must from the start have an idea behind it — a type of spiritual content that is conveyed to the listener.

And it is completely unimportant how exactly it is conveyed: whether the composition is actually heard or only read and mentally played, for example, while looking at a score. The most important thing is that the idea embedded in the music is translated using musical speech, in a non-verbal form.

As we know, the cerebral hemispheres take on different functions. The left (logical) part of the brain controls speech, while the right (imaginative) part is responsible for comprehending concrete images and signals from the outside world, and, in part, for **musical activity**.

The most recent research indicates that any information located in the human brain lies within its own neuro-dynamic carrier. When it leaves the environment for the brain, it is re-coded. "We have a basis for believing that the **form of the code** used for verbal and non-verbal information flows are **different**" (M. Bonfeld).

But after the non-verbal information is accepted by a person, it takes on a meaning for that individual, i.e., music **always** "re-codes" itself, transforming into new ideas and images in the mind of the recipient.

Thus, music is a type of mental activity performed on a non-verbal (non-lingual) basis. In other words, people can think in music.

"Psychologists call such information **mental non-verbal,** underlining in that term not only the non-verbality of music, but the presence of a definite **idea**, i.e., its ability to serve as a stimulus for mental (intellectual) activity. Of course, solving image-related, constructive,

---

[1] The quote here and later quotes are from composer and musician Moris Bonfeld.

and other tasks where verbal activity is either limited or outright impossible is considered by psychologists as activity of the **non-verbal intellect**" (M. Bonfeld).

A typical person receives loads of non-verbal information from the outside world.

Using this information, people can, for example, estimate weather conditions or discover a defect in the work of a complex mechanism. Based on such non-verbal information, a person creates a hairstyle, a smell, a photograph, a geometric figure, music, etc. The question of how and why exactly the process of understanding image-based information is different in different people is one that is being studied by a number of researchers from such varied areas of specialty as psychology, linguistics, art, mathematics, biology, etc.

It was discovered long ago that the non-verbal information during communication among people is often more important than the actual verbal dialog. It is expressed, for example, as gestures, mimicry, intonation, pauses, etc.

The significance of non-verbal information is first of all the fact that it is convincing (as opposed to words, non-verbal information reflects the internal state of the speaker). Second, it is able to more fully express certain nuances of communication that can't be conveyed in words.

Non-verbal thinking has its own specific features, and is being actively studied today by modern psychologists.

So, in creating music on the computer, you need to remember what is most important: this re-coding of the non-verbal idea can only happen when there is an actual idea in the original piece.

The Musical Context

The connection between mental processes and musical-speech activity is a relevant theme today. There are certain research projects going on that are trying to compare musical language and speech.

It was noted that these two phenomena have much in common. M. Bonfeld writes that "music is speech on a non-verbal basis".

And it's true: a word, which is a sign, receives a new value in various contexts. In just this manner, each of the smallest elements of musical language (subsigns) is also "exclusively defined by a context" (M. Bonfeld).

It's impossible to conceive of communication between people as just the mechanical pronunciation of words without intonation. That is: just like communication (in a wider context) is impossible without words, it is also impossible without the idea behind those words, which the person gives to them. Sometimes, even the meaning of a word — an interjection, for example — depends solely on the intonation with which it is pronounced.

Chapter 1: "Live" Music and Non-Verbal Intelligence

Intonation is the most important, most basic element of expression in music. It connects all sides of the musical fabric — the theme, the height, the volume, the rhythm, the timbre, and the articulation and phrasing. If this connection is absent, then the listener cannot receive the united idea, which means that the musical composition created will recall uncoherent speech in its "senselessness". And thus communication between the composer (performer) and the listener is impossible.

Without an idea, intonation can't exist; it dies. And if the intonation "dies", the music dies as well.

The process of creating a musical composition with the help of a computer contains certain difficulties. Often, the lack of knowledge of how to work with musical software leads to the idea of the composition getting lost during recording or during the performance.

The computer today is a new (and relatively complex) instrument for creating music. "Playing" it is something that must be learned, just as with any other musical instrument.

The computer can accurately perform a complicated passage, but it can't place the accents, increase or decrease the volume, or speed up or slow down the tempo by itself. No matter how fast your machine, it is simply an obedient performer of the author's ideas. It is not able to express itself using those variations on the norm that separate a virtuoso from a "mechanical collection of sounds". The musician must explain to the "electronic performer" all the nuances of his or her idea, i.e., enter into the computer all the aspects of playing the piece using the proper commands. But regardless of this complexity, the ability to create music on the computer is a huge step ahead in the historical sense.

Before, a composer had only one way of giving music to the performer — using notation, which hasn't changed for centuries and was always imperfect. Traditional notation can come very close to expressing the idea of a musical composition. And describing the artistic image of the composition is also impossible using notation, since the richest palette of nuance remains beyond the scope of the paper.

We could say that a musical composition written with notes is always different from the version performed, the same way that a play printed on paper has little in common with its performance on the stage.

> **NOTE** In theatrical drama, performance of a play necessitates the work of many different people: the writer, the director, actors, artists, musicians, costumers, lighting specialists, etc. The members of each of these professions bring with them their own take on the play (on the theatrical incarnation of the writer's idea written into the play). Each one creatively approaches his or her "part", but works within the framework of the general idea.

Just like the theater play, music is a compilation of many components. The notes are simply the "text of the play" to which the performer must add "life". In other words, the performer must get across to the listener not only the composer's idea, but also convey the wealth of artistic and image-based means of the piece with the creative idea. The more multi-faceted the "text" of a musical composition, the more interesting it is to perform, and the more musicians will attempt to tackle a concrete interpretation.

Humankind has always valued talented performers who are not only able to discover the creative idea of the composer, but who can also enrich the creation itself. In the "pre-computer" era, any musical composition was performed by people — conductors, musicians, vocalists, etc. — who participated in the composition on the same level as the composer.

Thus, music from time immemorial has been the *sum of the labor* of many people — or at least two: the composer and the performer, the author of the idea and the person who interprets and plays (sings) the idea presented. But in creative work with the computer, these two roles often end up being played by the same person. Although, if we were to look at it from another angle, the creative process includes two participants: a person and a "smart machine". However, this is not really accurate. It's very important to keep in mind at all times that the machine **cannot** participate in co-creation on the same level as a person; it can't create an interpretation of the composition. And so this is why, when creating "life-like" music with a computer, a *person* must be both the *author* and the *interpreter* of the composition.

Keep in mind that in order to get a "live" musical composition from the computer, it is not enough to just "enter the notes into the computer". You need to create an image, a *musical context*, within which the sound will, first of all, be filled with a definite idea, and second, will go along with the general idea of the composition. If this is not the case, music "born" by the computer will **always** sound "dead" and mechanical.

Musical Context

By *musical context*, we mean the set of those musically expressive means that the author and the performer have chosen and included into a *concrete* musical composition in order to express its idea, to convey the concept, and to create an image.

Although the term musical context is actively used in real conversation, we haven't been able to find it in academic dictionaries. (But as you know, dictionaries simply back up the norms of a language, and this always happens with some delay.)

In our opinion, musical context has a lot in common with poetic context. "Poetic context influences the element included in it: there is an accenting of particular semantic features in a word, a joining together of facultative features, a suppression of elements of the idea, and a joining of ideas".

Second, linguistic intuition has much in common with musicality: "What does linguistic intuition consist of? Well, it is certainly not in the ability to directly observe the truth, but probably rather in the ability to distinguish new contexts from impossible ones... to create convincing context for your contemporaries" — as said a linguist L. V. Shcherba.

Chapter 1: "Live" Music and Non-Verbal Intelligence

The musical context consists of the coordination of individual means of the idea's musical expression, the concept, and the image of the composition. The most important part of it is the musical intonation. Intonation in music, just as in speech, fills whatever is said (played) with an idea.

It's no secret that, in order to express an artistic image or idea for a composition, each author and performer chooses strictly defined musically-expressive means: the ones that, out of the wealth of those available — in their opinion — make the most sense, are the most expressive, etc.

As a result, various performers create their own, unique musical contexts of the same composition. And "the fate and the life" of a composition, as well as the popularity of the author or performer, depend on how much the image is keeping along with the listeners ideas, to what extent they accepted the interpretation of the composition, and whether or not the musical context was understood.

Computer software is now ready and able to present the user with new tools for creating "life-like" and not mechanical music. It is this kind of music that is fully able to convey feelings, emotions, ideas, and energy to the listener.

The "rules" of "live" music are made by nature itself. In nature, unjustified repetition doesn't exist. Every one of its creations is unique. And all the processes that go on in these creations have a purpose, an idea, and are subordinate to the tasks of the living organism.

Chapter 2

MUSICAL LANGUAGE AND COMPUTER TECHNOLOGY

Chapter 2: Musical Language and Computer Technology 13

> A musical composition created or realized in sound is always geared towards the listener and is the translation of a particular idea.
>
> *Moris Bonfeld*

It's hard to disagree with the statement that it is the idea that makes a composition artistic. But unfortunately, a large number of modern examples of mass computer music often seem to lack any kind of "human" idea. You might get the impression that in the creative process of creating music on the computer, the computer takes the lead. Putting the person in the background, the computer may sometimes seem to set its own rules for the musician to follow.

Throughout time, music has not only reflected the life surrounding humanity, but also has made the listener empathize, feel, and think. This happens due to the fact that the composition reflects the intellectual activity of the creator.

Today's mixing of accents in the role of the musician and the computer does not allow us to call the result "music" in the traditional sense of the word, since when listening to such a machine-like "composition", there are no ideas or emotions that come out of it — at least not for a person.

Many centuries of music history have proven the fact that the spiritual content of each **truly** artistic composition is unique and unimitable.

We won't bother making a comparison between modern music and so-called classical music. But we do want to mention that, for the hundreds of years that classical music has been in existence, for some reason, it is still in demand: musicians love to perform it, listeners want to hear it, and many people dream of creating something like it.

This is because "real" music not only reflects the world around us, but is in itself a new phenomenon, a new thing to be valued, since it gives birth to ideas that did not exist before, and after whose creation, compositions began to exist within its framework. Each unit of the common musical legacy contains an idea that is characteristic to it alone.

NOTE "Thus, any musical composition, like a linguistic sign, represents a complete material-ideal formation...This means that when a musical composition is played (its material form), it is connected within the mind of the listener to a set of concepts, impressions, emotions (spiritual essence) that only exist in that particular composition, and that differ from the playing of the composition itself, but that are united with it in a specific, indissoluble unit, which is what allows the music to be perceived as having a definite content, or idea." (M. Bonfeld, 2.0.3).

Means of Musical Expression

In order to convey something with the help of music, you need to know its language. A composer who has mastered the art should be acquainted with musical traditions of various epochs.

The term *musical language*, in music tradition, means the entirety of all *means of musical expression*.

Musical language is specific both for a particular epoch, type, style, and composer's style, and for each individual composition.

In the process of learning a "different musical language", there is no need to learn a bunch of foreign words. You become acquainted with it by entering into a new musical world, attaching yourself to a new culture, a new way of experiencing the world.

To do this, you need to listen to as much different, good-quality music as possible. It should of course be performed well, too. If you listen and learn to listen, you will be able to hear their various features.

Means of musical expression consist of two groups of components: relatively stable ones, and mobile ones.

The *relatively stable components* are: the key system, types of facture, tonal-harmonic parameters, structural types, etc. These components keep their basic features for a relatively long time (historically speaking). They are continuously collecting certain new properties that lead to a reformation — a significant, sometimes even cardinal, transformation.

Thanks to these relatively stable components, the music is able to do without a "translation", since they are based on fundamental properties of human nature, on the culture created by humans. This is the reason for the international and timeless influence of music.

Mobile components are unique elements that belong to one composition. An example of one of these is a melodic picture that has no analog in other compositions. If the melody is copied, words like imitation, borrowing, and plagiarism immediately spring to mind.

A real artist is one who can, along with creating special, unique mobile components for his or her composition, is also able to modify some of the relatively stable components as well.

Changing relatively stable components — if, of course, they are stable, purposeful, and content-rich enough — is considered to be one of the major aspects of the individual style of a composer.

How to Listen to a Musical Composition

The perception of a musical composition can vary. Each epoch listens to music in its own way; each person also perceives the same piece differently depending on his or her psychological state at the time.

Note that listeners **always** compare a new composition to ones they have heard before, and then, consciously or (more often) subconsciously, includes it into a context that they are familiar with. If the new music has clear characteristics (for instance, is of a popular genre), it will invoke certain images (ones associated with that genre) in the imagination of the listener.

If the composition is so unfamiliar, unusual, and unexpected that it doesn't recall any kind of context with the listener, it **will not be accepted** as artistically rich music.

This idea, unfortunately, relates to both masterpieces and the most mediocre compositions. In both cases, the sound and the idea don't go together for the listener. And only later — when a context is created in which the composition will be perceived as familiar and modern — will time put all things in place.

This rule is applicable not only to music, but to all areas of art and science as well.

It's interesting to note that the speed of change in musical language since the early middle ages up until today has been constantly increasing. Whereas in the eighteenth century stability was found even in the most mobile component — melody, and in the nineteenth century key harmonic factors and the form of the composition did not change much at all, composers in the twentieth century began to actively look for ways of creating "their own musical language". This process of searching for new forms of self expression is gradual, but is undoubtedly gaining speed. This is why the only thing we can call basic stable components these days is the actual use of musical sounds and their main properties; everything else are changeable, mobile elements.

We'd like to remind "musical revolutionaries" that trying to implement cardinal changes into stable components (the key system, the facture, the parameter harmony, etc.) may make your composition difficult for your contemporaries to understand. This is especially true if the music is so intense as to be far outside the framework of musical evolution. A long time might pass before these "revolutionary" means of musical expression are accepted by listeners as a stable component of musical language.

You might be soothed a bit by the fact that, first of all, evolutionary and revolutionary transformations of the basic stable components of musical language occur more quickly than they do in speech, and second, no type of variability will keep you from enjoying a true artistic musical composition.

If You've Got the Desire, You'll Find a Way

This is exactly how we could answer the question: How can you create "live" music on a computer?

The market of musical equipment and software for PCs is relatively large. Some of these tools are obvious, while others are not so obvious, some are easy to use, while others are not. Different programs have different qualities. The most important thing, however, is that there is lots of software available for creating "life-like" music on a computer. There's plenty to go around: enough for beginning musicians and for professionals, for computer specialists and computer novices.

We are convinced that, depending on the task that needs to be completed and the level of your musical and computer erudition, each person can find musical software that is right for his or her individual needs.

This book aims to describe some of these programs. We will only be able to touch on certain features, without going into a detailed explanation.

- ❐ The first program that we'll look at in the book is SAWPro. Our decision to begin with it was not arbitrary. In our opinion, it is the best program for those musicians who are just beginning their acquaintance with the computer, as well as for those who need quick and high-quality recording capabilities for, for example, a simple project. One undoubted advantage of this program is its high reliability level. It allows you to go almost 100 steps back (i.e., it has 99 undo levels). SAWPro is very convenient for recording an acoustic instrument(s), a vocal, or a composition containing speech and music (like, for example, a audio commercial, a "soundtrack" for a prom, a radio program, etc.). When you become more acquainted with SAWPro, you will begin to appreciate its features and its professional possibilities.

- ❐ **Cool Edit Pro** is a high-quality professional multitrack editor that, in our opinion, is best for processing sound under home computer studio conditions. This program has a number of advantages: an large selection of its own internal virtual effects of professional-level quality, and the ability to create *your own processing algorithms* (which allows you to automate sound processing to a significant extent), to name a few. It also has an understandable interface, with pop-up hints, a "tip of the day", etc.

- ❐ **Samplitude 2496** (versions 5.55—5.57) also presents us with a wide range of possibilities for recording and processing a live performance on acoustic and electric musical instruments. This package is a complete virtual studio with very high sound quality and a high virtualization level. In it, for instance, you can connect effects directly to the object (a clip with certain properties). Also, all the settings of the object will be saved after performing any kind of operation with it (moving, copying, etc.). In Samplitude 2496, you can place various types of objects on one track: both MIDI objects and AUDIO objects. Even with all of its advantages, the program requires relatively few of the computer's system resources.

- ❐ In the chapter dedicated to **Cubase VST 24**, most of the attention is focused on describing the mechanisms and means used in the area of "enlivening" a computer "performance". Basically, these are the capabilities that allow you to "breathe life" into the sound, and to remove as much as possible the effect of the computer's mechanicality. Special attention is given to such instruments as **Groove Quantize**, which allows you to move the positions of notes and set the accents so that they correspond to a certain template taken from a "live" performance (from an audio recording, for example). Another example is the **Styletrax** module, which lets you create a virtual "group" of musicians with which you can improvise using the MIDI keyboard in real time.

In conclusion, we'd like to say a few words about sound quality. Throughout time, this has been a hugely important consideration for musicians. It's not just for love of beauty that a good musical instrument was and is always valued much more than just a regular one.

The basic musical computer creation is digital sound. But the fact that the sound is digital is not a guarantee of quality. It's necessary that you understand the nature of digital sound and the specific features of processing it. This is one theme that we will be spending much time on in this book.

Chapter 3

THE SAWPRO PROGRAM: LIVE RECORDING IN A VIRTUAL STUDIO

Description of the SAWPro Interface

General Information about the Program

We begin this book with the SAWPro (Software Audio Workshop Professional) program, from Innovative Quality Software (**http://www.iqsoft.com**). We do so because SAWPro seems to us to be the best option for a newcomer to the realm of computer music, due in part to its "patience".

From our point of view, this program was designed to be used by people of any profession, age, or education level that wish to record music. No special musical or computer education is required to work with SAWPro.

We have attempted to lay the SAWPro program out in a way that would be intelligible for as wide an audience as possible, sometimes even by simplifying algorithms for actions to make them easier to understand.

This is done mainly for those who are fond of singing or playing musical instruments, and would like to record — alone or with accompaniment — high-quality live music using a home computer.

To find out about additional capabilities of the SAWPro program, an inquisitive reader can always refer to the **Info** menu. This is traditionally in the top right screen corner, and always ready to help.

Despite its simplicity, SAWPro might very well attract the interest of more advanced users too, since it allows for results of reasonably good quality, and gives the music a "live" sound. You end up with far more than just an assemblage of infinitely repeating fragments that turns out as more of a caricature of music, or a formless veil of noise (no offense to admirers of this kind of music).

Owing to its combination of reliability, ease of use, and professional multifunctionality, SAWPro is the optimal variant of a convenient "multitrack tape recorder" for users of all levels.

This program is perfectly suited for a first acquaintance with the world of computer-aided music creation; on the other hand, it still meets the high standards of sophisticated professionals in this field.

But strangely enough, in spite of all its advantages, SAWPro is like the Cinderella of the computer world. Why, then, is it still underestimated by users?

The answer is simple. Every extraordinary thing has its characteristic traits, and this program is no exception. One of its features can be compared to the strange and unexpected "face" of an intelligent robot, which may scare you off at first glance.

Believe it or not, the authors of this book were bewildered at the beginning too. When you launch it for the first time, the "honest" SAWPro program exhibits all its rich potentialities at once (Fig. 3.1), by displaying on the screen six of the seven possible windows ALL AT THE SAME TIME.

22   Live Music on Your PC

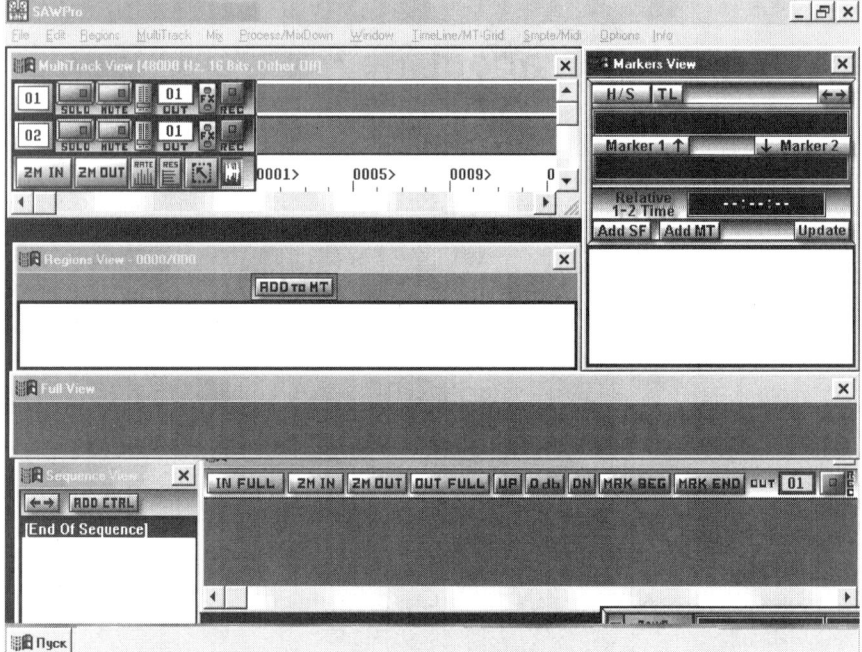

Fig. 3.1. SAWPro's **Main Screen**

This much information may shock even those used to such things. And since edgy and easily stressed people are not warned not to look at screens during initialization, many of them never come back to this program. Such a shame!

The readers of this book will learn many secrets. For instance, this "scary" screen can and should be transformed at once into a useful and handy set of windows. Another thing is that, due to its rather poor graphics, the program's creators were able to economize computer resources and direct them towards the main program function, i.e., producing sound. This in particular allows the user to experiment without being wary of fouling up the result.

Surely, from the point of view of someone who is creating a musical product using his or her home computer for the first time, one of the essential advantages of SAWPro is that the program nearly ideally guards against possible mistakes. Think of it like this: what are the basic problems run into by a person who is doing something for the first time? Obviously, while mastering something new, one makes mistakes. These errors can be quite annoying, hinder the work, and waste a lot of time.

The SAWPro program enables you to undo 99 (ninety nine!) actions, if you need to. Although, looking ahead, we have to mention one imperative requirement: never modify your sound file irreversibly. (We will discuss this in detail later, in the "*Destructive Editing*" section.)

This means that whenever you think what you have done could have been done better, or if you simply want to redo something, SAWPro lets you return almost to the beginning of your work.

This is highly convenient for a user of any level, while for a beginner it's priceless — with the ability to cancel previous actions, you use the trial and error method with no risk of losing something you cannot restore.

This is in contrast to other programs, which resemble a stroll along a minefield: they allow you one mistake, that is, you can cancel only ONE action (the last one)! Tell me, what kind of creative work is without mistakes.

One more advantage of the SAWPro program is that it is fit for recording live music (instruments or voice parts).

If you need to be the musician, singer, and soundman all in one, your faithful assistant SAWPro will help you re-record a bad fragment easily and quickly. Moreover, you can work with any time-value (including the minimal one, i.e., one note), and, what is especially important, the border will not be distinguishable by ear!

If you have never recorded music using a computer before, and have only used your computer for information storage, or used to think that only a professional was able to correctly use a musical program, but still have always dreamed of making your own high-quality sound recordings, then you should really try the SAWPro program. Working with it is not particularly complicated, and can at times be very interesting.

SAWPro Installation

The installation procedure is quite easy. Start the Setup.exe file from your distribution package and follow the installation instructions. By default, SAWPro will be installed in a folder of the same name. The **Programs** section of the Windows main menu will receive a shortcut with a tape-recorder depicted (Fig. 3.2).

Fig. 3.2. The SAWPro program icon

Recommendations for Configuring SAWPro to Work with Your Sound Card

To configure SAWPro for a certain sound card, open the **Options** menu and click **Audio Hardware Setup**. This will produce the **Audio Hardware Setup** window (Fig. 3.3).

Since SAWPro supports 12 devices, in the setup window you will be offered 12 drop-down lists in which you should make your choices. The program will allow you to work with a number of sound cards simultaneously, for example, one for recording and another for playback. To control this, use the **Out/In Device Toggle** in the top of the window.

A typical user, as a rule, has only one multimedia sound card installed in the computer. Accordingly, the recommendations below are applicable only for a case where there is just *one* sound card.

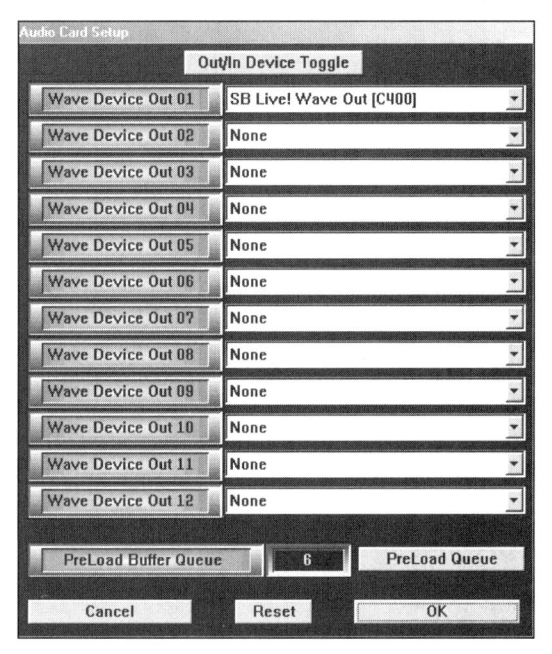

Fig. 3.3. The sound card configuration window

The program invites you to decide what you will use to record sound and what device will be used to play it back. To decide these issues:

1. Open the first drop-down list (Fig. 3.3) by pressing the button to its right, with the triangle. You will see your sound card's name with the word Out, and the word None across from it. Choose the field with the sound card's name and click on it.

2. Specify the input device. First, press the **Out/In Device Toggle** button. This will cause your sound card name, this time with the word In, to appear in the uppermost field. No device is assigned by default (**None**). Choose the line with the sound card's name and click on it.

3. Press **OK** in the bottom of the window.

4. Fix the current configuration: open the **File** menu, choose **Save Preferences**, and press **OK** when prompted.

The sound card configuration is now done.

Creating a Comfortable User Environment

Now that the program has been installed, it decides to proudly demonstrate its **Main Screen** with six windows for you. What you need to do is compose profiles, choosing one, two, three, or more windows, according to your preferences.

By the way, as well as choosing the windows, you can configure their size and appearance to fit your needs.

On the CD-ROM attached to this book, we offer a number of such configurations that we think may be of use. Find the Sawpro.prf file in the SAWPro directory of the CD-ROM, and copy this file into the folder on your hard drive where the SAWPro executable resides, overwriting the existing file.

NOTE If SAWPro is running, close it first before copying.

If you follow our suggestion and employ these ready-to-use workspace configurations, then, at least in the first stages of your work, you will not have to configure the windows yourself.

However, for those readers who are downright computer novices, we recommend that you read the next section in order to know what to do in case of emergency (such as when the screen configuration is somehow unexpectedly changed).

Creating a Working Screen

You can create your own working screen configuration like this.

First, *select the screen components* — that is, define the windows you need from the default set of those offered you by the program. Then, close all other (unnecessary) windows.

NOTE Windows are closed in the normal manner, by clicking on the x in the top-right corner of the window. After that, if necessary, *resize the selected windows*.

To do this:
1. Place your mouse cursor on any corner of the window.
2. When the cursor becomes a small, two-headed arrow, resize the window by dragging the frame in or out while holding the left mouse button pressed.

> **NOTE** Windows have a minimum size; the program will not allow a window to be made any smaller than this.

To *move* a window around the screen:
1. Place the mouse cursor on the window's title bar.
2. While holding the left mouse button, drag the window to the desired position. This is how to create the working screen that is most convenient for the individual user.

An Example of Creating a Screen Using the *MultiTrack View* Window

Shown in Fig. 3.4 is an example of simple screen; in our opinion, it is also the most convenient. As you can see, we have decided to leave only one of the windows the program offered us in the beginning — **MultiTrack View** (view all tracks for recording). This window has been expanded to fill the whole screen. We advise that you begin mastering the SAWPro program with this window. If you set it to one of the function keys, the window will pop up each time you press this key.

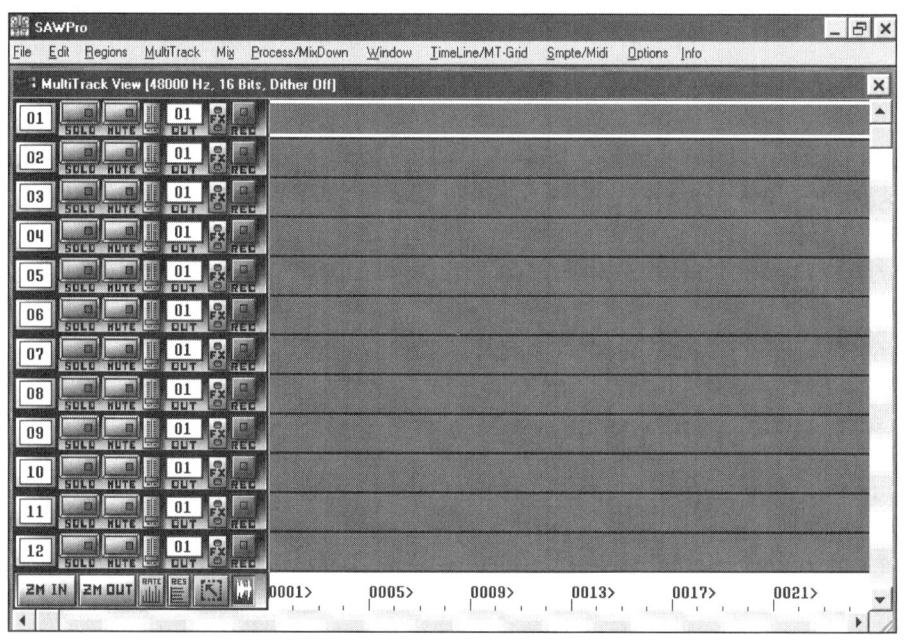

Fig. 3.4. An example of the main working screen with an active **MultiTrack View** window

> **NOTE** For instance, if you associate the **MultiTrack View** window with the <F1> key, pressing it will always result in the appearance of the main screen as seen in Fig. 3.4.

We shall later go into detail on how to associate a window with a function key.

Associating a Screen with a Function Key

Suppose you have configured the screen following the suggestions given above. Now it would be wise to bind the settings to a specific key, so that you can always get the screen you configured by pressing this key.

You can choose any function key from <F1> to <F12>. To assign the key, press it while pressing <Shift>.

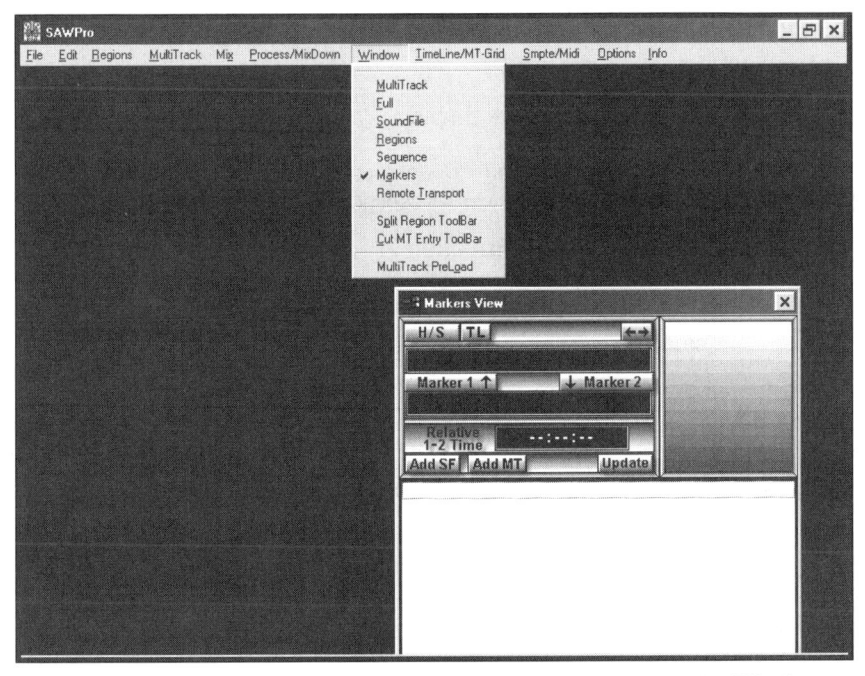

Fig. 3.5. An example of the **Markers View** window opened using the **Windows** menu

To create a new working screen, repeat the operation sequence described above:
1. Press an unused key (<F1>, ..., <F12>).
2. Close unnecessary windows.
3. Neatly place the windows you have left on the screen.
4. Associate the result with a key by pressing <Shift> + an unused key (<F1>, ..., <F12>).

Calling Windows Using the *Window* Menu

The working screen can be configured using the **Window** menu. For each of the windows to be included into a given configuration, do the following (Fig. 3.5):
1. Open the **Window** menu.

2. Choose the window.
3. Activate the window by clicking it in the menu.

Modifying the Working Screen

If you decide to change a working screen that you have already created and associated with some function key, proceed as follows:

1. Activate the screen to be modified.
2. Open the **Options** menu.
3. Execute the **Refresh All Windows** command.

> **WARNING** Be careful. If you by mistake use the similar looking **Refresh All Function Keys** command, you will cancel all your previous settings.

4. Press **OK** in the dialog box for confirmation.

> **NOTE** Here you will see the default **Main Screen** instead of the windows you have created.

5. Go back to the algorithm for creating a working screen, and then associate it with the same function key.

Invalidating All Screens Associated with <F1>, ..., <F12> Keys

This operation releases ALL function keys from current settings. It involves these actions:

1. Open the **Options** menu.
2. Execute the **Refresh All Function Keys** command.

Saving the Settings

Saving your settings spares you the trouble of configuring all the windows each time you start the SAWPro program.

Saving settings is just as easy as deleting them. After you create the appropriate configuration, do the following:

1. Open the **File** menu (Fig. 3.6).
2. Execute the **Save Preferences** command.

This way, SAWPro allows you to create up to 12 different comfortable working environments.

However, you will not likely use that many in practice. And for the first exercise, a simple working screen with only the **MultiTrack View** window is quite sufficient.

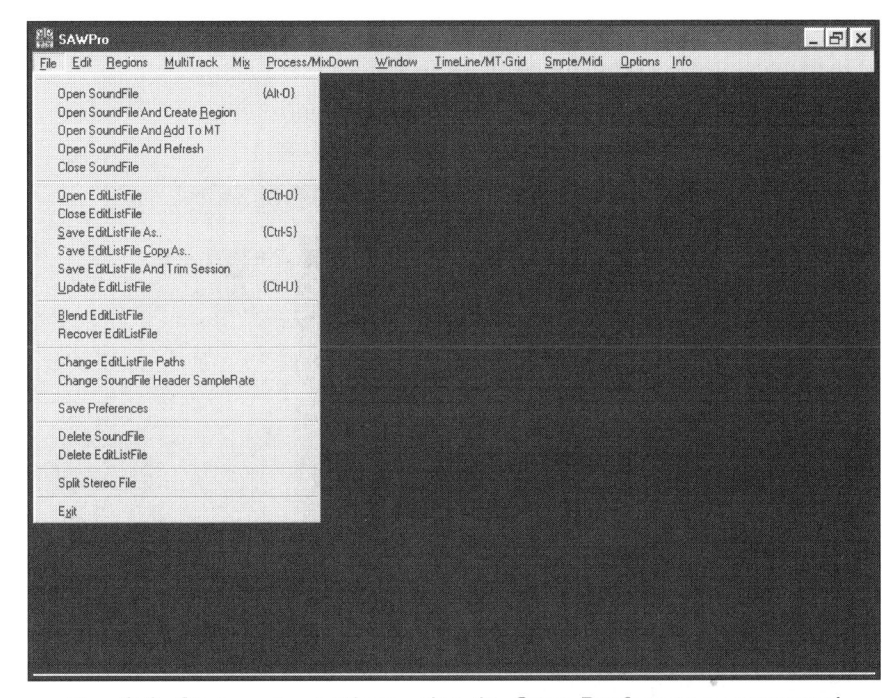

Chapter 3: The SAWPro Program: Live Recording in a Virtual Studio

Fig. 3.6. Saving your settings using the **Save Preferences** command

Custom Configuration Options

Before working with the program, it should be configured to execute those operations we need it to.

In other words, only relevant configuration options should be included.

We propose here the configuration most suitable for a beginner.

Here is how to set up this configuration:

1. Open the Options menu.
2. Turn on the recommended options, selecting them and clicking on them (Fig. 3.7) one by one.

NOTE To turn an option off, click on it once again (the check next to its name should disappear).

Some options are activated by the program by default.

- **SoundFile View Playback Tracking** — controls the correspondence between the visuals and the moving cursor in the **SoundFile View** window

❐ **MultiTrack View Playback Mixer Tracking** — animates the mix controls (*faders*); for slower machines, it is recommended that this option be disabled

❐ **GamePort Switch Toggle Mode** — for remotely controlling the SAWPro program through the game port

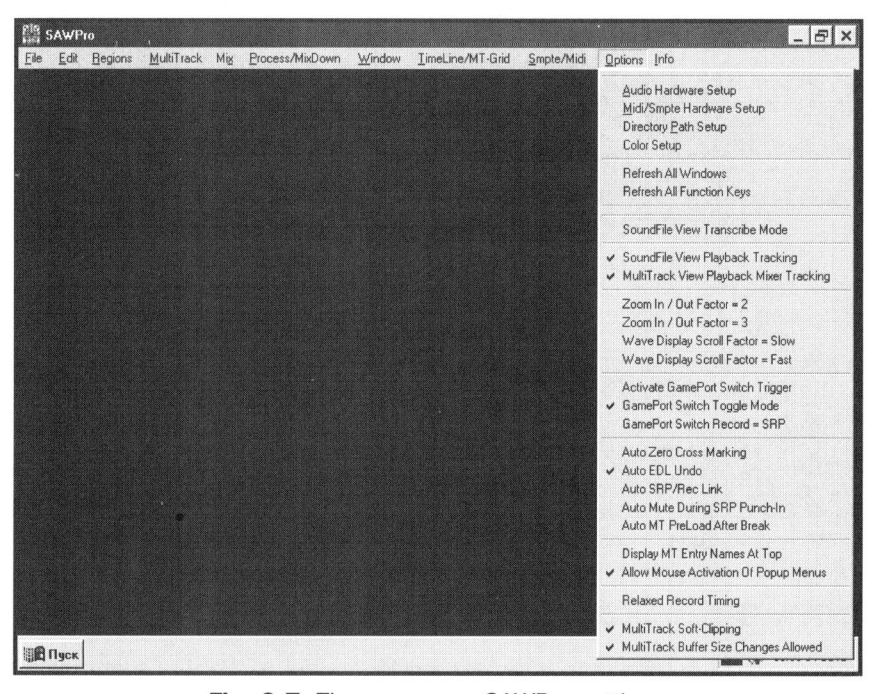

Fig. 3.7. The necessary SAWPro settings

And here are some options that we recommend be turned on, based on our own experiences when using the program:

❐ **Auto EDL Undo** — allows you to cancel up to 99 operations

❐ **Allow Mouse Activation Of Popup Menus** — allows you to call menus by simultaneously pressing the left and right mouse buttons

❐ **MultiTrack Soft-Clipping** — softly limits the volume level

❐ **MultiTrack Buffer Size Changes Allowed** — allows you to vary the multitrack buffer size

The SAWPro File Formats

The main file formats that the SAWPro program deals with are sound files with the WAV extension and project files with the EDL extension (EditListFile).

Chapter 3: The SAWPro Program: Live Recording in a Virtual Studio 31

SAWPro is actually a multichannel sound editor that can be used for both creating new sound files and editing existing ones. Project files keep all information about sound fragments' location in the **MultiTrack View** window, attached virtual effects, settings for the virtual mixer, and also data concerning the location of sound files on the hard drive.

> **WARNING** *Losing* an EDL file will occasionally put the music fragments *out of sync* and, consequently, make it impossible to easily reconstruct the project.

Setting the Number of Undos

So as to be able to erase occasional errors after you make them, set the highest number (99) of SAWPro undos beforehand. To do this:

1. Open the **Edit** menu.
2. Choose **Set EDL Undo Levels**. This will open the dialog box shown in Fig. 3.8.

> **WARNING** These actions clear the current undo stack.

3. Enter 99 in the text field.
4. Press **OK**.

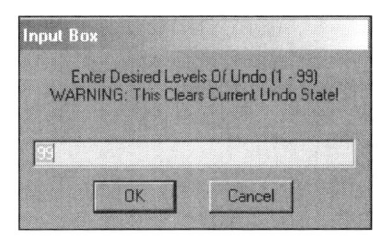

Fig. 3.8. The undo level setting window

After each of your actions, SAWPro creates a new copy of the EDL file (99 times if you allow for 99 undos). Each copy is assigned a numbered name automatically. For instance, if your file is called Song.edl, subsequent copies will receive these names: Song.u00, Song.u01, etc., up until Song.u99. Moreover, a file with a smaller number (*.u00) will reflect the most recent undo operation.

You can load one of the copies in one of two ways.

The first method is to execute the **Open Edl Undo History** command.

1. Open the **Edit** menu.
2. Select **Open Edl Undo History**.

3. In the dialog box that appears (Fig. 3.9), choose the necessary copy of the file.
4. Press **Open**.

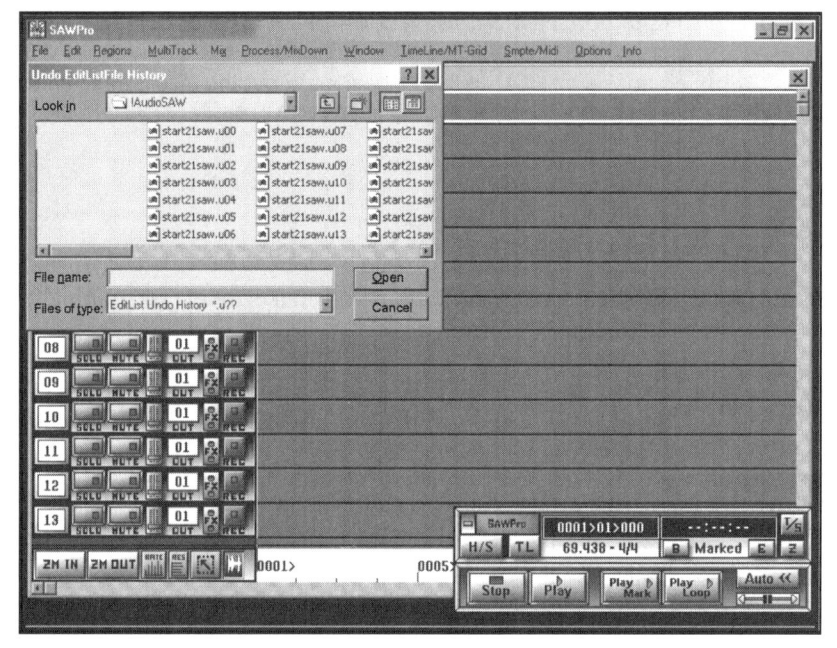

Fig. 3.9. The **Undo EditListFile History** window

The second way is to use another main screen menu item, **Recover Edit List File**:
1. Open the **File** menu.
2. Choose **Recover Edit List File**.
3. In the dialog box that appears (Fig. 3.10), choose the necessary copy of the file.
4. Press **Open**.

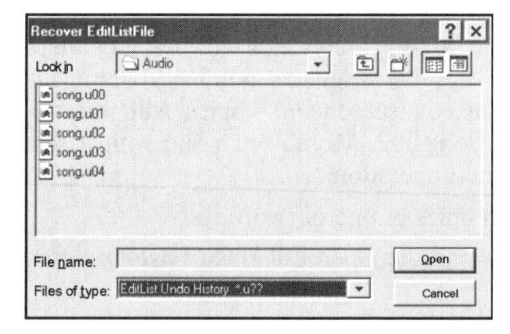

Fig. 3.10. The **Recover EditListFile** window

Description of the *MultiTrack View* Window

We can now begin the real work with sound. Let's investigate the **MultiTrack View** window (see Fig. 3.4).

It consists of 44 horizontal tracks, or a multitrack. At the top are 32 tracks for recording and playing the sound. Below these are 12 output tracks.

Tracks follow in the order of their numbers: 1—32 are normal tracks, and then the next 12 (1—12) are output tracks. These groups differ not only in their purpose and set of functions, but also in color.

There is not enough screen space to display all the tracks at the same time, but this is not necessary anyway.

> **NOTE** To see the tracks that do not fit on the screen, you can use the traditional procedure of scrolling: click on the upper (or lower) triangle on the scrollbar on the right side of the screen, which will allow you to scroll the window up (or down). By moving the scroll box on the scrollbar, you can look through all tracks quickly.

Most likely, when recording your first projects, you will only need one or just a few of the 32 tracks provided by the SAWPro program.

However, because a home computer sound card, as a rule, only allows you to use ONE *output track* (the first of the 12, or **Output Track 01**), we suggest that you place it next to the tracks you choose for recording, for convenience' sake. We'll tell you how to do this after describing the difference between the two kinds of tracks.

Normal and Output Tracks

A track and an output track are similar at first glance. However, the difference is substantial.

A track is used for recording and playback.

An output track is a track designated for mixing sound taken from regular tracks.

> **NOTE** For mixing, see the "*SAWPro Mixing and Mastering*" section.

In Fig. 3.11, you can see the boundary between the tracks of two types, where the last (32nd) normal track meets first output track. Their exterior distinctions are obvious.

As we stated before, using output tracks in a home studio has its restrictions. This depends on the number of sound cards installed on the computer, as well as their capabilities.

Fig. 3.11. A track and an output track

Normally, a few (or even just one) regular tracks are enough for recording and playback.

Using output tracks on a home computer is limited by technical restrictions. If there is only one multimedia sound card installed on your machine (which most often is the case), only ONE output track will be available in the SAWPro program. This output track's number will correspond to the number of the device defined in the sound card's configuration window (Fig. 3.3).

Even when comparing the two types of tracks visually (Fig. 3.11), you can somewhat see their functional differences. Table 3.1 lists the controls of these tracks and their purposes.

Table 3.1. Track and Output Track Button Functions

Button	Track	Output track
Track number	Number only	Number with arrow (1>)
SOLO button	Enables sound (Solo mode)	Enables sound (Solo mode)
MUTE button	Disables sound	—
Fader button	Launches the volume level control	Launches the volume level control
Device number	**(01) OUT** — points to a device	—
FX	Calls the window for including sound effects	Calls the window for including sound effects
REC	Calls the virtual tape recorder panel	—

Here are some explanations of these differences.

❐ As you can see from the comparison table, output tracks have no **MUTE** button, so the sound cannot be switched off on these tracks.

❐ The **SOLO** button on an output track disables the sound on all 32 regular tracks and at the same time turns on the playback of the sound file of the output track. If there is no file on the output track, then, of course, you will hear no sound.

❐ There are two **FX** buttons on every output track. This is done to duplicate the function for setting sound effects. With these two identical buttons, the user can assign sound effects to the output track TWICE: for instance, *before* and *after* adjusting the volume level. This opportunity enables you to noticeably enrich the final result.

Chapter 3: The SAWPro Program: Live Recording in a Virtual Studio   35

NOTE Effects attached using the purple **FX** button are processed with the help of the sound card's bit resolution. Those plug-ins attached by yellow **FX** buttons provide the highest 24-bit processing precision. (We shall come back to the problem of digital sound quality in *Chapter 8*.)

Moving Tracks around the Screen

A track can be easily moved to another place on the screen:

1. Place the cursor over the NUMBER of the track you wish to move.
2. Holding the left mouse button, move the track vertically to a new position.

NOTE The track number and function remain the same when the track is moved.

From our perspective, it is best that the track to be mixed (**Output Track 01**) be situated at the top of the screen, as depicted in Fig. 3.12.

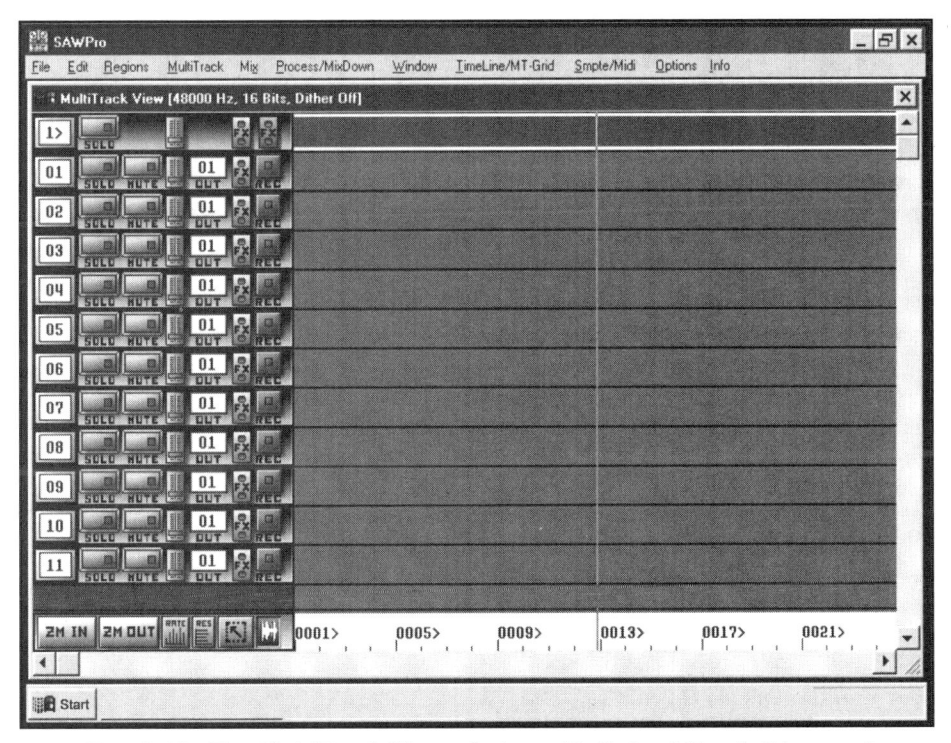

Fig. 3.12. The **MultiTrack View** window with **Output Track 01** moved

NOTE If you find this track arrangement convenient, you can save it — along with any subsequent settings — as an EDL file. The "*Saving a Project*" section explains how to do this.

The *Multitrack* Cursor

Pay attention to the vertical line that crosses all multitrack tracks (Fig. 3.12). This is the *Multitrack* cursor. As you record or playback sound, this cursor moves from left to right, indicating the current position.

The Track. Description of Tracks for Sound Recording and Processing

Now that you have created a suitable screen with the tracks placed to fit your preferences, it's time to learn how these tracks work.

As you might have noticed, each track is supplied with an identical set of 7 buttons (Fig. 3.13).

Fig. 3.13. A track for recording and processing sound

The track number is the leftmost button. This number never changes, and besides identifying the track, it is also a "handle" used for dragging the track to a new place.

The following two buttons turn the track's sound on or off.

The **SOLO** button turns the sound on, while automatically turning off ALL tracks that don't have this button pressed.

The **MUTE** button turns the sound off for each track individually.

By switching these buttons on and off, you can listen to music recorded on different tracks in various combinations.

The **Fader** button (the one with the picture) calls the virtual mixer panel (the **Fader and Pan Control** window). If these panels are opened on a number of tracks, the active, **Hot Track**'s fader will be on top of all the others.

Button **(01) OUT** is the device number.

Button FX displays the **Effects Patch Builder** window.

The **REC** button calls two virtual recorder panels.

Let's explore these controls in the order of their appearance on the track.

Chapter 3: The SAWPro Program: Live Recording in a Virtual Studio 37

The *Fader* Button (Volume and Pan Control)

This calls a virtual device (the mixer) for the sound's volume and pan control (Fig. 3.14).

> **NOTE** Clicking on the **Fader** button again will remove the mixer panel from the screen.

There is a **Fader** on every track, making it possible to adjust the volume level or panorama center at every specific point on the track. Besides which, the program remembers these data and creates a curve of volume or pan changes at these points. The resulting fade curve may be employed at different stages of work. We shall discuss this in detail in the "*SAWPro Mixing and Mastering*" section.

In the bottom of the **Fader** panel, you see a slider for adjusting the volume level. This may be controlled in either of two ways: by moving the knob up and down with the mouse, or by clicking the scale's tickmarks or its up and down arrows.

Fig. 3.14. The **Fader** virtual mixer (for volume and pan adjustment)

> **NOTE** Adjustment is less accurate when you drag the slider. When you click the tickmarks or arrows, the volume level increases (or decreases, depending on whether you click above or below the knob) in steps of 0.25 dB[1] per click.

---

[1] Decibel, a unit for measuring volume.

The Slope of Volume Level Changes

Let's ask ourselves, "If we increase the volume level to +10.00 dB abruptly, will the volume change at this point in the track be smooth or spasmodic?"

The **Slope Zone** is what answers this question. The **Slope Zone** is found above the volume level readout, between two slashes (one forward and the other back). Clicking on the **Slope Zone** displays a window where you can assign an appropriate volume level change slope, from the slowest (**Slope 1**) to the fastest (**Slope 10**).

> **NOTE** We recommend that you not alter this parameter unless it is absolutely necessary, leaving the program's default value — **Slope 5**.

Adjusting Pan

Above the slope is the **PAN** button, used for panorama adjustment. This is done in the same way as volume adjustment: either by moving the slider with the mouse, or by clicking on the area above the knob. In the latter case, adjustment is more precise.

Altering the Fade Curve

Suppose you have adjusted the volume or pan at some points. You now have a curve, which can be clearly seen if you choose the appropriate zoom level to expand the track width.

> **NOTE** Press <Page Up> to expand the track width and <Page Down> to contract it.

However, you might not be satisfied with the result after listening to it, and decide to cancel the curve. Use the **CLRALL** button (Clear All) to do this.

On the other hand, if you like the nuances of the settings, but wish to modify the whole fade curve in general (for example, to amplify the vocal track level), this can be easily done using the **OFFSET** button.

The **OFFSET** button shifts ALL fade curve points by the same value. After this button is pressed, you can move the volume or pan knob to make changes to the whole curve.

More about Adjusting Volume and Pan

Here we briefly describe some editing methods as a preface to the mixing and mastering section.

The **OFFSET** button is often used when adjusting the general volume level of an **Output Track**. The reason is that when mixing a number of tracks, the audio signal level can grow too high, causing the sound's distortion.

Chapter 3: The SAWPro Program: Live Recording in a Virtual Studio

While on the somewhat important subject of limiting the signal (clipping) on an output track, we wish to note once more the **MultiTrack Soft-Clipping** setting in the **Options** menu, which we recommended that you enable in the "*Custom Configuration Options*" section.

This option provides *automatic soft* limiting of occasional output signal amplitude peaks that exceed 100%. By the way, this was not possible with earlier SAW generations of the program.

Nevertheless, using this function alone is certainly not sufficient if you want to avoid distortion. The output signal should also be controlled manually, reducing the overall level if necessary.

In the **Mix** menu of the program's main window (Fig. 3.15), there are options that allow for different volume and pan editing actions.

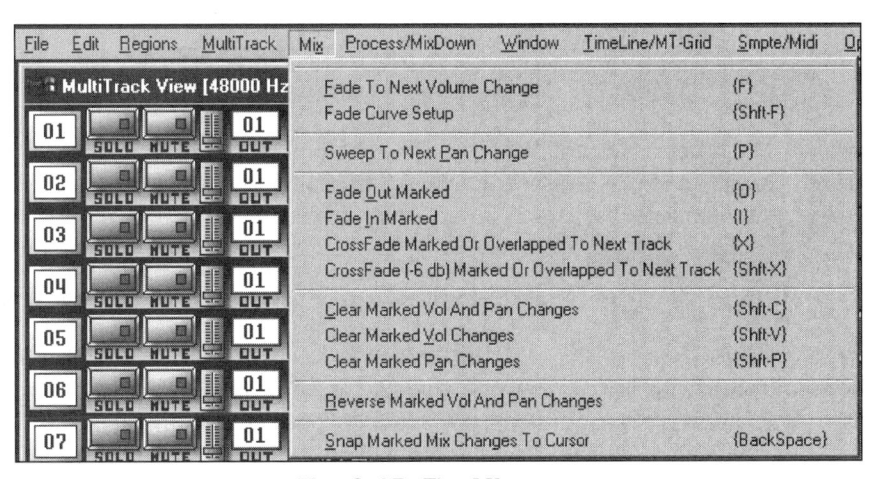

Fig. 3.15. The **Mix** menu

Some of these are listed below.

- **Fade To Next Volume Change** (the <F> key) — sets a smooth volume change from the current point to the next point of the track fragment
- **Fade To Next Pan Change** (the <P> key) — sets a smooth panorama change from the current point to the next point of the track fragment
- **Clear Marked Vol Changes** (keys <Shift>+<V>) — cancels volume changes in a marked area
- **Clear Marked Pan Changes** (keys <Shift>+<P>) — cancels panorama changes in a marked area
- **Clear Marked Vol And Pan Changes** (keys <Shift>+<C>) — cancels volume and panorama changes (at the same time) in a marked area

- **Fade Out Marked** (the <O> key) — fades out (smoothly reduces the volume level) within a marked area
- **Fade In Marked** (the <I> key) — fades in (raises the volume level smoothly) within a marked area
- **Fade Curve Setup** (keys <Shift>+<F>) — allows you to choose the fade curve shape and step (Fig. 3.16)

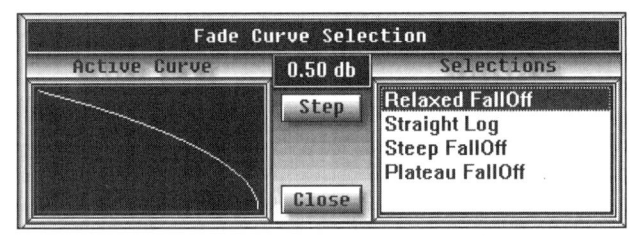

Fig. 3.16. The **Fade Curve Selection** dialog box

Besides what is listed above, the SAWPro program offers you the opportunity to relocate your favorite settings (curves) to other places on this or another track. This means that the volume or pan changes you made can be easily copied and moved (see the "*SAWPro Mixing and Mastering*" section).

The *NEXT* Button. Moving the Cursor along Certain Points in the Track

The upper button, **NEXT**, is designed with two arrows on purpose. Pressing this button moves the cursor along the volume or pan change positions on the track in either direction. If you look closely, you will notice small notches on this button, marking the middle. Clicking to the right or left of the middle causes the cursor to move to the next position in the corresponding direction.

The *Effects Patch Builder* Window

The **Effects Patch Builder** window for including virtual sound effects is called using the **FX** button (Fig. 3.13).

The importance of virtual effects for sound processing cannot be overestimated. The user can produce original sounds using various combinations of them.

Processing sound using virtual sound effects is such a large subject that we would need an entire book to even begin to tackle it correctly. Moreover, we dare say that applying these effects is more art than technology.

The first program implementations of *plug-in* effect modules were made mostly for sound editors that supported the VST and DirectX standards (such as WaveLab). The SAW program in its first releases could not work with plug-ins of these standards. In this regard, one

Chapter 3: The SAWPro Program: Live Recording in a Virtual Studio

should realize that interaction between SAWPro and sound plug-ins may be somewhat puzzling. To understand the reasons for this, let's go off on a historical tangent.

Early SAW generations were only compatible with their own Saw Native standard plug-ins. No DirectX or VST program modules produced by other vendors could be patched into SAW. For that reason, the number of applied sound effects was very limited.

Later, in 1998, more powerful processors with enough resources to handle sound in real time emerged on the market. Hardware performance and functionality were also extended, which allowed various manufacturers to develop and produce plug-in sound effects program modules intensively.

At the height of this blossoming of the plug-in market, the creators of SAWPro developed special connecting modules of the linker type that enabled SAWPro to work with DirectX and VST sound effects. These modules are **DirectX Linker** and **VST Linker**.

The appearance of these linkers was almost certainly what caused SAWPro's breakthrough to the top of the music software market: this program became a first-rate virtual studio with an unusually wide capacity for applying sound effects.

Now, the **DirectX Linker** and **VST Linker** modules are an integral part of the SAWPro program, in which you can use sound effects of the two standards, DirectX and VST, *at the same time*. Only three music editors: SAWPro, WaveLab, and Cubase VST offer this opportunity.

We won't pretend that in this book we will be able to give a detailed report on how the SAWPro program processes sound using effects.

However, we will stop at the most essential points of this subject twice: in this section, and in "*Processing Sound in SAWPro*".

In the section dedicated to processing sound, we will learn the existing standards in more detail, give the reader general recommendations on dealing with sound effects, and describe the effects that, from our point of view, are worth particular notice when working with SAWPro.

For a while, we will stick to the aspects that are important, from our perspective, for understanding the text that follows.

The latest SAWPro versions work with the following kinds of sound effects:

- Seven plug-in effects of SAWPro's *own internal standard*, Saw Native, from IQS (Innovative Quality Software)
- Plug-in program modules that are patched into the SAWPro program *directly*, that is, those that do not require linker modules, since they support the Saw Native standard (for example, DSP/FX Virtual Pack)
- Plug-ins that are patched using the **DirectX Linker** or **VST Linker** modules

The difference in speed between plug-ins that are patched directly and those using a linker is considerable. SAWPro is definitely much more productive when working with directly joined plug-ins. The difference is especially noticeable when you employ a number of effects simultaneously.

However, one should not reject plug-ins that need linkers, since the application of such plug-ins significantly extends your capabilities.

WARNING

Here, without going any deeper, we wish to warn our readers about the fact that plug-in sound effects may generally behave capriciously. Plugins of the DirectX standard best agree with SAWPro, while VST modules may often work incorrectly or cause the program to give an error.

There is a regularly updated list of SAWPro-compatible VST plug-ins at **http://www.iqsoft.com**.

Patching Sound Effects Directly

Let's look at the mechanism for including sound effects. We'll start with *direct patching* (i.e., with no connecting modules involved) via the **Effect Patch Builder** window, which appears on the screen when you click the **FX** button (Fig. 3.18).

NOTE Sound effects are applied to the track for which you have pressed the **FX** button. After an effect is attached, this button looks different: a vertical bar crosses it (Fig. 3.17).

Fig. 3.17. The appearance of the **FX** button when effects have been patched

The **Effect Patch Builder** window, in turn, includes two interrelated lists: **Effects Choices** and **Current Patch** (Fig. 3.18).

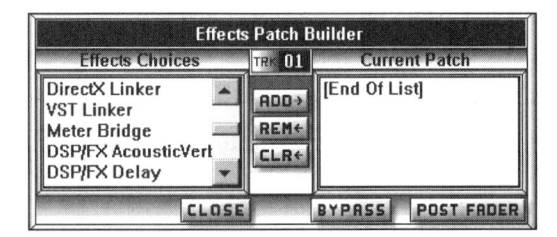

Fig. 3.18. The **Effect Patch Builder** window (called by the **FX** button on a track)

Chapter 3: The SAWPro Program: Live Recording in a Virtual Studio

The buttons between the two lists allow you to move the selected effects:
- **ADD** (adds an effect)
- **REM** (removes a previously selected effect)
- **CLR** (removes ALL previously selected effects)

The **BYPASS** button is used for listening to the track without the effect, without removing the effect or its settings.

NOTE When you press the **BYPASS** button and have effects attached, the vertical bar over the **FX** button breaks (Fig. 3.19).

Fig. 3.19. A view of the **FX** button with attached effects in the **BYPASS** mode

TIP The BYPASS function, in particular, helps you save computer resources. We suggest that you bypass effects as much as you can when making recordings, so as not to slow down the CPU (processor).

The **POST FADER** button causes the effect to be processed after processing volume and pan changes.

There are two ways of going through the procedure of processing an audio signal.

- The audio signal from a track first undergoes effect processing, and then volume and pan adjusting
- The audio signal first has the volume and pan adjusted, and only after that are the effects applied (when the **POST FADER** button is pressed)

Sometimes the signal's processing sequence is essential.

When using a reverber or a *noise gate*, it's recommended that effects be applied to the signal before adjusting the volume.

When working with the **Meter Bridge**, *always* use the second scenario — i.e., press the **POST FADER** button. Otherwise, you won't be able to see the changes you make reflected on the screen.

Without going into the **Meter Bridge**'s details, we'll just mention that it should be attached through **POST FADER** for implementation reasons. That is, the **Meter Bridge** is realized as a plug-in module, just like effects, although it is *not* an effect. This was done to allow for faster functioning and convenience in programming.

We should say that plugging in meters as effects is a practice employed by various plug-in makers. Examples are the oscilloscope and the spectrum analyzer.

To connect a plug-in, do the following:

1. Select an effect from the **Effects Choices** list by clicking it.
2. Click the **ADD** button. This will move the selected effect to the **Current Patch** list on the right side.

Patching Sound Effects via Connecting Modules

The **Effects Choices** list contains linker connecting modules as well as plug-ins. This can be clearly seen in Fig. 3.18.

If, having attached a linker, you double-click its name in the **Current Patch** list, a **Patch Builder** window — for either DirectX or VST effects — will open.

As an example, we patched the **DirectX Linker** module to the **Effects Patch Builder** window (Fig. 3.20). A new **DirectX Patch Builder** window (for applying DirectX sound effects) thus opens.

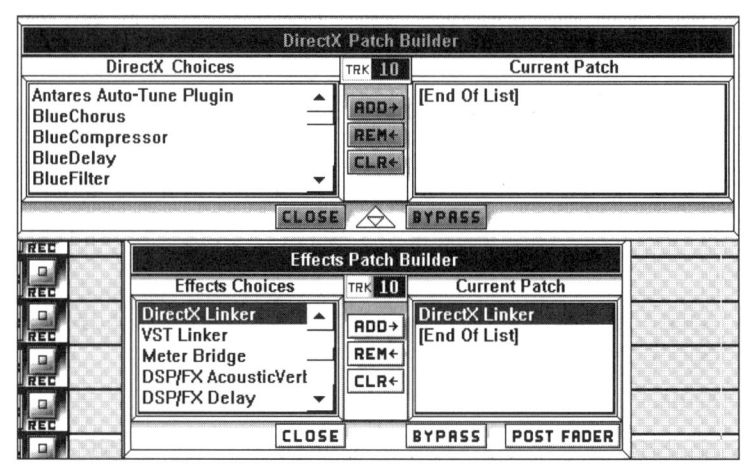

Fig. 3.20. The **DirectX Patch Builder** window called from **Effects Patch Builder**

The composition of this new window entirely mirrors that of the previous one (**Effects Patch Builder**). It too contains two interrelated parts: **DirectX Choices** (choose from all available effects) and **Current Patch** (active effects).

Patching Plug-ins via Linker Connecting Modules

To attach plug-ins using connecting modules, the following sequence of operations should be performed:

1. Choose a module from the **Effects Choices** window by clicking it.

Chapter 3: The SAWPro Program: Live Recording in a Virtual Studio

2. Press the **ADD** button, which will cause the chosen linker to appear in the **Current Patch** list.
3. Double-click the module's name in the **Current Patch** list.
4. Choose the required plug-in in the new window.
5. Press the **ADD** button and watch the name of the selected effect appear in the **Current Patch** list.
6. Double-click on the effect's name in the **Current Patch** list to call this effect's control window.

You can find more information about managing sound effects in the "*Processing Sound in SAWPro*" section.

The *REC* Button

The **REC** button displays a virtual tape recorder that consists of two panels (Fig. 3.21).

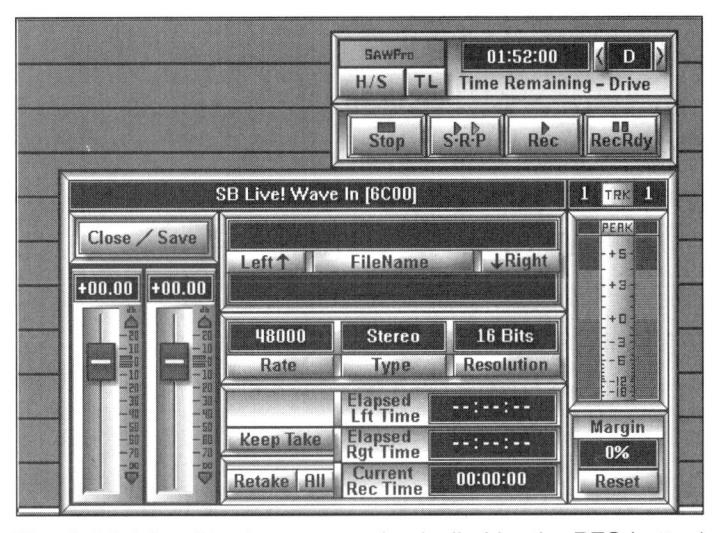

Fig. 3.21. The virtual tape recorder (called by the **REC** button)

The **Record Remote Transport** panel, the smallest of the two, is used for controlling the recording.

The other, **Record Panel**, sets and controls the recording level.

These two panels can be moved about the screen independently.

The panels, as you have seen, are opened simultaneously (using the **REC** button on a track), and close together as well (by pressing the **Close/Save** button).

Maintaining the virtual tape recorder is discussed in detail in the "*Description of the Virtual Tape Recorder*" and "*Recording a Live Performance*" sections.

Marking off a Clip Fragment in the *MultiTrack View* Window

A *clip*, also referred to in SAWPro as a *MultiTrack Entry (Entry)*, is an audio file fragment placed on a track.

> **NOTE** We will use the general term *clip* later when describing similar program interface elements.

The easiest way of marking off an area of a clip is to drag the mouse while holding the left button along the bottom of the **Time Line** display in the direction that the cursor moves during playback.

Another way of marking off an area is as follows.

1. Position the cursor at the beginning of a fragment.
2. Press <B> on the keyboard (for 'Begin').
3. Position the cursor at the end of a fragment.
4. Press <E> on the keyboard (for 'End').

Clearing a Selected Clip Fragment

To clear (unselect) a selected clip area, click the right mouse button any place within the **Time Line** display in the bottom of the screen, or press the <C> key.

Changing Fragment Boundaries

The boundaries of a selected fragment can be moved using the mouse.

- Clicking *inside* a the selected area *reduces* its size, i.e., the boundaries move towards the center
- Clicking *outside* a selected area *expands* its size, and the boundaries move outward

Listening to a Selected Fragment

To listen to a certain marked-off fragment in either of two modes, click on the appropriate button on the **Remote Transport** panel (see Fig. 3.30).

- **PlayMark** lets you hear the fragment ONCE
- **PlayLoop** plays back the fragment REPEATEDLY

> **NOTE** To play back a marked-off fragment in a loop, you can also use the <Ctrl> + right mouse button click combination.

Chapter 3: The SAWPro Program: Live Recording in a Virtual Studio   47

Importing Sound Files to SAWPro

There is a set of operations under the general name of **Open SoundFile** that is provided for using pre-prepared sound files in multitrack (such as previously recorded files or files copied from a CD-ROM).

Importing sound files to the SAWPro program is done using the **File** menu (Fig. 3.22).

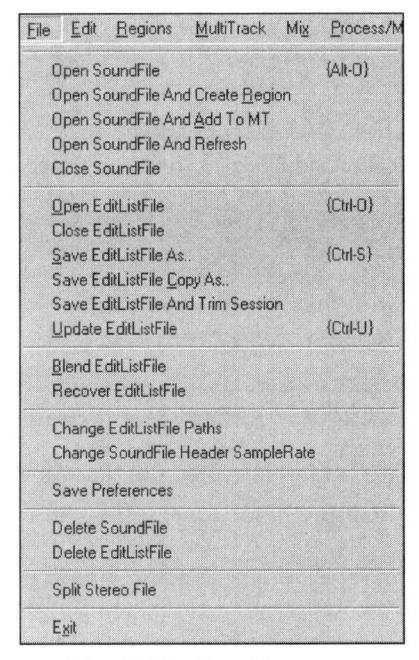

Fig. 3.22. The **File** menu

The *Open SoundFile* Window

The **Open SoundFile** command opens an audio file *for playback*.

This requires that you do the following:

1. Click the **Open SoundFile** menu item.
2. In the **Open SoundFile** dialog, choose the necessary file (Fig. 3.23).
3. Click **Open**.

This will produce the **SoundFile View** window on the screen.

Fig. 3.24 depicts a stereo sound file.

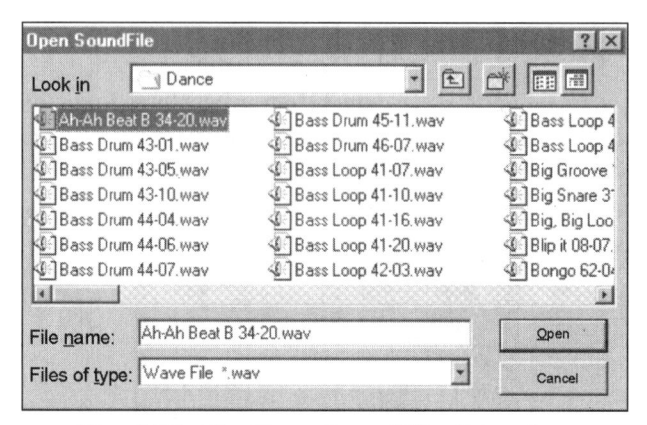

Fig. 3.23. The **Open SoundFile** dialog box

Fig. 3.24. The **SoundFile View** window

In the **SoundFile View** window, you can either listen to the whole file or just a fragment of it.

❐ There are three ways to switch the mode for listening to a *whole* file on (or off):
- Right-click on the waveform field
- Press the spacebar on the keyboard
- Click the **PLAY** button on the **Remote Transport** panel

❐ To listen to a file *fragment*, mark it and start playback.

> **NOTE** To mark off an area, drag the mouse along the **Time Line** display in the bottom of the **SoundFile View** window in the direction that the *tracking cursor* moves during playback. Areas are marked off in the **SoundFile View** window in the same way as in the **MultiTrack View** window.

In addition, we'd like to note that in the **SoundFile View** window, the program provides not only for playing an audio file, but also for creating *regions* of various length.

Creating a Region in SAWPro

A *region* is a fundamental notion in the SAWPro program. A special section, "*The Regions View Window*", will be dedicated to regions. Here, as an introduction, we will define a region as a *file area* labeled by the program in a certain way that may be used in various actions without destroying the original file. When creating a region, a file area is marked off so that it may be employed later many times in different places of one or more tracks. Speaking allegorically, a region is a photo of a sound file fragment.

SAWPro is capable of managing a great number of regions at once.

One Way to Create a Region

1. Mark off an area in the **SoundFile View** window.
2. Position the cursor on the selected area by clicking.
3. While holding the <Shift> key, click on the fragment. This will cause a different multitrack cursor to appear on the screen, now in the form of a dashed rectangle (which is the same size as the region being moved) and an arrow with a white brick (Fig. 3.25).

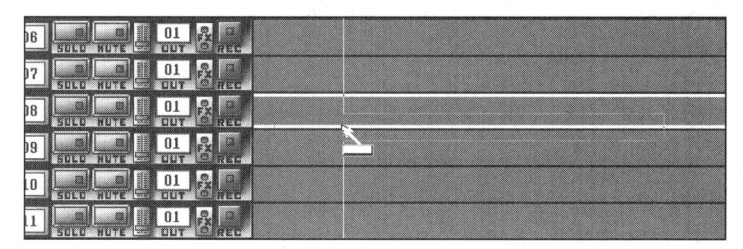

Fig. 3.25. Copying a region

4. Place the fragment anywhere on the multitrack (on any part of any of the 32 tracks) and lock its position by clicking again.

> **NOTE** When you place a region on the multitrack, keep in mind that regions must not overlap one another on the same track.

The "*Regions View Window*" section provides more information on regions.

Opening a Sound File and Creating a Region

The **Open SoundFile And Create Region** command opens an audio file and automatically creates a region of the same length.

Opening a Sound File, Creating a Region, and Adding It to the Multitrack

Performing the **Open SoundFile And Add to MT** command allows you to open a file, create a region of equal length, and immediately place this region onto the multitrack.

The sequence of operations in this case is as follows:
1. Before you begin, position the cursor where you want the new region to begin.
2. Open the **File** menu.
3. Click the **Open SoundFile And Add to MT** menu item.
4. In the **Open SoundFile** dialog box that appears (see Fig. 3.23), press **Open**.

Opening a Sound File and Refreshing the Waveform

The **Open SoundFile And Refresh** command opens an audio file and modifies its waveform.

When might you need this?

Imagine that you created a file using the SAWPro program, and then processed your file with some other program (for instance, SoundForge, WaveLab, or CoolEdit) without *renaming* the file.

WARNING Don't change the sound file's name when editing the file using other programs, because if you do, SAWPro won't be able to recognize it afterwards.

And naturally, when the sound of a file is changed, the waveform is changed, too.

Each sound editor creates its own waveform files. In SAWPro, for example, these files have the WPD extension.

Therefore, since the processing was done in another program, the waveform of the modified file is there too.

So if you open your file again in SAWPro after working with another program, the file's graphical representation on the screen (the waveform) will remain the same as before, in spite of the new sound.

This difference between the sound and its image causes discomfort, and may lead you to make editing errors. **Open SoundFile And Refresh** is used to eliminate this disharmony.

Closing a Sound File

The user can close a sound file with the **Close SoundFile** command.

However, the empty **SoundFile View** display remains visible (Fig. 3.26). Just close it.

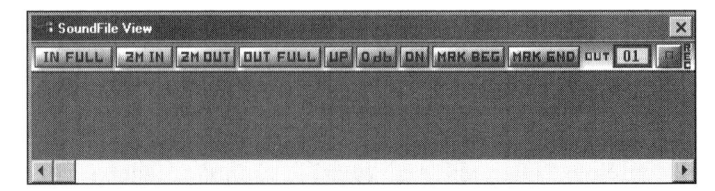

Fig. 3.26. The **SoundFile View** window after the sound file is closed

Some Suggestions on Importing Sound Files

In conclusion, we'd like to give you a few useful recommendations on maintaining external sound files imported to SAWPro.

One should copy sound files from a CD-ROM to the hard drive. If you have a file on a CD-ROM only and don't have it on your hard drive, this may cause a program fault when importing. It's handy to keep files in the Audio folder created in the SAWPro folder during setup.

If you plan to modify (edit) a file, you should make the file available for editing after copying it. To do this, you'll need to remove the Read Only file attribute:

1. Open the **File** menu.
2. Execute the **Open SoundFile** command.
3. Right-click anywhere in the empty space of the window that appears.
4. Choose **Properties** from the context menu.
5. In the new dialog box, clear the **Read-only** checkbox of the **Attributes** group (pointed to with an arrow in Fig. 3.27).

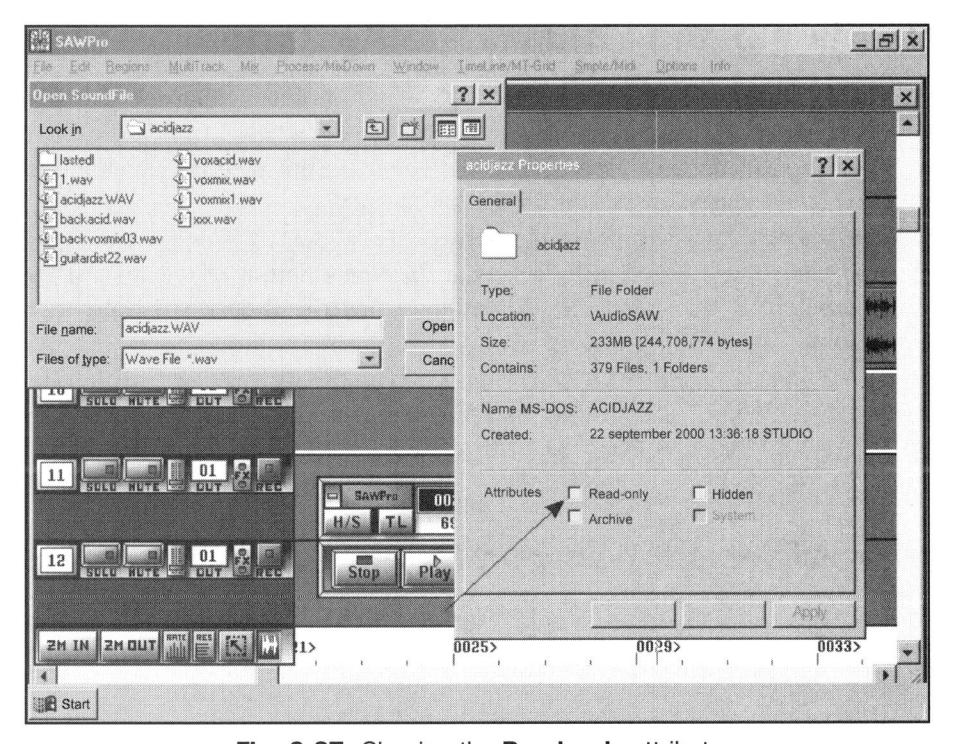

Fig. 3.27. Clearing the **Read-only** attribute

Only files with the WAV extension are recommended for import to SAWPro.

NOTE The SAWPro program can accept files with other extensions as well (for example, MP3), but only after attaching special plug-ins. However, we advise you not to do this to avoid a loss in sound quality.

If you still need to import a file with a different format, convert it using a sound editor, and import the resulting WAV file to SAWPro.

We suggest that you use a sample rate of at least 44.1 kHz (standard CD quality), or more, if your sound card allows it. The higher the sample rate, the better the sound. SAWPro can, however, work with a wide range of sample rates.

Imported files should have at least 16 bits per sample (according to current AUDIO CD quality level).

NOTE We will discuss notions of sampling and the number of bits per sample in detail in the "*Recording Live Performances*" section.

Both mono and stereo audio files may be imported.

Description of the Virtual Tape Recorder

The virtual tape recorder is activated by the **REC** button and contains two panels (see Fig. 3.21).

Before proceeding to a detailed report about the upper (in this picture) panel, let us draw your attention to the **FileName** button on the lower panel.

The reason for this is that before recording anything in SAWPro, the sound file to be created should be named first. This is what the **FileName** button of the **Record Panel** is for. The parameters of the sound file are defined using the **Rate** (for sample rate) and **Resolution** (for bits per sample) buttons.

If you try to record a nameless file, you will see a warning with an exclamation point in a yellow triangle. Then you'll have to press **OK** to confirm that you are agree to the conditions, and assign the file a name using the **FileName** button. The file name *must* be *ASCII*[1] only, since SAWPro does not support local national alphabets.

The *Record Remote Transport* Panel

The smaller part of the virtual tape recorder is the **Record Remote Transport** panel (a tape deck). It controls the two recording modes: *regular* (the **Rec** button) and *Simultaneous Record and Play* (the **S-R-P** button).

---

[1] The American Standard Code for Information Interchange.

Chapter 3: The SAWPro Program: Live Recording in a Virtual Studio 53

Let's examine the panel buttons more closely (Fig. 3.28).

Fig. 3.28. The **Record Remote Transport** panel of the virtual tape recorder

Four buttons in the lower row on this panel carry out recording functions. Some of these are functional duplicates of a normal tape recorder's buttons.

- **Stop** — stops recording
- **Rec** — starts recording
- **RecRdy** — pauses the recording
- **S-R-P** — allows you to listen to other tracks while recording a new one (when you press the **Rec** button). The next section provides more details about this mode.

> **NOTE** You can use the **Rec** and **RecRdy** buttons or the <Enter> key to start and stop recording.

At the top of the **Record Remote Transport**, there is a *clock* that indicates the remaining recording time, taking into account the amount of free space on the logical drive denoted next to the clock. The **H/S** and **TL** buttons are used for hiding the SAWPro window.

We won't stop here for long in order not to confuse beginners. More information on this topic can be obtained in the program's description.

Preparing for Recording

Please note that before recording, all necessary devices should be connected to the computer. If you play the synthesizer, its output signal should be fed to the line input of the sound card. If you plan to record a voice or an acoustic instrument via a microphone, plug it into the microphone input.

To get a better quality recording, we advise you to put an autonomous analog mixer between the microphone's output and the sound card's line input.

The *Full Duplex* Mode. The *S-R-P* Button

Full Duplex is the mode of simultaneous recording and playback.

All modern sound cards support the **Full Duplex** mode. Moreover, this mode is extremely important for musicians, since it allows for recording in sync with existing audio material.

The **Full Duplex** mode is enabled by the **S-R-P** button of the **Record Remote Transport** tape recorder panel.

When recording in this mode, all tracks with their **SOLO** buttons pressed (or their **MUTE** buttons released) will play.

Note that in **Full Duplex** mode, tracks will be played back with applied virtual effects if these effects are attached through **Effect Patch Builder**. This consumes a considerable amount of computer resources during recording, which in turn may affect the recording quality. It is therefore strongly recommended that you unburden the computer when using this mode, namely:

- When recording, exclude tracks whose playback is not necessary (by pressing the **MUTE** button on each of those)
- During the recording, limit playback with effects as much as possible (using the **BYPASS** button on each track that you can)

The suggestions given above may be ignored only if your computer is very powerful.

Setting the Recording Level

Before you start recording in **Full Duplex** mode, you will have to set the recording level. As a rule, this is adjusted beforehand (before starting recording), when the level meter is activated, i.e., when the **RecRdy** button is pressed.

Please remember that you should try your best to adjust the recording level so that the average meter indications are as high as possible, but only individual high peaks should reach the red area.

For more details on setting the recording level, see the "*Connecting to the Sound Card; Adjusting the Recording Level*" section.

Selecting the Volume Control Regulator

If you control the record volume level using the SAWPro virtual volume control, take care, because using it incorrectly may affect the sound's quality.

It is best to control the recording level from the sound card's mixer.

Thus, the SAWPro virtual recording level control should be set to zero (the default) or **−1.0 dB**.

For more details on this, see the "*Connecting to the Sound Card; Adjusting the Recording Level*" section.

The *Full Duplex* Mode Recording

There are two recording modes in the SAWPro program.

- Regular recording (without playing back any track). This mode is enabled by the **Rec** button on the **Record Remote Transport** panel.

❏ **Full Duplex** recording (with simultaneous playback of one or more tracks). This is done by pressing **S-R-P** and then **Rec**.

Normally, no trouble occurs when using the first mode, so we'll focus on the sequence of operations when recording in **Full Duplex**.

This mode can only be applied after producing a recording (that is, when there is some audio information on the multitrack).

Let's look at the following example. Suppose you have recorded an instrumental part fragment that consists of a song's introduction and one couplet on track **01**. Now a vocal part that you will record onto track **02** has to be added to the composition.

Preparatory Steps

1. Call the virtual tape recorder for track 02 (press the **Rec** button on this track).
2. Name the new file. (For more details about file names, see the "*Preparing for Recording*" section.)
3. Position the cursor on the beginning of the multitrack (press the <Home> key).
4. Click on the S-R-P button. While the cursor is sliding forward, track 01's instrumental part will play.
5. During the entrance, the singer tries out his or her voice, and the recording level is adjusted.
6. Before the couplet begins, click on the **Rec** button on track 02.

NOTE Data is written to the hard drive *from the moment you press the* **Rec** *button* (and not earlier).

If you want to determine the optimal recording level for a *complete* voice part, trace it during the recording to the very end. To do this, just run through the whole part while keeping the **S-R-P** button pressed. (Don't press the **Rec** button of **Record Remote Transport** during this rehearsal in order to avoid recording.)

Two typical recording algorithms will be introduced below. The first one is aimed at sequentially recording a number of musical parts. The second algorithm is for recording a moderate-size fragment on a marked-off area of a track.

These algorithms have been formulated for readers who think that they have already gained enough information to start experimenting.

You can read more about recording methods in the "*Recording a Live Performance*" section.

Algorithm 1. Recording Several Musical Parts

Recording the first part:
1. Open the **MultiTrack View** window.
2. Press the **Rec** button on a selected track to activate the virtual tape recorder.
3. Press the **FileName** button, assign a file name in the **Record Sound File** window that appears, and **Save** the file.
4. Press the **RecRdy** button and adjust the recording's volume level in the same way as with a normal tape recorder.

> **NOTE** The level may be adjusted using the virtual control on the **Record Panel** or, better yet, with the sound card mixer's control.

5. Press **Rec** on the virtual tape recorder panel.
6. Perform the musical part.
7. Stop the tape recorder by pressing the **Stop** button.
8. Close the tape recorder panels for this track with the **Close/Save** button.

> **NOTE** The tape recorder panels cannot be closed if the **RecRdy** button is pressed instead of **Stop**.

9. Record the second part. Call the virtual tape recorder panels for another track by pressing **Rec** on that track.
10. Name the new file (see point 3).
11. Put the multitrack cursor at the beginning of the recording.
12. Click on **RecRdy**.
13. Adjust the recording level (see point 4).
14. Start recording by pressing first the **S-R-P** button, and then the **Rec** button.
15. Perform the second part. Press the **Stop** button.
16. Press **Close/Save** to close the tape recorder panel on this track.

To record additional parts, repeat the sequence of operations described in points 9 to 16. You can record as many tracks as you need like this.

> **TIP** SAWPro possesses capabilities that make a musician's work notably easier. For example, if you mark off a segment of the first part on a track and order the program to play back only this segment, you can rehearse a fragment of another part. Then you can do a number of takes for the second part and choose the best one. If you are not satisfied with the result, you can clip recorded takes and combine them in to a new one that has no faults.

The *Record Panel* (the Second Part of the Virtual Tape Recorder)

The virtual tape recorder **Record Panel** (Fig. 3.29) is used for a number of operations.

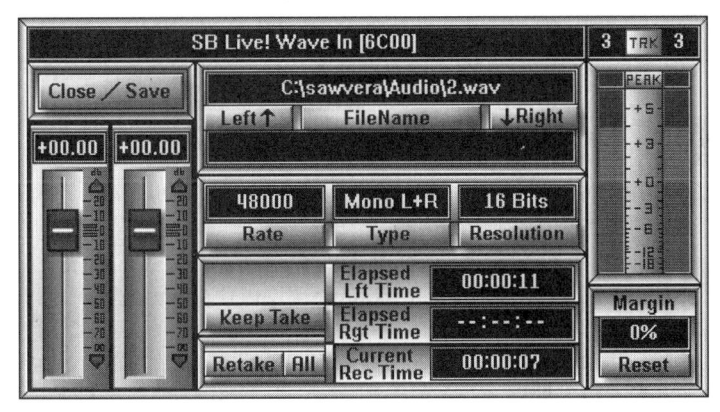

Fig. 3.29. The virtual tape recorder **Record Panel**

First of all, as we mentioned, this panel contains the **FileName** button that calls the **Record SoundFile** window.

Secondly, the other buttons of this panel allow for the following operations with versions of recorded fragments:

- **Keep Take** saves the recorded fragment in the region list and in the sound file, and removes this region from the track
- **Retake** removes the last recorded fragment
- **All** removes all recorded fragments

WARNING Be careful when pressing this button!

Thirdly, two volume control sliders for the left and right channels are situated on this panel next to the digital readouts. They can be manipulated using the mouse:

- For a rough adjustment of the volume level, move the slider up and down
- To fine-tune the volume (by increments of 0.25 dB), click on the triangles (up and down) at the ends of the scale

For mono sound, the levels of the right and left channels will be the same.

Separate adjustment of the recording levels in the channels is only possible in the *Multi Channel Record mode*, which is enabled by a command of the same name in the **MultiTrack** menu. This mode is effective when working with multiple sound cards.

In the right side of the panel (under the number of the track for which the virtual tape recorder has been called), there is a recording volume meter that remembers the highest (peak) level.

The last highest value can be reset by the **Reset** button.

The *Remote Transport* Window

The SAWPro program provides a convenient recording method that is especially valuable for those musicians working alone.

This method allows you to start playback in advance (before recording begins), and only later, when the cursor reaches a selected fragment on the recording track, the program will start recording automatically. When the cursor reaches the end of the marked-off area, the recording terminates. This is fully described in "*Algorithm 2*" after we give an account of the **Remote Transport** window, which controls the playback process (Fig. 3.30).

The **Remote Transport** window is activated through the **Window** menu.

This panel is capable of playing back a marked file fragment in different modes.

The buttons on the lower row are responsible for:

❐ **Stop** — stopping playback at any time

❐ **Play** — starting playback from the cursor position

❐ **Play Mark** — playing back the selected fragment once

❐ **Play Loop** — playing back the selected fragment repeatedly, until **Stop** is pressed

❐ **Auto** (Auto-rewind) — re-positioning the cursor (after it stops) back to the last starting point

❐ The slider — moving the cursor quickly in either direction

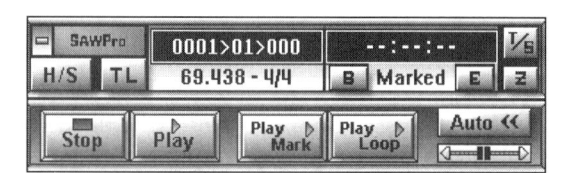

Fig. 3.30. The **Remote Transport** panel

Among the buttons in the upper row, only three are used for moving the cursor and marking off areas:

❐ **Z** — returns the cursor to the multitrack beginning (to the zero position)

Chapter 3: The SAWPro Program: Live Recording in a Virtual Studio

☐ **B** and **E** — position the cursor at the beginning and end of the selected area, respectively

> **NOTE** The **T/S** button alters the counter's format. This format depends on the **TimeLine/MT-Grid** menu settings. The left counter in the top precisely reflects the multitrack cursor's coordinates. If you enter a new numerical value in this counter, the cursor will take that position. (For more details, see the "*Snapping to the Musical-Meter and Tempo*" section).

The counter above the **B** and **E** buttons indicates the length of the selected fragment.

Algorithm 2. Recording to a Selected Area

This algorithm is used when, for example, an unsuccessful fragment needs to be overdubbed.

> **NOTE** The special *Punch* mode is described in detail in the "*Punch Mode Recording*" section (in "*Record Manual*").

Points 1 and 2 refer to preliminary operations (as in *Algorithm 1*), and points 3 to 8 refer to recording in the selected area.

1. Call the virtual tape recorder panels on the selected track with the **Rec** button.
2. Click on the **FileName** button, name the file in the **Record SoundFile** dialog that pops up, and **Save** the file.
3. Define the place on the track where the fragment to be recorded will be put. To mark off an area on the track, drag the mouse along the **TimeLine** strip at the bottom of the screen.
4. Position the cursor on the track *before the marked-off area* by clicking on the appropriate place in the track.
5. Press the **S-R-P** button on the tape recorder panel. The cursor starts moving towards the marked-off segment.
6. Start performing the musical part right before the cursor crosses the selected fragment's boundary.

> **NOTE** The recording starts and stops automatically when the cursor crosses the front and back boundaries of the selected fragment, respectively. Therefore, the musician can concentrate on performing without worrying about how not to damage the previously recorded material beyond the marked-off area.

7. Play the musical fragment.
8. Stop playback with the **Stop** button.

Non-Destructive Audio Editing

Editing always implies some changes. These changes can be of two kinds: *reversible* (when one can come back to the original version) or *irreversible*, when no restoration is possible.

SAWPro permits two kinds of sound file editing. These changes, being reversible and irreversible by nature, are called, respectively, *non-destructive* and *destructive*.

We will discuss non-destructive editing in this section.

The essence of this (as you might conclude from the name) is that the original audio material remains unaffected.

A natural question arises: how can anything be changed without disturbing the original?

We'll depict this mechanism with a simple example. If you cut an apple, this changes it irreversibly. In terms of the program, this is a destructive change. However, if you cut a photo of this apple, this change will be non-destructive with regard to the original, since the apple remains in the same condition.

Unlike the example with the apple, where the photo is very different from the original (a fruit), in the virtual world of SAWPro, the original and its image are quite the same. In other words, when editing non-destructively, you can make as many copies of the original as you want and edit those as you wish.

Non-destructive editing is justified not only by the fact that it spares the user (who is thus guaranteed against errors) from undue worry, but also by the fact that it saves a lot of disk space. That is, if users worked with original sound files instead of these file images, they would be short on hard drive space, and there would also be the constant hazard of occasionally losing or damaging audio material.

Non-destructive editing was invented to solve these very problems. It must be mentioned that such an advanced method has surfaced thanks to advanced computer technologies.

When editing non-destructively, the program works not with the files themselves, but with their imprints (or references), which are called regions in SAWPro terms. When dealing with regions, the program "knows" which audio file fragment should be played, and when, where, and how many times it must be repeated.

Let us stress that it is these audio file regions that reside on the multitrack, and not their source files. Thus, the same sound file may be employed many times, i.e., have a theoretically unlimited number of regions.

We should remind you that the technique used for creating a region was discussed earlier in this chapter, in the section dedicated to importing audio files to SAWPro.

Now let's focus on working with regions.

Copying a Region in the *MultiTrack View* Window

Let's look a typical situation: you have an audio file region whose replica you decide to place in another place on the multitrack. How can we create a new region that is exactly the same as the original one, without fault? Or, in computer language, how can we copy it?

Before describing the sequence of operations for copying, we'll take some time to discuss the concept of a clip in more depth.

SAWPro was created as a professional's instrument. This is why all the program's operations are absolutely transparent: the user can watch everything the program does. While this is very important for specialists, information concerning interrelation among clips and regions may seem redundant to an amateur user. However, we feel it is important to explain to the reader the difference between the key notions of region and clip, in order to avoid any confusion or possible misunderstanding due to having the wrong idea.

A region that is placed on the multitrack can be referred to in another program as something different. The SAWPro developers use the notion of **Entry** (*MT Entry*). However, we think that the term clip better expresses this idea.

A *clip* is a region, or a file fragment, that is placed on the multitrack. To rephrase this, a clip is the image of the region on the multitrack.

We wish to note that giving different names to nearly the same instances is not just a word game. The definition of a clip as a region placed on the multitrack is important for understanding the nature of the actions the program performs.

So we'll now go into the most convenient method of copying a region (or creating a new clip).

Double-click on the multitrack clip that you intend to copy (indicated by the arrow pointing upward in Fig. 3.31). At the bottom of the screen, you will see the **SoundFile View** window with the original file. The portion of this file that is in gray is the replicated region (in Fig. 3.31, indicated with the arrow pointing downward).

To copy the selected region to a new place, do the following:

1. Holding the <Shift> key, click the marked region in the **SoundFile View** window. A vertical cursor with a rectangle and an arrow will appear. The rectangle represents the clip that will be placed on the multitrack. This rectangle can be freely moved around the whole multitrack using the mouse (Fig. 3.32).

2. After you choose the place for the clip on the multitrack, fix it by clicking the mouse.

The method described above allows you to position any region formed in the **SoundFile View** window on the multitrack, i.e., to create a new clip.

> **NOTE** Keep in mind that a clip can be set either to any audio track point (without binding to the meter), or exclusively to specific points. This depends on whether the **Snap to Grid** mode (snapping to the bar grid, or musical tempo) is on or off in the **TimeLine/MT-Grid** menu settings. We'll return to this to go into more detail in the "*Snapping to the Musical Meter and Tempo*" section.

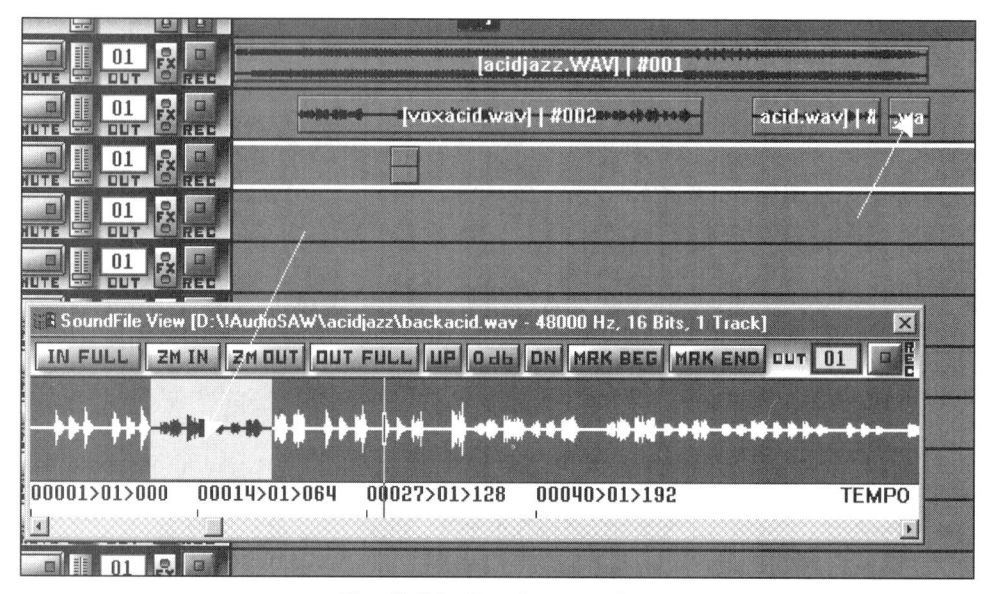

Fig. 3.31. Copying a region

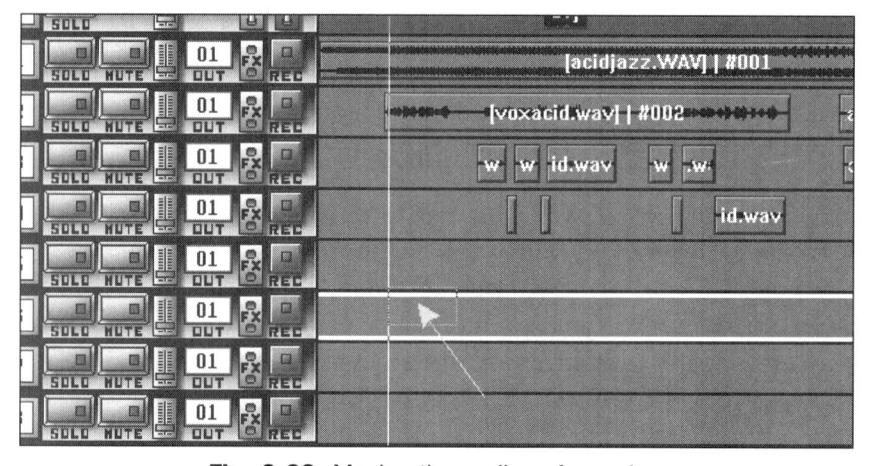

Fig. 3.32. Moving the replica of a region

Clip Handling Techniques; Toolbars

After you place clips on the multitrack, you will very likely need to modify these somehow: to divide, move, or delete them.

All these operations can be done using the **Split Region Tools** and **Cut MT Entry Tools** toolbars.

Chapter 3: The SAWPro Program: Live Recording in a Virtual Studio

There are two ways to activate these toolbars. It's up to you to choose which one you'd like to use.

- Press <Esc> on the keyboard
- Press the left and right mouse buttons at the same time

In either case, you will then see a context menu on the screen (Fig. 3.33).

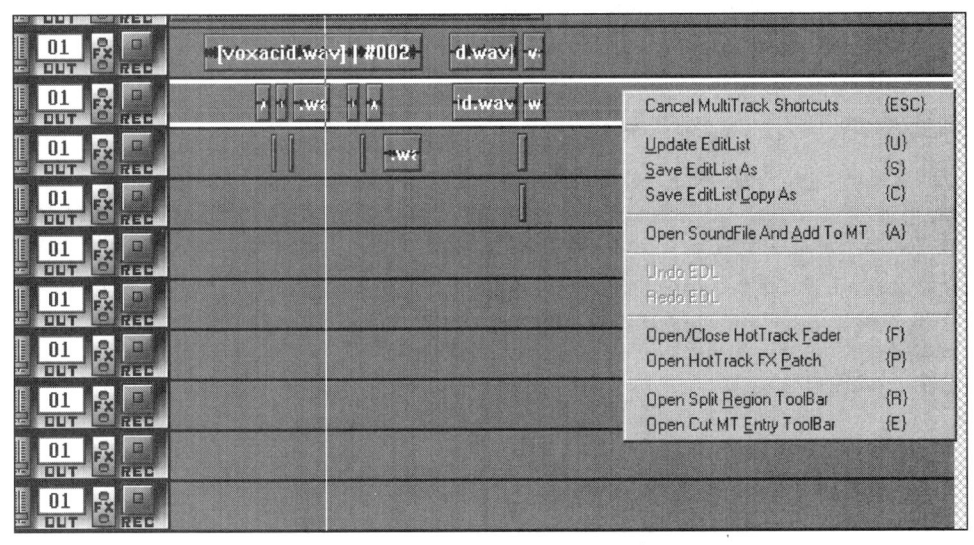

Fig. 3.33. A context menu for calling toolbars

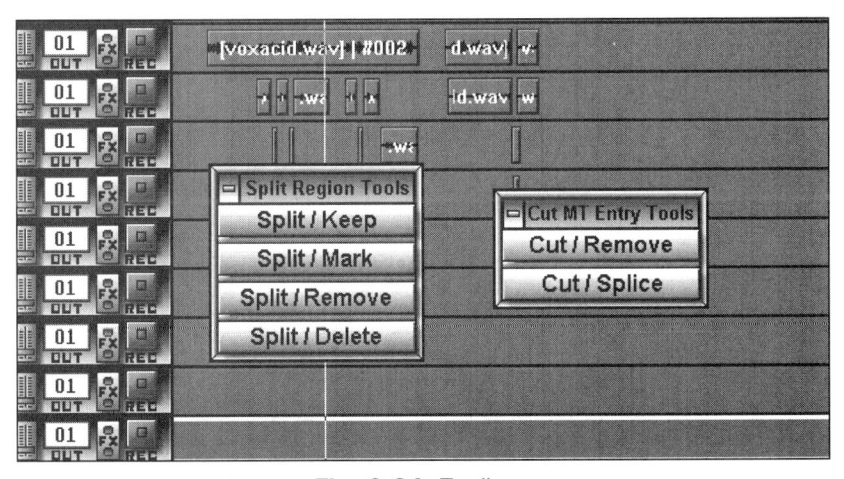

Fig. 3.34. Toolbars

In this menu, we are interested in the last two items, **Open Split Region ToolBar** and **Open Cut MT Entry ToolBar**.

> **NOTE** After the context menu is displayed, you can also execute these two commands using the <R> and <E> hotkeys.

So, after clicking the right context menu item (or pressing the corresponding hotkey), you see the **Split Region Tools** or **Cut MT Entry Tools** toolbar on the screen (Fig. 3.34).

The *Split Region Tools* Toolbar

Let's examine the **Split Region Tools** toolbar's functions first. As you can see from Fig. 3.34, the toolbar contains four buttons: **Split/Keep**, **Split/Mark**, **Split/Remove** (throw out without shifting), and **Split/Delete** (throw out and shift).

Because we will mainly be talking about operations applied to the hot track (the active track, indicated by two white lines), keep in mind that there can only be one hot track on the multitrack, which looks something like Fig. 3.35.

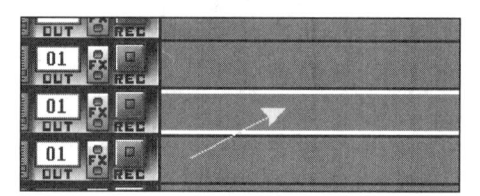

Fig. 3.35. The hot track

Any track can be made "hot" by clicking it once.

Now let's pause for more details on all of the listed operations.

- ❒ **Split/Keep** splits a clip in two at the point where the cursor line is. It also creates and saves the two new regions on the hot track (Fig. 3.36). The **Split/Keep** operation can also be accomplished by pressing the <K> key.

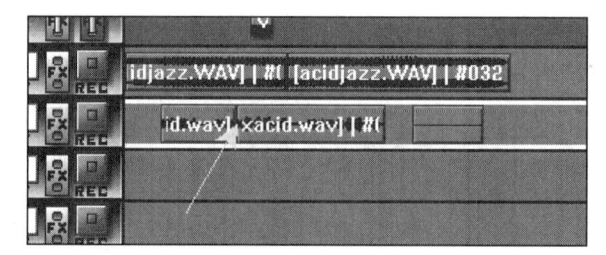

Fig. 3.36. The **Split/Keep** operation

Chapter 3: The SAWPro Program: Live Recording in a Virtual Studio 65

- **Split/Mark** duplicates **Split/Keep**, and also marks the segment *to the left* of the split line. This is only available in the **Select Mode**.
- **Split/Remove** splits the clip and removes the segment that is *to the left* of the split line.
- **Split/Delete** duplicates **Split/Remove**, except that the rest of the track (the area to the right of the split line) is shifted left by the length of the deleted fragment.

> **NOTE** If you execute any of the listed above **Split...** operations while pressing <Ctrl> on the keyboard, this operation will be applied to *all tracks below the hot track*.

To split *all clips* on the tracks situated below the hot track by the cursor line, use the <Ctrl>+<K> key combination.

The *Cut MT Entry Tools* Toolbar

We'll now proceed with inspecting SAWPro's clip-handling capabilities.

Suppose that a fragment of an executed musical part is found to be unsuccessful, and you have to throw out this ill-fated fragment. The **Cut MT Entry Tools** toolbar can assist you in this task.

The toolbar contains these two buttons: **Cut/Remove** and **Cut/Splice** (Fig. 3.37). The operations associated with these buttons can *only* be applied to a selected fragment of a clip.

- **Cut/Remove** (or the <Alt>+<R> key combination) removes the marked-off area of a clip (see Fig. 3.37).

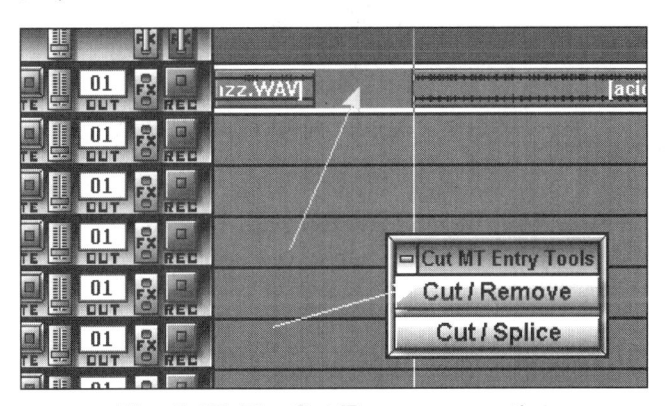

Fig. 3.37. The **Cut/Remove** operation

- **Cut/Splice** (or the <Alt>+<S> key combination) cuts the selected fragment from a clip and splices the ends together (Fig. 3.38).

> **NOTE** This makes all clips on the track to the right of the cursor shift left by the length of the area cut.

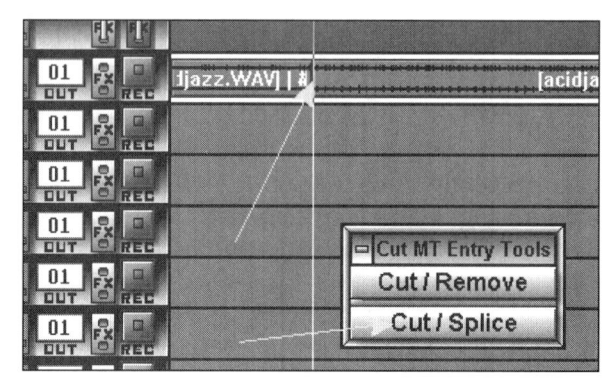

Fig. 3.38. The **Cut/Splice** operation

Select Mode

In SAWPro, various manipulations with clips can be done using the special Select mode.

This mode is enabled in one of two ways:

- With the **Select Mode Toggle** button (the one with the arrow in a dashed square (Fig. 3.39)
- With the <S> key

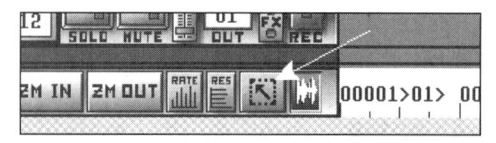

Fig. 3.39. The **Select Mode Toggle** button

When this mode takes effect, the mouse cursor changes its layout to an arrow in a dashed frame (Fig. 3.40). If you move this cursor over to the clip and click, this will *select* the clip. The clip will be also highlighted in blue.

Here is some useful information to note.

- When copying a clip in Select mode, only a new clip is created (and not a new region). This will be important in the future, when we examine the **Regions View** window.
- In Select mode, all the clips in the **MultiTrack View** window can be selected at once by pressing the <A> key.
- To cancel a selection, click the right mouse button or press <C> on the keyboard.
- To select all clips of the track situated to the right of the one selected before, press the <End> key. Pressing the <Ctrl>+<End> combination selects all clips to the right of the selected one and all clips below the hot track.

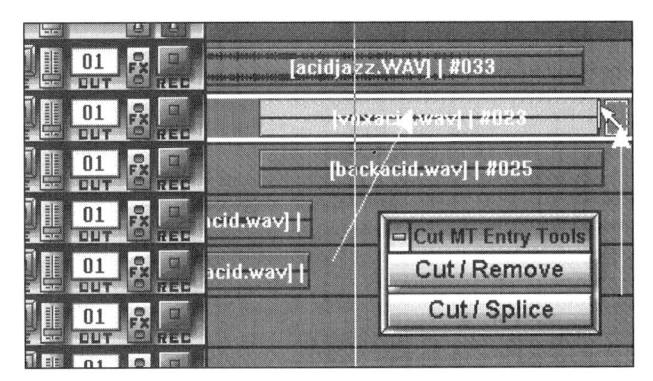

Chapter 3: The SAWPro Program: Live Recording in a Virtual Studio

Fig. 3.40. Selecting clips

Moving a Selected Clip

A selected clip can be moved in different directions.

❐ Horizontally (within a track)
   1. Position the cursor over a selected clip.
   2. Press (and hold) the <Shift> key.
   3. Drag the clip along the track.

❐ Vertically (from track to track)
   1. Position the cursor over a selected clip.
   2. Press (and hold) the <Ctrl> key.
   3. Drag the clip to another track.

❐ Free movement all over the multitrack
   1. Position the cursor on a selected clip.
   2. Press (and hold) the <Shift> and <Ctrl> keys.
   3. Drag the clip to a new place.

> *NOTE* The SAWPro program does not support clip overlapping.

Copying a Selected Clip

Clips are copied much in the same way as they are moved, but with an essential difference towards the end:

1. Position the cursor over a selected clip.
2. Press (and hold) the <Shift> and/or <Ctrl> keys.

3. Press the left mouse button.
4. Drag the clip to the multitrack, *but don't drop it!*
5. Still holding the left mouse button, click the right one.
6. Release the left mouse button and the key(s).

It was not by chance that the program developers came up with such sophisticated algorithms for moving and copying working objects.

Thanks to these operations, the user is reliably protected against relocating a clip unintentionally while editing. This is one of the insurance measures against accidental errors that assure the program's reliability and professional level.

The question might arise as to why this is such a difficult process. What has "live" music got to do with this? The gratitude of SAWPro users should be able to fully answer this question.

Despite the fact that the material introduced here may seem pretty complicated at first glance, these instruments very much ease your work. When recording live music, this is particularly true.

We'll supplement what was said with an example. The select, move, and copy operations are necessary for saving successful takes. In a way, these operations let us catch hold of a lucky creative moment.

After all, music is a fine art, alive in both time and space.

Every musician knows how difficult it sometimes is to repeat a part that has just been well performed with the same quality.

SAWPro helps you not only to save the godsends that happen while recording, but also to edit them after recording is done.

The mechanics described above may be also used in technically complicated cases. For example, say you record a masterly instrumental solo in fragments, and then you want to choose the best ones and link them conveniently. This is when you will need the **Split/Keep** and **Cut/Remove** operations.

You can also simplify things for the musician by recording a sequence (a looped musical fragment) of the necessary length, and copying the created region the appropriate number of times. Let us remind you that all these operations can only be done when editing non-destructively.

If you yourself are both the musician and the soundman, we hope you will appreciate the real value of this approach that never destroys the originals.

A more detailed discussion of live performance recording techniques can be found in the section specially dedicated to it.

Additional Non-Destructive Editing Tricks

Shown in Fig. 3.41 is a typical **MultiTrack View**. As you already know, the rectangles of different length on the multitrack are clips. Some of the rectangles (the smaller ones) represent small sound files.

Chapter 3: The SAWPro Program: Live Recording in a Virtual Studio 69

TIP Remember that small clips (especially adjoining ones) is evidence of the user saving disk space by not "recording silence". It's not at all necessary to cram the disk by recording every musical part from the beginning to the end, including rests and empty portions.

Clips are played back as soon as they are reached by the multitrack cursor (the vertical line), and the program keeps all clips playing in sync.

Pauses between clips are "absolutely" silent. This means that if you place the cursor in this area, you can start a new recording here (Fig. 3.41). Just remember that if there is a "border conflict" when recording, the new clip might "squeeze out" the old one.

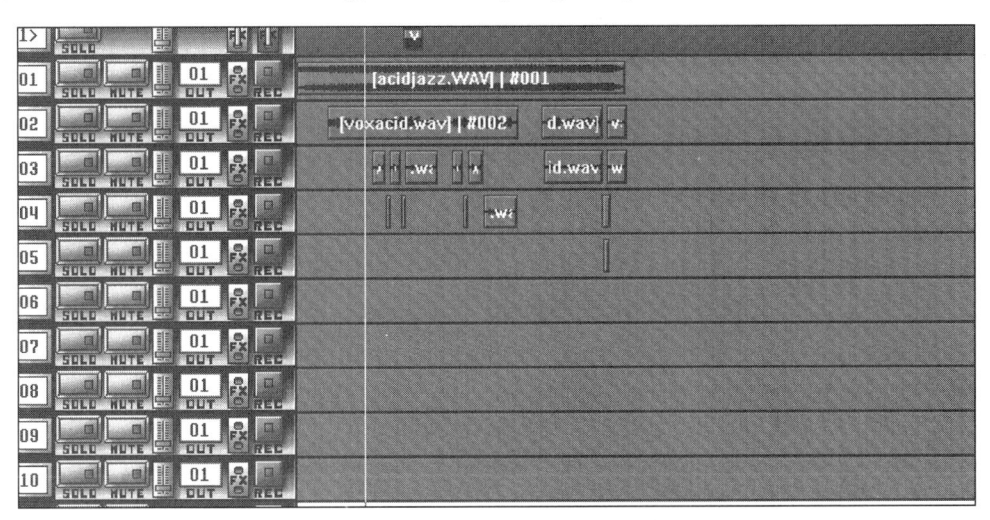

Fig. 3.41. An example of a project

Let's look at one more typical situation. Suppose that the recording starts before the execution of the musical part, and thus irrelevant noise is recorded in the very beginning of the clip. This can be a creak, a sigh, etc. For just such circumstances, SAWPro has a truncating operation in the SAWPro big toolkit (Fig. 3.42).

Fig. 3.42. Truncating a clip

The Truncate Operation

To use truncation, do the following:

1. Move the cursor to the necessary portion of a clip.
2. Press and hold the <Shift> key and the left mouse button.
3. Drag the clip's boundary.

The clip will be changed in length, or truncated to the size you need. By the way, using the same method, you can stretch out (enlarge) a clip within the sound file's physical boundaries. These actions with clips (truncating and stretching) may be done without any fear, since these never alter the sound file itself. What *is* altered is the sound file's "visible" and "audible" components, that is, the clip.

Removing a Clip

To remove a clip from the multitrack:

1. Position the cursor on the clip by clicking the latter.
2. Press the <Delete> key.

There are also more radical operations in the SAWPro program. These remove groups of clips, so one should be very careful when applying such operations. Some of these are executed from the **Regions** menu.

- The **Clear All Regions** command removes all regions from the **Regions View** list and, accordingly, all the clips from the multitrack.

> **NOTE** Apply this operation only if you are confident about removing ALL your results. The project's content will be completely erased and you can begin working from the beginning.

- The **Clear All Unused Regions** command removes all regions that are not placed on the multitrack.

> **TIP** You can use this at the end of your editing work, when a large amount of regions in the **Regions View** list is a hindrance.

Other actions with clips are accessed through the **MultiTrack** menu.

- The **Clear Entries On Current Track** command removes all clips from the hot track only.
- The **Clear Entries On All Tracks** command removes all clips from the multitrack. However, this does not affect the regions in the **Regions View** window; hence, the project can be restored, if necessary.

Moving a Clip

There is also the **Snap Selected to Cursor** operation used for moving a clip to any point on the multitrack (the beginning of the chosen clip snaps to the cursor position). The following steps should be followed:

1. Enable the Select mode in either of two ways:
   - Click on the arrow-in-a-dashed-frame button (Fig. 3.43)
   - Or press the <S> key

   NOTE The mouse cursor's appearance will change to look like the arrow in the frame.

2. *Select* the chosen clip (move the cursor to it and click).
3. Determine the new place for your clip by moving the cursor to a point on the **TimeLine** display (at the bottom of the screen) and clicking.
4. After that, press <BackSpace> on the keyboard to move the clip.

   NOTE To restore the former cursor appearance, click on the **Select mode** button in the bottom of the screen, or press the <S> key.

Fig. 3.43. The **Select mode** button

Creating a Sequence

If you create a musical sequence (i.e., a musical phrase consisting of repeating pieces), you can use this sequence of operations:

1. In the SAWPro program, record an audio file (or import it).
2. Mark off the repeating section (that will form your sequence) in the sound file, using the **SoundFile View** window. A new region is thus created.
3. Name the region, after which it will be registered in the **Regions View** list. A dialog box for naming the region (Fig. 3.44) is called by either:
   - The <Shift>+<N> key combination
   - The **Create New Region** command from the **Regions** menu

   NOTE Be careful when naming a region. Unfortunately, SAWPro allows you to assign identical names to different regions, which can cause confusion.

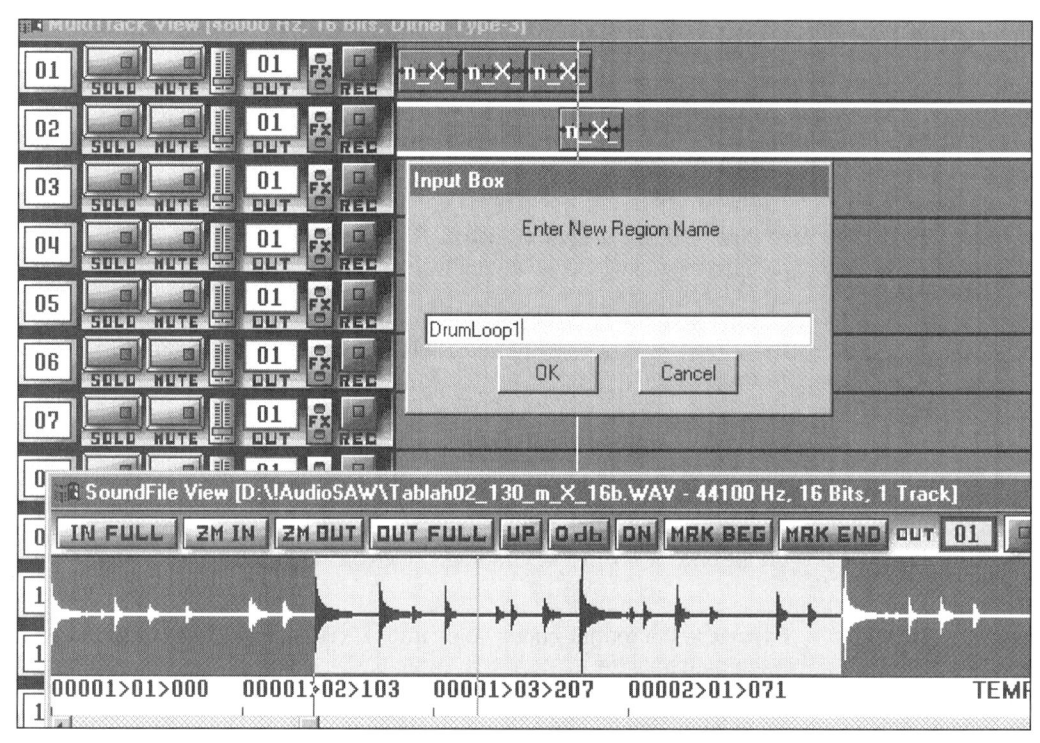

Fig. 3.44. Assigning a name to a region

4. Then, place the created region on the multitrack. You can do this in either of two ways:

   - In the **Regions View** window, select your region from the list and click on the **Add to MT** button
   - Select your region from the same **Regions View** list, and press the <A> key while the **MultiTrack View** window is active

   NOTE Every time you press **Add to MT**, the next clip is added onto the hot track. Each new clip emerges at the cursor position. This way, clips are adjoined to one another, forming a sequence (Fig. 3.45).

A sound file may be recorded not only in the **MultiTrack View** window, but also in **SoundFile View**. To do this, call the virtual tape recorder by pressing the **Rec** button in this window (Fig. 3.46). When recording in the **SoundFile View** window, unlike in the first method, you will have to lay out the recorded fragment on the multitrack yourself (by creating a region).

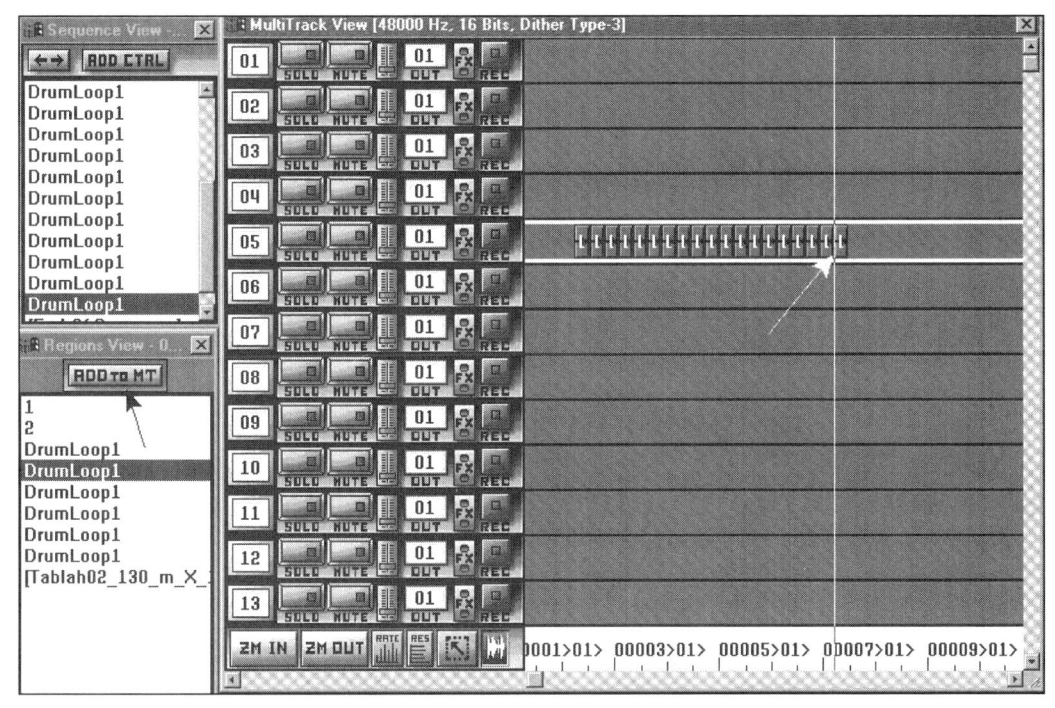

Chapter 3: The SAWPro Program: Live Recording in a Virtual Studio 73

Fig. 3.45. Creating a sequence

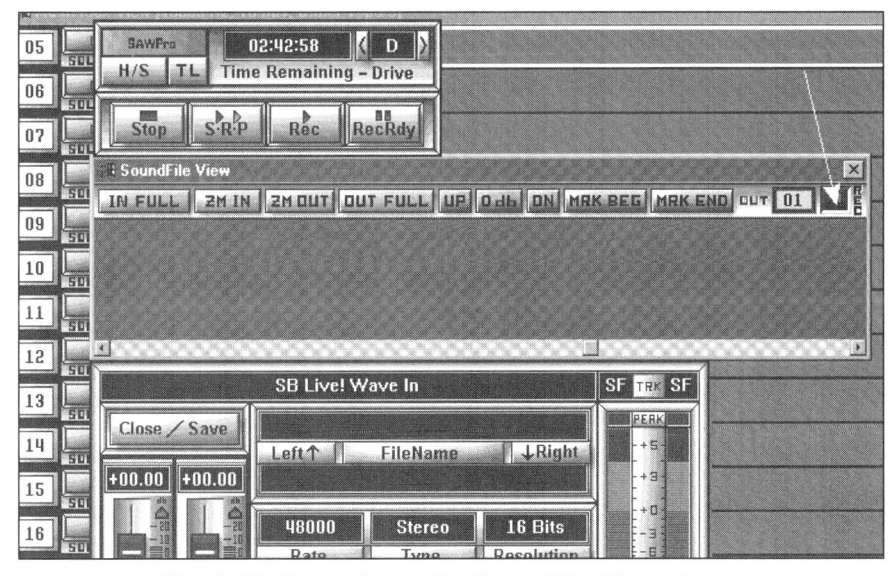

Fig. 3.46. Recording in the **SoundFile View** window

Playback of Recorded Material: A Description of the *Remote Transport* Panel

A special **Remote Transport** panel (see Fig. 3.30) is provided for the convenience of maintaining the recorded audio material. In all honesty, this panel is nothing more than a tape deck.

The **Remote Transport** panel can be controlled in any of these ways with the same comfort: either using the buttons situated on the panel, or by combinations of keys and mouse buttons.

A Brief Description of the *Remote Transport* Panel Buttons

In the "*Description of the Virtual Tape Recorder*" section, we acquainted you with the **Remote Transport** panel (see Fig. 3.30). Now we shall examine this panel in more detail, including the key combinations that you can use as an alternative to the buttons.

- **Stop** (or right-click) — halts playback
- **Play** (or right-click) — starts playback (from the cursor position)
- **Play Mark** (or <Shift> + right mouse button) — plays back a selected fragment
- **Play Loop** (or <Ctrl> + right mouse button) — loops a selected fragment

> **TIP** We recommend that you use the **Play Loop** mode intensively when fashioning virtual effects. The reason for this is that it's very handy to test the sound of an effect (using trial and error) while playing it in a loop.

- **Auto** — toggles the auto-rewind mode on and off. When you press this button, the cursor returns to the beginning of the last area to have been played back automatically
- **Z** — moves the cursor to the beginning of the multitrack
- **B, E** — sets the cursor at the beginning or end of the selected fragment, respectively
- **T/S (Time/Samples)** — alternates time units: **Measure/Beat/Tick** or **Samples**

> **NOTE** The **Time** measurement mode consists of the **Time Mode** and the **Tempo Mode**.
>
> We believe that **Tempo Mode** (**Measure/Beat/Tick** measuring) is much more important for a home studio than **Time Mode**. Therefore the latter is not covered in this book.
>
> **Tempo Mode** is enabled through the option of the same name in the **TimeLine/MT-Grid** menu. We'll come back to the issue of measurement units in the "*Snapping to the Musical Meter and Tempo*" section.

Ways of Working with the *Remote Transport* Panel

In this section, the information offered on the topic of working with the **Remote Transport** panel aims to help musicians to be as independent of the computer as possible when creating their music.

From our perspective, the process of creating things on the computer consists of two subsequent and interrelated stages: allowing oneself to become wrapped up in the creative work, and precise interaction with the program's interface.

When absorbed by his or her artistic work, a musician fully concentrates on creating a musical image. If the right moment is missed, the final product is nearly always soulless, and ends up being just noise and nonsense.

However, the performer is a human being, vulnerable to error. Therefore, the situation where playing back a recorded take reveals technical, stylistic, or compositional imperfections is quite typical.

This is where the technical arrangement of the record (during the musician's dialog with the program interface) is inestimable. Here, all the attention is focused on sound directing and the computer's richest capabilities of treating the musical piece. We can say that there are three basic steps in this stage: the elimination of defects in the recording, assembling the parts, and processing the sound.

The following two modes are recommended, to keep you from getting distracted by trying to deal with computer problems when recording.

Auto-rewind (the **AUTO** button) lets you return to the recording's start point easily, so that you can, for example, overdub a part if you find it not up to par. This action is not complicated, so it rarely gets in the way of the musician's inspiration.

Recurrent playback of a marked fragment (the **Play Loop** button) allows you to practise a part in real-time mode, while other parts are played back. This might actually be very useful for band members as an extra rehearsal method.

Please note that when there is this much automation, the performer can concentrate entirely on the music, and does not have to think about technical details (like where to click the mouse or what key to press).

SAWPro's reliability level (especially when running under Windows NT) guarantees the user that the results of his or her work will be safe, no matter what "dirty tricks" the computer plays (such as freezing, "illegal operations", etc., which can destroy the outcome of long hours of work).

The SAWPro developers have compensated for the low reliability of Microsoft operating systems by designing additional security levels to protect your production. However comical it seems, a user can be repelled by the same complexity of control that is necessary for providing such protection. Let us remind you that every step of yours is reliably fixed by the program on the disk. One of the consequences of this is that you are able to undo the last 99 operations.

We suggest that you *disable virtual effects* when recording, as they cause the program to slow down considerably. The computer's load during playback can be determined using the **Pwr Rsrv** resource reserve indicator (Fig. 3.47). This indicator is on the **Remote Transport** panel and displays the load as a percentage. If the indicator shows zero, it means that the CPU's resources are exhausted, and it cannot give the application the necessary power.

Fig. 3.47. The **Play** mode, 95% resource reserve

Continuing now with the advantages of the program, know that even if the computer is overloaded, nothing like the program crashing or the computer freezing should happen. SAWPro will simply inform you that the computer cannot run fast enough to execute the task you requested. This warning will appear on the screen (Fig. 3.48).

Fig. 3.48. An abortion message

MultiTrack View Hotkeys

In SAWPro, there are two traditional ways of control: by the keyboard and by the mouse.

As we know from experience, clicking the mouse continuously can become very tedious when working, although this device is handy for positioning the multitrack cursor and working with playback start and stop.

For other operations, we advise you to use the so-called hotkeys of the keyboard as much as possible. Hotkeys duplicate program interface buttons.

We talked about using certain hotkeys in the "*Custom Configuration Options*" section. In this section, we discussed the usage of hotkeys for configuring screens when forming a comfortable workspace. As you hopefully remember, switching between screens is done with the <F1>, ..., <F12> function keys.

Chapter 3: The SAWPro Program: Live Recording in a Virtual Studio

In this section, we will talk about the hotkeys that, from our point of view, are most often used when working with the multitrack. Please note that every pull-down menu in SAWPro provides a hotkey combination for executing the command in parentheses next to the menu item text (Fig. 3.49).

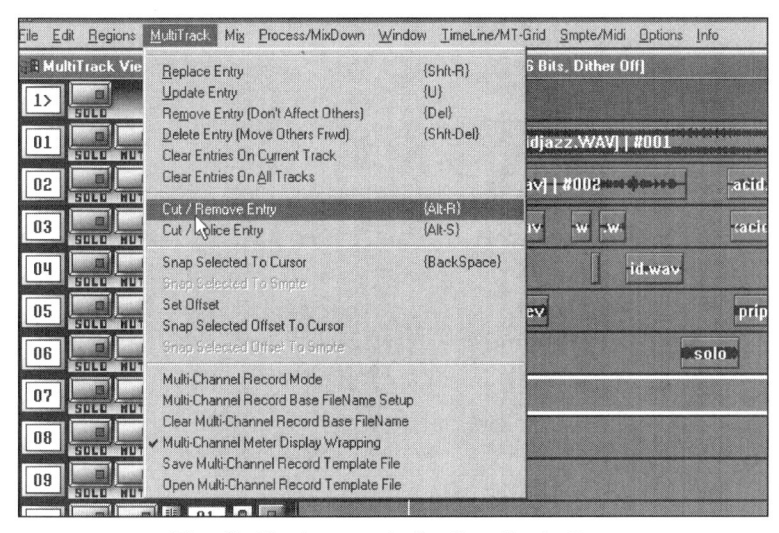

Fig. 3.49. A menu indicating the hotkeys

Some Hotkeys

Experience shows that the knowledge of hotkeys significantly speeds up work in SAWPro. It may seem at first glance that it is impossible to remember so many key combinations. But believe us, there is nothing difficult here, since it seems that the program designers tried to make hotkey combinations both convenient and self-evident.

Changing the Scale

When recording and editing, one often has to re-scale the multitrack using the **ZOOM IN** and **ZOOM OUT** operations. The reason for this is that sometimes a track fragment must be seen "blown up", and sometimes, especially when editing, the whole track should be seen at once (low-scaled). Using hotkeys for zooming in and out is particularly convenient. These are the <-> and <+> keys of the numeric keypad.

SAWPro allows you to stretch tracks out vertically as well. For this purpose, the program uses the <Page Up> and <Page Down> keys. These, just as in the previous case, change the scale step by step (Fig. 3.50).

- <Page Up> — widens the track
- <Page Down> — narrows the track

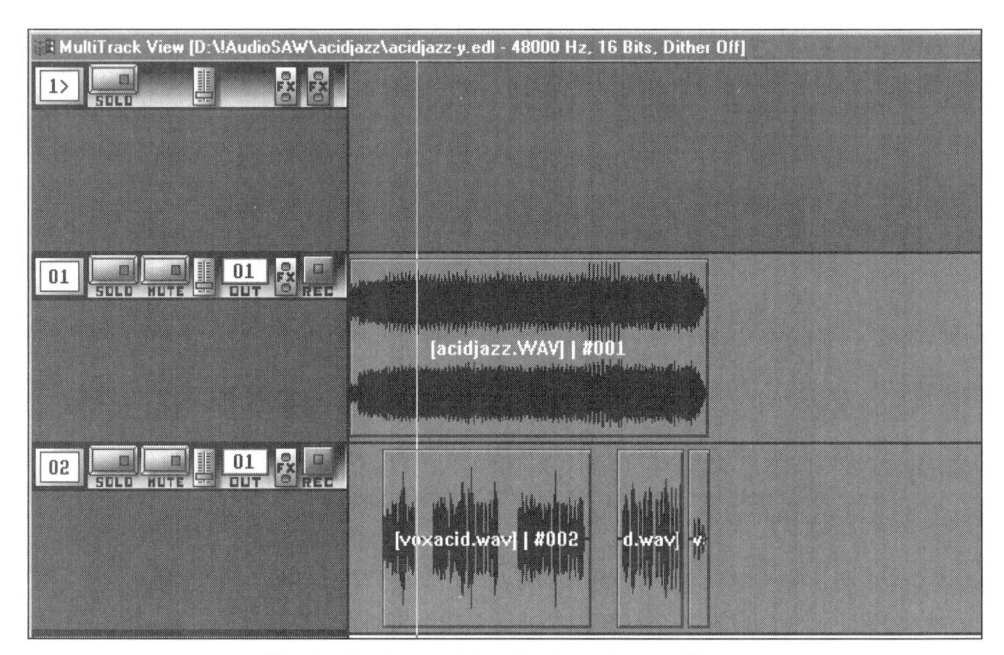

Fig. 3.50. Magnifying the track's amplitude

Moving the Cursor

There are three ways to set the cursor to the beginning of a project.

- <Home>
- <Shift>+<Left arrow>
- <Ctrl>+<Left arrow>

> **NOTE** Mnemonics: the direction of the arrows is the same direction towards which the cursor moves.

To move the cursor to the end of the project, use the <End> key. By the end of the project, we mean the end of the very last clip.

The following keys and key combinations are designated for vertical movement within the multitrack:

- <Up arrow>
- <Down arrow>
- <Shift>+<Up arrow>
- <Shift>+<Down arrow>

Chapter 3: The SAWPro Program: Live Recording in a Virtual Studio

- <Ctrl>+<Up arrow>
- <Ctrl>+<Down arrow>

NOTE Combinations with <Ctrl> work faster than those with <Shift>.

The <Tab> key lets you move the cursor precisely, according to clip boundaries. The <Z> key positions the cursor to the nearest zero offset point of a clip on the hot track, which allows you to split and splice clips without a clicking sound appearing.

Selecting Clips

One more group of hotkeys provides additional capabilities when selecting clips.

- The <S> key enables the Select mode.
- The <A> key (in the Select mode) selects all clips on the multitrack.
- <Tab>+<B> and <Tab>+<E> precisely mark a clip's boundaries (Fig. 3.51). This combination is easy to remember: 'B' is for Beginning, and 'E' for End.

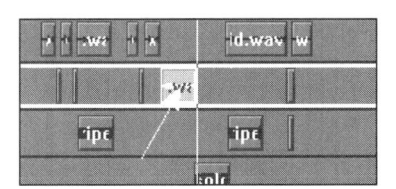

Fig. 3.51. Precise clip marking

NOTE The SAWPro program will not allow you to edit a clip if you accidentally indicate an area that is larger than the clip itself.

Selecting clips using the keys is much more exact and much easier than positioning the mouse cursor on the clip's beginning and ending points in the **TimeLine** display.

Skills in precise clip marking will serve you well when learning destructive editing (i.e., altering the original).

NOTE Looking ahead a bit, the idea behind destructive editing goes something like this. Because computer resources are not infinite, the opportunity to destructively edit is provided in SAWPro. This kind of editing irreversibly associates the file with the effects applied (or patched) to it. Disabling the effects afterwards significantly frees up CPU resources.

Pay attention to the fact that precision when marking a whole clip or a portion of one (Fig. 3.51) is extremely important when editing destructively.

Changing the Waveform's Scale

In practice, we often refer to the waveform, or graphic representation of the sound wave. To see the waveform, you can press the "wave" button (Fig. 3.52).

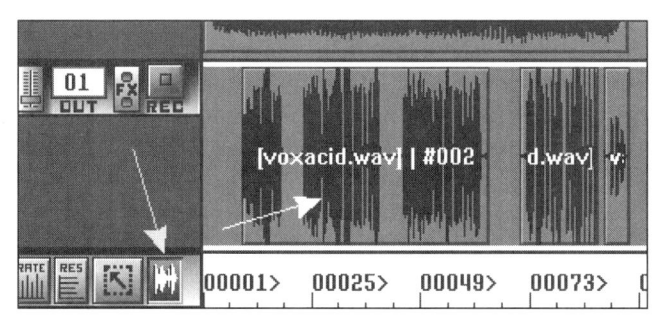

Fig. 3.52. Displaying tracks as waveforms

However, using hotkeys often turns out to be more convenient.

- The <W> key (for wave) toggles the clips' waveform display mode on and off
- <Shift>+<Page Up> enlarges the hot track clips' waveform display scale
- <Shift>+<Page Down> decreases the waveform display scale

Canceling Commands

To cancel a command, use the following:

- <Ctrl>+< < > (the 'less than' sign) undoes the last action. Using this hotkey repeatedly will cancel all commands one by one.
- <Ctrl>+< > > (the 'greater than' sign) redoes an action (cancels the *last* Undo), i.e., restores the command history step by step.

> **NOTE** Mnemonics: the signs < (less than) and > (greater than) indicate the direction of tracing the command history: to the beginning of the project, where there were *less* actions performed, or to the end of the project, where the number of actions is *greater*.

Splitting a Clip

Clips can be split at the cursor line as follows:

- The <K> key splits the clip on the hot track
- <Shift>+<K> splits all clips below the hot track

Calling a Context Menu

A context menu (see Fig. 3.33) can be gotten in either of these two ways, both convenient:

❏ The <Esc> key
❏ Simultaneously pressing the left and right mouse buttons

The *Full View* and *SoundFile View* Windows

In the "*Creating a Comfortable User Environment*" section, configuring the program's working screens was discussed. However, we mostly went over work in the **MultiTrack View** window. Now it's time to get acquainted with the others.

In Fig. 3.53, you can see a screen configuration convenient for practical application that has two windows, **Full View** and **SoundFile View**, stacked one on top of the other.

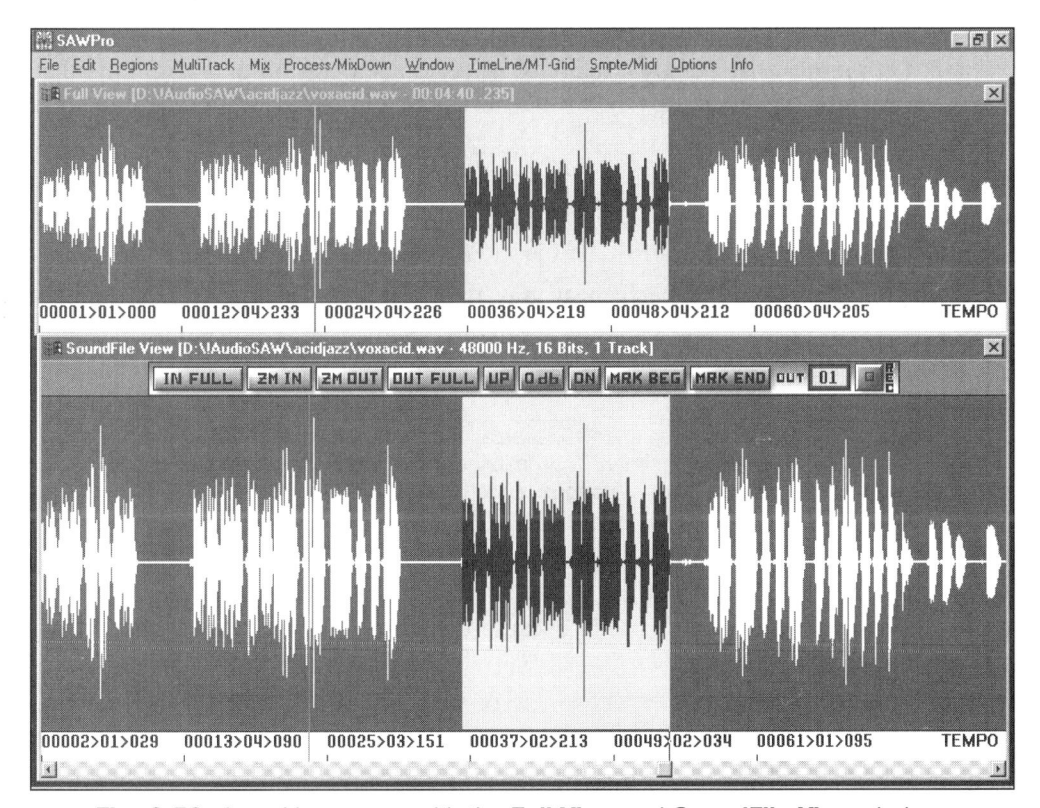

Fig. 3.53. A working screen with the **Full View** and **SoundFile View** windows

The **Full View** window reflects the entire imported or recorded audio file, and assists in quickly navigating the file.

The SAWPro developers created the **Full View** window to allow you to find the necessary file fragments easily.

In the **Full View** window, you can, for example, perform the following operations:

❒ Start playing a sound file from any point. To do this, click on the place where you want to position the cursor, and then click the right mouse button.

❒ When playing a file, move to another position quickly. In this case, without resuming playback, click on a new place. The playback will immediately proceed from the new point.

The **SoundFile View** window is mostly used for creating regions. It is also used for destructive editing (the **Edit** menu).

Creating a Region; Problems with the Final Result

In "*Importing Sound Files to SAWPro*" section, general information about regions was presented. Let's recall what exactly a region is. A region is a portion of a sound file that is marked by the program in some way so that it can be employed by the user afterwards (one or more times).

Let's look at how a region can be used practically.

Having marked a fragment of an executed musical part, you can copy it later. It is very important that you can never destroy the file itself when creating a region.

After the region is created, you can repeat it as many times as you wish to make a loop.

Sometimes, the need for loops — i.e., completely identical part fragments — arises in musical works of different genres.

> **NOTE** For instance, in the classical barcarole (the Venetian gondolier's song), the accompaniment that imitates the rhythmical lapping of waves requires the performer to produce "a monotonous landscape sound".

In practice, modern musicians are using pre-prepared musical fragments created by other performers more and more.

We shouldn't judge this habit, especially because there are raw products of different quality on the audio production market.

However, it's worth noting that excessive use of such fragments, especially in electronic music, inevitably makes the final product mediocre.

Our point here has little to do with our personal preferences. The answer is beyond the issue of music. Our hearing is such that repeating the same phrase first causes a slight

Chapter 3: The SAWPro Program: Live Recording in a Virtual Studio

irritation, in the same way that a skipping record does. Then, our perception dulls due to the lack of new musical events, and the "looped and overworked" music migrates to the category of regular noise.

As you know, everybody hears noise, but NO ONE tries to LISTEN to it.

Nevertheless, there are times where repeating a looped fragment is the essential point in a composition. This is mainly for DJs, those who construct music "from bricks". But this is usually dance music (for dancing to, and not usually for listening to).

We dare suggest that the product of such a constructive approach should be called the computer noise background for the modern technical era, rather than music (no offense to dance music fans).

So what should be done, and whose fault is it? The answer is short: it's not the method's fault, but rather the fault of those who use it incorrectly, i.e., the murderer is guilty and not the gun.

Despite the tendency of the music to sound robotized because of the looped fragments, there are many examples of using looping to create interesting, "live" pieces.

For instance, a well-known English musician, Robert Fripp, has used looped fragments in his work for a long time. He managed to create Soundscapes, a series of sound landscapes, which have very little in common with DJ-like loops!

Here is a quotation from modern music history: "In the early '70s, Fripp mastered a device invented by Brian Eno, which consists of two tape recorders with looped tapes, and functions so that the mixed playback of one tape and the guitar is recorded to the other tape. When the cycle reaches the end, the recorded tape is played back, while the other one is recorded, and so on. Named after its first user, this machine was called the Frippertronic. Later, Robert began using similar devices, now digital ones though, to create his soundscapes. This is loop-based, ambient, improvised music." (Maxim Volgin).

The quote was used first of all to give you a better understanding of the possibilities that the SAWPro program provides you with when working with regions, and secondly, to show the colossal difference in the possible results.

This is all to say that SAWPro is capable of providing a "live" sound when using "bricks". However, you have the choice of creating these "bricks" yourself, or selecting them very carefully from the many loops offered on the market, and then applying your creative efforts to integrating these loops into your project, rather than utilizing them mechanically.

Loop creating is very simple: play a part with your musical instrument, select a fragment to be looped, and then create a region with the <Shift>+<N> key combination.

It's best to generate fragments of considerable length (but yet still different) and vary them. The main idea is to escape the trap of mechanically repeating something, e.g., a rhythm, a melodic phrase, or a harmonic series, *without need for it*.

When creating MUSIC, bear in mind that there are no repetitions in nature. Anything natural will not stand soulless cloning.

OK, let's finish with this "lyrical" discourse, and proceed to the description of the **SoundFile View** window.

The Graphical Representation of the Sound File

The *SoundFile View* Window

This window includes three parts (Fig. 3.53). The main part is in the center. Residing in it is the sound track. The **TimeLine** display is in the bottom, like in the multitrack window. At the top, there is a line of buttons.

- **IN FULL** displays the sound file at maximum zoom along the time axis
- **OUT FULL** displays the whole sound file
- **ZM IN**, **ZM OUT** zooms the file display in or out in regard to the time axis
- **UP**, **DN** changes the waveform's amplitude gain up or down
- **0 dB** displays the signal with a scaling factor of 1:1
- **MRK BEG**, **MRK END** marks the beginning and the end of a fragment
- **REC** starts recording in the **SoundFile View** window

NOTE Recording is carried out through the virtual tape recorder panel, though without forming a clip on the multitrack.

Marking a File Area in the *SoundFile View* Window

The *first method* is the same one used in the **MultiTrack View** window. To mark an area, drag the mouse along the **TimeLine** display (Fig. 3.54). To cancel the selection, right-click on this display.

The *second method* is as follows: position the cursor at the starting point and press **MRK BEG**, then select the end point and press **MRK END**. The area you mark will turn gray (Fig. 3.54).

Area boundaries may be corrected (moved) in the **Play Loop** mode. Just click on the waveform to start making corrections.

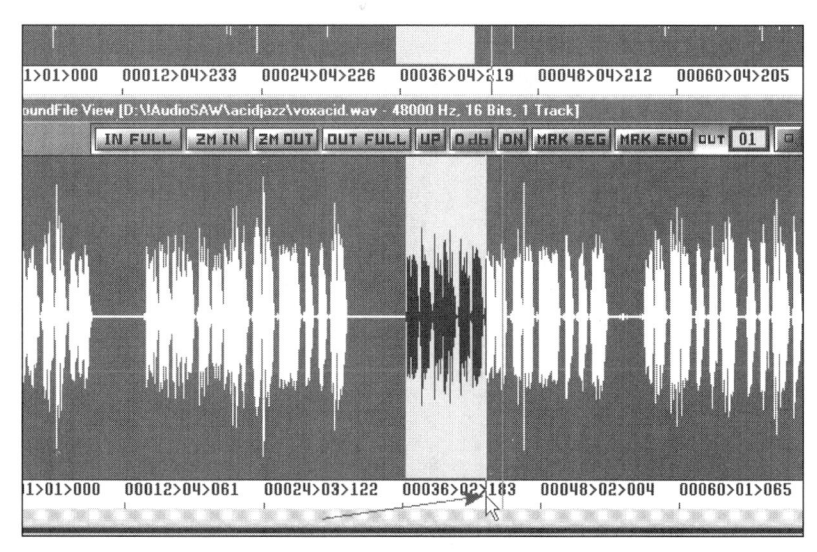

Fig. 3.54. Marking an area

Registering a Selected Area in the Region List

After you mark an area successfully, the result should be registered, that is, placed on the region list.

To do this, execute the **Create New Region** command from the **Regions** menu (or press <Shift>+<N>), and name the region in the dialog box (see Fig. 3.44).

As we mentioned earlier, an unlimited number of regions can be prepared from the same audio file, in theory.

NOTE It should be noted that the **TimeLine** display, similar to the one in the **MultiTrack View** window, displays time in either of two modes: **Time** (Measure/Beat/Tick) and **Samples**. These modes are switched by the **T/S** button on the **Remote Transport** panel. To make this possible, the **Tempo Mode** option should be checked on the **TimeLine/MT-Grid** menu.

Displaying Regions: the *Regions View* Window

The **Regions View** window is, in a manner of speaking, the SAWPro database, since it displays all non-destructive editing operations executed on the multitrack as regions.

For example, when importing or recording a file and creating a region, splitting a clip, or copying a region, all these actions are represented in the SAWPro region list (Fig. 3.55).

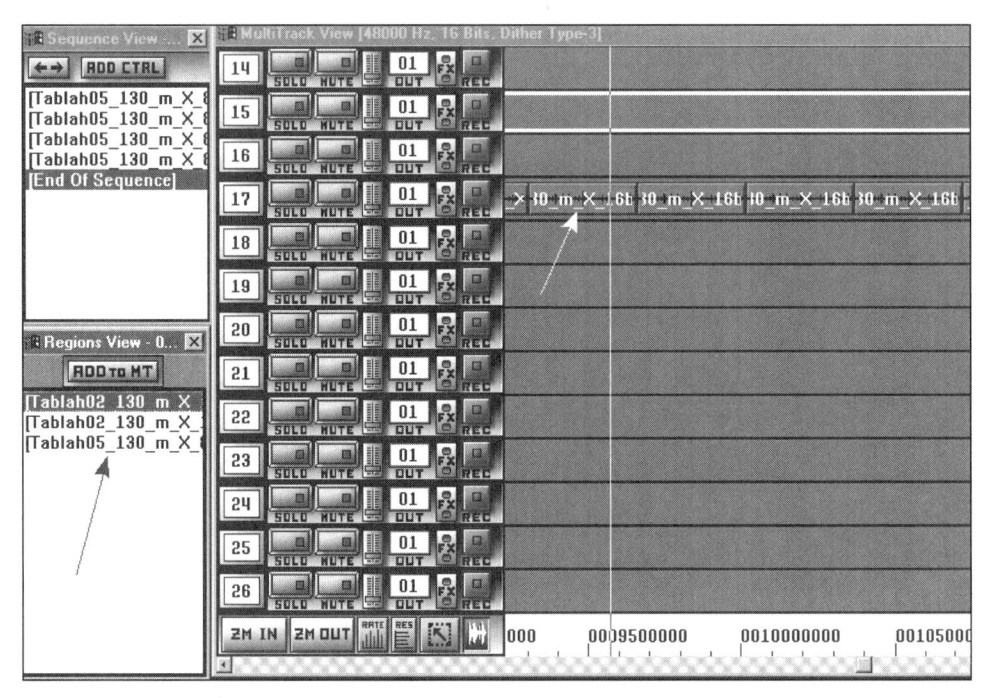

Fig. 3.55. The **Regions View** window on the working screen

As a matter of fact, the very regions and their position on the multitrack is the heart of the concept of the SAWPro virtual project itself.

If for some reason you don't name a region, the program will do it itself. It assigns every region a default name that consists of the sound file name and an ordinal number (Fig. 3.56).

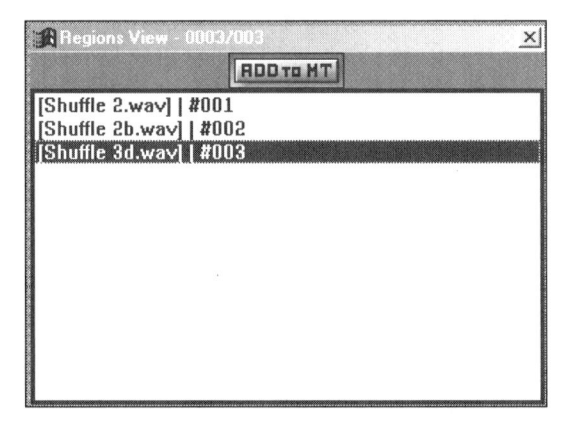

Fig. 3.56. The list of regions created by default in the **Regions View** window

Chapter 3: The SAWPro Program: Live Recording in a Virtual Studio

When creating regions with the **Create New Region** command (<Shift>+<N>), you appoint them names that are then displayed in the region list (Fig. 3.57).

NOTE Names should only consist of ASCII letters, since SAWPro does not recognize national alphabets.

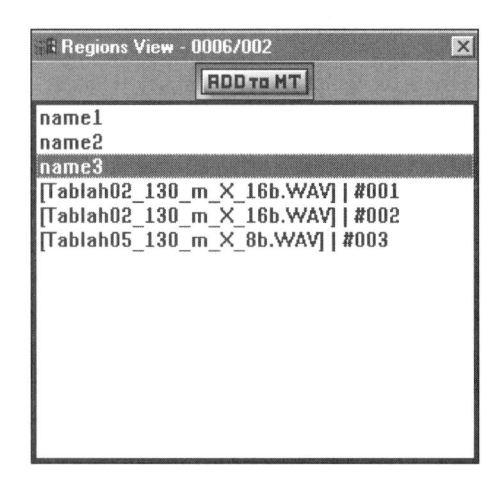

Fig. 3.57. Examples of region names created by the user

The actions listed below can be performed on regions in **Regions View** window.

❒ *Select a region* by clicking it. The region will be highlighted in black (see the **name3** region in Fig. 3.57).

❒ *Listen to the selected region.* This can be done in one of three ways:
  - Use the right mouse button
  - Use the **Play** button on the **Remote Transport** panel
  - Use the **Play Loop** button on the **Remote Transport** panel

If you press **Play Loop**, the region will be played back repeatedly.

❒ *Transfer a region to the multitrack.* To do this:
  1. Select a region.
  2. Position the cursor at the point of the multitrack where you intend to transfer the region. The beginning of the future clip will coincide precisely with the cursor's position.
  3. Press the **ADD TO MT** button, situated over the region list.

❒ *Add multiple copies of a region.*
  1. Select the region in **Regions View**.

2. Change to the **MultiTrack View** window.
3. Press the <A> key.

Every time you press <A>, the program inserts the region on the multitrack (at the cursor position).

❒ *Delete a selected region from the region list* using the <Delete> key.

> **NOTE** If a number of windows are displayed on the working screen simultaneously, you can switch windows by clicking the one you need once.

The Hot Track Clip List: the *Sequence View* Window

While in the last studied window, **Regions View**, the user could see all created regions ordered chronologically (by time of creation), the **Sequence View** window is intended for local use. This has been done so that the user can conveniently work with clips in just the one track (the hot track).

In **Sequence View**, the whole hot track clip list is displayed, from the first clip to the last one.

The list is terminated with the **[End Of Sequence]** line (Fig. 3.58).

The upper panel of the window is supplied with a button with two arrows (see Fig. 3.58). By pressing it, you can easily vertically resize the window, or restore the default window size.

The **ADD CTRL** button adds special commands to the clip list. A description of these is beyond the scope of this book, since using these commands in one's home computer studio makes little sense.

All operations with regions in the **Sequence View** window (selection, playback, removal, etc.) are executed in the same mode as in the **Regions View** window.

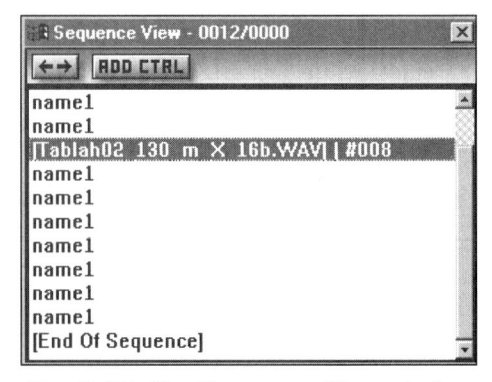

Fig. 3.58. The **Sequence View** window

Chapter 3: The SAWPro Program: Live Recording in a Virtual Studio 89

In **Sequence View**, there is a remarkable function: synchronized connection with the **MultiTrack View** window. As soon as you click on one of the clips in **Sequence View**, the cursor in the **MultiTrack View** window changes its position. It will point to the *beginning* of the hot track clip that corresponds to the selection in the **Sequence View** window (Fig. 3.59).

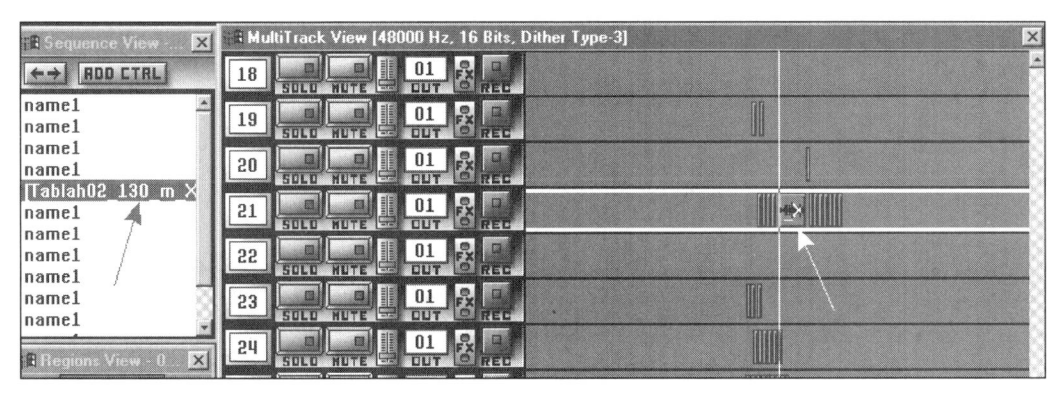

Fig. 3.59. The **Sequence View** window's connection to the **MultiTrack View** window

Pay attention to the difference in how the cursor moves about hot track clips in various windows.

- In the **MultiTrack View** window, the cursor is moved from clip to clip using the <Tab> key. The cursor stops at all clip boundaries.
- In the **Sequence View** window, when you go along the region list, the multitrack cursor moves along the *beginning boundaries* of the clips only.

Both methods are acceptable if the hot track clips are spliced (with no pauses).

However, if there are gaps between clips, it is recommended that you use the first method for moving the multitrack cursor, that is, the <Tab> key. This is the only way to set the cursor to the end boundary of a clip.

Working With Markers: the *Markers View* Window

Markers View is a window for bookmarks (markers) that allow you to quickly return to the necessary part of the project.

The ability of instantaneously jumping to the required place on the multitrack is, undoubtedly, an advantageous program function. Alas, we have to state the sad fact that markers are poorly arranged in SAWPro.

Nevertheless, this shortcoming can be partly compensated with a certain window configuration (Fig. 3.60).

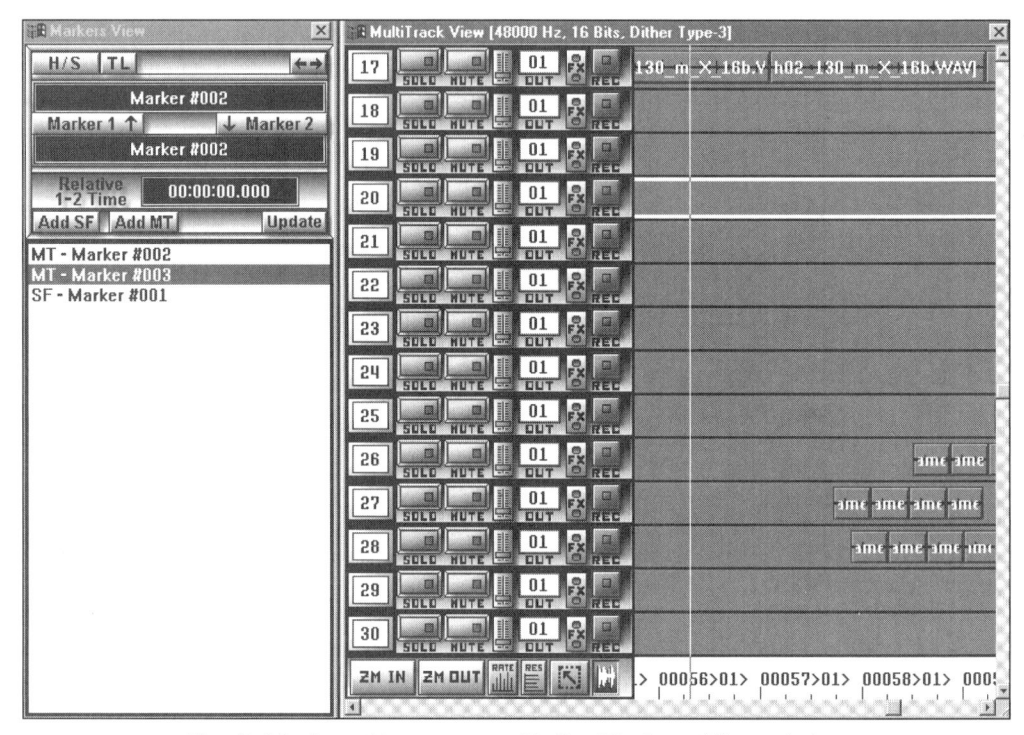

Fig. 3.60. A working screen with the **Markers View** window

The technique for working with markers is relatively simple. There are several possibilities.

❐ Create a marker for the **MultiTrack View** window:
   1. Place the cursor on the selected point of the multitrack.
   2. Press the **ADD MT** button.

❐ Create a marker for the **SoundFile View** window:
   1. Place the cursor on the selected point of the waveform.
   2. Press the **ADD SF** button.

A faster method of creating markers for **MT** and **SF** is to use the <M> hotkey.

❐ Name a marker:
   1. When you press **ADD MT** or **ADD SF**, a dialog box opens.
   2. Assign a name to the marker.

NOTE By default, markers receive names consisting of the three parts: a window name abbreviation (MT for multitrack and SF for **SoundFile View**), the word **Marker**, and an ordinal number (Fig. 3.60).

Chapter 3: The SAWPro Program: Live Recording In a Virtual Studio

- Select and delete a marker from the list. This is done by following the same rules as for regions in the **Regions View** window:
  1. To select a marker, click on it. The marker will be highlighted in black (see **MT—Marker#003** in Fig. 3.60). When selecting a marker, the cursor *automatically moves* to the correct position of the multitrack or sound file.
  2. Delete the selected marker from the list using the <Delete> key.
- Change a marker's position:
  1. Place the cursor in a new position (on the **MultiTrack View** or **SoundFile View**).
  2. Press the **Update** button.
  3. In the dialog box that appears, press **OK.**
- Rename a marker:
  1. Select the marker.
  2. Press the **Update** button.
  3. In the dialog box that appears, rename the marker.
  4. Press **OK.**
- Measure the time interval between any two markers:
  1. Select the first marker from the list.
  2. Press the **Marker1** button.
  3. Select the second marker from the list.
  4. Press the **Marker2** button.

The **Relative 1—2 Time** counter will indicate the value of the time interval between the two markers.

Saving a Project

A *project* is the preliminary result of the work done in creating the final version of a stereo audio file. Speaking allegorically, this is the program's "spy report" of all your actions.

In SAWPro, projects are saved in files with the EDL extension. This stands for **EditListFile**.

Such a file contains each and every project setting you have appointed:

- Lists of regions
- Clip positioning on the multitrack
- The fader sliders' positions

- ❐ Lists and settings of patched virtual effects
- ❐ The sound file folder path

SAWPro remembers each of the last 99 actions you have performed. Thanks to this, you can always come back to any of them. Every edit operation is saved as an EDL file with an extension consisting of two parts: letter 'u' (for **Undo**) and a two-digit index, according to the operation's ordinal number.

> **NOTE** This way, a file with the extension .u00 (MySong.u00) will contain the last edited version, while the u99 file (MySong.u99) reflects the very first version.

To get to any of the 99 project files, do the following:

1. From the **Edit** menu, execute the **Open EDL Undo History** command.
2. Choose the correct version in the opening dialog box.
3. Press **OK**.

The last version of the project (u00) can be loaded from the **File** menu using the **Recover EditListFile** command.

Projects are saved through the **File** menu as well.

- ❐ **Save EditListFile As** saves the project under an alternate name. The hotkey combination is <Ctrl>+<S>.
- ❐ **Save EditListFile Copy As** creates a copy of a project under an alternate name.
- ❐ **Save EditListFile And Trim Session** re-assembles the project and saves it as a new entity. That is, only the sound file areas from which regions have been removed are automatically selected and copied into the new project. The program copies those areas interacting with the user through a dialog box. The old project can be deleted along with old sound files. It's worth saying that the operation discussed here allows you to save disk space.

> **WARNING**
> Apply the **Save EditListFile And Trim Session** function with caution, since no region can be stretched after it is applied. Delete nothing before the final mixing and mastering of the project, unless you really have to.

- ❐ **Update EditListFile** saves the project in its current state (Fig. 3.61). This operation remembers the intermediate project stage. This means that the EDL extension is assigned to the proper file instead of the u00 working extension. The hotkey combination is <Ctrl>+<U>.

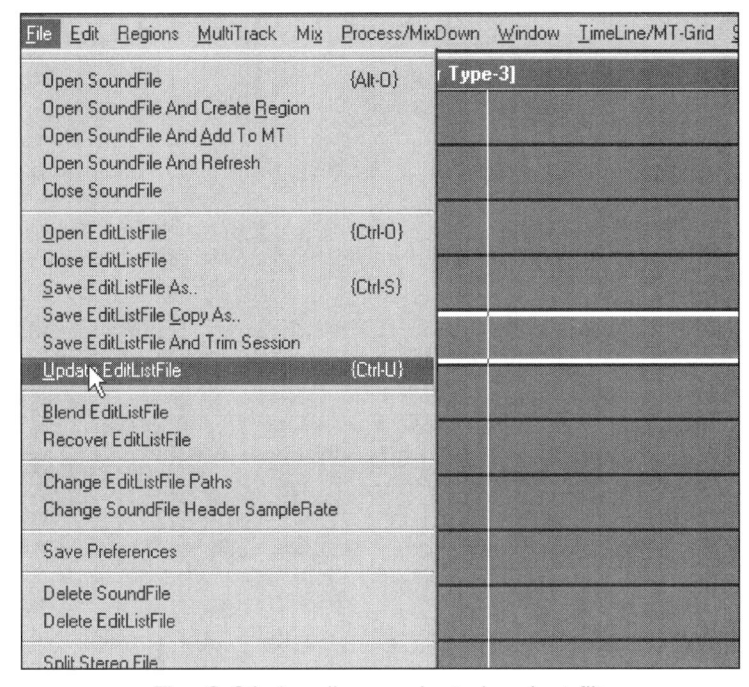

Fig. 3.61. Loading a selected project file

Recording a Live Performance

SAWPro & Computer Configuration: General Advice for Beginners

In our age, technical progress moves forward at a rapid pace. Only a few years ago, digital audio recording was the domain of professionals, but nowadays, modern computer technologies present a world of opportunities in digital multichannel recording for everyone who's interested.

Today, a typical home computer can easily be turned into a multichannel digital tape recorder, if the user so desires. This device, in turn, will be able to hold not only a virtual mixer, but also a set of programmed sound effects.

You should note that multimedia configurations that are insufficient for many modern computer games more than adequately meet the needs of a beginning musician who wishes to master computer sound technologies.

From our point of view, the minimal system requirements for running SAWPro in a home audio studio are as follows: a Pentium 200 MMX or something similar, 128 MB of RAM, a 6.4 GB HDD, and a Sound Blaster Live sound card. (However, a 256 MB RAM is preferred.)

If your computer meets these requirements, SAWPro is ideally suited for two of the main stages of project development in particular: recording the live performance and mixing the recording. Although mastering, which is the final project stage, is also quite feasible.

> **NOTE** *Mixing* is the process of transforming a multichannel (multitrack) recording that has been mixed and processed into a stereo (two-channel) or mono (one-channel) recording.
>
> *Mastering* is the final phase of processing the mixed material in order to get a high-quality sound.
>
> (For more details, see the "*SAWPro Mixing and Mastering*" section.)

The reason why SAWPro uses relatively few computer resources is that it is a program specially intended for multichannel recording directly onto the disk. Thus, SAWPro is actually a specialized multitrack HDD recorder.

> **TIP** To improve speed and reliability, we recommend that you setup SAWPro in Windows NT/2000 operating systems.

Of course, no program is perfect. The fact of the matter is that, in spite of the variety of existing software for creating music, there is no one program that is fit for solving every problem equally well. Namely, this concerns the problems that a user faces when creating a full-scale musical project and trying to achieve demo CD-standard quality.

This is why we describe different programs in this book, drawing the reader's attention to the advantages of each.

At each stage of project creation, it makes sense to use the software that will get the best, high-quality result.

> **NOTE** If you plan on working with an electronic musical instrument that has a MIDI interface (Musical Instrument Digital Interface), you would be better off using a sequencer program.
>
> A sequencer program allows you to record and edit music in the MIDI format. In our opinion, the best sequencer program at the moment of writing is Cubase VST 24 (version 3.7). We shall look at some capabilities of this program in *Chapter 6* in the context of the topic discussed there.
>
> After a MIDI project is created in a home studio using a sequencer program, such a project should be converted to audio files with the WAV extension. Afterwards, the project is developed in an HDD–recorder-class program, such as SAWPro or Samplitude 2496. In *Chapter 7*, we will examine this in more detail.

Coming back to SAWPro, we are of the opinion that this program is more suitable for recording live performances and mixing sound tracks than any other.

The SAWPro interface is convenient in that you can record either yourself or another musician with equal comfort.

In order to concentrate on the creative process, it's better if the artist be required to give only a minimal amount of attention to controlling the computer. The recording process should thus be as automated as possible, and this the SAWPro program does. While working with this program, you will feel the computer transforming from a piece of furniture, a video game terminal, or a CD player into your faithful ally and a friendly musical instrument that saves and guards all your creative achievements and discoveries.

Let's examine these benefits of the SAWPro program using practical examples.

Connecting to the Sound Card; Adjusting the Recording Level

To connect a microphone or an electronic musical instrument to the sound card, you'll need to have these devices and components: a microphone, connecting cables, and a device that performs the function of a preliminary amplifier, such as a mixer.

NOTE If you want to perform live on an electronic musical synthesizer, this instrument can be connected by the proper cable to the LINE IN sound card input.

The Microphone

Choosing a microphone is a subtle matter. In a home environment, one can start with a microphone that costs about $35 or more. Such a microphone has a mandatory differential output; as a rule, one can find these in specialized shops for professional and semi-professional audio equipment. The microphone should be fed to the external mixer's microphone input.

NOTE There is a detailed description of sound recording using a microphone in the book by Roman Petelin and Yury Petelin "*PC Music Home Studio: Secrets, Tips, & Tricks*", A-LIST, 2002.

The Mixer

If you want to record an amplified guitar with no intermediate processing devices, i.e., with no effects, we recommend that you use a preliminary amplifier.

An analog mixer will work best in this situation. This device is indispensable not only in a professional studio, but when recording at home as well.

> **NOTE** Today, the market offers a relatively large number of mixers. When determining which mixer to choose to work with with SAWPro, consider the following.

The SAWPro program possesses a 32-channel virtual mixer. This number is enough for solving the basic problems. Thus, an external mixer with a large number of inputs can be excessive, since many of inputs will be unnecessary when working with SAWPro, not to mention that the price of the mixer grows proportionally with the number of these inputs.

Home Studio Setup

The setup of a home studio for beginners is simple.

- A *signal source* is fed to the analog mixer.
- The *analog mixer* is connected to the LINE IN sound card input.
- The sound card output is connected to the *amplifier*. It is best if the amplifier is supplied with acoustic monitoring systems (for listening to the result).
- If no acoustic system is attached, *headphones* should be plugged into the amplifier.

> **NOTE** The headphones also should be of good quality. Otherwise, any work with the sound becomes senseless if there is distortion due to the headphones.

Sound insulation in one's dwelling can be a problem, too. For this reason, and also in order to suppress the microphone's self-excitation, all recording process participants should use headphones. Therefore, if you aren't working alone, make sure you have extra headphones: a pair for the soundman and a pair for the performer.

- There is an *internal hardware mixer* embedded in all modern sound cards (Figs. 3.62 and 3.63).

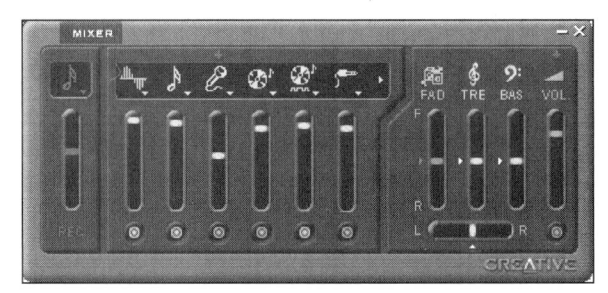

Fig. 3.62. The MIXER console for the Sound Blaster Live sound card

> **NOTE** As a rule, there is a hardware mixer accessible through **Start | Programs | Accessories | Multimedia | Volume Control** (a standard Windows program).

In sound cards of a more advanced level (like those from Creative Labs, Inc.), the internal hardware mixer employs its own specialized driver program (Fig. 3.62).

Adjusting the Recording Level

Let's talk about the methods of volume level adjustment using the standard Volume Control Windows program that works with most sound cards.

Controlling Recording: the *Record Control* Window

Depicted in Fig. 3.63 is the **Record Control** window. Its controls are divided into four groups: **CD Audio** (for recording from a CD), **Line-In**, **Microphone**, and **MIDI** (for recording from the internal MIDI synthesizer of the sound card).

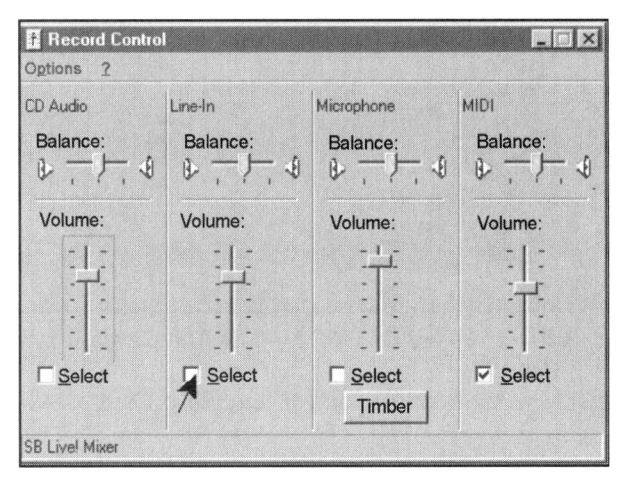

Fig. 3.63. The **Record Control** window. The record mode

To prepare for recording from an external source, follow these steps:

1. In the **Record Control** window, check the **Select** checkbox of the **Line-In** control (see Fig. 3.63). That is, *select* the **Line-In** input.
2. In the window for the playback mode, clear the **Mute** checkbox of the **Line-In** control (Fig. 3.64). That is, *unmute* the **Line-In** input.

To switch between windows, use the **Options | Properties** menu of the Volume Control program. If the **Line-In** input is selected but left mute, recording still will be done, but you won't hear it.

Playing Back the Recording: the *Play Control* Window.

A particular instance of the **Play Control** window is shown in Fig. 3.64. This window contains five groups of controls: **Play Control**, **CD Audio**, **Line-In**, **Wave/DirectSound**, and **MIDI**.

98   Live Music on Your PC

NOTE   The number of groups may differ in different versions of Windows and for different sound cards. **Wave/DirectSound** is the name for the Sound Blaster Live sound card. For other devices, the names will be different, even though their functions are similar. The recommendations provided below refer to sound cards that support independent input and output adjustment.

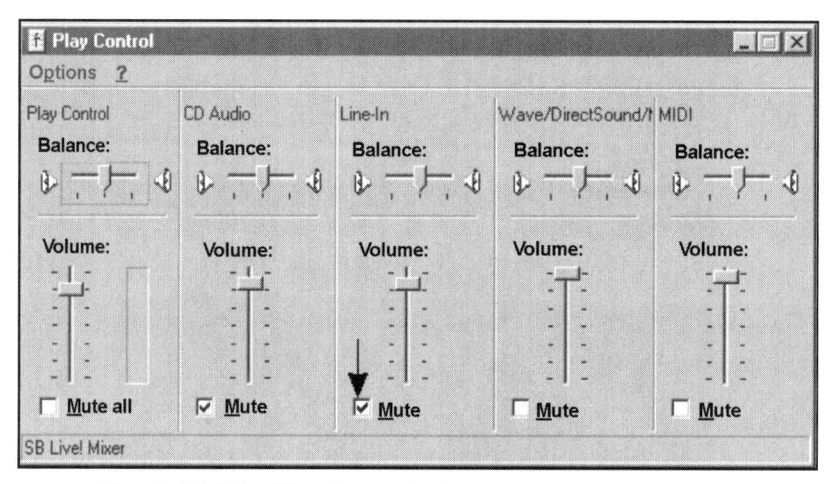

Fig. 3.64. The **Play Control** window. The playback mode

Please note that sliders in the **Record Control** and **Play Control** windows behave *independently*.

Adjusting the Volume Level When Recording

Controlling the recording volume level sets two tasks before of the user.

- ❐ **Creating comfortable conditions for the performer.** The performer will be more comfortable with a proper adjustment of the volume controls. To do this, set the performer's **Line-In** channel slider in the **Play Control** window higher than the **Wave/DirectSound** multitrack playback volume level. The performer will then be better able to hear his or her part against the background of the accompaniment. This does not affect the recording signal.
- ❐ **Adjusting the recording level.** The recording level can be adjusted using the external mixer (master) output signal control or the recording level control of the sound card mixer.

The SAWPro Recording Level Control

In the SAWPro **MultiTrack View** window, the **Rec** button calls the virtual tape recorder panel for a track (Fig. 3.65).

Chapter 3: The SAWPro Program: Live Recording In a Virtual Studio

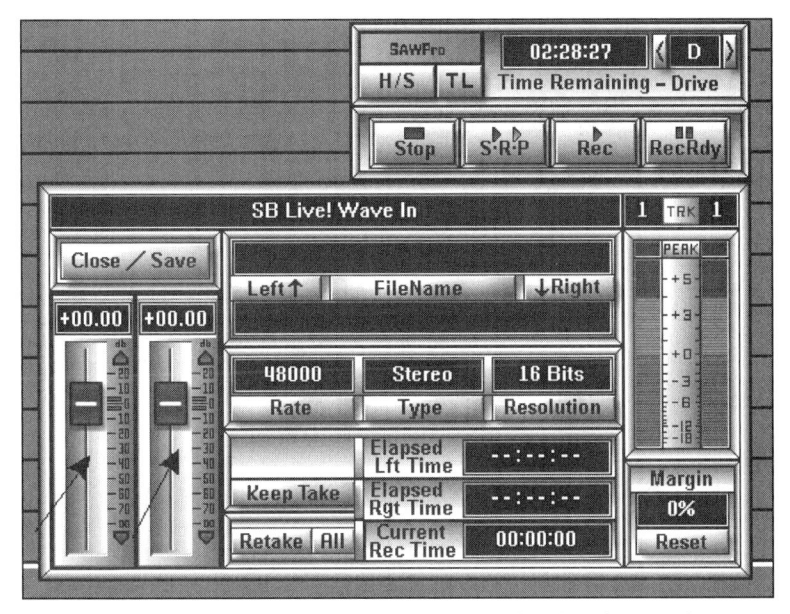

Fig. 3.65. The SAWPro virtual recording level control

The recording level is indicated on the *recording level meter*, situated on the virtual tape recorder panel.

The *highest* (*peak*) level on the meter is registered in the **Margin** numeric display as a percentage. The last peak level is kept on this display until it is exceeded by a higher one.

The peak value can be cleared by the **Reset** button.

One specific feature of digital recording is that, first of all, when the recording level grows too high, the sound quality abruptly worsens. That is, if the level exceeds 100%, this causes much more distortion than if the same excess took place under analog recording conditions.

Second, if the volume level is insufficient for digital recording, this makes the sound hard and less transparent due to the quantization noise.

NOTE   For an in-depth look at quantization noise, see *Chapter 8*.

The Amplitude Peak Limiter

We included this information on the specifics of digital recording in order to better comprehend the value of one of SAWPro's remarkable features. Namely, the program includes a *limiter* — an embedded amplitude peak clipper for the signal being recorded (Fig. 3.66) that functions in real-time mode.

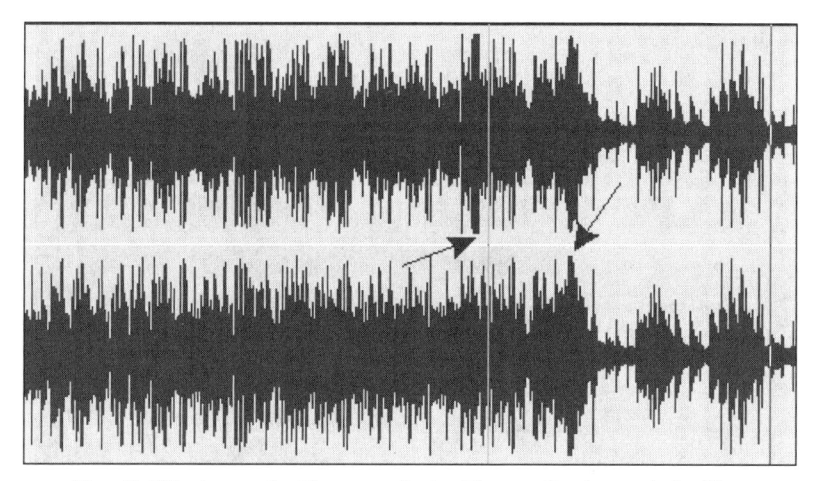

Fig. 3.66. An audio file recorded with amplitude peak limiting

The limit threshold is set by the virtual recording level control (Fig. 3.67).

NOTE The limiter program only turns on when the recording level is negative. The algorithm is outlined so that samples are scaled and limited by amplitude simultaneously.

The value the authors recommend is −1.0 dB, which is approximately 89% on the **Margin** display. With this value, the SAWPro program guarantees that the level of the signal you record will not exceed 89%.

If the recording level is controlled by the sound card mixer control, the ideal situation is for the signal to only reach that level occasionally (Fig. 3.67).

This property allows us to record (at home) acoustic musical instruments and voice parts with a much wider dynamic range (i.e., the relationship between the loudest and quietest sounds) than parts performed on electronic instruments.

To enable the recording level adjustment mode in SAWPro, you need to first press the **Rec Rdy** (pause) button on the virtual tape recorder panel.

When recording a solo part, it is better to use the **S-R-P** (simultaneous recording and playback) button. Using it, you will be able to quickly adjust the recording level, while the soloist rehearses his or her part to the accompaniment recording. As you may remember, recording does not start unless the **Rec** button is pressed. (For more details, see the "*Description of the Virtual Tape Recorder*" section.)

NOTE Let us remind you that before adjusting the recording level, you should name the future sound file (the **FileName** button).

If the **S-R-P** button is pressed, the virtual recording level control is *blocked*, and so the level is adjusted by the sound card mixer.

Chapter 3: The SAWPro Program: Live Recording In a Virtual Studio 101

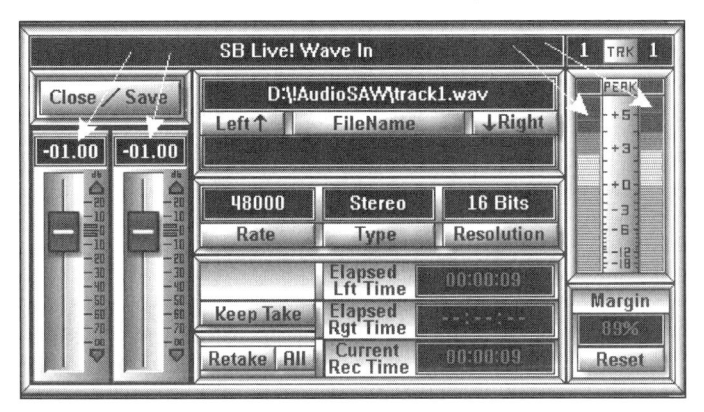

Fig. 3.67. Suggested threshold settings

The Project Sample Rate and Bit Resolution

In the bottom-left side of the **MultiTrack View** window, we see the **RATE** and **RES** buttons (see Fig. 3.70).

By pressing these, you open one of the menus used for setting the project's *sample rate* in Hz (see Fig. 3.69) or *bit resolution* (see Fig. 3.70).

NOTE Please forgive us technicians, but we're going to try to explain what sample rate and bit resolution are to the folks that are not as acquainted with the technical aspect of things.

When magnified a certain number of times, the sound file waveform looks somewhat like a zigzag curve (Fig. 3.68).

The smoother this sound curve, the better the sound.

The curve's smoothness depends on two factors. The first is how frequent the nodes are positioned horizontally (i.e., along the time axis). Their frequency is measured as the number of them per second, and is expressed in Hz. That is, 44,000 of these nodes per second is equal to a *sample rate* of 44,000 Hz.

The second factor is the precision of measurement of the vertical node coordinates. This depends on how many parts the vertical scale is divided into. For instance: if it is divided into 65,536 parts, then the amount of information necessary to express one coordinate value in the binary form will be 16 bits. This parameter is called *bit resolution* (and is counted in bits).

The general rule is, the higher the project sample rate and bit resolution, the better the sound. However, there are some restrictions on setting these parameters, namely, the technical capacities of the specific sound card.

Most sound cards support a recording format of 44,000 Hz and 16 bits, which is typical audio CD quality.

Sound Blaster Live sound card owners can increase the sample rate, setting it to 48,000 Hz.

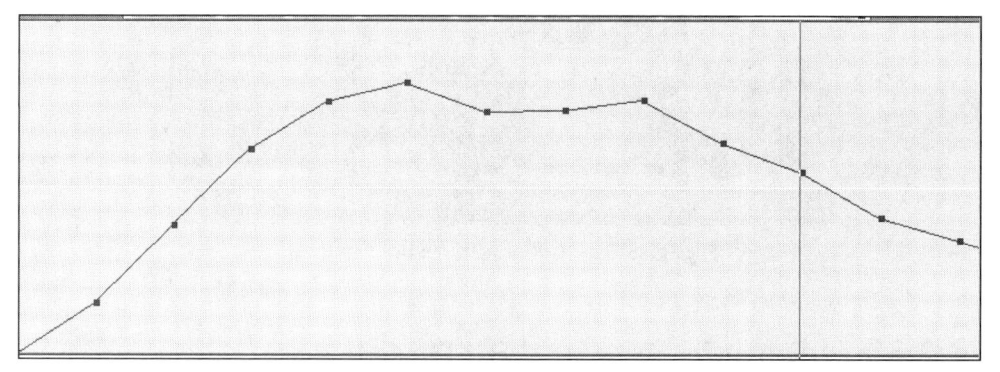

Fig. 3.68. A waveform view

The sample rate and the bit resolution are set for the whole project once, in the very beginning, by the **RATE** and **RES** buttons in the **MultiTrack View** window (Figs. 3.69 and 3.70).

NOTE In SAWPro, the *dither* option can also be enabled (Fig. 3.69). We'll tell you more about the dithering algorithm in *Chapter 8*.

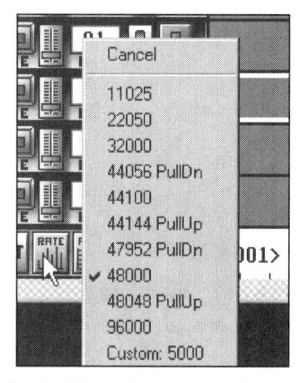

Fig. 3.69. Setting the project's sample rate

Every time the virtual tape recorder is activated by the **REC** button, the sound file sample rate and bit resolution are set in the **Record Panel** window automatically, and are equal to those of the project.

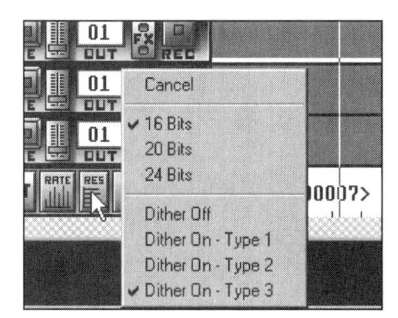

Chapter 3: The SAWPro Program: Live Recording In a Virtual Studio   103

Fig. 3.70. Setting 16-bit resolution

For the sake of the recording quality, it is not recommended that you alter the rate and resolution audio file parameters in the **Record Panel** window.

Mono and Stereo Recording

Hard disk space is wasted when stereo-recording mono signals. Therefore, if the problem of managing computer resources an important one for you, record amplified guitar parts, voices from a microphone, etc., in mono audio file format.

The **Type** button on the virtual tape recorder panel is used to select the audio file type: **Stereo** or **Mono**.

TIP — Keep in mind that the **Mono** button (<L>+<R>) allows you to record a mono signal that is supplied to both channels into an economical mono file.

Ways of Recording

Overdubbing

This is to remind you that basic information on recording methods is provided in the sections "*Importing Sound Files to SAWPro*" and "*Description of the Virtual Tape Recorder*".

Here we will stress the moments that may be important when working with multiple recording takes. You can see the controls used for overdubbing in Fig. 3.71.

1. The first record is naturally done on track **01**. However, if this is undesirable for some reason, any of the 32 tracks intended for this purpose in SAWPro will suffice.
2. After the track is chosen, place the multitrack cursor at the beginning. The fastest way to do so is the <Home> key.
3. To begin recording, press the **REC** button on the virtual tape recorder panel.
4. When recording subsequent tracks, place the cursor in the selected position. To record while listening to previous tracks, press **S-R-P** and then the **REC** button.

5. After you finish recording, if the quality of the fragment is acceptable, press **Stop** and then **Close/Save**.

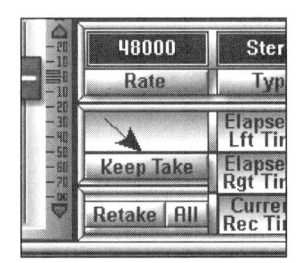

Fig. 3.71. Overdubbing control buttons

If, however, the recorded fragment needs to be overdubbed, SAWPro also possesses the necessary tools. Here we'll give an explanation of them.

Takes

This term is taken from professional sound-recording and cinema montage.

A *take* is a fragment that is performed by a musician, and which is, as a rule, recorded a number of times so that the best variant can be chosen. Moreover, using SAWPro's editing capabilities, a new variant can be arranged on the basis of existing ones.

Doing a Take

In SAWPro, every time you press the **REC** and **Stop** buttons, a new take is completed. The program will create a region that corresponds to this take.

Listening to a Take

To listen to a recorded take, click the right mouse button (without closing the virtual tape recorder panel).

Removing a Take

If a fragment has been executed so poorly that there is no sense in keeping it, press the **Retake** button on the virtual tape recorder panel (Fig. 3.71). The previous recording will be erased.

Removing all Takes

As a last resort, all previously recorded takes can be removed. This is done using the **ALL** button. As a result, only the sound file name will remain, while all file data will be deleted.

Reserving a Take

If a take was not perfect, but still has its good moments, you might wish to keep it just in case, using the **Keep Take** button.

This is what happens in such a case: the clip is removed from the track, but the program will remember its position so as to be able to restore the recording if necessary.

NOTE Next to the name of this take in the region list, both this take's number and its start position on the multitrack are indicated.

Don't get confused by the numbers: this is the way SAWPro records the take's starting position — using samples for the time count.

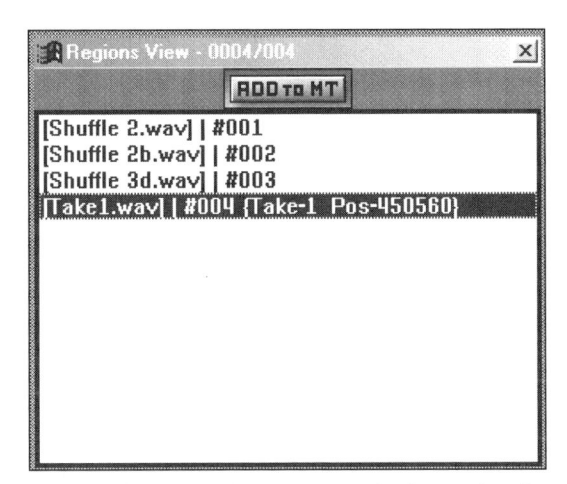

Fig. 3.72. A special take entry in the region list

Restoring a Take

To restore a take to the multitrack, there is a special command that is executed as follows: while holding the <Ctrl> key, click on the **ADD TO MT** button in the **Regions View** window.

This command places any region from the list on the hot track in the same position where the region was when recording, no matter what the current cursor position is.

NOTE However, this command cannot be applied to regions created in the **SoundFile View** window.

Choosing the Best Take

To choose the most successful take from all the ones recorded, lay out the saved takes on free tracks. Placing a take on the multitrack is done in the same way as restoring one: holding the <Ctrl> key, click on **ADD TO MT**.

Since all takes have been recorded at the same time position, they will be arranged one precisely under the other (Fig. 3.73).

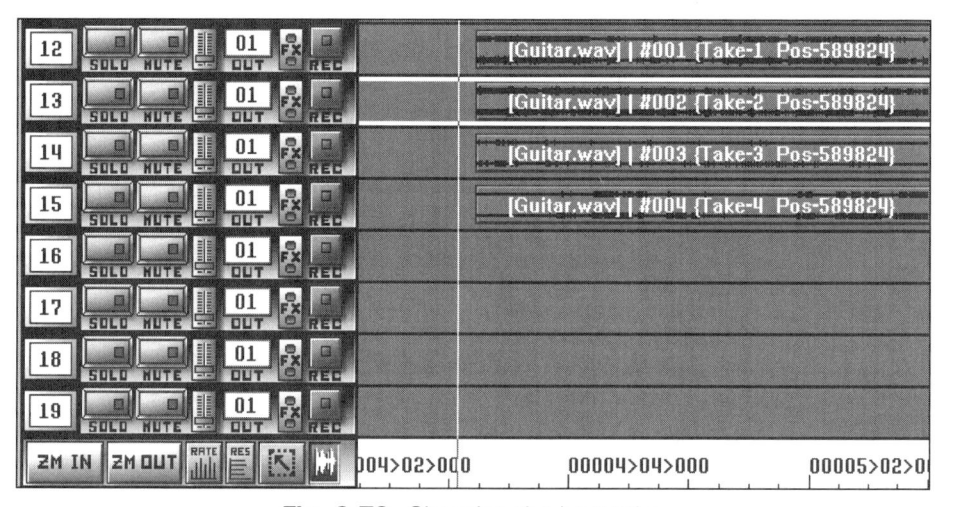

Fig. 3.73. Choosing the best take

The best one is selected like this:

1. Using the **SOLO** buttons, make active those tracks that you want hear.
2. Exclude non-essential tracks, pressing the **MUTE** button on each of them.
3. Listen to one take a time, using the track's **SOLO** button to play the take.

Bad takes detected while listening to the takes can be easily deleted. This is done as follows:

1. Initiate the Select mode either by:
   - Clicking the icon with the arrow in the bottom left corner of the **MultiTrack View** window.
   - Pressing the <S> key (you will watch the mouse cursor change its form to an arrow in a square). To get the normal cursor back again, repeat either of these operations.
2. Position the cursor on the clip and click it. The clip will be selected.
3. Press <Delete>.

Punch Mode Recording

Punching means inserting fragments into the content of a track during playback.

By giving two "punches" to the track — Punch In (initial) and Punch Out (final) — we delimit the area for recording.

The importance of this function is really tremendous. It allows us to insert fragments of *any* length, one note or one word long.

All this happens on a track segment whose boundaries have been defined beforehand. That is, during playback, when the take reaches the Punch In point, recording starts automatically and lasts until Punch Out.

This mode is unavoidable in cases when you have to:

❐ Insert a musical phrase on a ready track

❐ Insert local corrections while recording a voice (correct just one word)

In practice, it goes like this: the performer plays (or sings) a fragment somewhat bigger than the one used for overdubbing. Punch recording is turned on automatically only at the segment that must be re-taken.

It is nice to know that, with this technology, the insertion boundaries are not audible at all.

Note that there are no visible signs of the Punch mode's presence in the program, such as captions, buttons, keys, etc. Therefore, if you were to look for it on your own, it would probably take a while to find.

For Punch mode recording, follow these steps (Fig. 3.74):

1. Select the track fragment for overdubbing.
2. Execute the standard procedure of recording preparation (level adjustment, etc.).
3. Place the multitrack cursor somewhat before the selected area.
4. Press the **S-R-P** button.
5. Perform the fragment.

This sequence of operations will turn the recording on and off precisely at the selected area's boundaries.

In Fig. 3.75, you can see a practical result of using the Punch mode.

1. A fragment between two clips was precisely selected with the <Tab>+<B> and <Tab>+<E> hotkey combination.
2. The multitrack cursor was positioned a bit before the recording's start point.
3. **S-R-P** was pressed, and the fragment was performed.

As a result of these actions, you get an extremely accurate recording.

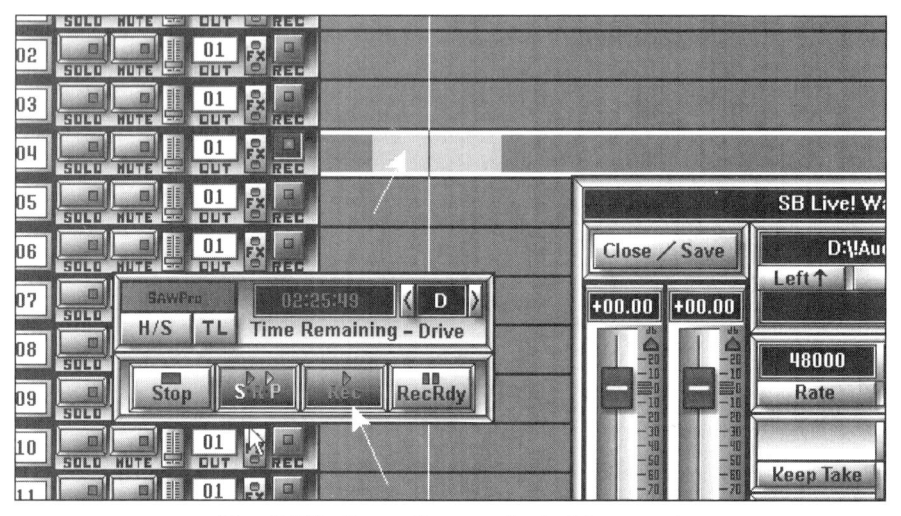

Fig. 3.74. Recording a selected fragment

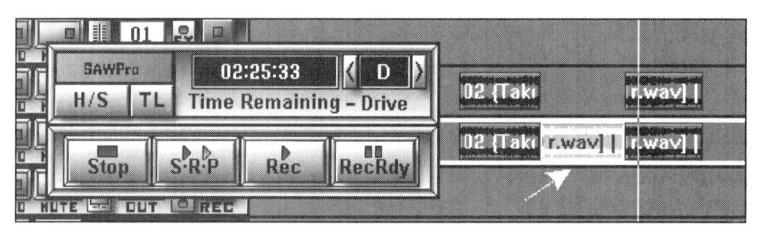

Fig. 3.75. A practical example of applying Punch mode recording

Using the Punch and Auto-Rewind Modes

If, dear reader, you ever have to perform musical part takes alone while controlling your computer, we suggest that you take the following into consideration.

When recording your takes, use both the Punch mode and the auto-rewind mode (the **AUTO** button on the Remote Transport panel).

With this combination, you need only perform one action with the mouse, and then just press the spacebar. The technique is as follows:

1. Select the track fragment in which you will record your takes.
2. Place the cursor at the starting point.
3. Press the **S-R-P** button, or the spacebar on the keyboard.
4. Record the take.
5. Press the spacebar to stop playback and automatically return the cursor to the starting point.

6. If this take failed, just press the spacebar once more and repeat the whole routine. The preceding take will be "dropped" to the region list, with the potential of being restored, which we discussed earlier (see Fig. 3.73).

> **NOTE** So as not to hear the previous take while recording the current one, check the **Auto Mute During SRP Punch-In** option on the **Options** menu.

As a result, the many computer control operations that divert your attention while performing music are reduced to one: pressing the "biggest" key, i.e., the spacebar. With this power of automation, one can pretty much ignore the computer and focus on the music itself.

> **TIP** If you have a large number of musical parts and fragments included in your work at the same time, we recommend, for your convenience, that you save each recording in a separate sound file with a distinct name.
>
> Don't hesitate to append fragments to a "ready" sound file. To be sure that you get the right audio file, choose its name directly after pressing the **FileName** button of the virtual tape recorder.

Recording a Complicated Instrumental or Vocal Part

To err is human, and this is especially the case when performing technically complicated musical pieces.

What should you do if your brain generates ideas whose complexity exceeds your technical level of performance?

You could, of course, ask a virtuoso musician for help. But you might not know a whole lot of them, so this might be somewhat problematic.

Eventually, you're going to have to figure it out for yourself. Here is where excellent non-destructive overdubbing and editing skill swill be required. The recording methods described below can help you a great deal. When using these methods, your motto should be something like the following: *anything complicated can be divided into simple parts and then performed and recorded.* So good luck!

❒ Start by dividing a long, complicated musical phrase into short parts that are easier to perform.
❒ If troubles occur when playing a keyboard instrument, record the parts for the left hand and those for the right hand separately.
❒ If it's easier for you to play the left hand part with your right hand, do so.
❒ Record a complicated guitar part in two or three parts.

> **NOTE** "Divide and record": this should be the policy for realizing of your musical plan. Remember that no rule restricts your creative activity. The computer will never "object" to any experiments you decide to perform.

- ☐ If it's easier for you to sing with a melody in the background, don't be afraid to use one. (Just don't forget to exclude it with the **MUTE** button before the final mixing of all tracks.)
- ☐ If you were not given a beautiful voice at birth, don't get upset. Use some "make-up" on your voice.

NOTE The easiest way to enrich the color of your voice is as follows. With a musical synthesizer, choose an instrument that resembles your voice in its timbre. Record the voice part, performed by this instrument, on a single track. After that, mix the two: the voice part track and the track with the same melody instrumentally. While doing this, find the proper volume ratio between the voice and the melody. This method allows you to strengthen the voice considerably when the sound is processed in a certain manner.

- ☐ Never hesitate to look for your own individual methods of working.
- ☐ By using many takes, you can create virtuoso-like music.

NOTE Fig. 3.76 shows the result of arranging a number of guitar solo takes. The fragments that remain on the track are the best pieces of each of four takes.

Afterwards, all the clips can be united onto one track in order to free up the other tracks.

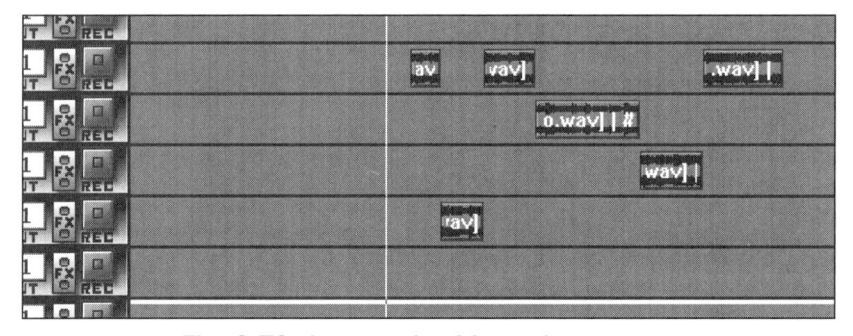

Fig. 3.76. An example of four-take montage

Snapping to the Musical Meter and Tempo

It's much easier to write evenly on ruled paper. Positioning clips on the multitrack, especially when mounting and editing, is easier when the multitrack is "ruled" as well. This is possible when you enable the *mode used for binding, or "snapping", the audio material to the time grid.*

Moreover, if you use pre-prepared musical fragments (loops), or if you have recorded a MIDI sequencer part to a sound file, you cannot manage without setting the meter and the tempo.

Enabling the Tempo Mode

This mode is set, as shown in Fig. 3.77, with the **Tempo Mode** option of the **TimeLine/MT-Grid** menu.

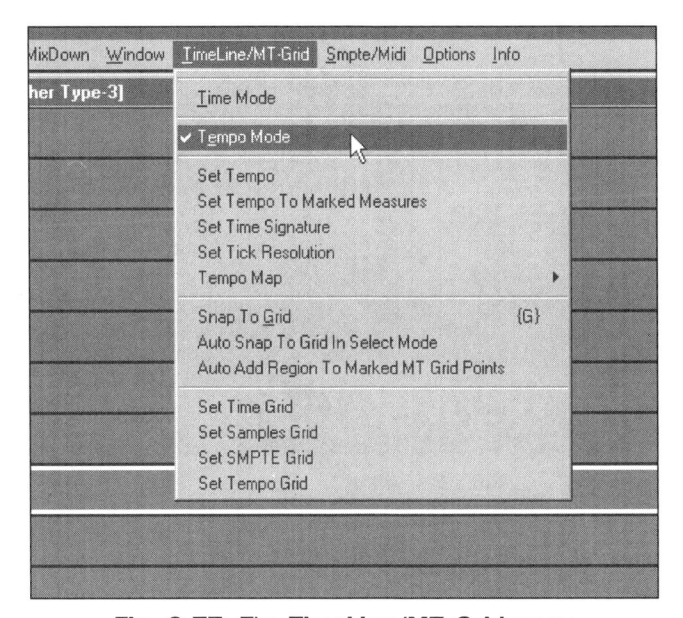

Fig. 3.77. The **TimeLine/MT-Grid** menu

To snap the project to the time grid, this grid's zero offset should be fixed to the first strong beat of your recording.

1. Among your records, choose a track that has clips containing pieces with a rhythmic pattern (for example, one with a rhythm section).
2. Then, place the cursor precisely on the first strong beat.
3. Press and hold the <Shift> key.
4. Click on the **Z** button on the **Remote Transport** panel.

The **TimeLine** reading will start from a strong beat in the rhythmic pattern (see Fig. 3.75). In Fig. 3.78, this strong beat coincides with the clip's beginning.

The zero offset can be reset by pressing the <Ctrl> key and clicking on the **Remote Transport** panel's **Z** button.

We stated above that there are two main options on the **TimeLine/MT-Grid** menu that reflect two different ways of measuring an audio file: the **Time Mode** and the **Tempo Mode**.

The **Time Mode** measures the audio file in units of time, SMPTE, and is required, for instance, for assembling advertisements.

The **Tempo Mode** measures the audio file using units that correspond to the note values: **Measure/Beat/Tick**.

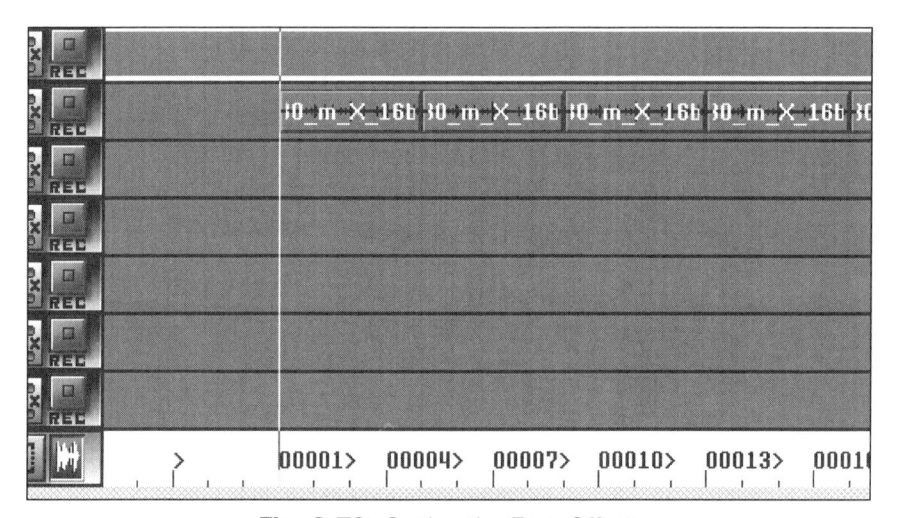

Fig. 3.78. Setting the Zero Offset

A *measure* and a *beat* are the exact same measurement units found in musical terminology.

A *tick* is the shortest time measurement unit. (It equals the result of dividing the value of a quarter note by the parameter defined by the **Set Tick Resolution** command of the **TimeLine/MT-Grid** menu.)

> **NOTE** We'll explicate these terms for non-musicians. A *measure* (or *bar*) is the distance between two strong musical beats. *Beats* are equal parts of a measure. For example, in a march, strong beats (every first one) alternate. Imagine the marching rhythm: ONE-two, ONE-two... In a waltz, the strong beat is every first of three: ONE-two-three, ONE-two-three.
>
> The distance between strong beats is exactly what a *measure* is. In a march, the measure is double (consists of two beats), while in a waltz it is triple (consists of three beats).
>
> It should be added that the tick is the minimal value for MIDI sequencers (such as the CakeWalk and Cubase programs).

The **Measure/Beat/Tick** time measurement mode is typical for MIDI (Musical Instrument Digital Interface) instruments.

The Tempo Mode Options

Let's investigate the **TimeLine/MT-Grid** menu options that relate to the **Tempo Mode**.

- **Set Tempo** — sets the tempo anywhere within the range of 20,000 to 350,000 beats per minute.
- **Set Tempo To Marked Measures** — sets the tempo by the selected musical measures. This is done as follows:
  1. Mark a distance of one measure on the clip (from one strong beat to another strong beat).
  2. Execute the **Set Tempo To Marked Measures** command.

The tempo is then calculated and set. This can be seen on the **Remote Transport** panel. (In Fig. 3.79, the tempo is about 129 beats per minute, with four-four meter).

> **NOTE** A different number of measures may be set for a selected area (from one strong beat to another strong beat) in the **Enter Marked Measure Count** dialog box, if you so desire. For instance, you can change it to two measures instead of one. In such a case, the tempo will be altered as well.

- **Set Time Signature** — set the musical meter (2/4, 3/4, 4/4, 6/8, etc.).

> **NOTE** March meter is 2/4, and waltz meter is 3/4.

- **Set Tick Resolution** — sets the number of ticks (shortest time intervals) per quarter-note (a note of a 1/4 value, or one beat).
- **Snap To Grid** — turns the mode of snapping to the time-beat grid on/off. The hotkey for this is <G>.

> **NOTE** When the *Snap To Grid* mode is on, two vertical bars appear on the **Remote Transport** panel (Fig. 3.79).

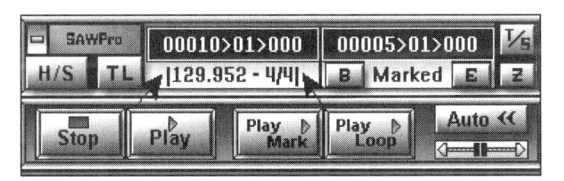

Fig. 3.79. The **Snap To Grid** mode indication

- **Auto Snap To Grid In Select Mode** — turns the mode of snapping to the time-beat grid on automatically when in Select mode.
- **Set Tempo Grid** — defines the grid interval in note values: 1/4, 1/8, 1/16, etc.

In SAWPro 2.1 or higher, there is an additional submenu — **Tempo Map**.

- **Set Tempo At Position** — changes (sets) the tempo at the cursor position
- **Set Tempo To Marked Measures At Position** — changes (sets) the tempo for a selected area of measures at the cursor position
- **Set Time Signature At Position** — changes the musical meter at the cursor position
- **Set New Measure Count At Position** — assigns a number to the measure at the cursor position
- **Clear Tempo Map** — cancels all changes in the tempo and meter
- **Clear Tempo Map Entry** — cancels all changes in the tempo and meter, at the cursor position

This way, if a musical piece includes tempo or meter alterations, the menu items described above will assist in bringing these changes into correspondence with the time grid, which will ease your subsequent work, like non-destructive editing, considerably.

In the "*Non-Destructive Audio Editing*" section, we discussed copying a region (see Fig. 3.31). In the example provided, a region image could move freely around the multitrack and take any place.

However, if the **Snap To Grid** mode is enabled, a region image can only occupy "correct" (in the synchronic sense) positions, or those that coincide with the grid's boundaries.

The region (clip) itself must be of standard size, i.e., be "truncated" to exactly fit the grid's boundaries, and must have the assigned tempo and meter.

If these conditions are met, it is easy to arrange a working composition from pre-prepared fragments. The **Set Tempo To Marked Measures** option may be useful when using ready fragments (loops) created by other musicians.

As a rule, the tempo in which a fragment was created is unknown or specified only approximately. It can, however, be "measured" with high precision using **Set Tempo To Marked Measures**.

With the **Snap To Grid** mode turned on, you can "slice" the fragment according to the musical note values. You can then experiment with these "slices", placing them on different tracks and applying virtual effects: for example, **Reverse** (playing backwards) or **Delay**.

To sum up, using the functions described above makes the SAWPro program more than a tool for multichannel audio recording to the hard drive; they make it a unique musical instrument.

Processing Sound in SAWPro

For quality sound producing, one should have the ability to listen to the project as a whole, with real-time sound effects. Files of the project can of course be processed with a separate sound editor, such as WaveLab. However, this requires a good imagination and a good ear in order to conceive of how the sound will be combined on the multitrack.

Attaching Sound Processing Program Modules

So as not to tire your imagination out, you can simply listen to and correct results in real time using SAWPro's **Effects Patch Builder** window to attach (patch) sound effects. This window is called by the **FX** button on the **MultiTrack View** window (Fig. 3.80; we saw it before in Fig. 3.18 when introducing the program interface).

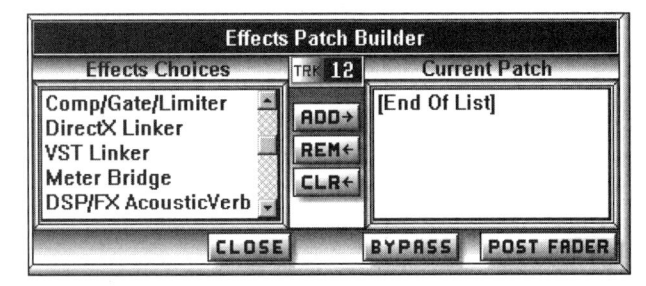

Fig. 3.80. The **Effects Patch Builder** window

We already learned the controls of the **Effects Patch Builder**, **DirectX Linker**, and **VST Linker** windows. Let's recall some tips.

On the **Current Patch** list, in the right side, you will find attached effects. When double-clicking on a selected list item, a specific window emerges for controlling this element's parameters. The **Reverse Phase**, **Reverse Audio**, and **CenterCh Eliminator** effects are an exception: they don't have configuration windows, since they have nothing to configure.

The list on the left contains all virtual effects that are used as built-in system modules.

In the **Current Patch** list, plug-ins are listed in the order in which they process the sound. The uppermost element of the list is the first effect that is applied to the signal. A new plug-in is always patched *before* the effect that is highlighted in the **Current Patch** list. To make an attached effect last in the chain, click first on the **[End Of List]** line of the **Current Patch** list. This rule applies to all plug-in patch windows.

An effect patched to a track functions for the entire length of this track.

To apply effects selectively — that is, to specific clips on a track only — clips that should not undergo processing have to be removed to a vacant track. Other ways of selective effect application to clips are destructive editing and preliminary reduction of selected clips (these will be discussed later).

To remove all effects on the multitrack, click on any **FX** button while pressing the <Ctrl> key.

Saw Native Standard Virtual Effects

The virtual effects of the Saw Native internal standard are included into the SAWPro installation set. These are: **VariPitch/Speed**, **Reverse Phase**, **Reverse Audio**, **CenterCh Eliminator**, **Graphic Equalizer**, **Echo/Delay**, **Comp/Gate/Limiter**, and two connecting program modules: **DirectX Linker** and **VST Linker**.

The **Meter Bridge** (the output level meter) is installed separately.

A Brief Description of Built-In SAWPro Effects

Unfortunately, virtual effects of the Saw Native standard are despairingly out of date and not able to compete with the world of plug-ins that has evolved before our eyes during the last three years. So we don't find it particularly necessary to give a detailed description of Saw Native's virtual effects. Let's just look at these briefly.

- **VariPitch/Speed** is an effect that shifts the pitch and the audio track playback speed. This is convenient to apply when adjusting percussion fragments of varying tempo.
- **Reverse Phase** inverts the track signal phase 180 degrees.
- **Reverse Audio** plays back the track backwards.
- **CenterCh Eliminator** forms the differential signal of the left and right stereo channels.
- **Graphic Equalizer** is a parametric graphical (or paragraphical) equalizer.

We shall make an exception for the **Graphic Equalizer** module, which we'll inspect in more detail (Fig. 3.81).

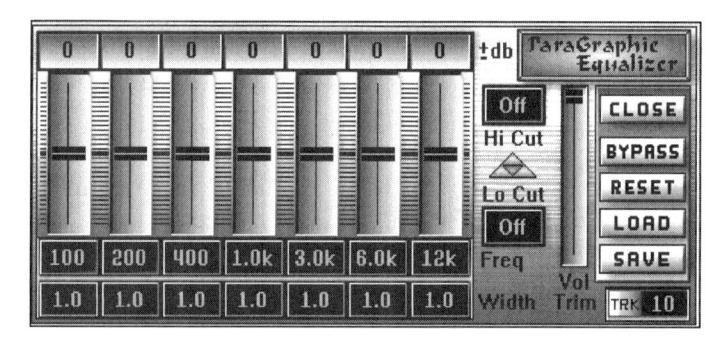

Fig. 3.81. A paragraphical equalizer window

This virtual device window contains high and low frequency filters, **Hi Cut** and **Lo Cut**.

The **Width** section controls the quality of equalizer frequency bands within a range from 0.5 to 2.0.

The equalizer adjustment range is +15 dB to −15 dB.

Chapter 3: The SAWPro Program: Live Recording In a Virtual Studio

Clicking with the right mouse button on the frequency indicator panel (the **Freq** section) disables the corresponding slider, so that the frequency indicator will read **Off**.

To enable the slider, repeat the operation.

To change the parameters of any readout, click on it and drag the mouse up or down. The **Vol Trim** slider allows you to reduce the volume if signal spike clipping takes place.

The **Reset** button turns the **Lo Cut** and **Hi Cut** filters off and sets the sliders in the center position. Current equalizer parameters can be saved in a file and loaded from that file using the **Save** and **Load** buttons, respectively.

> **TIP** We'll share some of our observations with you: other than the fact that they are not the fastest, TC Native EQ-G from TC Works (Fig. 3.82) and Q-Metric from Steinberg (Fig. 3.83) are the best equalizers to use. These equalizers are plugged-in through the **DirectX Linker**.

Let's now examine built-in effects.

- **Echo/Delay** provides the signal delay effect, repeated echo, and the effect of cross delay between the left and right channels.
- **Comp/Gate/Limiter** is a multifunctional module, combining a compressor, a noise gate, and an amplitude peak limiter (Fig. 3.84). This module also performs *normalization*, i.e., the highest possible amplification of the volume level without clipping the signal peaks.

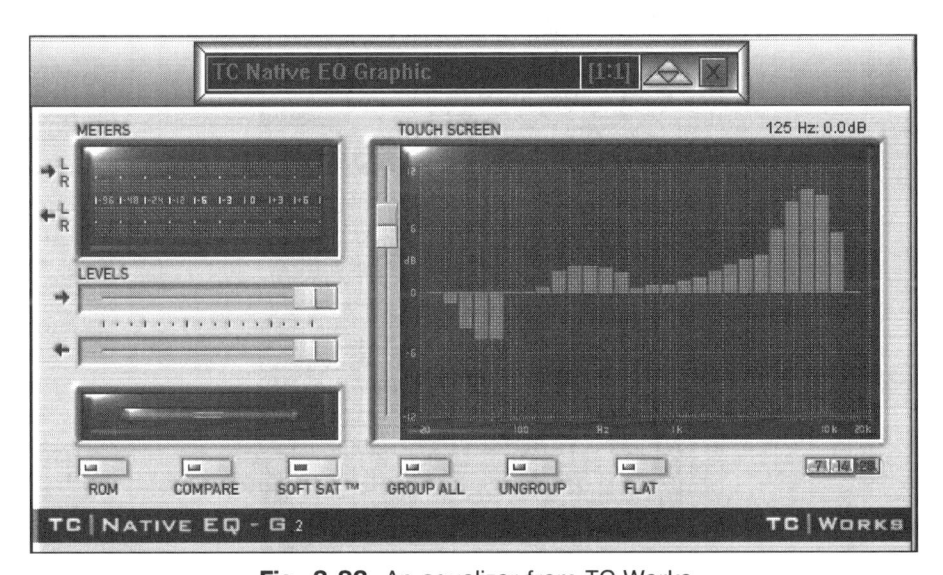

Fig. 3.82. An equalizer from TC Works

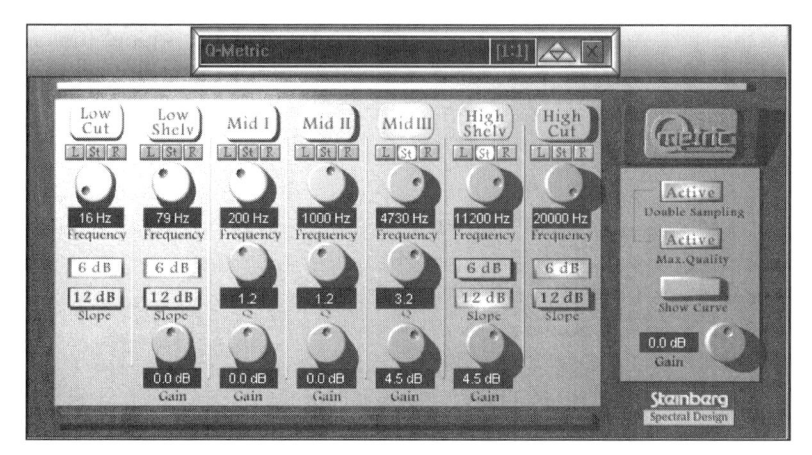

Fig. 3.83. The Q-Metric parametrical equalizer by Steinberg

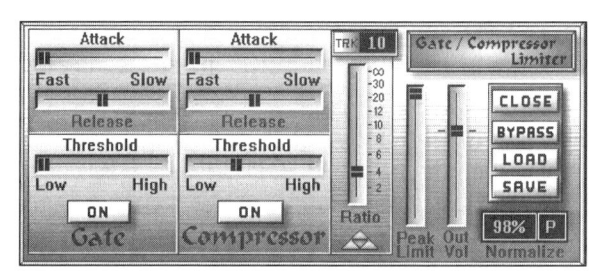

Fig. 3.84. The **Comp/Gate/Limiter** module window

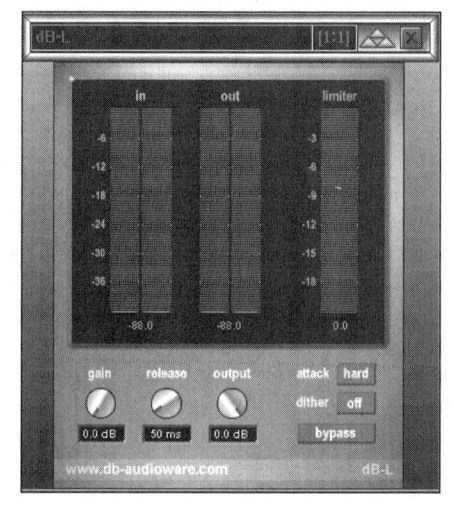

Fig. 3.85. The **dB-L** mastering limiter window

Chapter 3: The SAWPro Program: Live Recording In a Virtual Studio

Since this module cannot function in real time when normalizing or peak limiting, the **Force FX Pre-Scan/Playback** command (for scanning the effect preventively before playback) has been provided on the **Process/MixDown** menu.

This command is executed in two stages:

1. The sound file is scanned.
2. Playback starts when you see this: **Pre-Scan Complete. Click OK To Begin PlayBack**!

TIP — We suggest that you only use the **Normalize** function in the **Comp/Gate/Limiter** module.

NOTE — The **Comp/Gate/Limiter** module is described in detail in the book *Computer-Aided Sound Processing* by A. Zagumennov.

As an adequate alternative to the **Comp/Gate/Limiter** module, we can mention effects by Dave Brown: db-audioware (**http://www.db-audioware.com**), **dB-L** mastering limiter (Fig. 3.85), and the DirectX-standard **dB-M** multiband limiter.

A combination of a compressor and a noise gate can be also successfully realized, for instance, using the **C1+** DirectX standard module from the Waves company (Fig. 3.86).

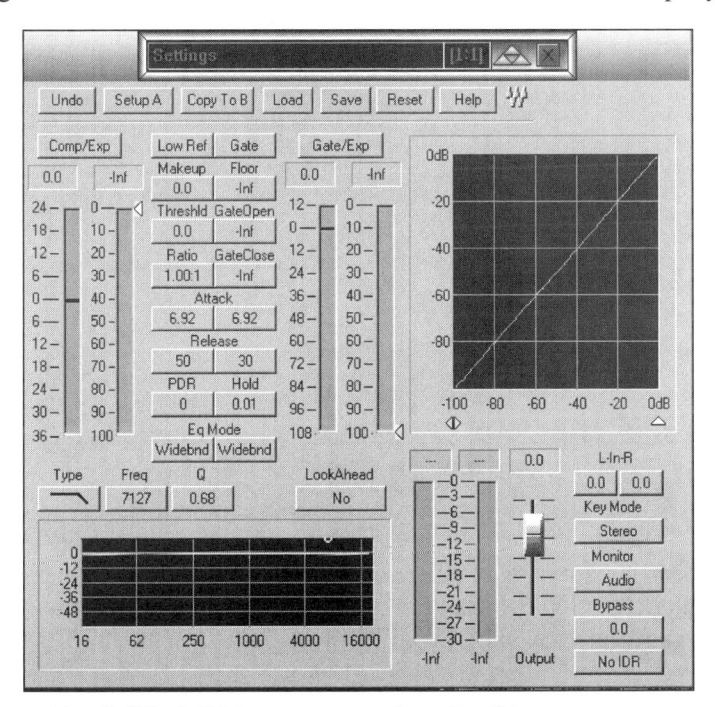

Fig. 3.86. A **C1+** compressor from the Waves company

Interaction between SAWPro and DirectX & VST Virtual Effects

Here we note once more that one of the attractive features of SAWPro when compared to other multichannel audio recording programs is its ability to apply DirectX and VST virtual effects simultaneously.

The scheme of interaction between SAWPro and plug-ins is simple and reliable. A list of available program modules is kept in the SAWProFX.ini file, which is located in the program's working directory (C:\SAWPro, by default).

An example of the content of the SAWProFX.ini file is depicted in Fig. 3.87. Each effect is organized as a dynamically linked module (a DLL module).

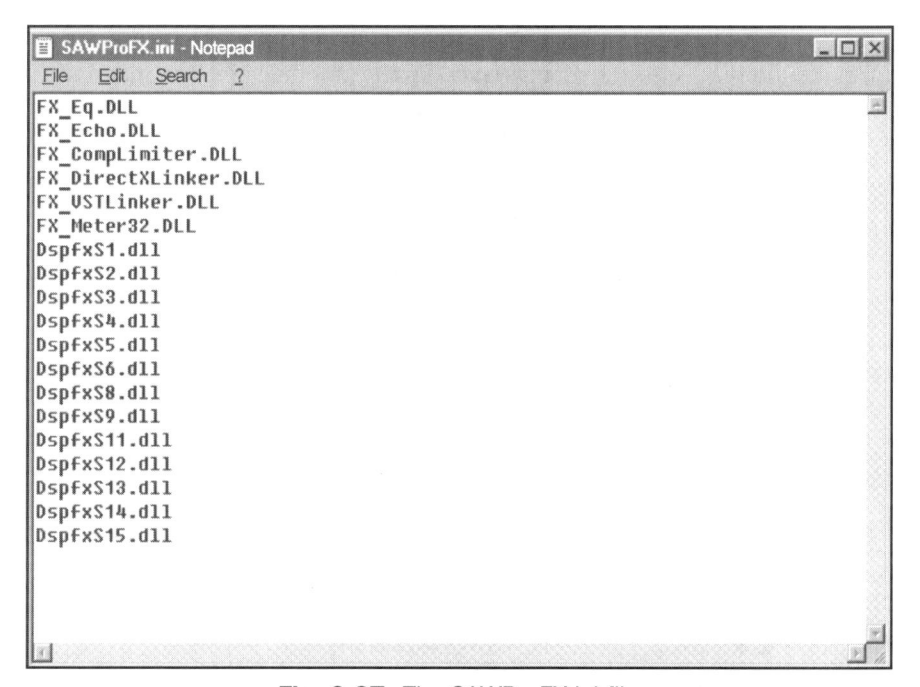

Fig. 3.87. The SAWProFX.ini file

All list items are program modules that can be linked directly to the program.

The **DirectX Linker** and **VST Linker** connecting modules are implemented in the FX_DirectXLinker.dll and FX_VSTLinker.dll files. These files must reside in the SAWPro program folder (Fig. 3.88), and must be included in the SAWProFX.ini DLL module list.

Meeting these conditions guarantees access to DirectX virtual effects.

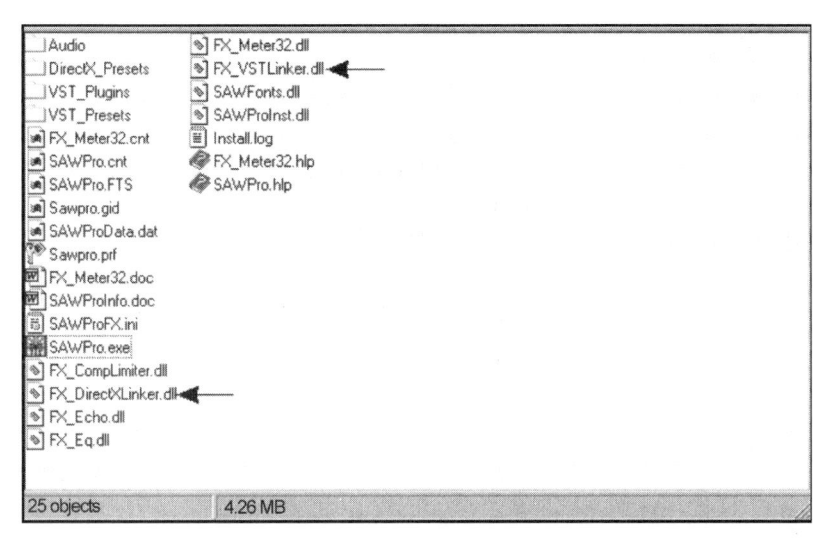

Chapter 3: The SAWPro Program: Live Recording In a Virtual Studio 121

Fig. 3.88. Files in the SAWPro folder

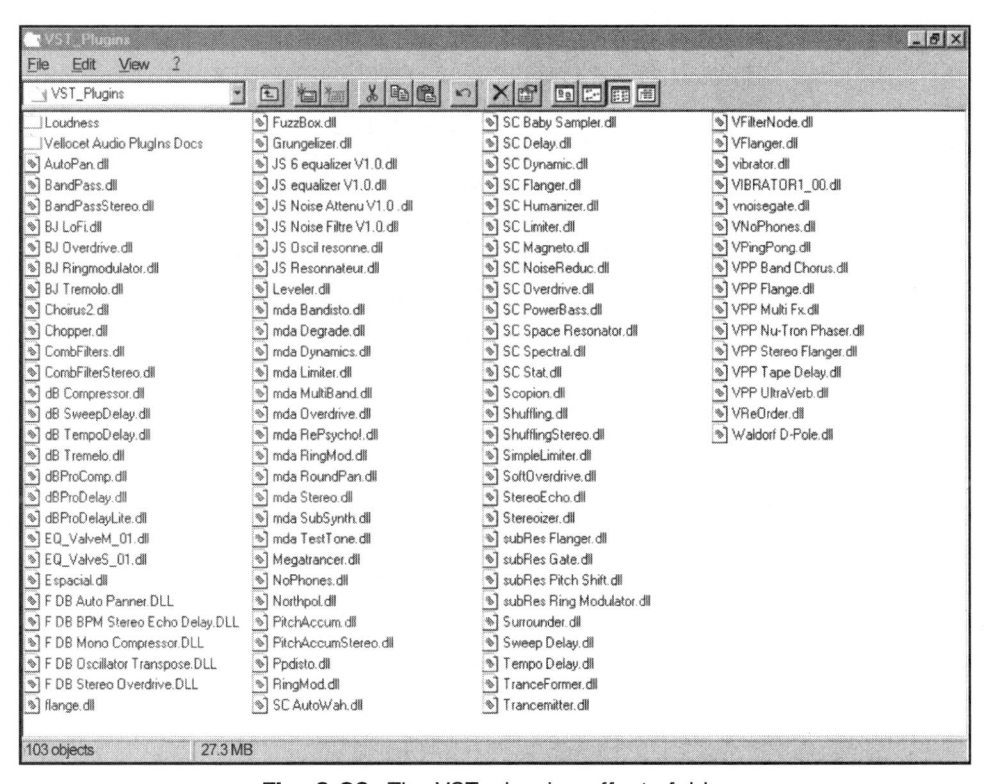

Fig. 3.89. The VST_plug-ins effects folder

With VST effects, the matter is somewhat more complicated. Due to their specific architecture, VST effects need to be installed in a special directory, VST_plug-ins, which is nested in the SAWPro working directory (Fig. 3.89). Some of the effects that are files with the DLL extension can simply be copied to the VST_plug-ins folder. Fig. 3.89 shows a typical set of DLL files that contain effects that can be used in SAWPro.

Some Distinctions between VST and DirectX Effects

VST effects require relatively modest computing resources. At the same time, they are considerably more varied and more music-oriented than DirectX effects.

This means that while DirectX effects are better for the sound processing itself (emulating hardware studio devices), some VST effects may be classified as supplementary musical instruments of a specific sort, or virtual arrangement tools.

VST effects constitute a large, separate topic that extends beyond the scope of the issues discussed here. We'll try to describe these effects in a separate book.

To access DirectX effects, the **DirectX Linker** module should be activated, i.e., added to the **Current Patch** list of effects in the **Effects Patch Builder** window (Fig. 3.90).

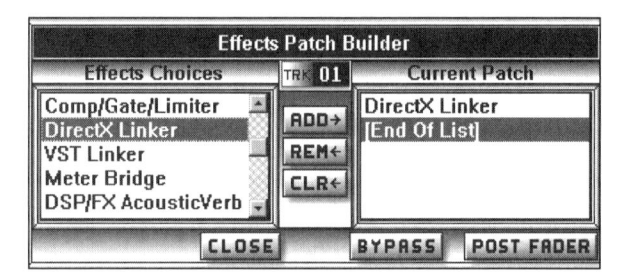

Fig. 3.90. Selecting the **DirectX Linker** module

In order to see a list of the DirectX effects themselves, double-click on the **DirectX Linker** line in the **Current Patch** list. This will open the **DirectX Patch Builder** window for attaching sound effects (Fig. 3.91).

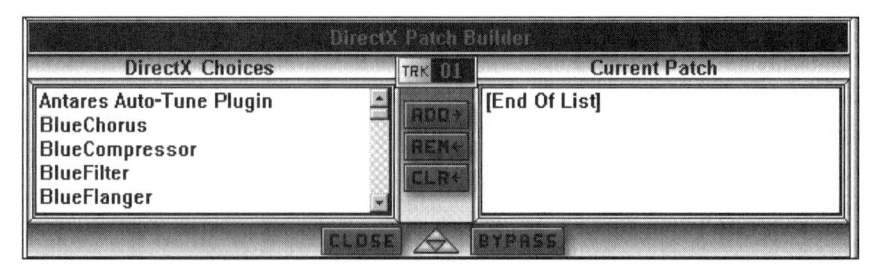

Fig. 3.91. The **DirectX Patch Builder** window

Chapter 3: The SAWPro Program: Live Recording In a Virtual Studio 123

The principle of attaching effects in the **DirectX Patch Builder** window is similar to that of choosing effects in the **Effects Patch Builder** window.

The **BYPASS** button lets you disable selected effects without unloading them from memory. Every DirectX effect is designed with an individual interface; however, there are common elements added by the SAWPro program (Fig. 3.92).

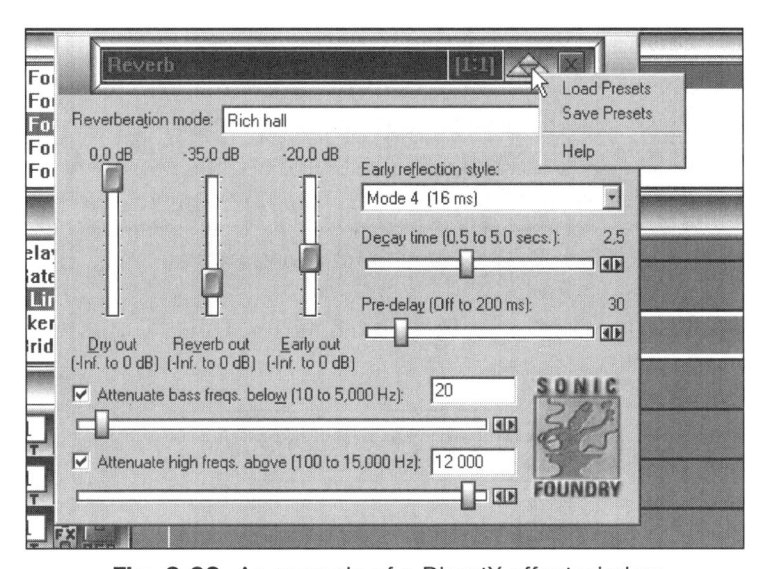

Fig. 3.92. An example of a DirectX effect window

These common elements are the following.

- An 'x' button for closing the window; this is the standard one used for Windows applications.

- The **Load Presets/Save Presets** pull-down menu icon, shaped as the IQS company logo.

Let's imagine a typical situation: having selected a fragment and looped its playback, you decide to use the virtual regulators to get the right sound (the **SOLO** mode can be turned on for this track).

When the effect is all set up, you save the project using the <Ctrl>+<U> key combination. All the effect's settings are placed into the EDL project file. You might, however, need this successful configuration afterwards, for instance, to process the next track.

This is what the presets menu is for. SAWPro is designed so that when saving the settings of an effect, an individual folder of the same name is automatically created for this effect in the **DirectX_Presets** folder (Fig. 3.94). For example, the **Sonic Foundry Reverb** effect will have a directory with the same name created for it (Fig. 3.93).

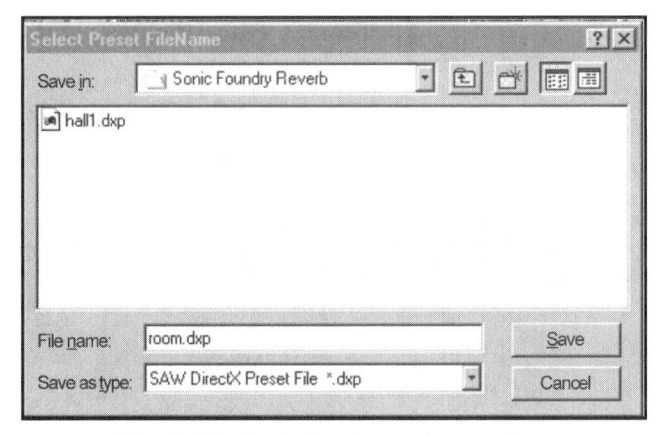

Fig. 3.93. A window for saving settings

The settings file has the DXP extension (standing for DirectX Presets), and occupies a small amount of space.

Fig. 3.94. Location of preset files

About Moving Preset Files

Preset files can be easily transferred from one computer to another, or set during SAWPro's setup, since they easily fit on a 1.44 MB floppy disk. You just need to copy the content of the **DirectX_Presets** folder into the folder of the same name on another computer. The corresponding DirectX effects should already be installed in the system.

To handle VST effects, the **VST Linker** must be activated in the **Effects Patch Builder** window. The **VST Patch Builder** for attaching VST effects is called by double-clicking on the **Current Patch** panel (Fig. 3.95).

The **DirectX Patch Builder** and **VST Patch Builder** windows have the same interface.

Chapter 3: The SAWPro Program: Live Recording In a Virtual Studio 125

You can call a window for adjusting a certain effect by clicking on the proper item of the **Current Patch** list (Fig. 3.96).

Unlike DirectX, some VST effects allow you to save not only presets, but also effect program banks (like with musical synthesizers). Preset files have the extension VSP, and bank files have the VSB extension. For every effect's presets, a folder of the same name is created. All VST effect configuration files are kept in the **VST_Presets** folder.

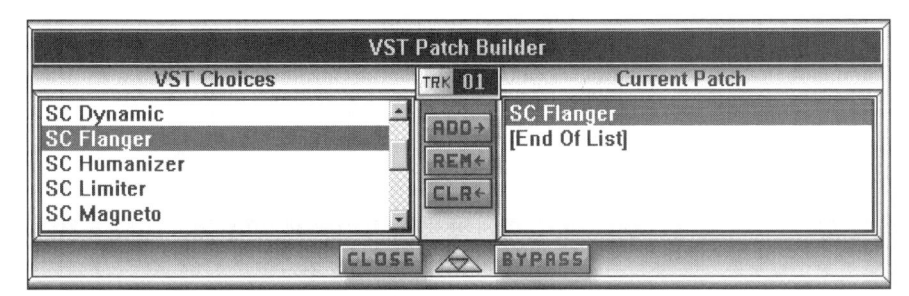

Fig. 3.95. The **VST Patch Builder** window

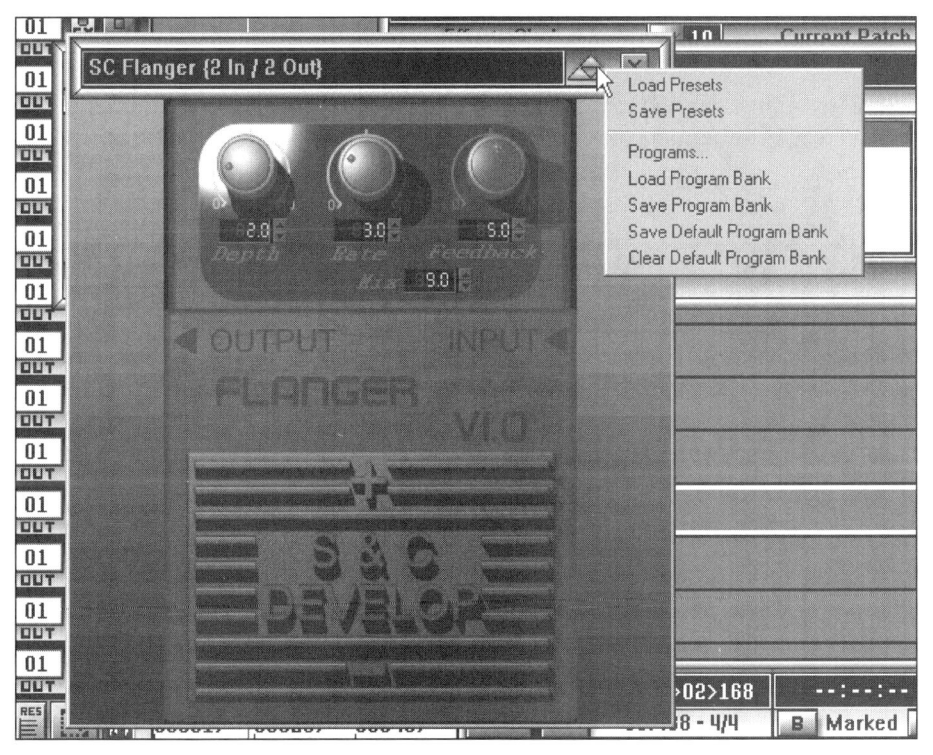

Fig. 3.96. The **SC Flanger** VST effect window

Types of VST Effects

VST effects can be of different types:

- One input — one output
- One input — two outputs
- Two inputs — two outputs

The last variant is best for a stereo signal. If other types of effects are used for a stereo signal, only the left channel will be processed. The list of SAWPro-compatible VST effects is constantly updated on IQS's site on the Internet: **http://www.iqsoft.com**.

Additional Settings

The same IQS logo can be found on the **DirectX Patch Builder** and **VST Patch Builder** windows. By clicking on this logo, the menu for additional settings is activated.

The menu (Fig. 3.97) contains the following items:

- **Save Preferences** saves the settings of the menu itself, as well as the **DirectX Patch Builder** (or **VST Patch Builder**) window's position on the SAWPro screen. Every time the window is opened afterwards, it will take the same position.
- **Continuous Adjustment Tracking**: this option being enabled, any parameter alteration for the effect is responded to with the shortest possible delay — almost immediately.
- **About** offers information about the program.

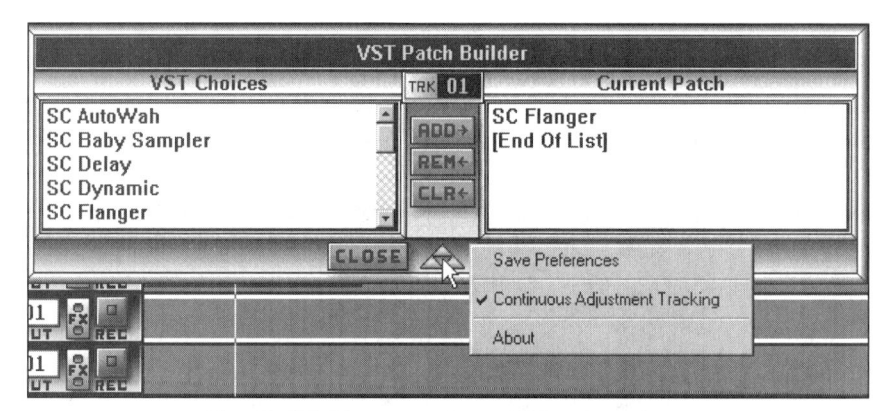

Fig. 3.97. The menu for additional settings

TIP We strongly recommend that you turn the **Continuous Adjustment Tracking** mode on in order to accelerate the effect adjustment, even despite the fact that **using this option requires extra CPU resources.**

Destructive Editing

Destructive editing modifies the sound file irreversibly, thus making it impossible to come back to the original state of the file.

Destructive editing is needed for fixing results during the intermediate stages of work. This procedure frees up computer resources considerably, because when editing destructively, all the applied sound effects are attached to the initial variant of the record for good.

Can One Do without Destructive Editing?

We became intrigued by this problem, and so we performed a few experiments with the aim of determining the productivity threshold for computers of different capacity, as far as SAWPro is concerned.

First, an "average" computer was tested, one with a Pentium III 450 CPU and 128 MB of RAM.

Running SAWPro on this computer, we saturated it as much as we could with the **TrueVerb** DirectX effect (a high-quality reverber) from Waves. The effect was patched to every track (from **01** to **XX**, where **XX** was the number of the last track before getting the overload message) using the MillenniumVerb preset.

With this configuration, the computer was able to stand up to seven simultaneously attached **TrueVerb** effects. Is this a little or a lot?

Let's count. For drums to sound "life-like", they need six to nine tracks allotted to them. The bass will require one or two. Three more tracks are necessary for guitars. Besides these, we also might have keyed instruments, wind instruments, a voice (voices), exotic percussion, etc., participating in the recording process.

We admit that the given calculation is not exact. Nevertheless, the conclusion is clear: a complete project with virtual effects cannot be played back in real time on a PIII-450 computer.

We began a new experiment, this time using the Pentium III 933 Coppermine CPU. Maybe with this "fast" machine, we would be able to manage without destructive editing?

This time, the test computer configuration was the following: Pentium III 933 Coppermine, 128 MB (PC 133) of RAM, and an AX34Pro motherboard by Aopen (other components are not listed, for the sake of brevity).

When testing with Samplitude 2496 (see *Chapter 5*), we managed to patch 17 **TrueVerb** effects (with the MillenniumVerb preset), one per *each* track of the project, which loaded the CPU 93%, according to the Samplitude program indicator.

NOTE The Samplitude 2496 requires more computer resources than SAWPro. In our tests, we used 16-bit stereo audio files with a sample rate of 44,000 Hz.

Of course, when the CPU is almost 100% busy, it is difficult, for example, to mix recordings. However, the results give us hope. Technology progresses rapidly, and the day when destructive editing becomes unnecessary is coming: the computer will manage alone with a large amount of sound effects *in real time*.

As for the results of our experiments, we've concluded the following.

There are several ways of solving the problem of "what needs to be done in order to record a full-fledged musical project at home". Here are four correct answers:

❏ Wait for the release of CPUs that function at the frequency of a microwave oven
❏ Connect digital hardware sound processing devices to the computer
❏ Use destructive editing
❏ Use intermediate mixing

Destructive Editing Techniques

This method has its advantages, despite the fact that it *always* modifies the source audio file. Among these advantages are freeing up computer resources and the possibility of applying different effects within one track, even on a limited track segment.

NOTE When processing a marked area destructively, the positions of the **Fader** volume and pan controls are taken into account. All clips and region copies of the processed fragment change their sound accordingly.

Applying an Effect to a Track Segment

As you may remember, effects attached through the **Effects Patch Builder** are valid along the whole track. However, you might come across a situation where the effect or its parameters need to be altered on a local segment of a clip. This can be done with destructive editing.

1. Mark off the area of the clip where you want to use destructive editing.
2. Go to the **Process/MixDown** menu.
3. On this menu, choose **Process Marked Area Back To Original File (Destructive)**.
4. Press **OK** or **OK/No Undo** in the dialog box that appears (Fig. 3.98).

After your confirmation (pressing **OK**), an indicator that the file is being processed will be seen on the screen.

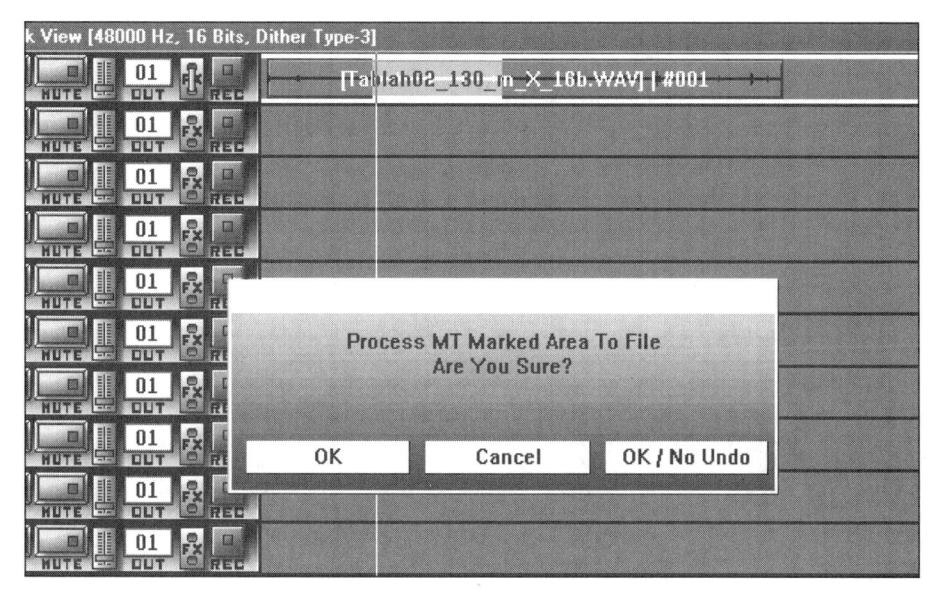

Chapter 3: The SAWPro Program: Live Recording In a Virtual Studio 129

Fig. 3.98. Destructive editing of a clip's marked area

Canceling the Last Operation When Editing Destructively

Only one undo of the last action is provided in SAWPro when destructively editing. This is accomplished using of the **Undo SoundFile** command from the **Edit** menu, or the <Alt>+<U> key combination.

Destructive Editing of Mono Files

Destructive editing of mono audio files has its own peculiarities. If an effect for transforming mono sound into stereo (like **Hyperprism DX Quasi Stereo by Arboretum Systems**, http://www.arboretum.com) is patched to a track where a mono clip is situated, a destructively processed file will not sound like stereo. This puts certain constraints on using mono files in a project. This obstacle may be overcome by using intermediate mixing (see the "*Intermediate Mixing*" section).

Destructive Editing in the *SoundFile View* Window

There are several additional opportunities for editing audio files in the **SoundFile View** window of the SAWPro program that are applicable to selected clip fragments. Let's talk about these.

Removing Unnecessary Fragments and Pauses

After a sound file is recorded in the **SoundFile View** window, unnecessary fragments and pauses can be removed (cut out). Choose the **Cut (Delete) Marked From SoundFile** command from the **Edit** menu.

Press the **Cut Snd File** button on the **Edit Cut Sound File** panel that will appear (Fig. 3.99).

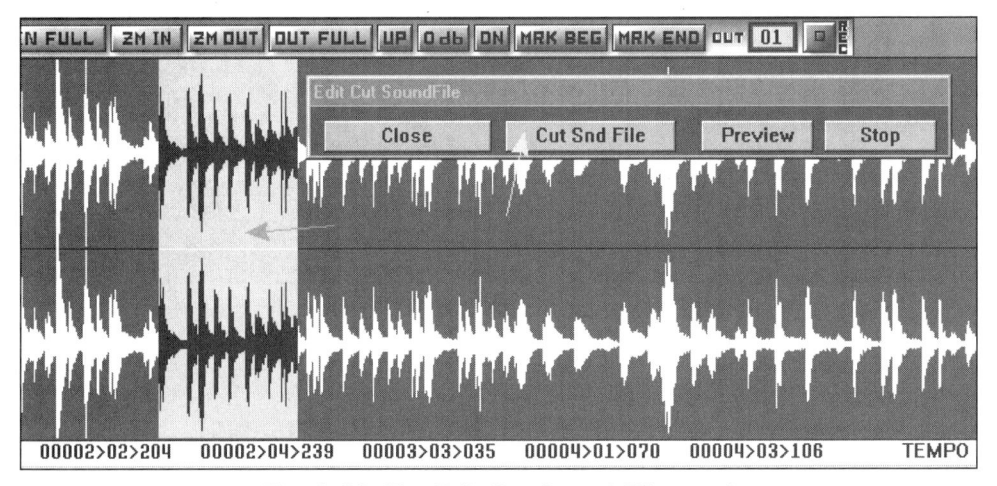

Fig. 3.99. The **Edit Cut Sound File** panel

WARNING You only can remove the material you don't need before regions are created in this sound file. Otherwise, the tracks will be out of sync afterwards.

NOTE The **Cut Snd File** button calls a dialog box that is similar to the one shown in Fig. 3.98. The difference is the absent **OK** button. This means that the operation can only be executed with the **OK/No Undo** button, i.e., with no opportunity to undo your actions.

Listening to a File without the Fragment to Be Removed

Before removing a clip fragment, the file can be listened to without the selected area. To do this, press the **Preview** button on the **Edit Cut Sound File** panel (Fig. 3.99).

You can stop playback using the **Stop** button on the same panel.

The **Edit Cut Sound File** panel is removed from the screen with the **Close** button.

Removing a Fragment without Changing the Recording's Length

All information in the marked fragment can be deleted without changing the length of the audio file (Fig. 3.100).

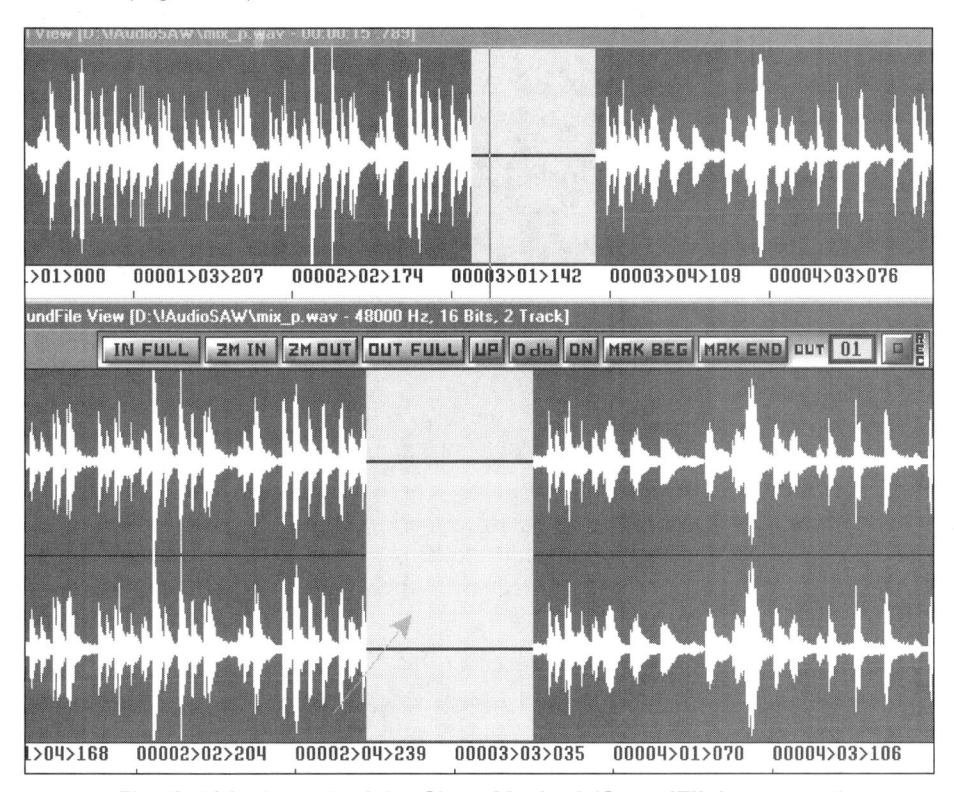

Fig. 3.100. A result of the **Clear Marked (SoundFile)** command

This is done using the **Clear Marked (SoundFile)** command of the **Edit** menu.

> *NOTE*   In sound editors, this operation is called **Silence** or **Mute**.

Editing the Waveform Manually

The waveform can be edited manually at the sample level in the **SoundFile View** window. This can help eliminate clicks, interference, and even signal distortion (Fig. 3.101).

To change to the manual editing mode:

1. Press the **IN FULL** button.
2. Press the **ZM IN** button a number of times to zoom in rapidly.

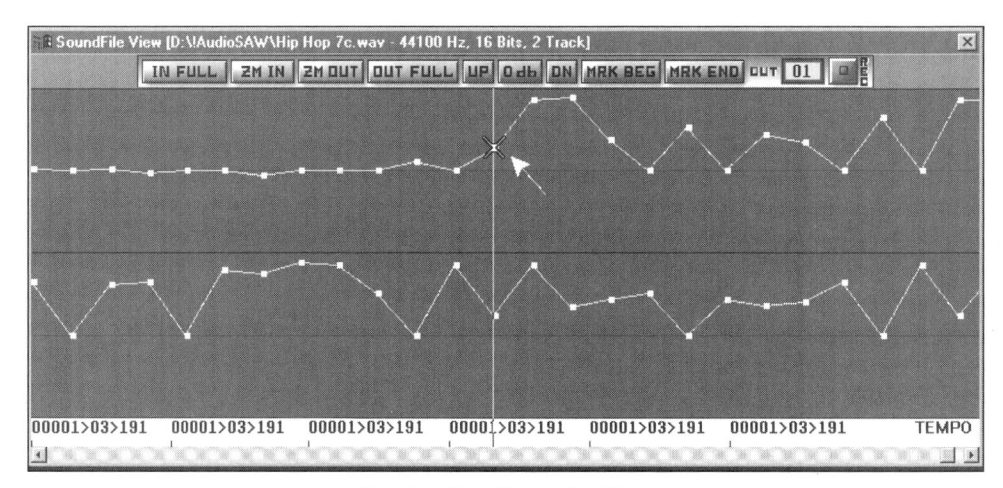

Fig. 3.101. Manual editing

You will see how the smooth waveform (see Fig. 3.101) begins to look like a bunch of small white squares (samples) connected by a string.

All samples are separated by the same distance. The distance between them is determined by the sample rate. Each sample contains information about the signal value at the moment of sampling. That is why the white squares in the diagram are all at different heights. Their vertical position, and consequently the signal value at the moment of sampling, can be altered using manual editing.

The manual editing process goes something like this:

1. Place the cursor at the point you want to edit (Fig. 3.101).
2. Press and hold the <Shift> key.
3. Drag the point to a new position (up or down).

TIP Manual editing is labor-consuming; therefore, you should only use it to correct isolated defects. To eliminate large masses of interference and distortion, it is better to use the various tools supplied in the Cool Edit Pro or Sound Forge sound editors.

Intermediate Mixing

Mixing is a special term that means that a multitrack (multichannel) recording is transformed by mixing and applying sound effects into a two-channel (stereo) or one-channel (mono) recording. This recording is what is then published on AUDIO CDs, audiocassettes, etc.

Intermediate mixing is reduction at a specific stage of work with the project. During intermediate mixing, as a rule, groups of tracks (channels) unified by a common feature, are processed (mixing). This could be, for example, a group of percussion tracks. The purpose of intermediate mixing is to disengage computer resources and tracks, and an individual case could be said to be the mixing of one track or a fragment of one in order to create a new sound file with virtual effects attached.

Intermediate mixing as a method of sound processing can be seen as an alternative to destructive editing. It allows us to save computer resources while keeping the most valuable part of the source material.

NOTE The only shortcoming of this method is the extra consumption of disk space.

Mixing Mechanics

Mixing in SAWPro results in a new sound file that is created, for example, from a number of mono and stereo files.

Uniting them is done using a program that considers all project parameters with mathematical precision, namely:

❐ Virtual effects

❐ Virtual mixer settings

❐ The status of all **MUTE** and **SOLO** buttons on *all* tracks in the **MultiTrack View** window

We can say that the program goes by the principle "what you hear is what you get after mixing".

In this regard, we wish to attract your attention to the following:

❐ Tracks whose **SOLO** buttons are enabled will be turned on during the mixing process

❐ Tracks whose **MUTE** buttons are enabled will be turned off during the mixing process

Thanks to the possibility of making such a choice, we can mix down as many tracks to the sound file as we wish.

For example, we can gather all percussion group tracks for intermediate mixing. This usually releases from five to nine tracks.

Then, the percussion part can be joined with the bass part, etc.

In SAWPro, intermediate mixing is referred to as *mixing down*.

The tracks that contain the results of mixing (**OutputTrack**s) are situated in the lower part of the **MultiTrack View** window.

NOTE For how to change a track's position, see the *"Description of the MultiTrack Window"* section.

It's not easy to recommend the ideal number of tracks in an intermediate mixing group.

This number depends on several factors:

- User's needs
- Musical production's genre and style
- Computer's speed

Therefore, the number of tracks to use in intermediate mixing is usually determined in each specific project on a trial basis.

There is also another way to use intermediate mixing: *mix one entire track,* or *mix a fragment of one track*, i.e., a clip or a part of a clip.

From our point of view, this method is preferable to destructive editing.

The reason is that, first of all, it provides for the safety of the original material. And additionally, this method allows you to convert a mono signal to stereo using DirectX or VST virtual effects.

Mixing Techniques

Depending on how the virtual effect is attached, intermediate mixing algorithms may be applied to both one and a number of tracks.

In the example that is provided here, we assume that virtual effects are already patched.

One-Track Intermediate Mixing Algorithm

Intermediate mixing for a fragment is done like this:

1. Press the **SOLO** button on the selected track. There must be no other track with its **SOLO** button switched on.
2. Precisely mark the clip by its boundaries. For exact clip marking, use the <Tab>+<B> and <Tab>+<E> key combinations.
3. If the fragment is inside the clip, it should be truncated along its boundaries using the <K> key (that is, a new clip should be created inside the first one). You can precisely position the cursor on the boundaries of the inside clip using the **B** and **E** buttons on the **Remote Transport** panel.
4. Open the **Process/MixDown** menu, and execute the **Build Mix To New SoundFile** command.

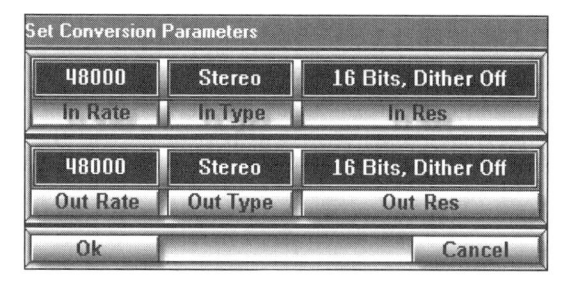

Chapter 3: The SAWPro Program: Live Recording In a Virtual Studio 135

Fig. 3.102. The **Set Conversion Parameters** dialog box

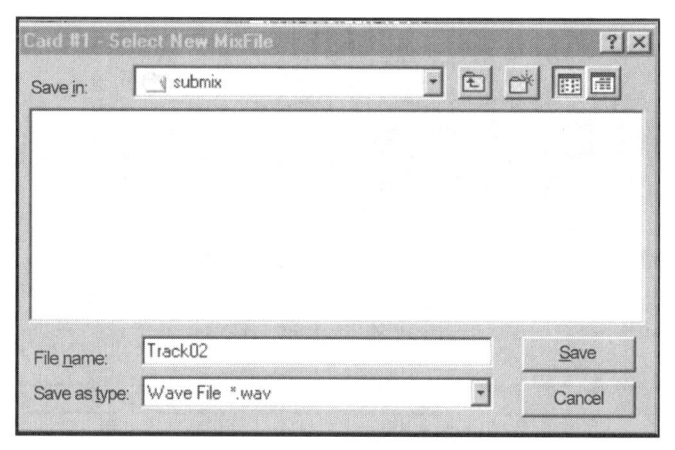

Fig. 3.103. A dialog box for saving a new file

Fig. 3.104. The mixing progress indicator

5. Press OK in the **Set Conversion Parameters** dialog box that appears.
6. Continuing the dialog in the **Select New MixFile** window, name the file (Fig. 3.103) and press **Save**. The mixing progress indicator will appear (Fig. 3.104). After the process is over, the **SoundFile View** window will be opened on the screen with the mixed file selected (Fig. 3.105).
7. Create a region for the mixed file using the <Shift>+<N> key combination.

   NOTE The program does not create a region for the mixed file automatically, so this operation needs to be done manually.

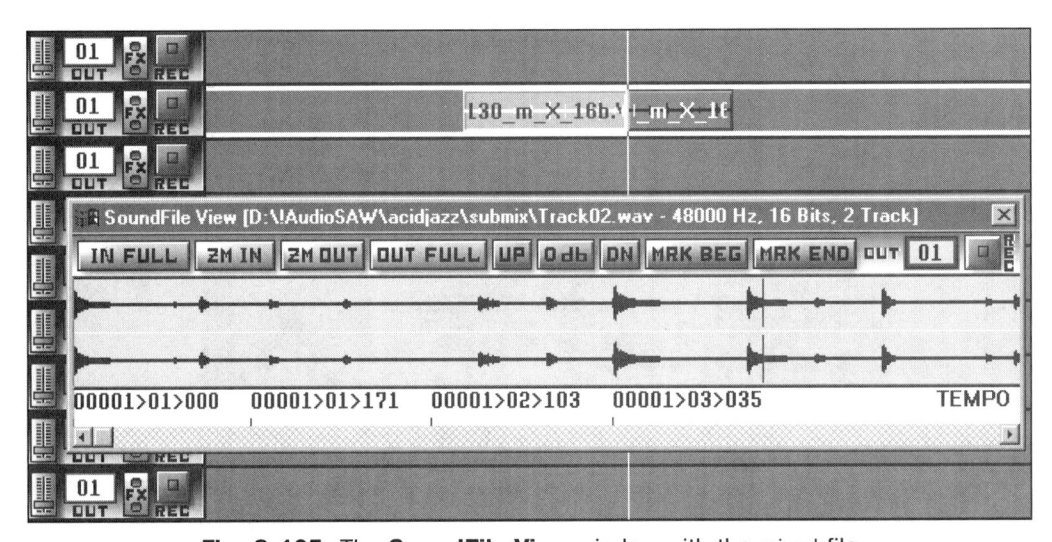

Fig. 3.105. The **SoundFile View** window with the mixed file

8. Substitute the old clip with the new (mixed) one as follows:
   - Click on the selected old clip; the multitrack cursor should cross the marked clip (Fig. 3.106)
   - From the **MultiTrack** menu, perform the **Replace Entry** command, or press <Shift>+<R>
   - When replacing the old clip with the new one, its exterior and the name above the clip are changed

   In Fig. 3.106, a mono clip is replaced by a stereo clip, according to the **Set Conversion Parameters** window settings.
9. The track's effects are to be disabled by the **CLR** button in the **Effects Patch Builder** window.

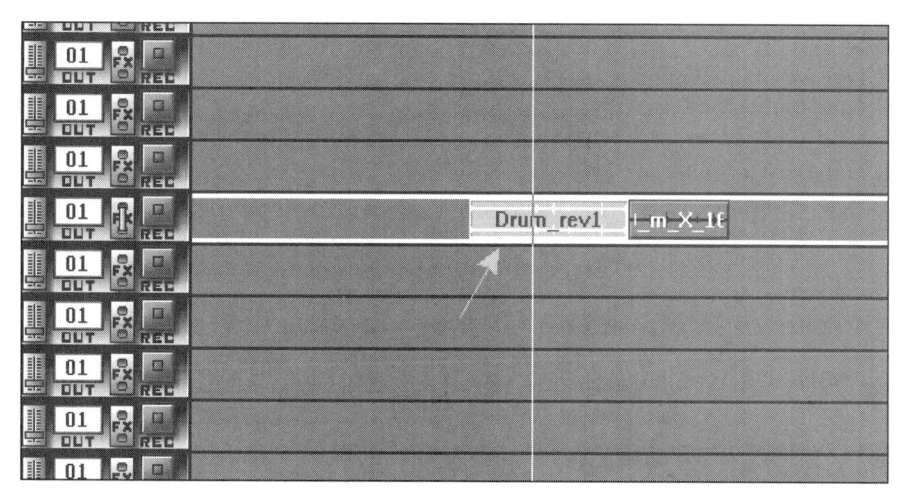

Chapter 3: The SAWPro Program: Live Recording In a Virtual Studio 137

Fig. 3.106. A modified clip after intermediate mixing

If you want to mix an *existing* file (with the **Build Mix To New SoundFile** command), the program can replace the previous file or append a new file to the existing one if you like (Fig. 3.107).

> **NOTE** In the **WARNING!** dialog box, choose the command you need. If you press **Yes**, the file will be replaced, while **No** will append the file.

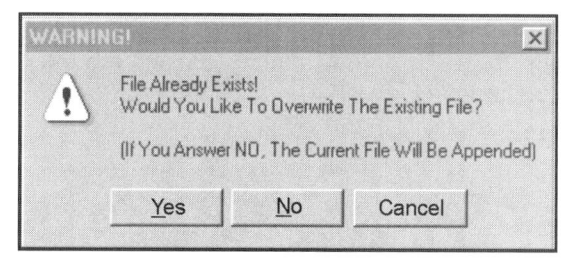

Fig. 3.107. A confirmation request dialog box (when mixing to an existing file)

This algorithm might seem complicated here on paper. In fact, this seeming complexity is just because of the detailed narration.

After trying this algorithm, you will probably learn to appreciate its advantages and will agree that it definitely eases the problem of final mixing.

This is especially true if you follow the system of naming the mixed file regions, as explicated in point 7, by giving parts and regions self-explanatory names that logically correspond. If you do so, the project interface in the **MultiTrack View** window will be much more friendly.

The reader can invent his or her own naming system. The program provides the freedom necessary for such experiments.

For clips that reside on one track, it is logical to create *one* intermediate mixing file, so as to append this file at every mixing stage by choosing **No** in the warning dialog box (Fig. 3.107).

For example, all the effects of the first track's fragments can be mixed to Track01.wav; all those in the second track to Track02.wav, etc. It is recommended that you keep these files in a separate folder, for example, with the name Submix.

An Algorithm for Intermediate Mixing to an Output Track

A simpler intermediate mixing algorithm exists, which uses the same first steps as the first one.

NOTE The difference is that when mixing to an output track, existing files CANNOT be appended with further mixing data.

The algorithm for intermediate mixing to an output track is described below.

1. Press the **SOLO** button on the selected track.
2. Select a clip.
3. On the **Process/MixDown** menu, choose the **Build Mix To Output Track File** option.
4. Press **OK** in the **Set Conversion Parameters** dialog box.
5. In the **Select New MixFile** window, assign a name to the mixed file immediately. This name ought to indicate the applied effect. Press the **Save** button.
6. After the mixing process is complete, remove the clip from the original track.
7. Move the mixed clip from the output track to replace the old one that was removed. This is done in Select mode (Fig. 3.108).
8. Disable the track's sound effects.

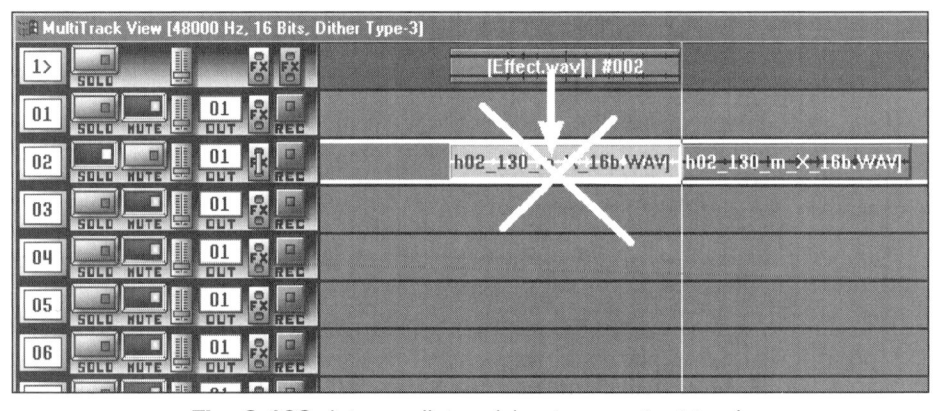

Fig. 3.108. Intermediate mixing to an output track

Mixing to an output track does not allow you to append further data to the created file, since SAWPro assumes that, in the end, the user wants to perform conclusive mixing that requires no appending.

On the other hand, using the first algorithm (one-track mixing) allows you to create files made of processed fragments, or clips (like Track01.wav, Track02.wav, etc.)

These files may then be processed in order to take on special audio effects in powerful sound editors such as WaveLab, Cool Edit Pro, or Sound Forge.

Doing this is not at all extraneous, since, even though SAWPro has many advantages, a specialized sound editor has many more possibilities available than any multitrack program.

WARNING When processing in such a manner, never change the audio file's length, or you will end up with synchronization problems on the multitrack.

Remember that both of the described intermediate mixing algorithms may be applied to both one and a *number* of tracks.

For instance, they can be used when:

❒ The same clip is copied to two (or more) tracks

❒ Different types of effects are patched to each track

❒ Tracks are mixed down

In such a case, both only the first step of these algorithms are changed: the **SOLO** buttons should be pressed on each of the tracks that you intend to mix.

SAWPro Mixing and Mastering

In the previous section, we talked about intermediate mixing in detail.

However, the process of creating an audio project does not end there.

The last step in of working with the recording will result in the final sound file with the WAV extension, properly processed. Moreover, its parameters should conform to the AUDIO CD standard, i.e., it should have a bit resolution of 16 and a 44,000 Hz sample rate.

Afterwards, this file can be recorded to a recordable compact disk in CD-AUDIO format using a CD-recorder device.

Special programs exist for working with CD-recorders, such as Easy CD Creator.

Multitrack programs allow you to record to an audio CD, too. For instance, Samplitude 2496 lets you create CDs directly from a virtual project (see *Chapter 5*). One may say that recording a CD is not a technical problem these days.

However, the sound file should be prepared beforehand, or mastered.

Mastering is a complicated mechanism for processing an audio file, which aims at reaching a high-quality sound. It includes such procedures as:

- Signal amplitude peak limiting
- Changing the frequency response
- Dithering and noise shaping (special algorithms that decrease quantization noise by "fooling" the ear)
- Special "tube" compression distorting to achieve a "warm" sound

Mastering is both a technical and a creative process. It depends on the human factor, that is, the style of the musical composition and to which kind of audience it is targeted to, as well as on technical parameters.

It should be clearly understood that no one, of course, can perform world-class mastering under the conditions present in a home computer studio. However, one can attempt to solve this problem by using the services of a professional studio. In this book, we'll share with you some tricks of home mastering that help to "double-cross" the ear.

> **NOTE** You can read about the subtleties of mastering in detail in *Chapters 8 and 9*.

To be fair, we should note that existing software allows you to create demo CDs of fairly good quality. Such quality is usually acceptable for radio broadcasting.

Applying the *Meter Bridge* Program Module to Indicate the Volume Level

The **Meter Bridge** program module is used to indicate the volume level of a track.

For commercial reasons, **Meter Bridge** does not belong to the standard set of SAWPro effects, so one has to purchase and install it separately.

Meter Bridge is a Saw Native standard module. It is attached through the **Effects Patch Builder** as a regular virtual effect.

> **NOTE** The **POST FADER** button in the **Effects Patch Builder** window *must* be pressed. Otherwise, the signal from the track is first fed to the **Meter Bridge**, and then to the **Fader** (the volume and pan control), and thus the results of regulation won't be indicated.

The **Meter Bridge** module is an important assistant during the mixing process, because it is not wise to rely on your hearing alone.

Chapter 3: The SAWPro Program: Live Recording In a Virtual Studio   **141**

One huge advantage of this indicator is its speed, considering its low level of computer resource consumption. **Meter Bridge** correctly reflects sound process dynamics, even on slow machines.

A remarkable feature of the SAWPro architecture in general, and the **Meter Bridge** module in particular, is an almost instantaneous response when indicating data, even if the project is heavily loaded with virtual effects.

> **NOTE** Here is some information for comparison. In Samplitude 2496, indicating the volume level is typically slow on slow computers throughout; on fast computers, indication is also delayed, but this only happens when attaching a considerable amount of virtual effects.

The *Meter Bridge* Configuration Menu

To open the module configuration menu (Fig. 3.109), click on the IQS logo.

> **NOTE** Fig. 3.109 shows the options that we recommend that you include as checked.

After you check the right options, press **Save Preferences**. The configuration parameters are saved in files with the PRF extension.

- **Help Contents** calls the help file
- **Save Preferences** is self-explanatory
- **Meter Display Wrapping** arranges the indicators in lines, one under the other

> **NOTE** This is a recommended option.

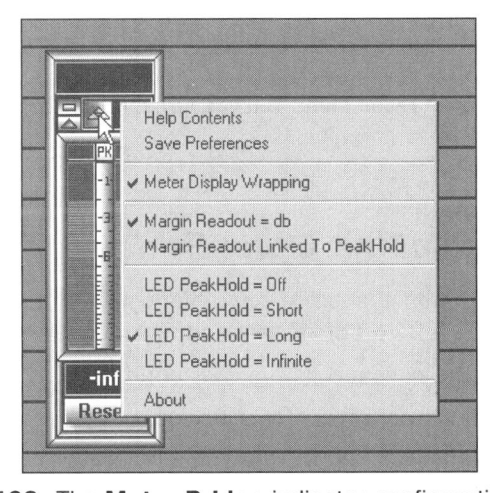

Fig. 3.109. The **Meter Bridge** indicator configuration menu

☐ **Margin Readout = dB** measures the maximum signal level (in decibels). In Fig. 3.109, **−inf** (silence) is indicated on the readout.

> **NOTE** This option is recommended. If it is disabled, the maximum level is indicated as a percentage.

☐ **Margin Readout Linked To PeakHold** keeps the **Margin Readout** in sync with the graphical indicator.

> **NOTE** We don't recommend that you turn this on, since the **Margin Readout** is used to trace the maximum signal level, and its value should not change often.

☐ **LED PeakHold = Off** disables the mode that holds back the amplitude peak indication.

> **NOTE** We don't recommend that you use this option.

☐ **LED PeakHold = Short** holds back amplitude peak indication for a short time.

> **NOTE** We don't recommend that you use this option.

☐ **LED PeakHold = Long** holds back amplitude peak indication for a long time.

> **NOTE** We recommend that you enable this option.

☐ **LED PeakHold = Infinite** holds back amplitude peak indication infinitely (until you press the **Reset** button).

> **NOTE** We don't recommend that you turn this option on.

Changing the Look of the *Meter Bridge*

To change **Meter Bridge**'s appearance to resemble a needle indicator, click on the icon with the triangle in the top left corner of the window (Fig. 3.109).

Another click will return the meter to its previous condition.

Fig. 3.110 depicts the two views of the **Meter Bridge**.

The button with a horizontal bar, above the triangle, is for removing the **Meter Bridge** module from the screen (Fig. 3.111).

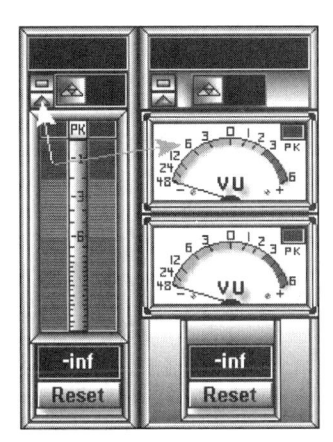

Chapter 3: The SAWPro Program: Live Recording In a Virtual Studio

Fig. 3.110. Changing the appearance of the **Meter Bridge**

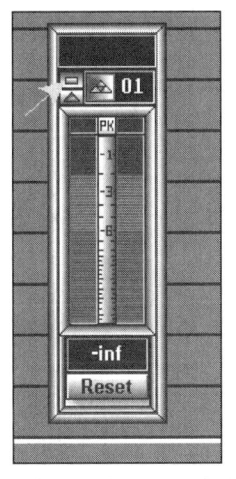

Fig. 3.111. The **Meter Bridge** window close button

The module can be easily dragged around the screen by grabbing it with the mouse cursor by the indicator columns. For your convenience, you can assign a name to the meter (Fig. 3.112).

To do this, click on the top field of the meter (which is initially black), and then enter the name from the keyboard and press the <Enter> key.

A newly called meter is adjoined to the others automatically. Adjacent **Meter Bridge** modules, when dragged with the mouse, move across the screen as a single block (Fig. 3.113).

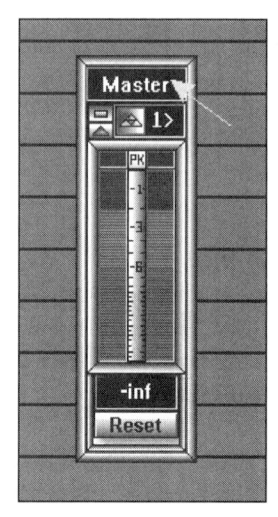

Fig. 3.112. A **Meter Bridge** named **Master**

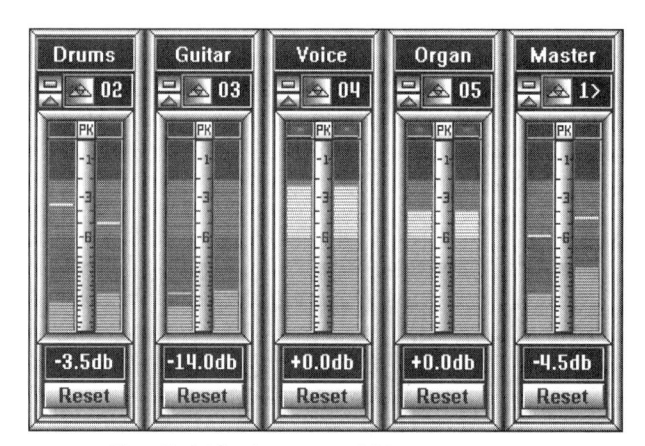

Fig. 3.113. A group of **Meter Bridges**

The Virtual Mixer

If you press a track's **Fader** button, the track will change its appearance, as shown in Fig. 3.114.

Next to it, you will see the **Fader** *virtual mixer* element (for adjusting volume level and pan).

The **Fader** interface was examined in the "*Importing Sound Files to SAWPro*" section.

Chapter 3: The SAWPro Program: Live Recording In a Virtual Studio

Here, we will turn our attention to the two horizontal lines that cross the clip. These lines are used to graphically represent the volume level and the pan as they change with time.

One of these, shown by default in yellow (in Fig. 3.114 it is the lower one), is the volume level line. The yellow color signifies that the level is set to **0 dB**.

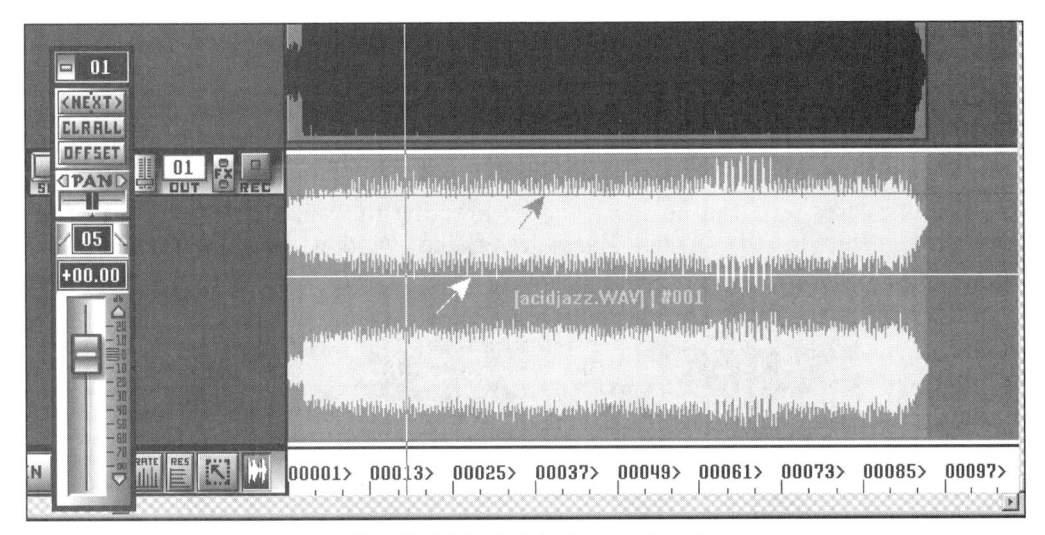

Fig. 3.114. A virtual mixer track

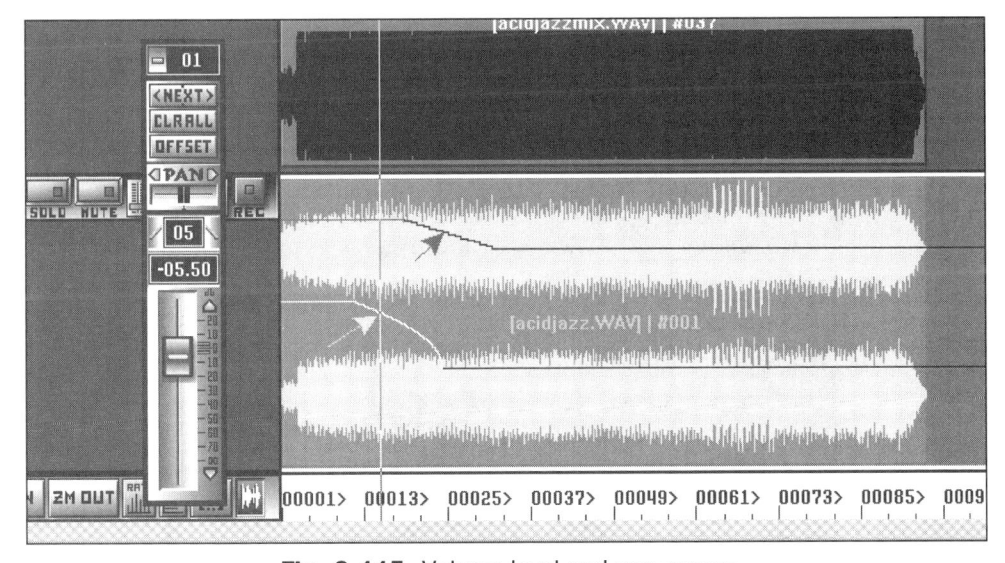

Fig. 3.115. Volume level and pan curves

When altering the volume level, yellow becomes gray.

The line that is red by default (the upper one in Fig. 3.114) is the pan line; if it is red, the left and right channels are equally balanced. When adjusting pan, the red color becomes gray (Fig. 3.115).

Volume level and pan can be controlled in real time.

To do so, you need just alter the **Fader** slider's position during playback.

Controlling these operations will require that you obtain certain skills, since it is only possible to hear the changes made after a delay of, normally, a fraction of a second. This is the time interval that it takes for the program to process the changes.

The response delay time can be shortened by lowering the value of the **PreLoad Buffer Queue** parameter in the **Audio Hardware Setup** window, in the **Options** menu (Fig. 3.116).

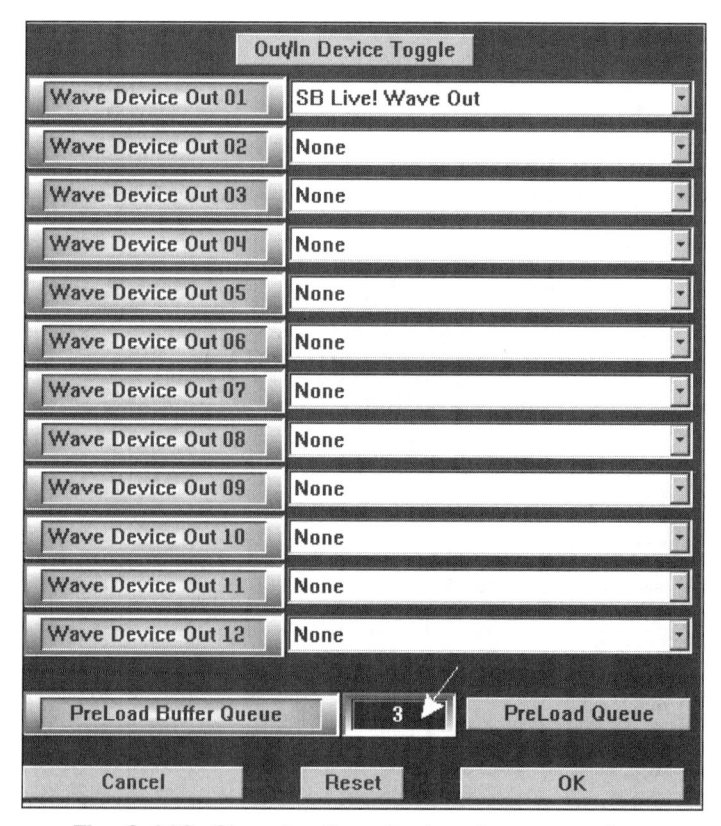

Fig. 3.116. Changing the adjustment response time

However, when reducing the control response time, remember that this *can* cause various errors during playback.

> *NOTE* Honestly, the response time does not decrease by much.

Adjusting in the *OFFSET* Mode

There is an **OFFSET** button on the virtual mixer (see more about it in the "*Importing Sound Files to SAWPro*" section).

With this button pressed on the **Fader** panel, the response delay does not matter much, since volume and pan curves are not changeable in this mode. Only the general parameter value for the whole track is altered.

Therefore, we recommend that you only use *real-time* adjustment in the **OFFSET** mode to preliminarily set the track volume levels before starting reduction. All other mixer editing should be fulfilled step by step at certain points, or by using automation (see below).

To adjust the volume level and the pan at a specific point (with the **OFFSET** button released), place the cursor in the desired position and adjust the slider. Then listen to the fragment and correct the parameter value if necessary.

To find a precise adjustment point, use the **NEXT** button on the **Fader** panel.

The volume level can be altered for an entire selected area of a track. For this, you need to change the volume slider's position after you have marked the fragment (Fig. 3.117).

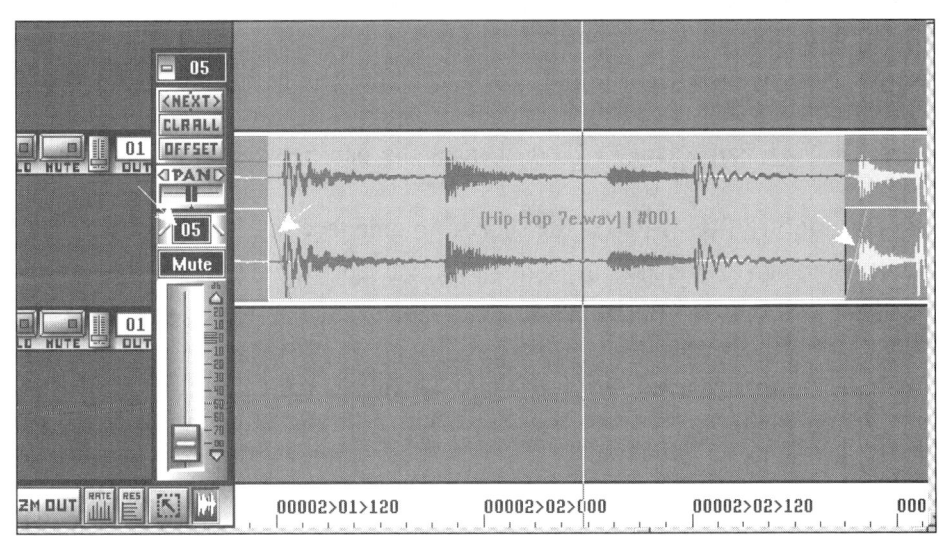

Fig. 3.117. Changing the volume level of a marked fragment

148   Live Music on Your PC

NOTE Remember that the volume level and pan change speed depends on the **Slope** parameter value (from the slow **Slope 1** to the fast **Slope 10**). The **Slope** parameter can be corrected at just one point or for the whole track in the **OFFSET** mode (Fig. 3.118).

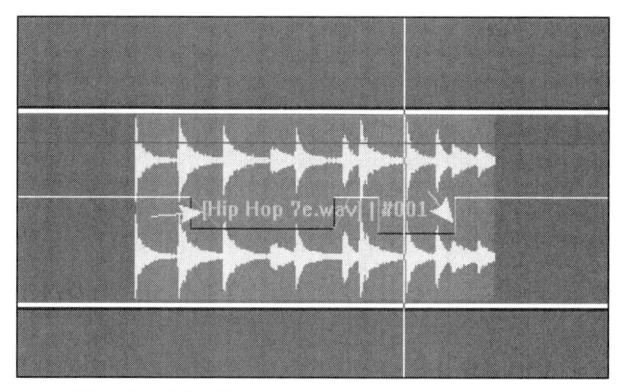

Fig. 3.118. Changing the **Slope** parameter

The new **Slope** parameter's value, set in the **OFFSET** mode, will affect new adjustment points only. A value that was applied before changing the **Slope** in the **OFFSET** mode will not affect certain adjustment points.

In the "*Importing Sound Files to SAWPro*" section, we discussed **Mix** menu commands.

Here we will note once more that it makes sense to replace manual adjustment with automation using these menu commands.

- **Fade To Next Volume Change** (<F>) changes the volume level between two adjustment points smoothly
- **Sweep To Next Pan Change** (<P>) changes the pan between two adjustment points smoothly
- **Fade Out Marked** (<O>) makes the signal's volume fade out in the marked area
- **Fade In Marked** (<I>) makes the signal's volume fade in in the marked area
- **CrossFade Marked Or Overlapped to Next Track** (<X>) is for cross volume level adjustment on two adjacent tracks
- **CrossFade (−6dB) Marked Or Overlapped to Next Track** (<Shift>+<X>) is for cross volume level adjustment on two adjacent tracks with a level of −6 dB at the point of the adjustment curves' junction

The **CrossFade** command implies the simultaneous execution of the **Fade Out** and **Fade In** commands for two overlapping clips on adjacent tracks, the upper one being the hot track.

Chapter 3: The SAWPro Program: Live Recording In a Virtual Studio   149

CrossFade is done over the entire area in which the clips overlap, unless a smaller area is marked off. The point of the adjustment curves' junction is defined by the cursor position.

CrossFade (−6dB) has the level at the adjustment curves' junction equal to −6 dB.

Examples to Illustrate Using Automation

☐ The **Fade Out Marked** command.

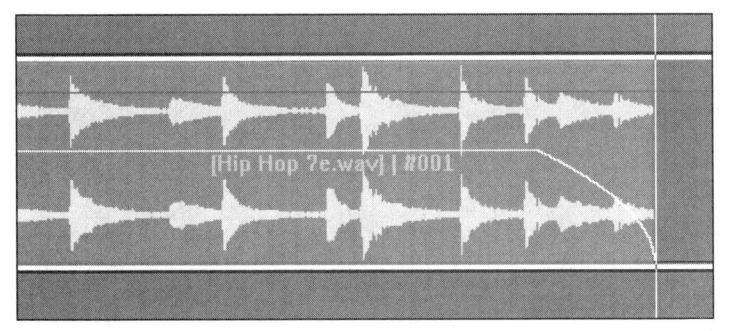

Fig. 3.119. Executing the **Fade Out Marked** command

☐ The **Fade In Marked** command.

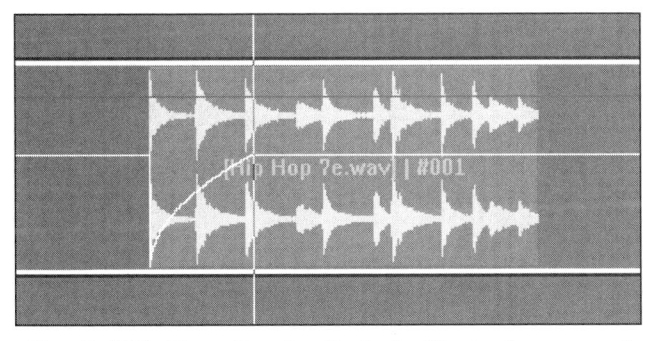

Fig. 3.120. Executing the **Fade In Marked** command

☐ The **Fade To Next Volume Change** command.
☐ The **Sweep To Next Pan Change** command.

Fig. 3.121. Executing the **Fade To Next Volume Change** command

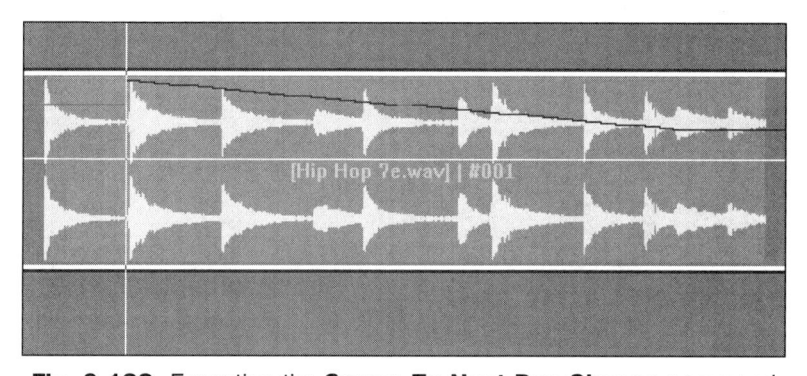

Fig. 3.122. Executing the **Sweep To Next Pan Change** command

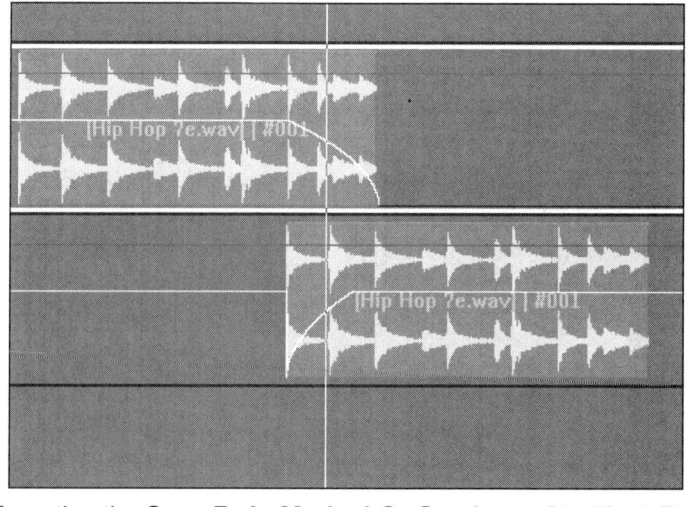

Fig. 3.123. Executing the **CrossFade Marked Or Overlapped to Next Track** command

Chapter 3: The SAWPro Program: Live Recording In a Virtual Studio 151

NOTE The **Fade To Next Volume Change** and **Sweep To Next Pan Change** commands are executed between two adjustment points, say, A and B. Before execution, place the cursor at point A.

- The **CrossFade Marked Or Overlapped to Next Track** command.

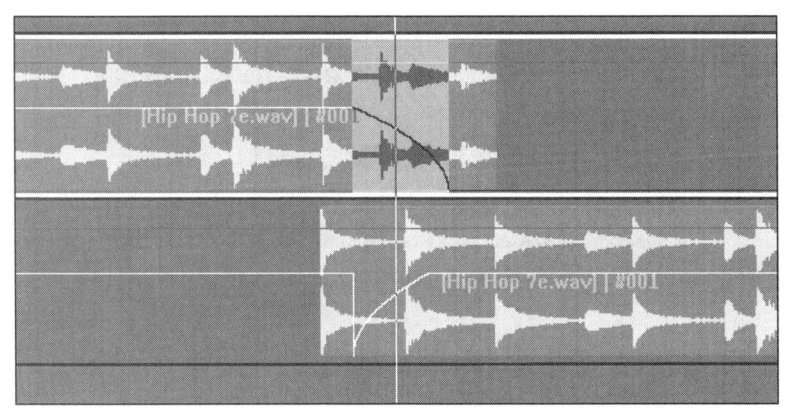

Fig. 3.124. Executing the **CrossFade Marked Or Overlapped to Next Track** command on a marked off area

- The **CrossFade (−6dB) Marked Or Overlapped to Next Track** command.

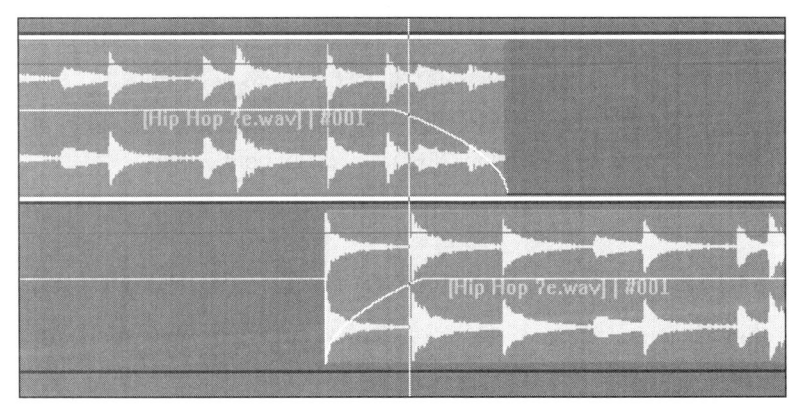

Fig. 3.125. Executing the **CrossFade (−6dB) Marked Or Overlapped to Next Track** command

Moving and Copying Volume and Pan Adjustment Curves

In practice, it often happens that a volume or pan adjustment curve needs to be copied or moved; for example, when handling clips whose time boundaries coincide.

You can move curves by simply dragging the marked area while pressing <Shift> and/or <Ctrl> (Fig. 3.126).

> **NOTE** The technology is the same one used for moving clips.

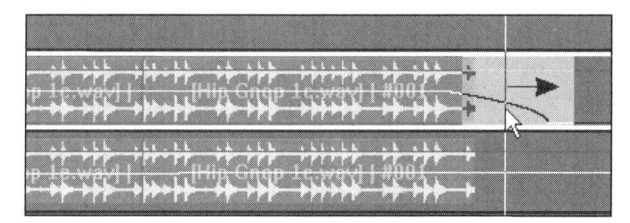

Fig. 3.126. Moving mixer adjustment curves

To copy, click with the right mouse button while holding the left one. Then release the left button.

Fig. 3.127 shows examples of copying mixer adjustment curves.

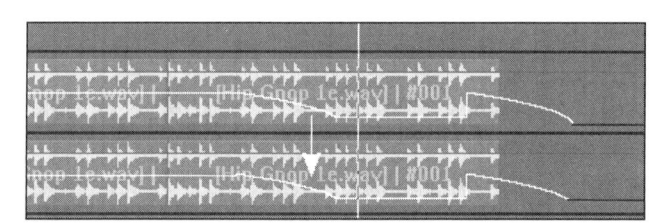

Fig. 3.127. Copying mixer adjustment curves

The Hot Track and Its Connection with the Virtual Mixer

When controlling a large number of tracks, **Fader** virtual mixer panels are situated one above the other, in a column.

If you spread the panels out over the screen, editing will be less convenient. One way to position the **Fader** panel that keeps the working space clutter-free is provided in SAWPro: this displays only one panel entirely, stacking all the others under it. To access the necessary panel, click on its track, thus making it the hot track. The **Fader** panel of this track will pop up automatically (Fig. 3.128).

> **NOTE** Plug-in patch windows are also connected with the hot track.

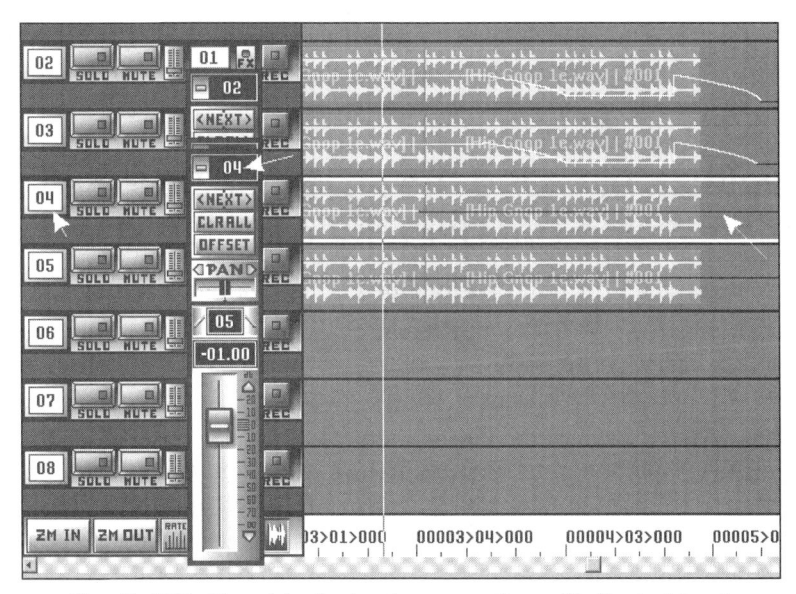

Chapter 3: The SAWPro Program: Live Recording In a Virtual Studio 153

Fig. 3.128. The virtual mixer's connection with the hot track

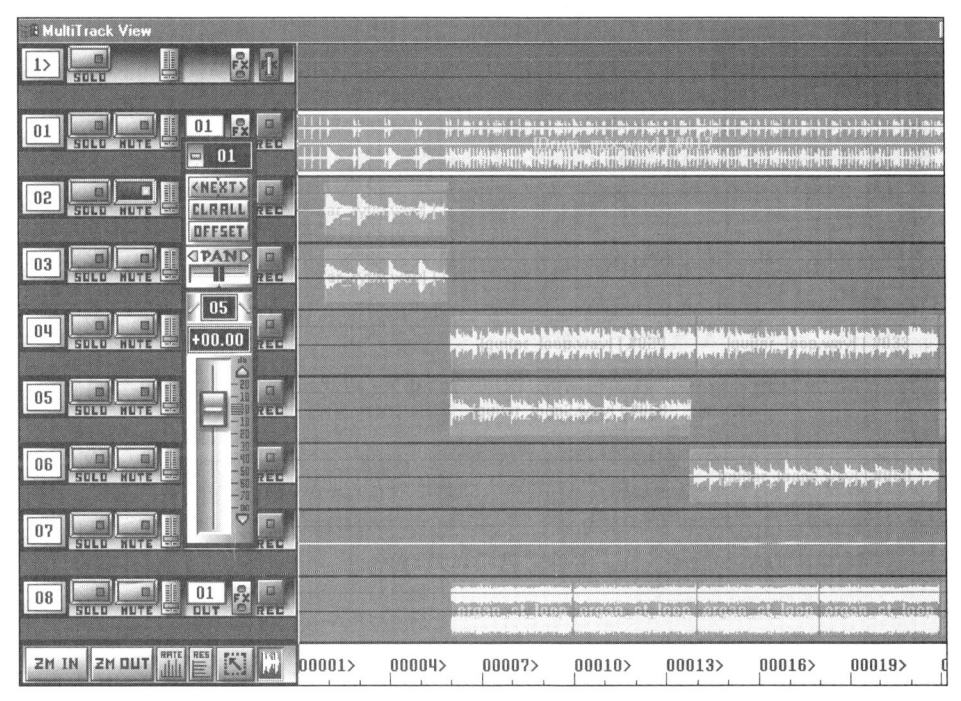

Fig. 3.129. The virtual mixer of the whole multitrack

All **Fader** panels of the multitrack can be opened by pressing the <Ctrl> key and clicking the **Fader** button. To close these, hold <Ctrl> and click on the button in the top left corner of the **Fader** panel (Fig. 3.129).

The Specifics of Using the *POST FADER* Button in the *Effects Patch Builder* Window

Please note that there are two, principally different paths a signal can take.

Remember that when the **POST FADER** button is pressed, the signal, after being manipulated by the **Fader** controls, is passed to the virtual effect attached in the **Effects Patch Builder** window.

When using the **Meter Bridge**, the signal should follow this very route, that is, use the **Fader** controls first, and only after that be processed by the effects. Otherwise, the meter will not be able to reflect the true situation, and no matter how you position the **Fader** slider, the signal volume level will be displayed as the same as it was before adjustment.

Now, if we attach the "*compressor*" effect, having the **POST FADER** button pressed, the situation changes. The compressor, as a dynamic range compressing device, will compensate for the adjustments made as you change the position of the **Fader** slider.

> **NOTE** The compression effect is described explicitly in the book *Computer-aided Sound Processing* by A. Zagumennov.

Due to these peculiarities, effects connected with dynamic range compression/expansion or non-linear amplitude response (FUZZ, OVERDRIVE) should be *always* connected *before* the **Fader**.

In these cases, the **POST FADER** button should be released.

We can give one rule of thumb: "All effects, except for the **Meter Bridge**, are attached with a released **POST FADER** button".

However, every rule has its exceptions. For example, if a signal needs to be panned before feeding it to an effect, press **POST FADER**.

So, in conclusion, we can note that you are free to try experimenting with this as well, but you should still have an idea of what processes the sound undergoes.

The SAWPro Mixing Technique

Preparing for Mixing

Some preparatory work should be done before final mixing.

Chapter 3: The SAWPro Program: Live Recording In a Virtual Studio   155

1. First of all, attach the **Meter Bridge** to each track using the **Effects Patch Builder** window (press the **POST FADER** button). This is necessary to observe the volume level of each track's signal.
2. Name the **Meter Bridges**. As we said before, it's best if these names correspond to the musical content of the tracks.

> **NOTE** Name examples are: **Drums** for the percussion, **Guitar** for a guitar part, **Master** for the output track, etc.

All **Faders** *must* be in the **OFFSET** mode.

Final Mixing

Let's examine this mixing algorithm using the example of a pop-music composition.

It is best is to start mixing with the rhythm section.

Let's say that this includes the following instruments: drums, a bass guitar, and a rhythm guitar.

You might want to follow these steps:

1. Press the **SOLO** button on the drums track (where the drums part is recorded).
2. Set a maximum level of about −1 dB for the drums track using the **Fader**. This is indicated in the **Margin** readout of the **Drums Meter Bridge**.
3. Set a maximum level of about −4 dB for the master output track. This is indicated in the **Margin** readout of the **Master Meter Bridge**.
4. Press the **SOLO** button on the bass track (bass guitar). The bass guitar volume level is adjusted by ear.

> **NOTE** If the highest level of the Master exceeds −4 dB, it should be decreased using the output track's **Fader** to the previous value.

5. Press the **SOLO** button on the rhythm guitar track. Its volume level is adjusted by ear as well.

> **NOTE** If you want, you can slide the guitar part to the left or right channel using pan adjustment. But make sure that you control the Master output signal and correct it if necessary.

All other tracks are adjusted in the same manner.

After the level of the *last* project track is set, you can increase the output track's maximum level to a value of −0.3 dB, release all **SOLO** buttons, and cancel the **OFFSET** mode on all **Fader** panels. From here, the project gets its finishing touches by adjusting specific points, the positions of which depend on the recorded audio material. Automation can be applied here also (the **Mix** menu).

The mixing technique for one track by adjustment points has been covered in the "*Virtual Mixer*" section. Applying this technique to all project tracks one by one, you can take the last step in mixing the whole project by changing the volume and pan slider positions in time all along the multitrack, from the beginning to the end.

We'd like to add that there has been a lot written on sound producing. And in principal, we agree with the following statement, taken from "*PC Music Home Studio: Secrets, Tips, & Tricks*" by Yu. Petelin and R. Petelin:

"Briefly speaking, we found no theoretical basis anywhere for giving recommendations such as: 'To create the hit of the season, turn the pan control N degrees and move the volume slider K notches'. This confirms once more that sound producing is more like a fine art than a science."

However, the following are some practical suggestions.

Some Practical Suggestions

- Signals with a wide stereo base should be shifted from the center using the pan control, so as not to merge when being superimposed.
- Voice and solo instrumental parts should not be lost in the background of the rest of the recording. If you don't bring them to the foreground by simply increasing the volume level, apply additional compressing. On the other hand, an excessively loud solo part worsens the impression of the recording. You have to realize that volume level adjustment is not a panacea. A solo might also sound like it is lost in the depths of the sound field, on the other hand. You may need a "basket" of effects made up of reverberation, compression, cross delay, and parametric equalizing in order to separate the solo part from an intense background.
- Try not to over-apply the reverberation and chorus effects, since a large number of these effects can make it hard to grasp the material as a whole.
- Don't hesitate to reject an effect for a part. Sometimes, a DRY sound is more suitable than a WET one (i.e., one with effects).
- If suddenly you feel the desire to add volume to a pre-mixed track, don't be too hasty. First, try to find the other track whose extra volume (most likely) aroused this desire in you. Start by reducing its volume level.

In conclusion, we'd like to say that the best advice will come from your own trained ear.

Listen to professional quality music on AUDIO CD and try to imagine the process of this recording's creation. Note the peculiarities of the soundman's work.

Analyze. Try to repeat things. Look for your own ways. Create.

Mastering in SAWPro

The SAWPro program includes the **Comp/Gate/Limiter** (compressor/noise gate/limiter) module, which we have already discussed.

> **NOTE** Unfortunately, the **Compressor/Gate** part has become obsolete and thus should probably not be used when creating high-quality recordings.

Some of this module's effects, such as **Peak Limiter** and **Normalize**, can provide real benefits.

Attaching the *Comp/Gate/Limiter* Module

To attach the **Comp/Gate/Limiter** module, do the following:

1. Associate **Comp/Gate/Limiter** to an output track (Fig. 3.130).
2. Adjust **Normalize** to a level of 98%.
3. Select the loudest multitrack fragment.
4. Mix the output track using the **Build Mix To Output Track File** option of the **Process/MixDown** menu.

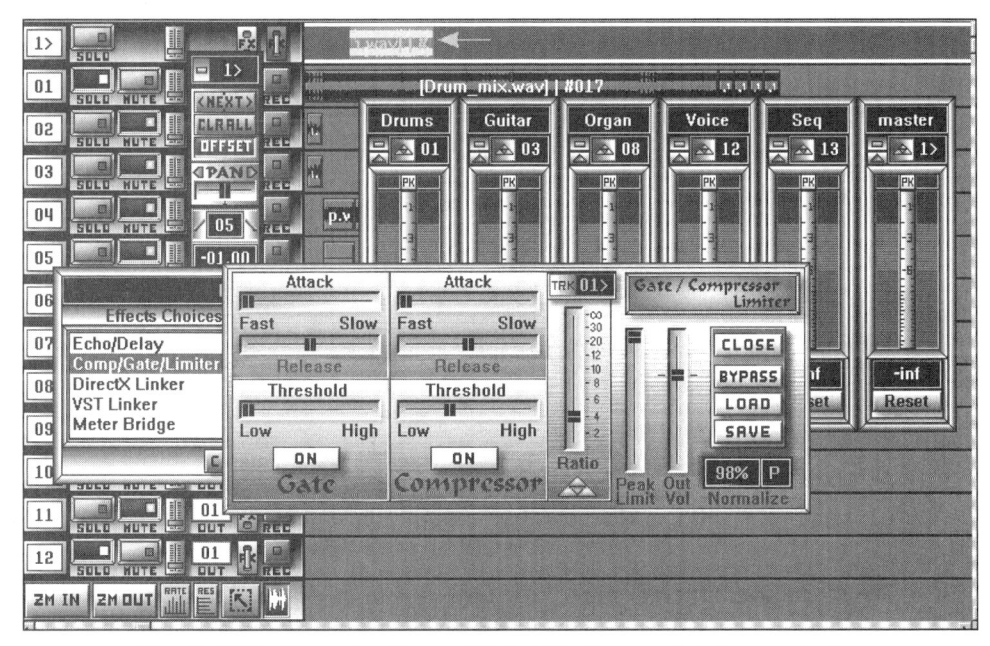

Fig. 3.130. Using the **Comp/Gate/Limiter** module for mastering

5. Double-click on the mixed fragment and go to the **SoundFile View** window.
6. Adjust the **Peak Limit** slider with the left mouse button.
7. During the adjustment, watch the state of the four vertical lines in the **SoundFile View** window. These are denoted with arrows in Fig. 3.131.

   NOTE   Try to attain a situation where only a few amplitude spikes exceed the threshold.

   Too low of a limit threshold may cause the signal's distortion.

8. After **Peak Limit** is adjusted, mix the fragment once again. Shown in Fig. 3.132 is a view of the final audio file (after repeated mixing).

Pay attention to the fact that using the **Peak Limit** and **Normalize** functions together assists in *increasing* the mixed sound file's volume level *as much as possible*.

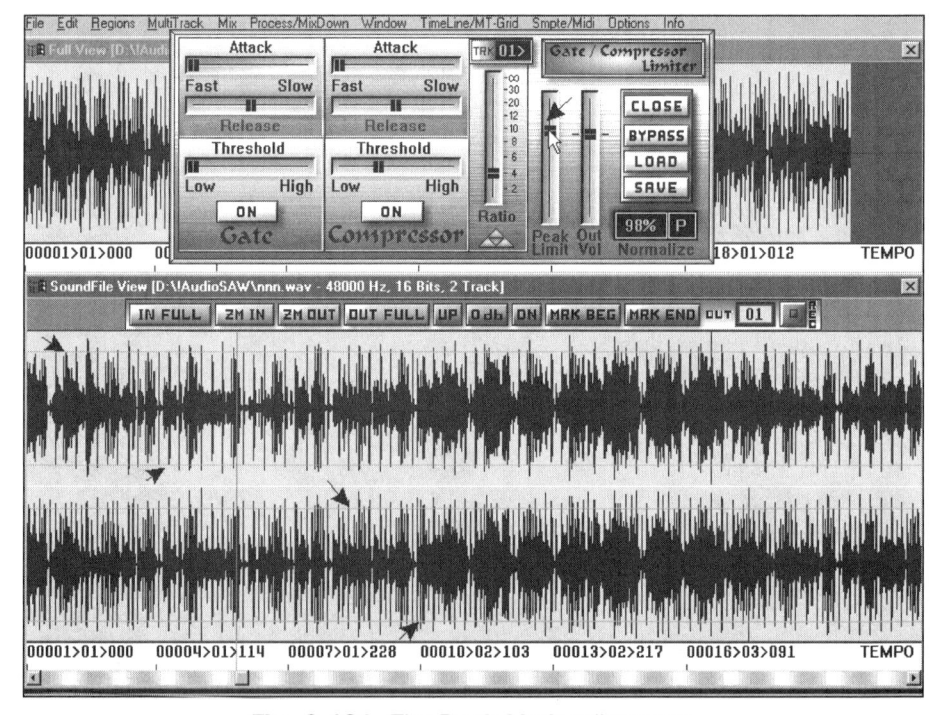

Fig. 3.131. The **Peak Limit** adjustment

You need the virtual output track mixer for *general editing* of the final file in the mixing stage (for example, to smooth out the volume reduction at the end of a piece, which is done using the **Fade Out** command.)

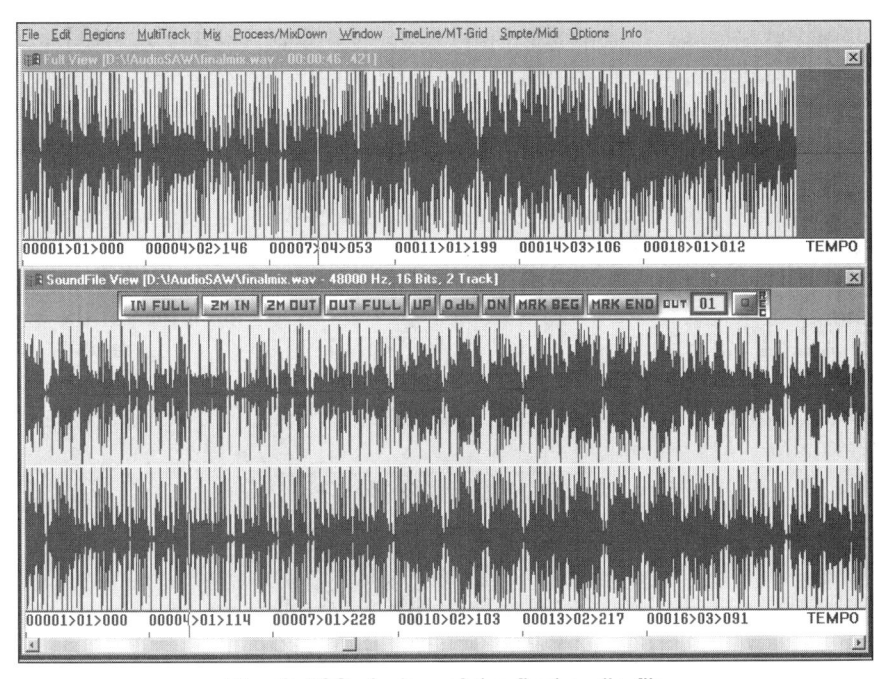

Chapter 3: The SAWPro Program: Live Recording In a Virtual Studio

Fig. 3.132. A view of the final audio file

Commercial Virtual Effects

Use plug-in effects by other vendors for faster and, what is most important, better-quality mastering in the mixing stage.

Here we are speaking of the db-audioware DirectX plug-in pack by Dave Brown (**http://www.db-audioware.com**).

Two modules, **dB-M multiband limiter** and **dB-L mastering limiter**, are of particular interest. These are patched together to the output track.

They are used like this:

1. Call the presets menu by clicking the left or right mouse button on the **dB-L** effect window. Choose the preset.

   TIP For novices, we advise you to work with a 3 dB loudness boost when working with **dB-L**.

2. Set the **dither** switch to the **type 1** or **type 2** position.

   TIP When experimenting with **dB-M**, we recommend beginning with the Bass/Treble boost.

The exterior view of these modules in working mode is depicted in Fig. 3.133 and 3.134.

At this point, we complete our introduction to the SAWPro program.

We are sure that after mastering the basic methods of controlling this program, you will fully appreciate its features, namely, the combination of sound reliability and professionalism, along with its utmost loyalty to the newcomer.

We hope that after you have some experience with SAWPro — a wonderful program, from our point of view — you will find its interface simple and obvious, despite the fact that it may make a strange impression at first glance because of its originality.

In concluding the chapter, we'd like to repeat once more the main idea of the book: your computer has all the capabilities necessary for recording "live" sound, and is practically begging you to use them.

The SAWPro program is perfectly suited to this task under the conditions of a home computer studio.

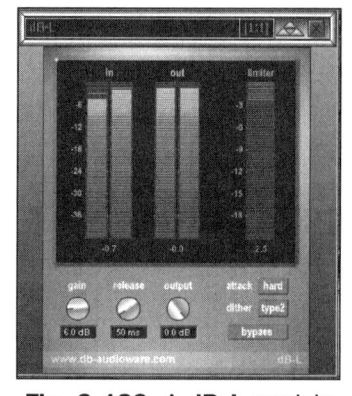

Fig. 3.133. A **dB-L** module

Fig. 3.134. A **dB-M** module

Chapter 4

COOL EDIT PRO AS A UNIVERSAL SOLUTION FOR HOME STUDIOS

Chapter 4: Cool Edit Pro as a Universal Solution for Home Studios

In the previous chapter, while discussing SAWPro, we touched on the idea that there is no "ideal" software for musicians working in a home studio.

And truly, currently there is no software on the market that would, while including the advantages of all the rest of the products, allow us to *ideally* create a musical project from start to finish in a home-based environment.

But despite this, there is a solution to our problem. We must figure out the strengths of each program, and then use each one for whichever stage of our work they best perform.

If it is more convenient to record, playback, and mix music in SAWPro, then obviously we should use it for this type of work. But since SAWPro is not very strong in the area of processing sound (unless you connect a slew of plug-ins), we would probably be better off using some other software better suited for this type of work.

On today's market, we find a huge variety of software created especially for sound processing. These make up a separate group, known collectively as sound editors. This basically means that these programs were developed specifically for editing sound files.

Among them, as you might expect, there is also a variety. Sound editors differ in their quality, their purpose, and in their features and ways in which they are used. This is why, when choosing a sound editor, you must always consider its advantages and disadvantages.

But, of course, the most important thing that is required of software intended for sound editing in a home studio environment is the following: it must be, on the one hand, relatively friendly to a non-professional, and on the other, it must have capabilities that allow you to edit sound and achieve a high-quality result.

Judging from these prerequisites, we'd like to turn your attention to the Cool Edit Pro program. In our opinion, it is the software best equipped for processing sound on a personal computer.

> **NOTE** The extended abilities of Cool Edit Pro (the fact that it uses a multitrack) do in fact allow you to create a musical project from start to finish in it.

In this chapter, we will describe version 1.2 of Cool Edit Pro, which is released by the Syntrillium Software Corporation, whose web page can be found at **http://www.syntrillium.com**.

Cool Edit Pro has a quite unique history. It was created as a run-of-the-mill sound editor, and originally called simply Cool Edit. Later, a multitrack containing 64 tracks was added to the program. This was obviously done to extend its capabilities and usage.

This addition was what inspired the tacking on of "Pro" (for "professional") to the name, and thus the enhanced version was called Cool Edit Pro, version 1. And today, it is exactly this combination — a powerful sound editor and a multitrack — that gives Cool Edit Pro its ample abilities when editing material.

> **NOTE** Undoubtedly, the newly-added multitrack has significantly expanded the functionality of Cool Edit Pro. But regardless of this, sound editing has remained the most important and best part of the program. Its new tool, the multitrack, is not quite on par with similar tools of other applications, especially those that were originally created for that purpose. This is completely understandable, and similar to Cool Edit Pro's own situation: it excels in that purpose for which it was developed — sound editing.

In the previous chapter, we pointed out the unfortunate fact that SAWPro's windows contain absolutely no help in the form of pop-up hints, etc.

In this sense, Cool Edit Pro is much more informative. First of all, it has a more standard form, and as a result, seems much more familiar to the user. Secondly, it includes pop-up hints, as well as a "Tip of the Day", which allows you to solve many problems that might arise, especially those that come up when just starting your work.

As for sound editing tools, Cool Edit Pro is relatively independent, meaning that it contains a large set of *its own*, internal virtual effects of professional quality (which, by the way, you can't connect to other sound editing programs). This set is usually enough for creating a full-fledged musical project. However, you can also plug in DirectX virtual effects if you so choose.

> **NOTE** However, we'd like to note here that Cool Edit Pro can not quite be considered a virtual studio, since the functions necessary for those types of programs — such as plugging in virtual effects directly to a sound track of the multitrack — are not available.

Thus we can say that Cool Edit Pro is completely autonomous, and, to a significant extent, self-sufficient.

One of the most attractive features of Cool Edit Pro is the fact that it allows users to create *their own algorithms*, which allows them to automate sound processing to a large extent. The **Scripts and Batch Processing** option is included in the program for this purpose.

> **NOTE** A *script* is the execution of operations in a certain order that can, if necessary, be performed automatically.
>
> For example, when editing sound, a script may consist of a chain of effects: first the compressor, then the reverber, etc.

If you create the necessary script, processing several sound files won't be as tedious, since you needn't directly participate in the process — the computer will execute the entire sequence of operations itself. This mechanism is particularly convenient for those with a "slow" machine: a computer that needs to "think about" each operation for a while when executing it.

Chapter 4: Cool Edit Pro as a Universal Solution for Home Studios 165

NOTE   Forming your own set of scripts and presets for virtual effects will considerably simplify your task. Immediately after recording a project, they can easily be put into action by using package processing, thus "handing over" control of all the routine actions of the computer. (Package processing is assigning a script to a group of files.)

After the computer has successfully finished working with them, you can move on to the next step, for example, mixing.

The next indisputable advantage of Cool Edit Pro is its reliable protection from errors.

Thanks to this function, Cool Edit Pro is able to fully recover the project, whatever may happen: for example, when such "real-life" problems such as a black out or the computer freezing up occur.

To conclude our little introduction, we'd like to express our hope that the reader that becomes acquainted with and obtains some experience using Cool Edit Pro will be able to appreciate the extent to which it lives up to its name — that it is truly a "cool" and professional editor.

After working with this program, you'll likely agree that Cool Edit Pro is without a doubt a high-quality, professional multitrack editor, which is a truly universal solution when it comes to sound processing in a home-computer studio environment.

A Description of the Cool Edit Pro Interface

Installing the Software

The process of installing Cool Edit Pro is not particularly difficult, since it is automated for Windows applications, and there are always installation instructions that come with the package.

Since this is the case, we'll only go over a few moments of the installation process.

While operating, Cool Edit Pro creates a temporary file that should be saved in a particular folder. Let's look at how to best place this file in the folder.

During installation, the user is asked to choose the location of the folder (directory) into which this temporary Cool Edit Pro file will be placed (Fig. 4.1).

When doing this, be aware that:

- If the hard drive is partitioned into logical drives, you should choose the one with the largest capacity
- If for some reason you can't choose the largest drive, you need to create two temporary files
- You can always change the location of the temporary file after installation. (you'll find more on this in the "*Configuring Cool Edit Pro. The* Options *Menu*" section)
- We recommend that you uncheck the checkbox that always associates Cool Edit Pro with those files that have the WAV extension (Fig. 4.2)

NOTE In our opinion, launching the program every time you address one of these files is not always justified (i.e., when performing such a common operation as double-clicking on the shortcut to a WAV file to listen to it).

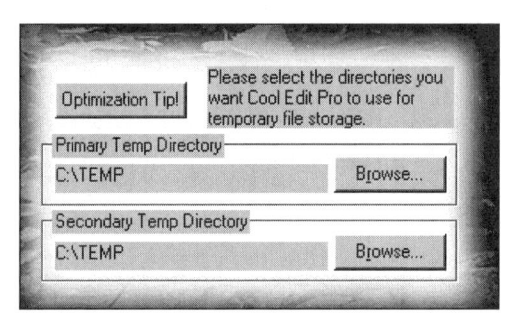

Fig. 4.1. Determining the directory for temporary files

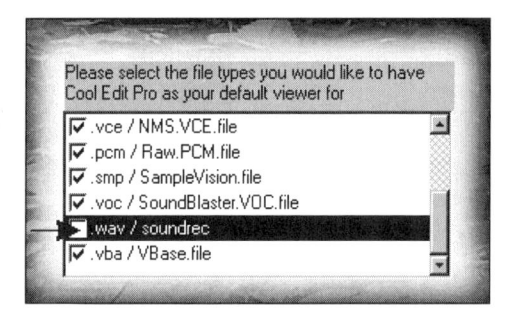

Fig. 4.2. Unchecking the **wav/soundrec** checkbox

As a sound editor, Cool Edit Pro is associated with various types of sound files upon its installation. For example, it will have this kind of connection with files with the VCE, PCM, VOC, and WAV extensions, and so on (Fig. 4.2). Each time you double click on a file with one of these extensions, Cool Edit Pro will start up.

Windows will create an easily recognizable shortcut for the program after it is installed. Cool Edit Pro's shortcut icon looks like a bobbin tape recorder next to the words **Cool Edit Pro** in the **Programs** menu (Fig. 4.3).

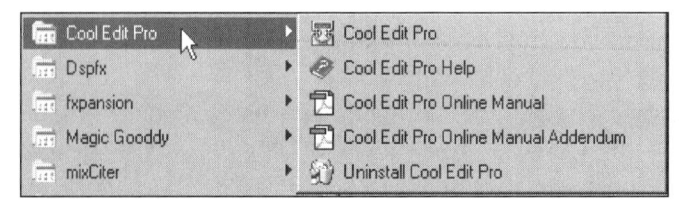

Fig. 4.3. The Cool Edit Pro shortcut

Configuring Cool Edit Pro. The *Options* Menu

When you first launch the program, you see on your screen the editing window — **Waveform View** (Fig. 4.4). Its upper part contains the traditional horizontal menu: **File**, **Edit**, ..., **Options**, **Window**, **Help**.

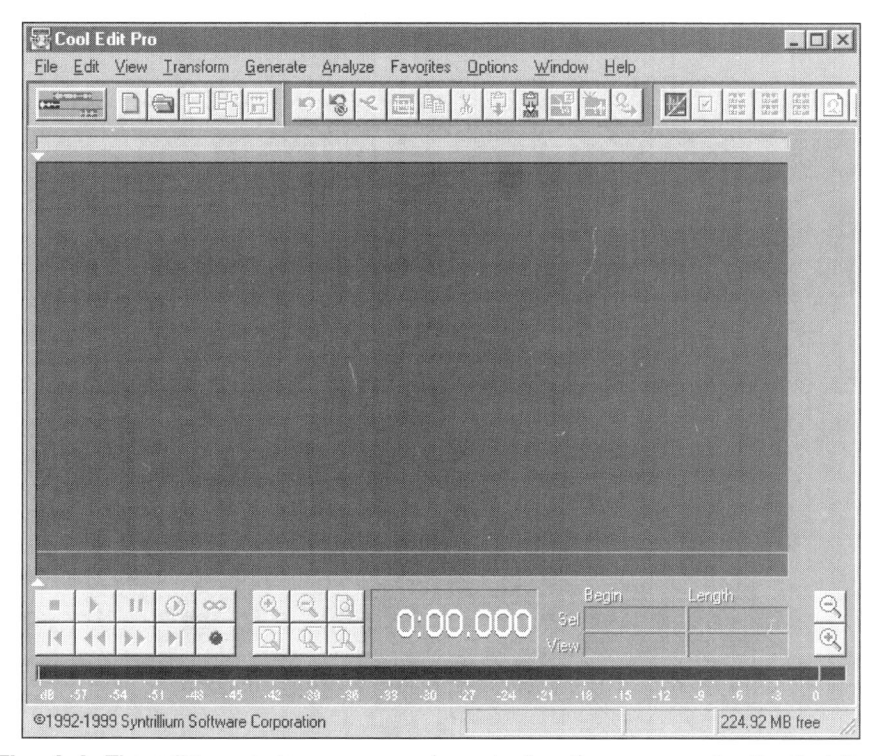

Fig. 4.4. The editing window you see when starting the program for the first time

In order for Cool Edit Pro to be maximally effective, you must set it up in a certain manner.

System settings are configured in the **Settings** window, which is called by:

1. Going into the **Options** menu.

2. And then choosing the **Settings** item.

> **NOTE** Another way of calling the **Settings** window is by pressing the <F4> hotkey.

Let's look at one of the tabs in the **Settings** window — the **System** tab.

The *System* Tab

The arrows in Fig. 4.5 point to those parameters to which we think you should pay the most attention: **Cache Size**, **Peaks Cache.../Block**, **Temp Directory**, **Secondary Temp**, and **Enable Undo...Levels (minimum)**.

We'll look at each of these in more detail.

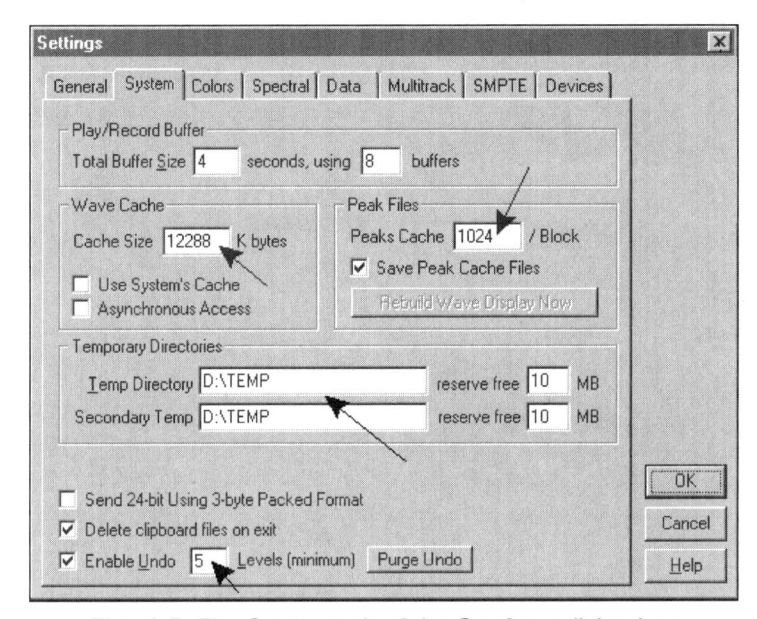

Fig. 4.5. The **System** tab of the **Settings** dialog box

The *Cache Size* Option (the Size of the Wave Cache)

You can significantly increase the performance of the program by choosing the optimal size of the **Wave Cache**.

> **NOTE** *Wave Cache* is the area of the RAM where a copy of the information recorded to the hard disk is stored. Caching is necessary for reducing the number of times that you have to address the device for saving information, since reading the data from the RAM is much faster than reading it from the hard drive.

Syntrillium Software Corporation — the company that releases Cool Edit Pro — recommends that you set the optimum size of the cache according to the size of the computer's RAM. This data is shown in the table in Fig. 4.6.

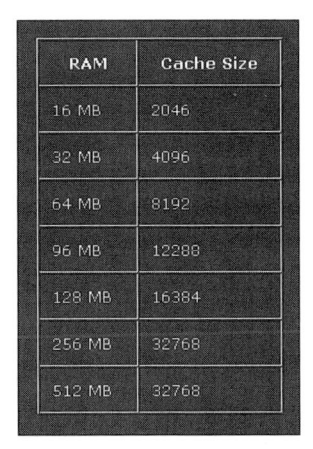

Chapter 4: Cool Edit Pro as a Universal Solution for Home Studios 169

RAM	Cache Size
16 MB	2046
32 MB	4096
64 MB	8192
96 MB	12288
128 MB	16384
256 MB	32768
512 MB	32768

Fig. 4.6. The table showing the dependence of the Wave Cache size on the size of the RAM

TIP — The **Asynchronous Access** option allows you to simultaneously read from and write to the hard drive. The Windows 95 operating system did not have this ability. We have tested this mode in Windows 98 and Windows NT (Service Pack 6), and recommend that you use it. Selecting the **Asynchronous Access** option considerably speeds up your work.

The *Use System's Cache* Option

This checkbox is left unselected in Fig. 4.5. Since the Wave Cache works a lot faster than the Windows system cache, it is recommended that you set the **Use System's Cache** checkbox only for computers with a RAM of 16 MB or less.

The *Save Peak Cache Files* Option

In the *"Importing Sound Files into SAWPro"* section of *Chapter 3*, we noted that each sound program saves images of the waveform in its own specific format.

Cool Edit Pro creates a file with the PK (PeaK file) extension.

If the **Save Peak Cache Files** checkbox is selected (Fig. 4.5), sound files will be loaded quickly, since you don't have to scan them again, nor do you need to create a new PK file.

The *Peaks Cache.../Block* Option (the Size of the Waveform File Cache)

The speed of redrawing the waveform on the screen when you are changing the scale depends on the **Peaks Cache** value. This value is measured in selections per block.

Increasing the size of **Peaks Cache** lowers the demands on the RAM when editing large sound files (those over 100 MB).

NOTE In these cases, you should increase the size of **Peaks Cache** to 2048.

You can change the size of the cache without unloading the edited file. To do this, you need to first enter the new value in the **Peaks Cache.../Block** field, and then press the **Rebuild Wave Display Now** button, which becomes available after changing the **Peaks Cache.../Block** parameter (Fig. 4.7).

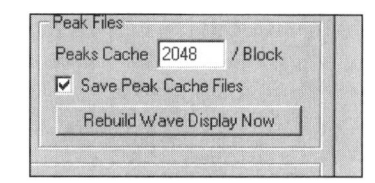

Fig. 4.7. Changing the **Peaks Cache** parameter

The *Temp Directory* and *Secondary Temp* Options

In the **System** tab (see Fig. 4.5) you can change the location of the temporary file folders by entering the paths to them in the **Temp Directory** and **Secondary Temp** fields.

TIP If the hard drive is partitioned, it is recommended that you create these directories on different logical drives.

More on temporary files can be found in the *"Processing Sound"* section.

The *Enable Undo ... Levels (minimum)* Option

This parameter is responsible for the minimum number of undo levels.

Cool Edit Pro makes a reserve copy of the edited file at each stage (level) of processing, which substantially reduces the free space on the hard drive. The **Purge Undo** button deletes all the undo levels except for the last *N*, where *N* is the minimum number of undo levels.

Configuring the Multitrack (the *Multitrack* Tab)

When you first begin using Cool Edit Pro, it's best to select the following options in the **Multitrack** tab (Fig. 4.8):

- ❐ **Default Rec** — the switches in this group should be set to **Stereo** and **16-bit**. If they are, recording in the **Multitrack View** window will be in stereo with a sound file resolution of 16 bits by default.

- ❐ **Mixdowns** — set the switch to **16-bit**. Accordingly, all mixdown operations on the multitrack will be done in a file with a resolution of 16 bits.

☐ **Playback Mixing** — choose the **16-bit Pre-mixes** button. When you do, all tracks of the multitrack will be mixed during playback with a resolution of 16 bits.

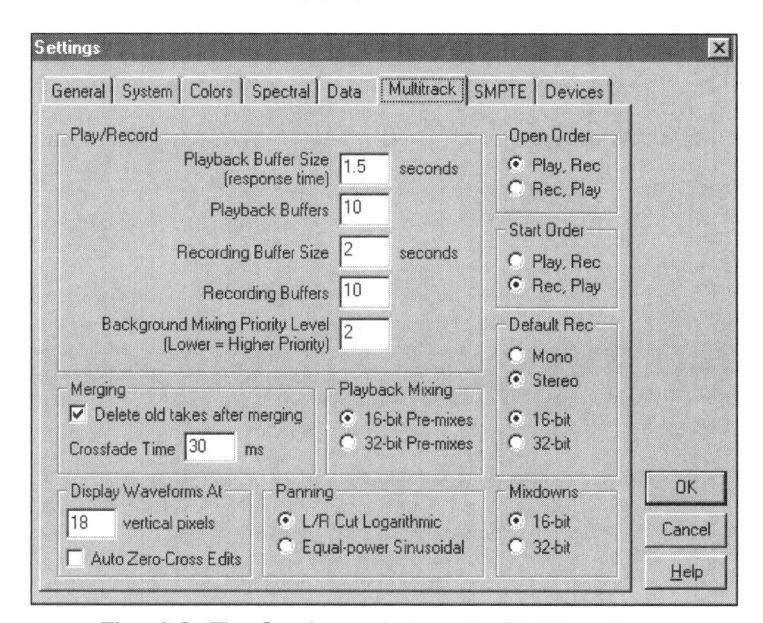

Fig. 4.8. The **Settings** window, the **Multitrack** tab

NOTE: Mixing multitrack tracks in Cool Edit Pro is done in background mode. Mixing is first done in a temporary file, which is then played as the output track in SAWPro.

The *Edit Waveform View Editing* Window

Cool Edit Pro has only two basic windows: the editing window **Edit Waveform View**, and the multitrack window **Multitrack View**.

Configuring the Toolbars

Fig. 4.4 shows the editing window **Edit Waveform View**.

When loading in the default mode, there is only one row of toolbars in the upper part of the window.

But the number of tools, and thus the number of toolbars that hold them, can be increased. This is done using a pop-up menu.

The pop-up menu for toolbars (Fig. 4.9) is called by right-clicking on any of the icons.

In this menu, you can set a check next to the name of the toolbar you need by clicking it with the left mouse button, or remove a checked (visible) toolbar that you don't need by doing the same.

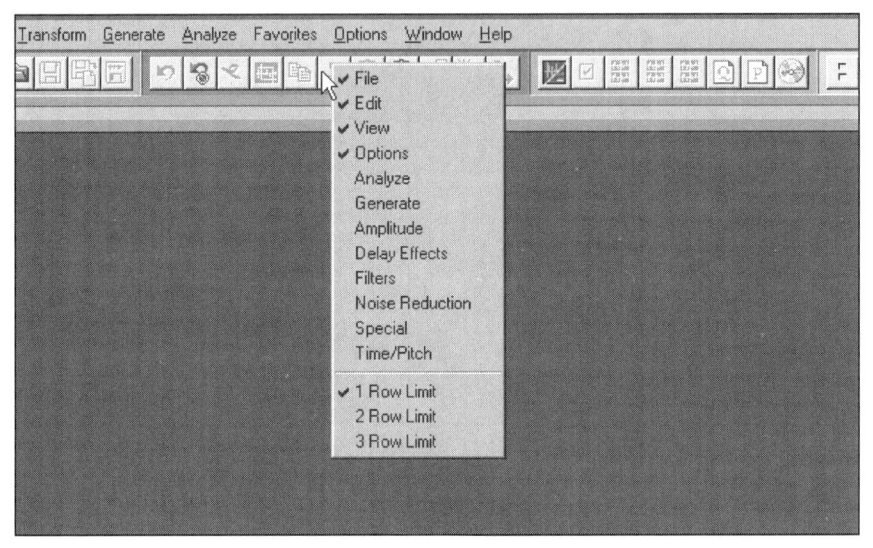

Fig. 4.9. The pop-up toolbar menu

NOTE The developers of Cool Edit Pro advise you to actively use these pop-up menus, of which there are more than a few in Cool Edit Pro. They are all called by right-clicking on the icons associated with them.

By putting a check next to the options you need, you can quickly create convenient, "personal" toolbars.

The Number of Toolbar Rows

In the lower part of the pop-up menu, you can assign the number of rows in which the toolbars you select will be situated:

❐ **1 Row Limit**

❐ **2 Row Limit**

❐ **3 Row Limit**

When choosing the **3 Row Limit** option, the window is able to hold the maximum number of buttons. But of course if you do this, the working area of the screen in which the image of the waveform is displayed will be smaller.

Chapter 4: Cool Edit Pro as a Universal Solution for Home Studios 173

One of the possible configurations — the middle one, with two rows — is shown in Fig. 4.10.

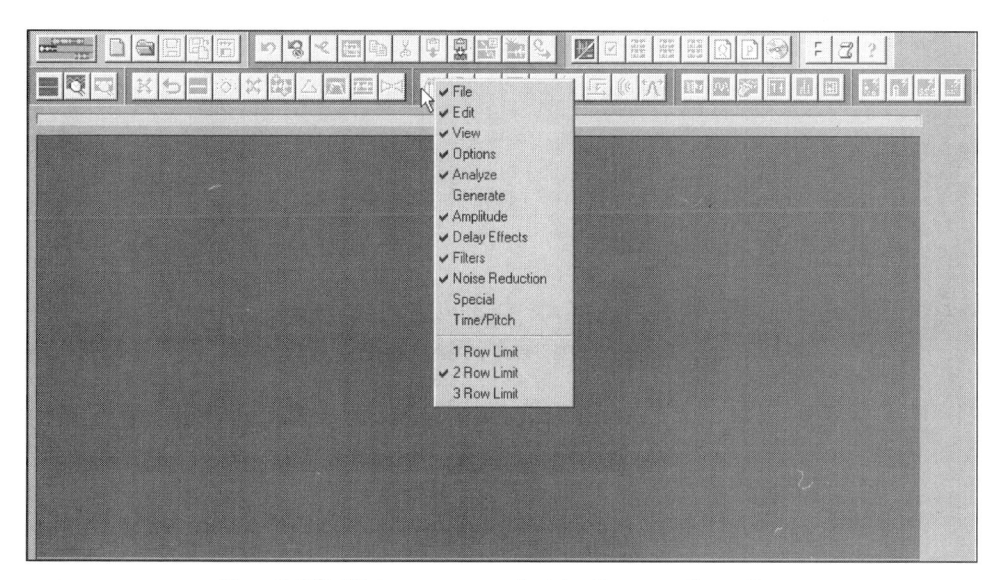

Fig. 4.10. The recommended toolbar configuration

Controlling Recording and Playback in the Editing Window

The **Transport Controls** toolbar is used for controlling the processes of recording and playback (Fig. 4.11).

Its functions are analogous to the **Transport** bar in SAWPro.

Fig. 4.11. The controls of the **Transport Controls** toolbar

The toolbar consists of ten buttons, whose functions are described below.

❐ The **STOP** button stops recording or playback.

> **NOTE** On the keyboard, the **STOP** function can be enacted by pressing the <Alt>+<S> key combination.

Fig. 4.12. The **STOP** button

- The **PLAY** button begins playback of only that fragment currently displayed on the screen (and also is used to play back selected fragments). Notice that:
  - If the multitrack cursor is on the left border of the window, the entire fragment will be played back
  - If the cursor has been moved, playback will begin later, at the point where it is located.

  NOTE On the keyboard, the **PLAY** button is duplicated by the <Alt>+<P> key combination.

  Fig. 4.13. The **PLAY** button

- The **PAUSE** button is used for temporarily stopping recording or playback.

  Fig. 4.14. The **PAUSE** button

- The **PLAY TO END** button begins playback from the cursor position, and continues:
  - Until the end of the *sound file* in the **Edit Waveform View** window
  - Or until the end of the *project* in the **Multitrack View** window

  Fig. 4.15. The **PLAY TO END** button

- The **PLAY LOOP** button turns on looped playback of the selected section or of the entire sound file.

  Fig. 4.16. The **PLAY LOOP** button

Using the Spacebar for Playback

If you activate the **PLAY**, **PLAY TO END**, or **PLAY LOOP** modes by clicking them with the mouse, you needn't press the buttons to begin playback — pressing the spacebar will suffice.

Chapter 4: Cool Edit Pro as a Universal Solution for Home Studios 175

❒ The **Go to Beginning** and **Go to End** buttons move you to the beginning or the end of the file.

> **NOTE** These buttons are duplicated on the keyboard by the <Shift>+<Home> and <Shift>+<End> key combinations, respectively.

Fig. 4.17. The **Go to Beginning** and **Go to End** buttons

❒ The **Rewind** and **Fast Forward** buttons are used for quickly moving the cursor along the sound file.

Fig. 4.18. The **Rewind** and **Fast Forward** buttons

❒ The **Record** button turns on the recording mode.

Fig. 4.19. The **Record** button

Recording

One peculiarity of the recording mode in Cool Edit Pro is that it has no virtual regulator of the recording level. Therefore, when regulating the recording level, you will have to use the sound card's mixer (you can read more on this in the section "*Connecting to the Sound Card. Setting the Recording Level*" in *Chapter 3*).

Controlling the recording level is done using the **Level Meters** indicator (Fig. 4.20).

Enabling the Mode for Setting the Recording Level

In order to turn on the mode for setting the recording level, you must:

❒ Press the <F10> key

❒ Or click the **Monitor incoming wave level** button (Fig. 4.20)

Since the icons aren't always able to clearly show the purpose of a function, use the pop-up hints when you are in doubt. To see one of these hints, just place the mouse cursor over the button and wait for a second or two (Fig. 4.21).

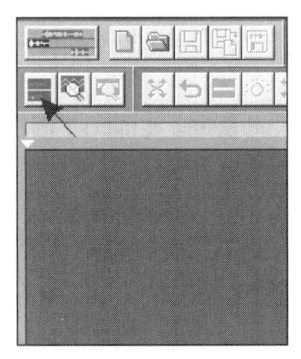

Fig. 4.20. The button for turning on the recording level indicator

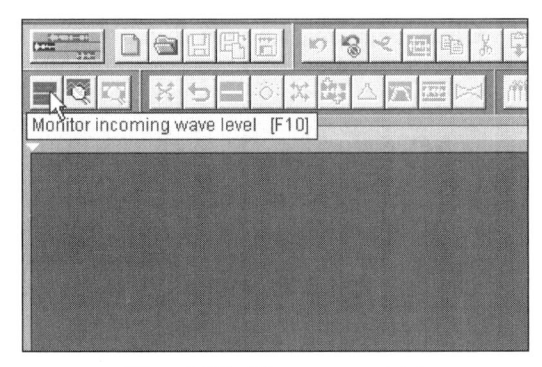

Fig. 4.21. The pop-up hint

When setting the recording level, you should remember that it must correspond to the indications on the horizontal scale at the bottom of the screen (Fig. 4.22).

> **NOTE** For a quality sound, the recording level should be set so that the indicator only reaches the zero level, i.e., the red column of the indicator should only touch the zero level occasionally, and not be there permanently (Fig. 4.22).

Remember that amplitude peaks higher than 0 dB are clipped.

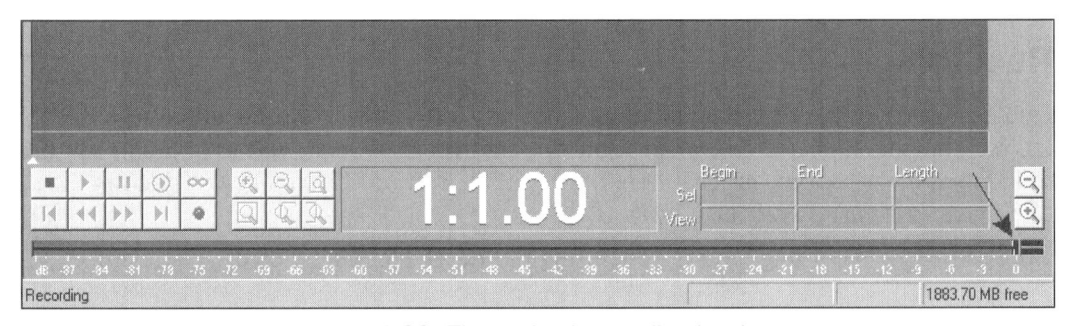

Fig. 4.22. The optimal recording level

Disabling the Mode for Setting the Recording Level

This operation can be done one of two ways:

- Pressing the <F10> key again
- Clicking the **Monitor incoming wave level button** (see Fig. 4.20).

Enabling and Disabling the Recording Mode

The recording mode is activated by clicking the **Record** button (see Fig. 4.19).

When you do this, the **New Waveform** dialog box opens. It contains the parameters of the future sound file — the sampling frequency and the resolution (Fig. 4.23).

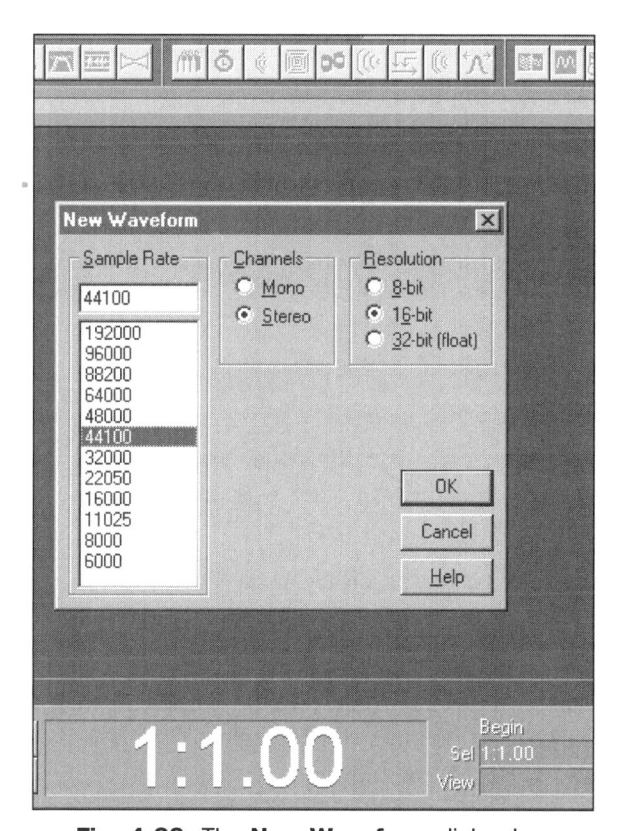

Fig. 4.23. The **New Waveform** dialog box

NOTE The **New Waveform** dialog box, when creating a new, empty file, is called using the traditional methods: either from the **File** menu, in which you should execute the **New** command, or by pressing <Ctrl>+<N>. Recording can only start after having created an empty file.

After configuring the necessary settings, click **OK**. Recording will begin.

You can stop recording with either the **Stop** or **Pause** buttons. Upon doing this, the fragment will be selected: you will see that it has a white background.

Visual Control of Recording with the Waveform

Controlling the recording level can be done visually, using the waveform that is displayed on the screen while recording. To turn this control on, you must check the **Live update during record** checkbox in the **General** tab of the **Settings** window.

Recording a sound file in Cool Edit Pro is always done following these simple rules:

- Recording always begins from the cursor position.

- If a fragment is selected, recording is automatically done only within that fragment. (This rule is also applicable in the **Multitrack View** window.)

WARNING When turning on the recording mode a second time, the new fragment will erase the previous one, and recording will stop automatically.

Selecting a Fragment

Moving the cursor in Cool Edit Pro is easily done. You can place it at any point you like (on the waveform image) by clicking that place with the left mouse button. There are two ways of selecting a fragment.

- Simply click the right mouse button either to the left or to the right of the cursor. The section of the file located to the left or to the right of the cursor, respectively, will be selected.

- Click the left mouse button, and while holding it pressed, drag the cursor to the left or to the right. The second boundary of the selected fragment will be located at the place where you release the mouse button.

Fig. 4.24 displays an example of recording a selected fragment.

Saving a Sound File

Saving a sound file is done using the **Save As** command of the **File** menu.

In the **Save Waveform As** dialog box that will open, the program will suggest that you go through the usual procedure: give the file a name and choose its format (Fig. 4.25).

We will look at the file formats supported by Cool Edit Pro below, in the "*Cool Edit Pro File Formats*" section.

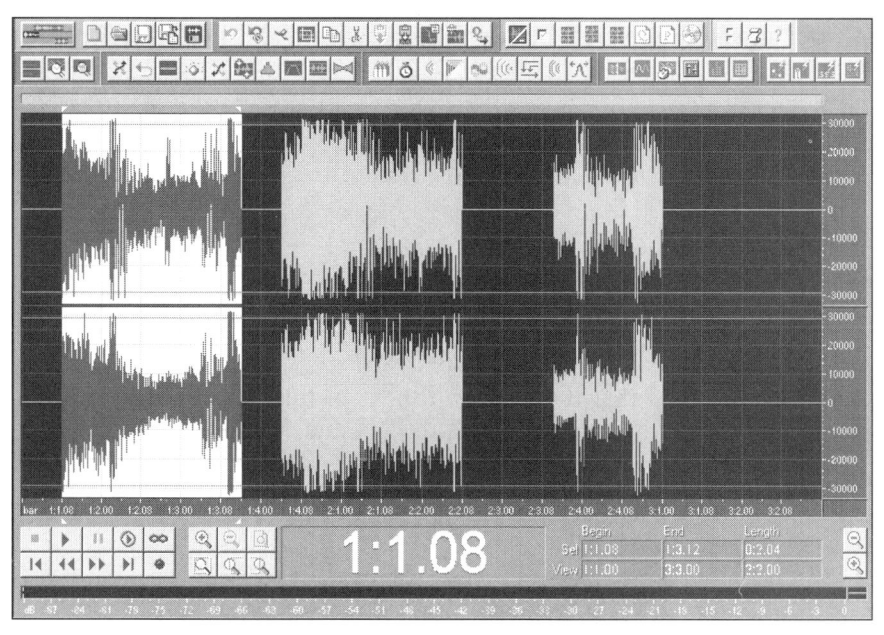

Chapter 4: Cool Edit Pro as a Universal Solution for Home Studios 179

Fig. 4.24. An example of recording a selected fragment

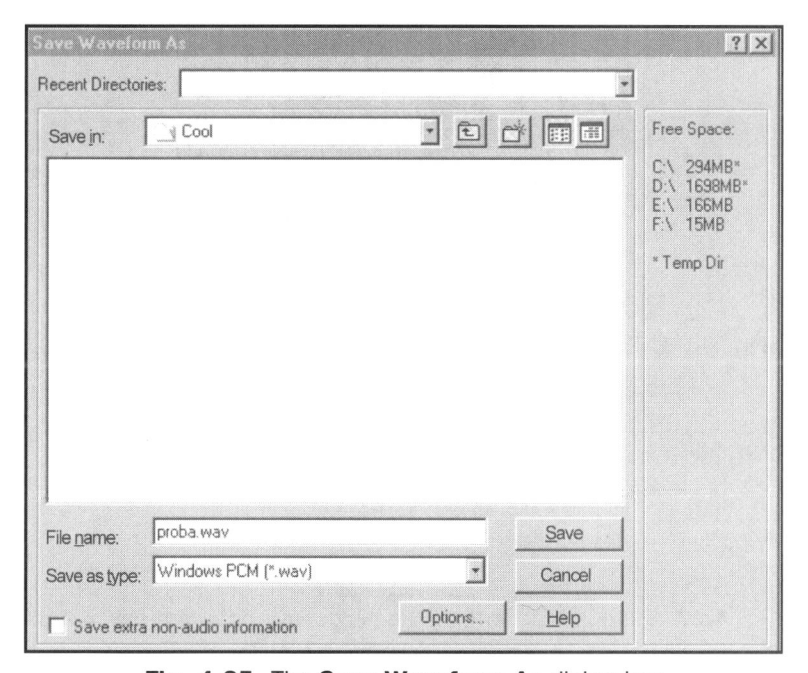

Fig. 4.25. The **Save Waveform As** dialog box

We'll now look at the features of the playback process in the **Edit Waveform View** window.

Cool Edit Pro provides various tools for changing the scale of the sound file's waveform. These tools are very user-friendly. Scaling the picture of the waveform allows us to do some truly intricate work: we can listen to a micro-fragment, and if necessary, edit it alone.

Changing the Scale of a Waveform

The buttons with which we can *vertically* change the scale of the waveform image are located in the lower right corner of the editing window.

We can see from Fig. 4.26 that they have on them pictures that clearly indicate the direction of the zoom (magnifying glasses with the "+" and "−" signs inside).

> **NOTE** The image can also be scaled using the <Ctrl>+<Up arrow> keys to enlarge, and the <Ctrl>+<Down arrow> keys to reduce.

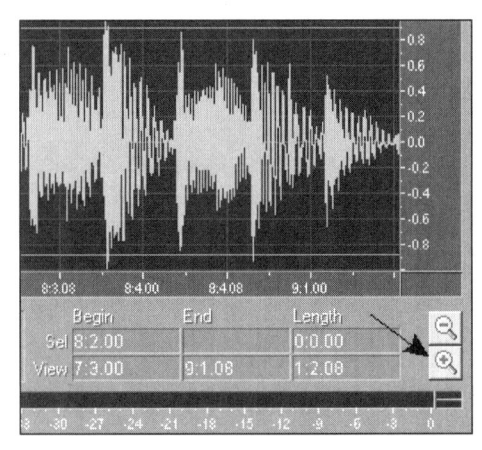

Fig. 4.26. The **Zoom In Vertically**, **Zoom Out Vertically** buttons

To set a new scale for the waveform image *horizontally*, you can use the block of six buttons found in the lower left part of the editing window (Fig. 4.27).

Fig. 4.27. Buttons for changing the horizontal zoom of the waveform

The functions of these buttons are described below.

Chapter 4: Cool Edit Pro as a Universal Solution for Home Studios 181

- The **Zoom In to Center** button increases the horizontal scale.

    NOTE The **Zoom In to Center** button is duplicated by the <Ctrl>+<Right arrow> key combination.

    Fig. 4.28. The **Zoom In to Center** button

- The **Zoom Out** button decreases the horizontal scale.

    NOTE The **Zoom Out** button is duplicated by the <Ctrl>+<Left arrow> key combination.

    Fig. 4.29. The **Zoom Out** button

- The **Zoom Out Full** button displays the entire file with a scale of 1:1.

    Fig. 4.30. The **Zoom Out Full** button

- The **Zoom to Selection** button blows the selected fragment up to full-screen size.

    Fig. 4.31. The **Zoom to Selection** button

- The **Zoom to Left of Selection** button increases the area next to the left-side boundary of the selected fragment.

    NOTE The **Zoom to Left of Selection** button is duplicated by the <Ctrl>+<Home> key combination.

    Fig. 4.32. The **Zoom to Left of Selection** button

- The **Zoom to Right of Selection** button increases the area next to the right-side boundary of the selected fragment.

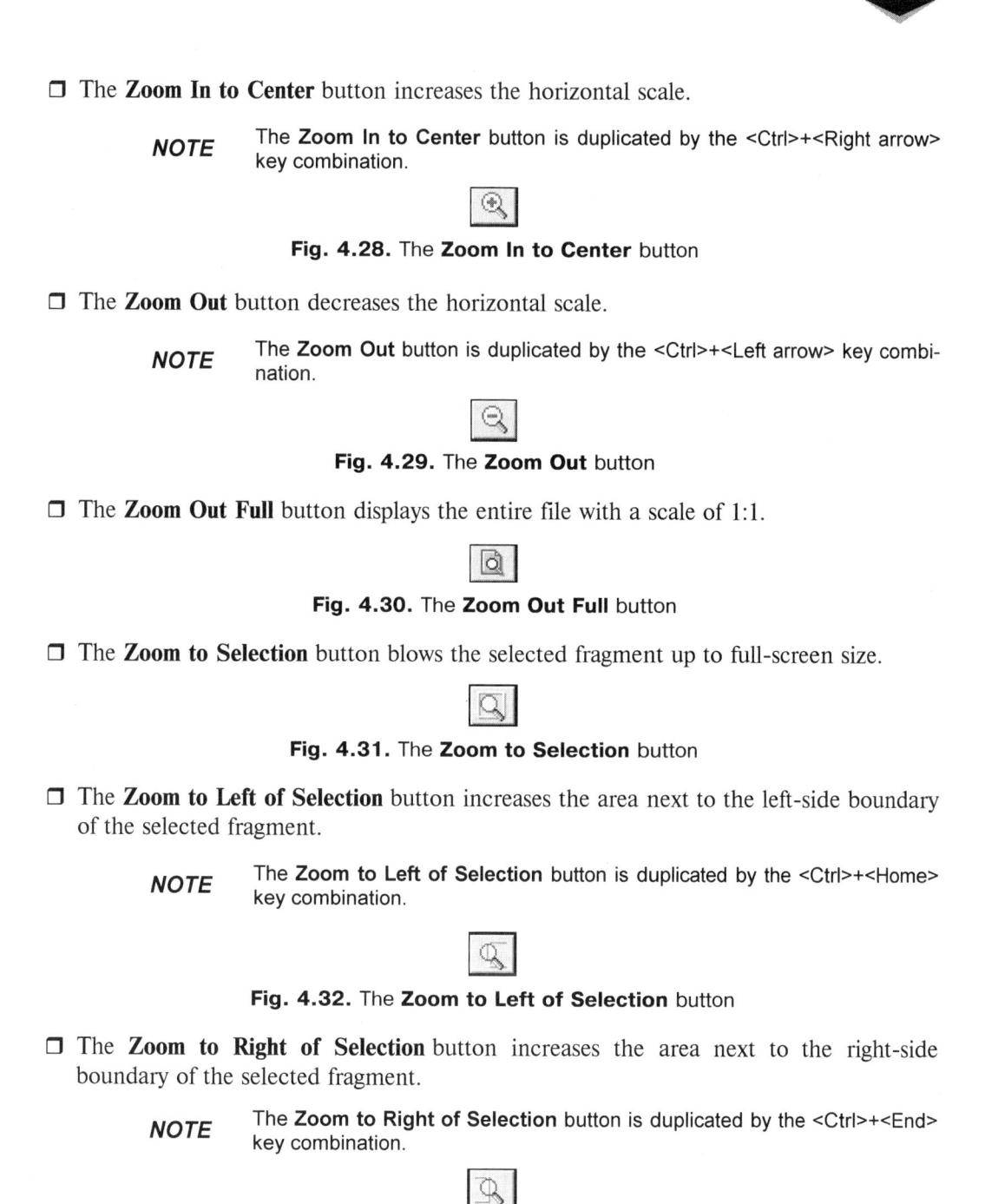

    NOTE The **Zoom to Right of Selection** button is duplicated by the <Ctrl>+<End> key combination.

    Fig. 4.33. The **Zoom to Right of Selection** button

Simultaneous Select and Zoom

Cool Edit Pro provides a convenient method of selecting a fragment and enlarging it to full-screen size. To do this, you need to select the fragment on the **Time Ruler** (Fig. 4.34), and not directly on the file's waveform.

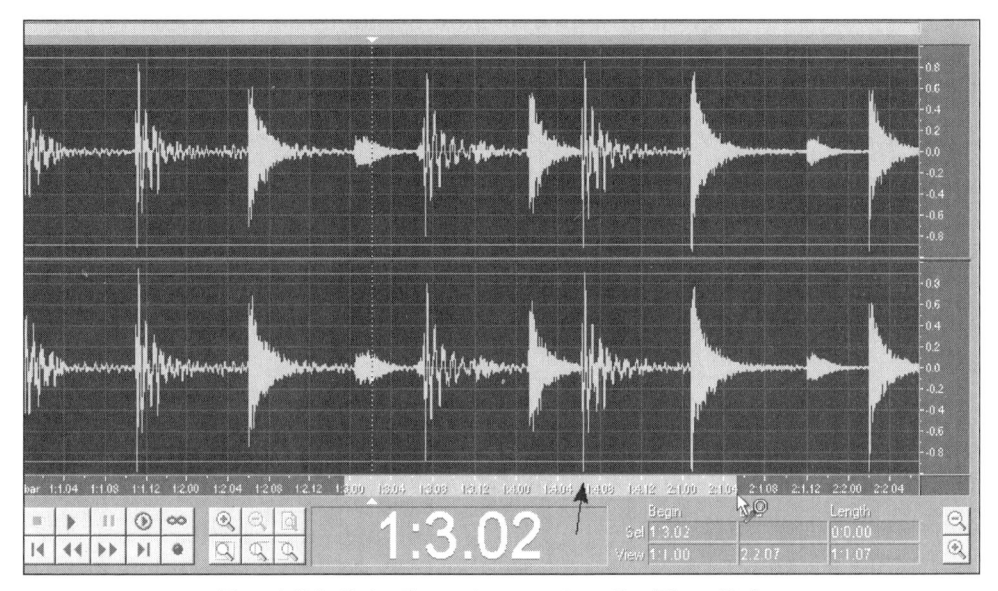

Fig. 4.34. Selecting a fragment on the **Time Ruler**

> **NOTE** The **Time Ruler** is a scale located in the bottom of the screen that displays time units for measuring the waveform.

To make such a selection:

1. Place the cursor at the position on the **Time Ruler** where the fragment begins.

2. Holding the right mouse button, move the cursor along the **Time Ruler** to the end of the fragment.

Each time you repeat this operation, the selected fragment will automatically be expanded to take up the entire screen.

Precise (Digital) Selection

When working with sound files, it is often necessary to not only change the scale, but also to be as accurate as possible in setting the boundaries of the selected file fragment or the one seen on the screen.

Chapter 4: Cool Edit Pro as a Universal Solution for Home Studios

For this we use the tools of the horizontal **Time Ruler** scale (Fig. 4.35).

Before we begin examining the **Time Ruler**, we'd like you to note how Cool Edit Pro indicates the cursor's current position.

The cursor coordinates are shown in two places: in large font on the **Time Window** counter, and in small font in the **Time Display Fields** (Fig. 4.35).

NOTE If no fragment is selected, the **Time Window** counter shows the cursor coordinates.

If there is a fragment selected on the screen, the **Time Window** will give the coordinates of the beginning of the fragment.

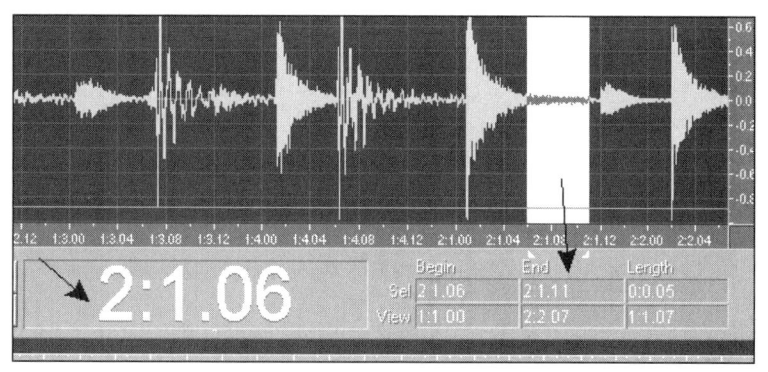

Fig. 4.35. The **Time Display** counter and the **Time Display Fields**

There are various units of measurement that can be used in Cool Edit Pro.

The horizontal scale can be divided into such units as samples, bars, and the like, just as in SAWPro (see *Chapter 3*).

NOTE You can change the units of measurement by right-clicking on the **Time Ruler**. You'll then see the **Display Time Format** pop-up menu, which is shown in Fig. 4.36.

Extensive information on the horizontal scale of the waveform display can be found in the **Time Display Fields**, which has three columns — **Begin**, **End**, and **Length**.

In the upper line, **Sel** (selection), you see all the information for the *selected* file. The lower line, **View**, contains information on the part of the file currently displayed *on screen*.

You can change the boundaries of the selected or visible fragment by entering new values in the corresponding cells of the **Time Display Fields** table. For this you need to:

1. Click on the field that you want to change.

2. Enter in the new value via the keyboard.
3. Press <Enter>.

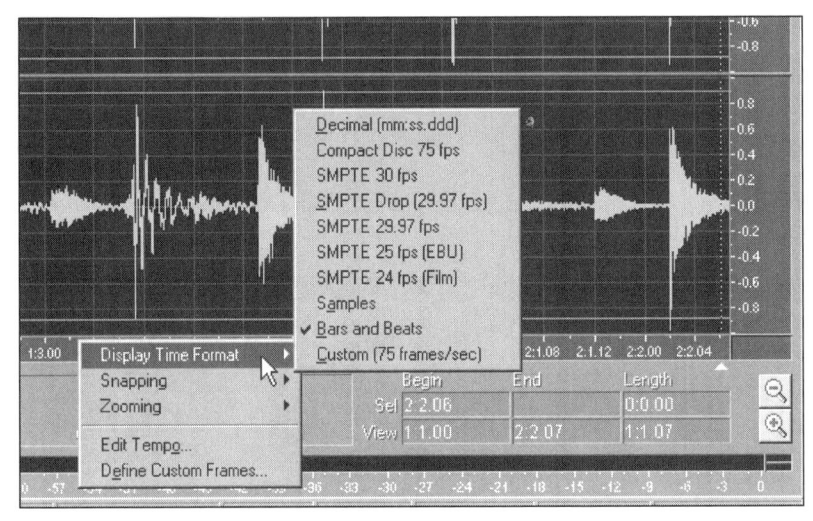

Fig. 4.36. The **Display Time Format** pop-up menu

The vertical ruler — **Amplitude Ruler** — indicates the amplitude of the signal.

The amplitude of the wave can also be given in various units of measurement: **Sample Values**, **Percentage**, or **Normalized Values**. When using **Normalized Values**, the maximum undistorted level (without clipping the amplitude peaks) is equal to one unit.

To change the units of measurement:

1. Right-click on the **Amplitude Ruler**.
2. In the pop-up menu that appears, put a check next to the units you wish to use (Fig. 4.37).

In Fig. 4.37, as in all of the previous examples, the sound signal on the screen is displayed as a *waveform*.

But Cool Edit Pro also allows you to display the signal in its *spectral form*.

The spectral display can be turned on from the **View** menu's **Spectral View** option (Fig. 4.38).

NOTE When processing stereo sound files in the editing window, you have the ability to independently edit the left and right channels. The <Ctrl>+<L> prevents you from editing the right channel, while <Ctrl>+<R> will prevent the editing of the left channel. <Ctrl>+<B> undoes the previous command, and allows you to work with both channels at the same time.

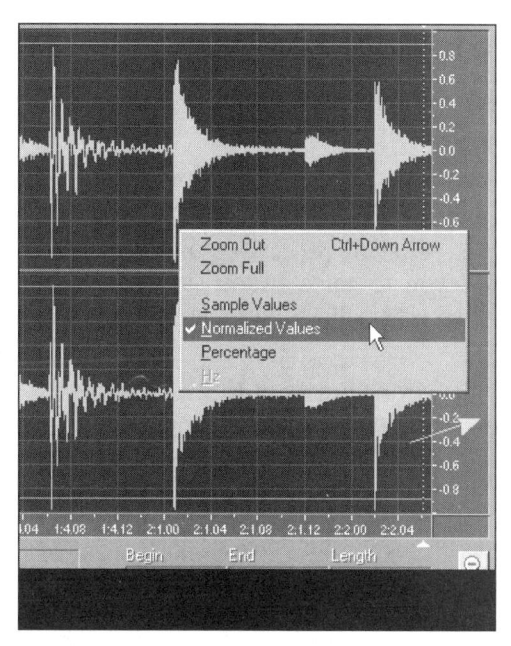

Chapter 4: Cool Edit Pro as a Universal Solution for Home Studios 185

Fig. 4.37. The **Amplitude Ruler**'s pop-up menu

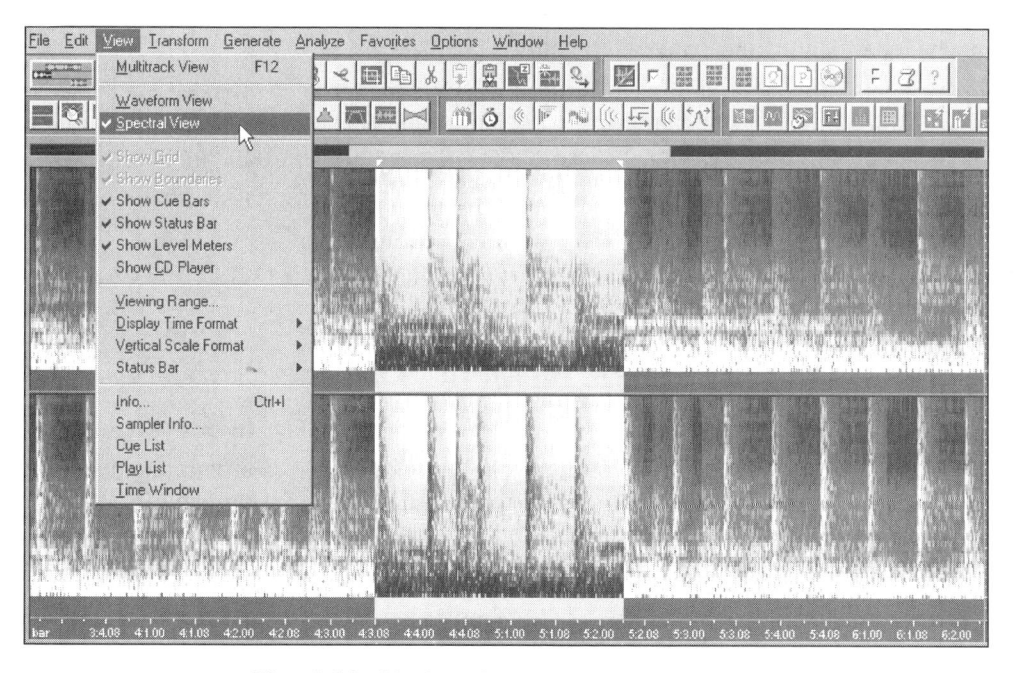

Fig. 4.38. Display of the signal as a spectrum

Audio Processing in Cool Edit Pro

Unfortunately, there is no software that is ideal for both recording and editing sound, and Cool Edit Pro is no exception to this rule.

As we mentioned in *Chapter 3*, the SAWPro software is the best choice for recording "live" music in a home studio.

However, Cool Edit Pro is better at processing under these conditions, since its set of instruments (effects) allows you to get a "warm" and "enlivened" sound at output. This advantage of the program is especially noticeable when recording acoustic musical instruments.

But when speaking about the strong points of Cool Edit Pro, we should also mention two of its disappointing weaknesses. Both of these are related to applying virtual effects.

- In Cool Edit Pro, you cannot plug an effect into a track and listen to it together with other tracks in real time. (You have to do the processing in the editor window.)
- You can't apply a group of effects simultaneously.

NOTE Note that SAWPro allows you to plug a large number of virtual devices in at the same time in the **Effects Patch Builder** window.

However, both of these features are compensated for by the high quality of signal processing and the friendly and convenient software interface.

The developers of Cool Edit Pro introduced a new concept — *delayed destructive editing*. This was done so that, while working with large multitrack projects, the user wouldn't notice or be hindered by the lack of destructive editing abilities when applying effects.

The idea behind this concept is that actually changing the original audio file is *delayed* until the saving action is performed.

Before saving the audio file or the project, it is not the file itself that destructively edited, but a copy. This copy is stored in a special *temporary* file.

Description of the *Transform* Menu's Effects

Using Cool Edit Pro's **Transform** menu, you can call audio effects to process the file.

Many of these effects support the **Preview** real-time mode. This is a definite advantage of the program, because it allows you to adjust the sound settings during playback.

Note that in the **Transform** menu we have the **DirectX** submenu, through which DirectX standard effects are plugged in (Fig. 4.39).

Before we start describing the effects of the **Transform** menu in detail, let's ask ourselves a question: is it necessary to know almost everything about the nature of sound signals in order to successfully produce sound in a home studio?

Chapter 4: Cool Edit Pro as a Universal Solution for Home Studios 187

A sound signal is a very complex object. A detailed description of the processes that take place during the processing of a sound signal is too much for us to cover in this book, and would be straying from our original purpose. But luckily — especially for those readers who are not at all interested in or who wouldn't understand the processes that are going on inside the computer — modern equipment allows anyone to be able to artistically process sound.

We can also mention that PC users who are not technicians have the same chance to achieve good sound processing results as technical experts.

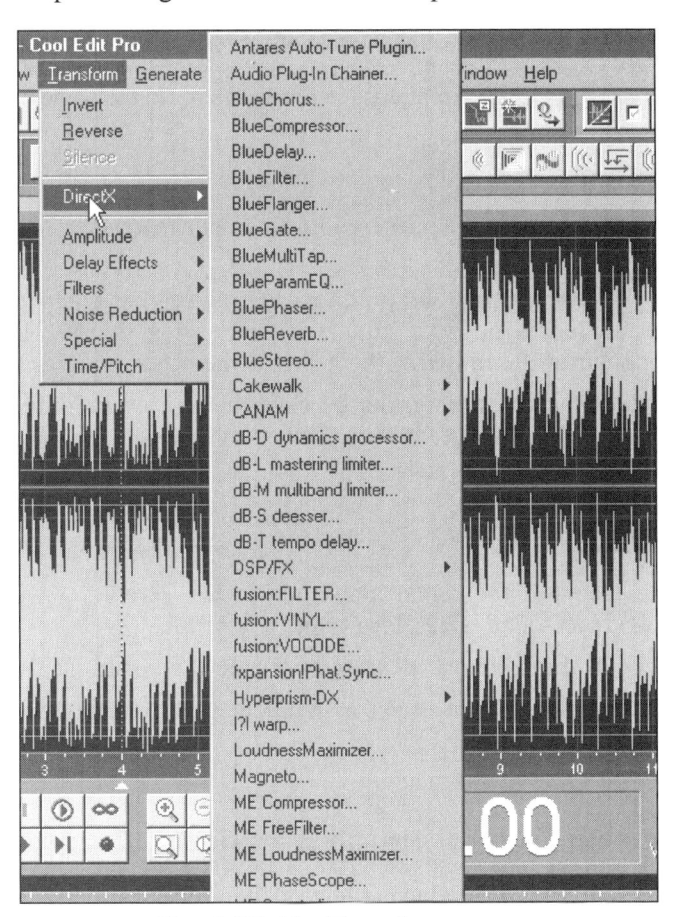

Fig. 4.39. The **Transform** menu

> **NOTE** There is a *general rule* you should know when applying effects: if the fragment is selected, the effect is applied to the fragment; if there is nothing selected, the effect is applied to the region of the audio file visible in the editor window. After the effect is applied, the region of the audio file remains selected.

The *Invert* Effect

This effect is applied very rarely, and only for special purposes.

The **Invert** effect makes all positive signal measurements negative, and all negative ones positive, i.e., the waveform becomes its own opposite.

The **Invert** effect may be useful when assembling various fragments, in order to avoid sharp changes in the amplitude.

> **NOTE** When applied to both channels of the audio stereo file, this effect is not audible. If you apply this effect for the channels separately, the **Invert** effect is basically equal to the acoustic systems being out of sync by phase. Applying this effect once again restores the previous state of the audio material.

The *Reverse* Effect

The **Reverse** effect allows you to play the audio fragment in reverse order, from the end to the beginning.

Reversing is a very amusing process. I'm sure you'll agree that when playing sounds in reverse order, you can come up with some very interesting things. This might be why reversing was so popular in the music of the '60s and the '70s.

Indeed, you can get some unusual results by experimenting with different noise effects and reversing "non-musical" sounds. If you apply the **Reverse** effect again, you'll restore the previous state of the audio material.

The *Silence* Effect

The **Silence** effect decreases the signal amplitude to the zero level within the selected fragment. Thus you get a "silent" area (Fig. 4.40).

You can use this effect when editing vocals to eliminate the noises in pauses.

It is fairly easy to implement: first select a fragment that contains no useful data, and then apply the **Silence** effect to it.

Effects Based on Transforming the Signal Amplitude

For non-experts to gain a better understanding of the processes that are taking place, we will equate the concept of *amplitude* to the concept of *volume*.

Cool Edit Pro provides a group of seven **Amplitude** effects. Their mechanism is based on changing the loudness of the signal. These effects are: **Amplify**, **Channel Mixer**, **Dynamics Processing**, **Create Envelope**, **Hard Limiter**, and **Normalize**. Now we'll describe them separately.

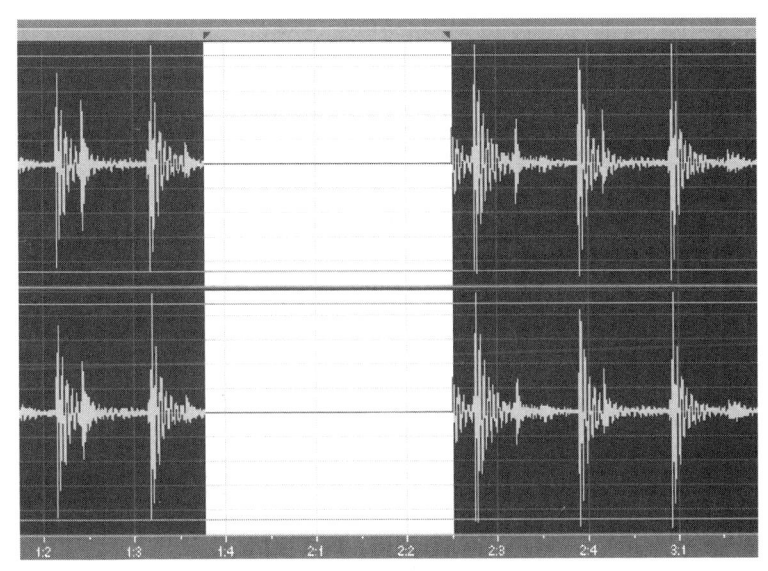

Fig. 4.40. The **Silence** effect

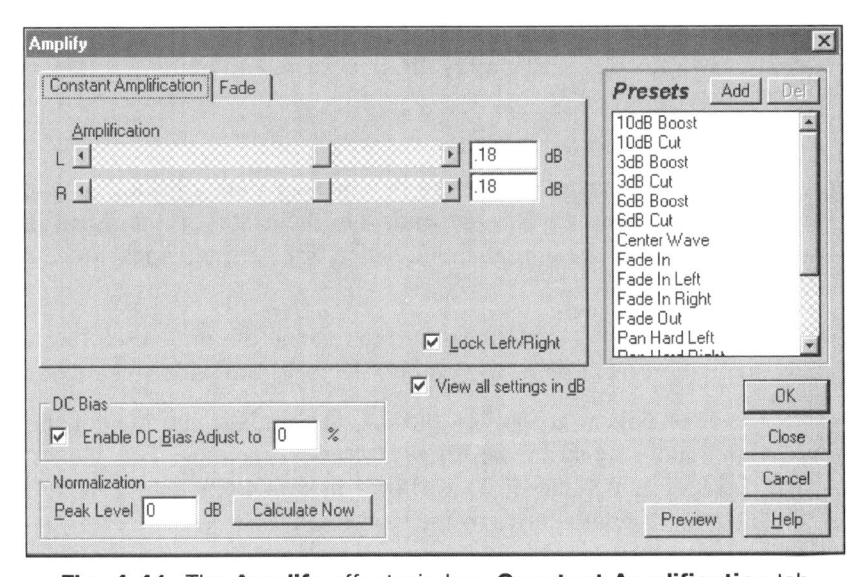

Fig. 4.41. The **Amplify** effect window, **Constant Amplification** tab

The *Amplify* Effect

The **Amplify** effect allows you to change the loudness of the signal. This effect is called by the **Transform | Amplitude | Amplify** menu command.

When the **Amplify** command is implemented, the control window for this effect appears. It contains two tabs: **Constant Amplification** (Fig. 4.41) and **Fade** (Fig. 4.42).

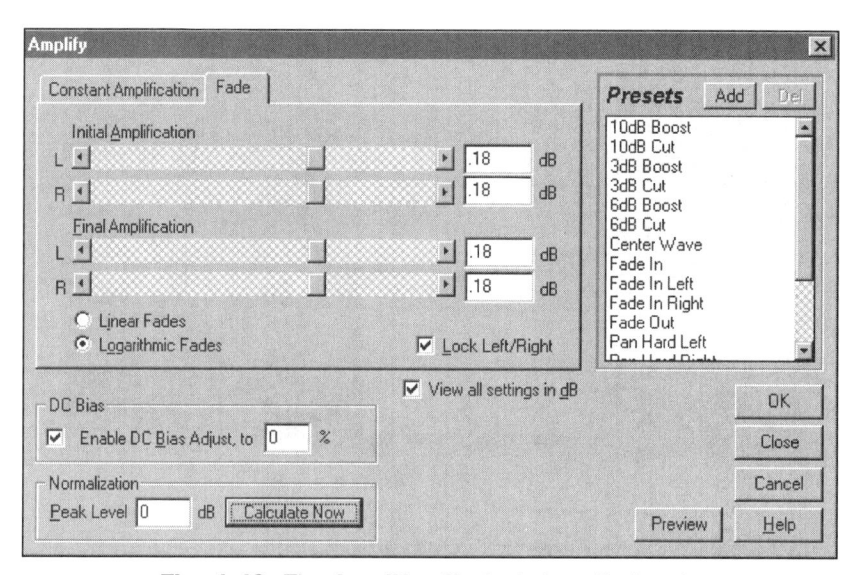

Fig. 4.42. The **Amplify** effect window, **Fade** tab

The settings of the first of these tabs are easy to understand.

- Regulating the amplification/reduction can be done separately in both channels, or in both channels simultaneously. This depends on the state of the **Lock Left/Right** checkbox. If it is checked, the amplification sliders for both channels move in concert with each other.

- The **View all settings in dB** option allows you to change the units used to measure the amplification/reduction from percentsages into decibels, and vice versa.

- The **Enable DC Bias Adjust, to** option allows you to adjust the bias of the constant component of the audio signal to the *assigned level* in percents. This means that if in the text field you specify a value of **0** (as shown in Fig. 4.42), the program automatically centers the audio signal relative to the zero level.

Bias over the DC

Bias over the DC can occur due to the audio card or external musical equipment. You should eliminate this bias as soon as it appears, since it can cause errors in the application of sound effects.

Chapter 4: Cool Edit Pro as a Universal Solution for Home Studios

- In the **Normalization** section we see the **Peak Level** input field. In this field, you can specify the *maximum peak level* of the signal in decibels. When you press the **Calculate Now** button, the program automatically calculates the necessary increase or decrease in the signal at the set peak level in the selected units (percents or decibels). The position of the amplification/reduction regulators of the left and right channels changes accordingly.

- In the window of each virtual effect there is a list of **Presets**. They change the parameters of the effect. You can activate a preset by clicking on its name in the Presets list. When a preset becomes unnecessary, you can remove it by pressing the **Del** button. If you have to save the current configuration of the effect, you can create a new preset. To do so, press the **Add** button, and from the keyboard input the name of the configuration in the **New Preset Name** dialog box.

- When you go to the **Fade** tab (Fig. 4.42), the one pair of sliders is replaced with two: **Initial Amplification** and **Final Amplification**. These sliders are used to create the effect of a *smooth* amplification or fading of the volume. When these effects are applied, the loudness gradually changes from the position of the **Initial Amplification** sliders to the position of the **Final Amplification** sliders.

    NOTE Similar effects are found in the **Mix** menu of the SAWPro software: **Fade Out**, **Fade In Marked**, and **Fade To Next Volume Change**.

- The **Linear Fades** and **Logarithmic Fades** button groups determine the smoothness of the loudness change curve. To get a better understanding of this effect, you can experiment with its presets, set during the installation of the program.

    NOTE When you select **Logarithmic Fades**, loudness amplifying/fading takes less time.

- The **Preview** button allows you to assess the effect *before you apply it* to your sound material.

The *Channel Mixer* Effect

The **Channel Mixer** is intended for processing *stereo signals only*. Using this effect, you can create, for example, an "extended stereo" effect.

NOTE The **Channel Mixer** window is unavailable if a mono file is loaded into the editor.

The **Channel Mixer** settings window (Fig. 4.43) contains four level sliders, two in each group — **New Left Channel** and **New Right Channel**.

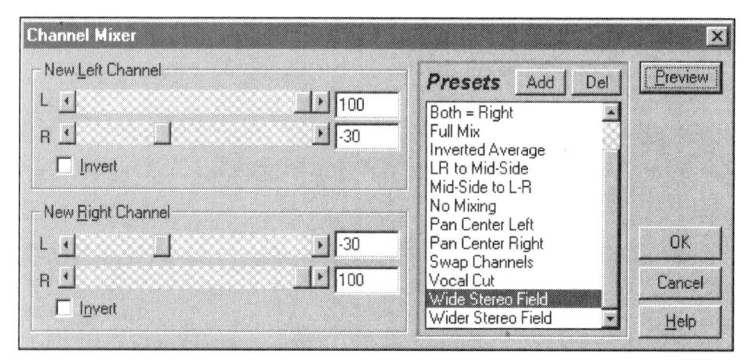

Fig. 4.43. The **Channel Mixer** settings window

The **Invert** options simply invert the output signal of the corresponding section (similar to the **Invert** effect). Each slider has a range from −100 to 100. If the slider is in a negative position, the signal is mixed with inversion. Settings in the **Wide Stereo Field** mode are shown in Fig. 4.43.

In the given example, the signals of the left and right channels are cross-mixed with inversion, which leads to the illusion of increasing the distance between the acoustic systems. This effect is called *widening the stereo base*.

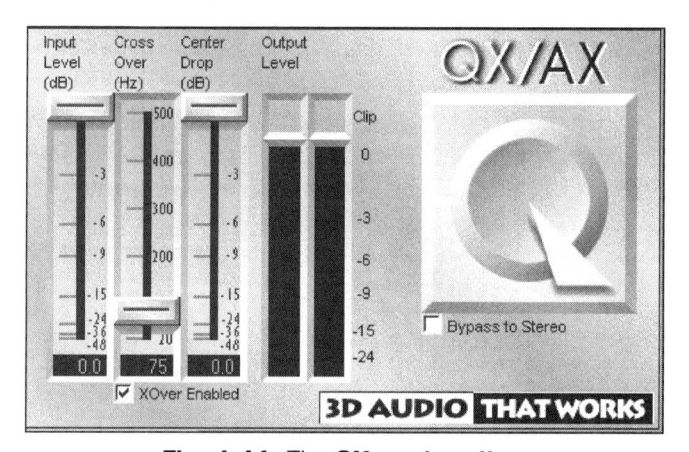

Fig. 4.44. The **QXpander** effect

TIP To get an expended stereo base and stereo sound, we recommend that you apply the **QXpander** DirectX effect (Fig. 4.44) from QSound Labs, Inc. (**http://www.qsound.ca**).

The **Vocal Cut** preset of the **Channel Mixer** effect allows you to partially remove the vocal part from the stereo signal. When you use this, the vocal part must have the same loudness in both channels.

The *Dynamics Range Processing* Effect

The **Dynamics Range Processing** effect is a multifunction virtual signal processing device that allows you to change the dynamic range.

> **NOTE** Remember that the dynamic range is the difference between the level of the loudest and the quietest sound in the logarithmic scale, or the logarithm of the ratio between the maximum and the minimum levels. The dynamic range is measured in dB. Digital sound with a 16-bit resolution has a dynamic range from −96 dB (lower limit) to 0 dB (upper limit), and thus equal to 96 dB. Compare this with the dynamic range of an orchestra: 45—55 dB.

The **Dynamics Range Processing** window has four tabs: **Graphic**, **Traditional**, **Attack/Release**, and **Band Limiting**. We'll now describe them in detail.

In the **Graphic** tab (Fig. 4.45) you can draw the curve of the dependence of the output signal level on the input signal level. The coordinates of each point are defined by the values along the X- and Y-axis. The input signal level (X) and the output signal level (Y) are specified in dB.

The position of the mouse cursor relative to each axis is displayed in the field located under the graph (see Fig. 4.45).

Draw the graph by using a combination of the following operations.

- *Creating a new point on the graph.* To do so, set the cursor on the desired point and click the left mouse button.

- *Moving the points on the graph in any direction.* This is done in the same manner in which objects are normally dragged: set the cursor on the point, press the left mouse button, and holding it, move the point to a new location.

- *Directly changing the point's coordinates.* Double-clicking on any point on the graph opens a dialog box in which you can specify the point's numeric coordinates on the X- and Y-axis by inputting them from the keyboard.

> **NOTE** In the Cool Edit Pro editor, for *all effects* that contain graphs, double-clicking on any point opens a similar dialog box with which you can change the coordinates of the point.

In the **Graphic** tab there is an optional element — **Splines**. It enables the spline approximation function that converts a "broken" line into a smooth one.

This ability may be useful when you process vocal parts, to "softly" regulate the "dynamics". This makes the voice sound more natural.

Additionally, the **Graphic** tab (Fig. 4.45) contains the **Invert** and **Flat** control buttons, and the **Create Envelope Only (preview as noise)** switch.

- The **Invert** button is used to invert the effect, and the curve on the graph is thus converted into its mirror reflection. The mirror reflection is done relative to the diagonal line that crosses the graph. This line is dashed in Fig. 4.45. The behavior of the effect also changes — it is replaced with the opposite effect (for example, the compressor is replaced with the expander, etc.).

- The **Flat** button cancels the effect. On the graph, it is displayed as follows: any curve is replaced with the diagonal straight line that is shown as dashed in Fig. 4.45.

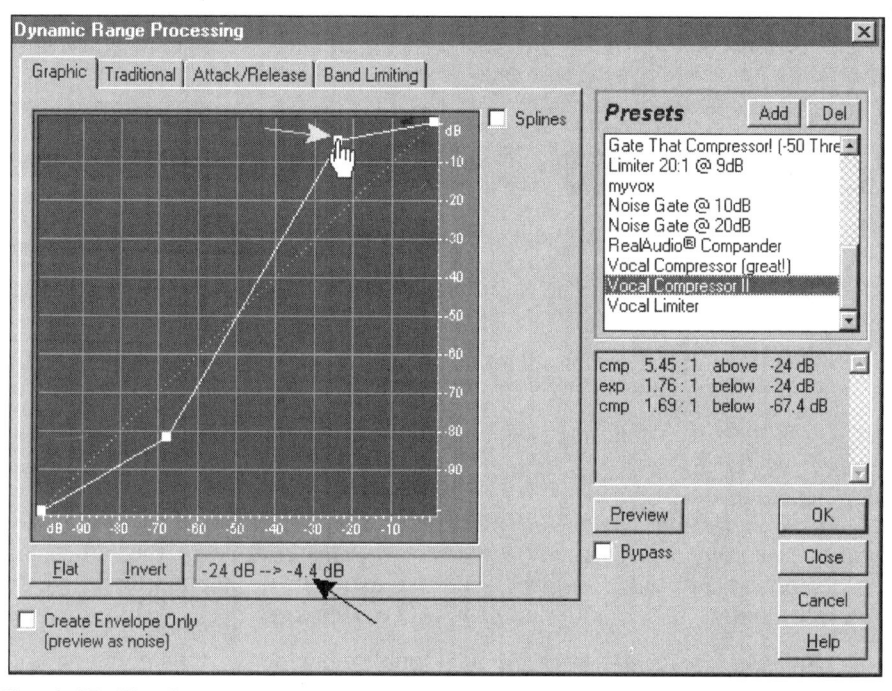

Fig. 4.45. The **Dynamics Range Processing** window with the **Graphic** tab open

- The **Create Envelope Only** (**preview as noise**) checkbox is intended only for special effects. Checking this checkbox selects the *envelope* of the sound signal. The envelope is the line that connects the *peak* values of the amplitude in the graph. You can use these data later on (**Edit** menu, **Mix Paste** item) to create the envelope of another audio signal. (We'll describe this in detail later.)

> **NOTE** You can gain some useful experience in drawing these graphs by correcting the supplied presets. You can start processing vocal parts from the Vocal Compressor II preset.

- The **Bypass** option allows you to compare the source and the processed signal.

> **NOTE** You can compare these signals only in the listening mode that is enabled by the **Preview** button.

Chapter 4: Cool Edit Pro as a Universal Solution for Home Studios 195

Now we'll turn to the next tab of the **Dynamics Range Processing** window. This tab is also responsible for changing the dynamic range.

The **Traditional** tab (Fig. 4.46) allows you to input numerical values and set the type of dynamic range processing at any point on the amplitude response.

A maximum of six points, or **Sections**, are allowed by Cool Edit Pro. In each of the sections, one of three types of processing is selected:

❒ **Compress**

❒ **Expand**

❒ **Flat** (without dynamic processing)

Compression and expansion ratios are specified in the **Ratios** fields, and the thresholds are specified in the **Thresholds** fields.

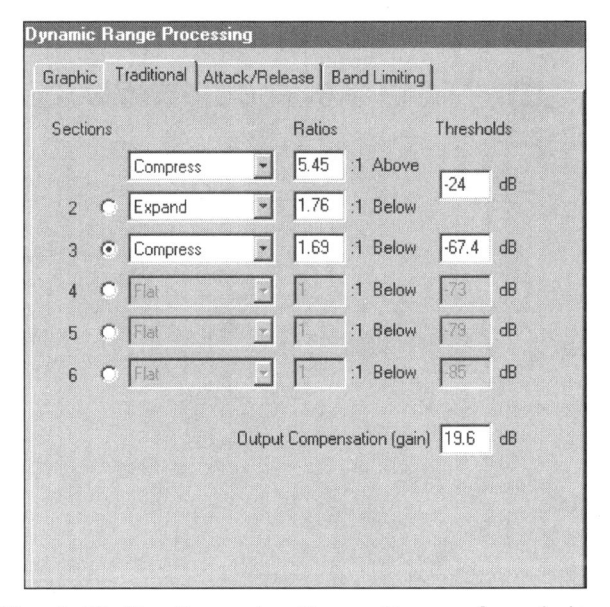

Fig. 4.46. The **Dynamics Range Processing** window, **Traditional** tab

NOTE To compensate for the losses to the input level that arise during dynamic range processing, you can specify the amplification ratio (in dB) in the **Output Compensation (gain)** field.

The **Attack/Release** tab is used to control the dynamic parameters of the effect (Fig. 4.47).

In the upper section, called **Gain Processor**, the following parameters are set:

- **Output Gain** — gain ratio at the output (in dB)
- **Attack Time** — attack time (in milliseconds)

  > *NOTE* The **Attack Time** parameter defines the reaction time of the effect to increasing the signal level.

- **Release Time** — release time (in milliseconds)

  > *NOTE* The **Release Time** parameter defines the reaction time of the effect to decreasing the signal level.

WARNING

An attack time that is too long may result in overloading, which is audible when the sound of percussion instruments is compressed. A release time that is too small also results in distortions — in the parasitic vibration of the signal.

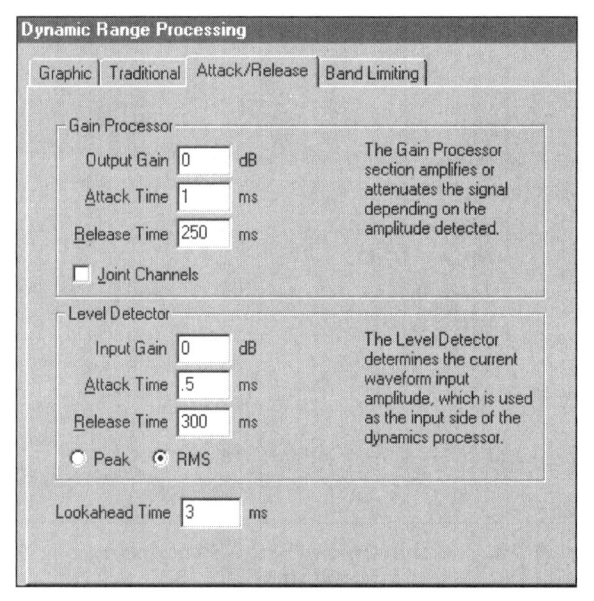

Fig. 4.47. The **Dynamics Range Processor** window, **Attack/Release** tab

The lower section called **Level Detector** is used to define the signal level at the input of the dynamics processor.

- The **Attack Time** and **Release Time** parameters of this section are similar to the parameters of the **Gain Processor** section with the same name

Chapter 4: Cool Edit Pro as a Universal Solution for Home Studios 197

- In the **Input Gain** input field, specify the gain ratio at processor input
- The **Peak** and **RMS** (Root Mean Square) group of buttons define the algorithm for changing the input level
- In the **Lookahead Time** field, you should specify the time span (in milliseconds) within which the dynamics processor should expect (detect) a sharp change in the signal level

The above facts about the **Attack Time** and **Release Time** parameters are true also for the level detector.

The developers introduced the ability to separately adjust the **Attack Time** and **Release Time** parameters for the **Gain Processor** and **Level Detector** parameters, since this significantly increases the abilities of the dynamics processor.

On the **Band Limiting** tab, you can set the boundaries of the frequency range in which the signal is to be processed (Fig. 4.48).

Eliminating Parasite Sounds

If, for example, you want to clear whistling sounds from the vocal part, you should apply the **De-Esser** preset.

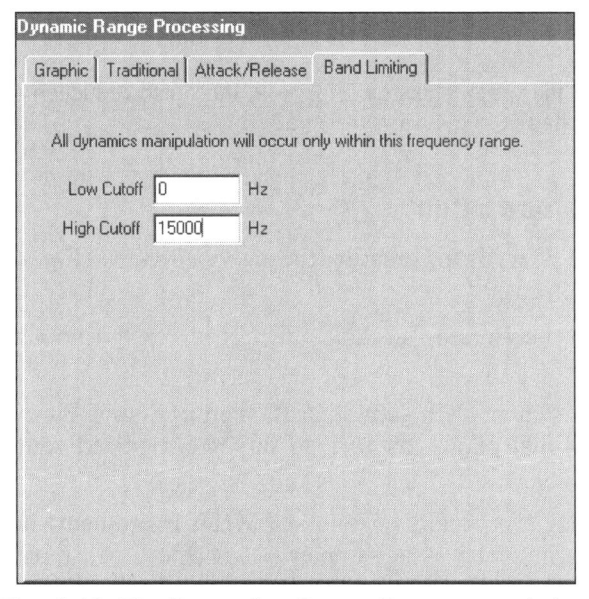

Fig. 4.48. The **Dynamics Range Processor** window, **Band Limiting** tab

The built-in **De-Esser** preset (that limits "s" sounds) provided by Cool Edit Pro is based on the principle of *narrow-band compression*, which compresses the dynamic range in the narrow frequency band:

- In the **Low Cutoff** field, a frequency of 4,000 Hz is set
- In the **High Cutoff** field, a frequency 12,000 Hz is set

The signal is not processed outside the specified range.

NOTE Repeated application of the "compressor" effect with various frequency bands set using **Band Limiting**, and with different compression ratios, provides for the high-quality, multiband compression of the same material. *Multiband compression* is a stage of mastering. It would be best to program the repeated application of this effect applications as a script (much like the scripts for multiband compression of the percussion, vocal parts, bass parts, etc.).

TIP The **Compressor/Gate** effect (Fig. 4.49) is created from the built-in "2:1 Compressor < 20 dB" preset.

We recommend that you apply this preset when processing the sound of an acoustic instrument recorded using a microphone (for example, a guitar).

When this effect is applied, the "noise" in the pauses is cut out, and quiet signals with a level below −20 dB become louder. This gives the sound the "breath of life".

To avoid quiet musical sounds being mistaken as noise and being cut out by the **Gate** effect, you should adjust the coordinates of the point at which the noise is cut for each particular recording.

For example, in the graph shown in Fig. 4.49, the noise reduction level is set at the point with the coordinates: X = −54 dB, Y = −36 dB.

The *Create Envelope* Effect

The **Create Envelope** effect is for creating the *signal envelope* (Fig. 4.50) — the line connecting the amplitude peaks.

The main purpose of the **Create Envelope** effect is to create samples for musical synthesizers.

The reason for this is that modern sound cards, such as Sound Blaster Live, are samplers. Samplers are devices that allow you to load any pre-digitized sound (sample) into the memory.

If the user plugs a MIDI keyboard (or another MIDI instrument) into a keyboard, he or she gets a complete synthesizer — a "sampler". This device can reproduce not only built-in sounds, but sounds loaded by the user as well.

However, before you input the new sound (sample), you should prepare it.

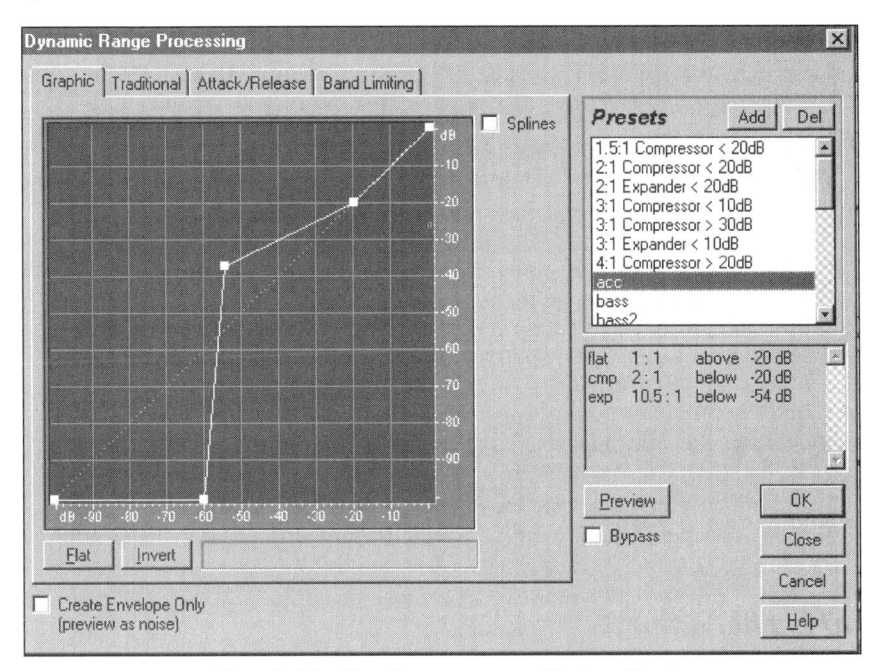

Chapter 4: Cool Edit Pro as a Universal Solution for Home Studios

Fig. 4.49. The **Compressor/Gate** effect

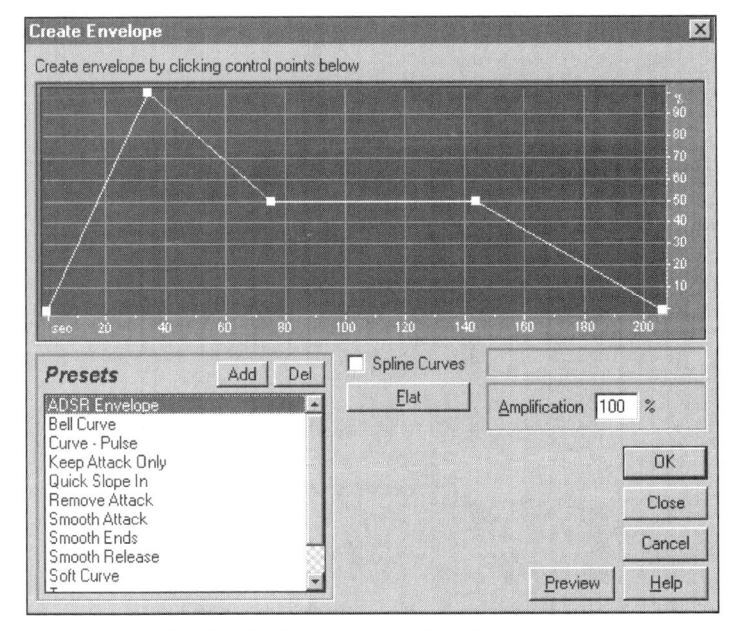

Fig. 4.50. The **Create Envelope** effect

One of the presets of the **Create Envelope** effect is called **ADSR Envelope**, which creates the standard envelope of the synthesizer. This abbreviation means: **Attack**, **Decay**, **Sustain**, **Release** (the sound after releasing a MIDI key).

The Vienna SoundFont Studio software was designed especially for sound cards by Creative Labs. This software completely prepares the samples, converts them into the SoundFont format, creates envelopes, and has many other features, too.

> **NOTE** Unfortunately, creating your own sounds is beyond the scope of this book. However, in future publications, we might describe the specific features of this amazing process of creating your own unique sounds for musical instruments. These could be done, for example, using the popular Sound Blaster Live sound card.

We should mention some other abilities provided by the **Create Envelope** effect. You can use it to smoothly change the volume level (**Fade In**, **Fade Out**) in the selected fragment.

> **NOTE** The curve of the **Create Envelope** effect is drawn in the same way as the curve of the **Dynamics Range Processing** effect in the **Graphic** tab.

The *Hard Limiter* Effect

The **Hard Limiter** effect is used for limiting amplitude peaks (Fig. 4.51).

The action of the **Hard Limiter** effect is similar to the **Peak Limiter** effect from the **Comp/Gate/Limiter** set in SAWPro, and it is applied during mastering of a recording for an AUDIO CD.

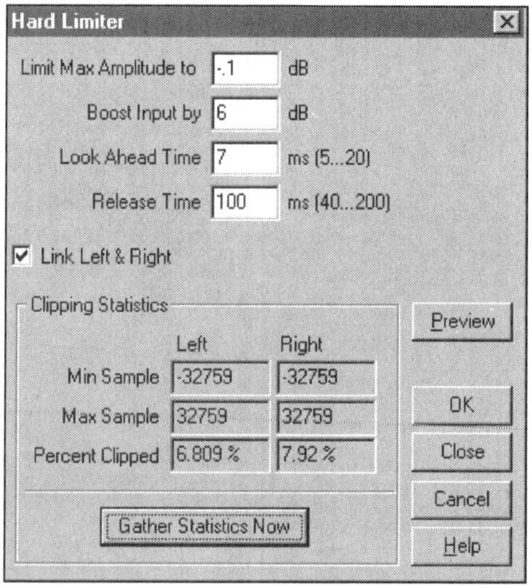

Fig. 4.51. The **Hard Limiter** effect window

Chapter 4: Cool Edit Pro as a Universal Solution for Home Studios 201

The **Hard Limiter** dialog box contains four fields (see Fig. 4.51). These are used to specify the following values:

- The maximum permitted amplitude of the waveform is specified (in dB) in the **Limit Max Amplitude to** field
- Additional amplification is specified (in dB) in the **Boost Input by** field
- The reaction's lag time is specified in the **Look Ahead Time** field

    NOTE The value of this parameter varies from 5 to 20 milliseconds.

- The time it takes to restore the signal is specified in the **Release Time** field

    NOTE The value of this parameter varies from 40 to 200 milliseconds.

- The **Link Left & Right** switch located in the center of the dialog box enables/disables the separate processing of the left and right channels
- The **Gather Statistics Now** button is used to get the statistics on the number of clipped amplitude peaks (as a percentage)

The *Normalize* Effect

The **Normalize** effect allows you to set the maximum (peak) level of the signal — in other words, to normalize it (Fig. 4.52).

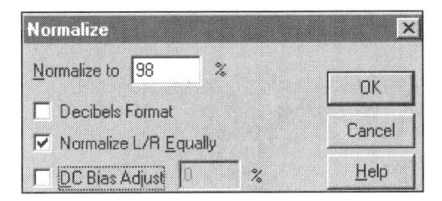

Fig. 4.52. The **Normalize** effect window

During normalization, the software first scans the audio file and finds the samples that are at the maximum level.

After that, the exact ratio is calculated and the signal is amplified or reduced to move its peak level at the specified value.

The signal level that is created after normalization is input in the **Normalize to** field. The units of measurement may vary, and depend on the state of the **Decibels Format** switch:

- As percentage (if the checkbox is unchecked)
- In decibels (if the checkbox is checked)

The **DC Bias Adjust** checkbox allows you to center the signal relative to the zero level.

NOTE This is done in the same way as for the analogous option of the **Amplify** effect.

The **Normalize L/R Equally** option, if checked, prevent the difference in the levels of the left and right channels that can appear during stereo signal normalization.

The *Pan/Expand* Effect

The **Pan/Expand** effect is used to dynamically change the width of the stereo base and the signal stereo panorama. This is as opposed to the **Channel Mixer**, which is not changed over time (Fig. 4.53).

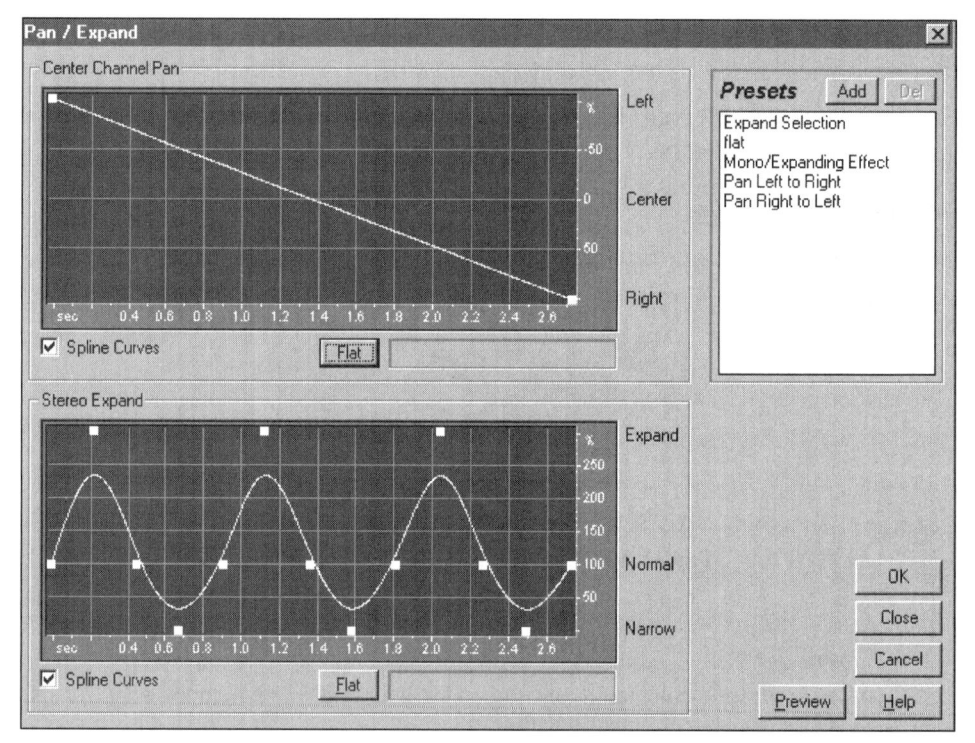

Fig. 4.53. The **Pan/Expand** effect window

In the **Center Channel Pan** and **Stereo Expand** sections, you can specify the required parameters graphically. For example, you can draw the curve of the change in the panorama or the stereo base widening/narrowing curve.

From the picture, you can see that the **Center Channel Pan** and **Stereo Expand** graphs use the following units of measure: the X-axis displays the time (in seconds), and the Y-axis displays the depth of the effect as a percentage.

In the **Stereo Expand** section, a value of 100% on the Y-axis corresponds to normal stereo.

You can adjust the effect's depth in the range from 0% **Narrow** (mono) to 300% **Expand** ("expanded stereo").

In the **Center Channel Pan** section, a value of 0% corresponds to the central location of the source of the signal.

You can move the panorama from the leftmost (**Left**) to the rightmost (**Right**) position.

> **The Stereo Vibrato and AutoPan Effects**
>
> The curve of change in the stereo base's width in Fig. 4.53 corresponds to the **Stereo Vibrato** effect, i.e., to the periodic change in the width of the stereo base with a certain low frequency (0.1–5 Hz). The analogous curve in the **Center Channel Pan** section creates the effect of periodic panning from one channel to the other (**AutoPan**). You can experiment with turning the **Spline Curve** off and on and with creating non-periodic curves. The frequency of the effect depends on the length of the selected fragment.
>
> The **Stereo Vibrato** and **AutoPan** effects can be used, for example, to enrich the timbre of the Electric Piano on musical synthesizers.

Effects Based on the Signal's Delay

Effects whose working principle is based on the delay of the signal (**Delay Effects**) make up a significant group among the sound effects.

We'll describe those effects provided by the Cool Edit Pro software that best go along with the theme of this book.

The *Chorus* Effect (Chorus)

From the name of this effect, you can probably guess that it imitates the simultaneous sounding of two or more sound sources. If these sources are voices, the effect imitates the sound of a chorus. The working principle of the **Chorus** effect is based on the signal's delay over time and adding the source signal to its delayed copies.

> **NOTE** We should note that this effect will not let you create the sound of a real chorus from just one voice.

Historically, the necessity of creating the Chorus effect arose in the time of analog sound synthesizers, when it was necessary to enrich their poor sound. It is notable that all the "cosmic" timbres of the electronic music of the '70s and '80s were created using the chorus effect. However, this was not the only application of this effect.

Currently, the **Chorus** effect is still used in various areas of sound processing. For example, you can use this effect to imitate the richer sound of a 12-string guitar from a regular 6-string guitar. You can also process a voice, varying it from unison to chorus. Chorus is even used in mastering, since it allows you to obtain a relatively "fashionable" sound. In short, we haven't yet come across any bad "side effects" when using **Chorus**.

> **NOTE** You should make sure to be accurate when applying this effect, because too much of it overloads the original sound.

Now, chorus is an integral part of a musical synthesizer. We'll now describe it in a bit more detail (Fig. 4.54).

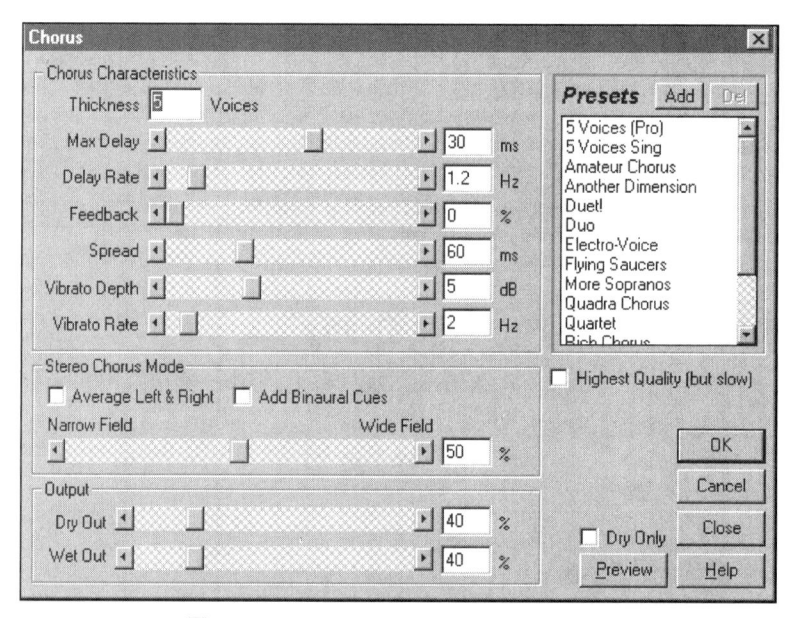

Fig. 4.54. The **Chorus** effect window

In the upper field, **Thickness ... Voices** (the number of voices), specify the number of sound sources created by the chorus.

> **WARNING**
>
> Increasing the number of voices will also increase the processing time.

Chapter 4: Cool Edit Pro as a Universal Solution for Home Studios 205

Six sliders are located under this field. You can change their parameters numerically (by inputting the values from the keyboard), or by moving them along the horizontal scale.

- **Max Delay** — sets the maximum delay of the entire processed signal

  > **NOTE** Too long of a delay time, when applied together with other adjustments, may result in non-musical distortions. Too short of one may eliminate the "brightness" of the effect.

- **Delay Rate** allows you to reproduce the sound of a poorly-tuned musical instrument

  > **NOTE** It is better to start experimenting by changing the value of the **Delay Rate** parameter using smaller values, since larger ones cause a very specific sound.

- **Feedback** — increases the "brightness" of the effect

  > **TIP** You should set the feedback depth to a value within the range of 10–25%, because larger values (see previous example with **Delay Rate**) may result in non-musical distortions, and even in the self-excitation of the effect.

- **Spread** — changes the delay time for each voice

  > **TIP** By using large values of the **Spread** parameter (in combination with **Feedback**), you can imitate the sound of a small auditorium.

- The **Vibrato Depth** and **Vibrato Rate** parameters define the depth and speed of the amplitude *vibrato* (the sound vibrating effect)

Two groups of controls are located under the sliders: **Stereo Chorus Mode** and **Output**.

The **Stereo Chorus Mode** section contains controls that considerably enrich the stereo sound.

- The **Average Left & Right** checkbox enables/disables the mode that averages the processing of the sound of the left and right channels

  > **NOTE** You cannot use this mode when processing original stereo sound when the location of the sound sources is *specified*.

- The **Add Binaural Cues** option is used for recordings that you plan on listening to through headphones *only*

- The **Narrow Field/Wide Field** slider changes the width of the stereo base of the processed signal

The **Output** section contains the **Dry Out** ("dry" output) and **Wet Out** ("wet" output) sliders, which allow you to mix the source and processed signals, respectively.

In finishing the description of the chorus effect, we should mention that, from the point of view of the quality of the result, it is not so simple.

That's why we recommend that you start applying this effect using the built-in presets provided by the developers of Cool Edit Pro.

The *Delay* Effect

Without the **Delay** effect, modern stereophonic sound could probably never have been achieved. The subjective feeling of the location (left or right) of the sound source is defined not only by the difference in the volume levels of the left and right channels (panorama), but also by the delay of the signal of one channel relative to the other. Users can experiment with the **Spatial Left** and **Spatial Right** presets of the **Delay** effect (Fig. 4.55).

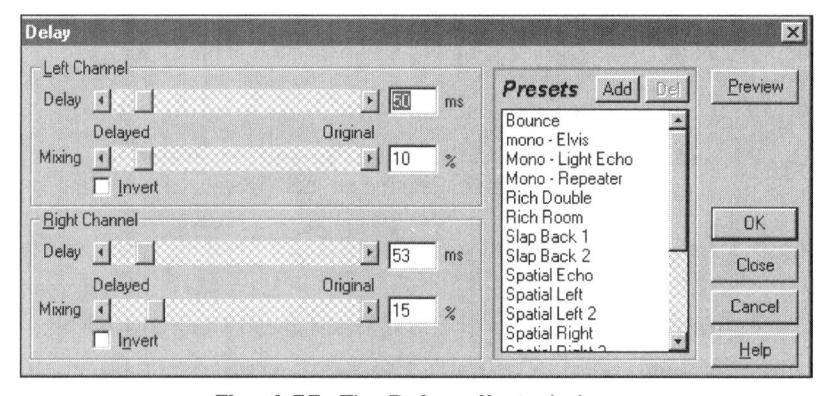

Fig. 4.55. The **Delay** effect window

The **Delay** sliders define the signal delay time for each channel (in milliseconds), and the **Mixing** sliders mix the direct and the delayed signals.

Note that in the **Delayed** position, only the processed signal is audible. The **Invert** option inverts only the delayed signal.

> **NOTE** If the **Mixing** slider is in the "50%" position, the direct and the delayed signals are equally loud.

In finishing the description of this effect, we'll remind you of a method that is often used to process sequences. It is the fine adjustment of the delay time to the music tempo (the **Tempo Delay** effect).

The *Echo* Effect

The **Echo** effect can be considered a complex version of the **Delay** effect. We'll now describe the various ways in which it can be set (Fig. 4.56).

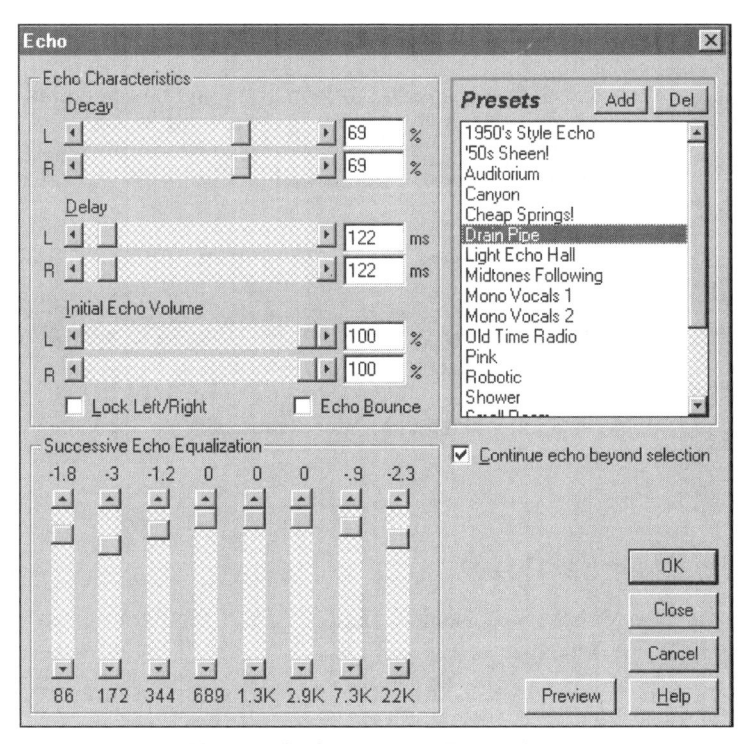

Fig. 4.56. Setting the **Echo** effect

The upper section — **Echo Characteristics** — contains three sliders and two switches.

❏ The **Decay** sliders change the echo fading separately for each of the channels

> **NOTE** If the sliders are in the "100%" position, there is an infinite repetition that results in the "eternal echo" effect.

❏ The **Delay** sliders define the signal's delay time

❏ The **Lock Left/Right** option enables/disables separate adjustment

❏ The **Initial Echo Volume** sliders define the loudness of the first "reflected" signal (the first repetition)

❏ The **Echo Bounce** option adds automated panorama movement from one channel to the other

208   Live Music on Your PC

> **NOTE** The position of the **Initial Echo Volume** regulator of one channel should be set to 0, while the position of the other **Initial Echo Volume** regulator should be set to 100%.

☐ The **Continue echo beyond selection** checkbox mixes the echo fade with the non-processed audio material outside the selected region

> **NOTE** The part of the file located to the right of the selected area within the fragment visible in the editor window is the part processed.

☐ The lower section — **Successive Echo Equalization** — allows you to create a frequency response for the fading echo signal

The equalizer consists of eight narrow-band sliders with an adjustment range from −15 dB to 0 dB.

The echo signal, when repeating, passes the *equalizer* (the multiband timbre regulator) multiple times. Each time it is repeated, the timbre changes.

> **NOTE** Pink Floyd often used this effect to process their vocal and guitar parts.

The *3-D Echo Chamber* Effect

We'll describe the next effect, **3-D Echo Chamber**, only briefly, since in our opinion it isn't of much use.

This effect allows you to model the acoustics of a rectangular room according to the dimensions you assign it.

However, the mathematical model of the actual spreading of the sound is much more complex than the virtual imitation created by this effect.

Artists that perform live know that the acoustic features of different halls, even though they have similar sizes, may be very different.

Due to all of the above, we won't describe the **3-D Echo Chamber** effect. As an alternative, we offer you the opportunity to *model the acoustics of a real room* using the so-called *impulse sound* (or simply impulse).

> **NOTE** An *impulse* is an audio file recorded using special methods in a room whose acoustics you are restoring using your PC. The sound in the *real* environment is based on this file.

This method is used in the Samplitude 2496 software and in the **Acoustic Mirror** DirectX module by Sonic Foundry, Inc. (**http://www.sonicfoundry.com**) (Fig. 4.57).

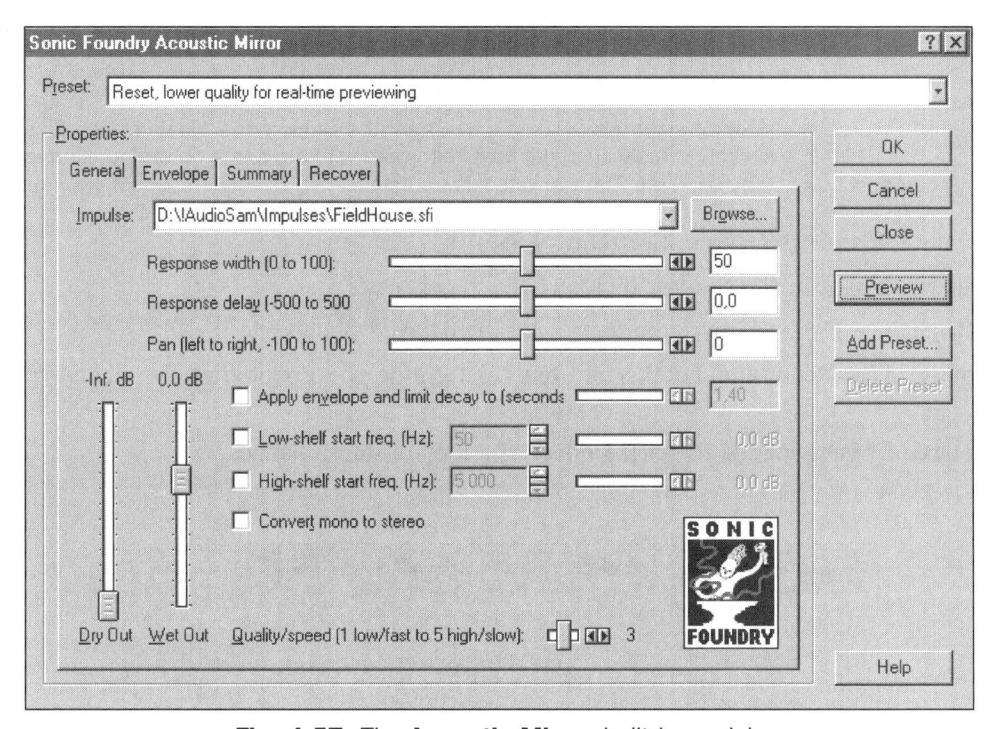

Fig. 4.57. The **Acoustic Mirror** built-in module

Besides special impulses (SFI files) by Sonic Foundry, you can use a WAV audio file as well. Using various short WAV files as impulses can serve as the basis for synthesizing unique, fantastic sounds.

> **TIP** In the **Preview** mode, some effects can make errors that will be audible, and sound like the sound being interrupted. You can avoid this by increasing the **Minimum Preview Buffer Size** in the **Settings** dialog box's **General** tab.

The *Flanger* Effect

Flanger is an effect of the sound "floating". Its working principle, as with chorus, is based on the signal's delay over time, and adding delayed copies of the source signal to the source signal itself.

> **NOTE** The name **Flanger** comes from the first analogous devices that were able to implement this effect. They were called flange filters.

Generally, there are no principal differences between the **Flanger** and **Chorus** effects.

We could say that flanger represents a specific case of chorus, one with a simplified technical implementation.

> **NOTE** Without using your PC, you can hear the illusion of a "floating" sound if you simultaneously start two tape recorders with the same recording. During the first seconds of playback, the **Flanger** effect is audible.

Here are the settings for this effect (Fig. 4.58).

In the upper part of the window there are five regulators:

- **Original — Delayed** mixes the direct and the delayed signals
- **Initial Mix Delay** and **Final Mix Delay** determine the boundaries for changing the delay
- **Stereo Phasing** is used to get the effect of a looped stereo flanger
- **Feedback** emphasizes the effect

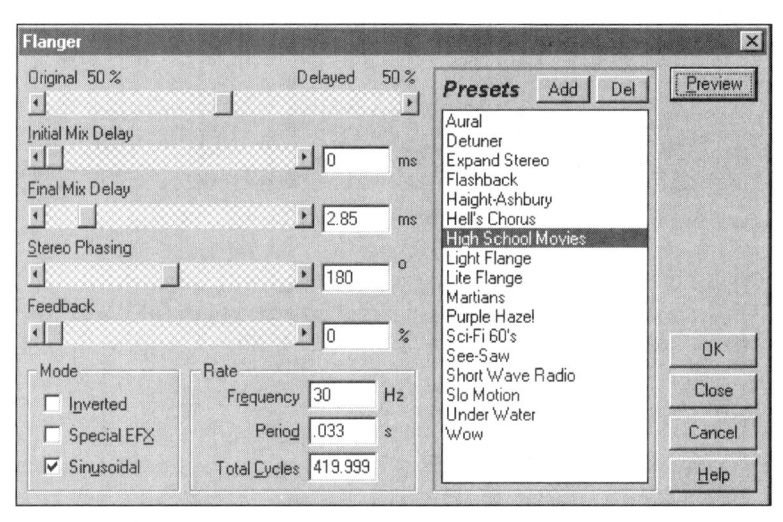

Fig. 4.58. The **Flanger** effect

In the **Rate** section, specify the speed of the delay time change (modulation).

> **NOTE** When you input a value in any of the three fields of this section, the values in the remaining fields are corrected automatically.

In the **Mode** section there are three switches.

- **Inverted** inverts the delayed signal.

> **NOTE** The sound of the effect is also reduced.

Chapter 4: Cool Edit Pro as a Universal Solution for Home Studios

- **Special EFX** (special signal mixing) enables a special mixing mode for the signal, in which the delayed signal is added and subtracted from the direct signal.

> **NOTE** When switching, the **Original — Delayed** switch is replaced with the **Original — Expanded** switch. This means that adjustment is made within the "direct signal — delayed signal" range, in the "expanded stereo" mode.

- **Sinusoidal** defines the curve of the delay time change. This checkbox is selected by default. When you uncheck it, the delay time changes linearly.

Reverberation Effects

Reverberation is the effect of the sound fading while it is being reflected around the room.

Without reverberation, it would be impossible not only to move the sound sources, but to get a natural and expressive sound as well.

Unfortunately, from our point of view, reverberation effects in Cool Edit Pro are not implemented as well as they are in similar plug-ins provided by other vendors.

Although this algorithm is rather "slow" (takes a long time to complete calculation), the result is no better than similar effects of the DirectX standard. In the **Reverb** effect in the **Preview** mode all the sliders are locked. For **Full Reverb** in this mode there are only three sliders available. Thus you cannot efficiently adjust the sound of these effects in real time.

That's why we won't be describing the effects "native" to Cool Edit Pro — **Full Reverb** and **Reverb** — but will rather look at an implementation from the Syntrillium Software Corporation — the fx:reverb Sonitus plug-in Ultrafunk reverber (**www.ultrafunk.com**), which uses the DirectX standard.

The interface of this reverber is simple and easy-to-use. Also, this effect does not require very many resources from your PC.

The **Ultrafunk fx:Reverb** reverberation module provides not only high-quality sound, but can also effectively react to changes made by the user in real time.

We'll now describe the controls of this effect (Fig. 4.59).

- In the upper part of the window, there are two LEDs: **L** and **R**. These are the overload indicators.

> **NOTE** These indicators should not always be flashing.

- The **Tail** button enables the mode in which the sound fades for a considerable amount of time.
- The **Stereo** button defines the output signal mode: mono or stereo.

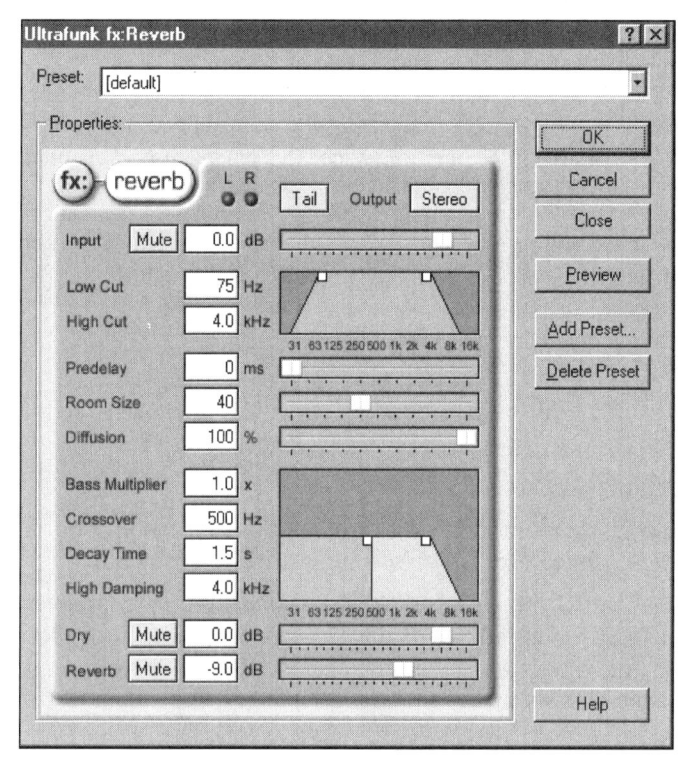

Fig. 4.59. The **Ultrafunk Fx:Reverb** window

- In the **Input** section, the signal output level is regulated before it is sent to the effect.
- The **Mute** button turns off the input.
- In the **Low Cut/High Cut** section, the frequency range of the signal is adjusted before final processing (reverberation).
- The **Predelay** parameter sets the delay time between the *direct signal* and the *first reflected* signal of the effect.
- The **Room Size** parameter sets the size of the virtual room: from a room to a large concert hall.
- The **Diffusion** parameter defines the nature of the reverberation.

> **NOTE** Small values of the **Diffusion** parameter correspond to a large number of clear reflections of the fading sound.
> When the value of the diffusion parameter is increased, reverberation sounds much like a noise (characteristic for rooms with a dome). This effect is often used by the group Enigma.

Chapter 4: Cool Edit Pro as a Universal Solution for Home Studios

- The **Bass Multiplier** parameter sets the reverberation's fading time for those signal frequencies that are under the crossover boundary (which is specified in the **Crossover** field)

   > **NOTE** Because the bass fading time is calculated as the product of the **Decay Time** (total decay time) and the **Bass Multiplier** ratio, the changes to the **Bass Multiplier** parameter result in increasing or decreasing the bass fading time (separately from the remaining signal), respectively.

- **Decay Time** is the reverberation decay time
- The **High Damping** parameters specify the absorption of high frequencies by the virtual room
- The **Bass Multiplier**, **Crossover**, **Decay Time**, and **High Damping** parameters are shown in a separate graph

   > **NOTE** By dragging the corresponding point on this graph, you can *simultaneously* change pairs of parameters: **Bass Multiplier** and **Crossover**; or **Decay Time** and **High Damping**.

- The **Dry** and **Reverb** switches are used to mix the direct and processed signal, respectively
- The **Mute** buttons allow you to switch off a signal (whether direct or processed)

   > **NOTE** Switching off the *direct* signal using the **Mute** button may be useful in certain cases — for example, to listen to the *processed* signal only.
   > In other cases, muting the direct signal may be useful when processing the copy of a fragment that is then added to the remaining data. We'll discuss this later on.

Besides the **Ultrafunk fx:Reverb** reverber, we recommend that you apply two other effects that are also DirectX modules:

- **TC Native Reverb** (Fig. 4.60) by TC Works Soft- und Hardware GmbH (**http://www.tcworks.de**)
- **Waves TrueVerb** (Fig. 4.61) by Waves Ltd (**http://www.waves.com**)

   > **TIP** Presets of the **Waves TrueVerb** module — **Drum room** and **Studio A** — are good for creating realistic acoustic environment effects when processing tracks.

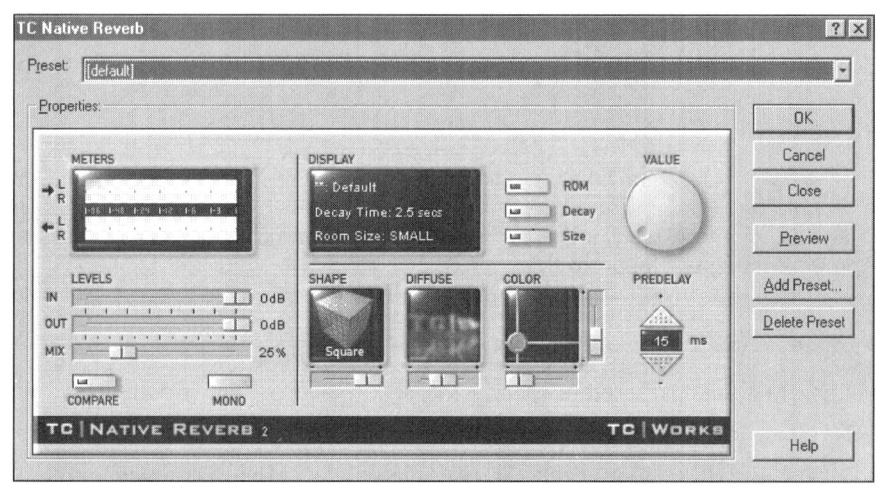

Fig. 4.60. The window of the **TC Native Reverb** module

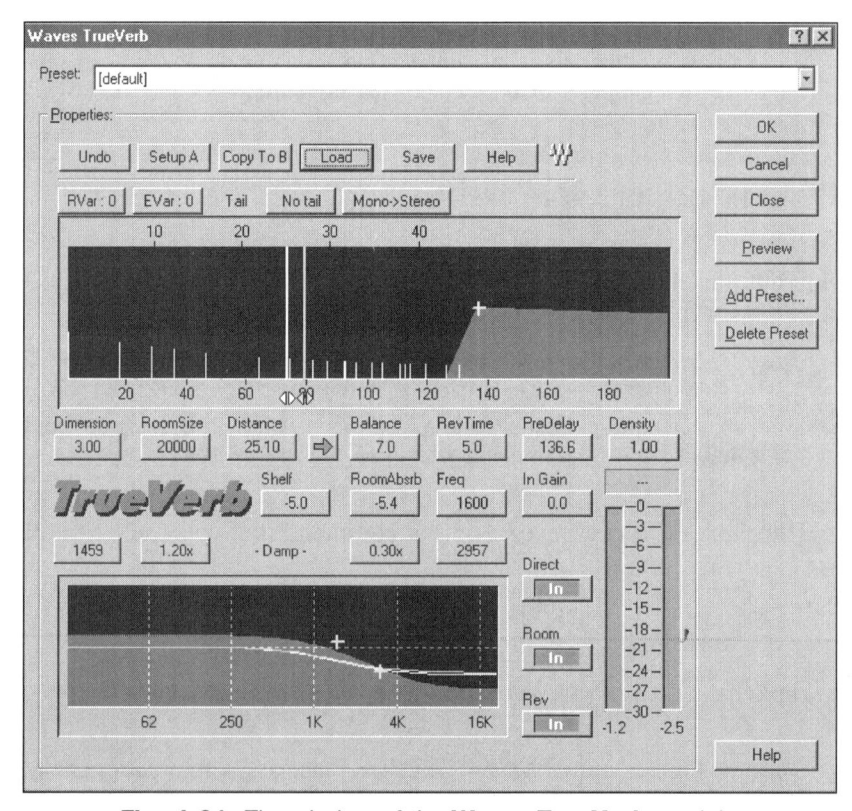

Fig. 4.61. The window of the **Waves TrueVerb** module

The *Sweeping Phaser Effects* Effect

The **Sweeping Phaser Effects** effect is also based on the signal's delay. In essence, **Sweeping Phaser Effects** is a particular type of **Flanger** effect in which the signal is only delayed for a very short period of time.

In our opinion, this effect's implementation in Cool Edit Pro is unusually successful.

However, we're not going to give you any advice on how to use it. We'll just say that you can boldly decide how you'd like to use it depending on your own tastes, since there are probably no specific instructions for its use, or any nasty "side effects" either.

Actually, this is much the same as the **Chorus** effect.

Let's look at the **Sweeping Phaser Effects** window, which contains the controls for the effect (Fig. 4.62).

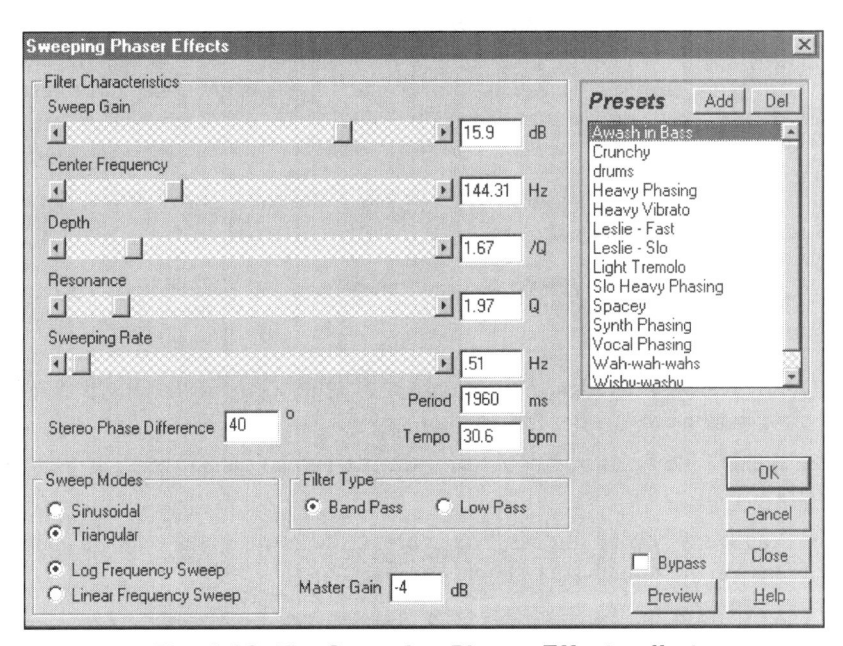

Fig. 4.62. The **Sweeping Phaser Effects** effect

In the upper block of parameters — **Filter Characteristics** — we see 5 sliders.

❐ In changing the **Sweep Gain** parameter, the process and direct signal are added together according to the given ratio

> **NOTE** The result of this directly depends on the value of the coefficient. If it is a positive number (dB), the processed signal is strengthened. If it is negative, the processed signal becomes weaker, since this indicates that the processed signal is subtracted from the direct signal.

- The **Center Frequency** slider sets the frequency at which the effect should be the most distinct
- **Depth** sets the "oscillation" depth of the "phasing sound" on both sides of the center frequency
- **Resonance** determines the *quality* (sharpness) of the resonance curve
- The **Sweeping Rate** slider sets the modulation frequency

One huge advantage of this effect is that it gives you the ability to set the **Sweeping Rate** slider to a modulation frequency that is a multiple of the tempo of the musical composition (that is, one that differs by several times).

Emphasizing the Rhythmic Features

It is exactly such "mathematical" tricks that are the "special touches" necessary to emphasize the rhythmic features. This is not a new method. It is used in electronic music, and can also be successfully used when processing rhythm guitar parts, percussion parts, sequencers, etc.

In the **Stereo Phase Difference** field, the phase difference between the left and right channels is indicated in degrees.

NOTE At a value of 180 degrees, the illusion of the sound being phased is created.

The options in the **Sweep Modes** section determine the form of the curve that represents the change (oscillation) of the central frequency:

- The **Sinusoidal/Triangular** radio buttons set the sinusoidal curve or the linear law of change (the "triangle")
- The **Log Frequency Sweep/Linear Frequency** radio buttons set either a logarithmic or a linear scale for the changes to the central frequency

The **Filter Type** section indicates which filter is to be used — **Band Pass** or **Low Pass**.

NOTE The **Low Pass** filter will give percussion instruments a brighter effect.

In the **Master Gain** field, you set the general level for the signal at output.

Effects that Correct the Frequency Response

The effects in this group are called *filters*.

The *FFT Filter (Fast Fourier Transform Filter)*

This effect is based on the *Fast Fourier Transform* algorithm (FFT).

Despite such a "frightening" name, this filter is very easy to use. It is used for constructing various amplitude-frequency response curves (Fig. 4.63).

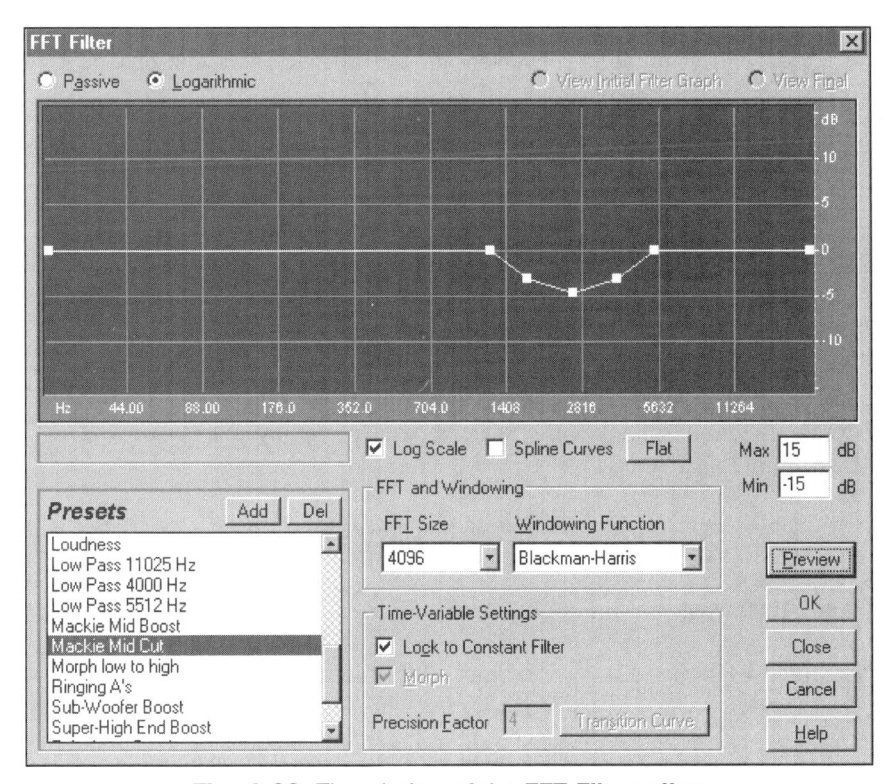

Fig. 4.63. The window of the **FFT Filter** effect

NOTE   The *amplitude-frequency response* is the dependence of the signal's amplitude on the frequency.

Note that the **FFT Filter** allows you to transform the amplitude-frequency response in time as specified by the parameters assigned.

Imitating the Sound of the Ocean

The mode for transforming the amplitude-frequency response is well suited for closely imitating the sound of the ocean. This is done by processing so-called "pink" noise using the filter (the **Generate** menu, **Noise** item).

Let's look at the controls of the **FFT Filter**.

Under the graph and to the left, you see two radio buttons: **Passive** and **Logarithmic**. These change the filter type.

- **Passive**. If you enable the passive mode, the values on the Y-axis will be indicated as percentages.

  > **NOTE** This mode is convenient for constructing filters that *only suppress* certain frequencies.

- **Logarithmic**. When you use the logarithmic filter, the values on the Y-axis will be given in decibels.

  > **NOTE** The logarithmic type is best for creating filters that not only suppress, but also intensify set frequency intervals.

Under the graph and to the right you'll find the **Min** and **Max** fields. Here you can set the minimum and maximum boundaries within which you can suppress/intensify the frequency.

The **Log Scale** checkbox changes the scale of the frequency display on the X-axis from linear to logarithmic and vice versa.

> **TIP** For wide-band amplitude-frequency responses, it's best to use a logarithmic scale.

The **FFT and Windowing** section contains two controls.

- The combined **FFT Size** list, which determines the quality of the filtration.

  > **NOTE** The larger the size of the selection, the higher the quality. But when increasing the quality, keep in mind that the calculation time is also increased.

- As for the **Windowing Function** parameter (used with data right before processing), we can say the following: the best criterion for determining each particular version is your own ear.

  > **TIP** But you can start with the **Blackman** or **Hamming** functions.

In the **Time-Variable Settings** sections, we find:

- The **Lock to Constant Filter** checkbox
- The **Morph** checkbox
- The **Precision Factor** input field

Unchecking the **Lock to Constant Filter** parameter opens up access to the switch connected with the beginning and final stages of transforming the amplitude-frequency response filter:

- **View Initial Filter Graph** shows the beginning graph
- **View Final** shows the final graph

The **Transition Curve** button calls the window of the same name (Fig. 4.64).

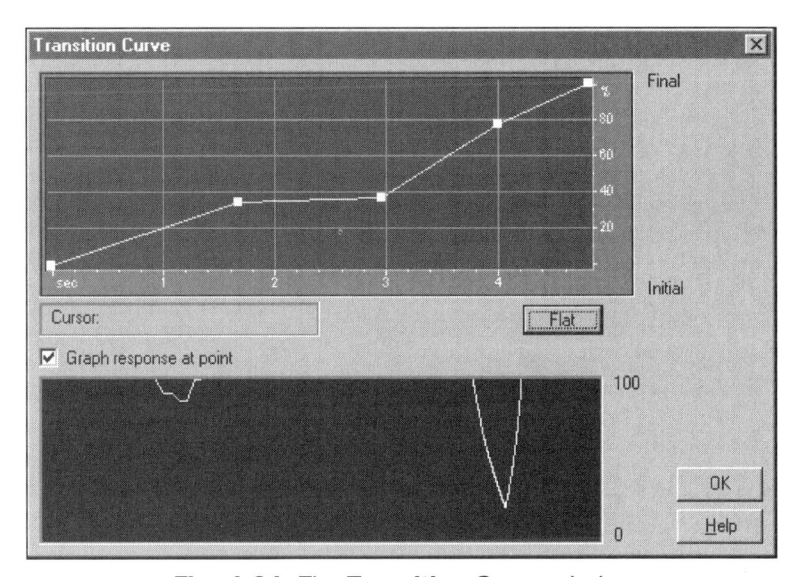

Fig. 4.64. The **Transition Curve** window

When you set the **Graph response at point** checkbox in this window, you can display the actual transformation of the amplitude-frequency response curve in the lower part of the window by dragging a point up or down on the transformation curve's graph.

> **NOTE** Thus, by creating and moving points of the graph, you can easily create your own amplitude-frequency response transformation curve.

Disabling the **Morph** option (see Fig. 4.63) prevents you from moving the amplitude-frequency response graph horizontally during the transformation process.

The *Graphic Equalizer* Effect

The *graphic equalizer* is a device used for forming the amplitude-frequency response while retaining fixed regulator frequencies (Fig. 4.65).

When it comes to the convenience of the interface and the sound quality, the realization of the graphic equalizer in Cool Edit Pro is clearly superior to any other.

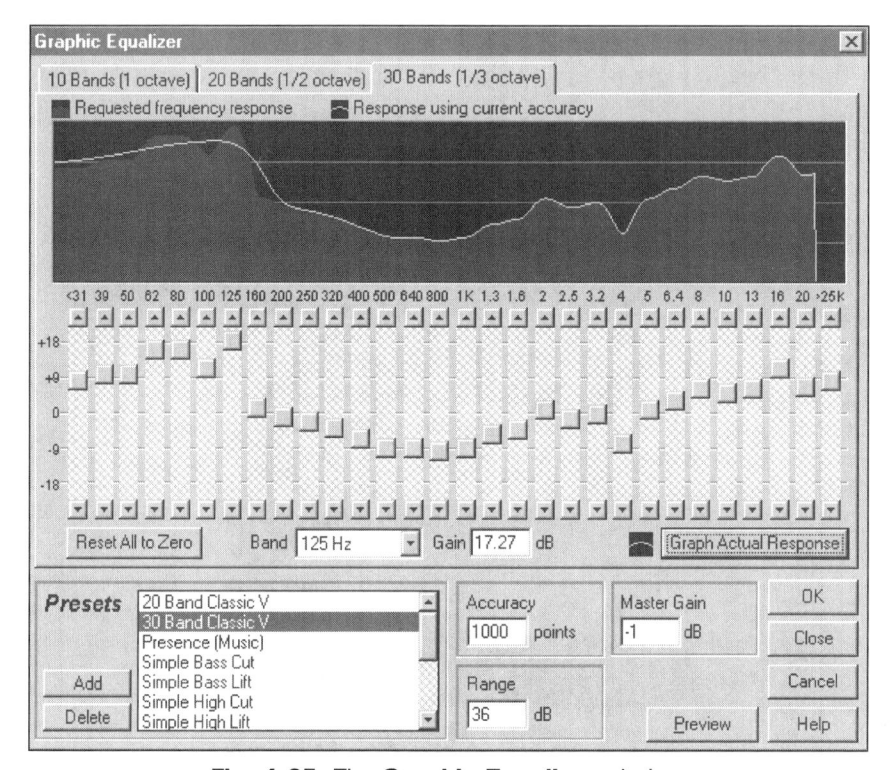

Fig. 4.65. The **Graphic Equalizer** window

The equalizer has three tabs that differ in the number of frequency bands (sliders).

Fig. 4.65 shows the **30 Bands (1/3 octave)** tab (30 bands with a width of 1/3 of an octave).

> **NOTE** An *octave* is the frequency interval within which the frequency doubles. An *octave* in music is the distance between two notes with the same name (for example, from the *A* of the one-line octave to the *A* of the two-line octave). The tempered octave order includes 6 tones and 12 semitones. Thus, the *A* of the one-line octave is 440 Hz, while the *A* of the two-line octave is 880 Hz.

Increasing the number of bands from 10 to 30 compresses the bandwidth of the slider from a whole octave to one third of an octave.

The contents of this tab are looked at below.

- The **Reset All to Zero** button sets all sliders to the 0 dB position
- In the **Band** combined list, you can choose the frequency band
- The **Gain** field determines the type of gain — positive or negative (in decibels)

Chapter 4: Cool Edit Pro as a Universal Solution for Home Studios 221

- The **Graph Actual Response** button enables the mode for calculating the curve corresponding to the actual changes made to the amplitude-frequency response, taking into account the settings of the equalizer

   > **NOTE** When the process of calculating the curve of the actual changes to the amplitude-frequency curve is finished, a blue line will be shown in the equalizer's window (in Fig. 4.65 it is the lighter line).

- In the **Accuracy** field, you set the accuracy with which the amplitude-frequency curve will be transformed

   > **NOTE** For fine regulation of the lower frequencies, you need to increase the **Accuracy** value. But keep in mind that the higher the accuracy, the longer the calculations will take.

- In the **Master Gain** field, a general gain is set to compensate for the general increase or decrease in the level by the equalizer
- The **Range** field is used to set the maximum depth of amplitude-frequency response correction

   > **NOTE** For example, a value of 40 dB set in the **Range** field means that the regulation range will be from −20 dB to +20 dB.

Notch Filter

The **Notch Filter** deletes parasite frequency components from the signal (Fig. 4.66). Such filters are often called "rejecting filters".

With this effect, we can, for example, easily cut out the background noise of an electric guitar.

> ### Eliminating the "Background Noise" of an Electric Guitar
>
> As you may well know, background noise (parasite electromagnetic components with the frequency of the industrial electricity network) is one main weakness of many electric guitars, especially homemade ones.
>
> The *rejecting* filter — a filter with a very narrow suppression band — is used for solving exactly these types of problems.

The filter is unique in that it suppresses not only the basic frequency of the electricity network (60 Hz), but also the *harmonics* (frequencies that are multiples of the basic frequency): 180 Hz, 300 Hz, etc.

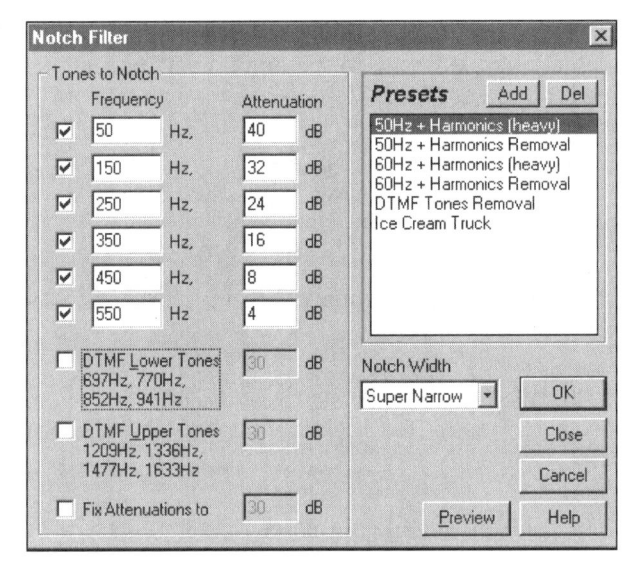

Fig. 4.66. The **Notch Filter** window

In the right part of the effect window, we see the smaller **Presets** window.

> **NOTE** In the US, the frequency of the industrial electric network is 60 Hz, therefore, to suppress background noise, you should use the presets that have "60" included in their names.

The *Parametric Equalizer* Filter

The *parametric equalizer* is the device that creates the amplitude-frequency response. It consists of selective filters with variable parameters.

> **NOTE** A *selective filter* is a filter that suppresses frequencies outside the bandwidth.

The **Parametric Equalizer** effect (Fig. 4.67) has five selective filters in which the center frequency and the bandwidth are adjusted separately.

- You can turn the filter on by checking the checkbox near the corresponding **Center Frequency** slider.
- In the **Width** field, specify the bandwidth (in Hz).
- The **Constant Q** (constant quality) and **Constant Width** radio buttons toggle the filter mode and the frequency display mode in the **Width** field.

Chapter 4: Cool Edit Pro as a Universal Solution for Home Studios 223

NOTE Since *quality* is the ratio of the center frequency to the band frequency at a level of −3 dB, increasing this parameter is equivalent to narrowing the bandwidth.

When you set the switch to the **Constant Width** position, increasing the center frequency results in increasing the quality (the amplitude-frequency response's sharpness).

When you select the **Constant Q** mode, increasing the center frequency results in widening the bandwidth, and the amplitude-frequency response's sharpness remains unchanged.

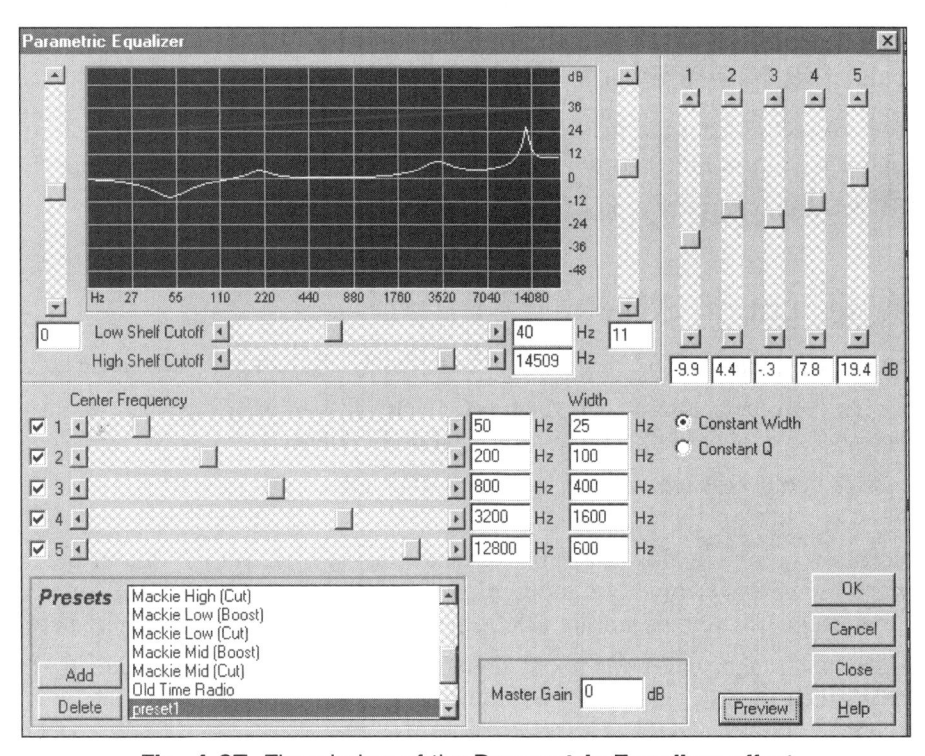

Fig. 4.67. The window of the **Parametric Equalizer** effect

In the upper right corner of the window, there is a section with five sliders that regulate the level of each band.

NOTE The bandwidth is emphasized when the amplification values are positive. When they are negative, the bandwidth is suppressed.

Additionally, the **Parametric Equalizer** effect has sliders that control the high-frequency and low-frequency timbre. They are located to the left and to the right of the graphic image of the amplitude-frequency response. Using the **Low Shelf Cutoff** and **High Shelf Cutoff** sliders, you can set the adjustment frequencies of the timbre for high and low frequencies separately.

The *Quick Filter* Effect

The so-called "quick filter" is the device that creates an amplitude-frequency response with fixed adjustment frequencies (Fig. 4.68).

NOTE We won't describe the controls of this window here, since they are similar to those used with the **Graphic Equalizer** effect (see Fig. 4.65). But **Quick Filter** operates using a simpler scheme than the one used by the graphic equalizer.

The Scientific Filters Effect

This effect correctly (from the mathematical point of view) creates standard types of filters (Fig. 4.69), such as the Butterworth filter, the Chebyshev filter, etc.

It is an effect that demonstrates just how "cool" the Cool Edit Pro software really is.

Noise Reduction Effects

In a home studio, you will never be able to completely eliminate outside noises.

This problem becomes more actual when you create "live" music, especially when you are recording a voice or acoustic instruments using a microphone.

These noises could be such outside sounds as the noise outside your window, or those from the next room.

The recording equipment also causes background noises, such as the noise of the amplifiers of the external mixer or the sound card, various clicking and crackling sounds in the connecting cables, as well as parasite electromagnetic sounds of the electricity network.

Also, some sound cards can bring about short-lived faults during sound digitizing (recording) that manifest themselves as extra-short impulses, heard as clicks.

To avoid these outside sounds, the Cool Edit Pro software provides a set of powerful tools for restoring the recorded material. They are found in the **Noise Reduction** menu. This group of effects is used for decreasing the noise level.

The *Click/Pop/Crackle Eliminator* Effect

The **Click/Pop/Crackle Eliminator** effect filters *impulse noises*.

NOTE *Impulse noises* are parasite signals with a very small duration. They are heard as clicks, pops, and crackles.

We'll now describe the algorithm for removing outside noises using the **Click/Pop/Crackle Eliminator** effect (Fig. 4.70).

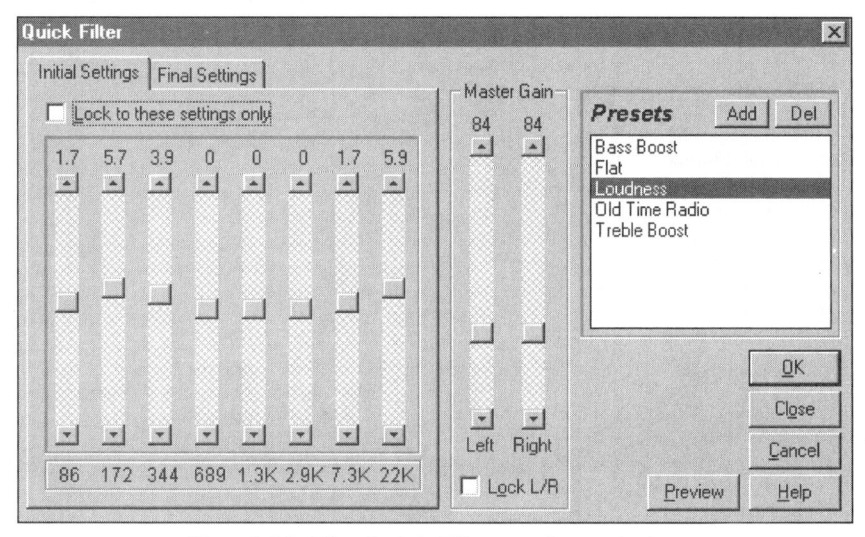

Chapter 4: Cool Edit Pro as a Universal Solution for Home Studios 225

Fig. 4.68. The **Quick Filter** settings window

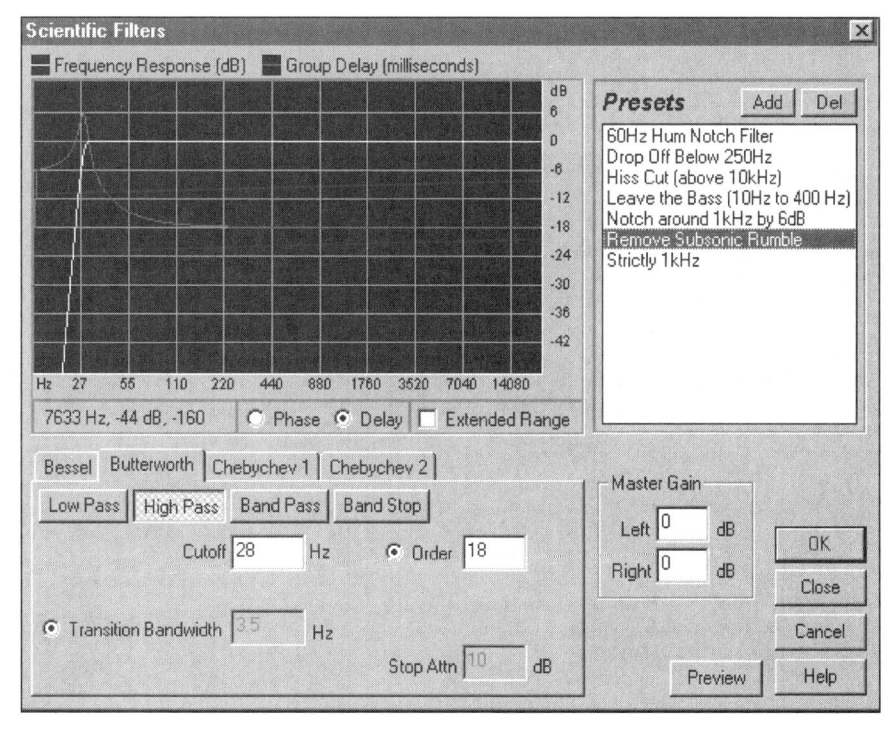

Fig. 4.69. The **Scientific Filters** window

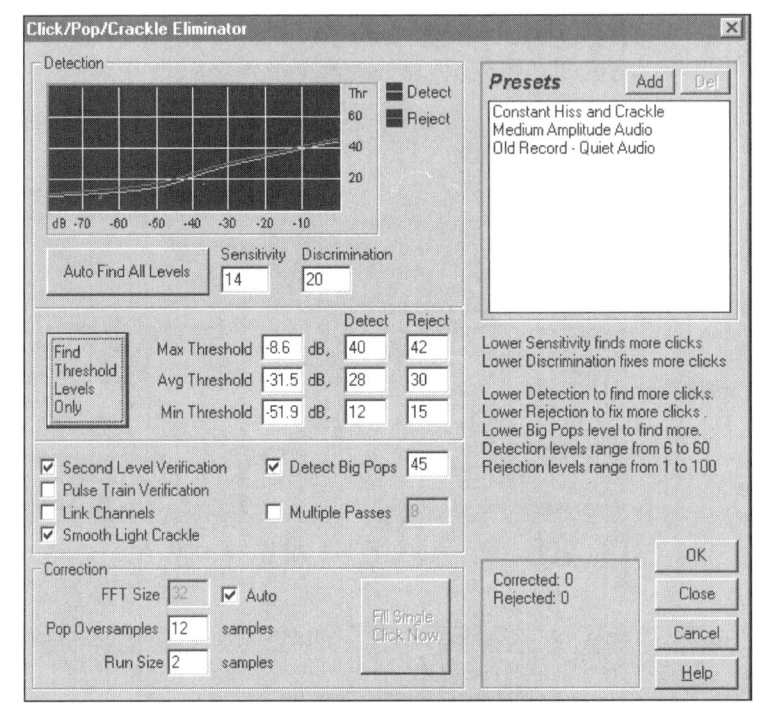

Fig. 4.70. The **Click/Pop/Crackle Eliminator** effect

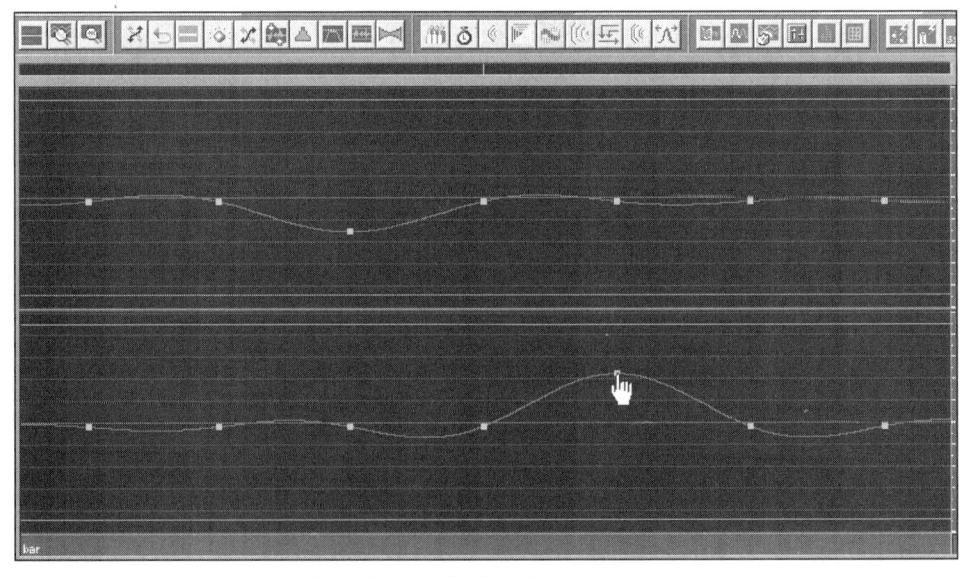

Fig. 4.71. Editing the samples

Chapter 4: Cool Edit Pro as a Universal Solution for Home Studios 227

1. In the first stage of the process of removing a noise (a click, for example) you should select a region in which it can be clearly heard.

   NOTE You should not apply this algorithm to the entire recording, because it may lead to distortions of the sound. Thus it is best to keep the size of the noise reduction areas as small as possible. Then apply the noise reduction algorithm to each of these areas separately.

2. Select the **Constant Hiss and Crackle** preset from the **Presets** list (see Fig. 4.70).
3. Press the **Find Threshold Levels Only** button.
4. After your PC has completed scanning, press **OK**.

The Cool Edit Pro software allows you to edit individual samples (Fig. 4.71).

This means that after you have increased the scale of the waveform image to its maximum size, you can "manually" remove the click (the same way as in the **SoundFile View** window of SAWPro).

   NOTE Manual editing is a painstaking process, with a low productivity level. It is therefore wise to only apply it occasionally, and not all the time.

You can enter the sample editing mode by repeating the **Zoom In** command until the waveform is displayed on the screen in the form of individual points, as seen in Fig. 4.71.

The *Clip Restoration* Effect

To successfully restore a signal with random amplitude clipping, you can apply the **Clip Restoration** effect.

The amplitude is clipped when the signal goes over the maximum allowed level of 0 dB.

The graphic images of the clipped amplitude look like waveforms with their peaks cut off.

This can occur when you are recording a "live" part, such as a vocal.

Here's how you can restore the amplitude after clipping using the **Clip Restoration** effect (Fig. 4.72).

Three input fields are located in the left part of the window.

- In the **Input Attenuation** field, specify the signal amplification before processing. We recommend that you start with a value of −6 dB.

- In the **Overhead** field, specify the part of the amplitude that was likely cut (as a percentage).

   NOTE You should control the value of the **Overhead** parameter experimentally, according to the minimum distortion level of the restored signal. It is controlled by ear.

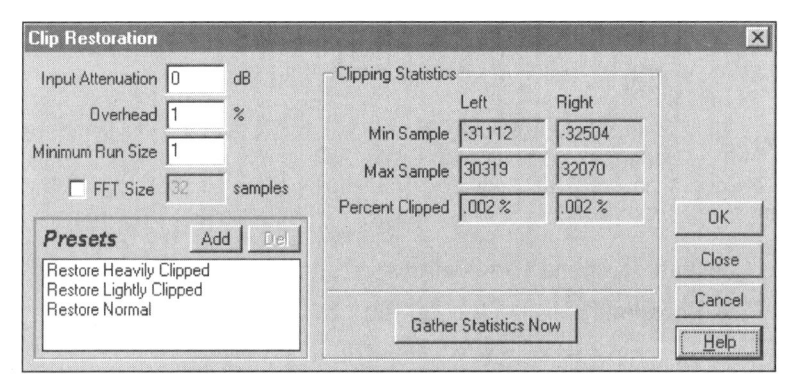

Fig. 4.72. The **Clip Restoration** window

☐ In the **Minimum Run Size** field, specify the number of neighboring measurements that are to be restored.

NOTE   A value of "1" means that *every* measurement that is cut is to be restored.

Depending on the type of distortion, you can obtain better results if you *slightly increase* this value. However, you generally need to experiment to be sure.

When you check the **FFT Size** checkbox, it is recommended that you set a value of 128 samples, because in most cases the least amount of distortions occurs when this value is set.

You can find out the percentage of clipped samples by pressing the **Gather Statistics Now** button.

TIP   Before you apply the **Clip Restoration** effect, we recommend that you center the signal relative to DC. You can do this by applying the **Amplify** effect, with the **Center Wave** preset.

It is better to apply all effects related to noise reduction and restoration in *32-bit* format. (We'll go into more detail on this later.)

The *Hiss Reduction* Effect

To avoid hissing noises (noises whose spectrum is in the high frequency area, Fig. 4.73), Cool Edit Pro provides the **Hiss Reduction** effect.

The following noises come under the category of high-frequency noises known as hissing noises:

☐ The noise of the magnetic tape of tape recorders

☐ The noise of the preliminary amplifier for a microphone or a piezoelectric sensor of a guitar

❐ The noise of the sound card, etc.

Noise Reduction

High quality noise reduction is a laborious procedure. You must be ready for a situation where it seems impossible to find the best relationship among the parameters, especially in the early stages. Improperly setting the **Hiss Reduction** parameters may lead to audible distortions that recall the **Flanger** effect.

However, noise reduction is not a hopeless case. To a certain extent you can always "fool" the human ear, which will not be able to hear the slight distortions that might result from a somewhat imperfect parameter configuration.

TIP We highly recommend that you perform *all* possible noise reduction operations during the initial stages of your work (just after you have completed the recording, and before special processing stages — i.e., application of such effects as reverberation, chorus, etc.).

The saying that an ounce of prevention is worth a pound of cure applies to sound editing as well. It is much easier to avoid noise than to correct it afterwards. Remember that computer algorithms cannot provide solutions for every problem. That's why it makes more sense to use relatively quiet preliminary amplifiers and make sure that you do a reliable screening than to have to resort to removing the noise afterwards, using mathematical methods.

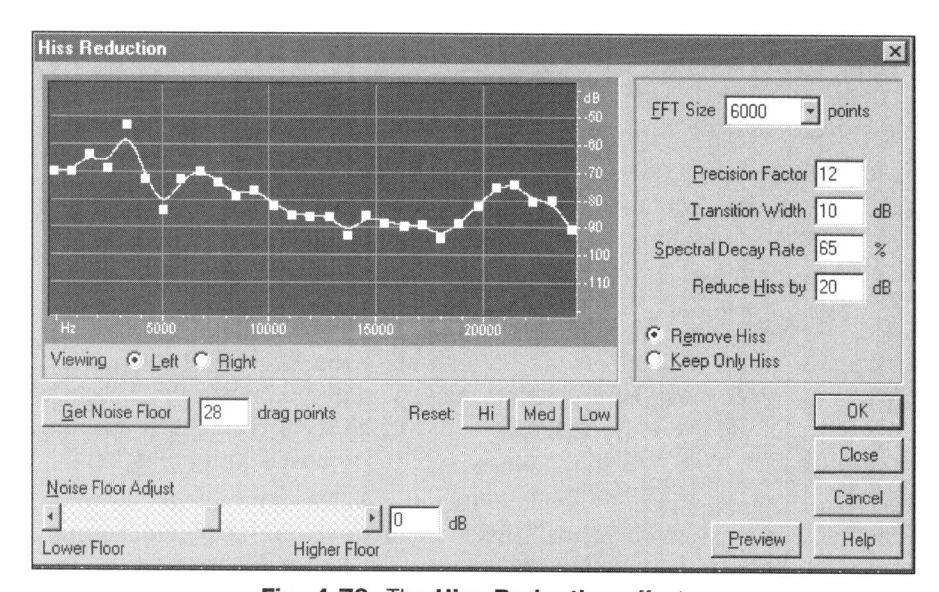

Fig. 4.73. The **Hiss Reduction** effect

Below we give the technique used for removing high-frequency noise.

Start the noise reduction procedure by selecting a fragment of the audio file in which only the noise component is present (a pause, or the beginning of the recording). Then, call the **Hiss Reduction** window and set the **FFT Size** parameter equal to 6000 points. This value is the optimal one in most cases. Next, in the **drag points** field, input the number of nodes that you want to be present on the graph of the dependence of the reduction *floor* on the frequency (the floor is the level below which the audio signal is weakened). By dragging the nodes, you can correct the floor level for a particular frequency. After that, set the **Noise Floor Adjust** slider to 0 dB. Press the **Get Noise Floor** button. After the statistics have been processed, the dependence of the noise reduction floor on the frequency is displayed on the graph. Then you should close the window of this effect (all of its parameters are preserved until the next change is made) and select the entire fragment that you intend to process. Then call the **Hiss Reduction** effect again and continue configuring. We recommend that you set the value of the **Precision Factor** parameter equal to 12.

NOTE The recommended values for the **Precision Factor** parameter are from 7 to 14.

The value of the **Transition Width** parameter is set experimentally. When you specify a value of 1 dB, a signal with a level 1 dB below the floor is sharply suppressed. This leads to audible distortions when noise reduction is done correctly. We recommend that you start with a transition width of 10 dB. The **Spectral Decay Rate** parameter describes the reaction of the noise reduction process to a quickly changed signal. When the value of this parameter is large (90%), noise "tails" will be present in the signal, since the reaction of the effect to the signal decay is slow. When the value is too small (3%), parasite vibrations are possible. Optimal values of the **Spectral Decay Rate** parameter are from 40 to 75%.

The **Reduce Hiss by** parameter determines the value by which the noise components will be reduced (in dB). We recommend that you start with a value of 12 and slightly increase it until audible distortions appear.

TIP For "fast" PCs, you can implement the **Preview** mode.

You can check whether the settings are optimal using the **Remove Hiss/Keep Only Hiss** switch. When in the **Remove Hiss** position, noise is reduced. When the **Keep Only Hiss** option is selected, only the noise remains — the signal itself is removed. Using this option, you can find out what part of the useful signal is removed with the noise.

The **Noise Floor Adjust** slider is used to offset the entire curve of the noise reduction floor. When the floor is passed in the **Higher Floor** direction, audible distortions of the useful signal can appear. Turning the regulator in the **Lower Floor** direction leads to an increase in the noise level.

A more effective way to adjust the curve of the noise reduction floor is by dragging the nodes on the graph. The noise spectrum is concentrated in the region of the upper frequencies of the sound range, so it makes sense to lower the noise reduction floor for middle and lower frequencies. You can also increase the noise reduction depth (the **Reduce Hiss by** parameter) without having distortions of the **Flanger** type appear.

> **NOTE** For a stereo signal, you can adjust the noise reduction floor using the nodes on the graph for each channel separately.

Thus, controlling the **Hiss Reduction** effect just means finding the optimal settings for a number of parameters.

The *Noise Reduction* Effect

The **Noise Reduction** effect can be used to remove *any* noise, and is based on a complex algorithm. First, statistics on the signal are collected in order to be able to recognize the noise, and then, based on an analysis of these statistics, all unnecessary components are removed from the signal.

> **NOTE** Music is a very complex signal; we might even say that it is simply logically organized noise. Removing any component from a musical signal — even random, "unorganized" noise — results in losing a part of the "useful" signal.

When losses are significant, this effect becomes audible. The sound is distorted and begins to sound similar to the **Flanger** effect. This happens in the same manner as in the **Hiss Reduction** effect.

Now we'll describe the settings of the **Noise Reduction** effect (Fig. 4.74).

Generally, the algorithms for applying the **Noise Reduction** and the **Hiss Reduction** effects are similar.

❐ Select a fragment of the recording that contains only noise

❐ To get the noise profile, press the **Get Profile from Selection** button

❐ You can save the noise profile as a file using the **Save Profile** button, and then load it using the **Load Profile** button

❐ In the **Noise Reduction Settings** section, you can select the **FFT Size**

> **NOTE** The higher the value of the **FFT Size**, the more precise the result, and the longer it will take to calculate.

❐ The functions of the **Remove Noise** and **Keep Only Noise** buttons are similar to the functions of the **Hiss Reduction** effect with the same name: they allow you to either clear the signal from noise, or remove the signal and have the noise remain

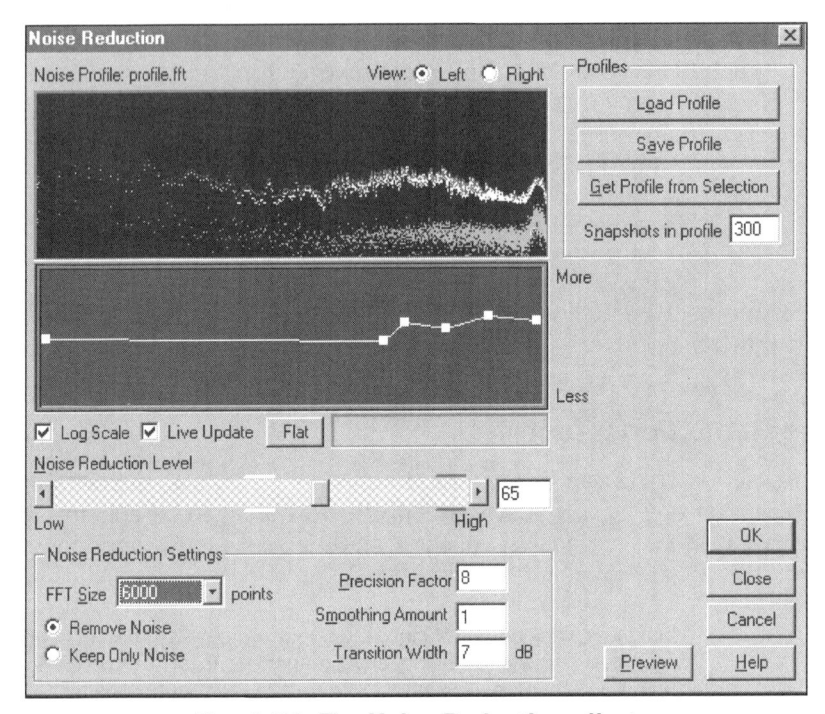

Fig. 4.74. The **Noise Reduction** effect

❐ It is recommended that you specify odd values in the **Precision Factor** field

> *NOTE* Large precision values (over 12) do not lead to audible results, but do result in a longer calculation time.

❐ In the **Smoothing Amount** field, you should specify the value on which the signal distortions (of the **Flanger** type) depend

> *NOTE* By increasing the **Smoothing Amount** parameter, you can reduce the distortions by increasing the total noise level.

❐ The **Transition Width** parameter determines the width of the noise reduction floor

> *NOTE* This parameter is described in detail in the description of the **Hiss Reduction** effect.

❐ The **Noise Reduction Level** slider sets the noise reduction level in dB

> *NOTE* By creating and moving nodes on the graph, you can change the noise reduction level for various frequencies.

Effects that Change the Duration and Pitch of the Sound
The *Pitch Bender* Effect

The **Pitch Bender** effect, which imitates a change in the playback speed, is used to change the pitch and duration of the sound (Fig. 4.75).

Using the **Pitch Bender** effect, you can smoothly *change the tempo or the pitch*. You select these options by changing the parameters in the input fields located next to the **Range** switch:

- **... semitones** — adjusts the tone pitch
- **... BPM,** (change the number of beats per minute) **with base of ... BPM** (set the base tempo in BPM) — changes the tempo

> **NOTE** BPM is the number of beats per minute. By creating and moving the nodes on the graph, you can create any ratio for changing the tempo or the tone pitch over time.

Remember that in both cases (for the tempo and the tone pitch) the duration of the audio fragment *always* changes. These changes are measured in various units.

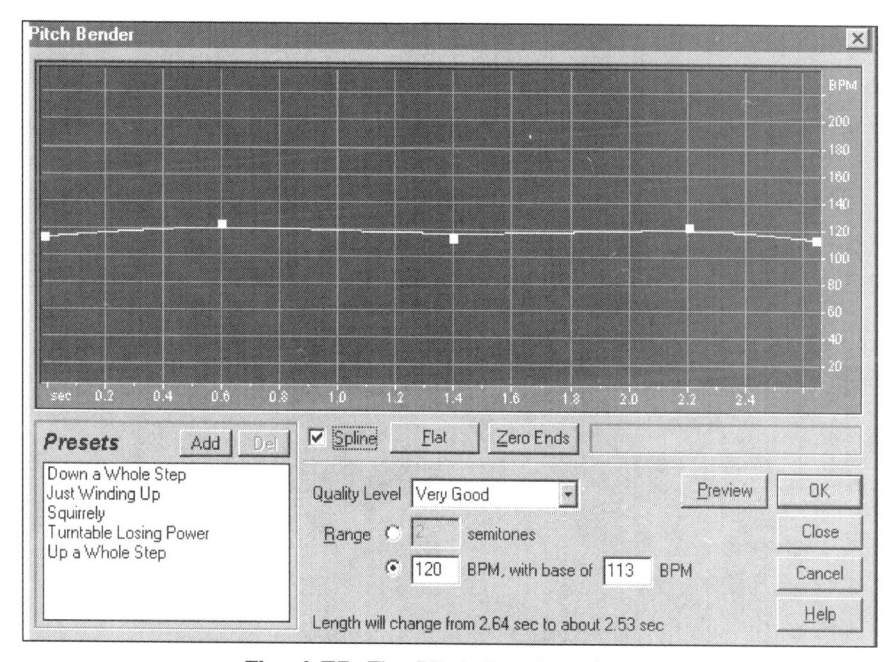

Fig. 4.75. The **Pitch Bender** window

The purpose of the other controls is as follows:

- ❐ In the **Quality Level** field, you specify the transformation precision
- ❐ The **Zero Ends** button, when pressed, resets the initial and final nodes of the graph to zero

Using the **Pitch Bender** effect, you can align the tempo of prepared fragments (loops) that have different tempos.

The *Favorites* Menu

As a rule, each user has his or her own preferences and "favorite" effects. It is much more convenient when the most frequently used effects are organized in a separate menu.

This is the reason that we are given a **Favorites** menu in Cool Edit Pro.

However, this menu is not just for storage of preliminarily selected effects. It also provides a number of actions that allow you to work with these effects conveniently.

For example, in the **Favorites** menu, you can set and save the necessary settings, appoint shortcut keys, call other applications from Cool Edit Pro, etc.

To set up the **Favorites** menu you will need to execute the **Edit Favorites** command (Fig. 4.76).

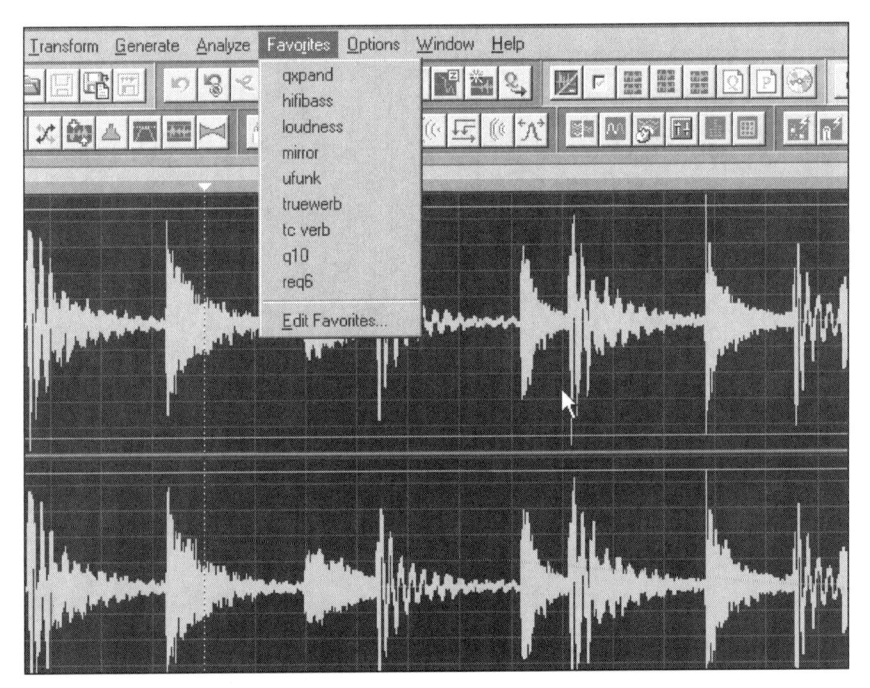

Fig. 4.76. The **Favorites** menu

Chapter 4: Cool Edit Pro as a Universal Solution for Home Studios 235

In the **Favorites** settings window (Fig. 4.77) you should supply the preset name, associate it with a shortcut key if necessary, and select the effect in the **Cool Edit Transform** list in the **Function** tab.

- The **Edit Transform Settings** button calls the window of the corresponding effect, in which you can make the necessary adjustments. When the **Use Current Settings** checkbox is checked, the last (current) settings of the effect are saved in the preset.
- The **Show Dialog** switch calls the effect window when the preset is selected in the **Favorites** menu. When the **Show Dialog** checkbox is unchecked, the effect with the saved presets is implemented at once, without filling in the options of the settings dialog box.
- You can add configurations to the **Current Favorites** list using the **Add** button.
- The **Up** and **Down** buttons allow you to change the order of the presets in the list. To do so, first select one of the presets by clicking on it.
- The **Delete** button removes the preset from the **Current Favorites** list.

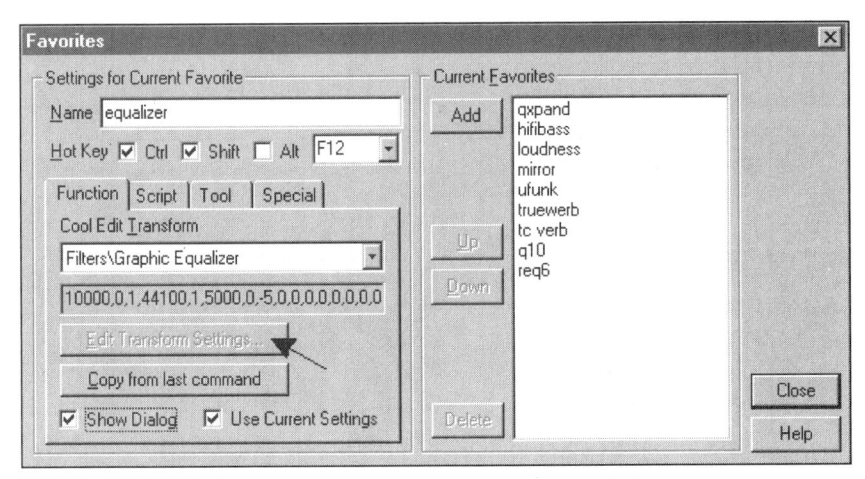

Fig. 4.77. The **Favorites** settings window

- The **Copy from last command** button allows you to create a preset with the last settings of the applied effect.
- The **Script** tab allows you to include script files into the **Current Favorites** list (we will discuss this later on).
- The **Tool** tab allows you to create a configuration for calling other applications (such as the sequencer or mixer of a particular sound card) directly from the **Favorites** menu. To do so, specify the path to this application (a file with the EXE, COM, or other extension) using the **Browse** button.

❐ The **Special** tab is used for organizing various submenus (Fig. 4.78 and 4.79). To do this, enter a submenu name that ends with the slash character (\) — such as **My Effects1** — in the **Name** field. To insert one submenu into another, separate their names with this character (see Fig. 4.78).

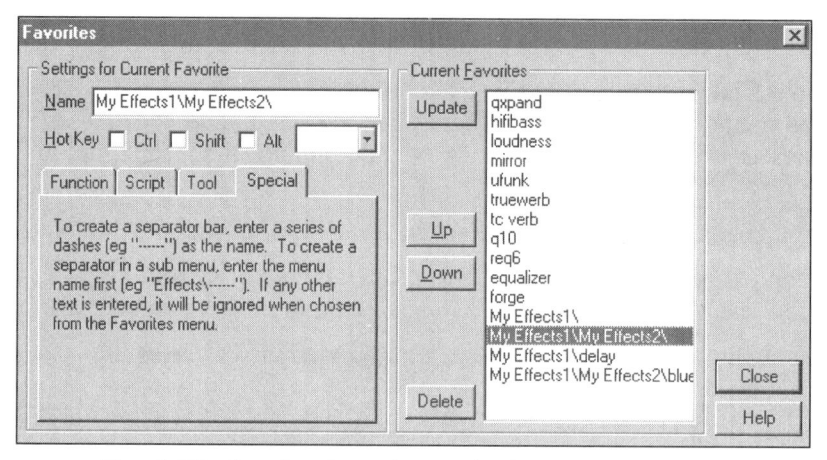

Fig. 4.78. Creating the submenu in the **Favorites** menu

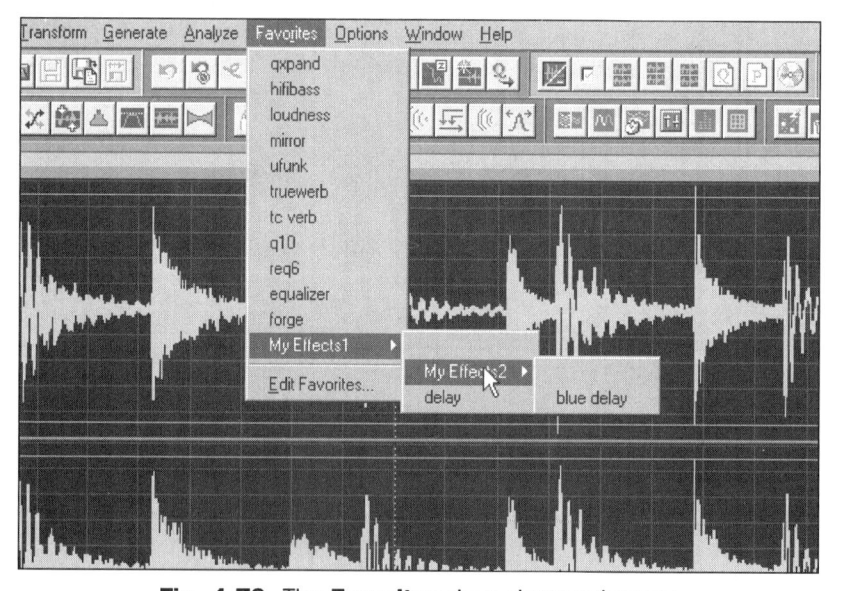

Fig. 4.79. The **Favorites** drop-down submenu

❐ The **Update** button is used to modify the preset. When you edit an element of the list, this button replaces the **Add** button.

Chapter 4: Cool Edit Pro as a Universal Solution for Home Studios   237

The Configuration File of Cool Edit Pro

All the settings of Cool Edit Pro — including the **Settings** menu, effect presets, and the configuration of the **Favorites** menu — are saved in the Cool.ini file. This file is found in the Windows (Winnt) folder. You can copy this file to a floppy disk, and then simply overwrite the existing file after the new installation of the program to restore the initial settings.

File Formats of Cool Edit Pro

The Cool Edit Pro software has a built-in converter that allows you to convert a number of different types of audio file formats.

You can make a sound file conform to the necessary format in the **File** menu, using the **Save As**, **Save Copy As**, and **Save Selection** commands.

NOTE The sound file's type is set in the dialog box you select (**Save As**, **Save Copy As**, or **Save Selection**) in the **Save as type** drop-down list, by clicking on it (Fig. 4.80).

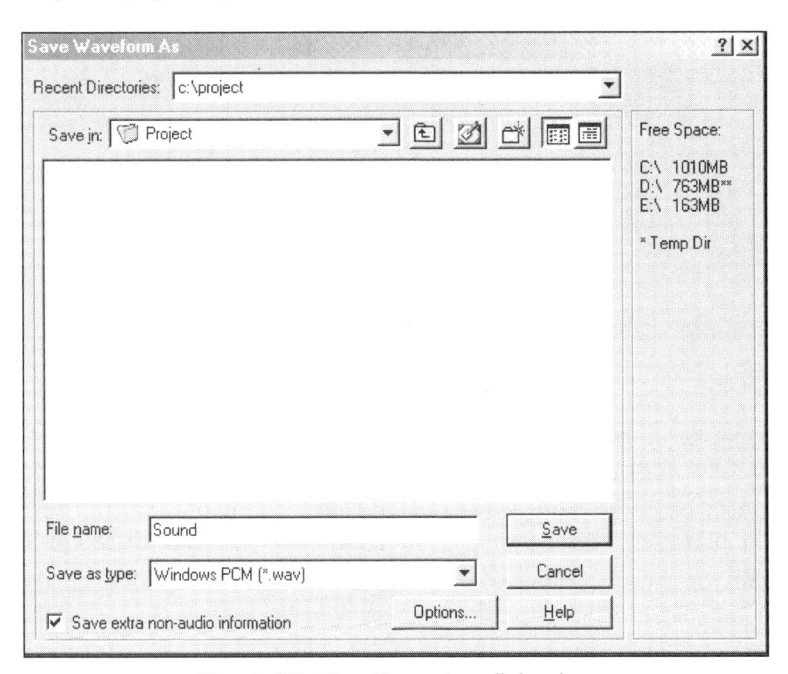

Fig. 4.80. The file saving dialog box

In this book, we will only describe the Windows PCM format (WAV files), which is standard for IBM PC-compatible PCs that operate under Windows 95/98/NT/ME/2000.

NOTE Remember that the AUDIO CD software that we described in *Chapter 3* works with the Windows PCM format.

In addition to the idea of creating a "live", pure, and transparent sound, we should mention another important feature of Cool Edit Pro: it supports 32-bit audio resolution.

In the **Settings** window on the **Devices** tab, you can assess the hardware abilities of the sound card (or sound cards) installed on your PC, as shown in Fig. 4.81. In the given example, in the **Waveform Playback** and **Waveform Record** fields, the word **Yes** is shown near the names of the audio formats supported by the sound card that differ in resolution and sampling frequency.

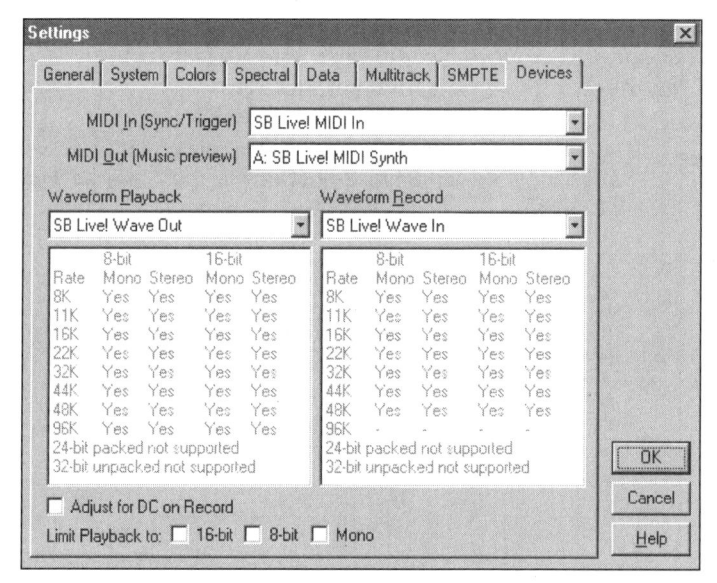

Fig. 4.81. The **Settings** window, **Devices** tab

32-bit processing is implemented in Cool Edit Pro in its own format, with a floating point. This allows you to convert 16-bit format into 32-bit format, and vice versa.

The program also has the ability to record and play audio files with a 32-bit resolution (32-bit files are played in 16-bit format if the abilities of the audio card are limited).

When 16-bit sound cards are used, the precision of audio digitization in 32-bit format is not increased (conversion into 32-bit format is done in real time, during the recording). Increasing the resolution affects the quality of the sound in further processing.

WARNING! *This Is Important for the Sound Quality*

Subjectively, the sound of a 32-bit recording, *after* it is processed by the effects of the **Transform** menu, becomes "deeper" and more transparent than a 16-bit recording.

Chapter 4: Cool Edit Pro as a Universal Solution for Home Studios

The developers of the Cool Edit Pro software highly recommend that you apply the 32-bit format of audio files for most processing algorithms, in order to reach the maximum quality of sound.

In *Chapter 8*, we will discuss the problems that arise when intermediate processing results are saved in 16-bit format.

In the **Data** tab in the **Settings** window, there is an option that automates transition to a higher resolution. This option is called **Auto-convert all data to 32-bit upon opening**.

Another conversion method is the **Open As** command of the **File** menu. After you select it, you can specify the parameters of the new 32-bit format (the **32-bit (float)** button of the **Resolution** switch) in the dialog box that opens (Fig. 4.82).

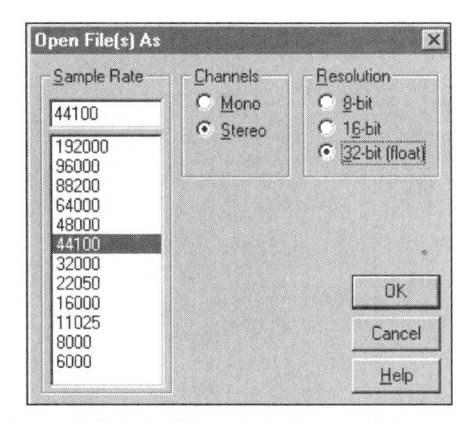

Fig. 4.82. The **Open File(s) As** dialog box

Preserving the "Dimension" and the "Transparency" of the Sound

In the **Data** tab of the **Settings** window, the **Dither Transform Results** option is enabled by default. (Dithering is described in detail in *Chapter 8*.)

Because Cool Edit Pro makes all conversions in the 32-bit format, the following stages must be completed when you process 16-bit data: audio conversion into 32-bit format, processing (application of the effect), and reverse conversion into 16-bit format.

When the "32-16" conversion takes place, lower order bits are truncated. This results in losing "subtle" information, such as transparency, dimension, "breath", etc., because of the quantization noise. (Quantization noise is described in detail in *Chapter 8*.)

Applying the dithering algorithm (adding pseudo-random noise) reduces quantization distortions and partially restores the transparency and dimension, of the sound. That's why the **Dither Transform Results** option *should most definitely be enabled*. However, this does not work when effects overlap many times. When effects are applied one after another, repeated "16-32" and "32-16" transformations are done along with dithering.

At each stage, "subtle" information resulting from 32-bit audio processing is lost during the reverse conversion into 16-bit format. This happens despite the application of the dithering algorithm, which reduces the quantization distortions, but does not restore the lost data.

The dithering itself is applied several times, although it is recommended that you apply it only once, in the final processing stage, such as when converting a 32-bit or a 24-bit recording into 16-bit format for AUDIO CD.

So, to get an "enlivened" sound, you should convert the audio material into 32-bit format, and process and save it in this format, until you finally get a 16-bit master file.

Another conversion method is the **Convert Sample Type** command in the **Edit** menu.

The dialog window with this name is a universal solution when it comes to changing the sampling frequency and the resolution (Fig. 4.83).

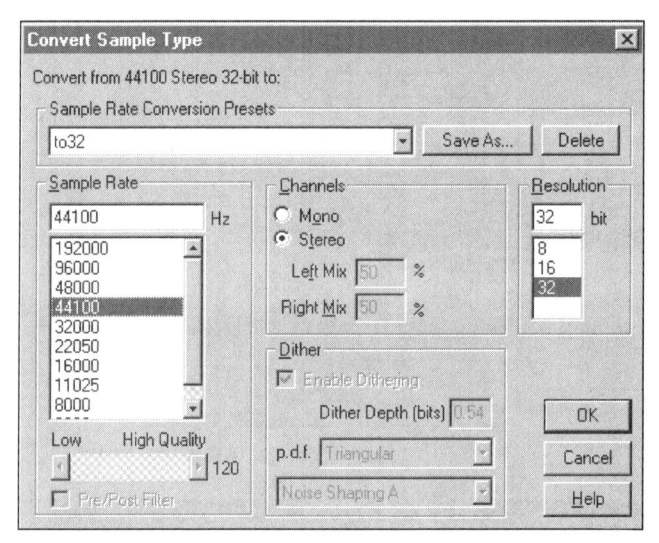

Fig. 4.83. The **Convert Sample Type** window

The Cool Edit Pro editor allows you to save its internal 32-bit data in the standard 24-bit and 32-bit formats so that it can be used by other programs (WaveLab, Samplitude 2496, SAWPro, Cubase VST 24, etc.).

Conversion is done using the same **Save As**, **Save Copy As**, and **Save Selection** options.

In the **Save** dialog box, the **Formatting for 20 to 32-bit samples** window pops up when you press the **Options** button (Fig. 4.84).

This window contains several radio buttons corresponding to the formats used. We will describe some of them:

- **32-bit 0.24 normalized float (type 3 — 32-bit)** — standard 32-bit format with floating point that is compatible with the WaveLab and Samplitude 2496 software.
- **24-bit packed int (type 1 — 24-bit)** — a packed 24-bit format compatible with WaveLab, Cubase VST 24, and SAWPro. The Samplitude 2496 software converts the

Chapter 4: Cool Edit Pro as a Universal Solution for Home Studios 241

24-bit packed int (type 1 — 24-bit) format into **32-bit 0.24 normalized float (type 3 — 32-bit)**, and vice versa.

> **NOTE** WaveLab, Cubase VST 24, and SAWPro convert 24-bit audio files into 16-bit resolution when they are played using a 16-bit sound card. For this purpose in theSAWPro software, the **RES** (resolution) parameter of the multitrack should be set to 16 bit (see *Chapter 3*).

❐ **32-bit 16.8 float (type 1 — 32-bit)** — an internal 32-bit format with floating point, used by Cool Edit Pro.

> **NOTE** The program performs all transformations in this format. By default, 32-bit files are saved in it (**File** menu, **Save** command).

The reverse conversion from 32-bit to 16-bit resolution in Cool Edit Pro is performed by the **Convert Sample Type** command of the **Edit** menu (Fig. 4.85).

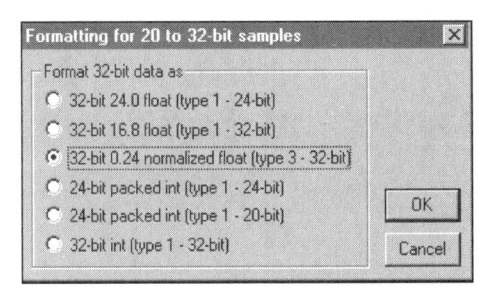

Fig. 4.84. The **Formatting for 20 to 32-bit samples** window

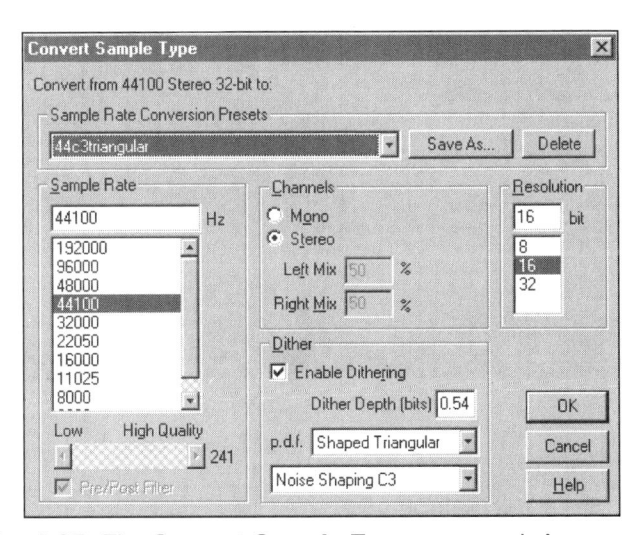

Fig. 4.85. The **Convert Sample Type** command. An example of conversion to a lower resolution

To get the quality of the reverse conversion into the "16 bits, 44,100 Hz" format, we recommend that you specify the following values of the parameters below:

- **Dither Depth (bits)** — 0.54 bit

- **p.d.f** (probability distribution function) — **Shaped Triangular**, **Noise Shaping C3**

The *Edit* Menu

The **Edit** menu is intended mainly for destructively editing the audio material (Fig. 4.86).

NOTE Remember that destructive editing is changing the file so as to destroy the initial data. (Destructive editing is described in detail in *Chapter 3*.)

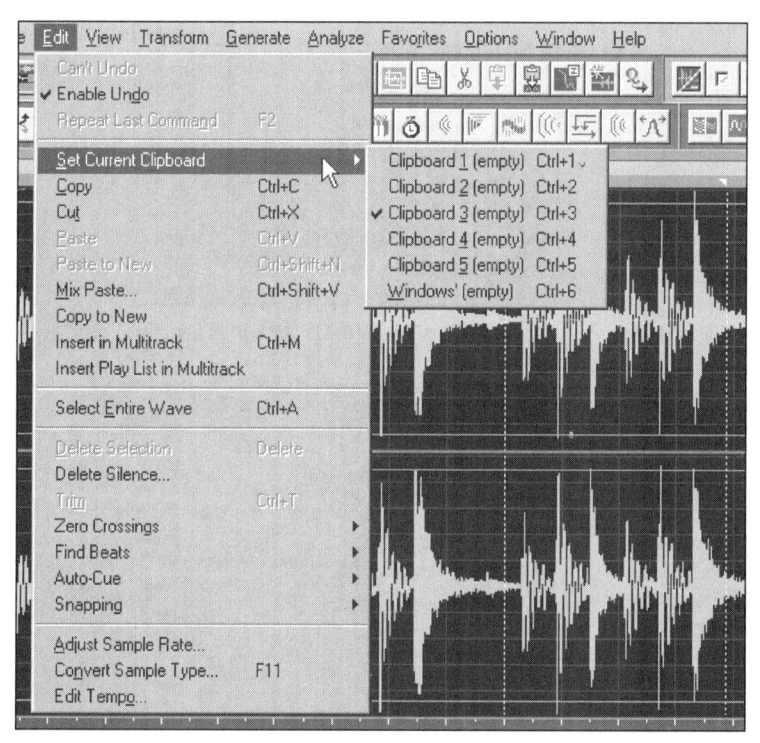

Fig. 4.86. The **Edit** menu

We'll now describe the options of the **Edit** menu.

- **Can't Undo** — disables the undo mode.

- **Enable Undo** — enables the undo mode.

Chapter 4: Cool Edit Pro as a Universal Solution for Home Studios

- **Repeat Last Command** ("shortcut" key <F2>) — repeats the last command and calls the dialog window to set the effect.

    NOTE You can repeat the last command without calling the dialog box by pressing the <F3> key.

- **Set Current Clipboard** — sets the current clipboard.

    NOTE The Cool Edit Pro software has five internal clipboards, plus the Windows clipboard.

- **Copy** — copies into the current clipboard.
- **Cut** — cuts into the current clipboard.
- **Paste** — pastes from the current clipboard.

    NOTE The **Copy**, **Cut**, and **Paste** operations can be associated with different clipboards — i.e., you can copy the data into one clipboard and paste data from another. To do so, you must make the desired clipboard current.

    The pasted fragment is placed in the cursor position.

    If the data format of the clipboard differs from the format of the file to which the fragment is pasted, Cool Edit Pro automatically adjusts the clipboard format.

- **Paste to New** — pastes into a new file. A new file called **Untitled** is created, and it has the same parameters as the contents of the clipboard.

    NOTE To switch between the files loaded into the editor, use the **Window** menu or the **Waveforms List** (<F9>) submenu in the **Window** menu.

    Switching between the files in the **Waveforms List** window (Fig. 4.87) is done by double-clicking on the filename. The **Close Wave** button closes (uploads) the file from the editor with a prompt to save changes. The **Open Wave** button opens the file (the same way as the **Open** option in the **File** menu does).

    The **Insert** button inserts the region (the waveform block) of the file selected in the list to the multitrack.

- **Mix Paste** — pastes while mixing from the current clipboard. The **Mix Paste** dialog box is also opened (Fig. 4.88).

    The **Mix Paste** box contains the following controls:

    - **Insert** — inserts from the current clipboard with the volume defined by the position of the **Volume** sliders.
    - **Overlap** (**Mix**) — the contents of the current clipboard is overlapped with the audio file that has its volume level defined by the position of the **Volume** sliders.

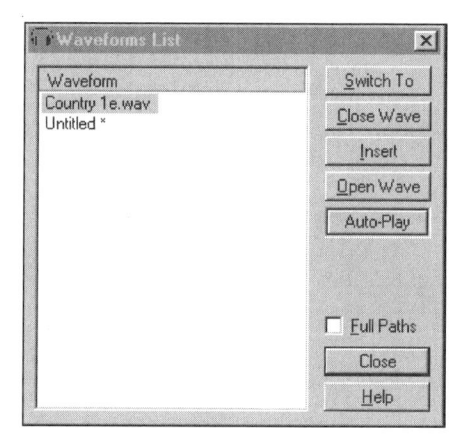

Fig. 4.87. The **Waveforms List** dialog box

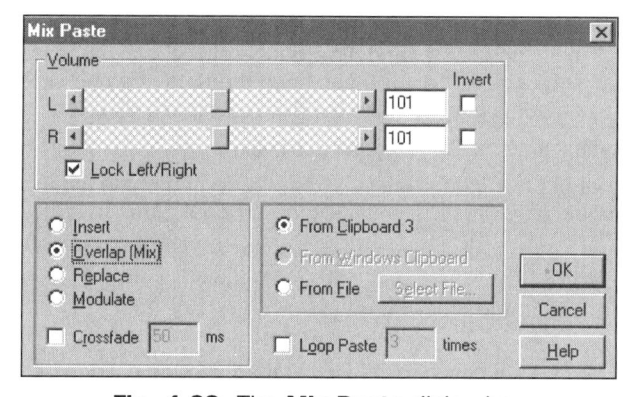

Fig. 4.88. The **Mix Paste** dialog box

- **Replace** — replaces an area of the audio file with the fragment from the current clipboard.

- **Modulate** — inserts from the current clipboard with the modulation of the area of the audio file. (This option can be used to overlay the amplitude envelope from another fragment made by the **Dynamics Processing** effect.)

- **Crossfade** — defines the transition smoothness at the boundaries of the pasted region.

- **Loop Paste** — allows you to repeat the paste operation (put it into a loop). The number of times the action is repeated is specified in the **times** field.

- **From Windows Clipboard** — pastes from the Windows clipboard.

- **From File** — pastes from a file. When this action is performed, the **Select File** button becomes available.

- **Invert** — inverts the clipboard data before pasting.

Chapter 4: Cool Edit Pro as a Universal Solution for Home Studios

- **Copy to New** — copies the selection into a new file.
- **Insert in Multitrack** — inserts the selection into the multitrack (shortcut keys <Ctrl>+<M>).
- **Insert Play List in Multitrack** — inserts the **Play List** list into the multitrack.
- **Select Entire Wave** — selects an entire audio file (<Ctrl>+<A>).
- **Delete Selection** — deletes the selection (<Delete>). (The deleted data are not copied into the clipboard. You can restore these by applying the undo operation (<Ctrl>+<Z>).)
- **Delete Silence** — deletes the pauses. The duration of the audio file is reduced by the time taken up by silence.
- **Trim** — deletes all the data outside the selected area (<Ctrl>+<T>).
- **Zero Crossings** — makes the boundaries of the selection equal to the nearest points of zero amplitude. (This function is used in assembling in order to avoid clicks on the boundaries of fragments.)
- **Find Beats** — finds rhythmically complete phrases; this option is recommended as a convenient tool for creating loops.
- **Auto-Cue** — automatically creates a list of notes (markers) to find musical phrases and rhythmic starting points.
- **Snapping** — attracts the cursor to certain points.
  - **Snap to Waves** — operates in the **Multitrack View** window only, and snaps to the beginning or the end of a clip. When the clip is copied or moved, the boundaries "stick together" (even if the clips are on different tracks) beginning from some minimum distance.

  ### Terminology

  In Cool Edit Pro and SAWPro, the same concept is known by two different names. An area located on the multitrack is called a *clip* in SAWPro and a *waveform block* in Cool Edit Pro. In the description of the interface of Cool Edit Pro, we have used the term "clip", which is clearer, in our opinion.

  - **Snap to Ruler (Fine)** — provides a *precise* snapping to the bar grid. If this snapping is in place, you can only position the cursor (or the selection boundaries) at numbered and intermediate points of the **Time Ruler** grid (and not just at any place on the multitrack).
  - **Snap to Ruler (Coarse)** — a *rough* attachment to the bar grid. In this mode, the cursor and the fragment selection boundaries are snapped only to the *numbered* points of the **Time Ruler**.

- **Snap to Cues** — snapping to markers, which allows you to move around the **Multitrack View** window, jumping from one set marker (cue) to another.
- **Adjust Sample Rate** — direct setting of the sampling frequency (without file conversion). This function allows you to listen to a file whose sampling frequency exceeds the abilities of the sound card installed on your PC. (This function is similar to switching between speeds on a tape recorder.)
- **Convert Sample Type** (<F11>) — converts the sampling frequency and the resolution of files.

> **NOTE** When the sampling frequency is decreased, it is recommended that you disable the **Pre/Post Filter** option and set the precision regulator to the **High Quality** position. This will slightly increase the conversion time, but will significantly improve the quality.

- **Edit Tempo** — allows you to measure the tempo and edit the musical measure of the selected fragment.

> **NOTE** To measure the tempo, press the **Extract** button. In the **Beats per Bar** field, you can specify the musical measure: 4 for 4/4, 6 for 6/8, 3 for 3/4. Specify the number of ticks per beat in the **Ticks per Beat** field. (It is best to set the number of ticks equal to the value set in the software or hardware MIDI sequencer.)

The *Multitrack View* Window

Remember that Cool Edit Pro allows you to work with two windows: **Edit Waveform View** and **Multitrack View**. Now that we have finished the description of the program in its role as an audio editor (in the **Edit Waveform View** window), we can now turn to the other window. Thanks to this window, the program can operate as a multitrack virtual tape recorder with the ability to non-destructively edit.

To switch between the editor window and the **Multitrack View** window, click the **Switch to** button (which is pointed to by the arrow in Fig. 4.89) or press the <F12> key.

The Session as an Analogy to the EDL File of SAWPro

Remember that an entire virtual project in SAWPro (lists of regions, the location of clips on tracks, settings of the virtual mixer, etc.) is saved in a file with the EDL extension.

Cool Edit Pro provides a similar ability. Because a virtual project is called a *session* in Cool Edit Pro, project files have the SES extension.

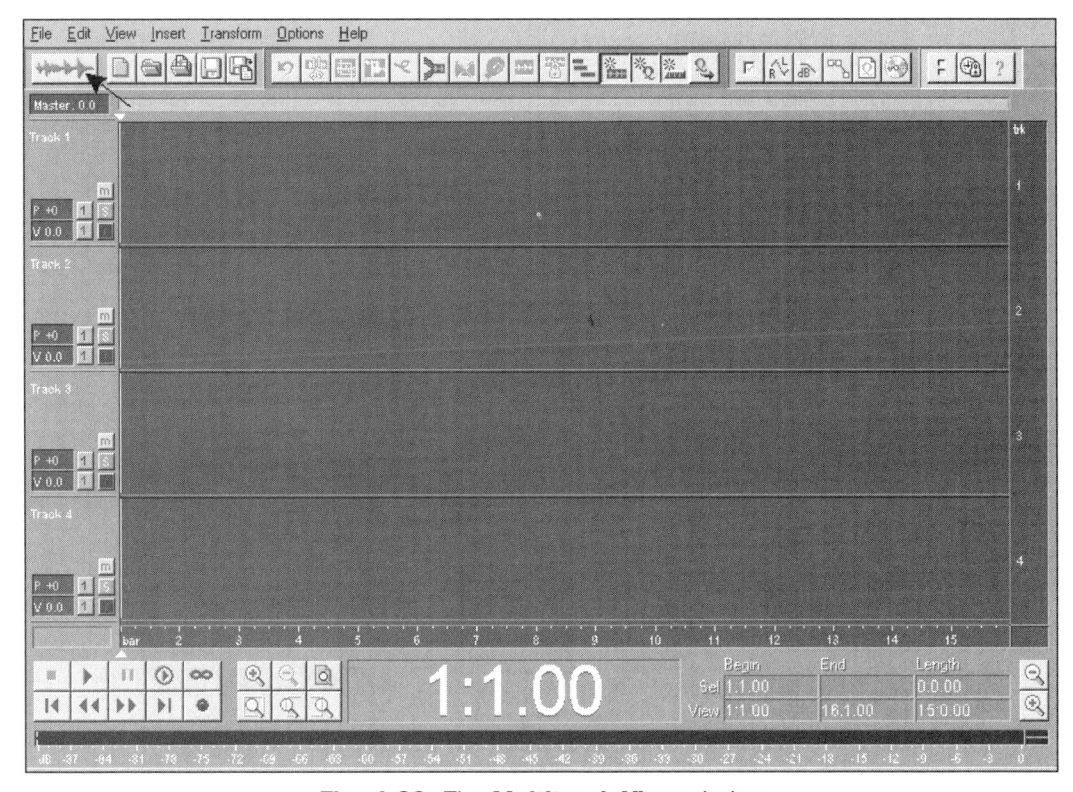

Chapter 4: Cool Edit Pro as a Universal Solution for Home Studios 247

Fig. 4.89. The **Multitrack View** window

In the **File** menu of the **Multitrack View** window, *sessions are created and saved* using the following commands.

- **New Session** (<Ctrl>+<N>) — creates a new ("empty") session. In the dialog box called by the program (Fig. 4.90), you should select the session format.

  NOTE When you work in 32-bit format, you should first change the following parameters in the **Settings** window in the **Multitrack** tab: **Default Rec**, **Mixdowns**, and **Playback Mixing**. They should be set to the 32-bit mode.

  Before importing 16-bit files into the project, check the **Auto-convert all data to 32-bit upon opening** checkbox (located in the **Data** tab of the **Settings** window).

- **Save Session, Save Session As** — saves the session.

  NOTE When you perform the **Save Session As** command, you can enable the **Save copies of all associated files** option in the dialog box. After that, besides saving all the SES files, it also creates copies of all files associated to this session.

❐ **Open Session** — opens a previously saved session.

NOTE The **Component Files** field displays a list of files that, all together, make up the session (the list is pointed to by the arrow in Fig. 4.91).

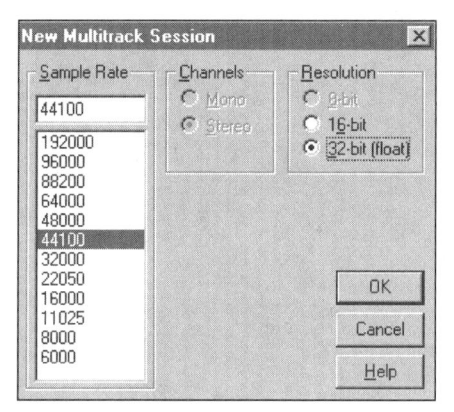

Fig. 4.90. The **New Multitrack Session** window

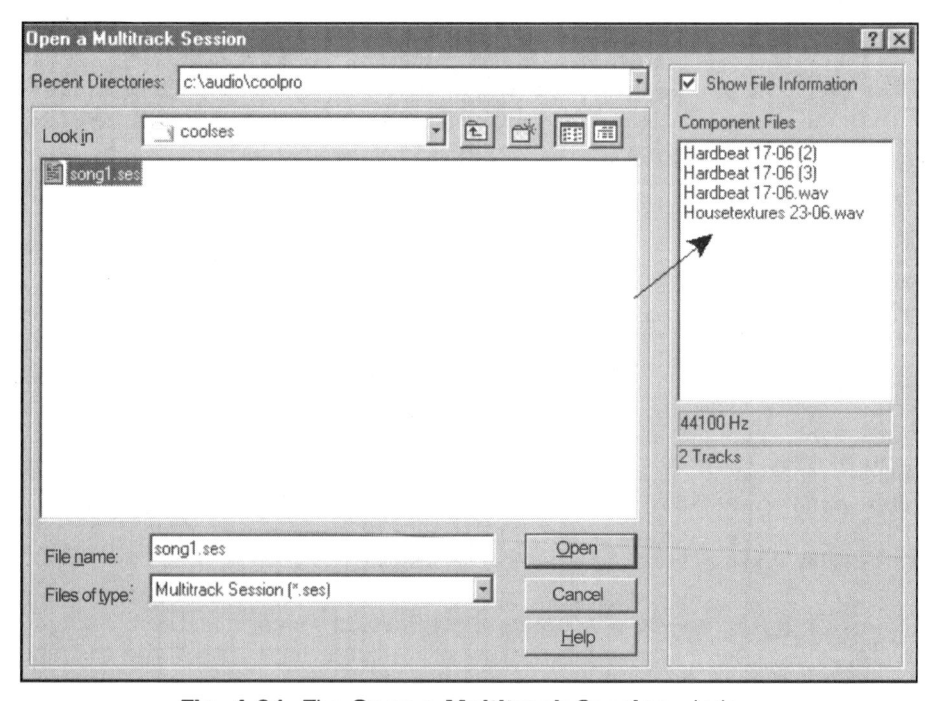

Fig. 4.91. The **Open a Multitrack Session** window

The *Track Info* Panel

The **Track Info** panel (Fig. 4.92) in Cool Edit Pro is used for the same purposes as the **Fader** panel in the SAWPro software: to control the volume and the panorama.

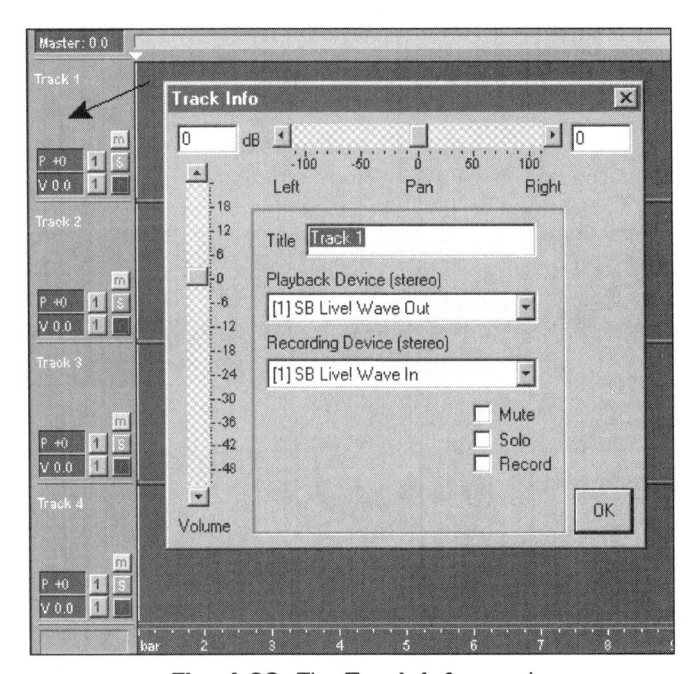

Fig. 4.92. The **Track Info** panel

The **Track Info** panel is called by clicking (one right-click or a left double-click) on the field with the **Track** caption. This field is pointed to by the arrow in Fig. 4.92.

The *volume and panorama sliders* are located on this panel. The values set by these sliders apply to the entire track.

> **NOTE** These sliders operate similar to the **OFFSET** mode on the **Fader** panel in the SAWPro software.

The **Title** field contains the track's name.

If several sound cards (or a multichannel sound card) are installed on your PC, you can select a device for each of them in the **Playback Device (stereo)** and **Recording Device (stereo)** fields.

The **Mute**, **Solo**, and **Record** checkboxes (duplicated by the **m**, **s**, and **r** buttons on the panel) are used for:

❏ Muting the track (**Mute**, **m**)

❏ Setting the playback mode for this track only (**Solo**, **s**)

❏ Enabling the recording mode (**Record**, **r**)

You can *adjust the volume and the panorama* directly on the panel. To do so:

1. Position the mouse cursor on either the **V** (volume) or **P** (panorama) field.
2. Press the left mouse button and, holding it, move the cursor up or down.

NOTE If you right-click (or left double-click) on the **V** or **P** field, the volume or the panorama slider, respectively, will appear on the screen (Fig. 4.93).

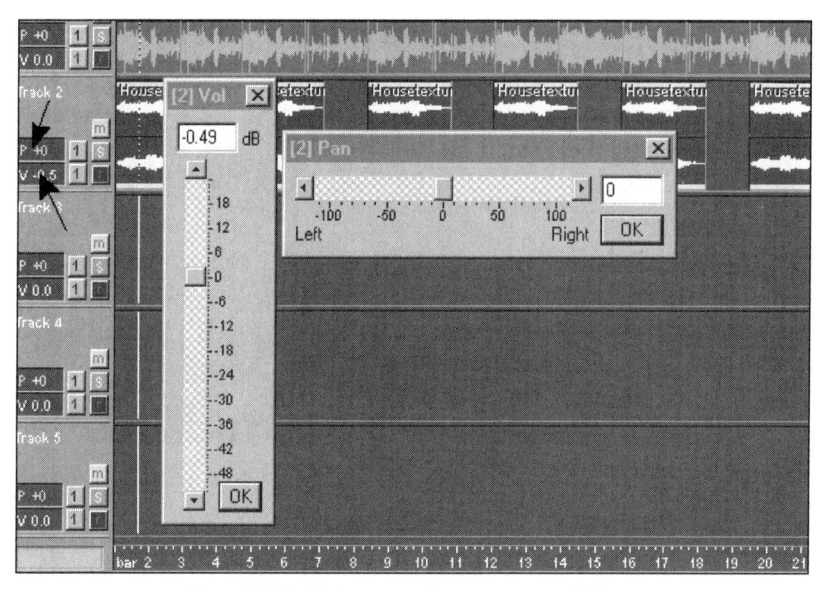

Fig. 4.93. Volume and panorama sliders

The blue and red buttons with a **1** allow you to efficiently select the recording (red button) or playback (blue button) devices.

NOTE The number **1** indicates the selected device (the first in this case).

When the red **1** button is pressed, the **Recording Device** dialog box appears (Fig. 4.94), in which you can change the recording parameters.

The **Same for All Tracks** checkbox sets the values you have selected for the remaining tracks as well.

Cool Edit Pro has no output track (as opposed to SAWPro's **Output Track**), but there is a general volume slider with similar functions. It is called **Master** (Fig. 4.95).

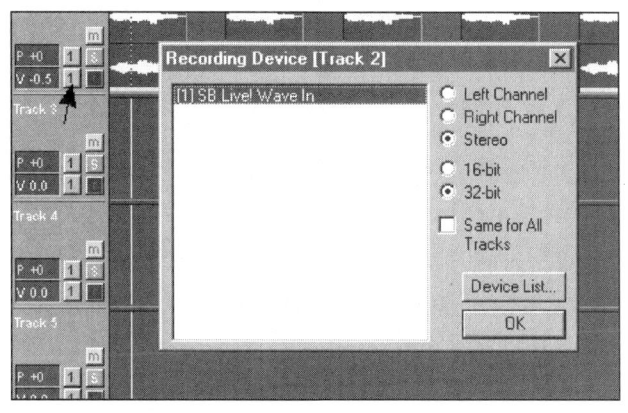

Chapter 4: Cool Edit Pro as a Universal Solution for Home Studios 251

Fig. 4.94. The **Recording Device** dialog box

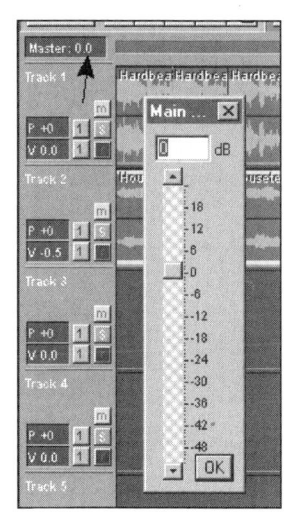

Fig. 4.95. The general volume slider — **Master**

Recording and Playback in the *Multitrack View* Window

Using Pop-up Menus

In both windows of the program — **Multitrack View** and **Edit Waveform View** — using pop-up menus allows you not only to organize your work but also to save time.

> **NOTE** Pop-up menus, though they are all rather different, are always called by right-clicking on the corresponding object.

As a rule, it is convenient to perform most operations with clips using the pop-up menus.

The Clip Pop-up Menu (*WAVE PROPERTIES*)

The clip editing pop-up menu is shown in Fig. 4.96. It is called by right-clicking on the clip image.

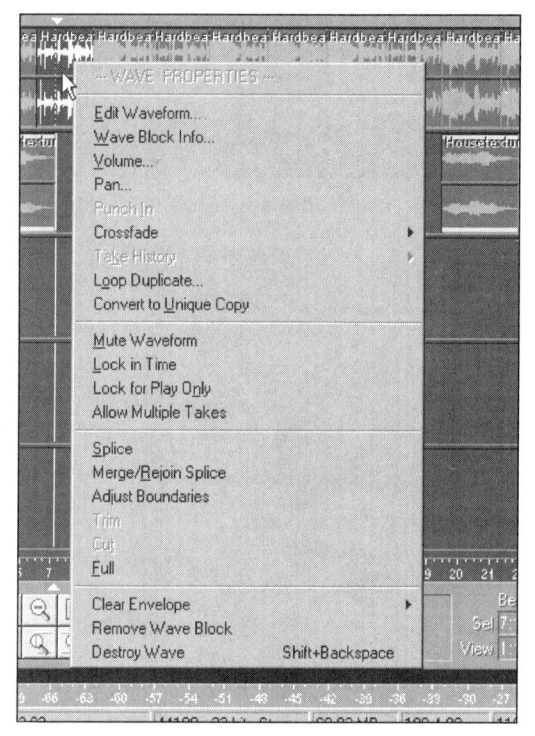

Fig. 4.96. The clip editing pop-up menu

> **NOTE** Of course, along with the pop-up menu, you can use the buttons located on the toolbar in the **Multitrack View** window.

We'll describe this menu in detail.

- **Edit Waveform** (or a double-click on the clip image) transfers the clip into the editor window for destructive editing.
- **Wave Block Info** calls the volume and panorama slider for the clip (Fig. 4.97), and opens a window (similar to **Track Info**, see Fig. 4.92) with the following controls:
  - The **Pan** and **Volume** sliders change the panorama and the volume for the given clip *only*

Chapter 4: Cool Edit Pro as a Universal Solution for Home Studios

- The **Hue** slider sets the clip's color
- **Mute** disables the playback of the given clip, and the clip turns black
- **Lock in Time** prohibits moving the clip along the time axis
- **Lock for Play Only** prohibits recording over the clip — i.e., during recording, a new file is created that is added to the current clip, but does not replace it
- The value in the **Time Offset** field transfers the clip to the assigned point of the multitrack over time

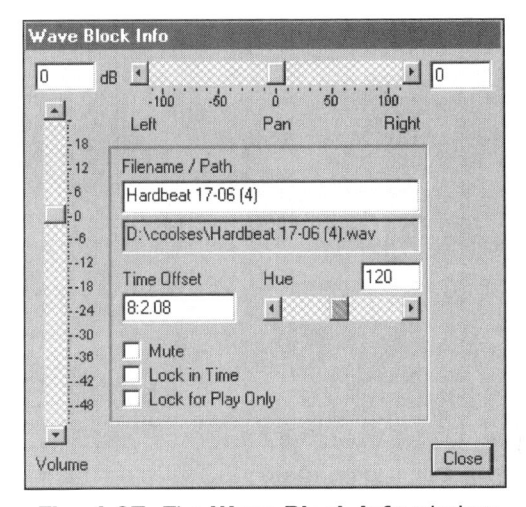

Fig. 4.97. The **Wave Block Info** window

- ❐ **Volume** calls the volume slider for the clip.
- ❐ **Pan** calls the panorama slider for the clip.
- ❐ **Punch In** enables the fragment recording mode (this command is available *only* for a *selected* fragment).
- ❐ The **Crossfade** submenu implements a smooth change of the volume in the selected region (Fig. 4.98) according to different change curves:
  - **Linear**
  - **Sinusoidal**
  - **Logarithmic In** and **Logarithmic Out**

> **NOTE** To select a clip, simply click on it.
> To select two or more clips, click on each of them with the <Ctrl> key pressed.

NOTE In Cool Edit Pro, the **Crossfade** function is universal: you can use it either as a **Fade In** and **Fade Out** on the selected fragment of one clip, as well as for a **Crossfade** on the selected fragment of two crossing clips.

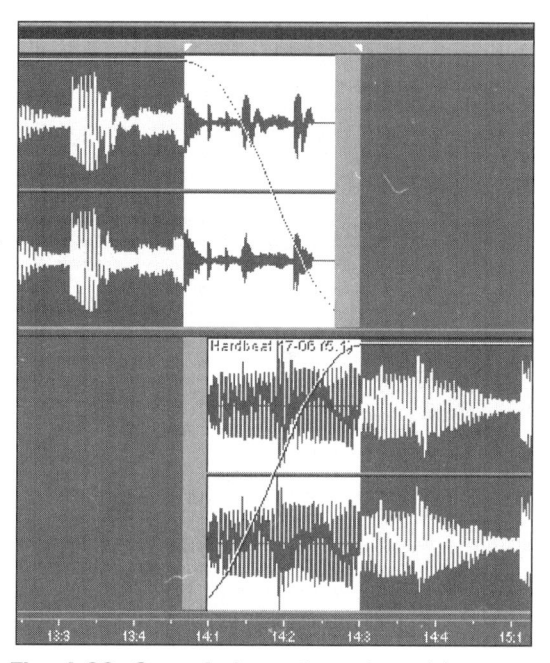

Fig. 4.98. Crossfade on the selected fragment

- **Take History** (the list of takes) is a list that is created when takes are recorded in the **Punch In** mode.

  NOTE The take selected from the list is "pasted" into the clip.

- **Loop Duplicate** — multiple copying of the clip (Fig. 4.99). In the window that opens when this command is performed, the following controls are used:
  - The **Duplicate waveform** field sets the number of copies
  - **No gaps — continuous looping** sets the mode for placing the copies without pauses
  - **Evenly Spaced** places the copies with equal time intervals between them (the value of these intervals is specified in the associated field)

- **Convert to Unique Copy** saves the clip in a separate file.

  TIP After an action is applied to the clip, such as **Loop Duplicate**, the destructive editing of one copy of the clip affects the sound of *all* copies. This is so

Chapter 4: Cool Edit Pro as a Universal Solution for Home Studios 255

because, physically, the same region of the audio file is processed. To avoid this situation, *before* you apply destructive editing, *convert* the selected clip into a physical copy using the **Convert to Unique Copy** command.

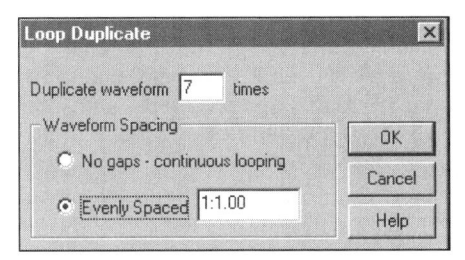

Fig. 4.99. The **Loop Duplicate** window

- **Mute Waveform, Lock in Time, Lock for Play Only** — components of the **Wave Block Info** window duplicated in the menu.
- **Allow Multiple Takes** allows you to save the previous copies when recording is performed over the clip.

   NOTE   You can restore copies using the **Take History** option.

- **Splice** — this non-destructive operation splices the clip along the cursor line or along the boundaries of the selected region.
- **Merge/Rejoin Splice** merges spliced parts of the clip (this action is the opposite of **Splice**).
- **Adjust Boundaries** — this non-destructive operation adjusts the boundaries of the clip to exactly match the boundaries of the selected region.

   NOTE   This action is similar to "trimming" the clip in SAWPro.

   If the clip was adjusted to a size less than its original one, selecting an area larger than the clip size and applying the **Adjust Boundaries** option moves the clip's boundaries.

- **Trim** non-destructively removes the parts of the clip that are outside the selected region.
- **Full** increases the clip size to the size of the entire audio file.
- The **Clear Envelope** submenu removes the nodes used for graphically editing the volume and panorama. Accordingly, it contains the **Volume Points** and **Pan Points** items.
- **Remove Wave Block** removes the selected clips from the multitrack.

- **Destroy Wave** removes all the selected clips from the multitrack and closes the audio files. The program prompts you to save the changes in the files to be closed.

Setting Shortcut Keys

The Cool Edit Pro software allows you to "program" shortcut keys. To do so, open the **Options/Shortcuts (Keyboard & MIDI Triggers)** menu, and in the dialog box that appears, select the correspondence between the hotkey and the program function from the list (Fig. 4.100).

The settings of the hotkeys you make are saved in the coolcust.ini file, located in the Windows (Winnt) folder.

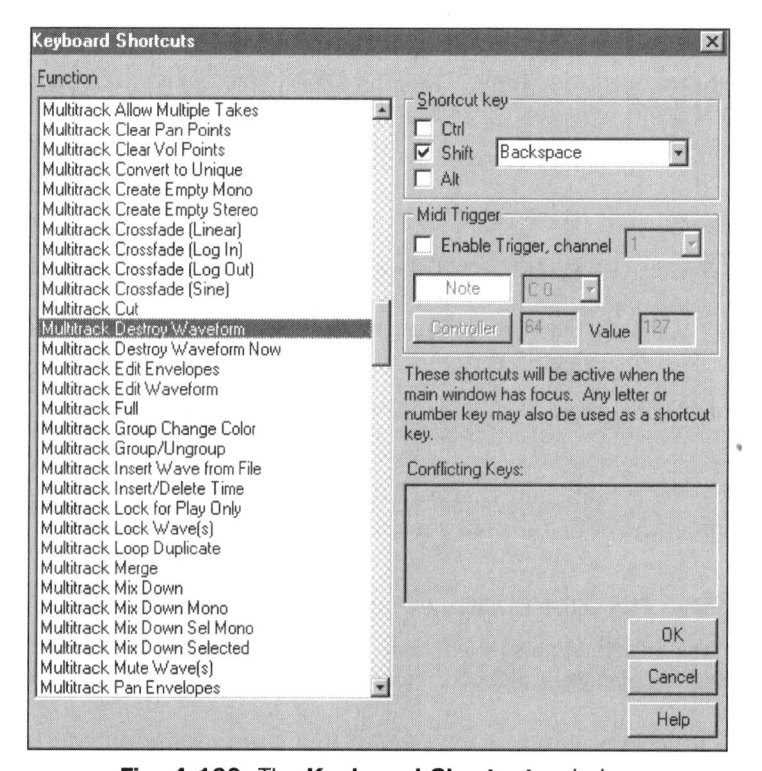

Fig. 4.100. The **Keyboard Shortcuts** window

The Track Pop-up Menu (*TRACK PROPERTIES*)

The track pop-up menu is called by right-clicking in any free space of the track (Fig. 4.101).

Chapter 4: Cool Edit Pro as a Universal Solution for Home Studios   257

Fig. 4.101. The **TRACK PROPERTIES** menu

The purpose of the most important items of the track's pop-up menu is described below.

❒ **Insert** submenu — creates new clips on the multitrack. This submenu contains:

- **Wave from File** — creates a clip of an audio file that is *not included* in the list of files opened by the program (**Waveform List**).
- **Waveform List** — the list of files opened by the program. Each file from this list can be located on the multitrack in different ways: entirely (**Entire Waveform**), the selected region only (**Current Selection**), or the region selected from the cue list (**Cue List**).

❒ The **Mix Down to Track** submenu creates the file for final or intermediate mixing in the *selected region* or on the *entire multitrack*:

- **All Waves** — all the clips included in the selected region are mixed *vertically*.
- **Selected Waves** — *only* selected clips (located on one or different tracks) are mixed. To make such a selection, it is convenient to use the <Ctrl> + left-click combination.

> **NOTE** The format of files after mixing (32-bit or 16-bit) depends on the state of the **Mixdowns** checkbox in the **Multitrack** tab in the **Settings** window.

❒ **Insert/Delete Time** — allows you to perform the following actions in the dialog box:

- Insert a time interval *in numerical representation*, or *equal to the selected region*
- Delete a time interval *equal to the selected region*

- **Mute**, **Solo**, and **Record** correspond to the **m**, **s**, and **r** buttons on the multitrack console.
- **Solo This Track Only** — enables the **Solo** *priority mode* in case the **Solo** mode is also enabled on other tracks.
- **Select All Waves in Track** — selects all clips located on the track (the same action is performed if you double-click the track).

Snapping to the Musical Measure and Tempo

In the **Multitrack View** window, the **Time Ruler** context menu is used for snapping to the musical measure and tempo.

In this menu, the units of measure (**Bar and Beats**) are selected, **Snapping** to the units of the grid or to the boundaries of another clip is performed, and the tempo and the musical measure of the composition are edited (**Edit Tempo**).

NOTE The mechanism of snapping to the musical measure and tempo in the **Multitrack View** window is the same as in the **Edit Waveform View** window.

The **Bar and Beats** units of measure are identical to the **Measure and Beat** units used in SAWPro.

An example of performing the **Snapping** function is shown in Fig. 4.102.

When you move a clip that crosses the boundaries of another clip (**Snap to Waves**) or the marks on the **Time Ruler** (**Snap to Ruler**), a vertical white line appears on the corresponding boundary of the clip. Its presence means that the clip is exactly aligned according to one of the **Snapping** methods.

The Fragment Recording Mode

Recording in the **Multitrack View** window is performed in the same way as in the editor window. The only difference is that you have to press the **r** (**Record**) button *beforehand* on the console of the track on which you want to record.

NOTE In **Multitrack View**, you can record on several tracks simultaneously, having pressed the **r** buttons on the corresponding consoles.

Remember that recording always starts from the place on the track where the cursor is positioned. If an area is selected, recording is done only in the selected area of the multitrack.

The *Punch In* Mode

In this mode, the order of actions you perform during recording is as follows:

1. You should first select the clip fragment in which recording is to be done.

Chapter 4: Cool Edit Pro as a Universal Solution for Home Studios 259

2. Then you should call the pop-up menu (by right-clicking on the clip) and select the **Punch In** command.

   NOTE The following changes are made: the selected region becomes red, and the **r** button on the console of this track "glows" (Fig. 4.103).

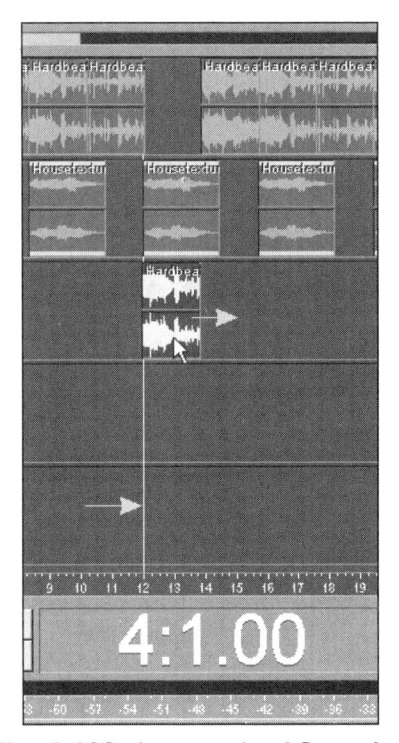

Fig. 4.102. An example of **Snapping**

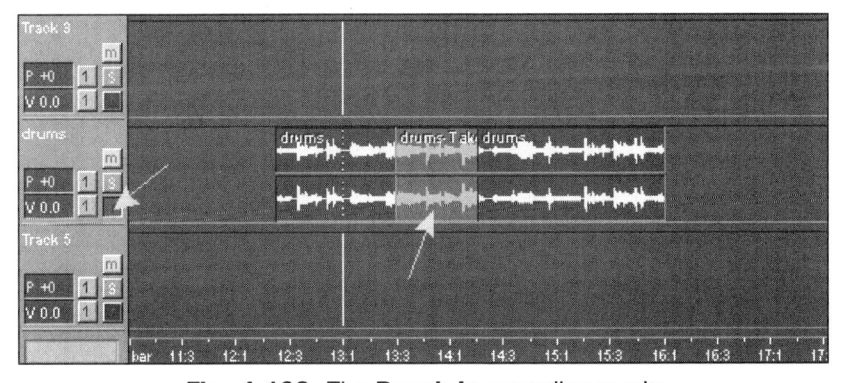

Fig. 4.103. The **Punch In** recording mode

3. Then, set the cursor to the beginning of the clip.

   NOTE It is best to preserve some distance before the selected region, as shown in Fig. 4.103.

4. Then press the **Record** button on the **Transport** panel. The recording automatically starts *on the selected region of the clip only*.

The above algorithm is very convenient for creating takes when you are recording a "live" performance.

NOTE The advantages of the **Punch** recording mode are described in detail in Chapter 3.

Using the *Take History* Submenu

The **Take History** submenu of the **WAVE PROPERTIES** window contains the list of takes. This list is used in two cases:

❐ If the recording was made in the **Punch In** mode

❐ If *multiple* recording over the clip was performed when the **Allow Multiple Takes** option was selected

In both cases, *all* the recorded takes are saved in the **Take History** list (Fig. 4.104).

NOTE The combinations of shortcut keys corresponding to the menu items (shown in Fig. 4.104) were set by the authors.

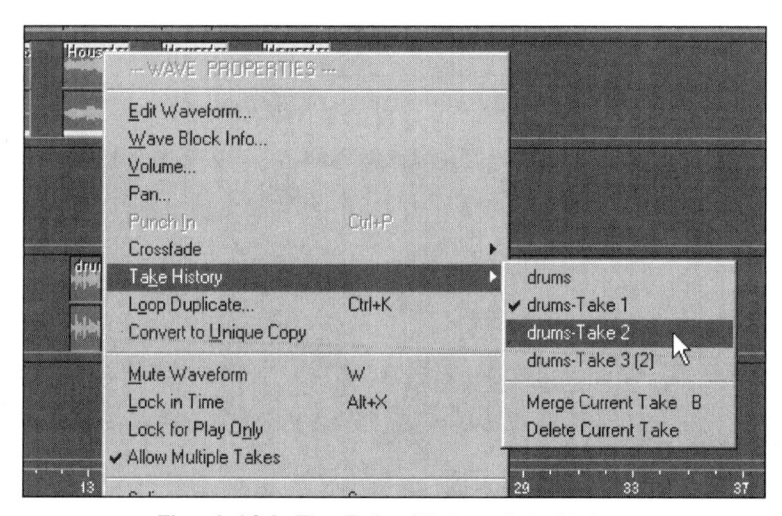

Fig. 4.104. The **Take History** list of takes

Chapter 4: Cool Edit Pro as a Universal Solution for Home Studios

To listen to a take, select it from the **Take History** list. To do so, check the checkbox near the take name.

The take selected in the list is placed into the track, and is called the **Current Take**.

You can perform the following operations on the selected (active, current) take: delete it using the **Delete Current Take** command, or "paste" it using the **Merge Current Take** command.

> **NOTE** The take is attached destructively when you apply the **Merge Current Take** command.

If the **Delete old takes after merging** option is selected in the **Multitrack** tab of the **Settings** window, old takes are deleted automatically after merging.

Using the *Loop Duplicate* Function

If the musical composition contains looped fragments, it is convenient to use the **Loop Duplicate** function (see Fig. 4.99).

> **NOTE** The **Loop Duplicate** function allows you to make multiple copies of the clip. The interface of this function was described in detail in the description of the **WAVE PROPERTIES** pop-up menu (see Fig. 4.99).

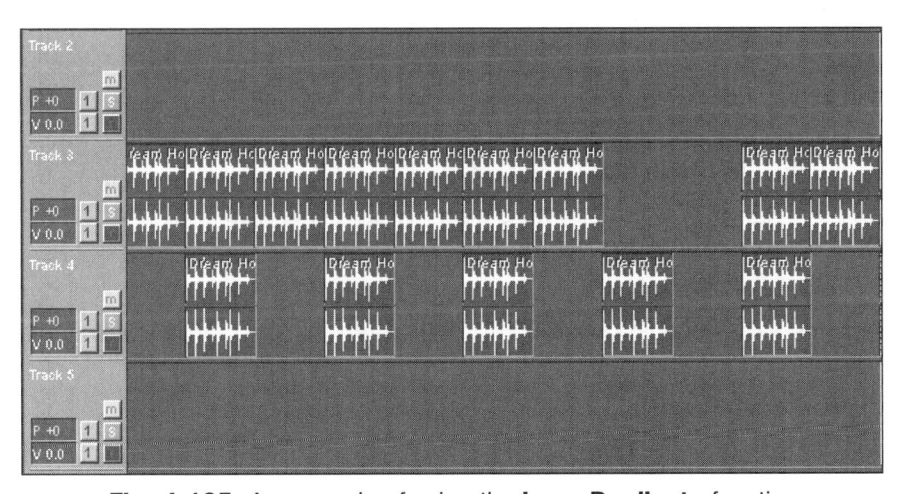

Fig. 4.105. An example of using the **Loop Duplicate** function

Remember that multiple copying of the clips may be performed both without pauses and with fixed pauses. In Fig. 4.105, an example of two variants of applying the **Loop Duplicate** function is shown.

Methods of Editing the Audio Material in the *Multitrack View* Window

Some non-destructive editing operations were described when we looked at the **WAVE PROPERTIES** pop-up menu. We will now describe some "workable" methods of editing the project.

> **NOTE** You can cancel any non-destructive editing operations in the **Edit** menu with the **Undo** command.

- *Moving a clip* is done by dragging with right mouse button inside the multitrack

> **NOTE** Remember that the **Lock in Time** option prohibits horizontal movement.

- *Moving a group of clips* is done in two stages:
  1. A group of clips is selected. To do this, with the <Ctrl> key pressed, click on each of the selected files (the color of the selected files changes and becomes brighter).
  2. Having released the <Ctrl> key, drag the group of clips with the right mouse button to the new location.
- *Copying a clip* is done by dragging with the right mouse button when the <Shift> key is pressed.
- *Copying a group of clips* — is done by dragging with the right mouse button while the <Shift> key is pressed
- *Copying a clip and creating a copy of the audio file* is done by dragging with the right mouse button while the <Ctrl> key is pressed
- *Copying a group of clips and creating copies of the audio files* is done by dragging with the right mouse button while the <Ctrl> key is pressed
- *Selecting all clips of one track*
  - First method — double-click on any empty point in a track (one *without a clip*)
  - Second method — with the <Ctrl> key pressed, double-click on *any clip* of the selected track
- *Undoing the selection of all clips of one track* is done by clicking on any empty point in the track
- *Transferring a clip into the editor window* (for destructive editing) is done by double-clicking on the clip
- *Creating a group of clips* (for further editing as one clip) is done using a special command of the **Group Waves** pop-up menu, applied to the group of selected clips

Chapter 4: Cool Edit Pro as a Universal Solution for Home Studios 263

Color and Graphical Differences in a Group of Clips

Clips that are edited the same way (within a group) are marked by two horizontal lines of the same color (Fig. 4.106). You can change the color of these grouped clips using the **Group Color** command of the pop-up menu.

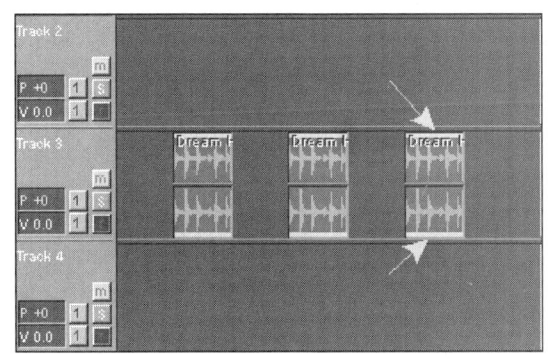

Fig. 4.106. An example of a group of clips

❒ To separate the clips, uncheck the **Group Waves** item of the pop-up menu.

TIP — ***How to accelerate changing the zoom.*** When you edit a large number of tracks, you often have to change the vertical and horizontal zoom (**Zoom**). Changing the zoom is a rather slow process, since redrawing the waveform of each clip takes a lot of time.

You can accelerate changing the zoom by limiting the height of the track when the waveform is displayed in detail. You can do this in the **Multitrack** tab of the **Settings** window, called from the **Options** menu. In this tab, you should change the value of the **Display Waveforms At** field and specify a value from 50 to 70 pixels vertically.

TIP — ***For inexpensive sound cards***, it is recommended that in the **Multitrack** tab in the **Open Order** and **Start Order** sections you set the switches to the **Rec** and **Play** positions.

TIP — ***Hotkeys.*** For frequently used commands of the pop-up menus, it makes sense to assign shortcut keys, since they both simplify and accelerate your work. You can do this using the **Options/Shortcuts (Keyboard & MIDI Triggers)** menu. It is best to use the first letter of a command, for example: **Volume** — <V>, **Pan** — <P>, **Splice** — <S>, etc.

Hotkey settings that we recommend are supplied on the disk that comes with the book, in the coolcust.ini file. If you want to use them, find this file in the Windows (Winnt) folder.

Graphically Editing the Volume and Panorama

Each clip of the multitrack can have independent settings for the volume and the panorama, which are copied when the clip is copied.

> **NOTE** The settings remain whenever either copying method is applied: both when a separate clip is copied, and when the "entire" clip is copied (*also creating a copy of the audio file*). We should mention that in the latter case, the clip settings remain, and the copy of the audio file is not destructively changed.

To create the curves of change for the volume and panorama, Cool Edit Pro uses graphic editing.

To switch to the volume and pan graphic editing mode, proceed as follows:

1. Select the following options from the **View** menu:
   - **Show Pan Envelopes**
   - **Show Volume Envelopes**
   - **Enable Envelope Editing**
2. Click on the corresponding button with the icon located on the toolbar where all these options are duplicated (their names are contained in pop-up hints).

After you have initiated the graphic editing mode, you can start editing the volume and panorama curves. The actions you perform are the typical ones (Fig. 4.107):

1. Click on the line, and a marker will appear. It is displayed as a white square.
2. Having pressed the mouse button, drag the marker to a new location (you can move the marker anywhere between two neighboring points).

> **NOTE** By default, the curves of the volume and panorama are positioned horizontally: the volume curve is on the top of the clip, and the panorama curve is in the middle (see Fig. 4.107).

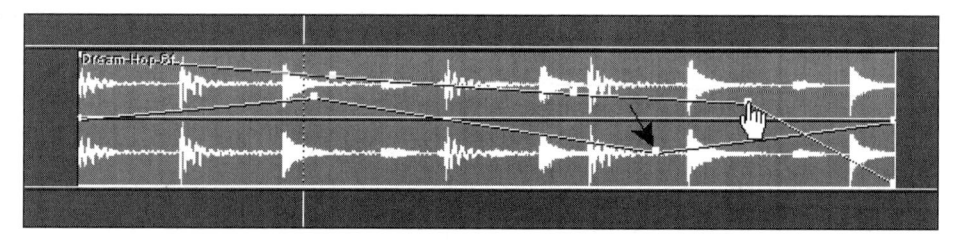

Fig. 4.107. An example of graphically editing the volume and panorama

You can remove the editing nodes. To do so, proceed as follows:

1. Select the region of the clip you want to delete.
2. Perform one of the following commands of the **WAVE PROPERTIES** menu:
   - **Clear Envelope/Volume Points**
   - **Clear Envelope/Pan Points**

> **NOTE** Do not be surprised when, after you delete the nodes, the curves of the volume and the panorama do not return to their initial *horizontal* state. They might become *slanted*, since the initial and final points of the clip are automatically connected when you cancel the editing. You can only restore the state of the slanted line manually.
>
> When the clip is copied, the graphic editing lines are also copied.

Applying the Effects of the *Transform* Menu

You should know that you can apply sound processing (effects) to the material recorded in the **Multitrack View** window only in the editor window — **Edit Waveform View**.

To perform such processing:

1. Double-click on the selected clip.
2. After you switch to the editor window, call the necessary effect from the **Transform** menu.

> **NOTE** The whole waveform included in this clip is displayed in the editor window.

Cool Edit Pro saves all physical copies of *each stage of editing*. This is done despite the fact that it takes up hard drive space, because it is part of the rules for delayed destructive editing. The **Free Hard Drive space** function of the **File** menu is used to control the free hard disk space.

This function opens a window whose elements we'll now describe in detail (Fig. 4.108).

- The **Waveform** list contains a list of the audio files of which the session consists.
- The **Undo History** list enumerates the destructive editing operations for the file selected from the **Waveform** list.
- The **Clear Undo(s)** button deletes previous copies of the file and frees hard disk space. However, you cannot return to the previous state of the audio file after this.
- In the **Reserve** (free) fields, the free (reserved) hard drive space is indicated (see Fig. 4.108).

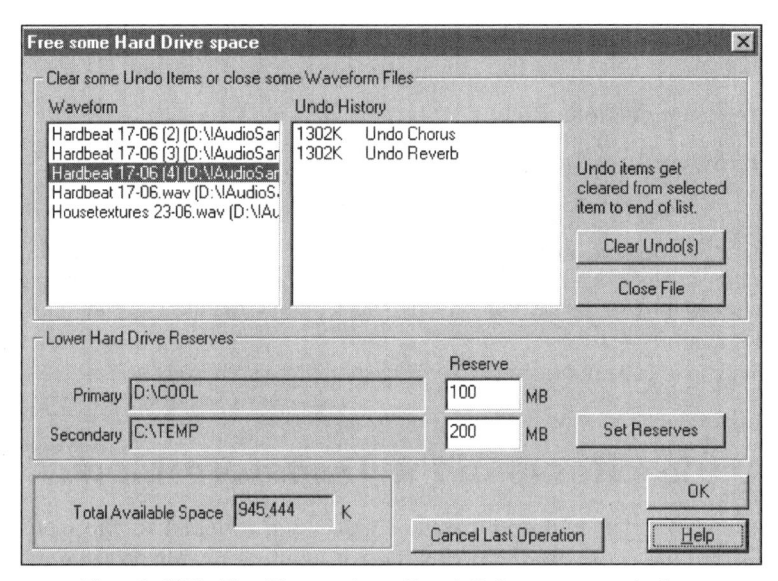

Fig. 4.108. The **Free some Hard Drive space** window

> **NOTE** If the hard disk is full (the free space is less than what is specified in the **Reserve** field), the warning window **Free some Hard Drive space** automatically appears on the screen.

- Using the **Cancel Last Operation** button, you can cancel the last destructive editing operation when the **Free some Hard Drive space** warning window appears.

- In the **Total Available Space** field, the total available hard drive space is displayed (in KB).

- The **Close File** button closes the audio file selected in the **Waveform** list.

> **NOTE** Cool Edit Pro prompts the user to save the changes made to the file, i.e., to apply delayed destructive editing.

The **Purge Undo** button (**Settings** window, **System** tab) removes all undo levels (all physical copies) besides the last few. (The number of remaining undo levels is specified in the **Levels (minimum)** field.)

> **NOTE** This means that if, for example, the initial undo level was 10, and you apply the **Purge Undo** operation with a minimum of 5 levels, you can only go five steps back after that, i.e., only the *last* 5 undo actions are saved.

Batch Processing in Cool Edit Pro

When you use destructive editing (apply effects), it often becomes necessary to apply them *in a certain order*.

NOTE For example, to process a vocal part, you may have to apply the following sequence of effects: **Dynamic Processing**, then **Graphic Equalizer**, then **Delay,** and so on.

The **Dynamic Processing** effect may be applied twice with different presets, such as **Vocal Compressor II** and **De-Esser Light** (to reduce "whistling" sounds).

Because such a processing sequence may be repeated a number of times, it makes sense to automate it. Cool Edit Pro provides you with this ability. Automating the application of effects is provided by means of user-defined macro programs. In Cool Edit Pro these are called scripts, and are set in the **Scripts & Batch Processing** window called from the **Options** menu.

NOTE Script files are regular text files with the SCR extension.

You will find the scripts folder in the coolpro folder, and there are some "built-in" script files stored in it. One SCR file may contain several scripts, so, according to the terminology accepted in the Cool Edit Pro software, it is correct to call an SCR file a *collection of scripts*.

It is better to start learning about scripts with the "built-in" collections (Fig. 4.109).

We'll now describe the **Scripts & Batch Processing** window.

- The **Run Script** button *starts* script execution.

- The **Pause at Dialog** checkbox interrupts the script execution before each operation is performed, i.e., it *calls a dialog box* in order to allow you to change the settings of the effect.

- **Alert when complete** — upon script completion, enables the output of a *completion alert.*

- **Executive Relative to Cursor** — defines the script execution area from the current cursor position to the end of file.

- The **Edit Script File** button allows you to edit an SCR file in the Notepad editor.

Scripts can be of three types.

NOTE The script type is indicated in one of the three lower sections of the **Scripts & Batch Processing** window (see Fig. 4.109) when the script is selected in the list in the left part of the **Script Collections** section.

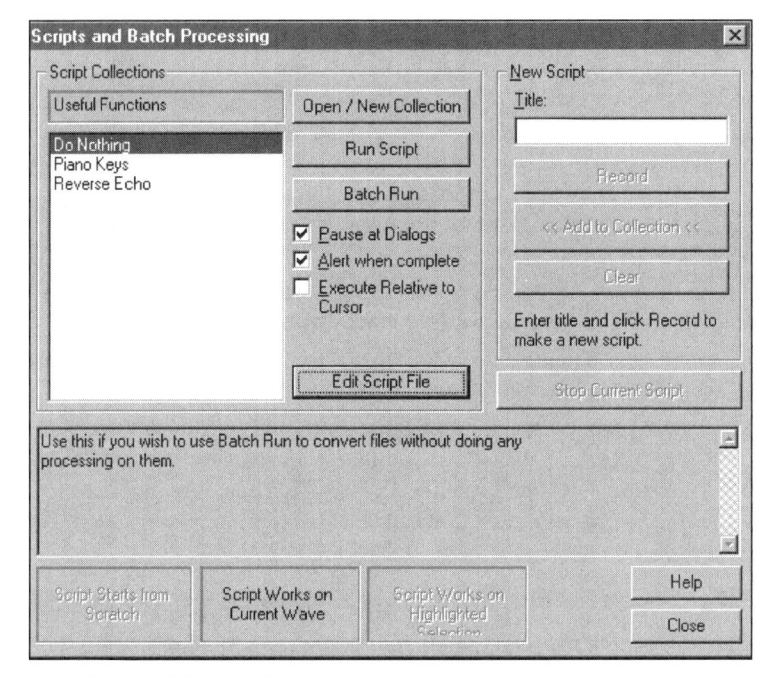

Fig. 4.109. The **Scripts and Batch Processing** window

- **Script Start from Scratch** — a script that starts with the creation of a new file (**File/New**). (Such a script is used to synthesize sounds.)

- **Script Works on Current Wave** — a script for processing the current waveform. The *entire audio file* is processed, without selecting any particular region.

> **NOTE** This is the only script type that can be used with **Batch Processing**.

It is for this script type that the **Executive Relative to Cursor** option is intended.

- **Script Works on Highlighted Selection** — only the selected region is processed.

> **NOTE** If you start script execution without selecting anything, the area from the current cursor position to the end of file is processed.

The **Open/New Collection** button calls the **Choose a script file** window (Fig. 4.110), in which you can open or create an SCR file.

After you have opened or created the SCR file, you can start recording the script. Proceed as follows:

1. Supply the script name in the **Title** field of the **New Script** section (see Fig. 4.109).

Chapter 4: Cool Edit Pro as a Universal Solution for Home Studios 269

2. Press the **Record** button in the same section, and perform all the editing actions in order.
3. After the last editing action has completed, press the **Stop Current Script** button.

> **NOTE** If a mistake was made while executing the script, you can clear the recording with the **Clear** button and repeat all the actions, starting with supplying the script name in the **Title** field.

If the script was recorded successfully, you can save it in a collection using the **<<Add to Collection<<** button (in Fig. 4.109 it is not available). If you do, the title of the new script will appear in the collection list.

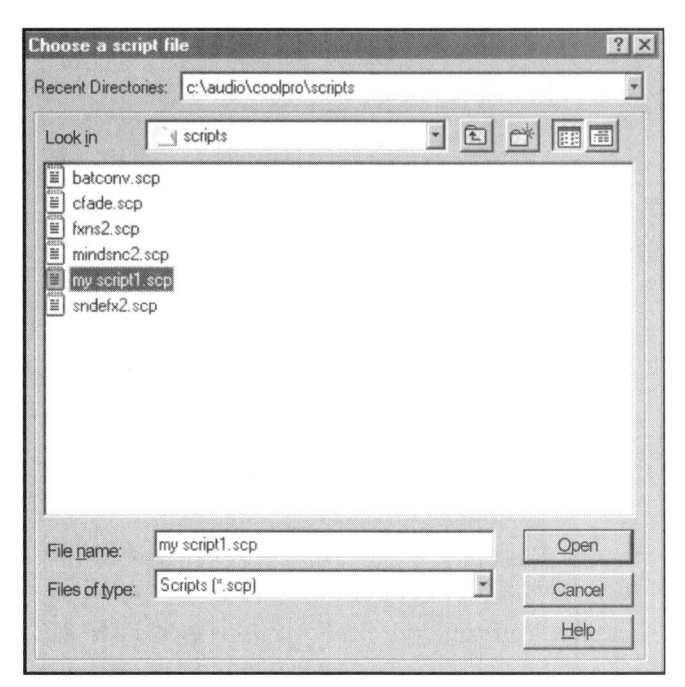

Fig. 4.110. The script file selection window

> **NOTE** Besides effects, various operations — such as changing the format, copying or deleting the selected region, etc. — may be recorded into a script.

DirectX effects are not available during the script's recording.

Batch processing assumes a higher level of automation — the application of *the same script to a group of files*.

To start the batch mode, you have to select a script of the **Script Works on Current Wave** type and start the processing by pressing the **Batch Run** button (see Fig. 4.109).

The **Batch Process** dialog box opens (Fig. 4.111).

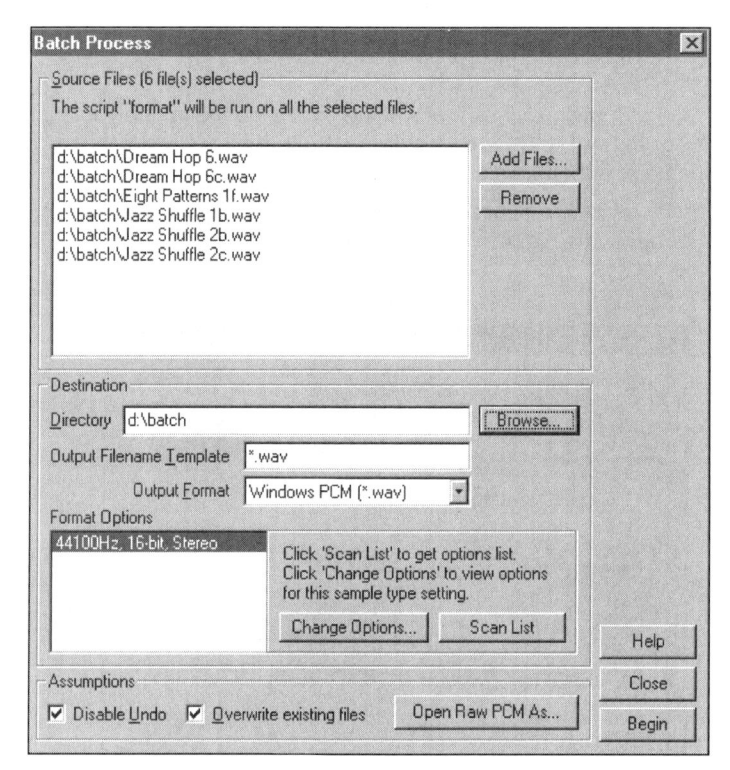

Fig. 4.111. The **Batch Process** dialog box

The list of files — **Source Files** — is located in the upper part of this box. This list displays the names of those files to which the batch processing is applied.

Initially, the box is empty. You can add files to it using **Add Files**, and delete files using the **Remove** button.

In the **Directory** field of the **Destination** section, specify the directory into which the processed files will be placed. You can use the **Browse** button for this purpose.

In the **Output Filename Template** field, you should specify the file extension. You can use additional letters and/or digits in the extension mask (for example, the *32.wav template converts the guitar.wav file into guitar32.wav).

In the **Output Format** list, select an output format that differs from the current format, if you plan on converting the files (in this book, we describe only the Windows PCM (WAV) format).

The **Change Options** button activates the format parameters window if these parameters are available for the selected type of files.

Chapter 4: Cool Edit Pro as a Universal Solution for Home Studios 271

The **Scan List** button scans the initial files and creates a list of their characteristics in the **Format Options** window.

The components of the **Assumptions** section — **Disable Undo** and **Overwrite existing files** — define additional settings of the batch processing.

❑ **Disable Undo** — batch processing is performed without the ability to undo

❑ **Overwrite existing files** — after processing, new files are written over the existing files

Mixing and Mastering in Cool Edit Pro
Background Mixing

The Cool Edit Pro software provides you with the ability to perform *background mixing*.

Background mixing means that all the tracks of the multitrack are continuously mixed into a temporary file, and only this file is played.

> **NOTE** Each editing action performed by the user (changing the volume, deleting, moving the clip) is traced by the software, and is considered during background mixing.

To help you track this process, the special **Mix Gauge** indicator is used (Fig. 4.112).

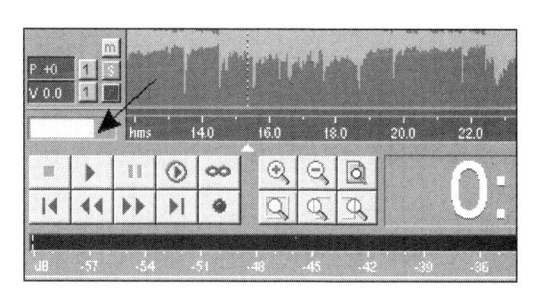

Fig. 4.112. The **Mix Gauge** indicator

When background mixing is complete, the **Mix Gauge** indicator changes — it becomes green.

However, you don't have to wait for the "green light" — you can edit the multitrack without the background mixing completion signal.

If a large number of editing actions are to be performed, you can disable background mixing. To do so, double-click on the image of the **Mix Gauge** indicator. Two crossed red lines appear instead of the indicator (Fig. 4.113).

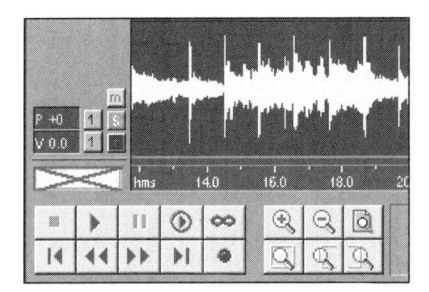

Fig. 4.113. Disabled background mixing

How to Avoid the Sound's Interruption

If you simultaneously edit many tracks, an effect of short sound interruption may appear. To avoid this, you can do one of the following. You could disable background mixing altogether. Or, you could increase the **Playback Buffer Size** or increase the number of such buffers (the **Settings** window, **Multitrack** tab).

Using the List of Markers — *Cue List*

Markers (or cues) add considerable convenience to your work.

The SAWPro software provides the separate **Markers View** window for markers, while in Cool Edit Pro, a list of markers — **Cue List** — is used.

You can add either separate points or track fragments to the list of markers.

NOTE In the list of markers, a point is indicated by one coordinate, and a selected area is indicated by two coordinates (Fig. 4.114).

For example, the cursor position can be indicated by a point, and a selected clip fragment can be indicated by two coordinates.

You can call the **Cue List** in two ways:

- With the **Cue List** command in the **View** menu

- With the **Open Cue List** button (Fig. 4.115) located on the toolbar

Navigation among the cues is implemented in a convenient manner. Double-clicking on any cue in the list (see Fig. 4.114) automatically moves the cursor to the corresponding point of the track (if the cue has one coordinate), or selects a fragment (if the selected area was associated with that cue).

You can *add a marker* to the list using the **Add** button in the **Cue List/Ranges** window, or using the **Add current selection to Cue List** button (Fig. 4.116) located on the toolbar.

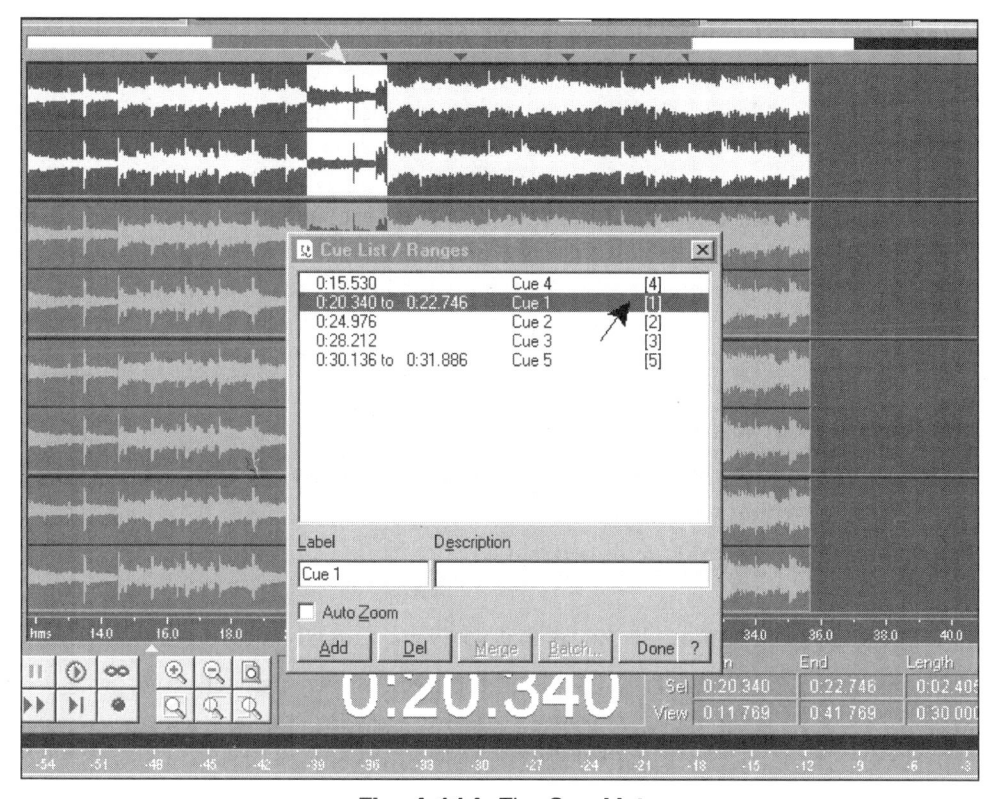

Chapter 4: Cool Edit Pro as a Universal Solution for Home Studios   **273**

Fig. 4.114. The **Cue List**

Fig. 4.115. The **Open Cue List** button

Fig. 4.116. The **Add current selection to Cue List** button

Specific Features of Mixing in the 32-Bit Format

If you intend to create a 32-bit project, you should set the following switches in the **Settings** window of the **Multitrack** tab:

❏ **Default Rec** in the **32-bit** position

❏ **Mixdowns** in the **32-bit** position

❏ **Playback Mixing** in the **32-bit Pre-mixes** position

This is very important, because it guarantees that there will be no decrease in the quality of the sound. Otherwise, "random" intermediate mixing into 16-bit format may lower the quality.

Due to this, you should definitely convert all 16-bit files that you plan on importing to the session into 32-bit format.

You can perform this conversion automatically. To do so, before you perform the conversion, check the **Auto-convert all data to 32-bit upon opening** checkbox (the **Settings** window, **Data** tab).

Because the 32-bit format makes more demands on the PC than the 16-bit format, you may need to increase the number of **Playback Buffers** and **Recording Buffers**. You can change their number in the same window, in the **Multitrack** tab.

Intermediate Mixing

The main purpose of intermediate mixing in Cool Edit Pro is to reduce the number of tracks in order to free up resources.

Intermediate mixing can be done in two ways.

The first method:

1. Press the **s** (**Solo**) button on the tracks that you want to mix.
2. Call the **TRACK PROPERTIES** menu on the free track by right-clicking.
3. Execute the **Mix Down to Track/All Waves** command in the pop-up menu.

> **NOTE** When this method is used, all the tracks (on which the **Solo** buttons are activated) are mixed, from the multitrack beginning to the last clip.

The second method:

1. Select only the clips that you want to mix.
2. Right-click on a free track to call the **TRACK PROPERTIES** pop-up menu.
3. Execute the **Mix Down to Track/Selected Waves** command in the pop-up menu.

> **NOTE** An example of intermediate mixing using this method is shown in Fig. 4.117.

In both cases, the tracks on which the **m** (**Mute**) button is pressed are not mixed, and neither are the clips for which the **Mute** command from the pop-up menu was executed.

If an area is selected on the tracks, intermediate mixing is performed only in this area (Fig. 4.118).

> **NOTE** A clip excluded from mixing (a clip for which the **Mute** command is applied) is in black.

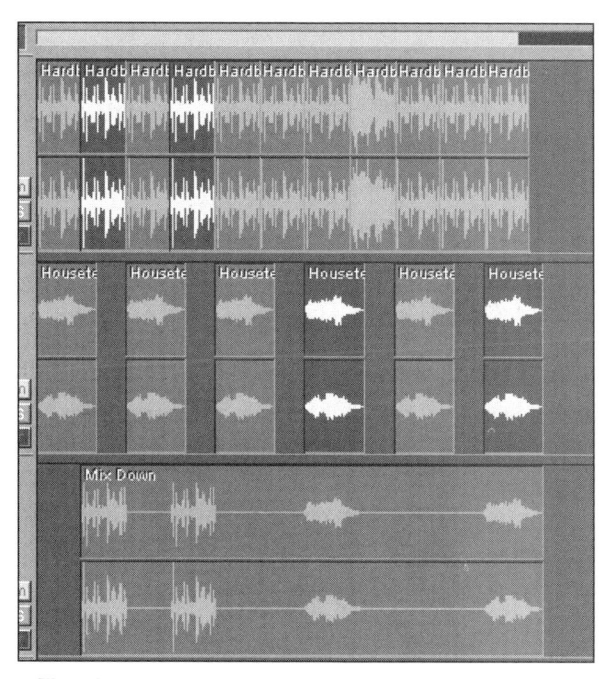

Chapter 4: Cool Edit Pro as a Universal Solution for Home Studios 275

Fig. 4.117. Intermediate mixing of selected clips

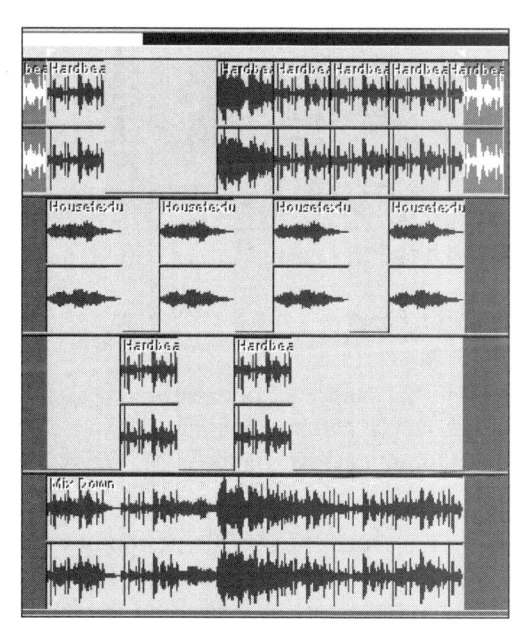

Fig. 4.118. Intermediate mixing of a selected area

Mixing

Unfortunately, Cool Edit Pro does not provide for separate indication of the volume level of each track (as opposed to SAWPro).

Thus, you have to rely solely upon your hearing.

You can control the general output level using the **Level Meters**.

NOTE **Level Meters** are described in detail in the "*Edit Waveform View*" section (*Fig. 4.20*).

The pop-up menu of the **Level Meters** settings is shown in Fig. 4.119.

The **Show on Play and Record** option enables the indication mode during recording and playback.

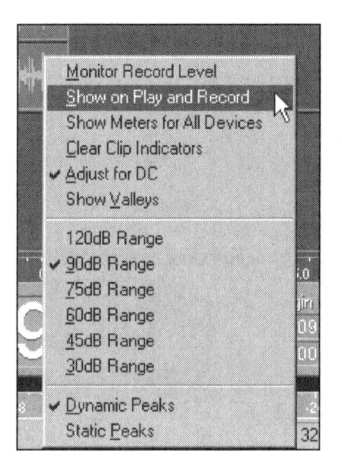

Fig. 4.119. The **Level Meters** pop-up menu

The mixing algorithm given in *Chapter 3* for SAWPro can be used with Cool Edit Pro, but in an even simpler manner.

1. To change the volume and the pan level in a particular area of the track, it is best to select this fragment in a *separate clip* by applying the **Splice** command. Then you can correct its volume and panorama (**Wave Block Info**).

2. You can adjust the volume and panorama each with a different precision. Clicking on the button below or above the slider changes the position by 0.01 dB. By clicking below or above the volume slider, you change the position by 0.5 dB. You can also input the values of the selected volume or panorama level from the keyboard into the slider's numerical field.

Chapter 4: Cool Edit Pro as a Universal Solution for Home Studios

3. You can control the output level of the track using the **Level Meters** by temporarily setting the **Solo** mode on this track.

4. The total level is controlled by the **Master** slider.

5. Final mixing is performed in the **Edit/Mix Down/All Waves** menu, and the resulting file is placed only in the editing window.

Mastering

In Cool Edit Pro, you should *always* perform mastering (final processing of an audio file) in 32-bit format. Even if the session has a 16-bit resolution, final mixing should be done to a 32-bit audio file.

> **NOTE** You can do this in the **Settings** window in the **Multitrack** tab by setting the **Mixdowns** switch to the **32-bit** position.

In *Chapter 8*, we will describe the specific features of mastering in detail. Here we should note that for mastering in Cool Edit Pro, you can apply the same DirectX module as in WaveLab.

Besides this, we recommend that you apply amplitude peak reduction effects provided by Cool Edit Pro, such as **Hard Limiting** from the **Transform** menu.

> **TIP** This effect is similar to the **Limiter** module of the **Comp/Gate/Limiter** set provided in SAWPro.

After you have completed mastering, you should convert the 32-bit format into 16-bit format for publication on an AUDIO CD.

To get a "transparent" and clear sound, we recommend that you set the following conversion parameters (Fig. 4.120):

- **Dither Depth (bits)** — 0.54

- **p.d.f.** (probability distribution function) — **Shaped Triangular**, **Noise Shaping C3**

Cool Edit Pro is first and foremost a powerful audio editor.

Its multitrack function is still considered just an addition.

Judging from experience in working with this software, we think that the multitrack of Cool Edit Pro is the best tool for creating a simple project that occupies no more than 8 tracks.

> **NOTE** The Cool Edit Pro software is very convenient for creating programs in which both an announcer's speech and music are present (radio programs, audio advertising, etc.).

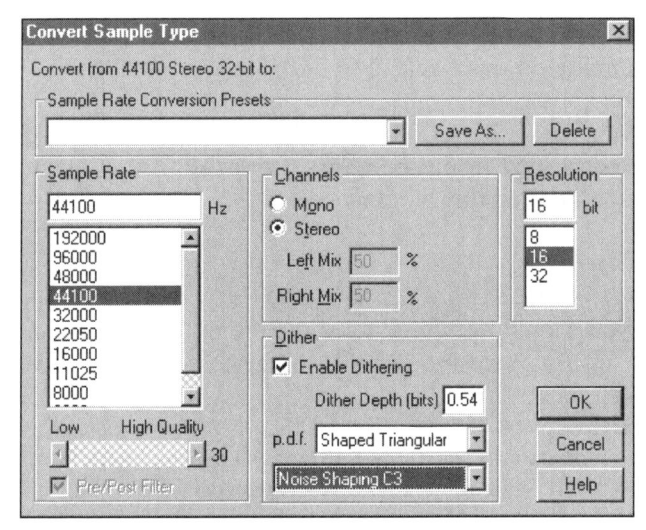

Fig. 4.120. Parameters of the conversion from 32-bit format into 16-bit format

All the above is connected with the basic principle of audio processing implemented in Cool Edit Pro — the principle of delayed destructive editing. For example, in SAWPro, when you have only one set of initial audio files that make up a project, you can create an infinite number of modifications of EDL virtual projects with different configurations of Direct-X and VST modules. In contrast, in Cool Edit Pro, you must save each new processing variation in destructively processed files. This takes much more free hard disk space, and limits the number of project modifications.

In *Chapter 5* we'll describe the Samplitude 2496 software, which, from our point of view, combines advantages of both SAWPro and Cool Edit Pro. In other words, Samplitude 2496 is at the same time a powerful professional audio editor and a virtual multitrack with an unlimited number of configurations of plugged effects.

NOTE The Samplitude 2496 software, despite all the advantages it provides, is not the "ideal" tool. As an audio editor, it has less processing algorithms than Cool Edit Pro, and, as opposed to SAWPro, it does not support VST plug-ins.

Chapter 5

THE SAMPLITUDE 2496 APPLICATION AS A HIGH-QUALITY VIRTUAL STUDIO

Chapter 5: The Samplitude 2496 Application as a High-Quality Virtual Studio

Experience shows that a user can always find a musical program to best suit a certain musical task. For the choice to be successful, the user must first state clearly his or her requirements for the final result, and second, take into account the features of the equipment used for recording.

In *Chapters 3* and *4*, we discussed the SAWPro and Cool Edit Pro applications and their advantages and disadvantages.

The Samplitude 2496 application (versions 5.55 to 5.57) discussed in this chapter extends the list of programs that, in our opinion, provide the user with many opportunities when recording and processing a "live" performance on acoustic and electronic instruments.

The SEK'D company (**http://www.sekd.com**), who developed this application, gives it the following description: "The 24-bit 96 kHz Mastering and Multitracking Software".

In other words, Samplitude 2496 is a self-sufficient, fully functional virtual studio, with very high sound quality. Moreover, the concept of virtuality put forward by SEK'D is unique. Unlike the previously discussed solutions, it doesn't include such notions as clips and regions. The developers of Samplitude 2496 extended these notions, and decided to use the concept of virtual *objects*. An object is a region of an audio file that is located on a multitrack. It allows you to connect virtual effects directly. The idea of non-destructive editing (editing that doesn't destroy the original audio file) was developed even further in this application.

Now, in a Samplitude 2496 *virtual project* (multitrack), you can not only connect channel effects directly to a track, but you can also connect them to an object itself, that is, to a clip that has certain properties. When being moved or copied, an object retains its sound, all its settings, and its internal configuration.

One advantage of Samplitude 2496 is that it is able to combine MIDI objects and AUDIO objects in one project. This allows you to easily import a MIDI project created, for example, in Samplitude 2496, and continue recording a "live" performance in the sound file format.

Despite its high potential, Samplitude 2496 poses relatively modest requirements to the system resources of the computer. For the program to work, a Pentium 200 MMX, 32 MB RAM, and any Windows-compatible sound card will suffice. The reliability and performance of Samplitude 2496 are higher on Windows NT 4.0 or Windows 2000. In order to work comfortably with the virtual mixer, you may wish to use a display with a resolution of 1024 × 768.

The developers of Samplitude 2496 optimized its code for Pentium III. This is why the internal virtual effects of the program have the highest performance level on computers with a Pentium III processor.

The number of tracks in a virtual project depends *only on the system resources of your computer*.

Another important advantage of Samplitude 2496 is *the ability to perform high-quality mastering* and create AUDIO CDs.

The Samplitude 2496 Interface

Program Installation

The installation of Samplitude 2496 is fully automated. For this reason, we aren't going to concentrate much on it, but we would like to give you some advice: if your hard disk is divided into logical disks, install the program in the largest of them.

> **NOTE** The application will always be able to use any files located on any partition of the hard disk.

The shortcut to Samplitude 2496 — a "sound wave" icon — is shown in Fig. 5.1.

Fig. 5.1. The shortcut to Samplitude 2496

The Main Window of the Program

No special settings are required to start Samplitude 2496. Immediately after the program starts, its main window opens (Fig. 5.2).

The first time the program starts up, the **Startup Screen** panel appears over the main window. It is designed to teach the user how to work with the application. This friendly component of the interface offers you several ways of learning Samplitude 2496 (according to the labels on the buttons). One of the options is **Open tutorial**. This loads an example of a training project from the Tutorial folder.

You can avoid the subsequent appearance of this panel by unchecking the **Always show on Startup** checkbox.

> **NOTE** Another panel — **About Samplitude 2496** — also appears at startup. It can be disabled in the same manner, by unchecking the **Show on Startup** checkbox.

Both the **Tutorial** and **About Samplitude 2496** panels can be accessed via the **Help** menu.

Chapter 5: The Samplitude 2496 Application as a High-Quality Virtual Studio

You should note that before a new project is created (or before an existing one is loaded), most buttons in the main window are unavailable. Only three buttons, which allow you to create or load a project, are active (Fig. 5.2).

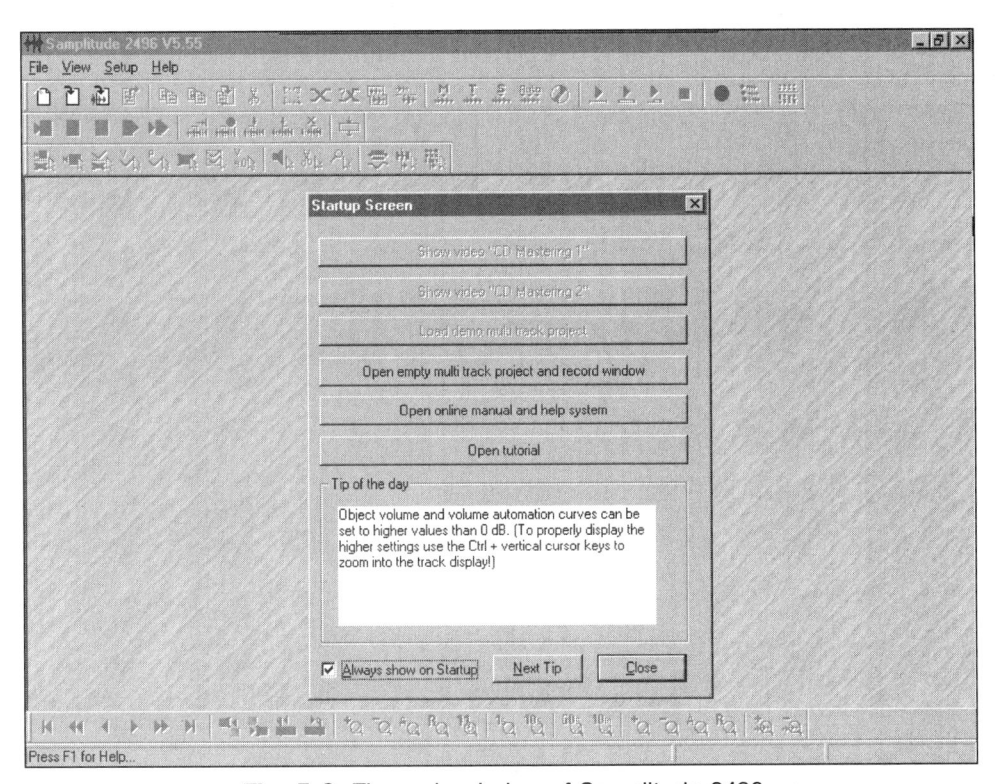

Fig. 5.2. The main window of Samplitude 2496

Immediately after a new project is created or an existing one is loaded, the application gives the user access to all the available menus.

> **NOTE** You can open a new project in several ways: with the **New Multitrack Project** item of the **File** menu, with the <E> hot key, or by clicking the corresponding icon. (Creating a new virtual project is discussed in the "*Types of Projects in Samplitude 2496*" section.)

Like Cool Edit Pro, Samplitude 2496 has a friendly interface, which includes both pop-up menus and pop-up hints. The latter appear in two places at once: immediately below the icon pointed to by the mouse, and in the status bar at the very bottom of the window (Fig. 5.3).

The program lets you create and edit various types of projects (for more detail on this, see "*Types of Projects in Samplitude 2496*").

All types of projects are located in the main window. Some of them can be maximized on the screen, the others traditionally remaining minimized.

In Fig. 5.3, you can see the NEW.VIP project in minimized form.

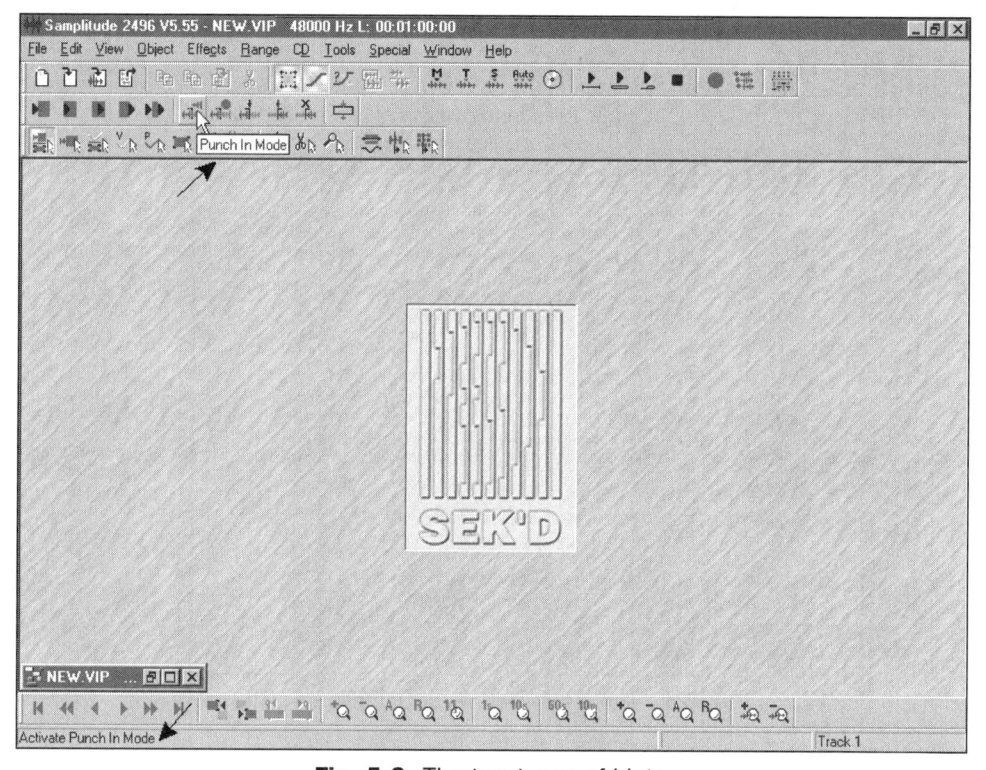

Fig. 5.3. The two types of hints

NOTE VIP stands for "VIrtual Project".

In the main window, you can create your own toolbar configuration.

This is very easy to do. After right-clicking at any place in the toolbar, the **Toolbar Settings** dialog box will open (Fig. 5.4), which allows you to add buttons to or delete buttons from the toolbar:

1. In the **Toolbar** list, click the toolbar button whose configuration you want to change. This selects the button.

Chapter 5: The Samplitude 2496 Application as a High-Quality Virtual Studio

2. In the **Buttons** list, click the necessary tool to select it.
3. Click the **Add** button to add the tool to the selected toolbar.

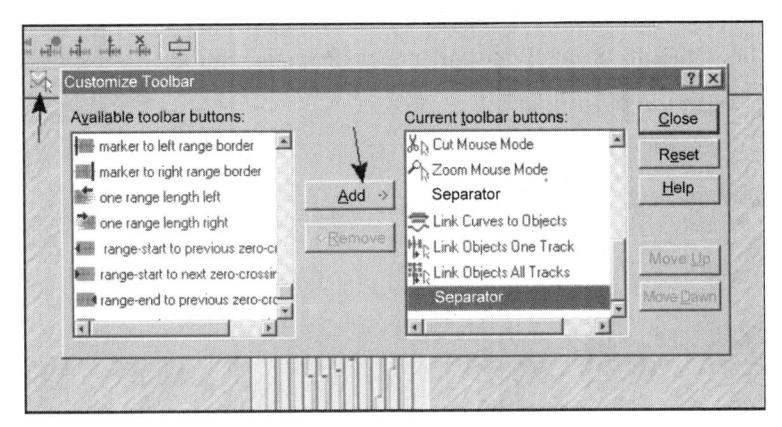

Fig. 5.4. Setting up a toolbar

NOTE The **Delete** button is used for the opposite operation.

If you wish, you can separate groups of buttons with a vertical separator line. For this purpose, add the separator at the desired place in the **Toolbar** list.

NOTE In the list, the separator for separating a group of tools is located above the first button of the group (Fig. 5.5).

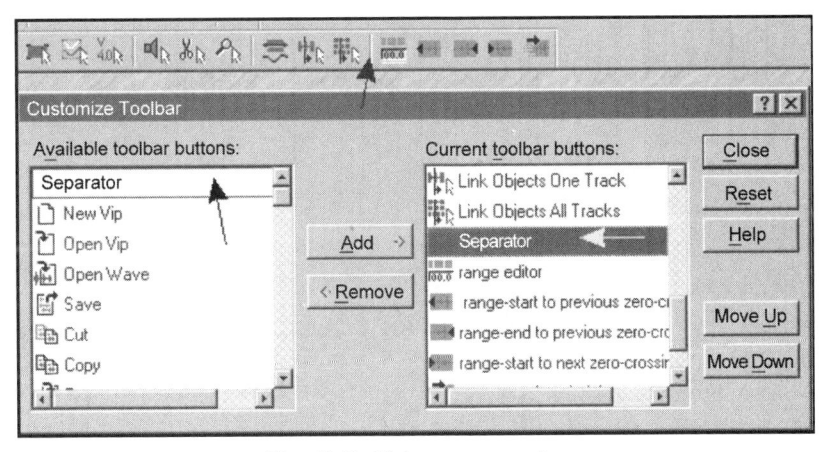

Fig. 5.5. Using a separator

All toolbars can be easily dragged over the window to any place you choose.

Fig. 5.6 illustrates a sample toolbar layout in the main window.

There is a special transport panel in Samplitude 2496. It is opened with the **Transport Control** command of the **Window** menu (Fig. 5.7).

Let's discuss the functions of the **Transport** panel (from left to right, as shown in Fig. 5.8):

- Set the cursor to the beginning of the project
- Rewind
- Reverse playback
- Stop
- Playback
- Fast forward
- Record

Like the Cool Edit Pro editor, Samplitude 2496 allows you to set shortcuts.

The dialog box where this procedure is performed is opened using the **Edit Keyboard Shortcuts** command of the **File|Preferences** menu.

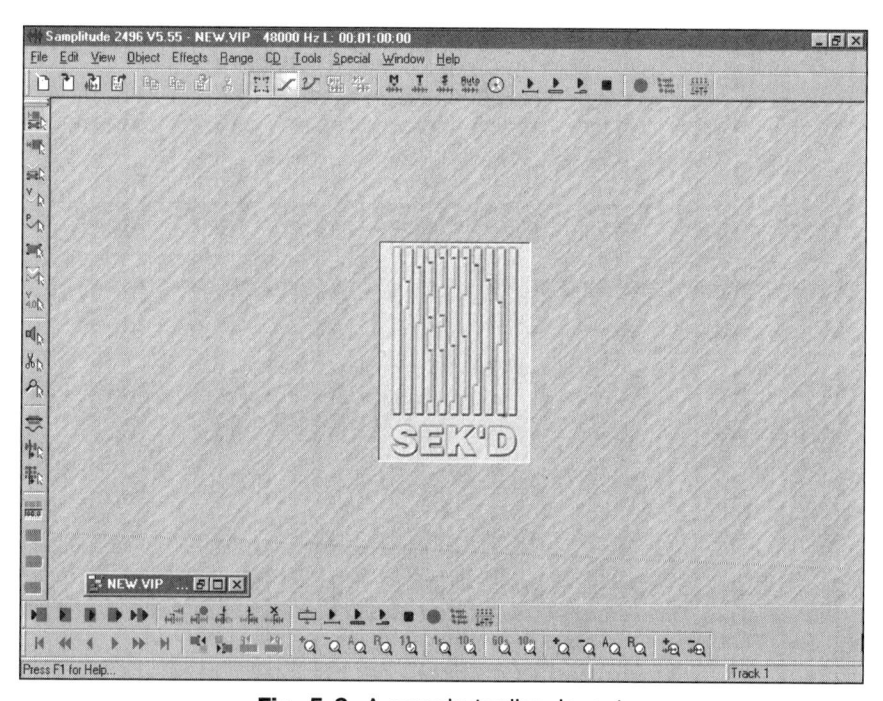

Fig. 5.6. A sample toolbar layout

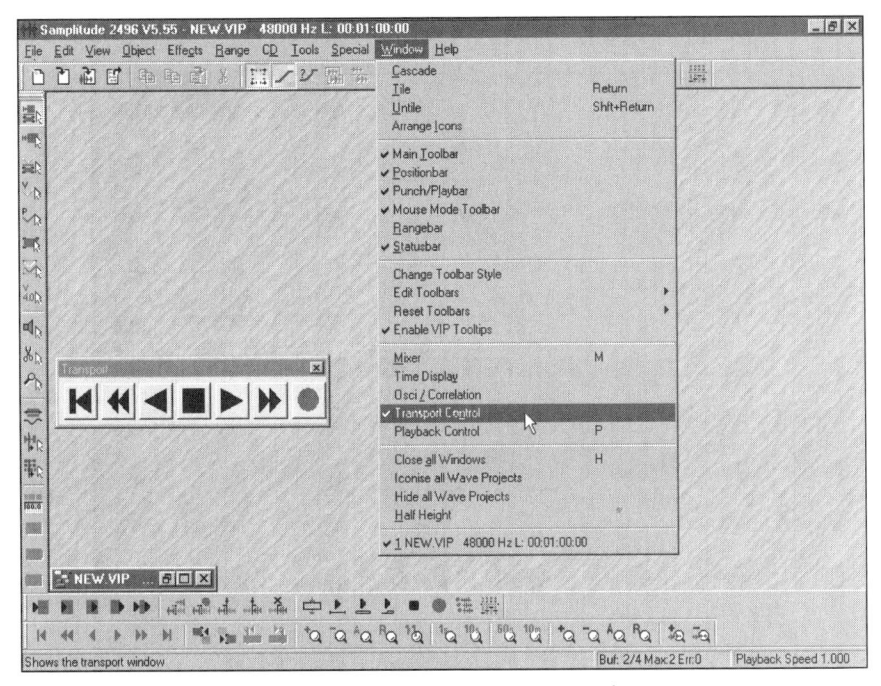

Chapter 5: The Samplitude 2496 Application as a High-Quality Virtual Studio

Fig. 5.7. The **Transport** panel

Fig. 5.8. The buttons of the **Transport** panel

In the **Edit Keyboard Shortcuts** dialog box, the items of all the menus of the program are listed (Fig. 5.9). To set up a correspondence between a shortcut and a menu item, proceed as follows:

1. Click the item in the list to select it.
2. Click the text box in the **New Shortcut** section.
3. Press the key or the key combination (for example, <Shift>+<F>) that will become the shortcut.
4. To conclude the procedure, click the **Assign new Shortcut** button. The shortcut will appear in the text box above the **Delete** button (indicated by the arrow in Fig. 5.9).
5. Click the **OK** button.

If the chosen key combination is already in use, a warning message will appear, suggesting that you either change the shortcut or cancel the operation.

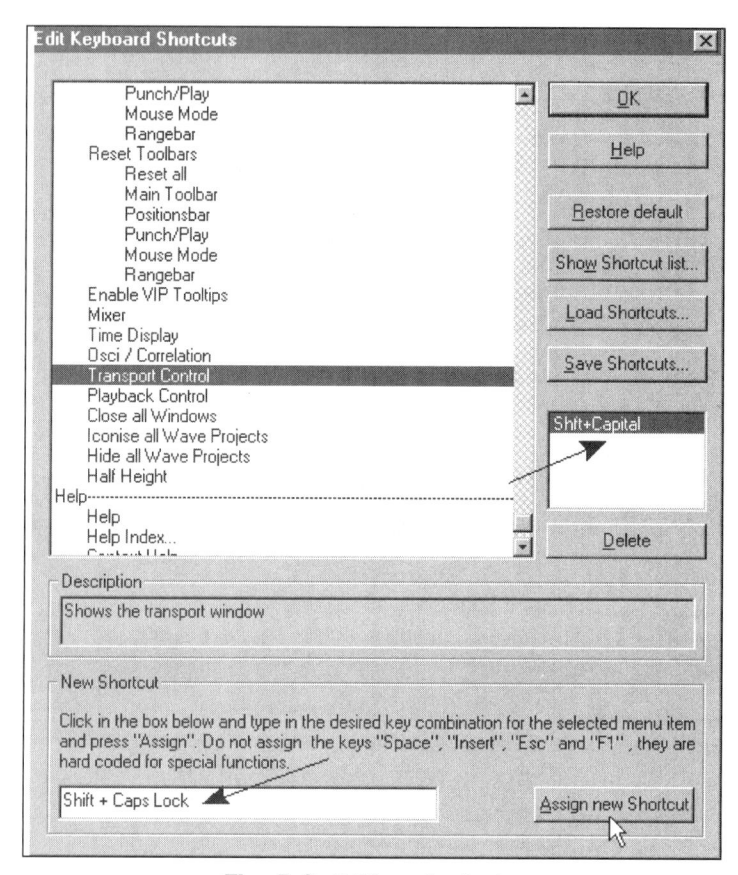

Fig. 5.9. Editing shortcuts

The *Shortcut List*

You can view all shortcuts if you click the **Show Shortcut list** button.

This list is saved in a separate file using the **Save Shortcuts** button, and loaded with the **Load Shortcuts** button (Fig. 5.9).

The **Restore default** button (Fig. 5.9) resets the list to its original state (before editing).

Files containing shortcuts have the SSC extension (Fig. 5.10).

Notice that the destructive and non-destructive editing methods in Samplitude 2496 go very well together.

NOTE Obviously, destructive editing will remain a "hot" topic until processors with a clock rate from the UHF range appear.

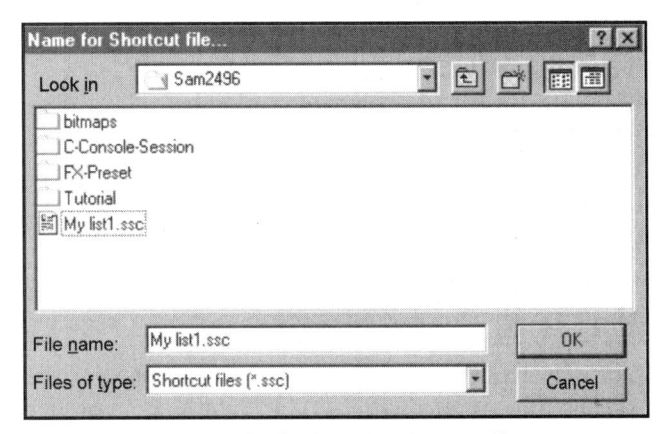

Chapter 5: The Samplitude 2496 Application as a High-Quality Virtual Studio 289

Fig. 5.10. Saving the shortcut list

When both editing methods are employed, the number and the properties of undo levels are of particular interest.

Samplitude 2496 allows you to setup the undo function independently for different types of editing. The maximum number of undo levels permitted (100) doesn't depend on the editing method used.

Setting the number of levels is done with the **File|Preferences|Undo definitions** menu in the **Undo Options** window (Fig. 5.11).

For *non-destructive* editing (or *virtual* editing, in Samplitude 2496 terms), the number of undo levels is set in the **Undo** field in the **Virtual** section.

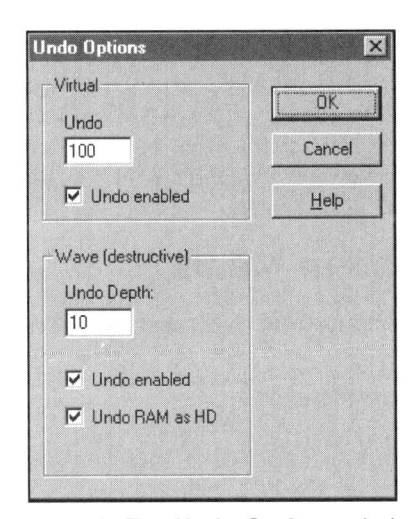

Fig. 5.11. The **Undo Options** window

NOTE The **Undo enabled** checkbox must be checked.

The **Undo Depth** field of the **Wave (destructive)** section specifies the number of the undo levels for destructive editing.

NOTE When setting the undo depth, you should keep in mind that every undo level of destructive editing is actually a physical copy of the audio file, which *reduces the free space* on the hard disk. This is why we don't recommend that you set values greater than 10.

The **Undo enabled** checkbox must be checked.

Getting a bit ahead of ourselves, we'd like to focus on the **Undo RAM as HD** option (see the checkbox in the **Wave (destructive)** section). The developers of Samplitude 2496 have provided for a special type of audio file — the RAM project. It is well known that data exchange between the RAM and the hard disk is much slower than inside the RAM.

NOTE A *RAM Wave project* is a sound file that is stored *in the hard disk* and is loaded into the *RAM* during startup.

Thanks to the fact that a RAM project uses a lot of random-access memory, Samplitude 2496 can achieve an astonishing performance level when working with virtual multitracks. Moreover, RAM projects can be edited destructively, just like common audio files.

NOTE However, this brilliant idea isn't free from drawbacks. First of all, the demands on the computer's memory are quite high. And second, information is lost when a power failure occurs.

Since the RAM's resources might be insufficient, a special setting is provided to save the undo levels (the copies of the RAM projects). It is called **Undo RAM as HD**. This option switches on the mode where the copies of the RAM projects are saved in the hard disk. We therefore recommend that you enable this option. RAM projects are more closely examined in the "*Types of Projects in Samplitude 2496*" section.

Setting up the System Menu

Before using any multitrack application, it is good to know the answers to the following "system" questions:

❐ How will the created files be named?

❐ Where will they be located?

❐ What are the system settings of the program?

❐ Where are the system settings located, and how can they be changed?

Chapter 5: The Samplitude 2496 Application as a High-Quality Virtual Studio

In Samplitude 2496, all the answers to these questions can be found in the **System** window.

If no project is loaded, the **System** window is available in the main window via the **System** command of the **Setup** menu.

After loading or creating a project, the **System** window can be opened either with the <Y> hotkey or through the **File|Preferences** menu.

In the upper part of the **System** window (Fig. 5.12), you can find fields that specify the locations of Samplitude 2496 projects. Notice that the project file locations can be arbitrary.

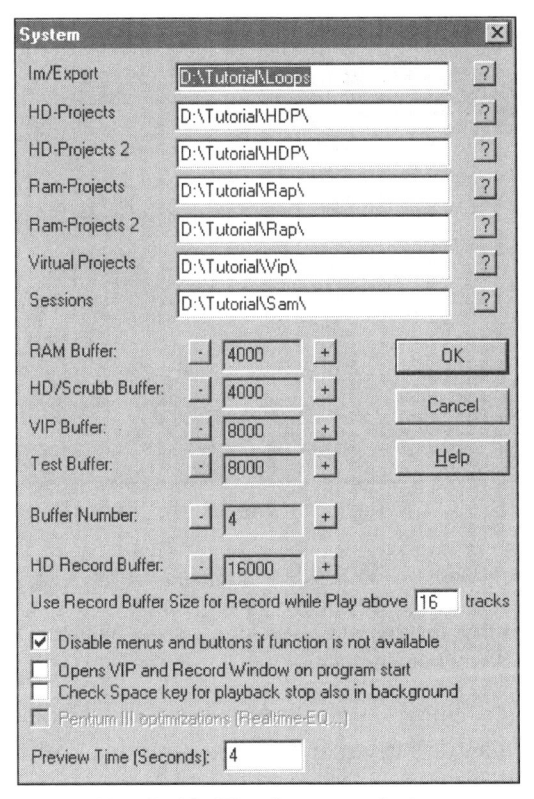

Fig. 5.12. The **System** window

NOTE In the example shown in Fig. 5.12, all projects are located in the Tutorial folder. This is done intentionally, in order to vividly demonstrate a certain system of placing the files. (All the folders containing various projects have appropriate names, and are included in the Tutorial folder.)

The button with the question mark (**?**) on it opens the **Path for import and export** window. There, you can not only browse through the folder, but also listen to the files contained in it by clicking the **Play** button (Fig. 5.13).

To use the disk space more effectively, you might want to place the HD-projects2 and RAM-projects2 folders on another logical (or physical) drive.

Here are the most important settings of Samplitude 2496.

- **RAM Buffer** is a reserved area in the RAM that is used during the playback of *RAM Wave* projects.

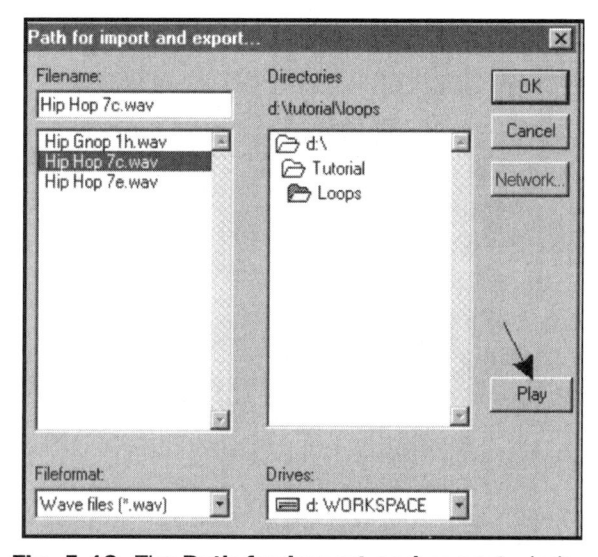

Fig. 5.13. The **Path for import and export** window

> **NOTE** The default value is 4,000 samples. Decreasing this parameter leads to a quicker response to the **Play** command during playback. However, you should keep in mind that failures are likely in this case. You can find the best value for the **RAM Buffer** parameter experimentally.

- **HD/Scrubb Buffer** is a buffer in the RAM that is used during the playback of *HD Wave* projects. By default, it is equal to 4,000 samples. Feel free to experiment with this parameter as well.

The Buffers

The **RAM Buffer** and the **HD Buffer** are used during the playback of RAM Wave projects and HD Wave projects, respectively.

When playing back a virtual project, the **VIP Buffer** is used.

Chapter 5: The Samplitude 2496 Application as a High-Quality Virtual Studio

- **VIP Buffer** is a buffer for virtual projects. It is used during the playback of multitrack virtual projects. Sometimes you have to change its size when editing a project.

    > **NOTE** The default value is 8,000 samples. However, with a large number of tracks and when using the virtual mixer, you'll need to increase the buffer size to 16,000 samples, or even more. When employing virtual effects, an insufficient size of the buffer can lead to CPU overload.

    On the other hand, an excessive VIP buffer size can slow down the response to the **Play** command during the playback of a VIP project.

- **Test Buffer** allows you to preliminarily listen to the virtual effects of the **Effects** menu in real-time mode. The default value of this parameter is 8,000 samples.

    > **NOTE** *Virtual effects* (enabled in the object editor or the virtual mixer) use the VIP buffer for preliminary playback in real time.

- **Buffer Number** sets the number of buffers used during the project playback. (When a RAM project is played back, this is the number of RAM buffers; when it is a VIP project, the parameter specifies the number of VIP buffers, and so on).

    > **TIP** The valid range for this parameter is from 2 to 9. By default, 4 buffers are used. When choosing a value, it is important to keep in mind that decreasing the number of buffers can lead to failures during playback, whereas increasing it slows down the response to the **Play** command. Moreover, larger numbers increase the requirements to the RAM size. This is why a middle value is the best.

- You can control the value of this parameter in the status bar of Samplitude 2496. During playback, the status bar is located in the lower part of the window (Fig. 5.14).

Fig. 5.14. The status bar

NOTE In the example shown in Fig. 5.14, the status bar reads **Buf:2/5 Max:3 Err:0**. This message means that 5 buffers are set, two of which are currently used. Also, a maximum of 3 buffers are active, and the number of playback errors is 0. Therefore, in this particular case, the total number of buffers can be decreased, say, to 4.

Since the most difficult mode for Samplitude 2496 is playback of a virtual project, it is necessary to choose the buffer number in this mode.

Buffer Size

The total buffer size of a virtual project is obtained by multiplying the *size* of one buffer by the *number* of buffers. (VIP buffer total = **Buffer Number** × **VIP Buffer**).

For example, if the buffer size is 16,000 samples, and the number of buffers is 2, the total value for the VIP buffer is 32,000 samples. 8 VIP buffers of 4,000 samples would also give us a size of 32,000 samples.

From the mathematical standpoint, the results are equal in both cases. However, as practice shows, the program's performance isn't the same.

In some cases, the best results are reached by increasing the *number of buffers*, whereas in other cases it is better to increase the *size of the VIP buffer*. You can control the ratio in the status bar that indicates the CPU load (Fig. 5.15).

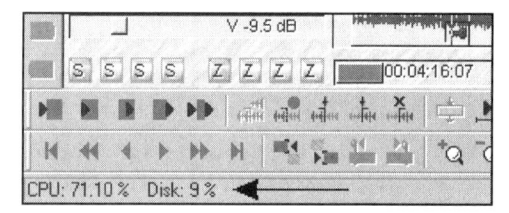

Fig. 5.15. The CPU status bar

- **HD Record Buffer** defines the length of the blocks of data recorded to the hard disk. The default value is 16,000 samples. As a rule, this parameter doesn't need any adjustment.
- **Use Record Buffer Size for Record while Play above ... tracks.** When recording and playing back simultaneously, if the number of tracks is greater than the value specified in this field, the **HD Record Buffer** value will be used. The default is 16.
- **Disable menus and buttons if function is not available.** When this checkbox is unchecked, an attempt to enable an unavailable mode or command will cause a warning message.
- **Open VIP and Record Window on program start.** This means that a new VIP is created, and the **Record Parameter** window is opened when the program starts.
- **Check Space key for playback stop also in background.** This means that the spacebar will be used to control playback in background mode.

Chapter 5: The Samplitude 2496 Application as a High-Quality Virtual Studio 295

> **NOTE** The spacebar can be used to start or stop the playback. If you turn on the listening mode and enter a *different* application (say, Microsoft Word), pressing the spacebar key in that application will stop the playback.

- **Pentium III optimizations.** If Samplitude 2496 is installed on a computer with the Pentium III processor, this checkbox will be checked automatically.

> **NOTE** This optimization significantly increases the program's performance as regards using virtual effects in real time.

- **Preview Time (Seconds)** sets the length of the fragment in the **Preview** mode for virtual effects.

> **NOTE** In this mode, the application first computes the musical fragment and then plays it back. This allows you to adjust effects that don't work in real time.

Additional Settings

In versions 5.55 to 5.57 of Samplitude 2496, certain settings that increase the performance of the application are available.

They can be accessed via the **File|Preferences** menu, by selecting its **TrackSpeed settings** item. This causes the **TrackSpeed settings** dialog box to appear (Fig. 5.16). Let's look at it more closely.

This dialog box demonstrates new features of Samplitude 2496 that were absent in earlier versions.

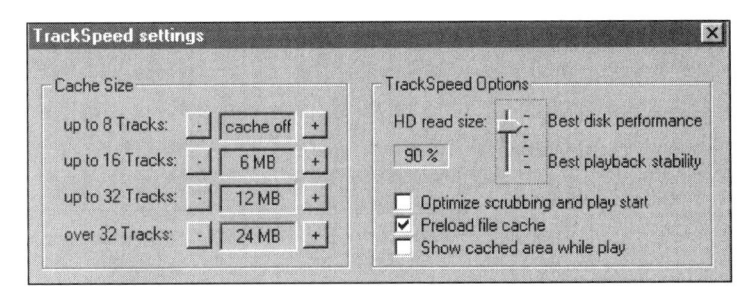

Fig. 5.16. The **TrackSpeed settings** dialog box

More specifically, this dialog box is designed to set the parameters for caching your virtual projects.

> **NOTE** Recall that the cache is an area in the memory (in our case) where copies of the data located in the hard drive are stored. Caching increases the program's performance, since it reduces the number of times that accessing the "slow" hard drive is necessary.

In the **Cache Size** section, projects are sorted by the number of their tracks. For example, if the **up to 8 Tracks** option is selected, the specified cache size will be valid for no more than 8 tracks.

> **NOTE** The size of the cache in each field can be changed using the **+** and **−** buttons located to the left and right of the field.

There are three checkboxes and a slider in the **TrackSpeed Options** section.

- The **HD read size** slider should be set to 100% (**Best disk performance**). If any failures occur, you may want to move the slider down one position. However, remember that failures might be caused by an insufficient size of the cache or the VIP buffer as well.
- The **Preload file cache** checkbox is used to switch on the mode where the cache is initialized before playback starts, that is, when the cursor is positioned at any point of the multitrack.

> **NOTE** Enabling this function can spare you errors when beginning the playback of a project with many tracks.

- When the **Optimize scrubbing and play start** checkbox is checked, it reduces the delay between the click with the left mouse key and the start of scrubbing playback.

> **NOTE** The scrubbing playback mode is discussed in the section "*VIP Mouse Editing Modes*".

- The **Show cached area while play** checkbox lets you visually control the effectiveness of caching.

Fig. 5.17 illustrates an example of the graphical representation of the cache for each track during the playback.

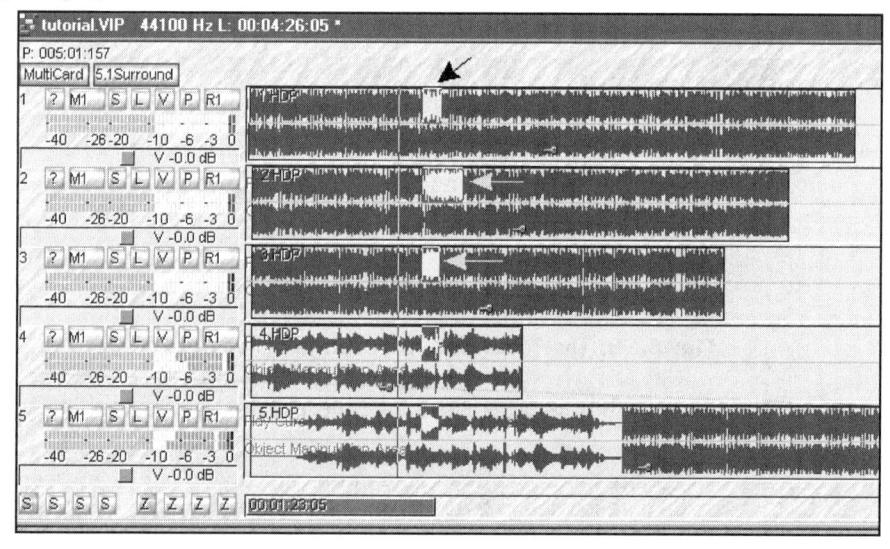

Fig. 5.17. A graphical representation of the cache

Types of Projects in Samplitude 2496

In Samplitude 2496, a project is a broader notion than in other applications, such as SAWPro.

A *virtual project* in Samplitude 2496 includes the multitrack, with all the settings and positions of the objects.

A *wave project* is an ordinary audio file recorded in or imported to Samplitude 2496.

Let's discuss the types of projects in more detail.

The RAM Wave Project

The RAM Wave project is a special type of wave project that is entirely stored in the RAM of the computer.

It is saved in the hard disk as a file with the RAP extension. The size of a RAP file with a playback of 1 second is equal to the size of a common WAV file of the same duration.

Since a RAM Wave project can be completely stored in the RAM, it doesn't encounter any problems typical to the relatively slow hard disk. On the other hand, the sizes of audio files are usually comparable to the sizes of the RAM of a home computer.

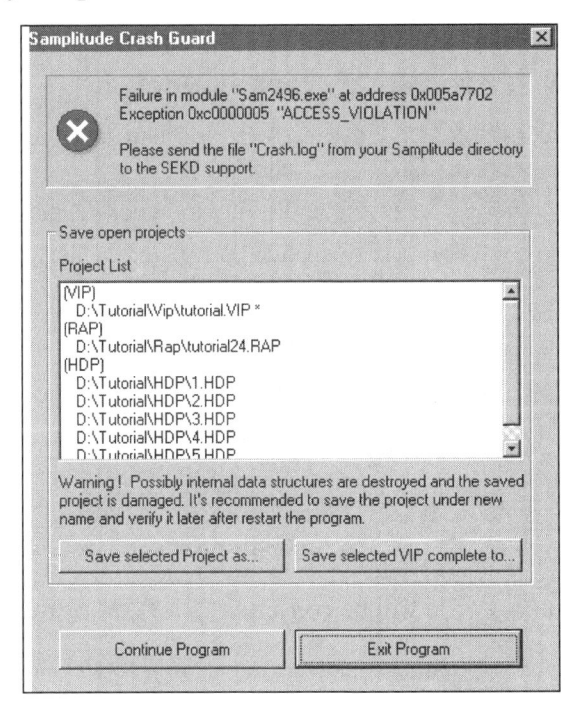

Fig. 5.18. Abnormal termination of Samplitude 2496

NOTE What happens when a RAM Wave project exceeds the size of the RAM?

Windows uses a so-called *virtual memory*. This means that the data from the RAM are transferred to a special *swap file* on the hard disk when the size of the RAM is insufficient. In Windows 9x, this file is called Win386.swp by default. In WindowsNT (Windows 2000), it is known as pagefile.sys.

The Windows swap file is used all the time. For example, when several applications are opened at once, the RAM contains only the data of the active (not minimized) application. If another application becomes active, the system will access the swap file.

If the size of the RAM Wave project *exceeds* that of the available memory, part of the project will be written to the *swap file*.

Since the swapping algorithm in Windows isn't intended for use with programs with such large amounts of inseparable data, errors or the abnormal termination of Samplitude 2496 are likely when playing back multitracks with large RAM Wave projects (Fig. 5.18). Besides this, when the swap file is used, the essence of the RAM Wave project is lost.

NOTE Failures are also likely when recording a RAM Wave project, for similar reasons.

Thus, for a RAM Wave project to be usable, it should have a size of a number of megabytes. This could, for example, be a loop.

Converting a WAV File to a RAM Wave Project

To convert a WAV file to a RAM Wave project, you can use the **Import Sample** command of the **File** menu (or the <Ctrl>+<I> shortcut).

In the **Import Sample** window, select the audio file and click **Open**.

The **Samplitude** dialog box (Fig. 5.19) will ask you to select the project type. Click the **Ram-Project** button.

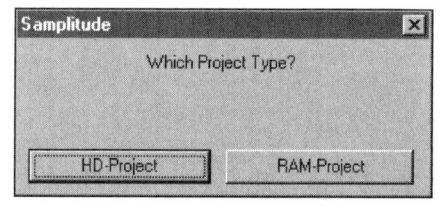

Fig. 5.19. The **Samplitude** dialog box

As a result, the original WAV file will be converted to a RAM Wave project (Fig. 5.20).

TIP On less powerful computers with smaller RAMs, it is recommended that you create RAM Wave projects only by converting original sound files (in other words, do not use direct recording).

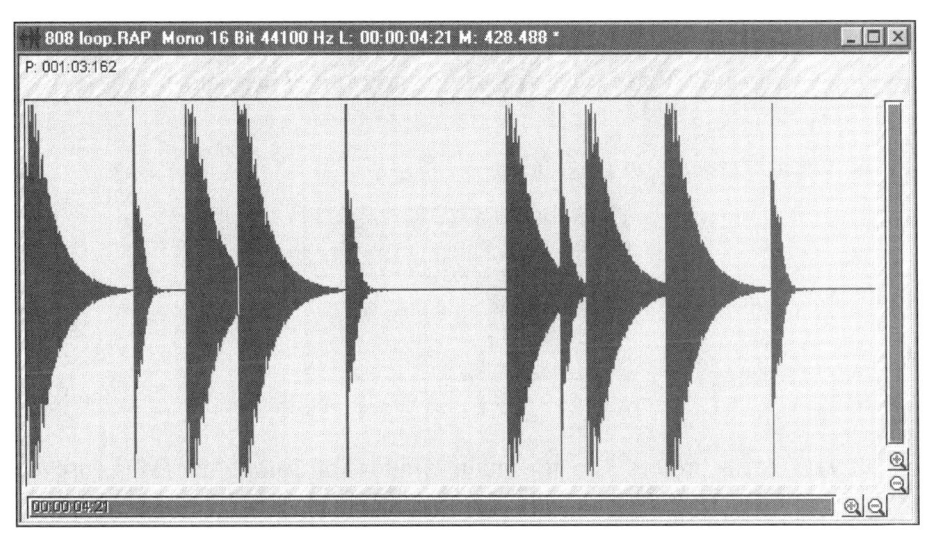

Chapter 5: The Samplitude 2496 Application as a High-Quality Virtual Studio   299

Fig. 5.20. The window of the RAM Wave project

To load a RAM Wave project into the main window of Samplitude 2496, use the **RAM** command of the **File|Open Project** menu (or the <L> hotkey).

Saving Projects

All types of Samplitude 2496 projects are saved in the hard disk with the **Save Project** or **Save Project as...** command of the **File** menu.

In the process, the window of the project being saved *must be active*, that is, on top of the other windows.

The HD Wave Project

An HD Wave project consists of three files:

- Audio file with the WAV extension
- Auxiliary identification file with the HDP extension
- Auxiliary file containing an image of the wave with the H0 extension

These three files are *always* created by Samplitude 2496, no matter whether an HD Wave project is recorded or an audio file is imported.

NOTE If the HDP file of a project is missing, it implies that all the objects of the virtual project that were created based on the HD Wave project are missing as well.

You can import an audio file into the application using one of the following methods:
- With the **Open Project Wave (*.WAV)** command of the **File** menu
- With the <W> hotkey
- With the **Open Wave** button (Fig. 5.21)

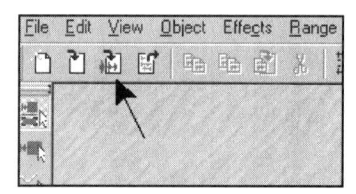

Fig. 5.21. The **Open Wave** button

To load an HD Wave project into the main window of Samplitude 2496, use the **HD** command of the **File|Open Project** menu (or the <Shift>+<L> shortcut).

The window of the HD Wave project is identical to that of the RAM Wave project (Fig. 5.20).

The Virtual Project

A *virtual project* is the *multitrack* itself, which contains objects, controls, level indicators, etc. (Fig. 5.22).

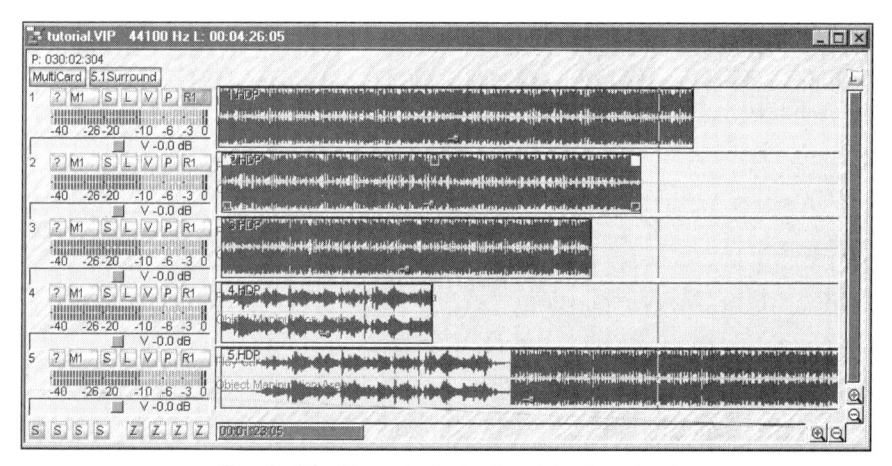

Fig. 5.22. The window of a virtual project

The virtual project is the main project type discussed in this chapter. Let's start the discussion with some general information.

Chapter 5: The Samplitude 2496 Application as a High-Quality Virtual Studio 301

The files of a virtual project have the VIP extension.

You can *create* a virtual project using one of the following methods:

- With the **New VIP** button located at the upper left corner of the main window (Fig. 5.21)
- With the **New Multitrack Project** command of the **File** menu
- With the <E> hotkey

> **NOTE** Each of the methods opens the **Setup for new VIP** window (we will go into more detail a little later in this chapter).

You can *open* a virtual project:

- With the **Open VIP** button (in the upper left corner of the main window between the **New VIP** and **Open Wave** buttons, as shown in Fig. 5.21)
- With the **Virtual** command of the **File|Open Project** menu
- With the <O> hotkey

Additional Types of Files

The following are additional types of files:

- Session files with the SAM extension
- MIDI files with the MID extension
- Object files with the OBJ extension
- EDL (Edit Decision List) files with the EDL extension
- TOC (Table Of Contents) files with the TOC extension

Let's look at each of these more closely.

The Session

This is used to save the configurations of all the windows of the application.

For example, several virtual projects, along with their corresponding RAM and HDP projects, can be opened in the main window. In such a case, you need only load the previously saved session (the SAM file) in order to restore the whole configuration. Besides which, SAM files contain the sizes of all the windows opened in the main window.

> **NOTE** The notion of *session* in Samplitude 2496 doesn't correspond to a session in Cool Edit Pro. A session in Cool Edit Pro is equivalent to a virtual project.

To *save* a session, either:

- Select the **Save Session** item from the **File** menu

or

❐ Press the <Ctrl>+<Alt>+<S> shortcut

To *load* a session, either:

❐ Select the **Load Session** item from the **File** menu

or

❐ Press the <Alt>+<S> shortcut

> **NOTE** In an empty main window, loading a session is done with the **Load Session** command of the **File** menu. However, if even one project is loaded or has been created, the session is loaded using the **Session (*.SAM)** command of the **File|Open Project** menu.
>
> The **File|Open Project** submenu also changes its appearance after at least one project is loaded or created. Nevertheless, the functions of its controls remain the same. For example, the **Virtual** command changes to **Virtual Project (*.VIP)**. In this chapter, the names of the items in the **Open Project** submenu are given for an empty main window.

The MIDI File

This is a recording of music in the form of a *command sequence* for a musical synthesizer (or a MIDI instrument). MIDI files can only be played back using equipment that supports the MIDI interface.

At present, all modern sound cards support the MIDI interface and allow you to record and playback MIDI files (the MIDI interface is described in detail in *Chapter 6*).

An important feature of Samplitude 2496 is the possibility of *simultaneous* playback of AUDIO and MIDI.

> **MIDI Sequencers**
>
> As a MIDI sequencer, Samplitude 2496 falls far behind such applications as Cubase VST 24 and Cakewalk Pro Audio.
>
> This fact can be explained by the history of the software's development. Cubase and Cakewalk were program MIDI sequencers from the beginning (more precisely, they were virtual MIDI studios). Later, they evolved from this point to digital sound processing.
>
> Unlike them, Samplitude 2496 was created for recording and processing sound. Playback of and synchronization with MIDI is just an additional feature of this application, though a very important one.
>
> Because of this, to obtain a high-quality result, you may want to first create a MIDI project in a specialized application, such as Cubase or Cakewalk. Then you can combine AUDIO and MIDI in Samplitude 2496. Examples of such combined projects will be examined in *Chapter 7*.

You can import a MIDI file into the main window of the application using:

❐ The **MIDI** command of the **File|Open Project** menu

Chapter 5: The Samplitude 2496 Application as a High-Quality Virtual Studio 303

or

- The <Ctrl>+<M> shortcut

Like AUDIO objects, MIDI objects:

- Are placed on the tracks of a virtual project
- Are subject to the general rules of editing objects on a multitrack

The Object

An object is a key notion of non-destructive (virtual) editing in Samplitude 2496.

> **NOTE** For you to better understand the processes that take place in the SAWPro and Cool Edit Pro multitrack editors, we'll use a well-fitting (in our opinion) term from Cakewalk: *clip*.
>
> It can be said that an *object* in Samplitude 2496 is a complex *clip* of SAWPro and Cool Edit Pro. Unlike a clip, an object contains not only information about the region, but also about some additional settings (such as volume, pan, DirectX plug-ins, etc.).
>
> Editing the properties of an object is discussed in the section "*Sound Processing in Samplitude 2496*".

Let's concentrate on the features of *objects* in Samplitude 2496.

- The objects of Samplitude 2496 can be moved beyond the boundaries of a virtual project. You can save them as files and copy them (by dragging) to another virtual project.

> **NOTE** Remember that it is possible to open several virtual projects in the main window of the application.

- To *save* an object in a file, you must first select the object in the virtual project (to select objects, see the "*Editing a Virtual Project*" section), then select the **Save Object** item in the **File** menu.
- To *load* an object, first select a short fragment on the VIP project track, and then perform the **Object (*.OBJ)** command of the **File|Open Project** menu.

Another way to achieve this is to drag the object file (with the OBJ extension) to the target VIP multitrack in Windows Explorer. In such a case, it is also necessary to select a short fragment on the VIP project track.

> **NOTE** In either case, the object will be put at the beginning of the selected fragment of the *currently active* virtual project. (If several VIP projects are open at the same time, the active one is on top of the others in the main window.)

> **TIP** You can create *a sound effect library* of object files. The point of this is that various configurations of DirectX plug-ins will be able to be attached to an object. The results can be stored as separate OBJ files.

EDL Files

An EDL file (where EDL stands for Edit Decision List) is a text file whose format allows you to save a virtual project in Samplitude 2496.

> **NOTE** Unfortunately, despite the fact that this file has the same extension as the project file in SAWPro, it is not compatible with it. The developers of Samplitude2496 designed it for other purposes, namely, for compatibility with the D-Vision *video editing* system.

TOC Files

A TOC file (Table Of Contents) is a text file that contains information about the positions of audio tracks on an AUDIO CD.

> **NOTE** Here is an example of a TOC file for three audio tracks:
> FILE D:\Tutorial\master.WAV AT 88200 FROM 0 TO 674803
> INDEX AT 00:02:00
> INDEX AT 00:07:13
> INDEX AT 00:11:22

Areas of Applying RAM Wave and HD Wave Projects

Samplitude 2496 gives the user the ability to choose the type of wave project by him- or herself. Before you make your choice between a RAM project or an HD one, you must first take into account the size of the RAM and the speed of data exchange between the RAM and the hard drive in your computer.

Today, a computer with 128 MB RAM, a 7200 rpm hard drive, and a UDMA/66 interface is quite a common configuration. With such hardware resources, you will be able to use *HD Wave* projects as the main ones and *RAM Wave* projects as auxiliary (for files several megabytes long).

Those who own one of the popular Sound Blaster Live sound cards use the RAM to load banks of musical instruments in the SoundFont format.

Top-quality musical instrument banks take up a lot of memory. This is why, when one virtual project combines both AUDIO and MIDI, *it is not recommended* that those with a Sound Blaster Live sound card use RAM Wave projects. This is because a certain area of the RAM will be allocated to the SoundFont banks.

Chapter 5: The Samplitude 2496 Application as a High-Quality Virtual Studio 305

NOTE We'd like to remind you of the main idea of the previous section: with smaller RAMs, there is no sense in using RAM Wave projects. Moreover, you should remember that if you do so, AUDIO and MIDI might become out of sync, and program errors are very likely.

The VIP Multitrack. Its Similarity to and Difference from the Multitracks of SAWPro and Cool Edit Pro

In Fig. 5.23, you can see an example of a VIP project consisting of two tracks.

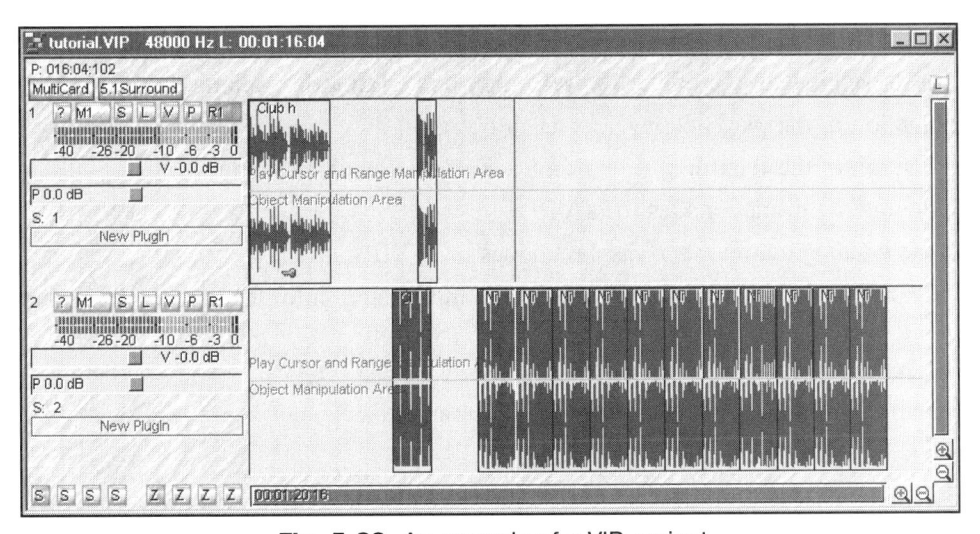

Fig. 5.23. An example of a VIP project

Let's consider the main similarities and differences between a VIP multitrack and the multitracks of SAWPro and Cool Edit Pro.

Similarities to SAWPro and Cool Edit Pro Multitracks

- The availability of volume and pan controls
- The ability to zoom in on the image of the tracks of a multitrack: **Zoom In** and **Zoom Out**
- The ability to zoom in on the image of the waveform of a clip
- The availability of the **Solo**, **Mute**, and **Record** buttons
- *Connecting a virtual effect* to a track (similar only to SAWPro)
- *Graphically editing* the volume and pan (similar only to Cool Edit Pro)

- *Adjusting* the pan and volume for each clip *separately* (similar only to Cool Edit Pro)
- The ability to edit non-destructively (snipping, copying, etc.)
- The ability to create a sound file region and place it on a multitrack (this is actually creating an object)

The Differences between Samplitude's Multitrack and the Multitracks of SAWPro and Cool Edit Pro

- The ability to change the number of tracks in the multitrack
- The ability to copy the tracks of a multitrack
- Illustrative changing of objects' waveforms when editing the volume
- Indication of the playback level for each track
- Indication of the recording level of a track in the **Punch In** mode
- Changing the display modes for a VIP
- Easy switching between two display modes for a VIP
- The ability to divide a virtual project (a multitrack) into sections (a maximum of three)
- The ability to simultaneously edit two or more virtual projects
- The ability to apply virtual effects directly to an object
- The ability to save an object (clip) in a file
- Eleven modes for editing a project using the mouse (the VIP Mouse Modes)
- The ability to create MIDI objects (clips)
- The ability to place AUDIO and MIDI objects on one track and have them overlap

When looking at the list of the main differences between the multitrack editing tools of SAWPro, Cool Edit Pro, and Samplitude 2496, one can conclude that Samplitude 2496 has fundamentally new features for editing a musical project.

Creating a New VIP Project

In Samplitude 2496, new VIP projects must be created in the following way:

1. Execute the **New Multitrack Project** command of the **File** menu.

    NOTE   This can be also done with the <E> hotkey.

2. Set the parameters in the **Setup for new VIP** dialog box that appears (Fig. 5.24).

Chapter 5: The Samplitude 2496 Application as a High-Quality Virtual Studio 307

This dialog box consists of many various controls for setting up a new virtual project. Let's examine them more closely.

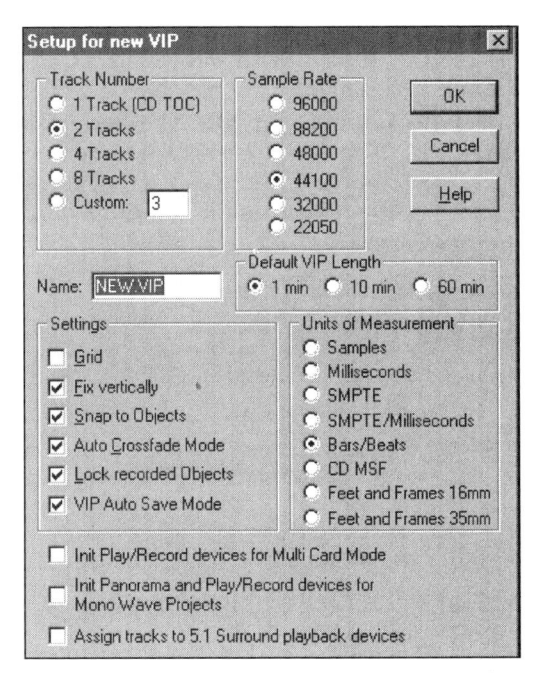

Fig. 5.24. The **Setup for new VIP** dialog box

The *Setup for New VIP* Dialog Box

The **Track Number** radio buttons set the number of the tracks in the new VIP project.

NOTE When editing a VIP project, this number can be changed if necessary.

In the **Custom** field, you can specify any number.

The Number of Tracks

In Samplitude 2496's documentation, it states that *the number of tracks* can be arbitrary. The maximum number you can enter in this field is 9999. However, despite this "promise", the application actually offers a much narrower range — from 0 to 1024.

You should be aware that the actual number of tracks is limited not only by the user's needs and common sense, but by the computer's resources as well.

Since you will be able to add new tracks if you need to, we recommend that you begin with a small number, such as 6.

Adding new tracks is done through the context menu of a track with the **Add one Track** or **Add several Tracks** commands of the **Track** submenu.

Notice that when importing a MIDI file, the number of tracks changes *automatically* (more details will be given later in this chapter).

A project consisting of *one track* (1 Track (CD TOC)) is designed for AUDIO CD mastering (see the *"Creating an AUDIO CD in Samplitude 2496"* section).

The **Sample Rate** section is used to set the sample rate for the new VIP project (for details on the sample rate, see *Chapter 3*).

The Sample Rate

Remember our basic rule: the larger the sample rate, the higher the sound quality.

To obtain AUDIO CD quality, set the sample rate to 44,100 Hz.

If you have a Sound Blaster Live sound cards, you should set the sample rate to 48,000 Hz. The maximum sample rate for this sound card is 96,000 Hz for playback, and 48,000 Hz for recording.

The **Name** field is used to enter the name of the new project.

The **Default VIP Length** radio buttons set the length of the empty VIP project being created. Later, the project gets longer automatically, both during recording and when importing RAM, HD, or MIDI projects.

In the **Settings** section, you configure additional settings of the VIP project.

❏ **Grid** shows/hides the vertical measure grid.

> *NOTE* The increments of the grid depend on the unit of time measurement (**Bars/Beats**, **Samples**, etc). For details on the grid and the units, see *Chapter 3*.

A function similar to **Grid** is performed with the **Show Grid** command of the **View** menu. The **Grid Setup** command of the same menu allows you to select the *appearance* of the vertical line of the grid.

❏ **Fix vertically** makes it impossible to select a vertical range.

> *NOTE* In Samplitude 2496, you can select both a vertical and horizontal range. Checking the **Fix vertically** checkbox prohibits vertical selection on the tracks of the VIP project. This feature is duplicated in the **View** menu.

❏ **Snap to Objects** switches on the mode where the objects "stick" to one another by their boundaries while moving or copying them. This "stickiness" is present even when

Chapter 5: The Samplitude 2496 Application as a High-Quality Virtual Studio 309

the objects are located in different tracks. Besides which, the range selection also "sticks" to the object boundaries.

- **Auto Crossfade Mode** turns on the automatic crossfade mode when objects are overlapped (Fig. 5.25).

    > **NOTE** The Auto Crossfade mode is described in detail in the "*Sound Processing in Samplitude 2496*" section.

- **Lock recorded Objects** provides for automatic locking of the objects saved in this VIP project. Locking is a very useful feature, since it protects objects from accidental moving along the multitrack.

    > **NOTE** The **Lock recorded Objects** feature doesn't work for imported objects.

- **VIP Auto Save Mode** turns on the mode for saving the project automatically.

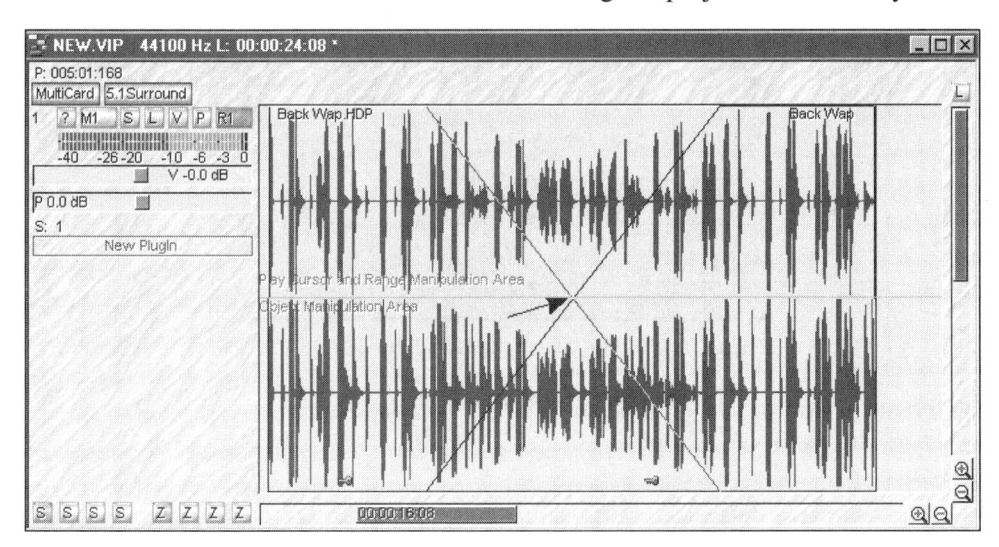

Fig. 5.25. An example of auto crossfading

- The **Units of Measurement** radio buttons set the unit of time measurement (**Bars/Beats**, **Samples**, etc.) on the multitrack.
- The **Init Play/Record devices for Multi Card Mode** checkbox turns on the Multi Card mode for sound cards having multiple inputs and outputs.
- **Init Panorama and Play/Record devices for Mono Wave Projects** prepares the VIP project to play/record the left and right channels as two *separate* audio files.
- **Assign tracks to 5.1 Surround playback devices.** Samplitude 2496 supports Dolby Surround 5.1 devices. This allows you to mix the project for this system.

Importing MIDI Files

Let's look at how to import a MIDI file to a VIP project of Samplitude 2496. To do this, you must:

1. Select a short area on the chosen track of your VIP project.
2. Perform the **Midi (*.MID)** command of the **File|Open Project** menu.

> **NOTE** You may also use the <Ctrl>+<M> shortcut.

The **Import MIDI File** dialog box will appear on the screen, as shown in Fig. 5.26.

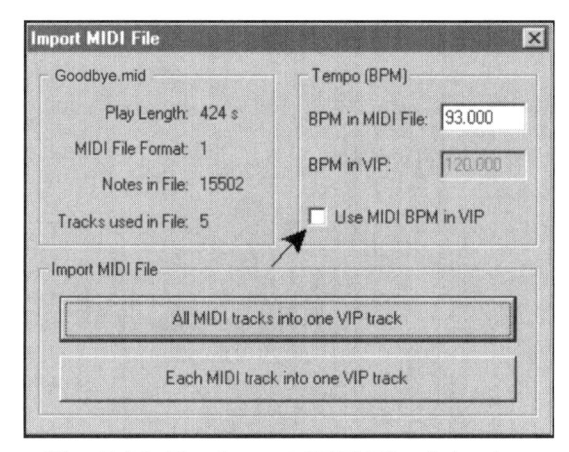

Fig. 5.26. The **Import MIDI File** dialog box

Let's look at the controls of the **Import MIDI File** dialog box:

☐ The **Use MIDI BPM in VIP** checkbox (indicated by the arrow in Fig. 5.26) is *very important*. It must be checked in most cases.

> **NOTE** You see, the tempo of the piece is always specified when creating a MIDI project. Therefore, the tempo must be retained when converting to AUDIO.

☐ There are two buttons in the **Import MIDI File** section:
- **All MIDI tracks into one VIP track**
- **Each MIDI track into one VIP track**

> **NOTE** Digitally processing a MIDI project created in Cubase VST 24 and then imported into Samplitude 2496 is discussed in *Chapter 7* in more detail.

To obtain a high-quality conversion of a MIDI project to AUDIO, you need to digitally process (record as AUDIO) each MIDI track separately, and only then mix them. For this purpose, you may use the **Each MIDI track into one VIP track** button.

Chapter 5: The Samplitude 2496 Application as a High-Quality Virtual Studio   311

If a MIDI project is used as a rhythmical "frame" to synchronize musical parts recorded in AUDIO form, it makes sense to place all the MIDI tracks into one track of a virtual project (the **All MIDI tracks into one VIP track** button).

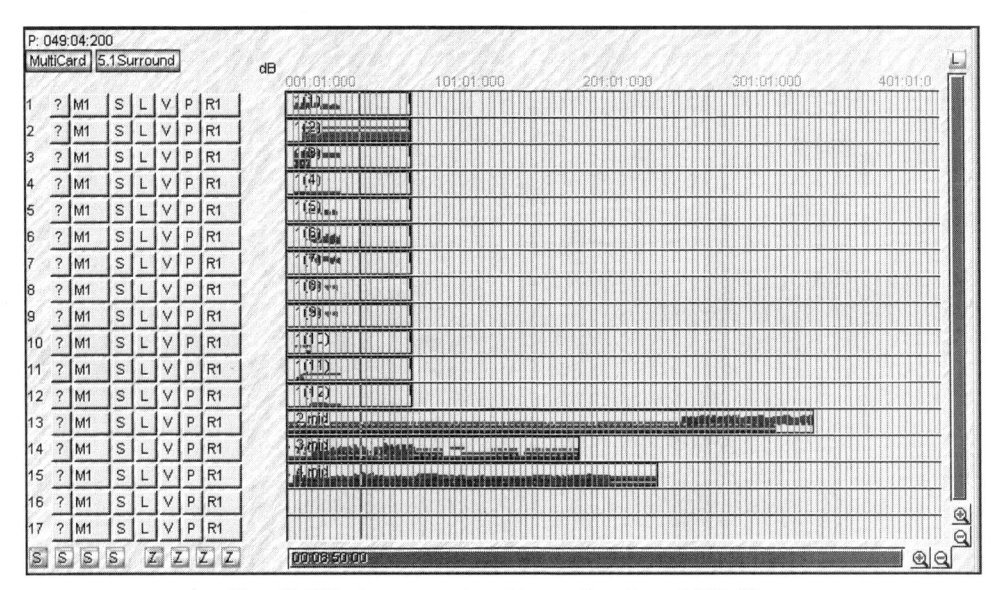

Fig. 5.27. An example of importing four MIDI files

Fig. 5.27 illustrates importing four MIDI files with two methods. Notice that the 1.mid file takes up 12 tracks of the VIP project, whereas the files from 2.mid to 4.mid take up one track each.

Recording and Playback in the VIP Window

The Purpose of the *?*, *M*, *S*, *L*, *V*, *P*, and *R* Buttons

In Fig. 5.28, you can see an example of a virtual project. Look at it closely.

The following controls appear in the left-hand side of the window: the level indicators, the **V** and **P** buttons to adjust the volume and pan, and track control buttons similar to those of SAWPro and Cool Edit Pro.

Let's focus on the track control buttons.

The **?** (Track Properties) button is designed for setting the track properties. When it is clicked, the **Track Info** dialog box with additional options will appear (Fig. 5.29).

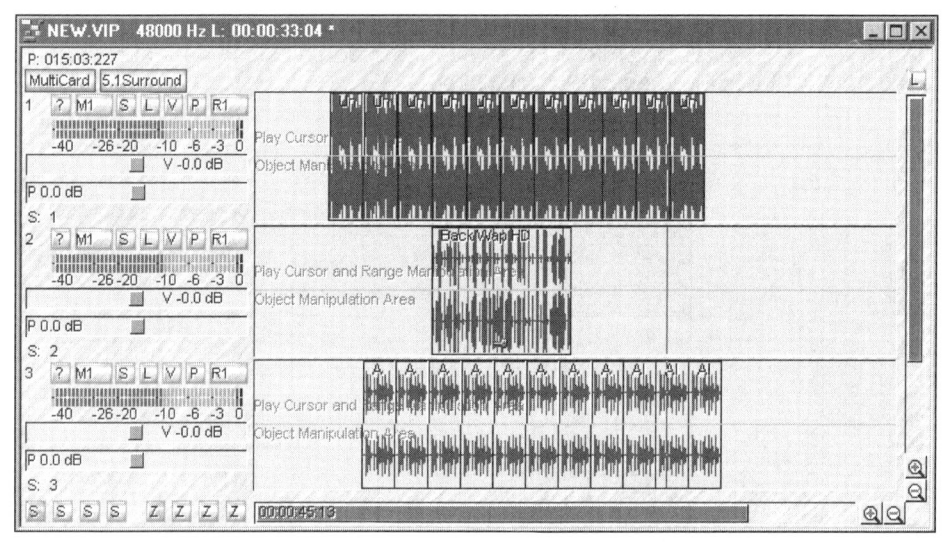

Fig. 5.28. An example of a virtual project

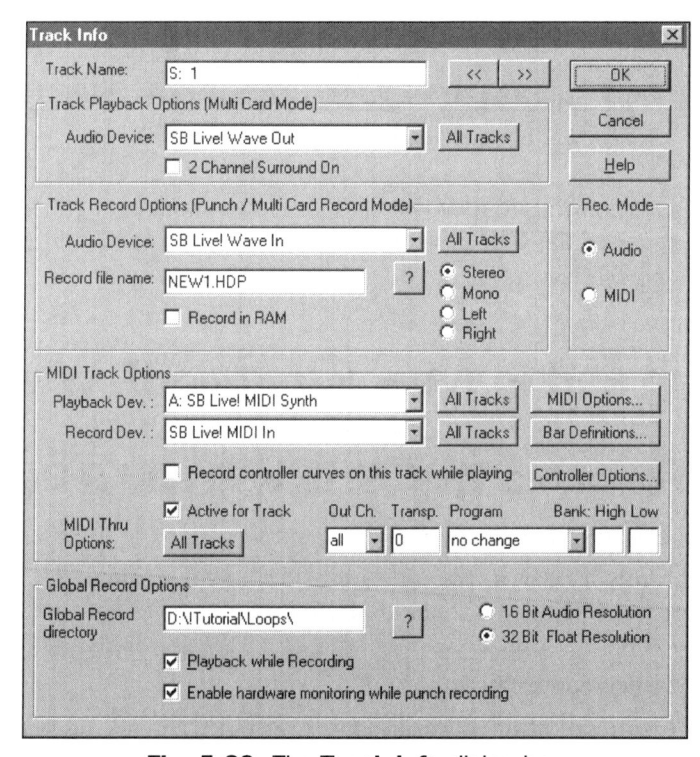

Fig. 5.29. The **Track Info** dialog box

Chapter 5: The Samplitude 2496 Application as a High-Quality Virtual Studio

The **Track Info** dialog box provides the user with various track settings.

- The name of the track is entered in the **Track Name** text box
- The << and >> buttons, located to the right of this text box, allow you to move to the previous or next track without closing the **Track Info** dialog box
- In the **Audio Device** drop-down list (in the **Track Playback Options** section), you can select a device for playback if a device that supports the MultiCard mode is installed
- The **All Tracks** button extends the current settings to all the other tracks

> **NOTE** The **2 Channel Surround On** checkbox turns the Surround mode of the Dolby Surround 5.1 system off and on for the track.

- In the **Audio Device** drop-down list (in the **Track Record Options** section), you can select a device for recording in the Punch/MultiCard Record mode
- The **Stereo**, **Mono**, **Left**, and **Right** radio buttons specify the type of HD or RAM Wave project that will be recorded on this track (stereo, L + R mono, L mono, R mono)
- The **Record file name** text box is used for the name of the HD or RAM Wave project
- With the **?** button, you can specify the folder where the project will be located
- The **Rec. Mode** radio buttons specify the type of the project (**Audio** or **MIDI**)
- The **MIDI Track Options** section is used to setup the mode of recording the MIDI project

The Possibility of MIDI Editing

Samplitude 2496 allows the user to record MIDI projects in real time from any MIDI source (for example, a MIDI keyboard). However, the editing of MIDI projects is *limited* in Samplitude 2496, in comparison to such specialized applications as Cubase VST 24 and Cakewalk Pro Audio.

For example, Cubase VST 24 provides special tools for transferring the rhythm from an AUDIO track to the "lifeless" MIDI sound, thus allowing you to "enliven" rhythmic parts. Besides which, Cubase VST 24 offers a unique **Drum Editor**, which has a very convenient interface and more varied features than the **MIDI Editor** of Samplitude 2496.

Since Cubase VST 24, which provides the computer musician with vast editing possibilities, is discussed in *Chapter 6*, we aren't going to describe the MIDI editing features of Samplitude 2496 here.

- The **Global Record directory** text box is used to enter the path to the folder where the files of the recorded projects will be located
- The **Playback while Recording** checkbox is self-descriptive

- The **Enable hardware monitoring while punch recording** checkbox should be used with sound cards that support the Punch recording mode, such as digital or analog studio tape recorders
- The **16 Bit Audio Resolution** and **32 Bit Float Resolution** radio buttons specify the format of the audio file

> **NOTE** The 32 Bit Float Resolution file format was discussed in *Chapter 4*, in the section entitled "*Cool Edit Pro File Formats*".

Let's now move on to other controls of a VIP project (Fig. 5.28).

- The **M (M1)** (Mute) button is used to turn off the volume for the corresponding track

> **NOTE** The number 1 after the letter **M** means that this track corresponds to the first audio device. If a Windows-compatible sound card is installed on your computer, *only the first device* is used at all times.

- The **S** (Solo) button turns on the solo mode, in which only this track is played back
- The **L** (Lock) button turns on the mode that protects objects from being moved accidentally along the horizontal axis
- The **V** (Volume) and **P** (Pan) buttons toggle the mode of volume and pan automation (Fig. 5.30)

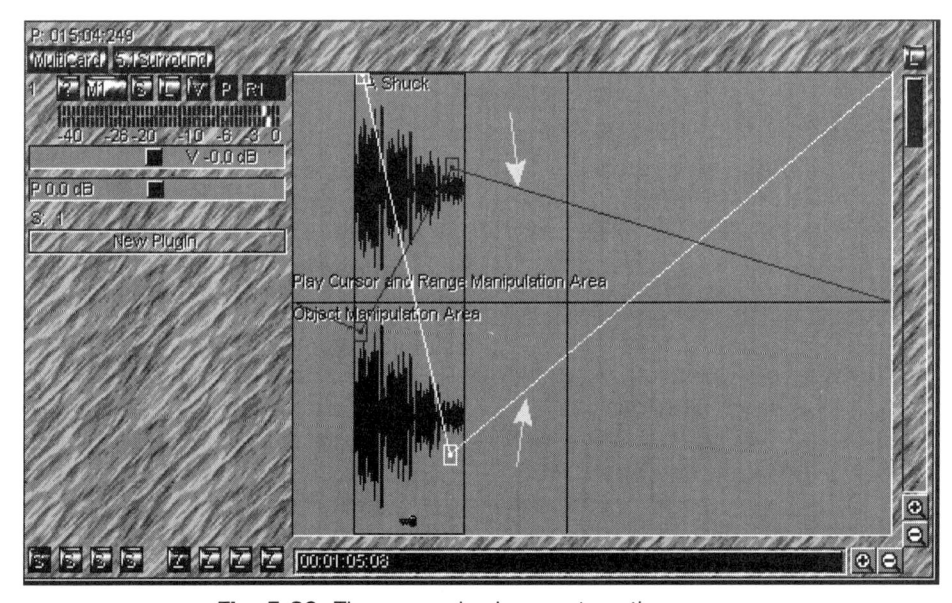

Fig. 5.30. The pan and volume automation curves

Chapter 5: The Samplitude 2496 Application as a High-Quality Virtual Studio 315

NOTE When the automation mode is *on*, curves for graphically editing the pan and volume are visible. During playback, the pan and volume of the track are changed in accordance with these curves.

When the automation mode is set to *off* using the **V** and/or **P** buttons, the previously edited curves are retained. However, automatic changing of the volume and/or pan stops. You can resume it by turning on the automation mode.

❐ The **R (R1)** (Record) button allows you to record to the selected track.

NOTE A right-click on the **R** button shows the *pop-up menu* (Fig. 5.31), where you can choose a device and the recording type (**Midi Record** or **Audio Record**). Samplitude 2496 supports the mode of simultaneous recording of AUDIO and MIDI on different tracks.

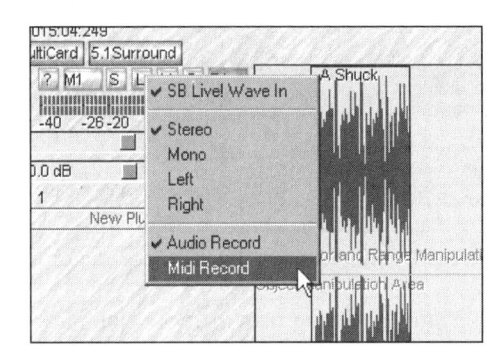

Fig. 5.31. The pop-up menu of the **R** (Record) button

Recording a Wave Project Using the *Record Parameter* Dialog Box

Before you start recording a RAM or HD Wave project, you must first click the **R** button on the selected track. Then turn on recording using one of the following methods:

❐ Click the **Record** button on the toolbar (Fig. 5.32)
❐ Click the **Record** button on the transport panel (Fig. 5.7)
❐ Select the **Record** item in the **File** menu
❐ Press the <R> hotkey

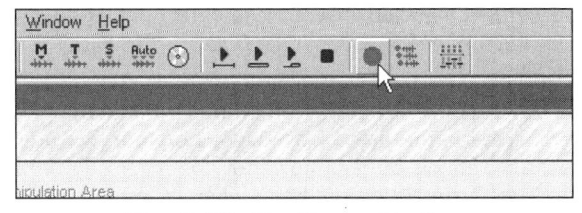

Fig. 5.32. The **Record** button

After clicking the **Record** button, the **Record Parameter** dialog box will appear (Fig. 5.33). Here you can select the *type* (RAM or HD) and *parameters* of the Wave project.

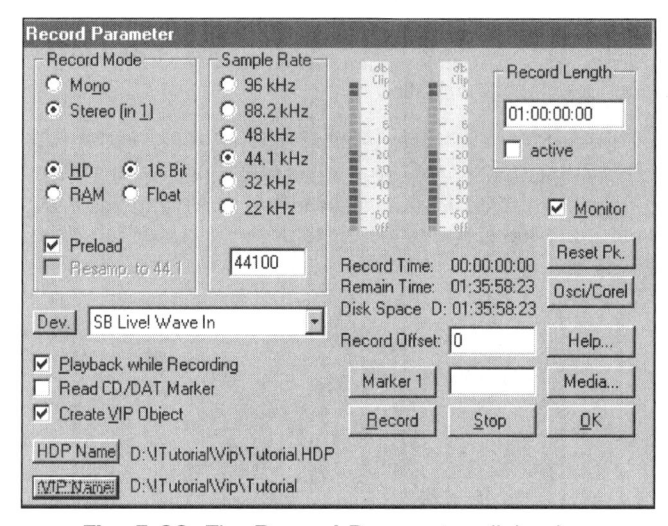

Fig. 5.33. The **Record Parameter** dialog box

Let's discuss the **Record Parameter** dialog box in more detail.

The **Record Mode** section contains a number of controls.

❏ The **Mono** and **Stereo (in 1)** radio buttons correspond to the mono and stereo recording modes.

❏ The **HD** and **RAM** radio buttons allow you to select the type of the Wave project.

> *TIP* We recommend that you *always* record your projects as HD Wave. Later, you will be able to convert them to RAM Wave if you wish.

❏ The **16 Bit** and **Float** radio buttons specify the format of the project.

The 32-bit Float Format

If a 16-bit sound card is installed in your computer, analog-to-digital conversion is performed in 16-bit format, *no matter which radio button* — **16 Bit** or **Float** — is selected in the **Record Mode** section.

When **Float** is selected, conversion from the 16-bit format to the 32-bit Float format is done in real time. This increases the processor load. Therefore, *we don't recommend* that you use the **Float** recording mode on less powerful computers, in order to avoid failures and sound distortions. These are especially likely when recording and playback take place *simultaneously*.

Chapter 5: The Samplitude 2496 Application as a High-Quality Virtual Studio 317

Conversion to the 32-bit Float format is *necessary* in order to minimize distortions when you plan on editing destructively (for example, using some virtual effect). In most cases, you cannot do without destructive editing. This is why, to obtain a high-quality, "live" sound, you should convert all audio files to the 32-bit Float format *immediately* after you record them in the 16-bit format. This can be done with either of the following methods:

- For an HD Wave project, use the **Float (32 Bit)** command of the **Special|Change Bit Resolution** menu. A 32-bit copy of the original file will be created (with the Filename_flt.hdp or Filename_flt.wav name). The conversion is done in the window of the HD Wave project.

- For an *object*, use the **Track Bouncing** command of the **Tools** menu. Also, the **Save in 32-bit (Float) Format** option must be checked, and the **Solo** mode must be chosen in the converted track. (Track bouncing will be discussed in more detail in the "*Non-destructive Sound Processing*" section.)

After the **Track Bouncing** procedure is finished, you may delete the 16-bit Wave projects with the **Remove unused Samples** command of the **Tools** menu.

Since Samplitude 2496 performs all conversions using the 32-bit format, it is better to mix the whole virtual project to a 32-bit file. The highest quality will thus be achieved. When mastering an AUDIO CD, Samplitude 2496 will perform high-precision conversion to the 16-bit format.

❏ The **Preload** checkbox enables preloading of all the buffers.

> **NOTE** Checking this checkbox makes it possible to start recording *immediately* after clicking the **OK** button of the **Preload** dialog box (Fig. 5.34).

If preloading isn't used, recording will start only *after* all the buffers of the virtual project are loaded, rather than just with a click on the **Record** button.

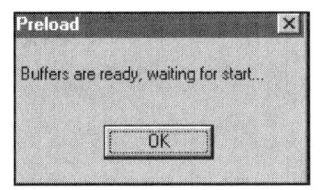

Fig. 5.34. The **Preload** dialog box

❏ The **Resamp. to 44.1** checkbox provides for the conversion of the sample rate to 44,100 Hz during recording (if the input data stream has another sample rate).

❏ The **Sample Rate** radio buttons allow you to select a sample rate other than the current sample rate of the Wave project.

❏ The **Playback while Recording** checkbox allows you to perform the two processes simultaneously.

❏ The **Create VIP Object** checkbox ensures that a new object is created on the multitrack immediately after recording ends.

NOTE If the **Create VIP Object** checkbox is unchecked, only the HD Wave project will be created.

- The **HDP Name** and **VIP Name** buttons allow the user to rename projects and/or change their locations on the hard disk.
- The **Monitor** checkbox turns on the recording level indicator before recording starts. This allows you to adjust the recording level.
- The **Record Length** section is used to automate the process of recording.

NOTE In the **Record Length** field, you can set the length of the fragment (in the SMPTE format) to be recorded. The **active** checkbox must be checked in this case.

- The **Reset Pk.** button serves to reset the indicator of the recording level peaks.
- The **Record Offset** field sets the offset (in samples) to compensate for a delay between the signals during simultaneous recording and playback that occurs with some sound cards.
- The **Media** button gives you access to a window where you can adjust synchronization with any MIDI or AVI file (Fig. 5.35).

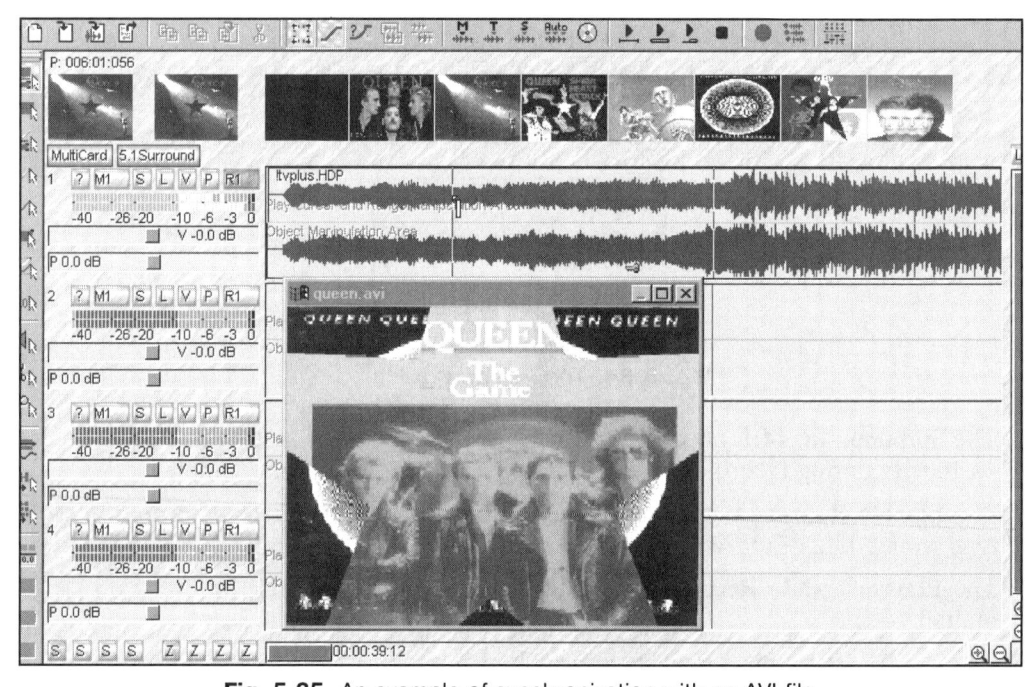

Fig. 5.35. An example of synchronization with an AVI file

Chapter 5: The Samplitude 2496 Application as a High-Quality Virtual Studio 319

> **NOTE** In our opinion, it is simpler to import a MIDI file *directly* to a VIP project.

The topic of synchronizing AUDIO and VIDEO in Samplitude 2496 is beyond the scope of this book.

- The **Record** button starts recording (or preloading of the buffers if the **Preload** mode is on).
- The **Stop** button stops recording and opens the **Recording finished** dialog box (Fig. 5.36).

> **NOTE** You can stop recording with the right mouse button.

Clicking the **Yes** button saves the take (the last version), while clicking the **Delete** button deletes it.

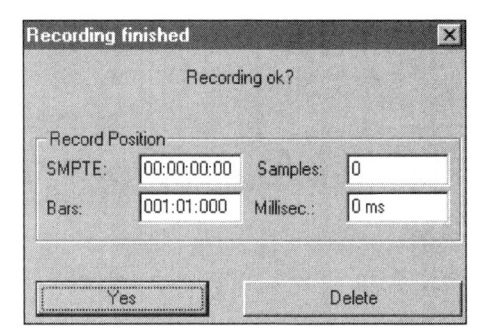

Fig. 5.36. The **Recording finished** dialog box

- The **OK** button closes the **Record Parameter** dialog box.

The beginning of a new object on a VIP track always coincides with the current cursor position.

> **NOTE** Notice that the cursor position cannot be changed when the **Record Parameter** dialog box is open.

In the **Record Parameter** dialog box, you can perform multiple recording by repeatedly clicking a sequence of buttons — **Record**, **Stop**, and **Yes**.

> **NOTE** In this case, the objects obtained will be placed sequentially: **Take 1**, **Take 2**, etc. (Fig. 5.37).

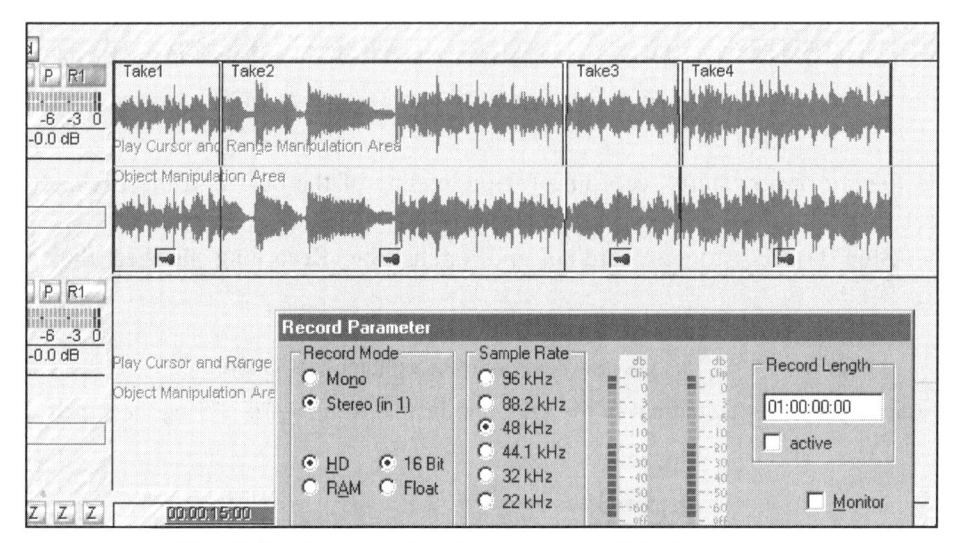

Fig. 5.37. An example of recording multiple fragments

How to Record Takes in the *Record Parameter* Dialog Box

To record takes in the **Record Parameter** dialog box, proceed as follows:

1. Select a loop (a fragment) in the VIP track.
2. Use the **Playback** command of the **Special** menu to turn on the **Play Loop** mode.

> **NOTE** You can achieve the same result by clicking the **Play Loop** button in the toolbar.

The toolbar section in which the various playback buttons are located (including the **Play Loop** one) is found to the left of the **Record** button (Fig. 5.32).

For more details, see the section entitled "*The Playback Modes*", and Fig. 5.46.

3. Click the **R** button on an empty track to open the **Record Parameter** dialog box (or press <R>).
4. In the **Record Parameter** dialog box, click the **Record** button (or press the <R> key again).

After this procedure, the selected fragment will be repeatedly played back in the mode of simultaneous recording and playback.

> **NOTE** We'd like to remind you that the **Playback while Recording** checkbox must be checked.

Chapter 5: The Samplitude 2496 Application as a High-Quality Virtual Studio 321

You can stop recording with the **Stop** button on the toolbar (or with the <S> key). All the takes will be placed in one object, one after another (Fig. 5.38).

This procedure allows you to record any number of takes. Thus you can concentrate on performing without being distracted by technical details.

> **NOTE** The number of takes is limited only by the free space available on the hard disk.
>
> You can easily delete bad takes and move the most successful take to the desired place in the project with the non-destructive editing methods provided by Samplitude 2496. These will be discussed in the "*Editing A Virtual Project*" section.

The proposed procedure can also be used with a separate VIP project created for this purpose. But first you must copy the objects of the selected loop from the main project to this VIP project. In this case, after editing the project, you need just drag the successful take to the main project.

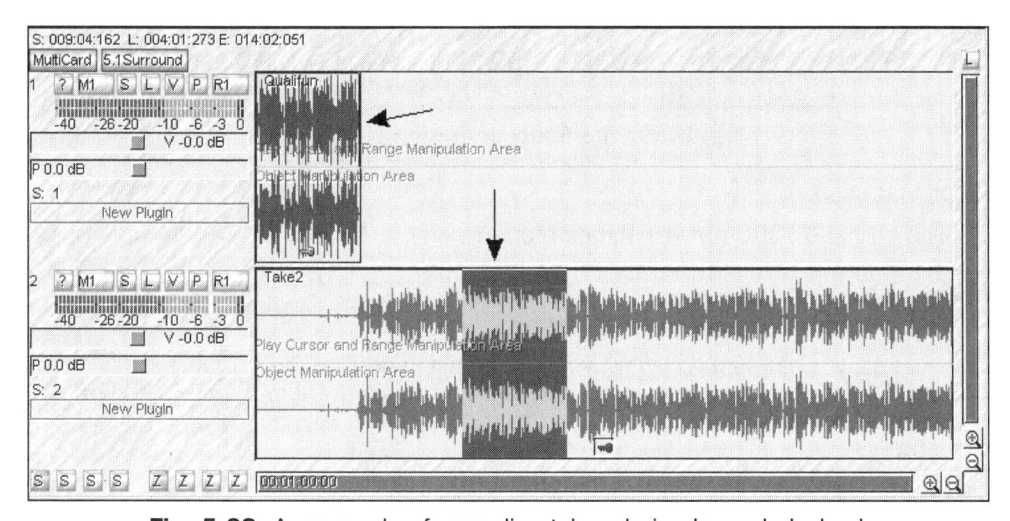

Fig. 5.38. An example of recording takes during looped playback

Even though it is a bit premature, we'd like to offer you a procedure that lets you *listen to* and *edit* recorded takes.

1. Select an object in the loop by dragging the mouse pointer (with the left mouse button pressed) between the vertical boundaries of the loop. In Fig. 5.38, the selected loop can be found in the upper track.

> **NOTE** To select an object *with the mouse*, you must first select the **Universal Mode** or **Range Mode** option of the **VIP Mouse Mode** switch. These

modes are examined in the "*VIP Mouse Editing Modes*" section. For now, notice that the **Universal Mode** is set by default.

The **Snap to Objects** checkbox, set in the **Setup for new VIP** dialog box while creating the VIP project, allows you to select the object accurately.

2. Execute the **Snap Setup** command of the **View** menu (or use the <Shift>+<R> shortcut).

3. In the **Snap definition** dialog box that will open (Fig. 5.39), click the **Get Range** button.

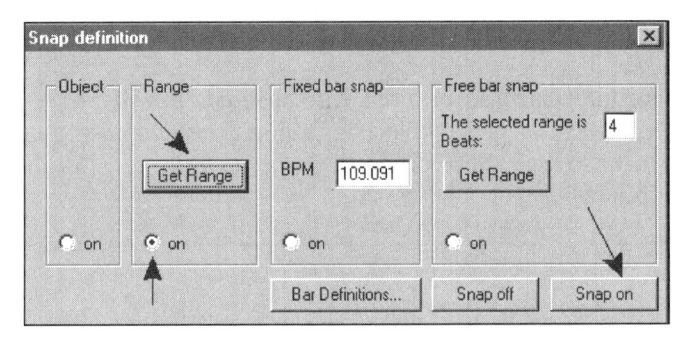

Fig. 5.39. The **Snap definition** dialog box

4. After that, click:

    - The **on** radio button in the **Range** section

   and

    - The **Snap on** button

    > **NOTE** Having done this, you will be able to position the multitrack cursor or select a range only in accordance with the grid, where the minimal distance between two points is equal to the length of the loop. This is why the multitrack cursor is automatically set only at the boundaries of the takes.

    Fig. 5.38 illustrates an example of this precise take selection.

5. After the take is selected, delete all the unused takes.

    - Click the portion of the object that is below the *horizontal line*. This is necessary in order to select the object that contains the takes in the **Universal Mode**. (The *horizontal line* can only be seen in **Universal Mode**.)

    - Apply the **Trim Objects** command of the **Object** menu to the selected object.

    > **NOTE** Alternatively, you may use the <Ctrl>+<T> shortcut.

You can free some space in the hard drive with the **Remove unused Samples** commands of the **Tools** menu. After this operation, only those fragments of audio files connected with the VIP project that are used as objects on the tracks of the multitrack will remain.

Chapter 5: The Samplitude 2496 Application as a High-Quality Virtual Studio 323

The *Punch In* Recording Mode

There are various recording modes in Samplitude 2496. One of them was introduced in the "*Recording a Wave Project Using the Record Parameter Dialog Box*" section.

Another technique — the **Punch In** mode — we will discuss right now.

NOTE Recall that the **Punch In** mode enables automatic recording only for a certain fragment during playback. This was covered in detail in *Chapter 3* (on SAWPro) and in *Chapter 4* (on Cool Edit Pro).

You can control the **Punch In** mode using either of the following methods: using the **Punch In/Live Input** commands of the **Special** menu, or with the special **Punch/Play** toolbar (Fig. 5.40).

Fig. 5.40. The **Punch/Play** toolbar

Here are the buttons of the **Punch/Play** toolbar (from left to right):

- Switch on the **Punch In** mode
- Record in the **Punch In** mode (**Punch In Record**)
- Set the **Punch In** marker (**PI**)
- Set the **Punch Out** marker (**PO**)
- Remove the **Punch In/Out** markers

Recording in the *Punch In* Mode

In the **Punch In** mode, you can record using one of three methods:

- "On-the-fly", that is, during playback
- With the help of *markers*
- "Punch in loop", i.e., loop recording

Let's examine these methods more closely.

The On-the-Fly Method

1. First, you need to enable recording on the selected track by clicking the **R** button.
2. Then switch on the **Punch In** mode (Fig. 5.40).
3. Start recording.

4. When the cursor has almost reached the desired place on the track, click the **Punch In Record** button on the **Punch/Play** toolbar.

> *NOTE*   The **PI** (Punch In) marker will appear in the VIP window (Fig. 5.41).

Notice that the beginning of the created object will be at the very point of the track where the **PI** marker is set.

Recording will continue until you stop it with the spacebar.

After recording stops, Samplitude 2496 will suggest that you either save or delete the recorded take. In particular, the **Recording finished** dialog box will appear in the same manner as it did when recording in the **Record Parameter** dialog box (Fig. 5.36).

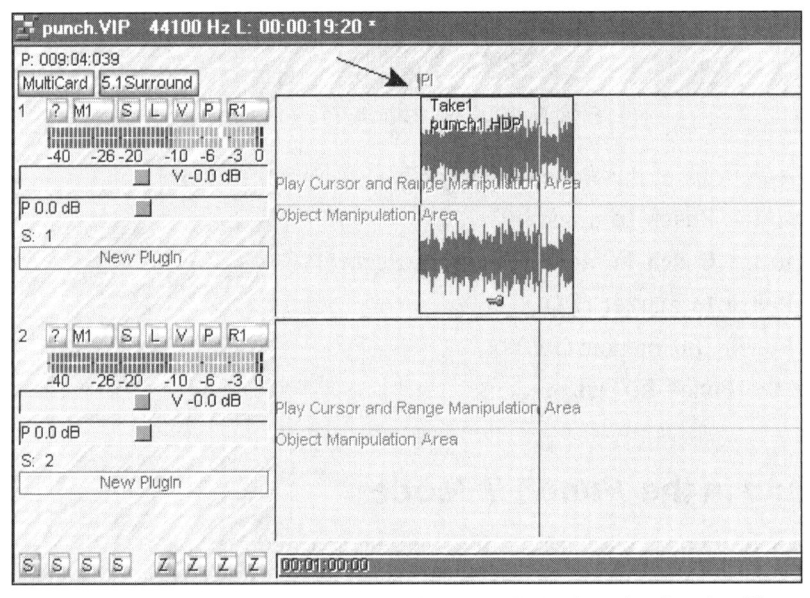

Fig. 5.41. An example of recording in the **Punch In** mode (using the On-the-Fly method)

Recording Using Markers

To record using the markers, proceed as follows:

1. Select the fragment where recording is to take place.

> *NOTE*   You might select, say, a fragment inside an object.

2. Click the **PI** and **PO** buttons (in any order).

Chapter 5: The Samplitude 2496 Application as a High-Quality Virtual Studio 325

> **NOTE** Two markers corresponding to these buttons will appear on the boundaries of the selected area.

3. Switch on the **Punch In** recording mode.
4. Set the multitrack cursor to a small distance to the left of the **PI** marker and click the **Punch In Record** button (Fig. 5.40).

> **NOTE** After the cursor passes the **PO** marker, the portion of the object between the **PI** and **PO** markers will disappear.

A new object will be created between the **PI** and **PO** markers (Fig. 5.42) after you stop the playback with the spacebar and click the **Yes** button in the **Recording finished** dialog box.

> **NOTE** If you click the **Delete** button in the **Recording finished** dialog box, the previous object will be kept. The **PI** and **PO** markers can be moved during recording.

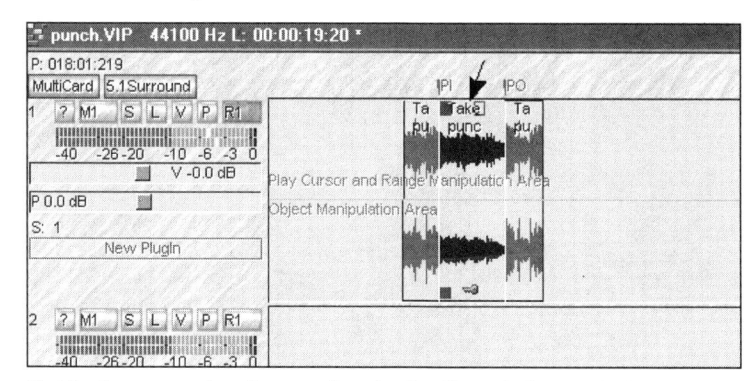

Fig. 5.42. An example of recording in the **Punch In** mode (using markers)

The *Punch-In-Loop* Recording Method

Punch In Loop is a method of loop recording in the **Punch In** mode. Using it, you can obtain a virtually unlimited number of takes on a fragment between the **PI** and **PO** markers.

Loop recording is very convenient, since it lets the musician concentrate on performing, leaving the routine work for the computer, which is ready to repeat the selected fragment and save the takes until the user stops the process or the free disk space is exhausted.

> **NOTE** You don't have to record takes of just one particular version of the performance. You may perform and create several versions and combine them into a separate VIP project, as we will demonstrate later.

The *Punch In Loop* recording procedure goes as follows:
1. Set the **Play Loop** playback mode.
2. Click the **R** button on the track of the multitrack where recording is to take place.
3. Using **PI** and **PO**, mark the fragment that you plan to replay.
4. Select a loop playback area wider than the marked one (Fig. 5.43).

> **WARNING** The playback area must *always* be larger than the marked one (Fig. 5.43).

5. Switch on the **Punch In Record** recording mode.

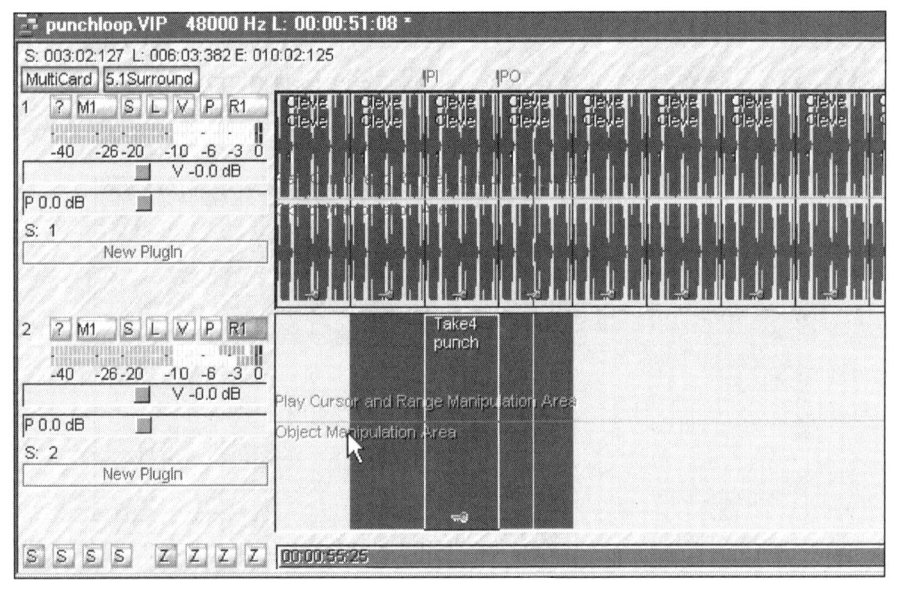

Fig. 5.43. An example of recording in the **Punch In Loop** mode

6. Having recorded the takes, stop the process with the spacebar.

> **NOTE** The **Recording finished** dialog box lets you either delete *all* the recorded takes (with the **Delete** button) or leave the object of the last take on the multitrack (the **Yes** button).

The *Take Manager* Dialog Box

Samplitude 2496 provides the user with a special tool to work with takes, **Take Manager**. The **Take Manager** allows you to organize the listening to, sorting, and selecting of recorded material.

Chapter 5: The Samplitude 2496 Application as a High-Quality Virtual Studio 327

NOTE The **Take Manager** is somewhat similar to the **Take History** tool of Cool Edit Pro, but its features are more powerful.

To call **Take Manager**, proceed as follows:

1. Select the object.

NOTE To select an object in the **Universal Mode**, click it below the horizontal line that divides the track of the VIP project.

2. Select the **Take Manager** item from the **Tools** menu.

The **Take Manager** dialog box will appear on the screen (Fig. 5.44). Let's examine it more closely.

A significant part of the dialog box is occupied by the Take list, that is, the list of all the recorded takes.

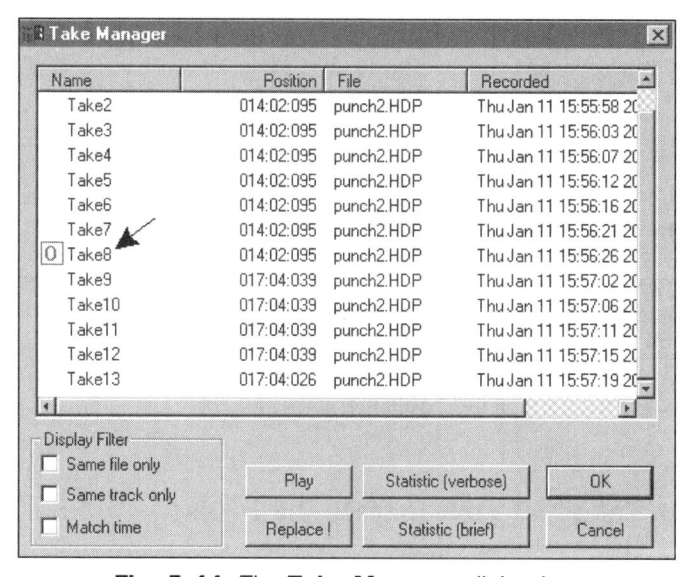

Fig. 5.44. The **Take Manager** dialog box

Marking the Last Take

Since Samplitude 2496 allows you to record multiple groups of takes (for example, for different fragments of composition), a *special marker* is provided to separate these groups.

The marker looks like parentheses inside a box (Fig. 5.44). It is automatically set next to the name of the last take of the object *currently selected* in the multitrack.

The checkboxes in the **Display Filter** section specify how the takes of the Take list must be displayed.

- **Same file only** displays only those takes that belong to one sound *file*
- **Same track only** displays only those takes that belong to one *track*
- **Match time** displays the takes that belong to one *time interval* on the track

Choosing the Best Take

To choose the most successful take, you should listen to all the recorded takes together with all the other tracks of the project.

To do this, proceed as follows:

1. Position the cursor of a VIP project at the beginning of the object that contains the takes.
2. Open the **Take Manager** dialog box.
3. Click the **Play** button and listen to the take.
4. Call the next take:
   - Click its name in the Take list
   - Click the **Replace** button
   - Click the **Play** button
5. Having made your choice, close the **Take Manager** dialog box. The selected take will remain on the multitrack.

> **NOTE** To free some space on the hard disk, use the **Remove unused Samples** command of the **Tools** menu.

Combining the Takes into a Separate VIP Project

All the takes in the **Take Manager** dialog box can be combined into a separate VIP project. This is done using the **Statistic (brief)** and the **Statistic (verbose)** buttons.

- The **Statistic (brief)** button creates a new VIP project where all the takes are placed *on one track*, one after the other
- The **Statistic (verbose)** button creates a new VIP project where all the takes are placed *on different tracks*, each just below the other (Fig. 5.45)

Working with takes results in:

- Either choosing the best take from all those performed
- Or creating a new take from the existing ones

Chapter 5: The Samplitude 2496 Application as a High-Quality Virtual Studio 329

NOTE The montage of a new take is performed in Samplitude 2496 in the same manner as in SAWPro. To be more precise, you use several takes as the material for one new take (using non-destructive editing).

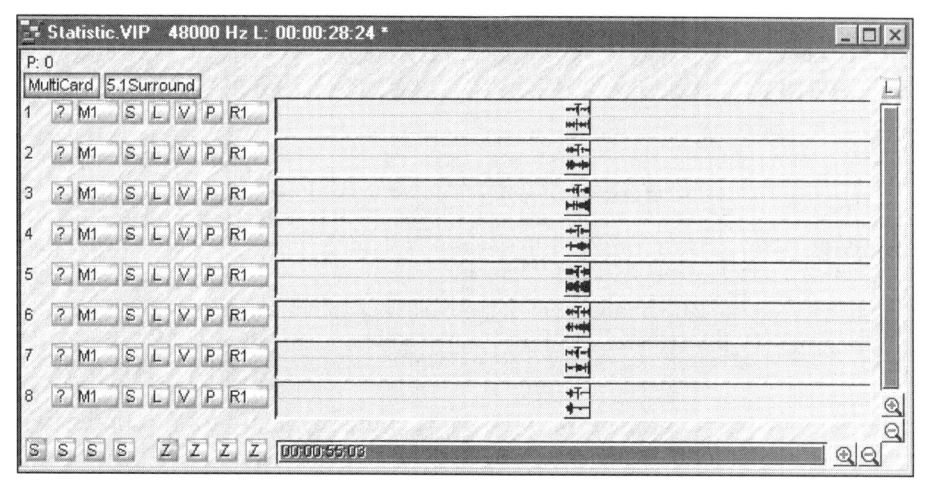

Fig. 5.45. The **Statistic.VIP** dialog box

By enabling various combinations of virtual effects, you can use the **Statistic.VIP** project as a collection of objects, or "blocks", so to speak, for building the composition of the main project.

The Playback Modes

This section covers such frequently used elements of the interface as the toolbars that are related to the project playback modes.

There are two such panels in Samplitude 2496:

- The **Play** toolbar
- The **Play to/from Cut** toolbar

The *Play* Toolbar

In this toolbar (Fig. 5.46), you can find all the buttons necessary to control the playback modes of the selected fragment.

Fig. 5.46. The **Play** toolbar

Here we give the functions of these buttons (from left to right):

- **Play Once** — play the selected fragment once
- **Play Loop** — play the selected fragment in a loop
- **Play into Loop** — first play from the beginning of the track up to the end of the selected fragment, and then play the selected fragment in a loop
- **Stop** — stop playback

> **NOTE** The **Play Once**, **Play Loop**, and **Stop** buttons are duplicated by the spacebar. Upon starting playback, this key "remembers" the previous playback mode. (For example, if this was **Play Once**, pressing the spacebar starts the one-time playback of the selected fragment.)
>
> The restart can be done at any point of the multitrack without stopping the current playback. To do this, click the desired point of the multitrack in the upper half of the track (in the **Universal Mode**).

Before we proceed with the other playback modes, it is necessary to introduce an important concept of Samplitude 2496 — the *range*.

The Range

A range in Samplitude 2496 is a selected area.

We've already discussed how to work with selected portions in SAWPro and Cool Edit Pro. However, in Samplitude 2496, the range is a self-sufficient notion.

It is subject to the following operations:

- Edit
- Invert
- Save
- Move
- Expand
- Narrow, etc.

To process the selected areas (ranges), a special menu is provided in Samplitude 2496. This is **Range**.

Working with Ranges

The features of Samplitude 2496 are quite vast. It would take a separate book to describe all of them, so only the main techniques are described here.

Range Mode

We'd like to remind you again that the **Universal Mode** for editing virtual projects is set in Samplitude 2496 by default. In this mode, every track of the multitrack is divided horizontally into two equal areas. The upper part is used for editing ranges (**Range Mode**), and the lower part is for editing objects (**Object Mode**). The appearance of the mouse pointer changes when it crosses the horizontal boundary between the two parts. To select a range, move the mouse pointer to the upper part of the track. To select an object, click it in the lower part of the track.

Let's consider the most important operations valid for ranges in the **Range Mode**.

- To *select* a range, drag the mouse pointer (with the left mouse button pressed) along the track in either direction from the current position.
- To *unselect* one, just click at any point outside of the range (in the upper part of the track).
- To *change the boundaries* of a range, position the cursor within the range, click, and drag the boundary (with the left mouse button pressed) to the new position.

> **NOTE**   The boundary "sticks" to the mouse pointer.

- To *move* a range along the track of the multitrack, position the mouse pointer within the range, press and hold down the <Shift> key, and drag the range horizontally to the new position.
- To *expand* a range vertically to other tracks, position the cursor within the range, click, and drag it up or down.

> **NOTE**   When creating a range, you can span multiple tracks all at once. Just move the mouse pointer diagonally.

- To *zoom* the image of a range, double click within the selected area.

> **NOTE**   The image will zoom in so that the selected area takes up the entire visible portion of the track.

- To *save* ranges, use the **Store Range** command of the **Range** menu.
- To *restore* a range at the same place (with reference to the time axis), use the **Get Range** command of the **Range** menu.
- To restore *the length of a saved range*, you can use the **Get Range Length** command of the **Range** menu. The position of a range is determined by the current position of the multitrack cursor.

How to Measure the Tempo of a Range

The tempo of a range is measured in the **Snap definition** dialog box (Fig. 5.39):

1. Select the range.
2. Open the **Snap definition** dialog box.

> **NOTE** To open the dialog box, you can use the <Shift>+<R> shortcut.

3. Click the **Get Range** button in the **Free bar snap** section.

The tempo will be shown in the **BPM** (Beats Per Minute) field.

The number in the **The selected range is ... Beats** field shows the number of beats in the selected range. This value determines what is shown in the **BPM** field.

The *Play to/from Cut* Playback Modes

The **Play to/from Cut** modes are additional playback modes in Samplitude 2496. They are used for various ways of listening to a selected range.

The functions of the buttons in the **Play to/from Cut** toolbar are clearly reflected by the icons (Fig. 5.47).

Fig. 5.47. The **Play to/from Cut** toolbar

These buttons are (from left to right):

- **Play to Cut Start** — playback of the fragment *before* the selected area

  > **NOTE** The cursor automatically stops at the starting boundary of the selected range.

- **Play from Cut Start** — playback of the fragment *from the starting boundary* of the selected range

  > **NOTE** Playback begins at the starting boundary of the range, and automatically stops after a while.

- **Play to Cut End** — playback of the fragment *up until the end* of the selected area

  > **NOTE** The cursor stops at the end boundary of the range.

- **Play from Cut End** — playback of the fragment *from the ending boundary* of the range

Chapter 5: The Samplitude 2496 Application as a High-Quality Virtual Studio 333

> **NOTE** The playback begins at the ending boundary of the range, and automatically stops after a while.

- **Play over Cut** — playback excludes the selected range

> **NOTE** Here, playback starts before the selected range, keeps playing up until the starting boundary, "jumps" over the range to its end boundary, and automatically stops playing after a while.

The **Play to/from Cut** modes make the process of editing sound material much easier and more convenient.

Additional Services of Samplitude 2496

The developers of Samplitude 2496 have provided users with a very convenient and unique interface, using which you can easily solve the tasks of multichannel recording and editing audio material.

> **NOTE** The approach of software developers to the interfaces and dialogs of their program products varies from one application to another. When you first encounter Samplitude 2496, you might feel confused by the abundant amount of buttons and its many unfamiliar terms. However, you will eventually understand that this seemingly excessive interface has no unnecessary elements.

In Samplitude 2496, it is possible not only to use the rich set of the features of its graphic interface, but also to program the user's own combinations of hotkeys. In other words, the musician can create his or her own environment based on the Samplitude 2496 interface in order to write music of any style.

Positionbar

Let's now discuss some additional services of Samplitude 2496.

The buttons for tools having similar functions are grouped together in certain panels (toolbars).

> **NOTE** We've already seen such toolbars — for example, the **Punch/Play** toolbar (Fig. 5.40), which is designed to record in the **Punch** mode.

Now let's look at some tools that make editing a project easier. They are collected in the **Positionbar**. Since this panel contains many buttons, we're going to look at them in groups.

The First Group of *Positionbar* Buttons

The buttons of this group (Fig. 5.48) allow you to adjust the zoom — that is, to zoom in or out, to display the whole project, or display a portion with a length of, say, 10 or 60 seconds.

Fig. 5.48. The first group of **Positionbar** buttons

This group can be divided into two sections (separated by the black vertical line in Fig. 5.48). On the screen, these sections differ by their foreground color: in the left section, the letters and digits are red, whereas they are blue in the right section.

The "red" (left) section is used to zoom *horizontally*, while the "blue" (right) one zooms *vertically*.

Here are the functions of the buttons in the "red" section (from left to right).

- **Zoom In** (with the "+" sign on the icon)
- **Zoom Out** (with the "−" sign on the icon)
- **Show entire project** (the letter **A**, denoting "all")

   NOTE Clicking this button zooms the project so that it is displayed on the screen in its entirety.

- **Zoom from range** (the letter **R**, standing for "range")

   NOTE The selected range will take up the whole screen.

- **One pixel = one sample** (with the **1:1** inscription).
- Four buttons (**Zoom = 1s, 10s, 60s,** and **10m**) set a zooming that corresponds to the specified time interval

   NOTE If you select **1s**, a portion 1 second long will take up the whole screen; if you select **10s**, the length of the displayed portion will be 10 seconds, etc.

The functions of the buttons in the "blue" section are the following (from left to right):

- **Zoom in vertically** (with the "+" sign)
- **Zoom out vertically** (with the "−" sign)
- **Show all vertically** (with the letter **A**)
- **Zoom in range vertically** (with the letter **R**)

Chapter 5: The Samplitude 2496 Application as a High-Quality Virtual Studio 335

- **Zoom Wave In** (with the "+" sign and the waveform icon)
- **Zoom Wave Out** (with the "−" sign and the waveform icon)

The Second Group of *Positionbar* Buttons

It is difficult to overestimate the convenience provided by the buttons of this group (Fig. 5.49). You can move along the project by steps of a certain size while moving a *section*.

Fig. 5.49. The second group of **Positionbar** buttons

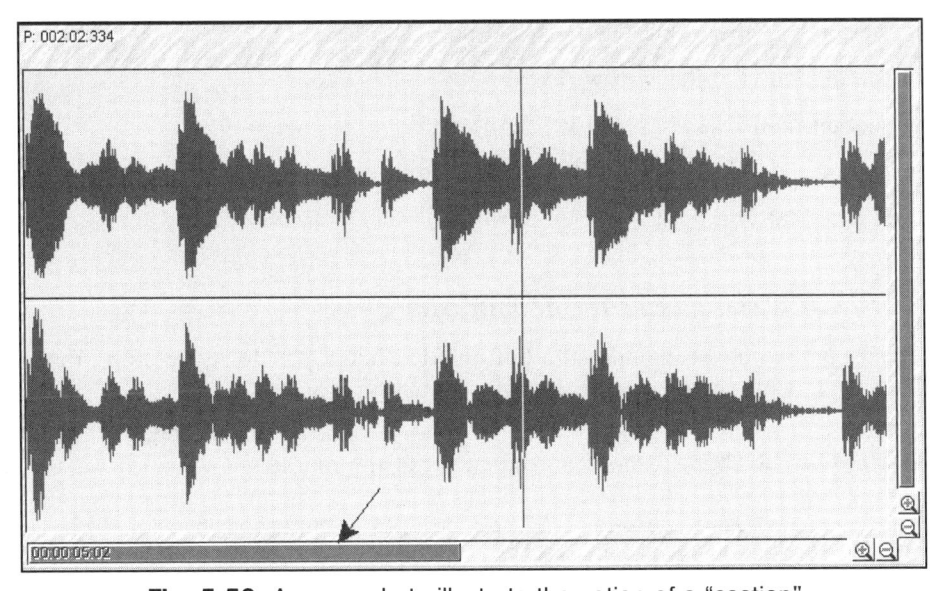

Fig. 5.50. An example to illustrate the notion of a "section"

The Section

In terms of Samplitude 2496, a *section* is the visible portion of a VIP project, or the visible portion of a sound wave in a RAM project window (or an HD Wave project window).

A *section* is a fragment of a project that is currently displayed on the screen.

The size of a section can be changed using any of the operations that zoom the track horizontally. Changes in a section's size are immediately reflected in the bottom of the window: the size of the scroll box changes with the number that shows the section size in seconds (Fig. 5.50).

The section size is inversely related to the zoom. In other words, when the picture is big, a short fragment can fit into the screen. On the other hand, you're able to view the entire project only when the wave picture is very small. This means that in the first case (the zoom and the picture are big), the section is small — just a portion of a second. In the other case, it is as big as possible (equal to the whole project).

Using the buttons of the second group of the **Positionbar**, you can easily and conveniently move along the project leftwards or rightwards. For example, you can go to the beginning or to the end of the project, or you can move by steps one section long or a half section long.

Let's look at the buttons of this group (from left to right):

- **To beginning** (the "bar and left arrow" icon)
- **One section left** (the "double left arrow" icon)
- **Half section left** (the "left arrow" icon)
- **Half section right** (the "right arrow" icon)
- **One section right** (the "double right arrow" icon)
- **To end** (the "bar and right arrow" icon)

The Third Group of *Positionbar* Buttons

The last group (Fig. 5.51) includes the buttons that allow you to move along the project in various ways: using the edges of the objects, or using markers.

The first two buttons of this group position the cursor exactly at the edges of the objects, whereas the other two buttons position the cursor at the markers.

> **NOTE** Using markers in Samplitude 2496 is discussed in detail in the "*Editing a Virtual Project*" section.

Fig. 5.51. The third group of **Positionbar** buttons

Here are the functions of the buttons of this group of the **Positionbar** (from left to right).

- **To previous object edge**
- **To next object edge**
- **To previous marker**
- **To next marker**

Chapter 5: The Samplitude 2496 Application as a High-Quality Virtual Studio

Additional Buttons of a Virtual Project

Let's discuss some additional groups of buttons found in the window of a VIP project (Fig. 5.52).

- The **L** button locks all the markers in the VIP project

   NOTE After this button is clicked, it is impossible to move the markers to the left or right.

- Two pairs of buttons with the "+" or "−" signs in magnifying glasses serve to zoom the image vertically or horizontally
- Four **S** buttons ("Store screen position and zoom level") allow you to store four values of these parameters and access them at a later time
- Four **Z** buttons ("Store zoom level") allow you to store and get zoom levels only

   NOTE You store parameters by clicking the **S** or **Z** button while holding the <Shift> key pressed.

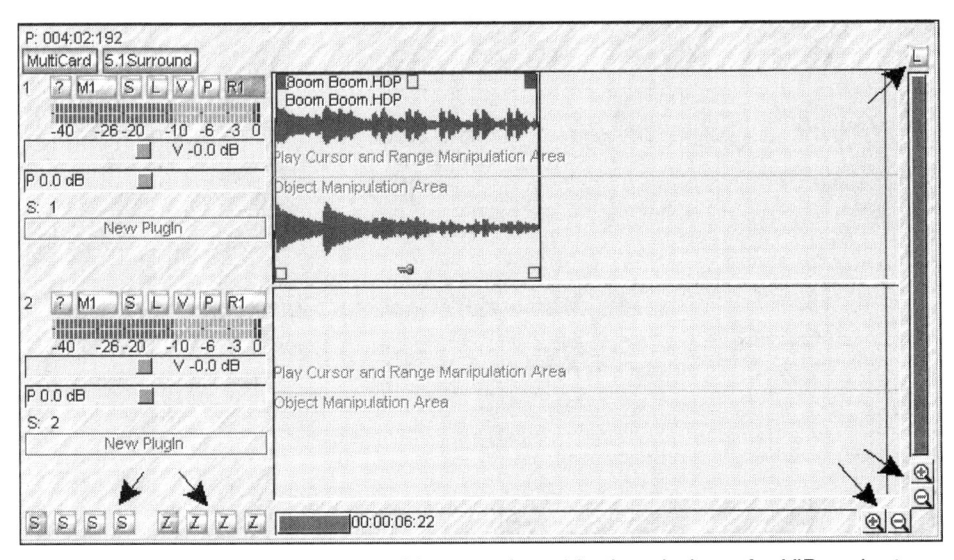

Fig. 5.52. Additional groups of buttons found in the window of a VIP project

Splitting the Project Window

You can also split the project window into two or three sections with the help of the **1**, **2**, and **3** items in the **Sections** submenu of the **View** menu (Fig. 5.53).

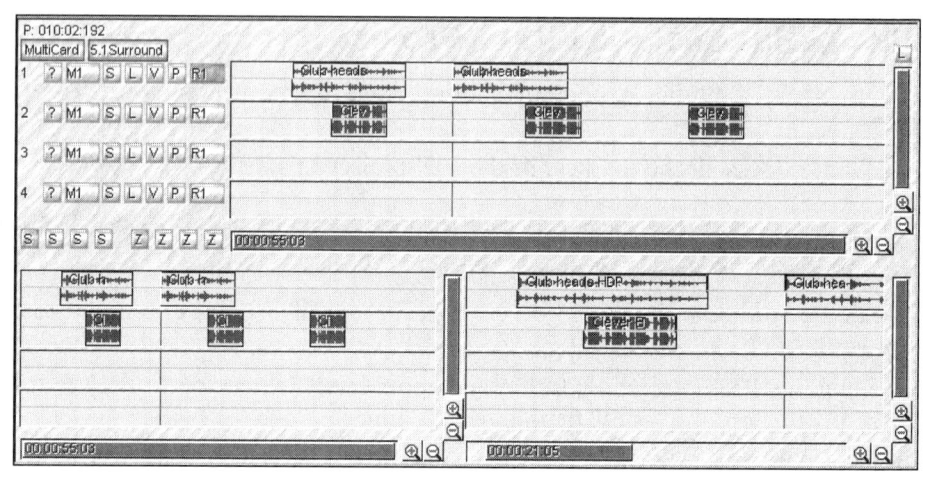

Fig. 5.53. Splitting the project window into three sections

To make loop editing more convenient, the **Range** menu provides the **Split Range** option (the <B> hotkey) (Fig. 5.54).

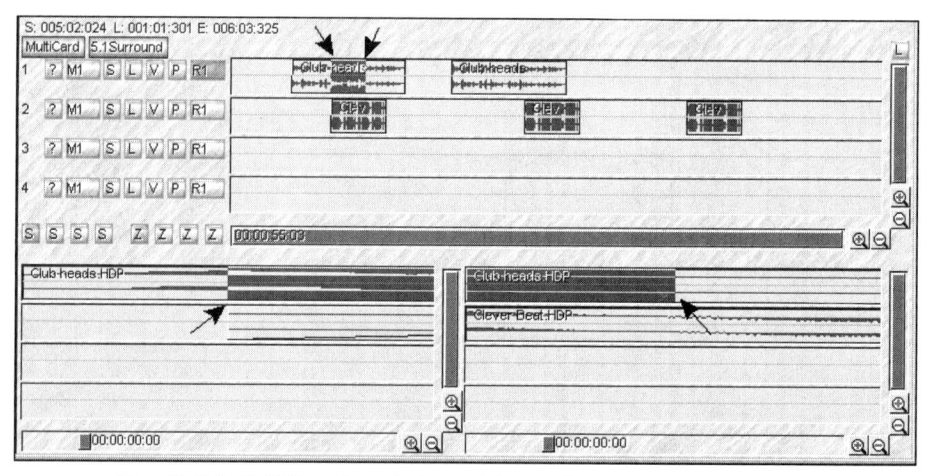

Fig. 5.54. Splitting the window with the **Split Range** command

The project window is split into three sections in such a way that the range in the lower left sub-window corresponds to the beginning of the range in the upper sub-window, and the range in the lower right sub-window corresponds to the end of the upper range.

To return to the whole window, press <Shift>+<R>.

The VIP Display Mode

Samplitude 2496 allows the user to have two screens for displaying a virtual project. Switching between them is done using the **Mode 1** and **Mode 2** commands of the **VIP Display Mode** submenu of the **View** menu. You may also use the <Tab> key.

To set up the display modes in Samplitude 2496, you must access the **Draw Mode/Properties in Virtual Projects** dialog box shown in Fig. 5.55.

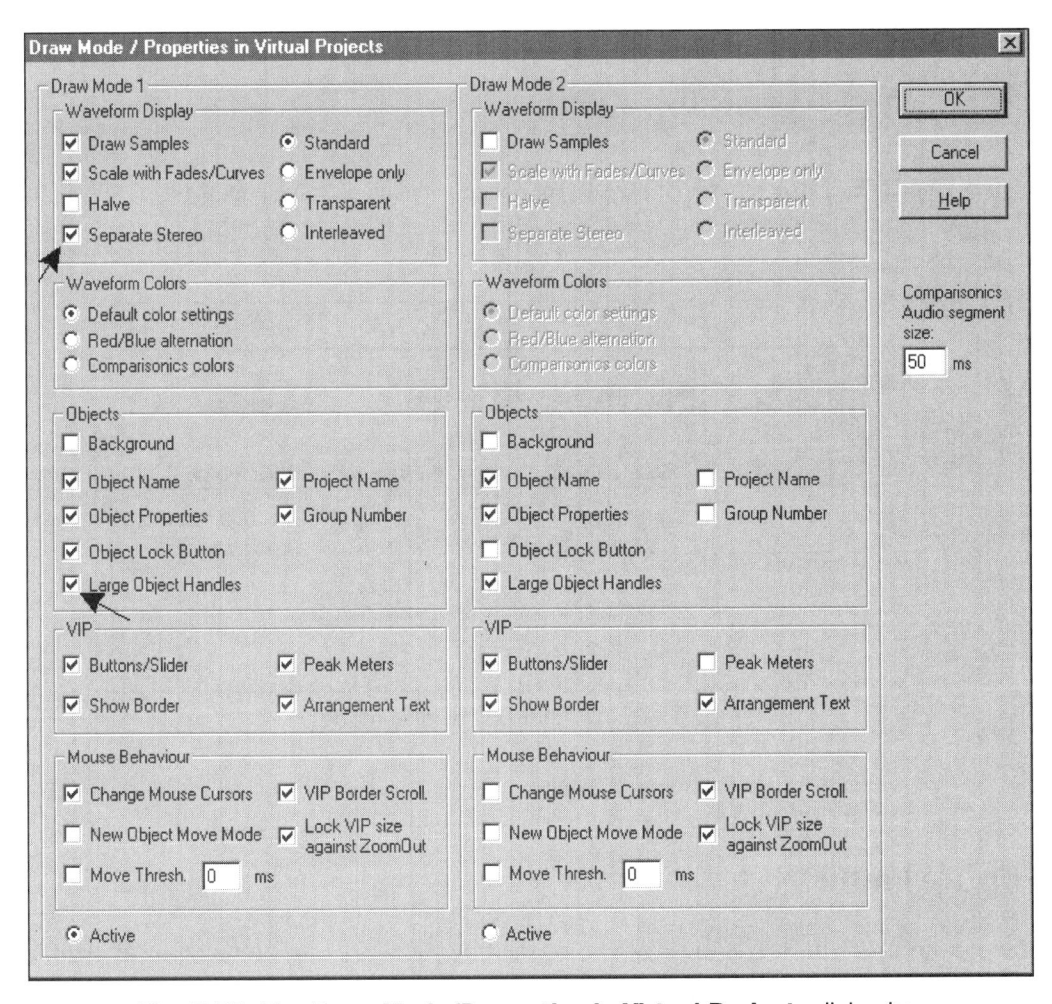

Fig. 5.55. The **Draw Mode/Properties in Virtual Projects** dialog box

This dialog box is opened using the **Definition** command of the **VIP Display Mode** submenu of the **View** menu, or with the <Shift>+<Tab> shortcut.

The default settings are quite appropriate, so we recommend that you leave most of them as they are. The only exception is for the **Separate Stereo** and **Large Object Handles** checkboxes (indicated by the arrows in Fig. 5.55 in the **Mode 1** section).

You should check them, since this will facilitate graphic editing and show you the visual differences between the mono and stereo objects.

The **Halve** checkbox enables a display mode where the waveform is halved horizontally (Fig. 5.56).

NOTE Such a mode is typical for earlier versions of Samplitude 2496.

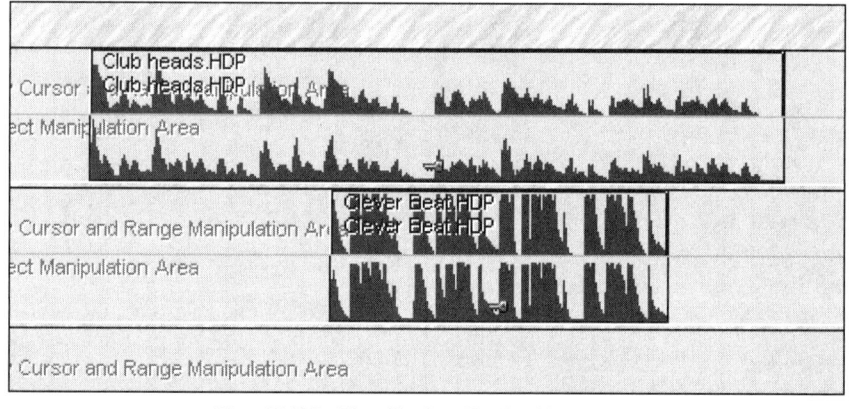

Fig. 5.56. The "halved" display mode

Pop-up Menu

The pop-up menu in Samplitude 2496 is opened by right-clicking on a graphical element of the interface (a button, a track, etc.), just like in Cool Edit Pro.

Sound Processing in Samplitude 2496

Non-Destructive Sound Processing

The Object

When discussing the programs that allow multitrack recording to the hard disk, we intentionally put the chapters that covered these programs in a certain order.

- In SAWPro, the multitrack includes a clip (called an "entry") that has no properties. However, any non-destructive editing operations can be applied to the clip.
- In Cool Edit Pro, a clip (called a "wave block") already has some "embryonic" properties. It has its own volume, pan, and color, and it can be turned off with the **Mute** button.
- In Samplitude 2496, a clip (called an "object") is a *virtual object* that has properties reflected by a great many individual settings.

The large number of properties implies the large number of possible settings. Let's concentrate on how to edit the properties of *objects* in Samplitude 2496.

> **NOTE** As we stated in the "*Playback Modes*" section, there are several modes for editing a virtual project, called **VIP Mouse Modes**. Each of them allows you to perform various operations on *ranges* and *objects*.
>
> The **Universal Mode** is set by default. The peculiarities of editing in the other modes will be discussed in the "*Editing a Virtual Project*" section later in this chapter.

In the **Universal Mode**, each track of a multitrack is divided horizontally into two halves (Fig. 5.57).

The upper half is called the **Play Cursor and Range Manipulation Area**. It is used for editing *ranges* and setting the *cursor* to a certain position.

The lower half — the **Object Manipulation Area** — is used for:

- Selecting
- Moving
- Copying
- Changing the *handles* of the object

Handles are the points of an object that are used to *change the boundaries of the region,* the *volume* of the object, and adjust the **Fade In** and **Fade Out** lines.

If you click an object in the lower half of the track, this object will change its appearance. Five handles will appear as little boxes along the perimeter of the object (indicated by the arrows in Fig. 5.57). When the handles are visible, the object is considered to be *selected*.

The "key" at the bottom of the object is designed to lock the object against being accidentally moved.

- When the "key" is red, the object is locked
- When it is yellow, the object is unlocked

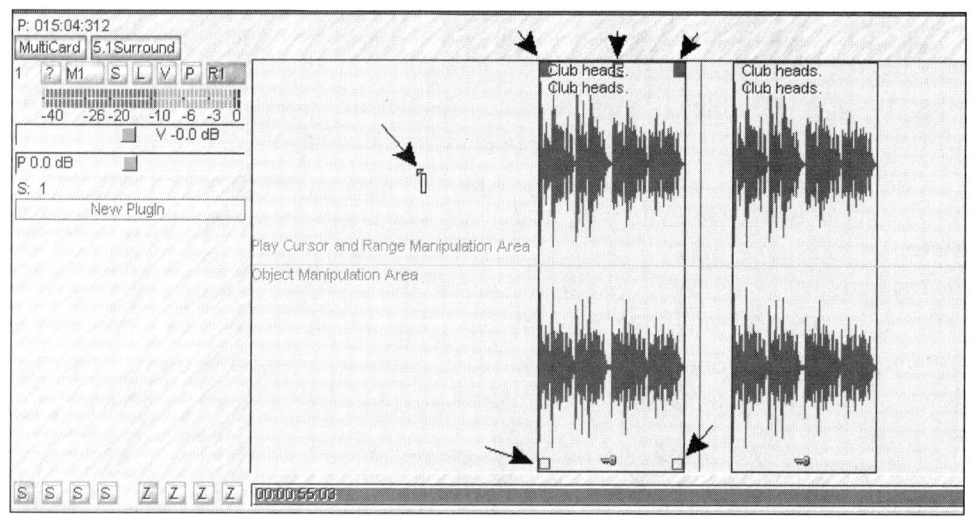

Fig. 5.57. An object in the VIP window

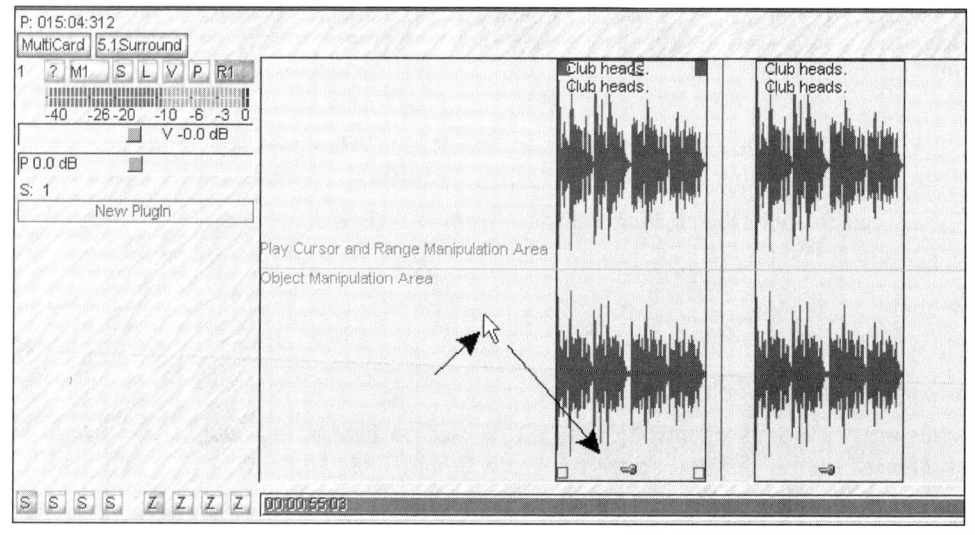

Fig. 5.58. Selecting an object

Chapter 5: The Samplitude 2496 Application as a High-Quality Virtual Studio 343

Every click with the left mouse button on the "key" changes the locking state of the object, thus changing the color of the "key" indicator.

> **NOTE** Notice that the mouse pointer looks different in the upper and lower parts of the track. In the lower part, it has its normal shape (Fig. 5.58), whereas it changes its appearance in the upper part (Fig. 5.57).

Object Handles

Let's consider the purpose of each handle. In Fig. 5.59, we give them numbers for illustrative purposes.

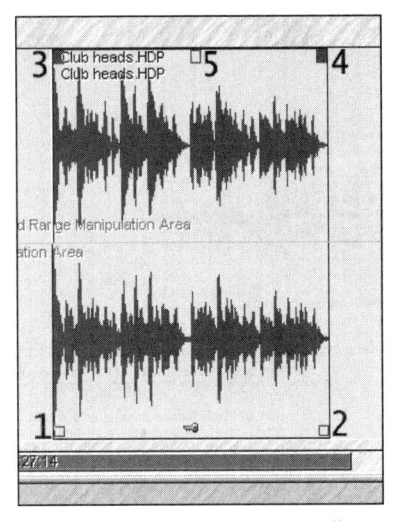

Fig. 5.59. The object handles

The Functions of the Object Handles

Handles 1 and 2 are used to change the boundaries of the object region (this is similar to the "trim" operation in SAWPro).

Changing the boundaries is done by dragging the handles to new positions (with the left mouse button pressed).

> **NOTE** If you position the mouse pointer on either handle, it will change its appearance and show you a *pop-up hint* (Fig. 5.60).

Handles 3 and 4 control the **Fade In** and **Fade Out** lines (Fig. 5.61).

These handles can be moved around the entire object, which changes the view of the waveform accordingly.

Fig. 5.61 shows the **Fade In** and **Fade Out** envelope lines of the waveform amplitude.

> **NOTE** The graphical representation of all the non-destructive operations that change the volume is a huge advantage of Samplitude 2496. It lets the user visually control the volume level of each object.

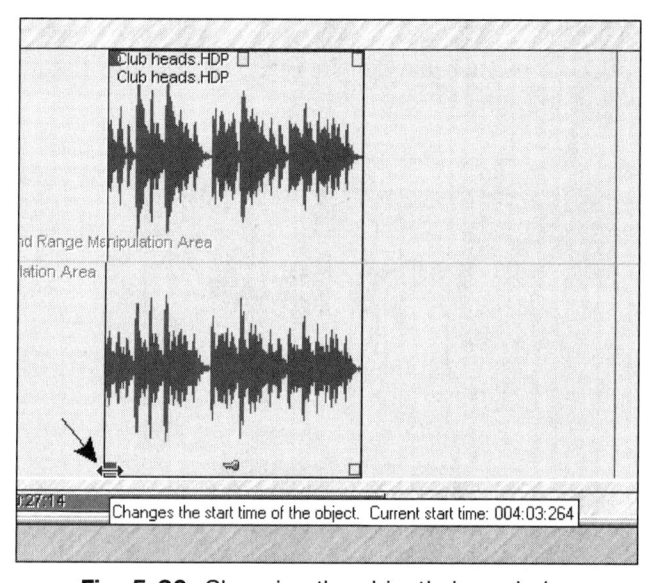

Fig. 5.60. Changing the object's boundaries

Handles 3 and 4 are also useful when linking objects, since a fade in/out of a few milliseconds eliminates unwanted clicking sounds when the amplitudes change.

> **NOTE** To set handles 3 and 4 with such precision, set the zoom level to **one pixel = = one sample (1:1)**.

Handle 5 is designed to control the volume level of the object (Fig. 5.62).

When the volume level of the object changes, the graphical representation of the waveform is updated accordingly.

The volume level of the object can be both decreased and increased (i.e., made higher than 0 dB, the upper line of the track). To increase the volume, proceed as follows:

1. Zoom the waveform representation out (using the **Zoom Wave Out** button, see Fig. 5.48) until you see red horizontal lines.

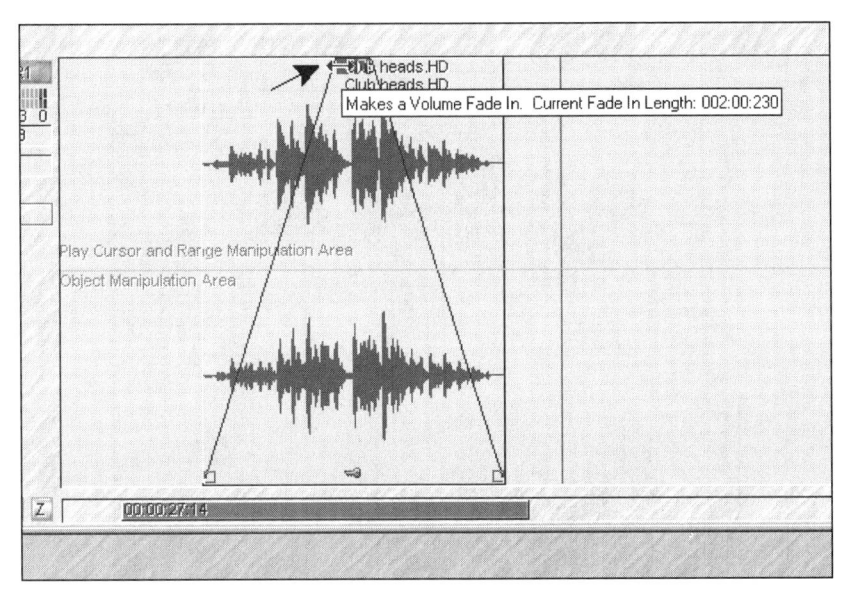

Chapter 5: The Samplitude 2496 Application as a High-Quality Virtual Studio 345

Fig. 5.61. Changing the **Fade In** and **Fade Out** lines

NOTE   Or, use the <Ctrl>+<down arrow> shortcut.

2. Stretch the object upwards (to the area with the red horizontal lines), as high as you need (Fig. 5.63).

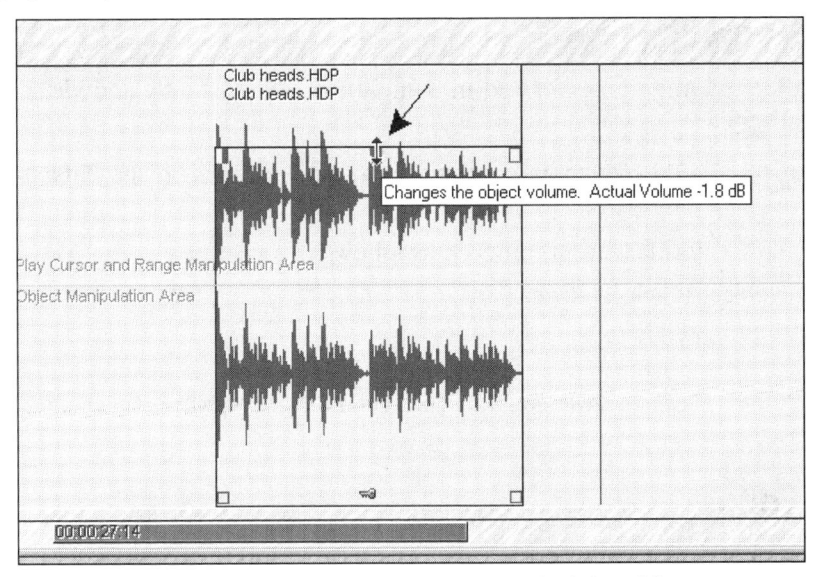

Fig. 5.62. Changing the volume level of the object

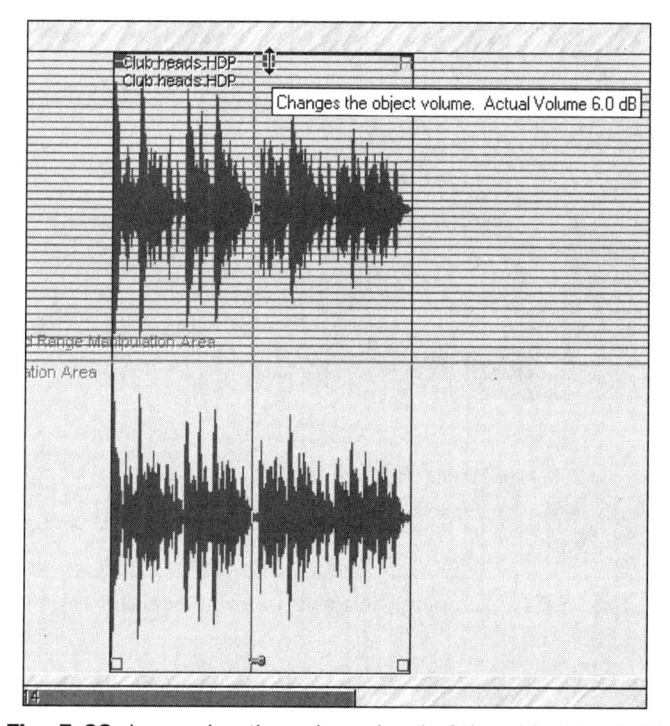

Fig. 5.63. Increasing the volume level of the object by 6 dB

Object Normalization

The **Normalize** operation is performed in Samplitude 2496 instantly and virtually (that is, non-destructively).

> **NOTE** The normalization commands can be found in the **Effects|Normalize** menu.

To perform object normalization, proceed as follows:
1. Select the object (click its lower part).
2. Press the <N> key.

> **NOTE** Destructive normalization is done with the <Shift>+<N> shortcut.

Object Editor

The **Object Editor** is the main tool of Samplitude 2496 for changing the properties of an object.

Chapter 5: The Samplitude 2496 Application as a High-Quality Virtual Studio

Using the object editor, you can set the length of an object, its volume and pan, and the dynamic range. You can also adjust the frequency-response curve, enable DirectX plug-ins, etc.

There are several ways to open the object editor.

❏ The first method is to double-click the lower part of the object (in the **Universal Mode**).

❏ The second method is to use the pop-up menu:
  - Right-click the object to open the pop-up menu
  - Execute the **Object Editor** command (Fig. 5.64)

❏ The third method is to use the **Object** menu.
  - Select the object
  - Execute the **Object Editor** command of the **Object** menu

In any case, the **Object Editor** window will open (Fig. 5.65), which we'll now discuss section-by-section.

The **Position/Length** section is used for entering the precise value for the *start position* and *length* of the object on the multitrack. These values are entered via the keyboard into the following fields:

❏ **Start (SMPTE)**   ❏ **Length (SMPTE)**

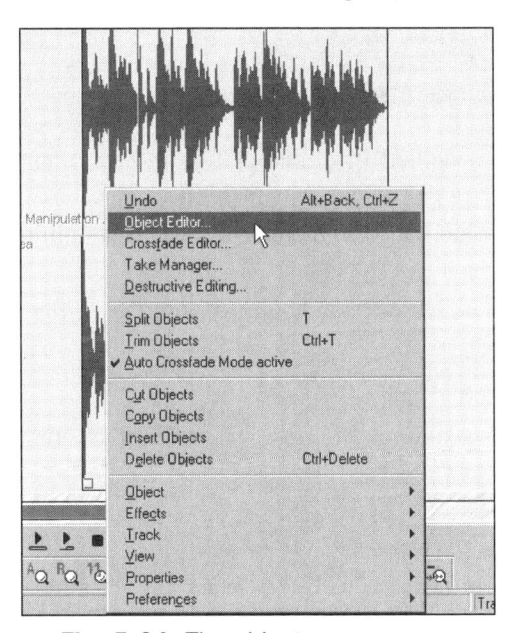

Fig. 5.64. The object pop-up menu

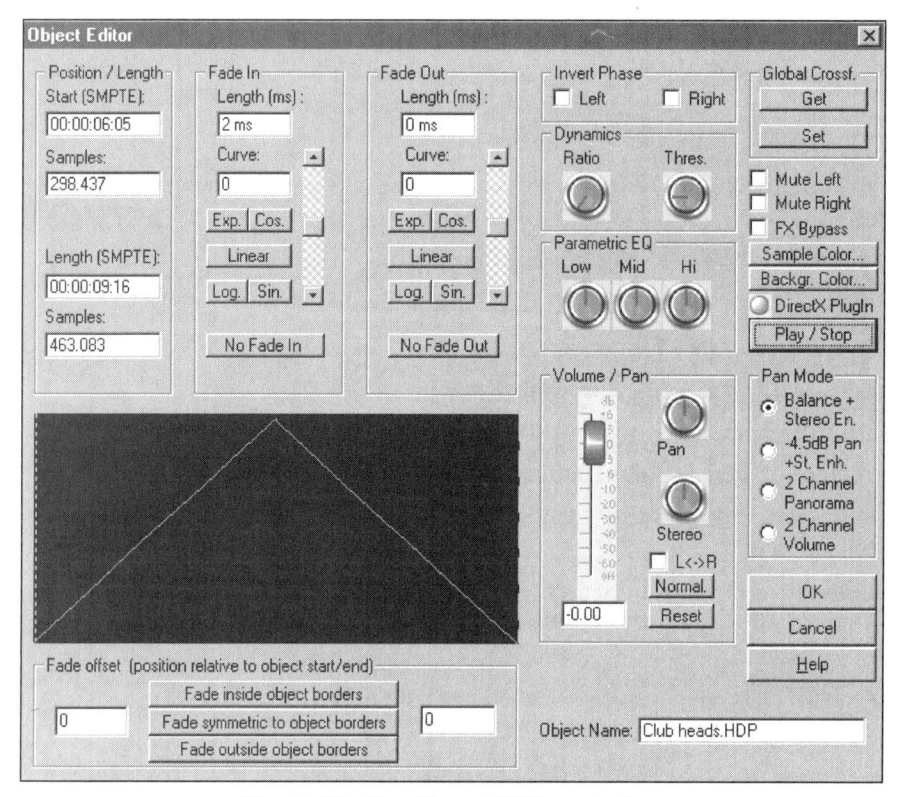

Fig. 5.65. The **Object Editor** window

Both parameters can be specified in either of two measurement units: in samples or in the SMPTE format (see *Chapter 7*).

The **Fade In** and **Fade Out** sections include buttons that allow you to adjust the fade in/out lines.

❏ In the **Length (ms)** field, the precise length of the *fade in/out area* is specified.

> *NOTE* Zero means no fade in/out.

❏ In the **Curve** field, the value of the positive or negative curvature of the **Fade** line is specified.

> *NOTE* The range of these values is from −100 to +100 units. Zero corresponds to a straight line.

The vertical scrollbars next to the **Curve** fields in both **Fade** sections allow the user to gradually change the curvature of the fade line. The curvature can be viewed in the display located under the **Fade** sections.

Chapter 5: The Samplitude 2496 Application as a High-Quality Virtual Studio   349

- The **Exp**, **Log**, **Cos**, and **Sin** buttons specify the mathematical function of the **Fade** line.

  > **NOTE** The values in the **Curve** field vary according to the curvature, from −100 to +100.

  If you turn the **Fade** line into a straight line with the **Linear** button, the value in the **Curve** field will be reset to 0.

- The **No Fade In** and **No Fade Out** buttons reset the values in the **Length (ms)** fields of the **Fade In** and **Fade Out** sections to 0.

The **Fade offset (position relative to object start/end)** section allows you to adjust this position.

- The **Fade inside object borders** button sets an offset of zero, which is the default setting.

- The **Fade symmetric to object borders** button sets the offset equal to half of the **Fade** line. In such a case, when handles **3** and **4** are moved, the length of the object will change. The **Fade** line will rotate around the point indicated by the arrow in Fig. 5.66.

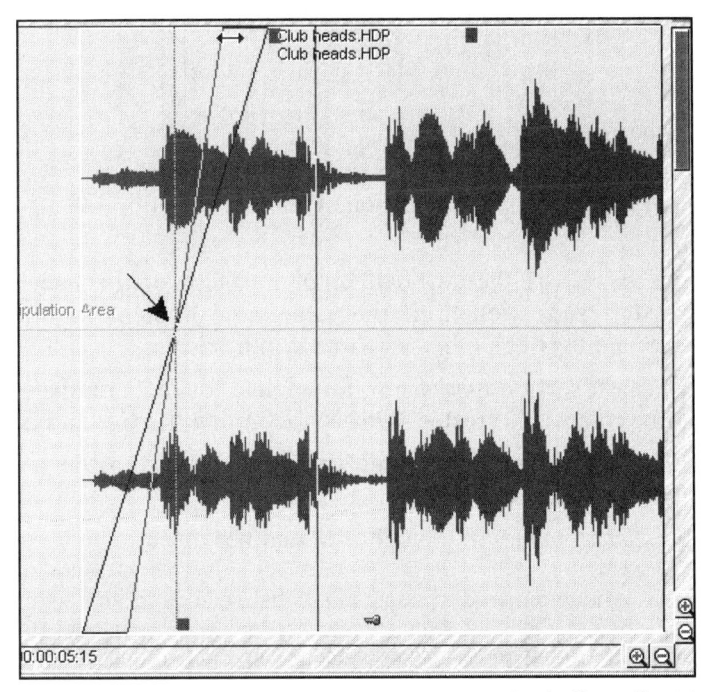

Fig. 5.66. An example of moving a handle with a **Fade** line offset by 0.5

❐ The **Fade outside object borders** button sets the offset equal to the length of the **Fade** line. Here, the length of the object can become equal to the length of the **Fade** line when handles 3 and 4 are moved (Fig. 5.67). The **Fade** line will rotate around handle **3** or **4** (indicated by the arrow in Fig. 5.67).

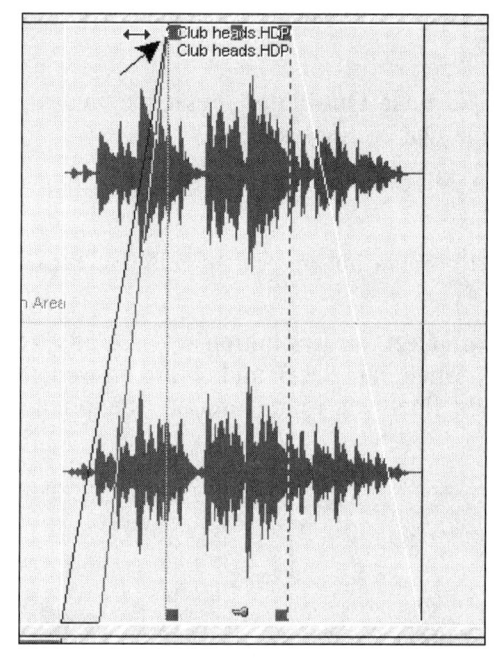

Fig. 5.67. An example of a **Fade** line offset by 1.0

You can enter the values via the keyboard into the fields of the **Fade offset (position relative to object start/end)** section. If the values are different for the left and right boundaries (say, 0.5 and 0.7), the offset won't be symmetrical.

❐ In the **Global Crossf.** section (Fig. 5.65), a template for the **Crossfade (Fade In, Fade Out)** lines of other objects is created. This is done using the **Get** and **Set** buttons.

- **Set** saves all the settings of the **Fade** line (that belong to the *selected* object) as *global settings* for other objects
- **Get** calls the *global settings* in the editor of another object

NOTE When you need to apply the global settings to an object that was created before the new template was saved, you must open the **Object Editor** window for this object and get the global settings with the **Get** button.

Objects created after the new template is saved get the global settings automatically.

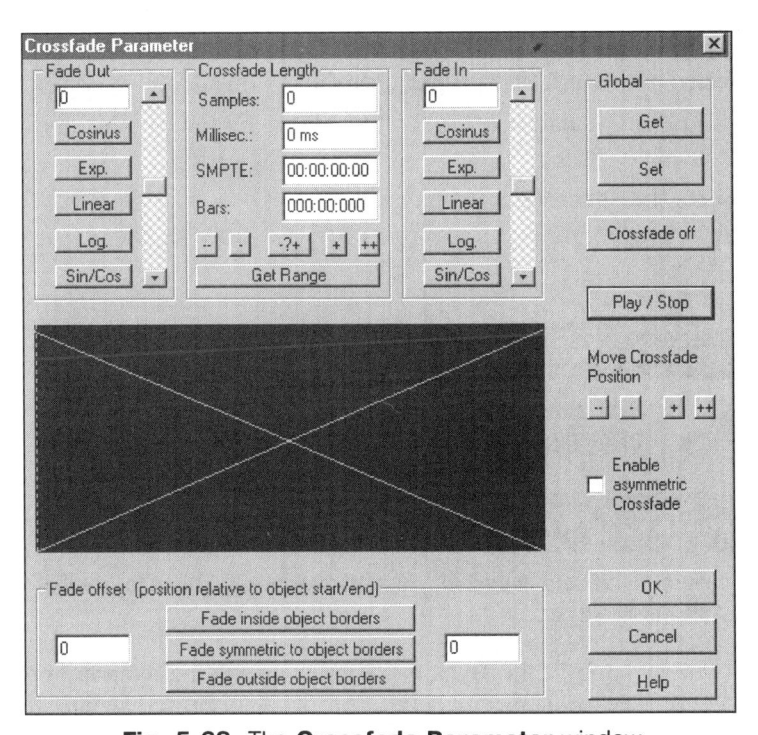

Chapter 5: The Samplitude 2496 Application as a High-Quality Virtual Studio 351

Fig. 5.68. The **Crossfade Parameter** window

Crossfade

Recall that when objects overlap, the **Auto crossfade** mode turns on automatically. In this mode, the sound of one object fades out while the sound of the other object fades in. This happens in the area where the two objects overlap. The **Auto crossfade** mode (Fig. 5.25) works only when the **Auto crossfade active** option is checked in the **Edit** menu. In the display, the crossfade looks like an intersection of the **Fade In** and **Fade Out** lines.

When objects overlap, the global settings of the curvatures of the **Fade In** and **Fade Out** lines create the **Crossfade** diagram (the intersection of these lines). This is why the global settings are called **Global Crossfade**. To adjust crossfade for a particular pair of overlapping objects, use the **Crossfade Editor**.

The **Crossfade Editor** is called with the command of the **Edit** menu with the same name.

NOTE The **Crossfade Parameter** window (Fig. 5.68), where the crossfade settings are determined, partially resembles the **Object Editor** window (Fig. 5.65). The **Fade In** and **Fade Out** sections have the same purpose as in the **Object Editor**, and the **Crossfade Length** section makes it possible to adjust the crossfade area length. The **Get Range** button writes the settings of the selected range to the fields of the **Crossfade Length** section.

- ❐ In the **Invert Phase** section of the **Object Editor** window (Fig. 5.65), the phase of the channel selected with the **Left** or **Right** checkbox is inverted.
- ❐ The controls in the **Dynamics** section of the **Object Editor** window are used to change the dynamic range of the signal.
  - **Ratio** adjusts the compression/expansion ratio
  - **Thres.** (Threshold) sets the *threshold* level relative to which the dynamic range is changed

> **How to Turn a Knob**
>
> To turn a knob, click it without releasing the left mouse button. With the button pressed, move the mouse pointer in the necessary direction (clockwise or counterclockwise).

> **How to Reset a Knob to the Default Position**
>
> To reset a knob to the default position, just double-click it. This rule is valid for all the control knobs of Samplitude 2496.

A right click on either knob in the **Dynamics** section opens the dynamic processor setting window (Fig. 5.69.). The processor will be thoroughly discussed when we examine the **Effects** menu later in this chapter.

- ❐ The **Parametric EQ** section of the **Object Editor** window (Fig. 5.65) is designed to control the frequency response curve of the signal.

  The equalizer includes three control knobs:
  - **Low**
  - **Mid**
  - **Hi**

  When a knob is turned, a number appears next to it indicating the adjustment depth (in dB).

  > **NOTE** A right click on any control opens the **Filter Adjustments** window, which is also discussed when describing the **Effects** menu.

- ❐ The **Volume/Pan** section (Fig. 5.65) is used to adjust the volume, pan, and stereo base of the object.
  - The volume slider changes the volume of the object within the range of −70 to +6 dB

    > **NOTE** You may also enter the volume value from the keyboard into the field located below the slider.

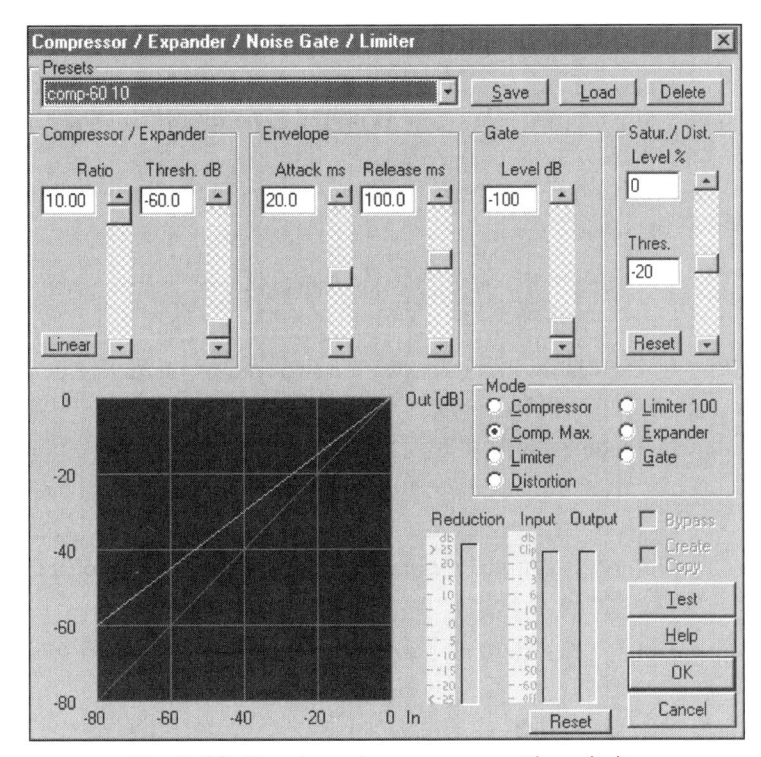

Chapter 5: The Samplitude 2496 Application as a High-Quality Virtual Studio

Fig. 5.69. The dynamic processor setting window

- The **Reset** button resets the volume to 0 dB
- The **Normal** button performs virtual normalization of the signal (similar to the normalization of an object in the VIP project window done using the <N> key)

> **WARNING** Virtual normalization of the signal *doesn't take into account* volume changes that come about as a result of sound processing by the parametric equalizer or dynamic processor.

- The **Pan** and **Stereo** control knobs adjust the pan and stereo base, respectively
- They work in the mode selected using the **Pan Mode** group of checkboxes

☐ The **Pan Mode** section is used to select one of the four modes for the controls in the **Volume/Pan** section.
  - **Balance + Stereo En.** sets the mode in which the **Pan** and **Stereo** controls of the **Volume/Pan** section act in the usual manner

  > **NOTE** The stereo base in this mode can be adjusted to anywhere within a wide range, from "mono" to "expanded stereo".

- The **−4.5 dB Pan + St. Enh** mode has the following features:
  - In *extreme positions of the pan control*, one of the channels gets an additional gain of 4.5 dB, whereas the other is muted. *The overall volume remains constant* at the 0 dB level.
  - When the pan control is in the *center position*, the volume of both channels is decreased by 4.5 dB.

  > **NOTE** This mode is best suited for panning mono signals when placing several mono sources in the stereo sound field.

- The **2 Channel Panorama** mode allows for two independent *pan* controls for each channel. The overall volume remains constant, just as in the previous mode.
- The **2 Channel Volume** mode allows for two independent *volume* controls for each channel.

  > **NOTE** All the controls have the following range: from a completely muted channel (silence) to a volume level 6 dB greater than that of the main **Volume** control.

☐ The **L <-> R** checkbox (in the **Volume/Pan** section) allows you to swap the left and right channels.

☐ The **Mute Left** and **Mute Right** checkboxes (located below the **Global Crossf.** section) turn off the left and right channels, respectively.

☐ The **FX Bypass** checkbox lets the user switch off signal processing by virtual effects. This makes it possible to compare the sound before and after processing (so-called dry and wet sounds).

> **NOTE** If the **FX Bypass** checkbox is checked, all the sections and controls become disabled (the **Invert Phase**, **Dynamics**, and **Parametric EQ** sections; the pan and stereo base controls; the **Mute Left** and **Mute Right** checkboxes; and the **DirectX PlugIn** button).

☐ The **DirectX PlugIn** button enables DirectX plug-ins.

A *right*-click on this button opens the dialog box for enabling plug-ins.

A *left*-click turns the DirectX plug-ins on/off. When these virtual effects are enabled, the **DirectX PlugIn** button is blue. Otherwise it is gray.

☐ The **Sample Color** and **Background Color** give access to the settings that allow you to select the color of the sound wave of the object and the color of its background.

> **NOTE** For the background color to appear on the screen, check the **Background** checkbox in the **Objects** section in the **Draw Mode|Properties in Virtual Projects** dialog box (Fig. 5.55).

Chapter 5: The Samplitude 2496 Application as a High-Quality Virtual Studio

> **WARNING! Saving the Settings in the Object Editor Window**
>
> After all the necessary settings in the object editor window are fixed, *make sure* that you click the **OK** button. All the changes made in the object editor take effect only *after* this button is clicked.

Using Virtual Effects of DirectX Plug-ins in the Object Editor

Unlike the previously described SAWPro and Cool Edit Pro programs, Samplitude 2496 provides many possibilities when processing musical material with virtual effects. This application allows you to connect virtual effects *directly* to each object.

For example, *a single track* of Samplitude 2496 can contain objects that have been processed:

❏ With various settings of one effect

❏ With various effects

❏ With various groups of DirectX plug-ins

> **NOTE** Recall that there were a lot fewer options open to us when combining multiple effects in SAWPro. SAWPro only allows you to connect effects to the entire track. When you need to use different effect configurations in SAWPro, you have to snip clips and place them in different tracks (the number of tracks in SAWPro, remember, is limited).

Due to the many possibilities when processing sound in Samplitude 2496, an object becomes a unique "building block" that can be used when erecting the "building" of a musical project.

Since configuring objects in Samplitude 2496 is a rather autonomous area (the sound is adjusted at the object level), the tasks of sound producing can be subdivided into just two stages:

❏ Setting the properties of each object

❏ Final mixing

> **NOTE** Making a comparison between Samplitude 2496's features and computer programming, one could say that editing objects vaguely resembles object-oriented programming.
>
> We'd like to remind you that the basic principle of non-destructive editing (non-linear montage) is the following: a *reference* to the original sound file (that is, a region) is changed, rather than changing the file itself. The number of references to one sound file is theoretically unlimited. Thus the number of objects corresponding to the same region is also unlimited. In other words, you can create an arbitrary number of objects with different properties that share a common region.

It should be noted that Samplitude 2496 also allows you to process sound using traditional methods. A special virtual mixer is provided for this purpose.

Creating an Object

In addition to directly recording onto a track of the VIP project, an object can be created using one of the following three methods:

- ❏ The first way is to simply drag a selected fragment (region) from the HD Wave project window to the VIP project window (Fig. 5.70)
- ❏ The second way is the following:
  1. First, select a fragment of the HD Wave project.
  2. Then select a small range in the selected track of the VIP project.
  3. Finally, execute the **New Object** command of the **Object** menu.
- ❏ The third way is to import an AUDIO (or MIDI) file into the virtual project

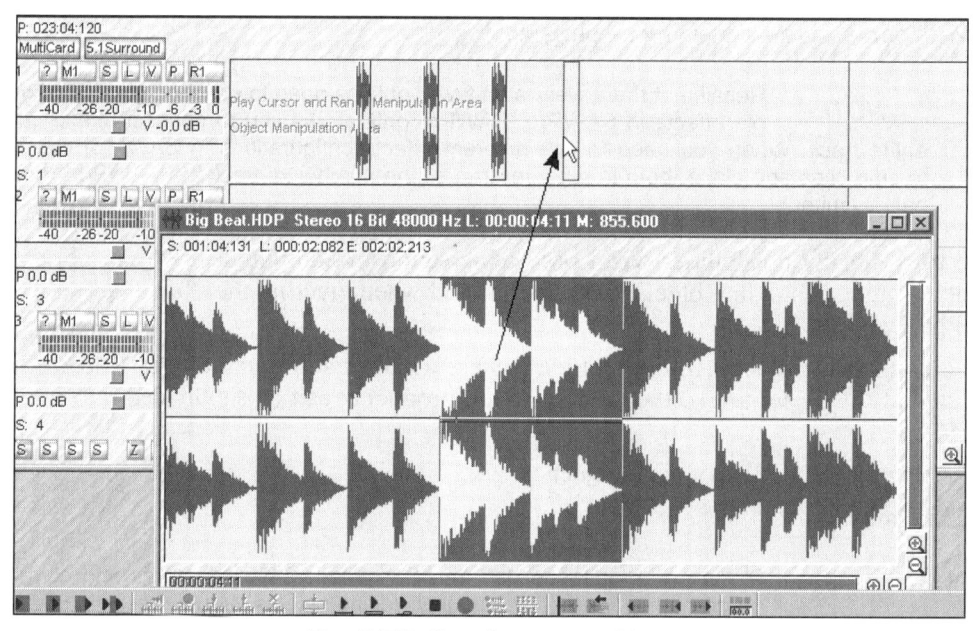

Fig. 5.70. Creating a new object

Samplitude 2496 allows you to process each object separately. In other words, you not only have the ability to create a configuration of settings for each *individual* object using the object editor, but you can also connect different DirectX plug-ins to different objects. As a result, the objects will sound different after such processing. This will take place

Chapter 5: The Samplitude 2496 Application as a High-Quality Virtual Studio

despite the fact that some objects were initially absolutely the same, since they were created based on the same fragment of the sound file.

Saving an Object

Every created object can be saved in a file with the OBJ extension. Later on, you can use it, say, in another VIP project.

OBJ Files

A file having the OBJ extension is strongly connected with the corresponding file of an HDP or RAM project. This is why you should keep in mind that deleting an HDP or RAM project file makes it impossible to use the corresponding OBJ file.

When a file of an HDP or RAM project is moved, Samplitude 2496 suggests that you perform a search (Fig. 5.71).

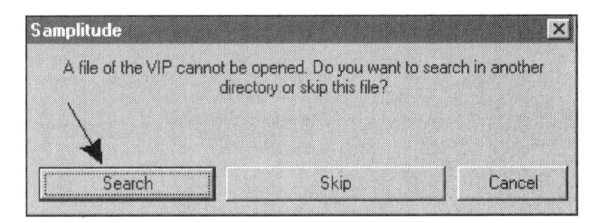

Fig. 5.71. The dialog box suggesting that you search for object files

Connecting a DirectX Plug-in to the Object

To connect DirectX plug-ins to the object, proceed as follows:

1. Open the **Object Editor** window (Fig. 5.65).

   NOTE This window is opened by double-clicking in the lower part of the object (in the **Universal Mode**).

2. Right-click the **DirectX PlugIn** button.
3. In the dialog box that opens (Fig. 5.72), enable the necessary effect.

Let's discuss the features of the dialog box used to enable virtual effects.

- ❏ In the **Presets** drop-down list, you can select previously created presets that contain the list of enabled DirectX plug-ins and their settings
- ❏ The **Save** button allows you to save a new project in a file with the PLG extension
- ❏ The **Load** button loads the preset from the PLG file

- In the **Installed DirectX Plug Ins** list, all the DirectX plug-ins installed in the system are shown
    - To connect a plug-in to the object, double-click the name of the selected effect
    - The names of the connected plug-ins will appear in the **Active Plug Ins** list
    - To delete a connected (active) plug-in, select it with a click on the **Active Plug Ins** list, and click the **Delete Selected Entry** button
- The **Switch Mute** button allows you to turn off the virtual effects selected in the **Active Plug Ins** list
- A muted effect is marked with the letter "M" next to its name (Fig. 5.72)
- The **Switch Solo** button disables all the effects in the **Active Plug Ins** list except the selected one

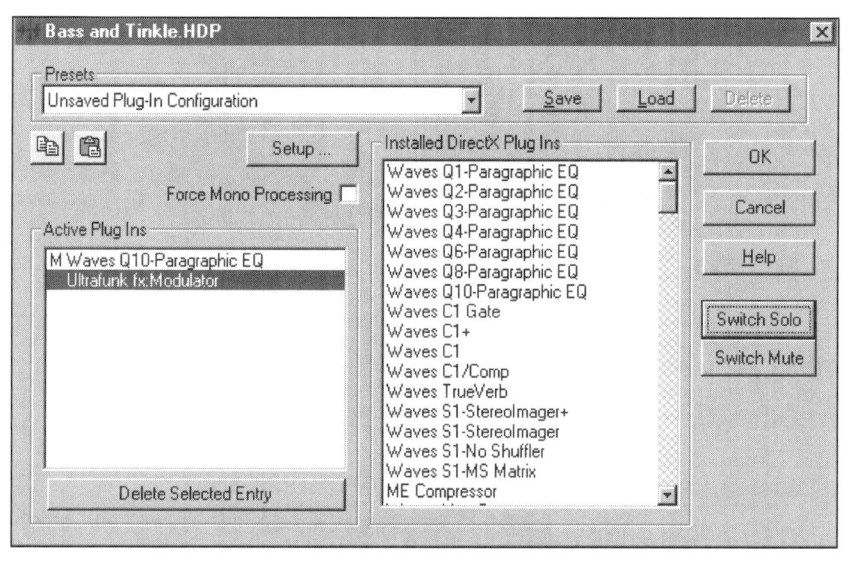

Fig. 5.72. The dialog box for enabling DirectX plug-ins

The buttons with the standard icons denoting data exchange with the clipboard, which are found below the **Presets** drop-down list, are used to copy a list from one DirectX plug-in dialog box to another one that belongs to another object.

NOTE Copying is done in the traditional manner (just as in MS Word): first click the "copy" button, and the DirectX plug-ins dialog box of another object will open. Then insert the contents of the clipboard by clicking the "paste" button.

Chapter 5: The Samplitude 2496 Application as a High-Quality Virtual Studio

- The **Force Mono processing** checkbox toggles the mode with the same name.

    NOTE This mode is recommended for less powerful computers, in order to increase the processing performance. However, you must be aware that all plug-ins do not support this mode.

- The **Setup** button opens the dialog box containing additional settings (Fig. 5.73). Its controls have the following uses:
    - The **Write DirectX Logfile** checkbox turns on the mode in which a DirectX logfile is maintained

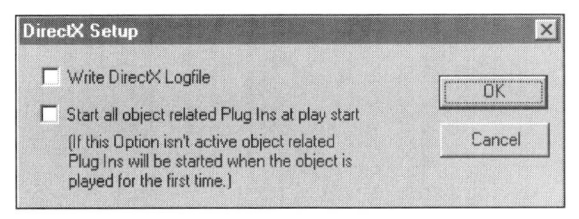

    Fig. 5.73. The dialog box with additional settings

    NOTE You may need to analyze the logfile if virtual effect errors occur. In most cases, this feature is of interest only to developers of virtual effects.

    - The **Start all object related Plug Ins at play start** checkbox ensures that all the enabled DirectX plug-ins will start to process the sound as soon as playback starts
    - If this checkbox isn't checked, the enabled plug-ins start processing the sound when the multitrack cursor crosses the beginning boundary of the object
    - If failures occur during playback of an object "overloaded" with effects, checking this option can help you cope with them, since sound processing will have been performed beforehand

Connecting DirectX Plug-ins to a Track of the Multitrack

In Samplitude 2496, you can connect virtual effects not only to objects, but to tracks of the multitrack as well (traditionally, you might say — like in SAWPro).

You can achieve this in several ways.

- The first way is to use the **New PlugIn** button (indicated by the mouse pointer in Fig. 5.74).

    NOTE This method isn't convenient when there are many tracks in the window and the **New PlugIn** button cannot be seen. In those cases, you have to zoom tracks in vertically.

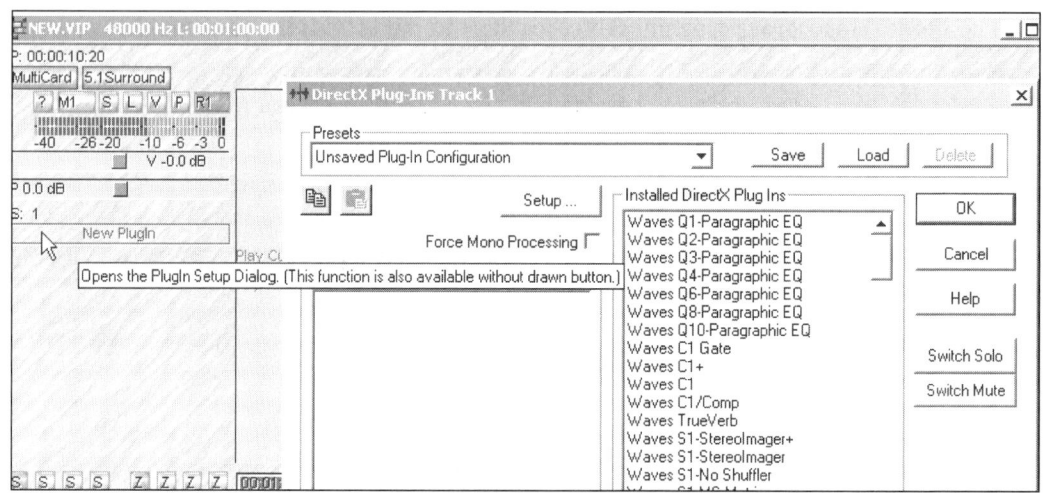

Fig. 5.74. Connecting virtual effects to a track using the **New PlugIn** button

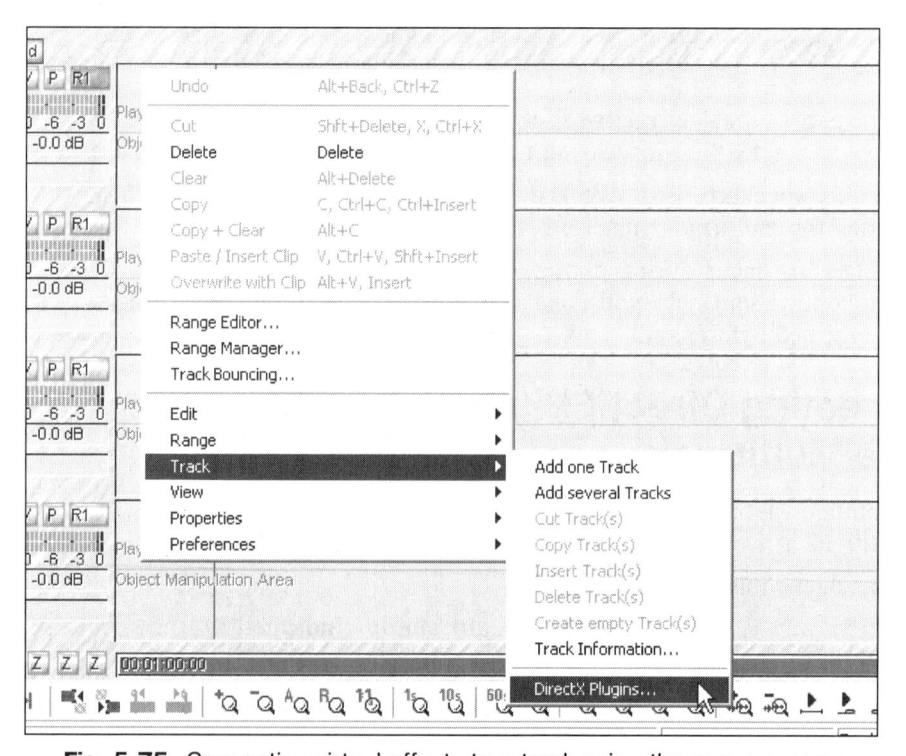

Fig. 5.75. Connecting virtual effects to a track using the pop-up menu

Chapter 5: The Samplitude 2496 Application as a High-Quality Virtual Studio 361

- The second way is to use the pop-up menu of the track. For this purpose:
  1. Open the pop-up menu by right-clicking the track.
  2. Use the **DirectX Plugins** command of the **Track** submenu (Fig. 5.75).

    NOTE This method is more convenient, since it doesn't require zooming in.

- The third way is to use the **Samplitude Mixer**.

    NOTE We're going to discuss this later, when describing the mixer.

The windows used to connect plug-ins to objects and to tracks are identical.

NOTE If you encounter any problems while using the **DirectX Plug-Ins Track** pane (Fig. 5.74), see the description of the **Object Editor** window (Fig. 5.65).

Effects connected to a track are valid along its entire length.

Controlling a Group of Effects on One Track

It should be mentioned that Samplitude 2496 provides quick and easy ways to both open the DirectX plug-in setting window and enable/disable the effects in a group.

All these operations can be performed with a single right or left click — that is, without opening the **DirectX Plug-Ins Track** window.

NOTE This advantage is especially noticeable when you need to change the parameters of two or more DirectX plug-ins at the same time.

In Fig. 5.76, you can see a group of effects connected to one track. Each DirectX plug-in has *its own* button (control panel).

- A *left* click on the effect name disables the effect without unloading it from the memory, i.e., it turns off processing of the signal by that effect. This is the bypass mode.

    NOTE A disabled effect is marked with the word **Muted**, and is written in a different color on the button (Fig. 5.76).

- The next *left*-click enables the effect.
- A *right*-click on the effect button opens its settings window.

The list of the connected DirectX plug-ins and their settings is saved in a PLG file (as in the object editor).

NOTE Later, you will be able to create your own collection of settings for original sound processing.

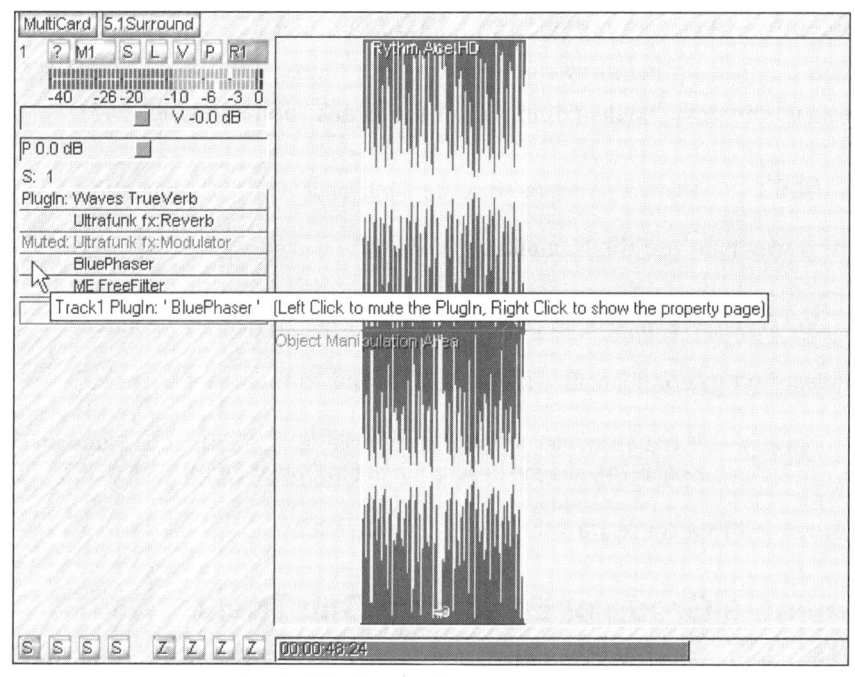

Fig. 5.76. Controlling virtual effects

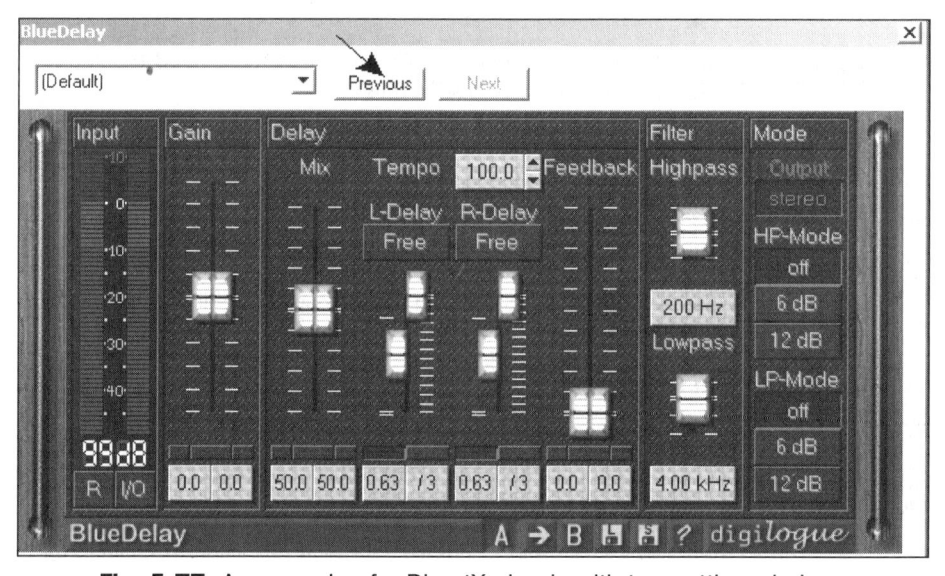

Fig. 5.77. An example of a DirectX plug-in with two setting windows

Chapter 5: The Samplitude 2496 Application as a High-Quality Virtual Studio 363

Some of the DirectX plug-ins have several settings windows.

For those effects, two buttons are available in the effect setting window. These are **Previous** and **Next**. They allow you to navigate the settings windows.

For example, the **Blue Delay** plug-in of Digilogue's Blue Line X set of plug-ins has two settings windows (Fig. 5.77).

Some Finer Points of Connecting VST Plug-ins to Samplitude 2496

At the end of *Chapter 4*, we mentioned that one disappointing drawback of Samplitude 2496 is that it doesn't allow you to connect a whole class of wonderful virtual effects, namely, VST plug-ins.

For those who appreciate VST plug-ins, we suggest that you use a linker program. One of these is is VST-DX Wrapper Lite (from Spin Audio Software), whose free version can be downloaded from Spin Audio Software's site **http://www.spinaudio.com**.

VST-DX Wrapper Lite is connected as an ordinary DirectX plug-in. At the program's startup, the **VST Plugin...** dialog box opens (Fig. 5.78).

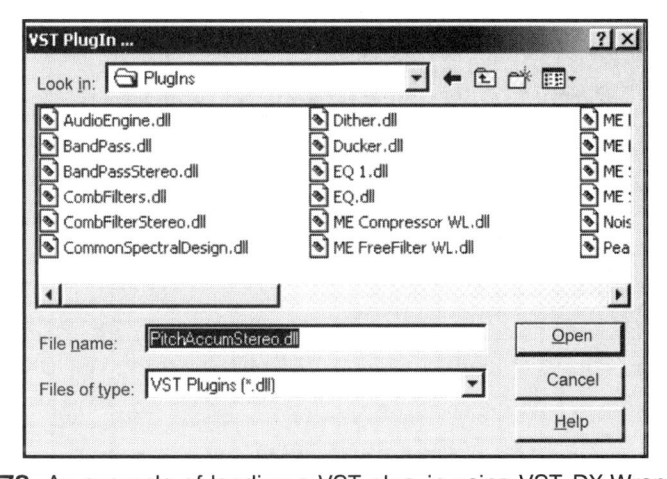

Fig. 5.78. An example of loading a VST plug-in using VST-DX Wrapper Lite

NOTE VST plug-ins are files with the DLL extension. They were discussed in *Chapter 3* in relation to the functions of the **VST Linker** module of SAWPro.

Having chosen a VST plug-in, click the **Open** button. If the selected DLL file isn't a VST plug-in, VST-DX Wrapper Lite will issue a warning message.

Where should we look for VST plug-ins? If they haven't been installed from their distributives into a separate folder (like VST_Plug-ins in SAWPro, see *Chapter 3*), they are usually located in such folders as Cubase Audio VST\Vstplugins or WaveLab\System\Plugins (if Cubase VST 24 or WaveLab are installed).

The free copy of VST-DX Wrapper Lite doesn't let you enable more than one VST plug-in in its window. (For details on this, visit **www.spinaudio.com**.) However, this limitation can be easily overcome by loading several VST-DX Wrapper Lite plug-ins and connecting each to a single VST plug-in (Fig. 5.79).

To conclude, it should be mentioned that VST-DX Wrapper Lite is a sort of **VST Linker** for applications that cannot use VST plug-ins directly.

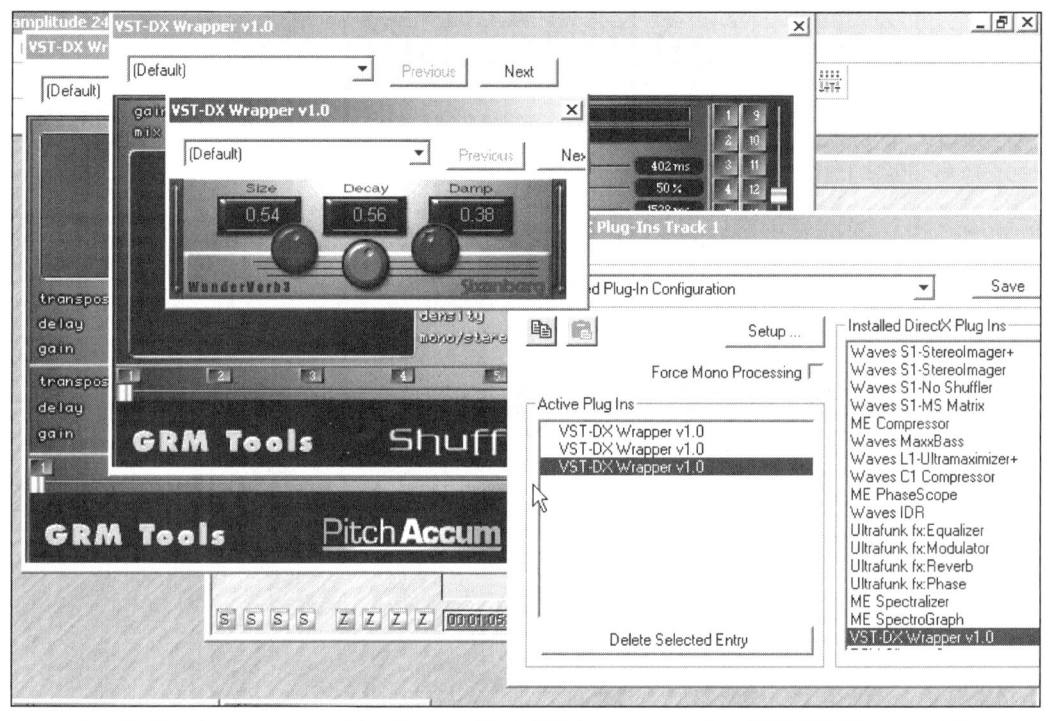

Fig. 5.79. An example of loading multiple VST plug-ins using VST-DX Wrapper Lite

The *Samplitude Mixer*, Built-in Effects of Samplitude 2496, and Enabling DirectX Plug-ins

Whereas the virtual mixers in SAWPro and Cool Edit Pro are combined with the multitracks, Samplitude 2496 allows you to mix both on the multitrack and with a separate virtual mixer — Samplitude Mixer.

The **Mixer** control panel can be opened in two ways:

❐ With the <M> hotkey
❐ With a click on the **Mixer** button (Fig. 5.80)

Chapter 5: The Samplitude 2496 Application as a High-Quality Virtual Studio 365

NOTE The next click on the **Mixer** button (or pressing of the <M> hotkey) closes the **Mixer** panel.

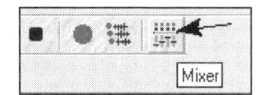

Fig. 5.80. The **Mixer** button

In Fig. 5.81, you can see the mixer of a virtual project for eight tracks. Using the horizontal scrollbar, you can also view the currently hidden seventh and eighth tracks (Fig. 5.81).

NOTE The **Mixer** control panel is resizable, just like any other window in Windows.

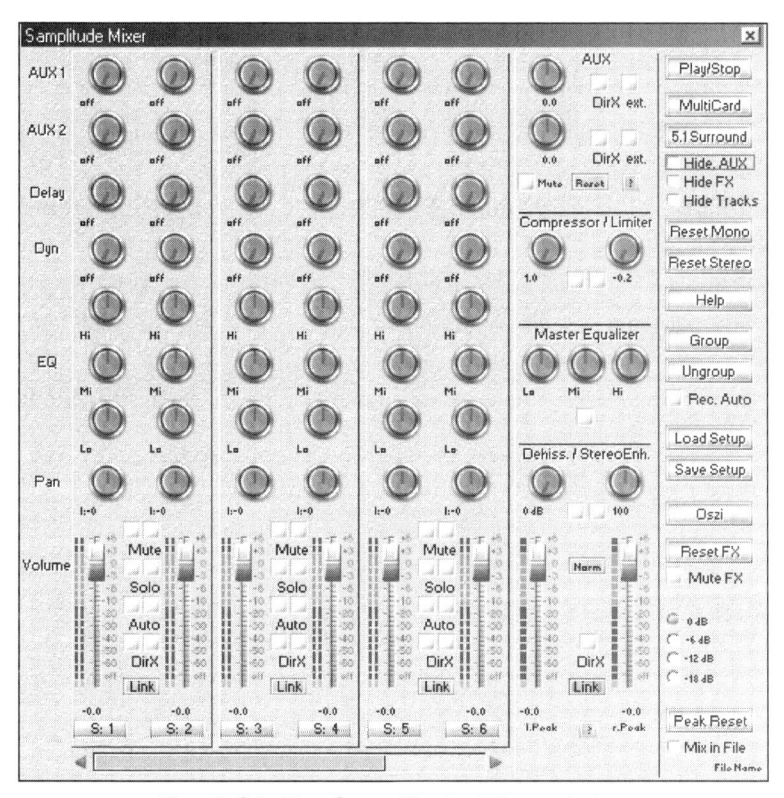

Fig. 5.81. The **Samplitude Mixer** window

Let's look at the **Samplitude Mixer** window in more detail.

The mixer is divided into vertical blocks, each of which contains two tracks.

The horizontal scrollbar located below the blocks allows you to scroll the mixer blocks.

The rightmost block is used for *global settings* and *controlling* the mixer.

Next to it is the *master* block, where general sound parameters for the entire multitrack are adjusted.

> **NOTE** The master block is functionally similar to the **OutputTrack** of SAWPro. This will be discussed in the "*Editing a Virtual Project*" section.

The number of virtual mixer blocks is related to the number of multitrack tracks. There are always half as many blocks as there are tracks.

> **NOTE** When the number of the tracks is odd, one of the blocks contains controls only for one track.

The output level indicators of the mixer tracks (LED meters) are identical to those of the VIP project tracks.

Let's look at the elements of the track blocks from bottom to top.

- The **S:1 (S:2, S:3)** buttons open the **Track Info** dialog box (Fig. 5.29) with the track properties
- All the buttons with the track numbers (**S:1, S:2**) are duplicated by the **?** buttons in the VIP project window
- The **Volume** slider is duplicated by a slider in the VIP project window (Fig. 5.82)
- The **Pan** control knob is also duplicated by a slider in the VIP project window (Fig. 5.82)

> **NOTE** Double-clicking a control knob of the mixer sets this knob to its default position.

There are two columns of buttons between the volume sliders of each block. Some of these buttons are duplicated in the VIP project window.

- **Mute** (the track is muted).

> **NOTE** This button is duplicated by the **M** button in the VIP project window.

- **Solo** (only this track is played).

> **NOTE** This button is duplicated by the **S** button in the VIP project window.

- **Auto** (automation is on).

> **NOTE** Switching on the automation mode is reflected by both the **V** and **P** buttons in the VIP project window.

The **Auto** mode makes it possible to record the changes to the volume and pan controls in real time, that is, during playback with automation line creation.

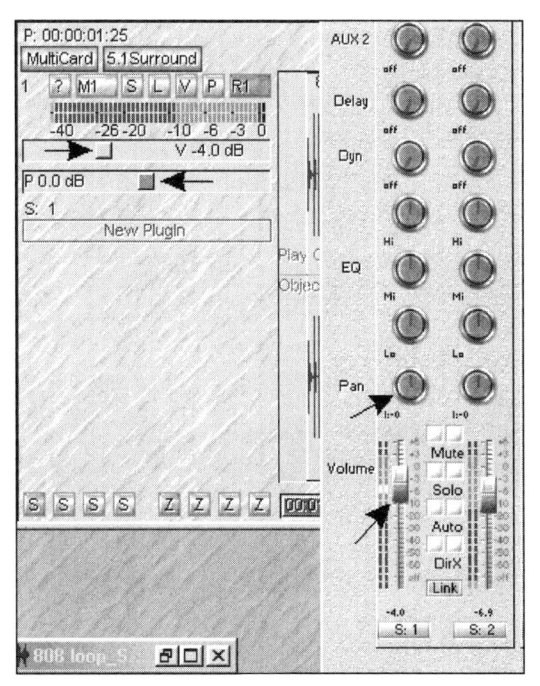

Chapter 5: The Samplitude 2496 Application as a High-Quality Virtual Studio 367

Fig. 5.82. The duplications of the volume slider and the pan control

- The **DirX** (DirectX) button is used to enable/disable DirectX plug-ins.

  A right-click on this button opens the **DirectX PlugIns Track** dialog box (Fig. 5.74).

  NOTE This is simply the third way of connecting a DirectX plug-in to a track of the multitrack.

  - When the **DirX** button is blue, it means that the signal is being processed by DirectX plug-ins
  - When the **DirX** button is gray, the "bypass" mode is on — this means that DirectX plug-ins are connected, but aren't processing the signal

- The **Link** button co-ordinates the controls within one block: when it is in the "pressed" state, controls of the same kind change *synchronously*.

  NOTE For example, when the pan of a track in the block changes, the pan of the other track changes correspondingly.

  The mode turned on with the **Link** button may be necessary when a stereo sound file is divided into two mono files, and these are laid along the neighboring track, that is, along the tracks in the same mixer block.

- The **EQ** controls refer to the parametric equalizer.

  NOTE The parametric equalizer of the virtual mixer is absolutely identical to that of the object editor.

A right click on any control in the **EQ** section opens the **Filter Adjustments** dialog box (Fig. 5.83), in which you can adjust the equalizer parameters.

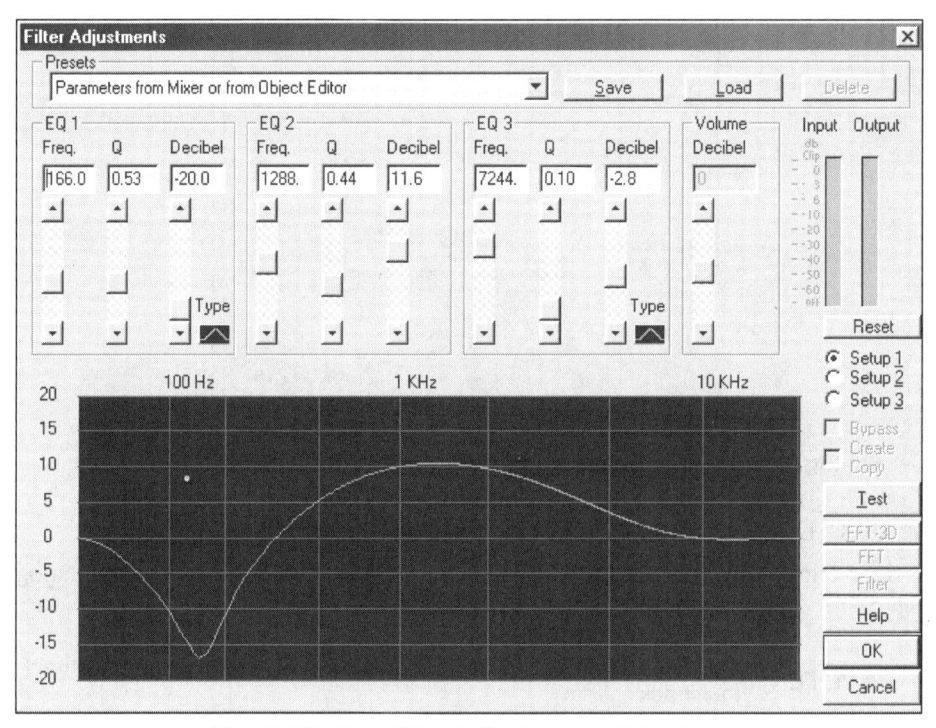

Fig. 5.83. The **Filter Adjustments** dialog box

NOTE Since the parametric equalizer is a built-in (internal) effect of Samplitude 2496, we're going to look at it when discussing the **Effects** menu.

Here we'll just mention that the **FFT-3D**, **FFT**, and **Filter** buttons are not available when the parametric equalizer is accessed from the object editor or the **Samplitude Mixer**.

- The **Dyn** (Dynamics) controls (Fig. 5.82) refer to the Samplitude 2496 dynamic processor.

  NOTE The dynamic processor in the **Samplitude Mixer** is identical to the dynamic processor of the object editor (Fig. 5.69). It is also a built-in effect, so it will be examined when discussing the **Effects** menu.

Chapter 5: The Samplitude 2496 Application as a High-Quality Virtual Studio

- The **Delay** controls are responsible for the **Wet/Dry Balance in %** ratio in the **Echo/Delay/Reverb Effect**.

  Right-clicking on a **Delay** control opens the **Echo/Delay/Reverb Effect** dialog box (Fig. 5.84).

  The **Echo/Delay/Reverb Effect** is also a built-in effect, so it will be examined when discussing the **Effects** menu.

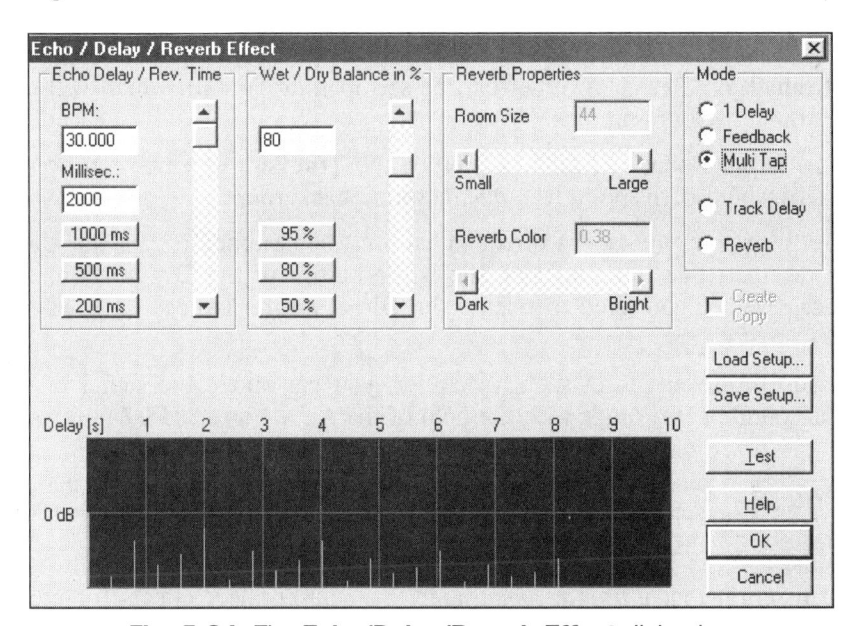

Fig. 5.84. The **Echo/Delay/Reverb Effect** dialog box

- The **AUX 1** and **AUX 2** controls (Fig. 5.82) are auxiliary controls to adjust the level of the track signal sent to the **Auxiliary Master Section**

  NOTE   AUX is short for "Auxiliary master section".

The *Auxiliary Master Section*

The virtual mixer of Samplitude 2496 — **Samplitude Mixer** — is a programmatic model of a hardware mixer. So one could say that its architecture involves a hardware-based ideology.

Not only can DirectX plug-ins be connected to the **Auxiliary Master Section**, but external hardware sound processing devices can as well (as in the case of a hardware mixer).

The **Auxiliary Master Section** panel is shared by all the tracks of the multitrack. And this is why all the connected DirectX plug-ins are shared by all the tracks.

As a rule, the *reverber* and *chorus* are used as "common" effects. In this case, the **AUX 1** and **AUX 2** controls allow you to send a signal from a track to the reverber and chorus, the signal level being determined by the necessary effect depth, i.e., by sound mastering.

Another instance in which you would use the **Auxiliary Master Section** is when connecting two DirectX reverbers. For example:

- The **TrueVerb** (from Waves) can be connected to **AUX 1**.
- The **Ultrafunk fx: Reverb** can be connected to **AUX 2**.
- The **Ultrafunk fx: Reverb** reverber can be set up as a big hall, which will correspond to a *far* sound background.
- Using the **Drum Room** or **Studio A** presets, the **TrueVerb** reverber can be set up as a room. This would correspond to a *middle* sound background.
- When setting up reverbers, the direct signal must be switched off. In the **Ultrafunk fx: Reverb** reverber, you have to click the **Mute** button in the **Dry** section, and in the **TrueVerb** reverber you need to release the **Direct** button (whose label will change to **Out**) (Fig. 5.85).

Having set up the reverbers in such a manner, you can move the signal of each track between the sound backgrounds with the help of the **AUX 1** and **AUX 2** controls.

NOTE Notice that the given examples shouldn't be considered the only proper solutions. They only give an example of a direction that your own experiments might take.

We should mention that it *isn't recommended* that you connect effects (or groups of effects) that strongly distort the sound to the **Auxiliary Master Section**. Such attempts can change the sound of the entire project (since these effects are shared by a large number of tracks).

It is best to connect effects that "add space" to the sound to the **Auxiliary Master Section**.

You can control the **Auxiliary Master Section** with the **DirX**, **Mute**, and **Reset** buttons (Fig. 5.86).

- **Mute** turns on the effects of the **Auxiliary Master Section**
- **DirX** enables DirectX plug-ins

NOTE DirectX plug-ins are enabled in the same manner as for a track.

- The **Reset** button resets the controls like so:
  - The **Master AUX** controls are reset to 0 dB
  - All the controls of the **AUX 1** and **AUX 2** tracks are reset to −40 dB

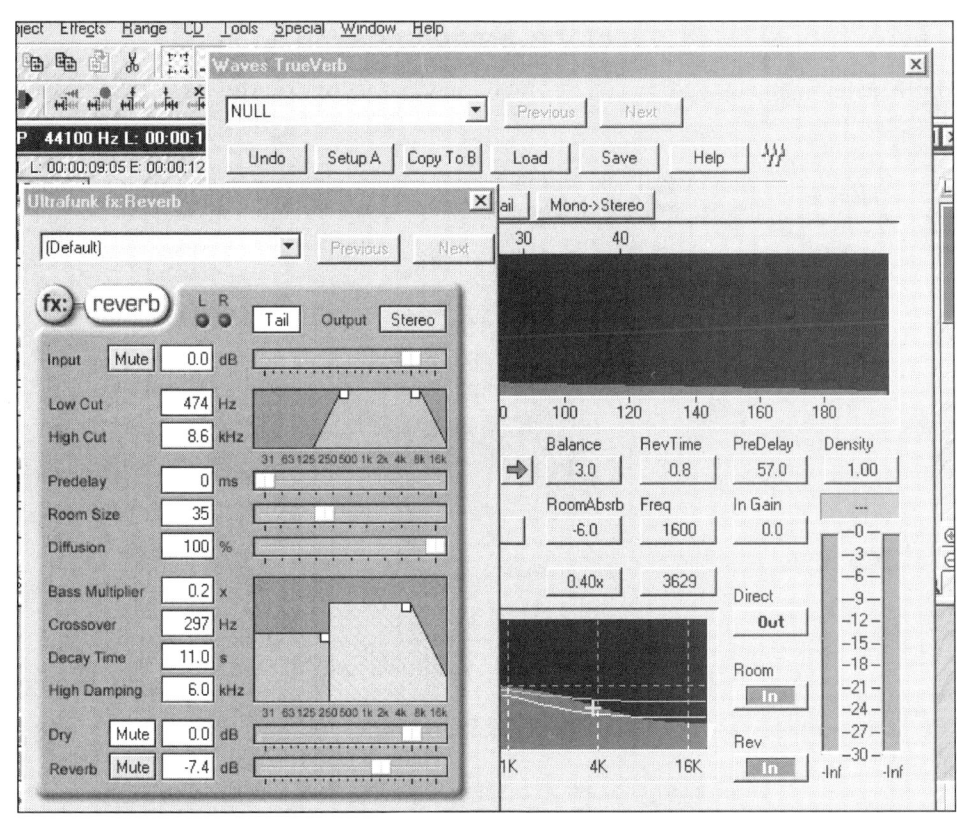

Chapter 5: The Samplitude 2496 Application as a High-Quality Virtual Studio 371

Fig. 5.85. An example of using two reverbers in the **Auxiliary Master Section**

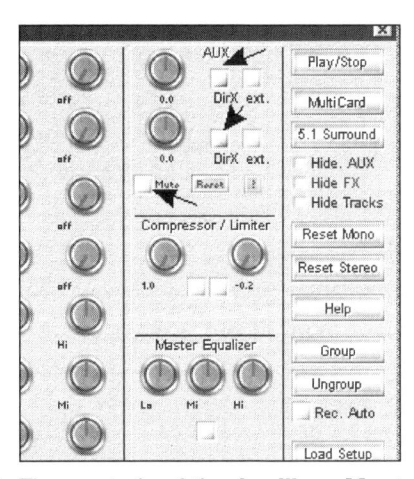

Fig. 5.86. The controls of the **Auxiliary Master Section**

Some Additional Features of the *Samplitude Mixer*

- The **Master Volume Fader** sliders are designed to control the **Master Output** level (Fig. 5.87)

    NOTE They are similar to the overall level sliders of other programs, namely, to the **Fader Output Track** in SAWPro and the **Master Gain** in Cool Edit Pro.

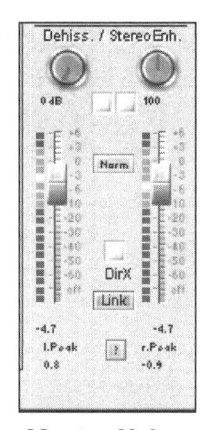

Fig. 5.87. The **Master Volume Fader** sliders

- The **Link** button links the sliders for the left and right channels together

    NOTE This is very convenient, since, if mixing has been done correctly, there is no need to separately adjust the channel volume levels.

- The **DirX** button is used to connect DirectX plug-ins that are used in final sound processing
- The **Norm** button serves to normalize the overall level of the VIP project

When the **Norm** button is clicked, the positions of the **Master Volume** sliders change automatically in such a way that the maximum level of the VIP project is 0 dB.

Normalization will be most accurate if you click the **Norm** button while the *loudest* fragment of the project is playing.

Let's look at the control block of the mixer more closely (Fig. 5.88).

- The **Play/Stop** button lets you start/stop the playback
- The **Hide Aux**, **Hide FX**, and **Hide Tracks** checkboxes allow you to temporarily disable entire sections of the mixer (that correspond to the labels of these checkboxes)

    NOTE Using these buttons, you can considerably decrease the dimensions of the mixer window.

Chapter 5: The Samplitude 2496 Application as a High-Quality Virtual Studio

- The **Reset Mono** button lets you configure the mixer for mixing mono tracks
- The **Reset Stereo** button lets you configure the mixer for mixing stereo tracks
- The **Group** button allows you to group together individual components of the mixer
- The **Ungroup** button separates a group into individual components of the mixer

Let's discuss the notion of a *group*.

Fig. 5.88. The mixer control block

Grouping Together the Components of the Mixer

There is a universal function in Samplitude 2496 that makes it possible to group *any kinds* of mixer components together (controls, buttons, etc.).

As a result, the positions of the components of a group can be changed with a single control.

Both a *direct* and an *inverse* relationship can be established between the components in a group.

The number of mixer components in a group isn't limited, and there can be multiple groups.

A group can include:

❐ Various controls (such as volume, pan, etc.)

❐ Components having *different initial* control points

❐ Controls of different tracks

To create a group, proceed as follows:

1. Press and hold down the <Ctrl> key.

2. Click the controls that are to be grouped together.

Each component included in the group will be boxed (Fig. 5.59).

Later, the black color of the box will change to red or blue to reflect the status of the component.

❐ A *black* box appears when the control is included in the group for the first time

❐ *Blue* boxes mean that there is a *direct relationship* set between the boxed controls

> **NOTE** In other words, increasing the parameter of one control increases the parameters of the other (blue) controls.

The black box changes its color to blue as soon as a new control is included into the group.

❐ *Red* boxes mean that there is an *inverse relationship* set between the boxed controls

> **NOTE** When the parameter of a red control increases, the parameters of the blue controls will decrease (and vice versa).

You can turn a box red by clicking any blue control while holding the <Shift> key.

After the group is created, you must secure it by clicking the **Group** button (Fig. 5.89).

You can thus create several groups of mixer components.

To ungroup, click any component in the group and click the **Ungroup** button.

Creating such groups can be useful, for example, when you mix your project to a file in real time with the **Mix in File** checkbox checked in the **Samplitude Mixer**.

If, for example, you wish to fade in one track while simultaneously fading out another, you can use a group where the volume controls of both tracks are inversely related to one another.

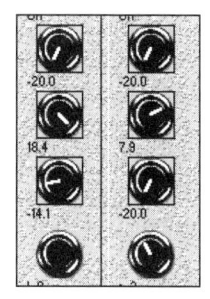

Chapter 5: The Samplitude 2496 Application as a High-Quality Virtual Studio   **375**

Fig. 5.89. An example of a mixer component group

You may also want to create a group in the following situation. Suppose you have set a certain balance of the levels of certain tracks. Later, you need to change the volume of the tracks (without changing this balance). For this purpose, you may bind the volume controls of these tracks into one group with a direct relationship.

Let's turn back to the control block of the mixer (Fig. 5.88).

- The **Save Setup** button allows you to save the mixer settings in a separate file with the MIX extension
- The **Load Setup** button is used to load the settings from a MIX file

Thus, thanks to these MIX files, you can use the mixer settings without regard to a virtual project.

These settings can be used in another VIP project, for example, for preliminary processing of similar tracks with vocal or instrumental parts.

> **NOTE** All the parameters of the enabled DirectX plug-ins are also saved in MIX files.

- The **Reset FX** button resets (to the default values) all the *internal* effects of Samplitude 2496 provided by the mixer control panel.

> **WARNING** The **Reset FX** button *has no effect* on *enabled* DirectX plug-ins.

- The **Mute FX** checkbox turns on the bypass mode for *all* the mixer effects *except for* DirectX plug-ins enabled in the master block (including the **Auxiliary Master Section**).
- The **Input Attenuation** switch consists of four radio buttons: **0 dB**, **−6 dB**, **−12 dB**, and **−18 dB**.

    These buttons serve to prevent the clipping of a loud sound signal as a result of digital-to-analog conversion.

- The **Peak Reset** button resets the peak level indicator of the master block.

❐ The **Mix in File** checkbox turns on the mode of *real-time* mixing in a 32-bit sound file during playback of a VIP project — in this mode, *all* settings of the virtual mixer that were set in real time during the playback are written to the output file.

> **NOTE** If the **Mix in File** checkbox is unchecked, the newly mixed file will replace the previous one (without creating a backup copy).

To create a backup copy, you need to click the **File Name** label and enter another file name.

Some "Tricks" in *Samplitude Mixer*

Every application has a number of "hidden" possibilities that the user might discover in the course of actual practice with it. We're going to concentrate on some of these nuances of the **Samplitude Mixer** in Samplitude 2496.

The values of the parameters set using the mixer components can be changed by entering numbers directly from the keyboard.

❐ There is a *numeric field* below each component where the value of the parameter is displayed.

- Double-clicking on this numeric field changes the appearance of this parameter, as shown in Fig. 5.90, and allows you to enter a new value via the keyboard

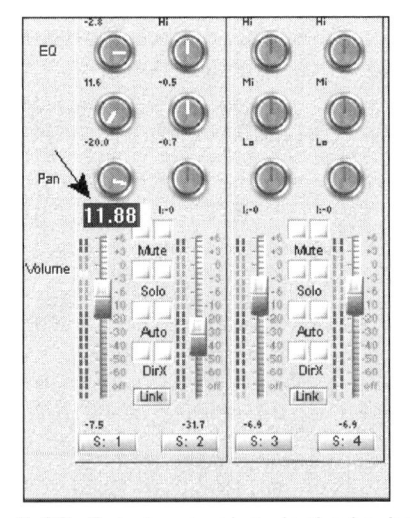

Fig. 5.90. Entering a value via the keyboard

- After you type a new value, press the <Enter> key
- Every component of the mixer has its own range of adjustment

Chapter 5: The Samplitude 2496 Application as a High-Quality Virtual Studio 377

> **NOTE** If you enter a number that is beyond this range, the value will be truncated to fit the range. For example, if you enter −70 for the pan control, this value will be truncated to −40 (the lower limit for the parameter).

Recall that double-clicking a component of the mixer resets it to the default position.

- The **Samplitude Mixer** can *automatically* gradually change the parameter value. To do this:
  1. Set the mouse pointer over the numeric field of the mixer component.
  2. Press and hold the left or right mouse button.

     > **NOTE** Pressing and holding the *left* mouse button gradually *decreases* the value until the mouse button is released.

     Pressing and holding the *right* mouse button *increases* the parameter value.

When mixing a VIP project in real time, using automation is often more convenient than "turning" the knobs with the mouse.

- For a frequently used *volume control*, an additional, very convenient method is provided for automatic parameter changing. The slider will automatically move to the mouse pointer. To accomplish this:
  1. Set the mouse pointer above or below the slider, on its trajectory (possible positions are indicated by the arrow in Fig. 5.91).
  2. Press and hold the left mouse key.

     > **NOTE** While the button is pressed, the slider moves in the corresponding direction, up to the end of the scale.

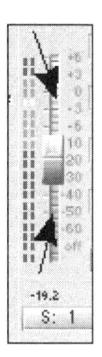

Fig. 5.91. Changing the volume gradually

Using the *Surround Panning Module*

A significant advantage of Samplitude 2496 is the possibility of adjusting panorama in the **Surround Panning** mode.

378 Live Music on Your PC

The difference of the **Surround Panning** mode from an ordinary pan control is in the geometry of the space around which the sound moves.

An ordinary pan control moves the sound source *only* along a straight line (connecting the left and right virtual acoustic systems).

In the **Surround Panning** mode, you can:

- Move sound sources over a vast virtual area in which are located five acoustic systems
- Change the diameter and the *soundfield character* of the sound source
- Create the trajectory of the sound source movement

> **NOTE** In the **Surround Panning** mode, it is possible to draw an arbitrary curve as the sound trajectory.

To turn on the **Surround Panning** mode, proceed as follows:

1. Open the control panel (with the <M> hotkey).
2. Right-click the pan control of the chosen track.
3. In the opened **Surround Panning Module Track 1** window, check the **2 Channel Surround On** checkbox (Fig. 5.92).

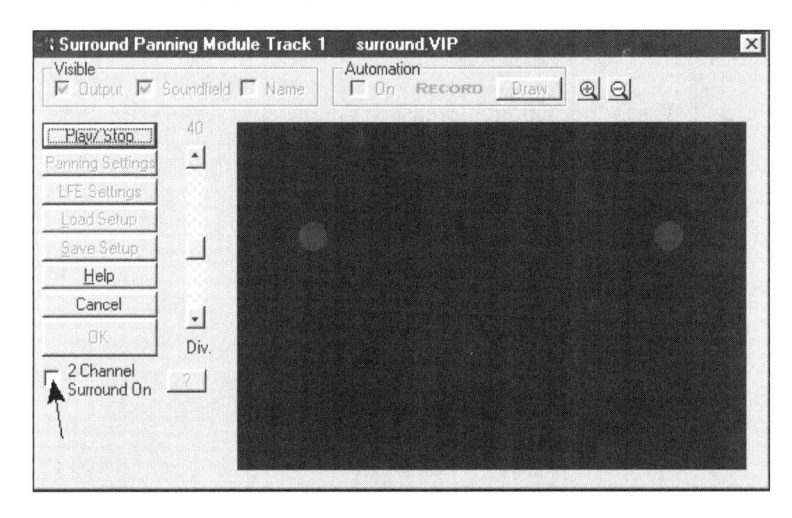

Fig. 5.92. The surround panning module in its inactive state

After switching on this mode, the appearance of the **Surround Panning Module Track 1** changes, as shown in Fig. 5.93.

> **NOTE** In the mixer, the pan control knob will be replaced by an icon showing six dots.

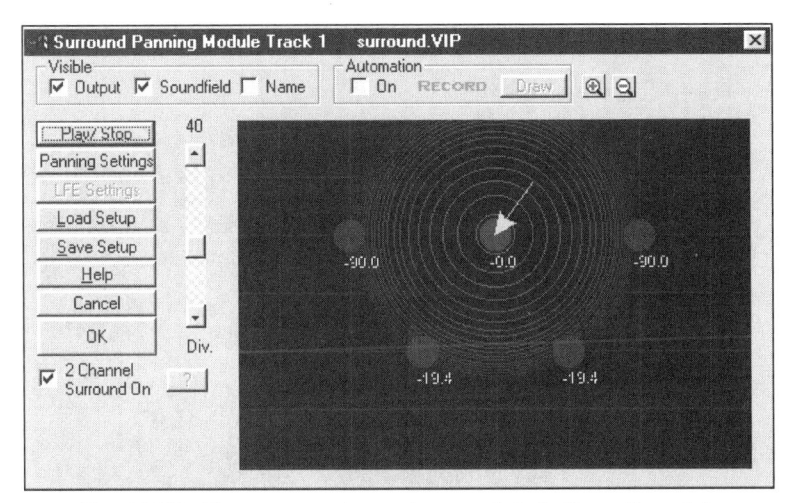

Chapter 5: The Samplitude 2496 Application as a High-Quality Virtual Studio

Fig. 5.93. The surround panning module in its active state

> **NOTE** In Fig. 5.93, the sound source coincides with one of the virtual acoustic systems (indicated by the arrow). This picture is displayed in the **Surround Panning Module Track** window by default.

One can say that the idea of surround panning is that the sound source is moved within a space (the black area in the window) in which five acoustic systems are positioned.

> **NOTE** To move the virtual sound source, you must press and hold the left mouse button.

The *Surround Panning Module Track* Window

Let's look at the checkboxes in the **Visible** section.

❒ **Output** reflects the signal level (in decibels) of the five virtual acoustic systems.

> **NOTE** When this checkbox is checked, numbers appear next to each acoustic system *on the screen* (these are shown as blue discs). The numbers show the signal levels in dB.

In Fig. 5.93, you can see that the central acoustic system has a signal level of 0 dB.

❒ **Soundfield** allows you to make the *sound field* of the source resemble *concentric circles* (Fig. 5.93).

> **NOTE** *Sound field* is the parameter that determines how the sound waves propagate from the source.

380   Live Music on Your PC

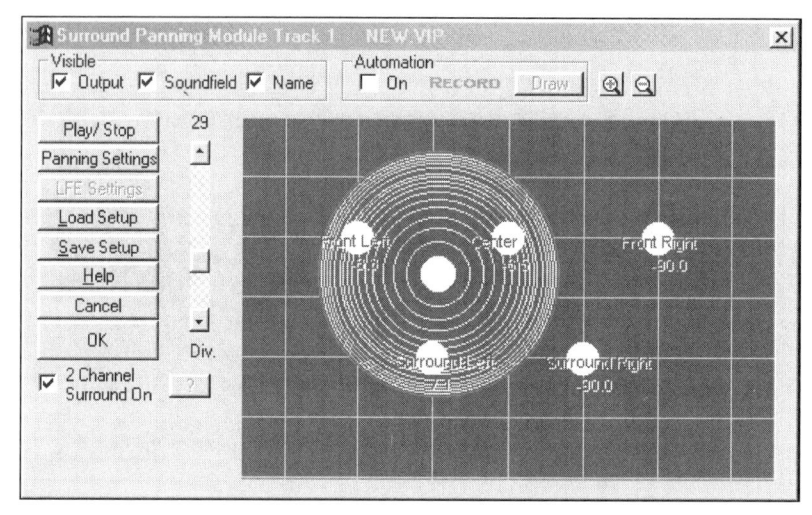

Fig. 5.94. The **Surround Panning Module Track** window with the **Name** checkbox checked

❐ **Name** allows you to display the names of the virtual acoustic systems in **Surround Panning Module Track** (Fig. 5.94).

The virtual acoustic systems are named according to their default positions:

- **Front Left**
- **Center**
- **Front Right**
- **Surround Left**
- **Surround Right**

Moving the sound source along a straight line between the **Front Left**, **Center**, and **Front Right** acoustic systems is the same as normal panning.

Moving the sound source "in depth" — that is, to the **Surround Left** and **Surround Right** acoustic systems — is surround panning.

❐ The **Div.** slider (Fig. 5.93) is used to change the diameter of the sound field (i.e., the diameters of the concentric circles).

> **NOTE** If you change the size of the sound field, the levels of signals emitted by the virtual acoustic systems will change correspondingly.

Notice that if the radius of the sound field increases, a listener with a conventional stereo system feels that the "power" of the sound source has increased as well.

❐ The **Panning Settings** button opens the **Surround Panning Settings Track** window (Fig. 5.95). Here you can adjust the *soundfield character*.

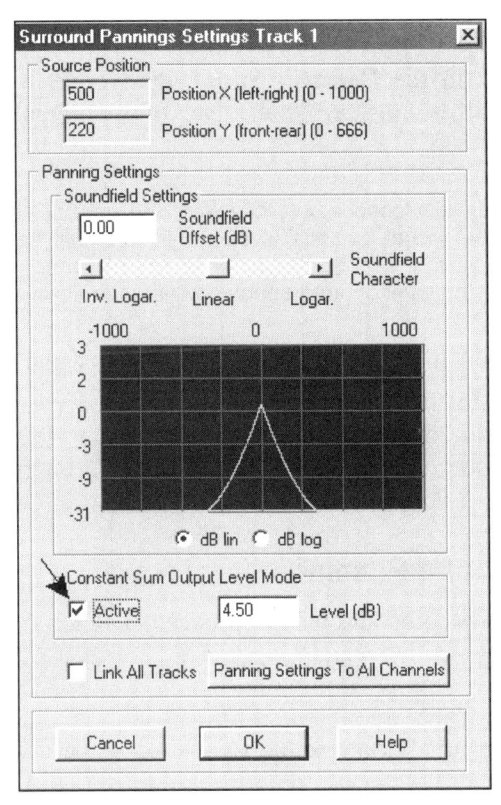

Chapter 5: The Samplitude 2496 Application as a High-Quality Virtual Studio 381

Fig. 5.95. The **Surround Panning Settings Track** window

The Decay of the Sound Wave

To describe the notion of the "soundfield character", we'd like to draw an analogy with the waves in water that are caused by a thrown stone. In other words, the *soundfield character* is determined by the wave amplitude's dependence on the distance from the source (that is, by the decay).

You can set the decay (whether it should be smooth or sharp) in the **Surround Panning Settings Track** window.

The curve shown in Fig. 5.95 is a graphic representation of the decay. Its upper point (with the X=0, Y=0 coordinates) is the sound source. The curves sloping down from the source determine the amplitude's dependence on the distance from the source.

❏ The **Soundfield Character** slider (Fig. 5.95) changes the type of the sound wave decay. It can be:
  - Linear
  - Logarithmic (the rightmost position)

- Inverse logarithmic (the leftmost position)

❐ The **Active** checkbox (in the **Constant Sum Output Level Mode** section) turns on a mode which maintains a constant total level of the signal emitted by the virtual acoustic systems.

> **NOTE** When this checkbox is checked, the *sum* of the numbers displayed next to the virtual acoustic systems (in dB) will be *constant*, no matter how the sound source moves (Fig. 5.94). In other words, when the signal level of certain systems decreases, the level of other sources will automatically increase.

❐ In the **Level** field, you can specify the level of the total signal (in dB).

The **Surround Panning Module** provides the *surround panning automation* mode, in which any changes in the sound source position (relative to the virtual acoustic systems) are memorized, and this trajectory is automatically repeated during playback.

Automation of Surround Panning

For surround panning to become automated, proceed as follows:

1. Check the **On** checkbox in the **Automation** section.
2. Turn on the playback mode.
3. Using the mouse, move the virtual sound source along the desired trajectory.

> **NOTE** All the movements of the sound source will be memorized, and the trajectory will be automatically repeated during playback.

Automation surround panning is displayed in the VIP project track by two lines: the panning automation line and the surround automation line.

Creating an Automation Line on a Selected Range

You can create automation curves of surround panning on a selected range of a multitrack track *without switching the playback on*. For this purpose, proceed as follows:

1. Select a range.
2. Click the **Draw** button in the **Automation** section.
3. Draw automation curves by dragging the image of the sound source (without switching the playback on) (Fig. 5.96).

The automation curves drawn will be applicable only to the selected range.

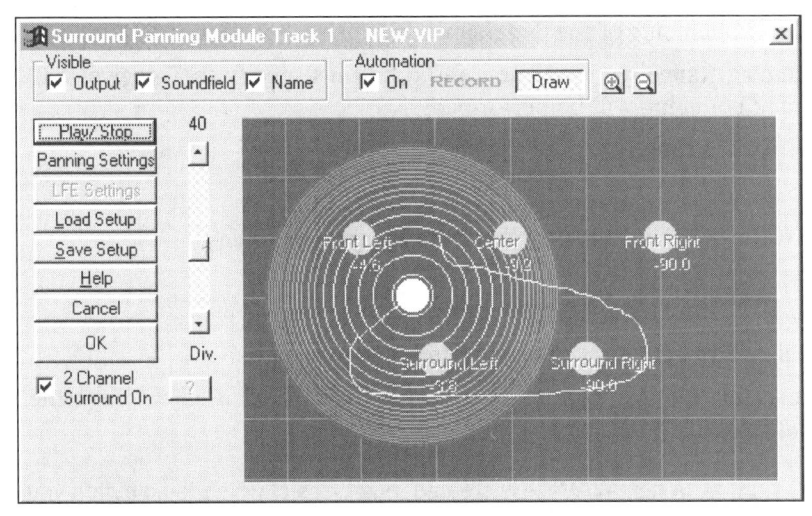

Chapter 5: The Samplitude 2496 Application as a High-Quality Virtual Studio 383

Fig. 5.96. Drawing the trajectory of the sound source

Intermediate Mixing Using Track Bouncing

In Samplitude 2496, you can perform intermediate mixing using the **Track Bouncing** command in the **Tools** menu.

> **NOTE** There was a similar function called **Mixdown** in SAWPro and Cool Edit Pro. However, unlike those applications, **Track Bouncing** in Samplitude 2496 has more powerful features.

Track Bouncing means converting a virtual project to a sound WAV file (an HD Wave project). This conversion takes into account all the settings of the virtual project:

- Pan and volume settings
- Plugged-in virtual effects of the track
- Plugged-in virtual effects of the objects
- Object properties, including **Crossfade**, etc.

> **NOTE** In other words, everything you hear during the VIP project playback will be saved in the newly created HD Wave project.

The **Track Bouncing** operation is carried out only for those tracks in the **Solo** mode. It doesn't apply to tracks in the **Mute** mode (just like when mixing down in Cool Edit Pro and SAWPro). If the **Solo** and **Mute** modes are off, *all the tracks* of the VIP project take part in the mixing process.

Let's look at the elements of the **Trackbouncing** dialog box (Fig. 5.97).

❐ The **Bouncing Range** section. These radio buttons specify the *range* of the VIP project where track bouncing will be performed.
- **Only marked range**

> *NOTE* This is the best choice for intermediate mixing.

- **From VIP Start to last Object End**
- **Complete Project** (from the beginning up to the end)

❐ The **Generating Option** section. These radio buttons are used to select the type of the *final result* of track bouncing.

> *NOTE* A new WAV file is created regardless of which radio button you select in the **Generating Option** section.

- **Only a Wave Project** — only an HD Wave project is created

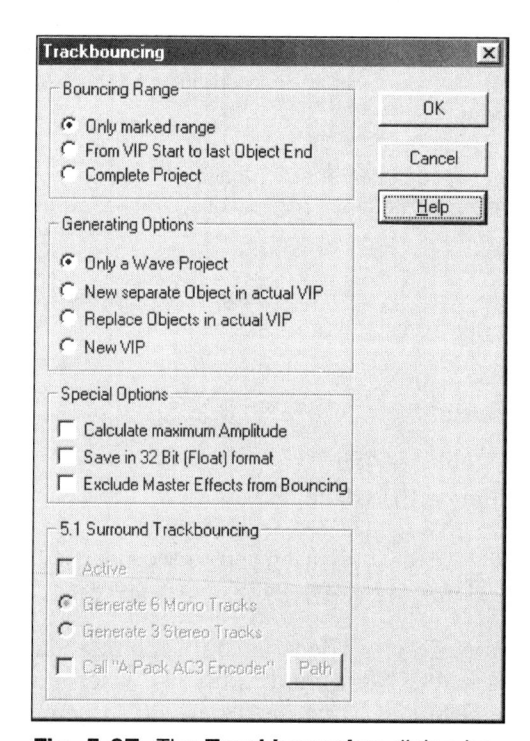

Fig. 5.97. The **Trackbouncing** dialog box

Chapter 5: The Samplitude 2496 Application as a High-Quality Virtual Studio 385

- **New separate Object in actual VIP** — a *separate* object is created in the same VIP project

    NOTE For this option, the new object created as a result of track bouncing is added to the existing ones.

- **Replace Objects in actual VIP** — the objects involved in mixing are *replaced* by the new ones obtained as a result of this process
- **New VIP** — a new VIP project containing the object created during mixing is created

❐ The **Special Options** section

- The **Calculate maximum Amplitude** checkbox

    NOTE At the end of track bouncing, a message is issued informing you of the value of the maximum amplitude

- The **Save in 32 Bit (Float) format** checkbox

    NOTE Samplitude 2496 performs all conversions (including mixing) in 32-bit format. Checking this checkbox allows you to save the 32-bit quality of intermediate mixing up until the final mastering stage, where conversion to 16-bit will take place.

- The **Exclude Master Effects from Bouncing** checkbox allows you to perform bouncing without processing by the virtual effects of the master block of the **Samplitude Mixer**.

    NOTE This checkbox is checked automatically when you select the **New separate Object in actual VIP** or **Replace Objects in actual VIP** radio button.

Intermediate Mixing

Intermediate mixing in Samplitude 2496 can be used for the same purposes as in SAWPro: to free up computer resources taken by sound in real time.

When performing intermediate mixing, the virtual effects of the master block must be disabled, since they will otherwise introduce unwanted distortions to the signal.

We use the **Replace Objects in actual VIP** feature to replace "heavy" objects with "light" ones. (Objects are "heavy" when they increase the computer load due to a great number of enabled virtual effects, whereas "light" objects are those created with intermediate mixing.)

When the **Replace Objects in actual VIP** option is selected, the original audio material isn't destroyed, since a new audio file is created during intermediate mixing in this case.

Replacing an Object

Replacing an object using the **Track Bouncing** operation is done in the following manner:

1. Select the object *accurately*. Additionally:
   - The **Snap Object** checkbox in the the **Snap definition** dialog box must be checked
   - The **Snap on** button must be in the pressed state (Fig. 5.39).
2. Click the **S** (Solo) button on the track where the selected object is located.
3. Open the **Trackbouncing** dialog box with the **Tools** menu, and select:
   - The **Only marked range** radio button, and
   - The **Replace Objects in actual VIP** radio button
4. Click the **OK** button in the **Trackbouncing** dialog box.
5. Give a name to the new HD Wave project in the dialog box that opens. Finally, click the **OK** button.

> **TIP** It is recommended that the name of the new HD Wave project reflect the processing method applied.

After track bouncing has completed, the older object will be deleted, and the new one will be placed on a new (empty) track. The **Solo** mode of this track will be switched on (Fig. 5.98).

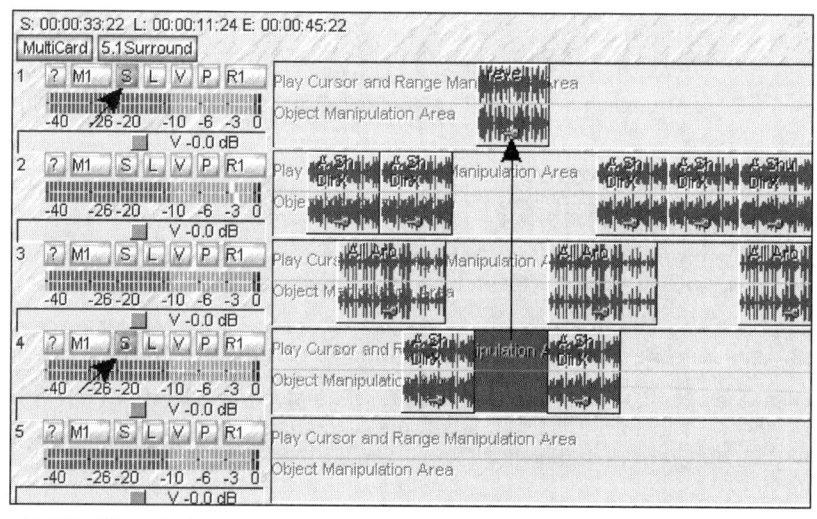

Fig. 5.98. The window of a VIP project after an object has been replaced using **Track Bouncing**

Chapter 5: The Samplitude 2496 Application as a High-Quality Virtual Studio

Destructive Sound Processing

As its name implies, destructive editing destroys sound files.

Destructive editing in Samplitude 2496 can be applied to the objects of a VIP project, or directly to wave projects (of the HD Wave and RAM Wave types). When destructively editing HD Wave and RAM Wave projects, Samplitude 2496 behaves as a sound editor, like Cool Edit Pro.

> **NOTE** Destructively editing the objects of a VIP project vaguely resembles destructively editing clips in SAWPro.

Destructively Editing the Objects of a VIP Project

Destructively editing the objects of a VIP project can be considered an alternative to intermediate mixing with the **Track Bouncing** operation.

> **NOTE** As we'll see later, neither method has much of an advantage over the other from the standpoint of saving disk space. The reason for this is that the destructive editing of an object must *always* be done by creating a physical copy of a sound file, and the very essence of **Track Bouncing** lies in always creating a new sound file.

When editing an object destructively, the action is applied to the portion of the sound file that is a physical copy of the region of this object.

Let's discuss this process in detail.

> **NOTE** The sound processing of an object is done using the **Effects** menu, whose items will be described later.

Destructively editing the objects of a VIP project is done in the following manner:

1. Select the chosen object by clicking it (in the **Universal Mode**, below the horizontal line).

   > **NOTE** Recall that a selected object displays its five handles.

2. Select any effect in the **Effects** menu (in our example, we have chosen the *parametric equalizer*) (Fig. 5.99).

   > **NOTE** You can also use the pop-up menu of the object: open the **Effects** submenu and select an effect there. (The pop-up menu is opened with a right-click on an object.)

3. Set up the effect in the **Test** mode (or in **Preview**). These modes will be discussed later.

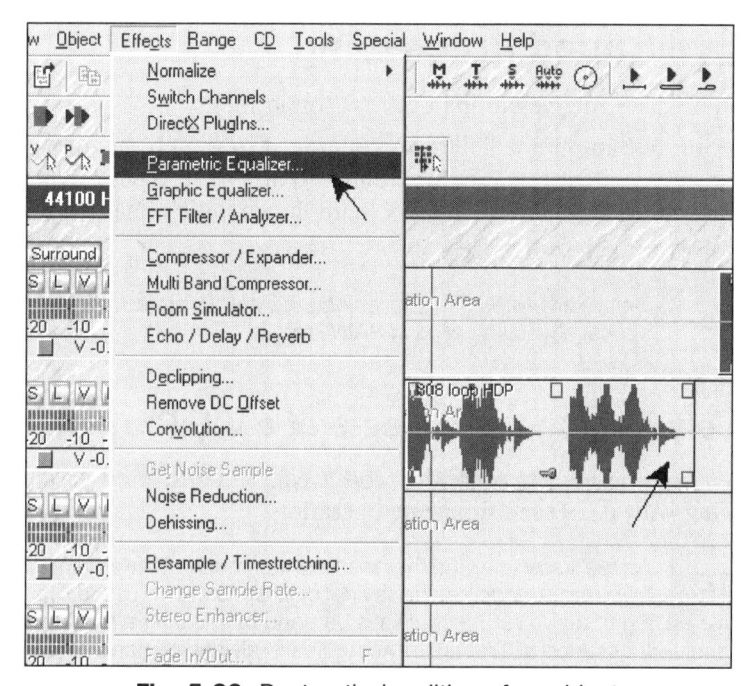

Fig. 5.99. Destructively editing of an object

4. After you finish with the settings, click the **OK** button in the *effect setting window*.

The Create Copy *Checkbox*

Notice that the **Create Copy** checkbox *must* be checked in the effect setting window (Fig. 5.100).

This is a default setting. This means that Samplitude 2496 creates a physical copy of the object region and appends it to the wave project (of the HD or RAM type) where this object region was created.

It is this copy that will be edited destructively (Fig. 5.101). Besides which, the object reference will be redirected to the edited copy.

Thus, if the object being edited has copies on the tracks of a virtual project, the changes of sound will only affect this object, i.e., the copies will have references to the original region.

Warning: if the **Create Copy** checkbox is unchecked, the *original* region will be processed, and *all* the related objects will change their sound.

The Marker of a Destructively Edited Copy of the Object Region

Notice that the program automatically marks the destructive editing operation performed (Fig. 5.101).

Chapter 5: The Samplitude 2496 Application as a High-Quality Virtual Studio 389

This is a very convenient feature, since the marker label allows you to access such information as the type of the applied effect (in the example, **Par. Eq.** stands for "parametric equalizer") and the time and date of destructive editing.

The stages of destructive editing are placed one after another, like physical copies of the region, at the end of the wave project. Each stage has a corresponding marker.

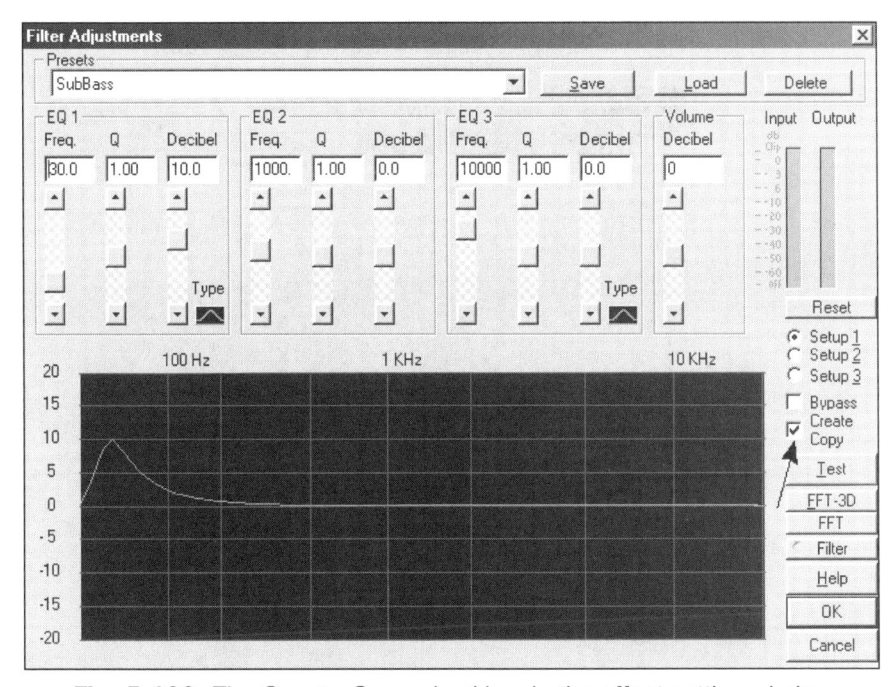

Fig. 5.100. The **Create Copy** checkbox in the effect setting window

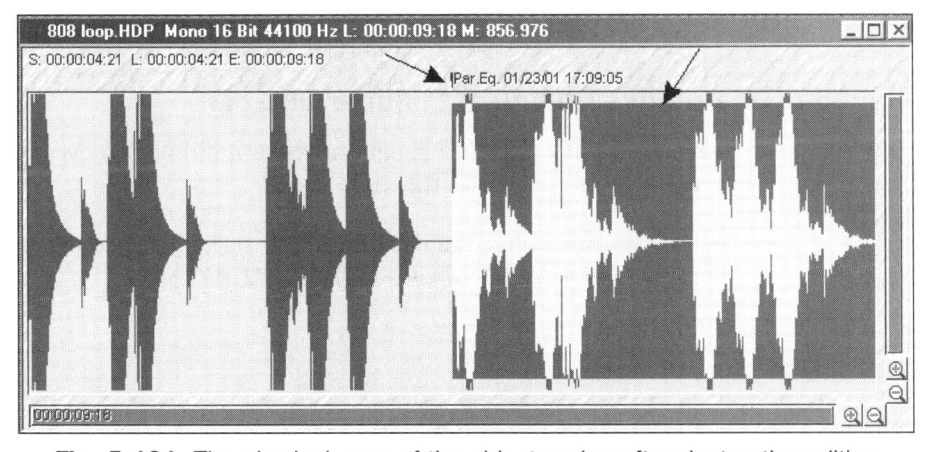

Fig. 5.101. The physical copy of the object region after destructive editing

❐ You can undo the results of destructively editing an object with the **Undo** command of the **Edit** menu

❐ The undo can in turn be undone with the **Redo** command of the same menu

It is possible to use the **Undo History** command of the **Edit** menu without interrupting playback. By selecting the operations in the **Undo History** list one by one, you can compare the sound of the project at different stages of editing (Fig. 5.102).

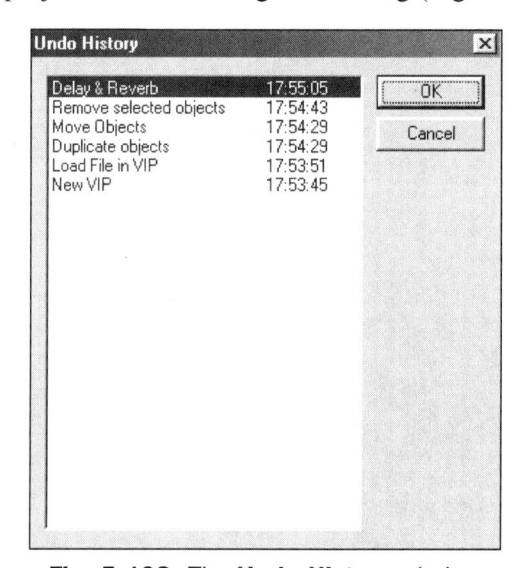

Fig. 5.102. The **Undo History** window

NOTE The **Undo History** window can also be used to undo the results of non-destructive editing.

Simultaneous Destructive Editing of Multiple Objects

Jumping a bit ahead, we're going to consider a situation where multiple objects from different wave projects are destructively edited at the same time.

NOTE This is very useful when you need to perform uniform processing for separately recorded fragments of the same part, say, a vocal.

The procedure is the following:

1. Select multiple objects all at once.

NOTE To select multiple objects, first press and hold the <Ctrl> key, and then click each object below the division line (in the **Universal Mode**).

Chapter 5: The Samplitude 2496 Application as a High-Quality Virtual Studio 391

2. Apply a virtual effect (or a group of DirectX plug-ins) of the **Effects** menu with the **Create Copy** checkbox checked.

A physical copy of the region that corresponds to the object is created in each wave project. All these copies will be processed by the same virtual effect. As a result, completely different objects will have the sound typical for the chosen processing algorithm.

Destructively Editing an HD or RAM Wave Project

One could say that in the destructive editing mode of a wave project, Samplitude 2496 behaves like a sound editor, such as WaveLab or Cool Edit Pro.

The window of an HD or RAM Wave project is opened with the **Destructive Editing** command of the object's pop-up menu (Fig. 5.103).

NOTE When this window opens, the region referenced by the object will be selected.

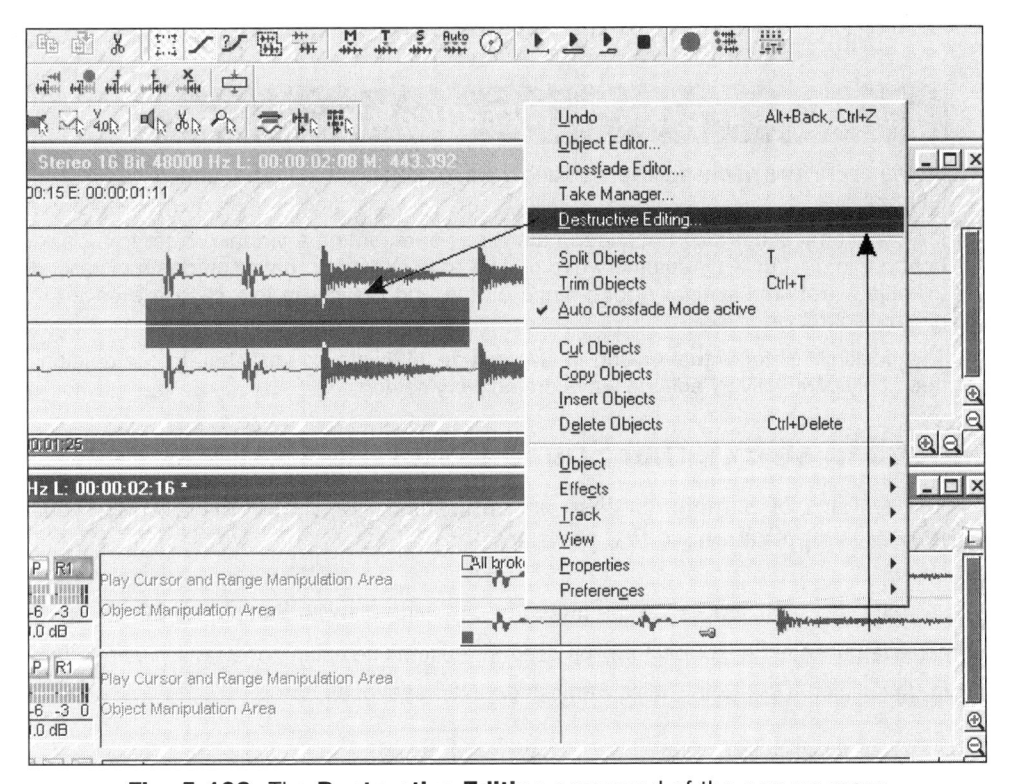

Fig. 5.103. The **Destructive Editing** command of the pop-up menu

You can apply virtual effects of the **Effects** menu to the automatically selected range. Also, you can select a range by yourself.

The Undo Levels

The difference between destructively editing a wave project and doing the same to an object is that the physical copy of the selected range is saved as an undo file rather than put at the end of the wave project (provided that the **Create Copy** checkbox is checked in the virtual effect window).

The same algorithm — where each undo level is a copy of the sound file — is employed in Cool Edit Pro.

In Samplitude 2496, the number of undo levels of destructive editing is specified in the window opened with the **Undo Definitions** command of the **File|Preferences** menu. More exactly, this number is set in the **Undo Depth** field of the **Wave (destructive)** section. You should keep in mind that increasing the number of undo levels reduces the free space on the hard disk.

Using **Undo** and **Redo** commands of the **Edit** menu, you can navigate through the stages of destructive processing. However, the **Undo History** command is unavailable.

Limitations of Destructively Editing a Wave Project

All the operations of destructively editing a *wave* project must be performed *before* creating a virtual project.

If a wave project has been obtained as a result of recording a virtual project to a track, it is best not to destructively edit the wave project at all. You'd be better off destructively editing an object. This is especially good since all the undo levels in this case are saved in the original sound file.

The possibilities for virtual editing in Samplitude 2496 are so vast that, in our opinion, you need only destructively edit the wave project very seldom.

Connecting an External Sound Editor

When the features of Samplitude 2496 are insufficient for destructive editing, you can connect external applications to this program.

NOTE No more than two programs can integrate with Samplitude 2496.

An external sound editor can only be used for destructive editing of an HD Wave project.

In our opinion, Cool Edit Pro fits Samplitude 2496 best of all.

To connect an external sound editor, proceed as follows:

1. Execute the **External Program 1** or **External Program 2** command of the **Special** menu.

Chapter 5: The Samplitude 2496 Application as a High-Quality Virtual Studio

2. Specify the path to the executable file of the external program. This is done in the **Path and File name for external program** field in the **Send wave file to external program** dialog box (Fig. 5.104).

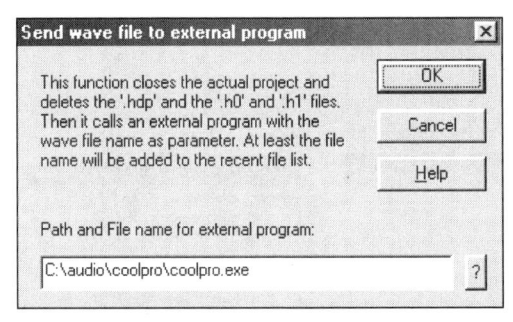

Fig. 5.104. The dialog box for connecting an external program

Using Plug-ins

Connecting a DirectX plug-in to Samplitude 2496 is always done using the same interface.

When editing destructively, DirectX plug-ins are connected with the **DirectX plugIns** command of the **Effects** menu, which opens the **DirectX Plug Ins** dialog box (Fig. 5.105). Unlike the **DirectX Plug Ins** dialog box of the object editor, this dialog box provides two additional buttons: **Test** and **Preview**.

❐ The **Test** button allows you to adjust the sound before destructively using an effect. It gives the user the possibility of listening to the project in real time along with the applied chain of DirectX plug-ins (if there are multiple effects).

> **NOTE** Plug-ins can be used like hardware devices, that is, when you adjust effects, all the changes are heard at once.

❐ The **Preview** button is mainly used to adjust DirectX plug-ins on less powerful computers, where using the **Test** button can overload the processor. This button acts a bit differently than the **Test** button.

- A small fragment is chosen as a sample and played back.

> **NOTE** The length of the fragment is set in the **Preview Time** field in the **System** dialog box (Fig. 5.12).

- At the same time, a new wave project with the **Preview** name is created. It can be played back in a separate window.

Destructively editing an object using DirectX plug-ins can be done in two ways.

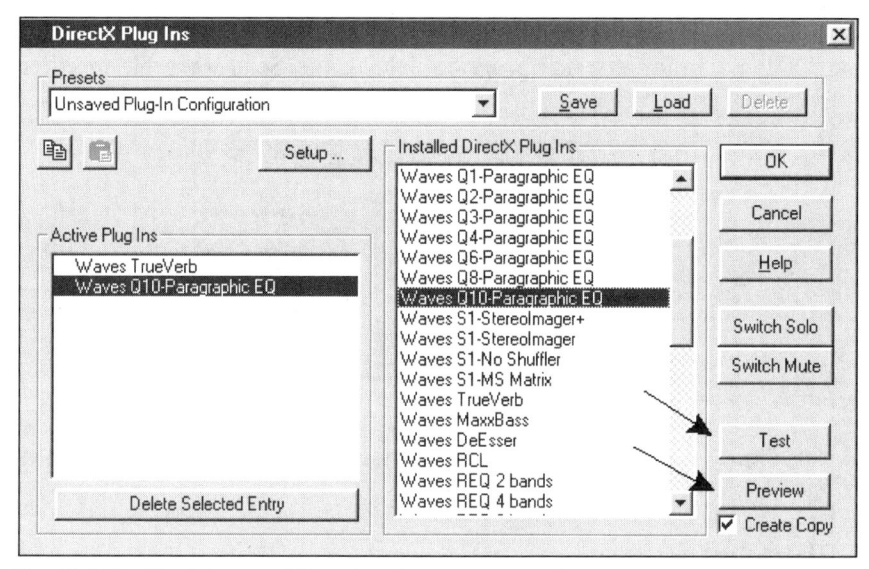

Fig. 5.105. The **Test** and **Preview** buttons in the **DirectX Plug Ins** dialog box

The first method:

1. In the object editor, connect a chain of DirectX plug-ins to the chosen object.
2. Adjust the sound in real time, along with the sound of the other tracks of the project.
3. Using the **Save** button, save the configuration in a file with the PLG extension (Fig. 5.72).

   > **NOTE** In the **Presets** list, a new preset with a name identical to the name of the PLG file will be created.

4. Using the object editor, delete all the DirectX plug-ins.
5. Execute the **DirectX plugIns** command of the **Effects** menu.

   > **NOTE** The configuration of DirectX plug-ins saved with the object editor will be available as a preset in the **Presets** list.

6. Select the previously saved preset.

   > **NOTE** This will start loading the whole chain of DirectX plug-ins with the preset parameters.

7. Apply destructive editing to the object by clicking the **OK** button.

The second method involves moving the configuration of the DirectX plug-in chains with the saved settings using the clipboard (Fig. 5.106).

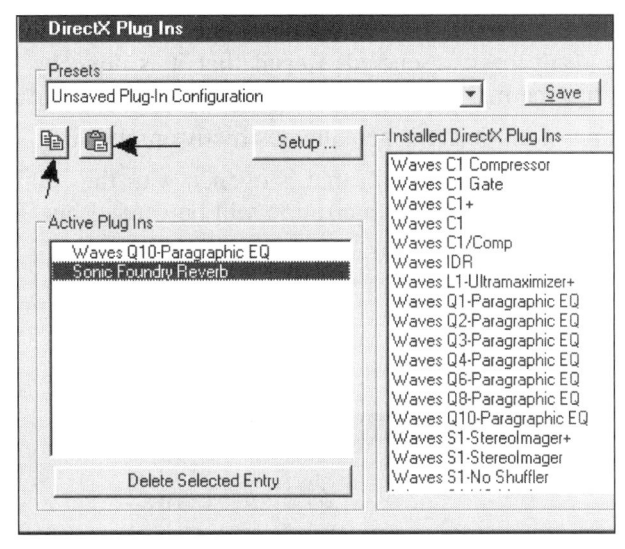

Chapter 5: The Samplitude 2496 Application as a High-Quality Virtual Studio 395

Fig. 5.106. The button for using the clipboard in the **DirectX Plug Ins** dialog box

In this case, you must click the "copy" button (the left one in Fig. 5.106) in the **DirectX Plug Ins** dialog box of the **Object Editor**, and click the "paste" button in the **DirectX Plug Ins** dialog box opened with the **Effects** menu.

Built-in Virtual Effects of Samplitude 2496

Samplitude 2496 provides a number of powerful tools for sound processing, and thus can almost be classified as a sound editor. The built-in virtual effects of Samplitude 2496 are called via the **Effects** menu.

Let's discuss them in detail.

The *Normalize* Effect

The **Normalize** effect allows you to normalize the maximum (peak) signal level, that is, to bring it to a certain level.

Normalization

When performing this operation, the sound file is first scanned to detect the samples at the maximum level. Then, after computing the gain, the program performs signal amplification or attenuation to bring the maximum (peak) signal level to the value specified by the user.

There are two types of normalization in Samplitude 2496: virtual and physical. *Virtual* normalization has already been discussed. Recall that it is done by simply pressing the <N> key, which brings the maximum sound level of the object to 0 dB.

Physical normalization of an object is actually destructive processing.

In the **Normalize** dialog box (Fig. 5.107) that is opened with the <Shift>+<N> shortcut, you can specify the level to which normalization will be carried out. This is done in several ways:

- Quickly — with the **100%** or **50%** button
- Precisely — by entering numbers via the keyboard
- Approximately — with the slider

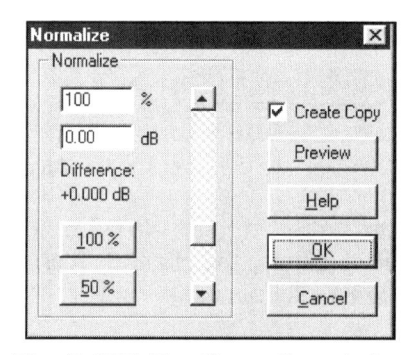

Fig. 5.107. The **Normalize** window

There is no **Test** button in the **Normalize** window. This can be explained by the fact that physical (destructive) normalization cannot be done in real time, since the program must first scan the samples of the wave project.

The **Preview** button lets you estimate the specified settings by ear. In the process, a wave project with the **Preview** name is created.

Prior to destructively processing an object with effects such as reverberation, it is necessary to perform physical normalization to a level anywhere from 50 to 70%; otherwise, signal peaks may be clipped.

You mustn't perform virtual normalization in this case, since destructively processing an object takes into account only the actual (physical) signal level of the wave project.

The *Switch Channels* Effect

The **Switch Channels** effect swaps the left and right channels. It can be used when the positions of sound sources are of great importance, for example, when correcting stereo recordings.

The *Parametric Equalizer* Effect

We already encountered the **Parametric Equalizer** effect when discussing the object editor and the virtual mixer. The version of parametric equalizer used for destructive editing has a few differences (Fig. 5.108).

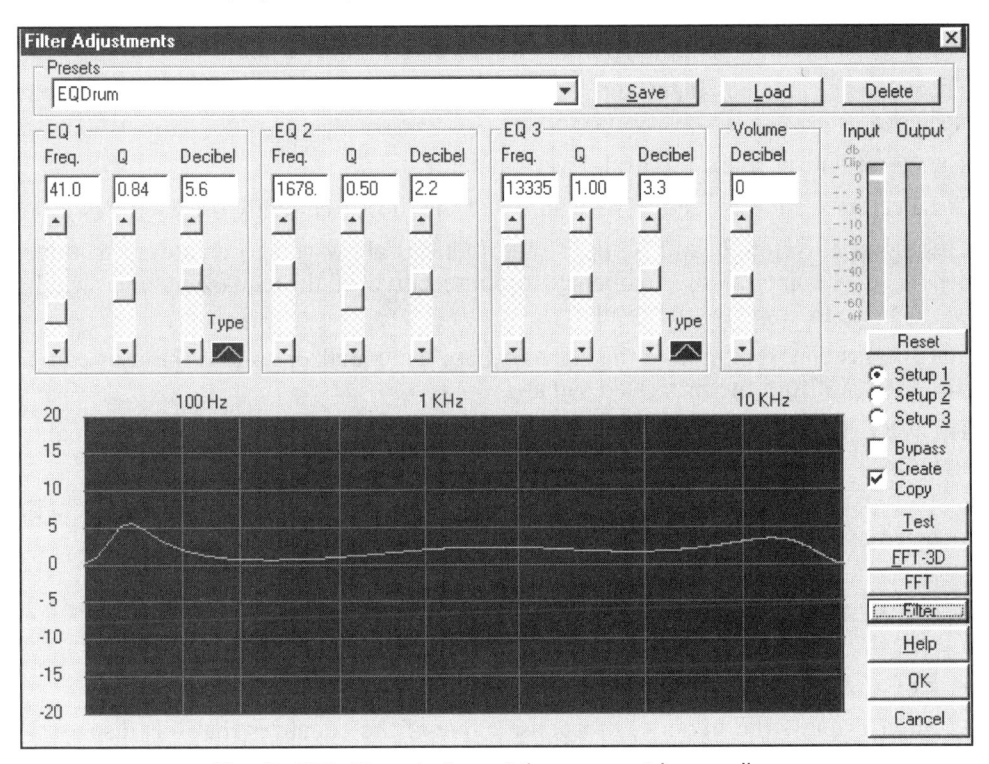

Fig. 5.108. The window of the parametric equalizer

The equalizer consists of four main sections:

- **EQ 1**
- **EQ 2**
- **EQ 3**
- **Volume**

Each **EQ** section includes three sliders:

- **Freq.** (frequency)
- **Q** (quality)
- **Decibel** — the amplification/attenuation sound level

The **Type** buttons change the character of the frequency response curve of the filter.

> **NOTE** The working principles of the Samplitude 2496 parametric equalizer are identical to those of the Cool Edit Pro equalizer.

The **Volume** slider is used to control the overall volume at equalizer output.

Let's look at the general components that are outside of these main sections.

- The equalizer includes **Input** and **Output** level indicators to monitor the corresponding signal levels
- The **Reset** button resets the peak level indicator
- The **Presets** section is used to save and load the most frequently used settings
- The **Setup 1**, **Setup 2**, and **Setup 3** radio buttons allow you to create up to three independent variants of the frequency response curve of the equalizer, and switch between them to compare the results
- The **Bypass** checkbox makes the signal bypass the equalizer so that the user can compare the "raw" and the processed signal
- The **FFT-3D**, **FFT**, and **Filter** buttons change the display mode in the equalizer window:
  - **FFT-3D** displays a 3D diagram of the results of spectral analysis of the signal processed by the equalizer

    > **NOTE** The letters "FFT" mean that spectral analysis is done using the Fast Fourier Transform method (see *Chapter 4*).

  - **FFT** displays a two-dimensional diagram of the results of spectral analysis
  - **Filter** displays the frequency response curve of the equalizer that was displayed initially, before pressing the **FFT-3D** or **FFT** buttons

The *Graphic Equalizer* Effect

The **Graphic Equalizer** effect is a 5-band parametric equalizer similar to the **Parametric Equalizer** effect.

The *FFT Analyzer/Filter* Effect

The **FFT Analyzer/Filter** effect of Samplitude 2496 is a special effect that provides unique possibilities for sound processing.

FFT Analyzer/Filter is a combination of a *spectrum analyzer* and an *FFT filter*.

FFT Filter

Recall that the FFT filter was already described in *Chapter 4*, which covered Cool Edit Pro. Let's focus on some of its advantages.

A characteristic feature of the FFT filter is that it is programmatically implemented as a filter with a finite impulse response.

Such filters can have a linear phase response. This feature ensures equal delays for all the frequency components of the signal that will be processed after it passes the filter. Therefore, phase signal distortions are excluded.

A necessary and sufficient condition for this is the symmetry or antisymmetry of the impulse response of the filter, depending on the filter's purpose. For example, a symmetrical impulse response allows you to implement classic selective filters, such as low-frequency and high-frequency filters, and band-pass and rejecting filters. With an antisymmetrical impulse response, it is possible to develop differentiators and wide-band phasers — for example, those approximating the Hilbert transform, which results in the phase shift of all the frequency components by $-\pi/2$.

Generally, the time it takes to process a finite impulse response filter is in direct proportion to the length of the impulse response. This is why using this filter in real time becomes more and more inconvenient with the increase of the length of the impulse response. This poses a certain problem when implementing impulse filters that have a long impulse response. However, there are a number of well-known, effective computation solutions to this problem that are based on the FFT algorithm.

Unlike finite impulse response filters, filters with an infinite imimpulse response (IIR filters) are always implemented with recursive methods (as they are known in digital signal processing). For this reason, the problem of the effectiveness of the computation isn't as urgent for IIR filters as it is for non-recursive, finite impulse response filters. At the same time, IIR filters are in principle unable to have a linear phase response. As a rule, the term "FFT filter" is used to specify the method of implementing a finite impulse response filter based on the FFT algorithm, rather than the type of the filter. As opposed to the filter programming method based on the convolution formula (which associates the output signal of the filter with the one processed using the impulse response), implementation of the filter using the FFT method allows you to decrease the filtration time by approximately $M/log(M)$ times, where M is the length of the impulse responses of the filter. This is why such a fast method of finite impulse response filter implementation is very effective for a large M. In literature concerning digital signal processing, such fast filtration methods are often called "fast convolution methods".

The impulse response of filters with a linear phase can be computed in several ways. One of the simplest is the frequency sampling method. It uses the fact that M sample values of the frequency response curve of a finite impulse response filter are actually the discrete Fourier transform of the impulse response of this filter. This is why, if such a filter is specified by setting M values of the frequency response curve, the impulse response can be obtained by an inverse FFT. It isn't inconceivable that software developers, when using the term "FFT filter", actually mean a fast filtration method combined with the filter computing method.

Readers interested in digital signal processing algorithms should have a look at the MatLab application.

400 Live Music on Your PC

An advantage of the FFT filter in Samplitude 2496 is that it is combined with a spectrum analyzer that uses the same FFT algorithm as the filter.

Thanks to this combination, the **FFT Analyzer/Filter** effect of Samplitude 2496 presents us with radically new features, as compared to the **FFT Filter** of Cool Edit Pro.

Let's now discuss this effect in more detail.

Like the **FFT Filter** of Cool Edit Pro, the **FFT Analyzer/Filter** effect can be used in two main modes — static and dynamic. Mode selection and switching between the starting and ending frequency response curves are performed with the **Filter Mode** radio buttons (Fig. 5.109):

- **Static** is the mode where the frequency response curve of the signal doesn't change with time
- In the dynamic mode, the frequency response of the signal changes from the *starting* to the *ending* frequency response curve:
  - **Dynamic Start** is the starting frequency response curve in the dynamic mode
  - **Dynamic End** is the ending frequency response curve in the dynamic mode

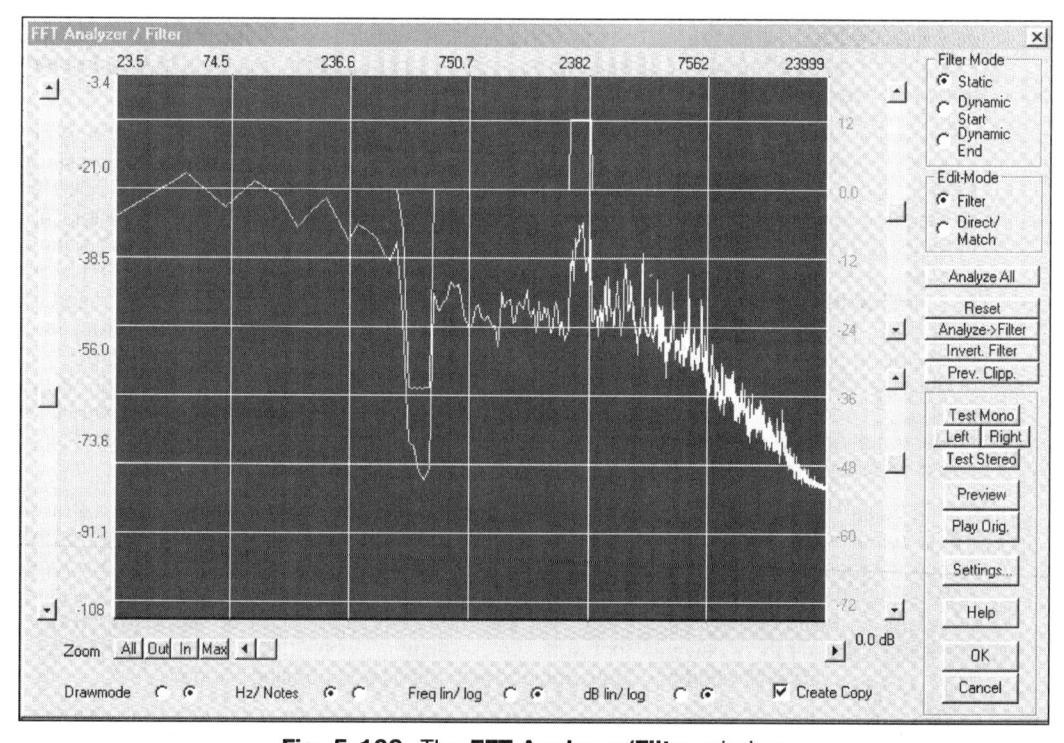

Fig. 5.109. The **FFT Analyzer/Filter** window

Chapter 5: The Samplitude 2496 Application as a High-Quality Virtual Studio 401

NOTE The length of the fragment analyzed by the filter upon first starting the effect can be changed. If you click the **Settings...** button (Fig. 5.109), the **Advanced Settings** dialog box will open (Fig. 5.110), where you'll be able to set the length of the analyzed fragment in seconds. This is done in the **Analysis Time(s)** drop-down list.

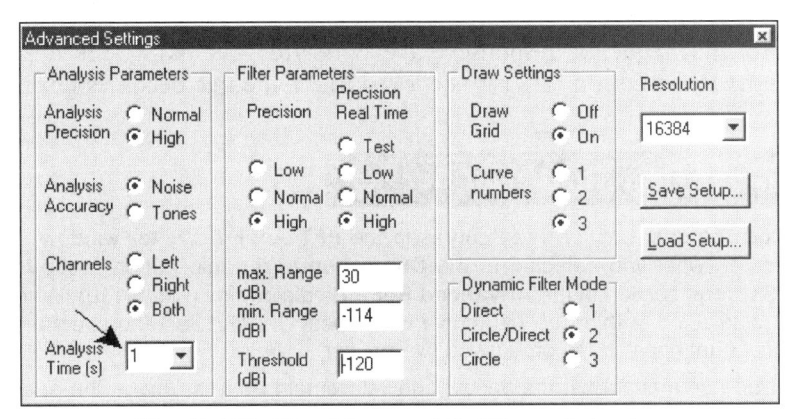

Fig. 5.110. The **Advanced Settings** dialog box

Let's consider how the **FFT Analyzer/Filter** effect works in static mode.

Static Mode

The mode for editing the filter is selected with the **Filter** and **Direct/Match** radio buttons in the **Edit-Mode** switch.

- The **Filter** mode lets you change the frequency response curve of the signal, and its spectrum will change accordingly.
- The **Direct/Match** mode acts in the reverse manner. Changing the signal spectrum leads to changes in the frequency response curve of the filter.

The *Filter* Editing Mode

In the **Filter** editing mode, two curves (of three possible) are displayed upon the first program start (Fig. 5.109).

- The *blue* curve (the lower one in the figure) is the result of *primary spectral analysis* upon the first start

The first time, a short fragment is always analyzed for the **FFT Analyzer/Filter** effect. For a full spectrum analysis — that is, to analyze the entire object — click **Analyze All**.

- The *red* curve (the upper one in the figure) reflects the *frequency response curve* of the FFT filter

Any changes in the *frequency response curve* of the filter change the result of the *spectral analysis*. In other words, every change of the shape of the red curve has an effect (immediately) on the shape of the blue curve.

This feature of the **FFT Analyzer/Filter** is very important, since it allows you not only to listen to the changes, but also to have them reflected on the display.

If the shape of the frequency response curve is not to your liking, the changes can be undone with the **Reset** button (after it is clicked, the red curve becomes horizontal).

Settings. The Number of Curves

There can be one, two, or three curves in the **FFT Analyzer/Filter** window. Their number depends on what you selected in the **Curve numbers** radio button group located in the **Draw Settings** section in the **Advanced Settings** dialog box (Fig. 5.110). When the **3** radio button is selected, a third (yellow) curve will appear. It will reflect the spectrum of the original signal (that hasn't been processed by the filter).

If the blue curve changes, the yellow one will remain as it is (this is the spectral analysis before editing).

We recommend that you always use the mode where three curves are displayed, since the deviations in the frequencies that have appeared while drawing the red filter curve are most vivid in this mode (Fig. 5.111).

Besides which, if the computer performance allows, it is recommended that you specify the high precision mode, as shown in Fig. 5.110.

The maximum valid value of the **Resolution** parameter is 32,768. In this case, the frequency range of the signal is divided into a number of bands that is half as large as the **Resolution** value.

The **Resolution** parameter is common both to the filter and the spectrum analyzer.

Filter adjustment can be done in real-time mode by clicking one of the following buttons:

- Left
- Right
- Test Mono
- Test Stereo

To listen to the signal *before processing* it with the filter, use the **Play Orig.** button.

If the obtained frequency response curve of the filter clips the signal peaks, you should perform automatic normalization, that is, click the **Prev. Clipp.** (prevent clipping) button.

Fig. 5.111 shows the red, blue, and yellow curves, as well as the **Fader** sliders, indicated by numbers (1 to 4).

Chapter 5: The Samplitude 2496 Application as a High-Quality Virtual Studio 403

These sliders have the following purpose:
- **Slider 1** changes the vertical scale for the blue and yellow curves (the dB level axis)
- **Slider 2** moves the display horizontally (along the Hz axis)
- **Slider 3** changes the vertical scale for the red filter curve only
- **Slider 4** adjusts the output signal level

The **All**, **Out**, **In**, and **Max** buttons (to the left of the horizontal scroll bar) serve to zoom the image horizontally (along the Hz axis). The **All** and **Max** buttons allow you to quickly switch between the minimum and maximum scales.

The **FFT Analyzer/Filter** allows the spectrum of one signal (such as the frequency-response curve of the filter) to influence the spectrum of another signal.

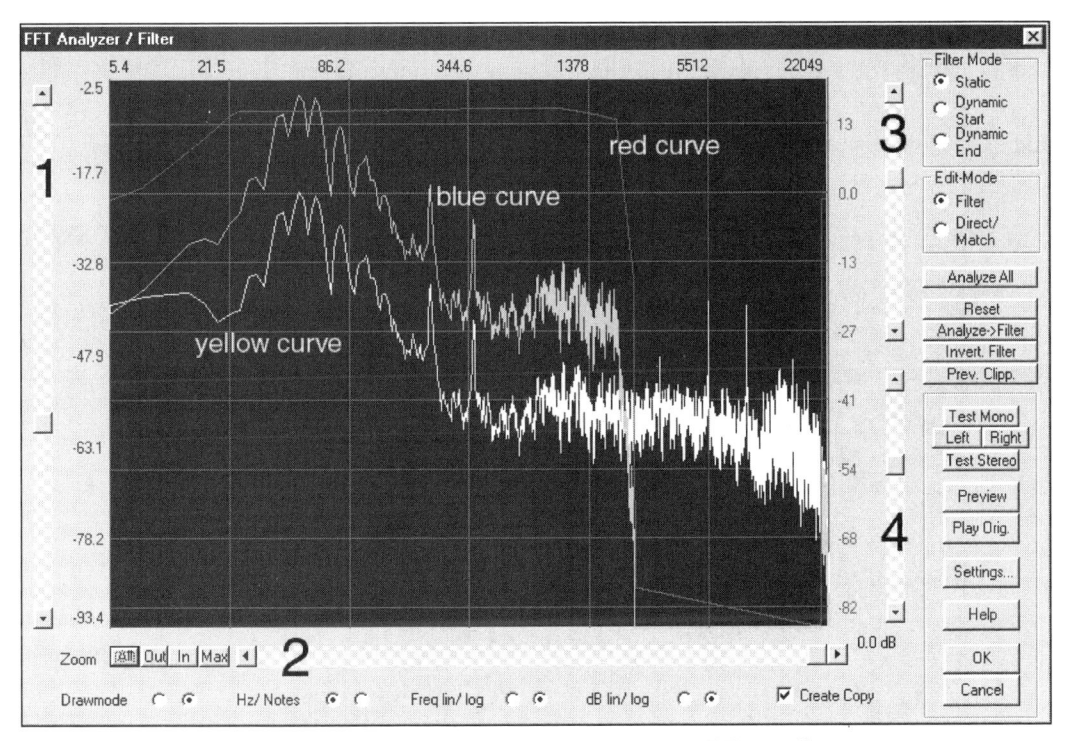

Fig. 5.111. Controlling the **FFT Analyzer/Filter** effect

This procedure is done in the following way:

1. Click the **Analyze -> Filter** button.

    > **NOTE** This is necessary in order that the frequency response curve of the original signal (the yellow curve) become the frequency response curve of the filter (the red curve).

2. Click the **Cancel** button to close the **FFT Analyzer/Filter** effect window (without destructive processing).
3. Then select the range (or the object) that you're going to process.
4. Again, open the effect window with the **FFT Analyzer/Filter** command of the **Effects** menu.

> **NOTE** The new material will be influenced by the previous frequency response curve of the filter that was saved in Step 1.

The **Invert. Filter** button inverts the frequency response curve of the filter horizontally.

The *Direct/Match* Editing Mode

In the **Direct/Match** editing mode (the **Edit-Mode** section), changes are made in reverse order — from the signal spectrum to the frequency response of the filter.

Here, the user has the ability to edit the signal spectrum (the blue curve — Fig. 5.112) directly, rather than drawing the frequency response curve of the filter (the red curve), as done in the **Filter** editing mode.

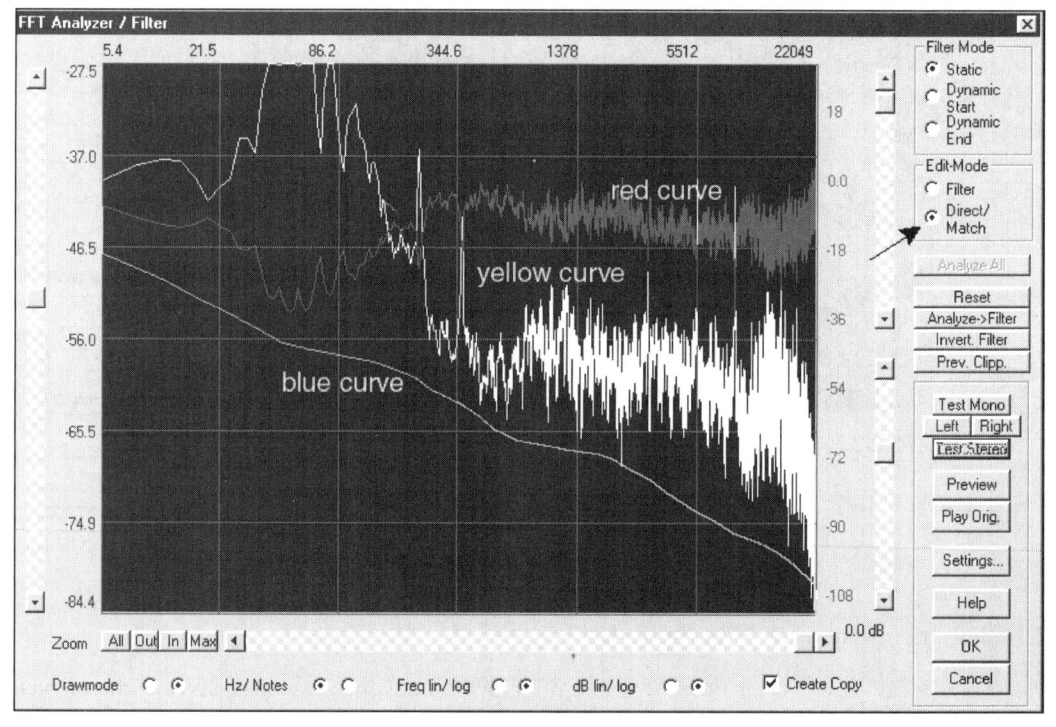

Fig. 5.112. The **Direct/Match** editing mode

Chapter 5: The Samplitude 2496 Application as a High-Quality Virtual Studio 405

As a rule, when the spectrum is changed directly, the shape of the frequency response curve of the filter (the red one) becomes very complex, resembling the result of a spectral analysis (Fig. 5.112).

The **Direct/Match** editing mode is convenient when you need to create a completely new, unusual sound for well-known musical instruments.

> **NOTE** For example, by experimenting with the bass spectrum, you can give new "coloration" to the sound of a bass guitar, or highlight the subharmonics of percussion instruments. It is virtually impossible to achieve such results with a conventional equalizer alone.

If you need to keep the natural sound when processing in the **Direct/Match** mode, maximize the horizontal scale (with the **Max** button).

To highlight the *harmonics* equal to the frequencies of musical notes, the **FFT Analyzer/Filter** effect provides the ability to display the frequency not only in Hz, but as notes or in the MIDI standard as well (for details, see *Chapter 6*).

> **NOTE** Harmonics are frequencies that are multiples of the main frequency of the signal. Subharmonics are frequencies that are "factors" of the main frequency.

To enter the mode that displays frequencies as notes, you must select the **Notes** radio button (Fig. 5.113).

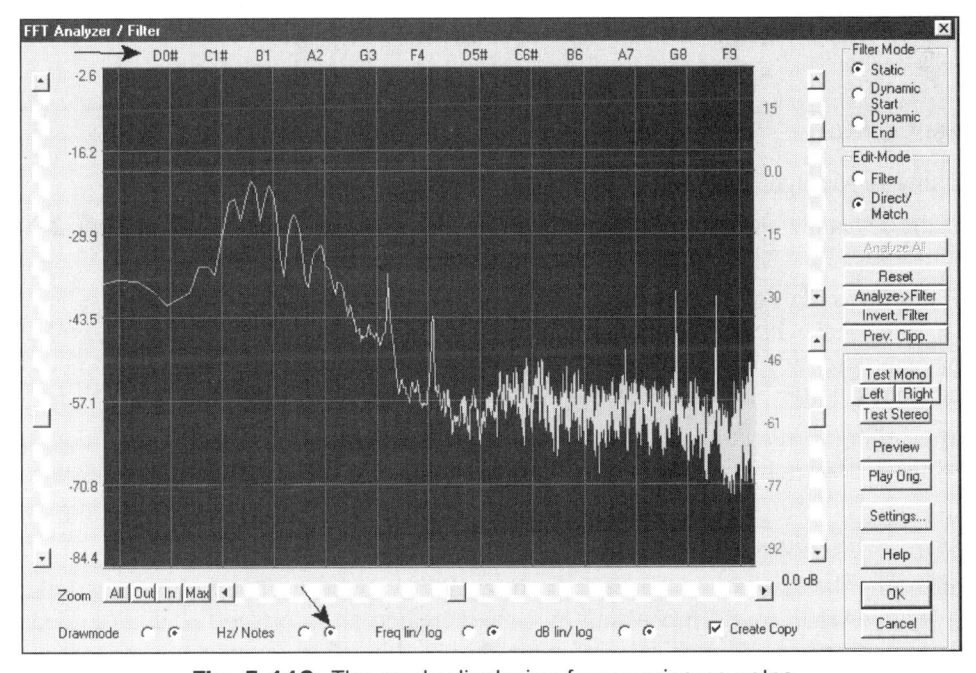

Fig. 5.113. The mode displaying frequencies as notes

One could say that in this mode, the effect becomes a musical instrument, since, with certain settings, you can make it resonate with a complex chord. In other words, you can create something similar to the **Harmonizer** effect.

In the **Direct/Match** mode, you can also influence the spectrum of one signal by the spectrum of another signal (such as the frequency response curve of the filter).

To do this:

1. Analyze the signal using the **Analyze All** button.
2. Using the **Save Setup** button in the **Advanced Settings** dialog box (Fig. 5.110), save the settings in a file with the FFF extension.
3. Close the **FFT Analyzer/Filter** window.
4. Select another object that you plan to process.
5. Open the **FFT Analyzer/Filter** window again, and load the settings from the FFF file using the **Load Setup** button in the **Advanced Settings** dialog box.

This procedure can be called the *new sound synthesizing algorithm*. Moreover, using the **Invert. Filter** button, you can get two filter curves — direct and inverse — from a single FFF file.

> **NOTE** A computer musician using the Samplitude 2496 program can form a collection of sound spectra consisting of FFF files.

Dynamic Mode

Switching to the dynamic mode is done with the **Filter Mode** radio buttons:

- In the **Dynamic Start** mode, you draw the spectrum or the frequency response curve of the filter that will correspond to the starting point of conversion.
- In the **Dynamic End** mode, you draw the spectrum or the frequency response curve of the filter that will correspond to the ending point of conversion. (For example, this might be the inverse of the curve created in the **Dynamic Start** mode, obtained using the **Invert. Filter** button.)

When listening to the conversion results with the **Test** button, you can correct the curves in real time by switching between the **Dynamic Start** and the **Dynamic End** modes.

Besides which, you may also experiment with the **Dynamic Filter Mode** radio buttons in the **Advanced Settings** window (Fig. 5.110).

Summarizing the features of the **FFT Analyzer/Filter** effect, we can say that the developers of this powerful sound processing tool have created an interface that fits the needs of computer musicians as much as is possible. Using this effect opens new horizons in the area of creating new sounds.

The *Compressor/Expander/Noise Gate/Limiter* Effect

The **Compressor/Expander/Noise Gate/Limiter** effect is a universal module of dynamic signal processing (Fig. 5.114).

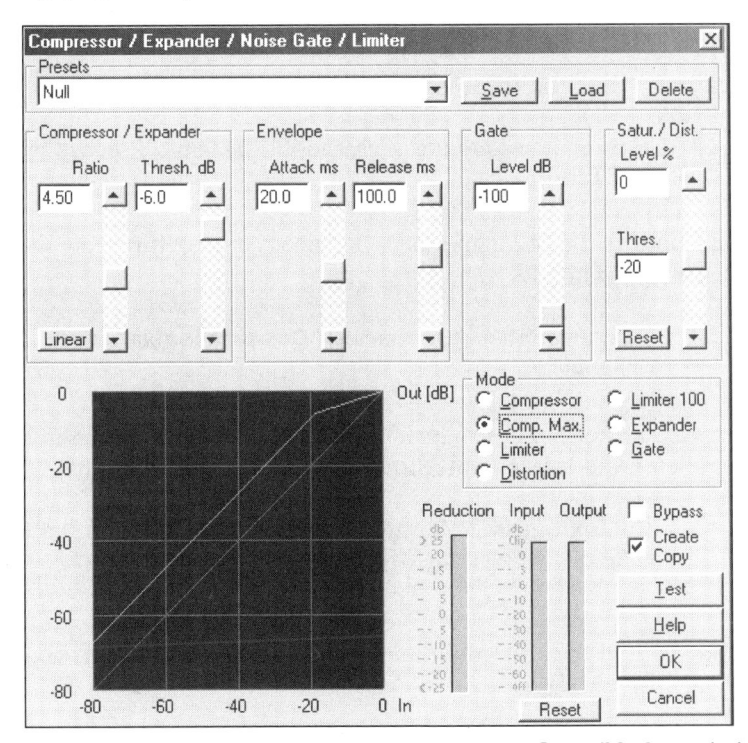

Fig. 5.114. The **Compressor/Expander/Noise Gate/Limiter** window

This module has seven working modes selected with the **Mode** radio buttons.

Let's take a closer look at these modes.

The **Compressor** radio button turns on the "classical" compressor.

> **NOTE** The curve in the effect display (Fig. 5.114) shows the input/output relationship of the signal level. In other words, it represents the *amplitude response* of the compressor.

The **Linear** button found in the **Compressor/Expander** section turns off the dynamic processing and makes the amplitude response linear.

In the **Compressor** mode, you can set up the following parameters:

❑ The compression ratio (**Ratio**)
❑ The threshold (**Thresh. dB**)

The changes are made in the **Compressor/Expander** section with one of the following methods: either by moving the corresponding sliders, or by entering numbers from the keyboard into the numeric field next to the sliders.

There are two sliders in the **Envelope** section that determine:

- The attack time (**Attack ms**)
- The compressor release time (**Release ms**)

> **NOTE** These parameters are similar to the **Dynamic Processing** parameters in Cool Edit Pro.

The **Comp. Max** button (the **Compressor/Maximizer** mode) turns on the mode where the signal level is maximized.

> **NOTE** This mode has two names: **Compressor/Maximizer** and **Loudness Enhancer**.

Unlike the **Compressor** mode, the **Compressor/Maximizer** mode has a direct relationship to the **Ratio** parameter: the larger the **Ratio** value, the higher the volume.

> **NOTE** The **Compressor/Maximizer** mode is the main one used to raise the volume of quiet objects. This is why it is the default mode for the **Dynamics** section of the object editor and the virtual mixer.

The **Limiter** mode is used to limit amplitude peaks of the signal that exceed the *threshold* (the level specified with the **Thresh. dB** slider).

> **NOTE** In all the applications discussed so far (SAWPro, Cool Edit Pro, and Samplitude 2496), the **Limiter** mode has the same purpose: to avoid signal distortions at amplitude peaks.

The **Distortion** mode allows you to introduce nonlinear distortions that simulate the effect of an overloaded amplifier.

In this mode, the **Compressor/Expander** section is switched off, and the depth of distortions is adjusted with the **Level %** slider in the **Satur./Dist.** section.

The amplitude response of such an overloaded virtual amplifier is reflected by the *red* curve.

The **Thres.** (Threshold) field in the **Satur./Dist.** section is used to enter a *negative* threshold value (in dB) via the keyboard.

> **NOTE** After you enter this value, click the **Level %** field. Otherwise, the entered value won't have any effect.

The **Reset** button resets the settings in the **Satur./Dist.** section.

The Satur./Dist. *Section*

The **Satur./Dist.** (Saturation/Distortion) section is also available in the other modes of the **Compressor/Expander/Noise Gate/Limiter** effect.

The settings of this section can be used to obtain a "dense" sound, or, as a variant, to imitate the sound of an amplifier that is a little overloaded at a concert with live sound.

The **Limiter 100** mode turns on the limiter of amplitude peaks of the signal that exceed the *threshold* (the level specified with the **Thresh. dB** slider). The difference between the **Limiter 100** mode and the **Limiter** mode is that the output signal level is increased to the max in the former.

The **Expander** mode turns on the mode in which the dynamic range is expanded. This expansion manifests itself in the fact that loud signals get louder and soft ones get even softer.

The expansion ratio of the dynamic range is specified with the **Ratio** slider.

The **Gate** (noise gate) mode is actually a noise suppressor that lowers signals whose level is below the specified threshold.

The noise suppression threshold is set with the **Level** slider in the **Gate** section.

The **Gate** mode is effective when you want to eliminate extraneous noise during pauses.

Separating the Noise and the Signal

The **Gate** section works in all the modes of the **Compressor/Expander/Noise Gate/Limiter** effect. This allows you to easily combine the noise suppressor with the **Compressor/Maximizer**.

As a result, you get the **Compressor/Gate** effect, which can be successfully used to separate the useful signal from the noise.

This is done in the following way: first adjust the **Compressor/Maximizer**, and then use the **Level** slider in the **Gate** section to find the optimum noise suppression threshold from the standpoint of a trade off between noise suppression and signal distortion.

The *Multiband Dynamics* Effect

The **Multiband Dynamics** effect is a virtual device for *multiband dynamic signal processing.*

This effect can be used as a main tool for processing the objects and tracks of a VIP project in order to obtain a "live" and expressive sound. This is due to the fact that this effect helps "liven up" the dull and lifeless sound of the MIDI synthesizers of some sound cards and of some cheap "home" models of Casio and Yamaha synthesizers that have simplified sound synthesizing algorithms.

The **Multiband Dynamics** effect is the main tool for recording mastering, and so it is included among other effects in the master block of Samplitude 2496's virtual mixer.

Multiband Dynamic Processing

Multiband dynamic signal processing means that the original signal is first filtered by frequencies to divide it into bands. Each frequency band is then processed by a separate dynamic processor, and the processed signals are summarized at the output.

Multiband processing allows you to avoid drawbacks of wide-band processing caused by a high signal level of a certain frequency band influencing the whole process.

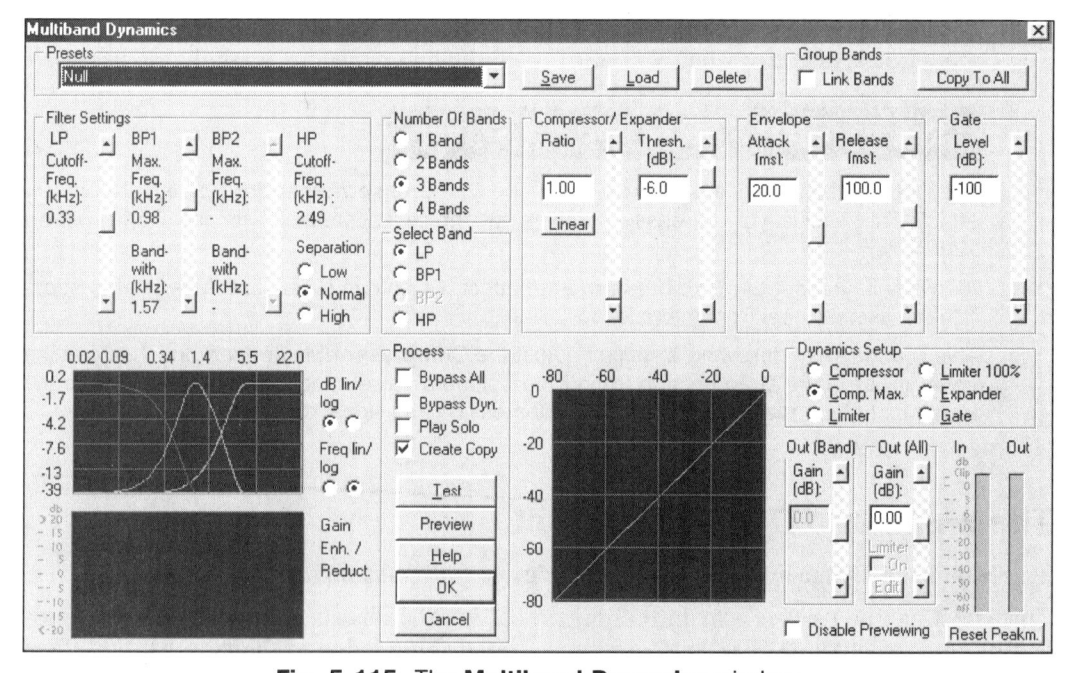

The **Multiband Dynamics** window can be opened using either of two methods: with the **Multi Band Compressor** command of the **Effects** menu, or by right-clicking the **Compressor** button in the **Compressor/Limiter** section of the virtual mixer's master block.

Let's consider the controls of the **Multiband Dynamics** effect (Fig. 5.115).

Fig. 5.115. The **Multiband Dynamics** window

Chapter 5: The Samplitude 2496 Application as a High-Quality Virtual Studio

The **Number Of Bands** group consists of four radio buttons: **1 Band**, **2 Bands**, **3 Bands**, and **4 Bands**. They specify the number of frequency bands for adjustment.

> **NOTE** You should bear in mind that on less powerful computers, the **4 Bands** mode might overload the processor.

The **Select Band** group allows you to select the *active* frequency band:
- **LP** low frequencies
- **BP1** middle frequencies (range 1)
- **BP2** middle frequencies (range 2)
- **HP** high frequencies

> **NOTE** The **Multiband Dynamics** window is divided into two parts: the filter block is to the left, and the dynamic processor control section is to the right (Fig. 5.115).

Each of the four bands has its own dynamic processor. The number of *working* dynamic processors is determined by the **Number Of Bands**.

Only one of the four dynamic processors is available in the effect window, namely, the processor of the *active* frequency band.

The *active* frequency band is presented in the display of the effect window as a *red* curve.

Thus, when selecting a frequency band (with the **LP**, **BP1**, **BP2**, or **HP** buttons of the **Select Band** switch), the user gets access to the settings of the corresponding dynamic processor.

The checkboxes of the **Process** section are used to change the modes of listening to the effect.
- **Bypass All** allows you to listen to the unprocessed signal — the filter block and dynamic processor block are bypassed

> **NOTE** This feature is used for quick comparison of the results of processing to the "dry" signal.

- **Bypass Dyn.** bypasses the dynamic processors and allows you to estimate the results of dynamic processing in a *single* frequency band

> **NOTE** This checkbox must only be used *in combination with* the **Play Solo** checkbox.

- **Play Solo** allows you to listen to the active frequency band

> **NOTE** When this button is checked, you can accurately adjust all the parameters of the filter and the dynamic processor for the active frequency band.

The **Filter Settings** section contains three sliders, using which you can change the *boundaries* between the frequency bands.

> **NOTE** Not all the sliders are available. The quantity depends on the number of the frequency bands selected in the **Number Of Bands** radio button group.

Three radio buttons from the **Separation** group — **Low**, **Normal**, and **High** — determine the steepness of the band filters.

> **NOTE** You should keep in mind that increasing the steepness increases the load to the CPU.

In the **Multiband Dynamics** effect, the dynamic processor of each frequency band is actually the **Compressor/Expander/Noise Gate/Limiter** effect (except for the **Distortion** mode) discussed earlier (Fig. 5.114).

Notice the new features acquired by the dynamic processors of frequency bands in the **Multiband Dynamics** effect.

- The controls in the **Group Bands** section allow you to synchronize the settings of different dynamic processors
  - The **Link Bands** checkbox links the controls of the dynamic processors. When it is checked, changes of *any* parameter of one dynamic processor leads to synchronous changes of the *same* parameters of the other processors.

    > **NOTE** For example, setting the **Attack** time to 10 msec for the *active* dynamic processor automatically sets the same attack time for the other dynamic processors.

  - The **Copy To All** button makes all the current settings of the *active* dynamic processor valid for the other processors.

- The **Out (Band)** slider is available only in the **Compressor** mode. It allows you to set the *volume level* for the active frequency band

  Separate Volume Adjustment in Each Frequency Band

  If the **Compressor** mode is selected in the **Dynamics Setup** section for *each* frequency band, it will be possible to set different volume levels for each of them using the **Out (Band)** slider.

- The **Disable Previewing** checkbox disables the "look-ahead" feature for signals with sharp amplitude peaks

  > **NOTE** When the **Disable Previewing** checkbox is unchecked, sharp amplitude peaks aren't smoothed out. Because of this, checking this checkbox can be useful for obtaining some specific distortions.

Chapter 5: The Samplitude 2496 Application as a High-Quality Virtual Studio   413

☐ The **Limiter On** checkbox and the **Edit** button are available in the **Multiband Dynamics** window only when it has been opened by right-clicking the **Compressor** slider in the master block of the virtual mixer

- Checking the **Limiter On** checkbox turns on the **Compressor/Expander/Noise Gate/Limiter** effect of the master block of the virtual mixer that is used in the **Limiter** mode
- The **Edit** button opens the settings window of the **Compressor/Expander/Noise Gate/Limiter** effect to set the limiting threshold

> **NOTE** The interaction between the **Multiband Dynamics** and **Compressor/Expander/Noise Gate/Limiter** effects is thoroughly considered in the section "*Creating an AUDIO CD in Samplitude 2496*".

The *Room Simulator* Effect

The **Room Simulator** effect allows you to simulate the acoustics of a room by its impulse response.

The **Room Simulator** effect is based on the following algorithm: first, an impulse response is recorded in a room with the required acoustics (for example, a clap is recorded); the musical material is then processed using this impulse response.

> **NOTE** In *Chapter 4*, we came across a similar DirectX plug-in — **Acoustic Mirror** from Sonic Foundry.

To record an impulse response, the standard configuration in Samplitude 2496 includes a special "impulse" VIP project, **IMPULS.VIP** (Fig. 5.116).

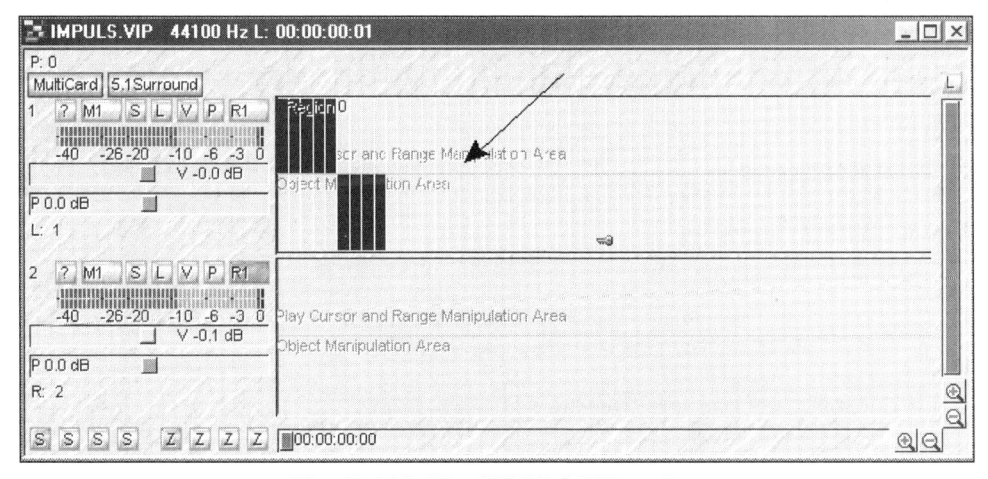

Fig. 5.116. The **IMPULS.VIP** project

The object indicated by the arrow in Fig. 5.116 is an impulse (heard as a click). In the recording mode (with the **playback while recording** checkbox checked in the **Record Parameter** window), you can fix the impulse response in the lower track.

Recording the Impulse Response

Impulse Response is the acoustic reaction of a room to an impulse sound — for example, to a click.

There are several ways to record the impulse response.

When working in a room (such as a concert hall, a palace, a temple, etc.), special hardware is needed (at the least, you'll need a computer with Samplitude 2496 installed, a microphone, and an amplifier with an acoustic system).

Another method is to get the impulse response from an external hardware reverb. In this case, you'll need to replace the microphone and amplifier with the hardware reverb connected between the input and the output of the sound card, and record the impulse response into the **IMPULS.VIP** virtual project. Taking into account the fact that hardware effect processors are quite expensive, such technology is quite "hot" today.

You can also use the ready-made collection of impulse responses delivered with Samplitude 2496. These are in the form of RAM Wave projects.

In general, any WAV file can be used as an impulse response, including a fragment of the sound material being processed. Interesting effects can be obtained when using noise signals.

In this regard, the **Room Simulator** effect can be treated as a tool for creating new sounds.

Let's discuss the **Room Simulator** effect in detail (Fig. 5.117).

❐ In the **Impulse Response Selection** section, you can select the impulse response from among files with the RAP, HDP, and WAV extensions. To load a file use the **Load** button, and to listen to it click the **Play** button.

❐ In the **Quality** section, you can set the sound processing quality:

- **normal**

or

- **high**

❐ In the **Impulse Response Envelope** section, you can use three sliders — **Early Reflect.**, **Late Reverb.**, and **Length: %** to adjust the parameters of the impulse response envelope within a wide range.

- **Early Reflect.** sets the level for early signal reflections

    NOTE The envelope curve is colored blue in the effect display. The **Early Reflect.** slider changes the attack of the envelope.

- **Late Reverb.** sets the level for late signal reflections

    NOTE In the effect display, you can see the decline of an envelope curve that is adjusted with the **Late Reverb.** slider.

Chapter 5: The Samplitude 2496 Application as a High-Quality Virtual Studio 415

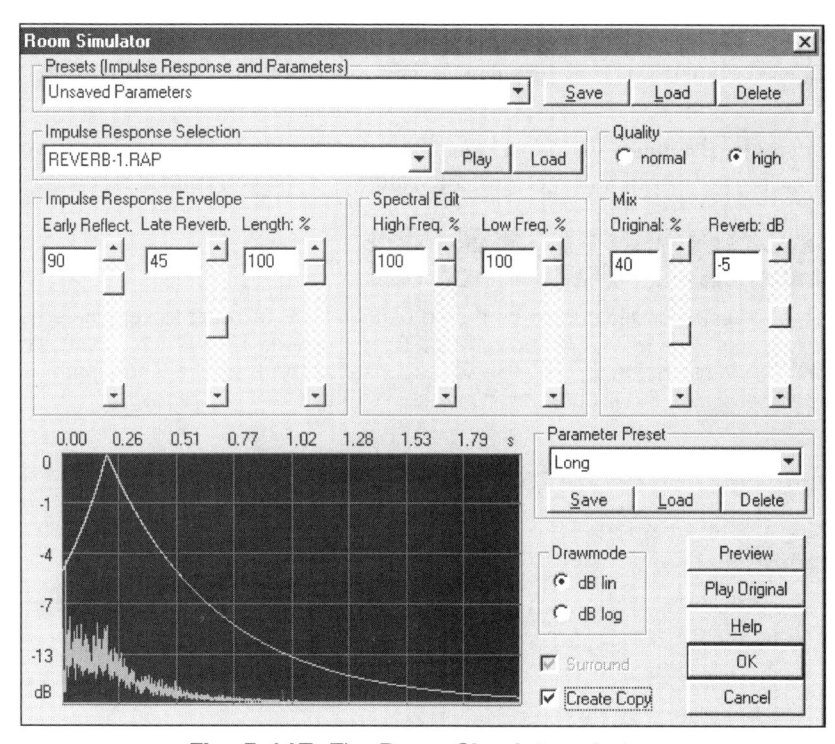

Fig. 5.117. The **Room Simulator** window

- **Length: %** specifies the reverberation length as a percentage

    NOTE Small values of this parameter (about 10%) can make the reverberation effect indistinguishable by ear.

☐ In the **Spectral Edit** section, you can set the degree of frequency absorption in the virtual room:

- The **High Freq %** slider changes the absorption of high frequencies (as a percentage)
- The **Low Freq %** slider changes the absorption of low frequencies (as a percentage)

☐ There are two sliders in the **Mix** section:

- **Original %** sets the relationship between the original and the processed signal level

    NOTE The valid values fall into a range from 100% (the original signal only) to 0% (the reverberation signal only).

- **Reverb: dB** specifies the reverberation signal level in dB

❏ In the **Parameter Preset** section, you can save, load, or delete a certain configuration of settings specified in the **Impulse Response Envelope**, **Spectral Edit**, and **Mix** sections.

❏ In the **Presets (Impulse Response and Parameters)** section, you can save, load, or delete a configuration of settings with the reference to the impulse response file used.

Storing Impulse Response Files

An impulse response file should be stored *only* in the FX-Preset folder located in the folder containing the files of the Samplitude 2496 application. This is important, since presets contain only a reference to the impulse response file, and not the whole path. So, if the file is in another folder, the program won't be able to find it.

Processing Impulse Response Files

By processing impulse response files, you can significantly extend the range of the **Room Simulator** effects.

Undoubtedly, introducing such changes is a creative task. Any recommendations are hardly necessary in this case. However, we'd like to draw your attention to some points that we think are important to note.

❏ To increase the sound quality:
- Convert impulse response files and the material being processed to **32 Bit Float** format
- Select the **high** mode in the **Quality** section

❏ An additional direction for your research into new sounds may lie in processing the impulse response file with the **FFT Analyzer/Filter** effect, especially in the dynamic mode.

Combining the **FFT Analyzer/Filter** effect in dynamic mode and the subsequent **Reverse** effect will lead to unusual recursive reverberation.

NOTE The **Reverse** operation is applied only to wave projects, and called with the **Reverse** command of the **Effects** menu.

❏ Using the **Resample/Time Stretching** effect allows you to change the sizes and frequency characteristics of the virtual room.

The *Echo/Delay/Reverb* Effect

The **Echo/Delay/Reverb** effect is a simple and easy-to-use tool for delay setting, which is also included among the other effects of the virtual mixer (Fig. 5.118).

Chapter 5: The Samplitude 2496 Application as a High-Quality Virtual Studio 417

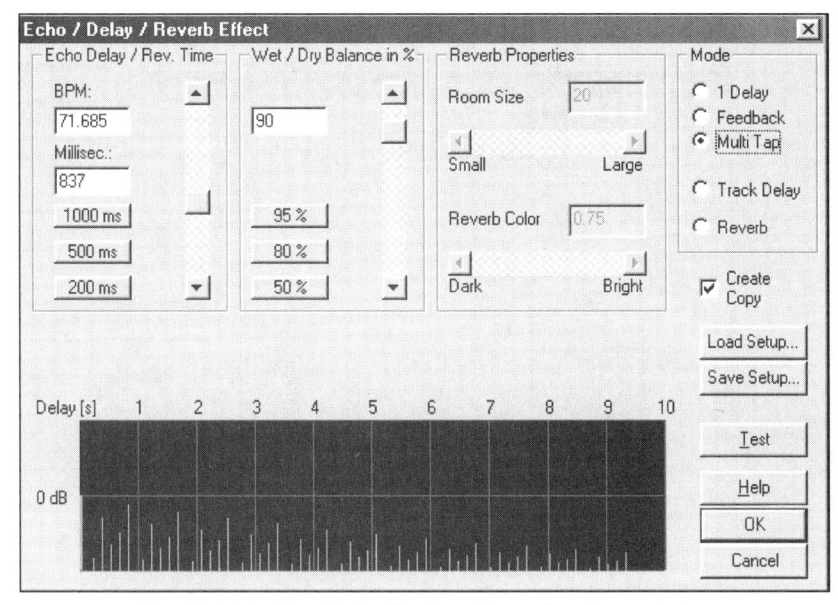

Fig. 5.118. The **Echo/Delay/Reverb** effect window

The delay time can be related to the tempo of the piece of music by setting the tempo in the **BPM** field in the **Echo Delay/Rev.Time** section.

NOTE   Also, the delay time can be adjusted within a wide range by the slider.

The slider in the **Wet/Dry Balance in %** section specifies the relationship between the direct and delayed signal.

The sliders in the **Reverb Properties** section are available only in the **Reverb** mode:

❐ The **Reverb Color** slider adjusts the degree of high frequency absorption during reverberation

❐ The **Room Size** slider changes the size of the virtual room

The working modes of this effect are selected with the radio buttons of the **Mode** sections. They should pose no difficulties to the user.

The *Convolution* Effect

The **Convolution** effect allows you to, so to speak, modulate one wave project with another.

The algorithms behind the **Convolution** and **Room Simulator** effects are similar. The difference between them is that the latter is optimized for reverberation.

In the **Convolution Sample** list, you can select a wave project for **Convolution** (Fig. 5.119).

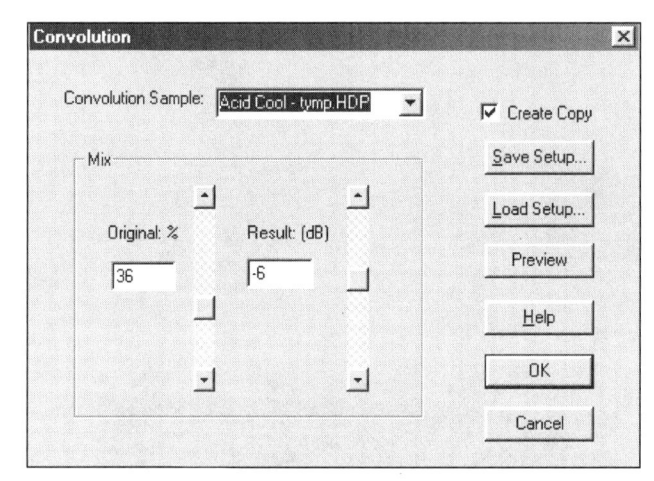

Fig. 5.119. The **Convolution** effect window

In this list, only those wave projects that are currently open in Samplitude 2496 are shown.

The **Mix** section works identically to the **Mix** section of the **Room Simulator** effect.

Like **Room Simulator**, this effect can be used to obtain unusual sound effects.

The *Noise Reduction* Effect

The **Noise Reduction** effect is designed for noise suppression.

> **NOTE** The noise suppression algorithm in Samplitude 2496 is similar to the one in Cool Edit Pro.

The procedure for noise suppression is the following:

1. Select a fragment of the sound material that contains *only* noise.
2. Use the **Get Noise Sample** command of the **Effects** menu.
3. Select the fragment to process.
4. Use the **Noise Reduction** command of the **Effects** menu. This will open a window with the same name.
5. In the **Noise Sample** section of the **Noise Reduction** window, select a noise sample, as shown in Fig. 5.120.

> **NOTE** If several wave projects have been loaded, they also appear in this list. It is the **Noise Sample** file that you must select.

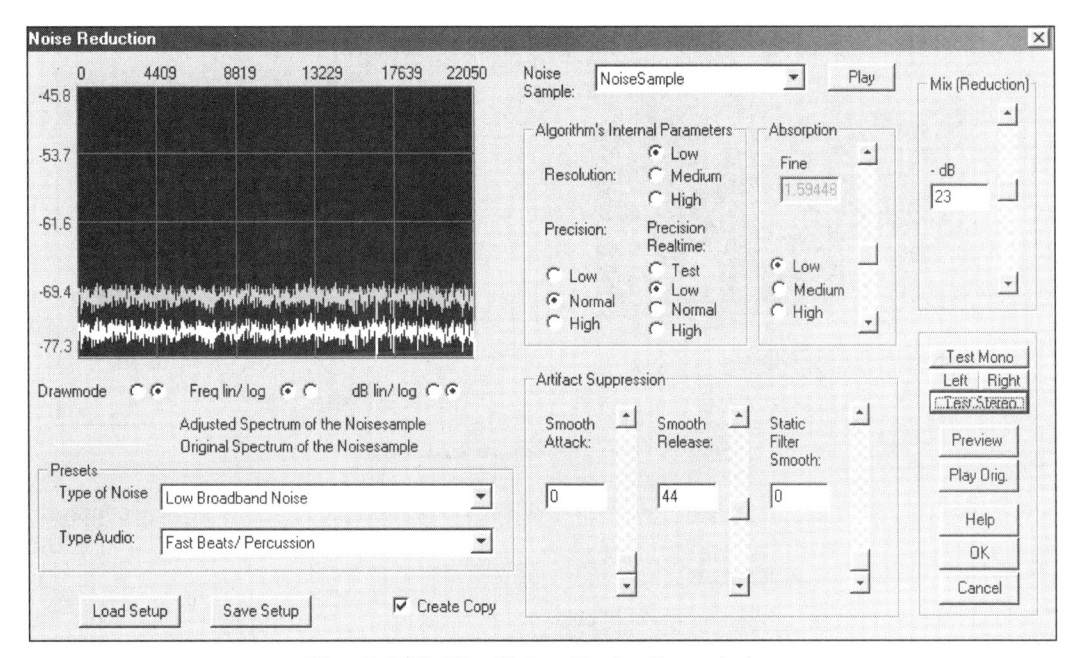

Chapter 5: The Samplitude 2496 Application as a High-Quality Virtual Studio 419

Fig. 5.120. The **Noise Reduction** window

6. In the **Test** mode, find a compromise between the depth of noise suppression and the distortions resembling the "flanger" effect. This is done using two sliders:
   - **Mix (Reduction)**
   - **Absorption**

   NOTE The **Absorption** slider shifts the blue curve, which reflects the noise spectrum (and is used in noise suppression) relative to the yellow curve, which reflects the initial noise spectrum obtained as a result of the **Get Noise Sample** operation. This shift is made by level (in dB).

Notice **the Static Filter Smooth** slider.

NOTE The **Static Filter Smooth** slider can diminish distortions that resemble the "flanger" effect. However, you must keep in mind that this operation can make the sound "harder" to some extent.

The *Dehisser* Effect

The **Dehisser** effect is provided in Samplitude 2496 specifically to remove high-frequency noise.

It is called in the usual manner, that is, with the **Dehissing** command of the **Effects** menu. This opens the **Dehisser** window (Fig. 5.121).

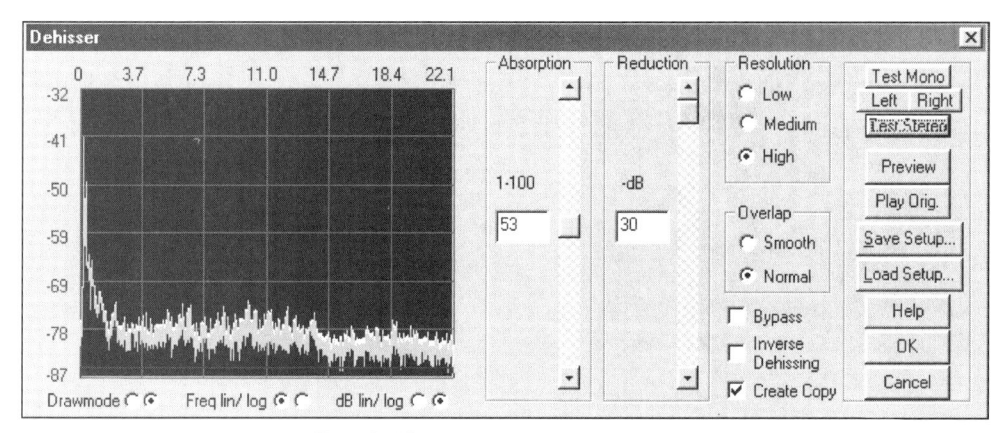

Fig. 5.121. The **Dehisser** window

The **Dehisser** effect is much less powerful and provides less quality than **Hiss Reduction**, an analogous effect of Cool Edit Pro. This is why we recommend that you use the **Dehisser** effect at low noise levels.

To find the optimum relationship between noise reduction and sound quality, you are only given two sliders to use in this mode:

❒ **Absorption**

and

❒ **Reduction**

The **Inverse Dehissing** checkbox allows you to eliminate the useful signal and listen to noise in order to check the correctness of settings.

The *Resampling/Time Stretching/Pitch Shifting* Effect

Resampling/Time Stretching/Pitch Shifting is a universal effect used to change the tempo, pitch, and length of a sample.

Using it, you can not only obtain an interesting sound, but also solve a practical task — adjust the tempo of one fragment to the tempo of the other when linking fragments with different tempos.

Let's look at the **Resampling/Time Stretching/Pitch Shifting** effect window more closely (Fig. 5.122).

❒ In the **Algorithm** section, the main algorithm (mode) of the effect is selected: **Resampling**, **Time Stretching**, or **Pitch Shifting**:

- In the **Resampling** mode, the *tempo and pitch* change simultaneously (just like they change when the playback speed of a tape recorder changes)
- In the **Time Stretching** mode, the *tempo* is set with the **Time Factor** slider, the pitch remaining unchanged

Chapter 5: The Samplitude 2496 Application as a High-Quality Virtual Studio 421

- In the **Pitch Shifting** mode, the *pitch* is set with the **Pitch** slider, the tempo remaining unchanged

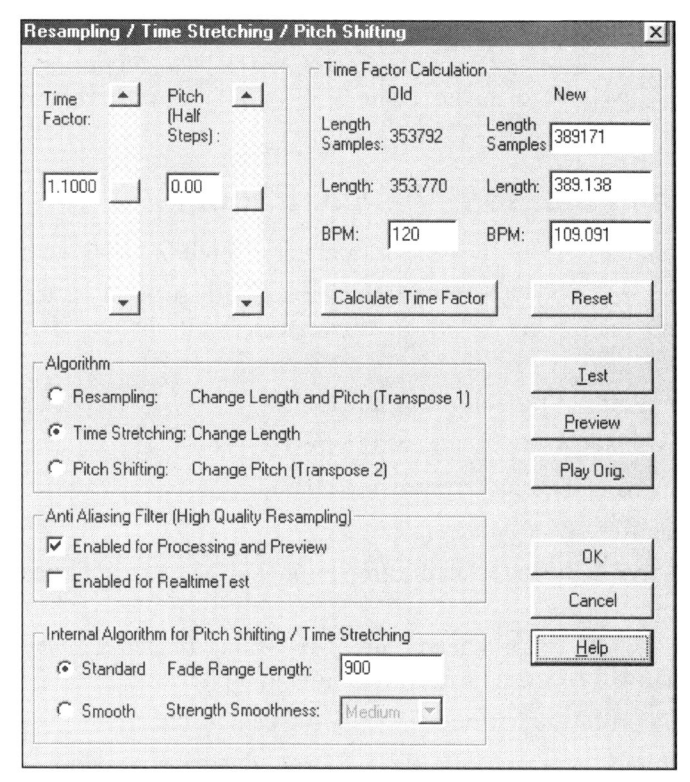

Fig. 5.122. The **Resampling/Time Stretching/Pitch Shifting** effect

❐ In the **Time Factor Calculation** section, it is possible to automatically calculate the time factor for precise tempo measurement. For this purpose:

1. Enter the new tempo value from the keyboard to the **BPM** in the **New** column.
2. Click the **Calculate Time Factor** button.

> *NOTE* The **Time Factor** slider will automatically move to the calculated value.

❐ In the **Internal Algorithm for Pitch Shifting/Time Stretching** section, you can select the processing algorithm.
  - **Standard**

  or

  - **Smooth**

NOTE Since the **Smooth** algorithm is much more complex than the standard one, it cannot be tested in real time.

To obtain high-quality sound when using the **Internal Algorithm for Pitch Shifting/Time Stretching**, it is better to use the **Smooth** specialized algorithm, whose **Strength Smoothness** parameter has five quality degrees, from **Very Low** to **Very High**.

The *Multi Band Stereo Enhancer* Effect

The **Multi Band Stereo Enhancer** effect is an effect of multiband stereo base correction.

This effect is designed to change the size of the stereo base, that is, to expand, narrow, and pan it. All the changes to the stereo base can be made independently, in three frequency ranges.

This effect can be useful in the following situations:

- Preliminary processing of the tracks of the mixed recording
- Correcting the errors that occurred during mixing

For example, using this effect, you can:

- Narrow down the stereo base in the low-frequency range to eliminate distortions in bass sounds
- "Free up some space" in the already mixed recording (called a *submix*) for additional instruments that will be mixed with the submix at a later time
- Shift the vocal part to the left or right from the center, etc.

The main components of the **Multi Band Stereo Enhancer** window are the filter and three sliders for stereo base and panorama settings (Fig. 5.123).

The filter of the **Multi Band Stereo Enhancer** effect uses an algorithm similar to the one used in the filter of the **Multiband Dynamics** effect, and has similar controls.

- The **Split-Freq 1** and **Split-Freq 2** sliders change the boundaries of the frequency range
- The **Separation** radio button group (in the **Filter Settings** section) specifies the steepness of the frequency response curve at the boundaries of the frequency ranges:
  - Low
  - Norm
  - High
- The **Band Stereo Width and Pan/Direction (3 Bands)** section includes six sliders, each frequency range having two sliders — one for the stereo base width and one for the panorama

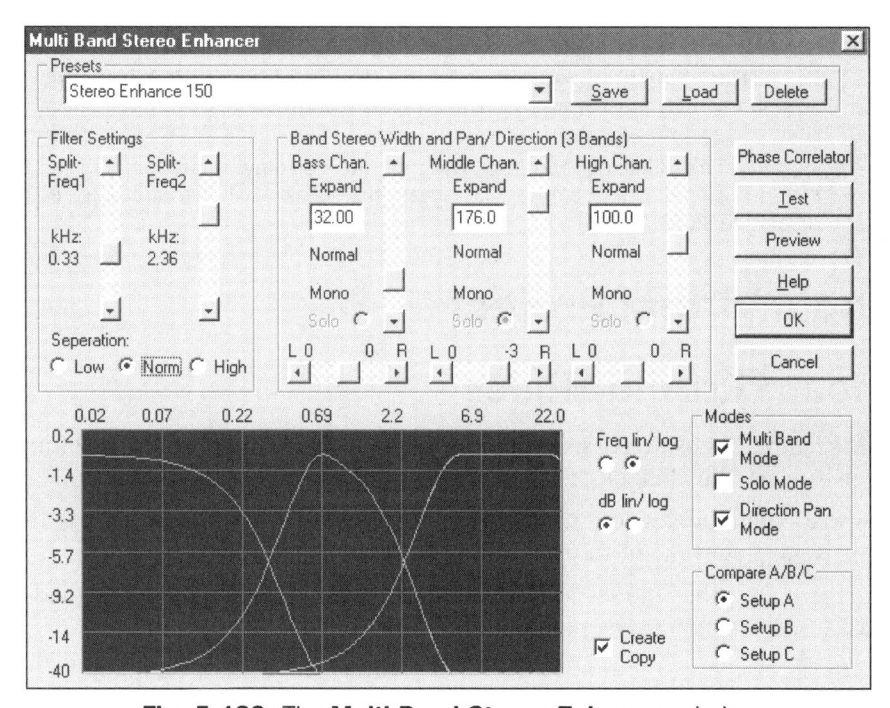

Chapter 5: The Samplitude 2496 Application as a High-Quality Virtual Studio 423

Fig. 5.123. The **Multi Band Stereo Enhancer** window

- The **Solo** radio buttons allow you to select the frequency range that will be listened to when the **Solo Mode** checkbox is checked in the **Modes** section
- The **Direction Pan Mode** checkbox turns on a special programming mode, where only the center (the sum of the signals of the left and right channels) is shifted in the selected frequency range

> *NOTE* This mode is convenient for panning the vocal parts in mixed audio material.

- When the **Multi Band Mode** is unchecked, the frequency range isn't divided into multiple bands
- The **Compare A/B/C** radio button group allows you to compare various configurations of the effect settings

> *NOTE* The application can remember up to three variants of the effect's configurations. You can switch between them using the **Setup A**, **Setup B**, and **Setup C** radio buttons.

❏ The **Phase Correlator** button opens the **Oscillograph/Phase Correlator** display, which allows you to *visually* estimate in the **Solo** mode the changes that took place in the chosen frequency range after applying the **Stereo Enhancer** effect

> **NOTE** The blinking vertical line in the display corresponds to the sum signal (*monosignal*), whereas the blinking horizontal line corresponds to the difference signal.

Editing a Virtual Project

VIP Mouse Editing Modes

In all the examples considered so far, the **Universal Mode** was used for editing virtual projects. It is selected by default at the first startup of Samplitude 2496.

The **Universal Mode** proves true to its name, since it is in fact *universal*. It is this mode in which it is most convenient to perform the majority of operations.

However, there are other modes in Samplitude 2496 that are specially designed to solve certain tasks, such as editing the pan and volume automation curves.

Let's discuss all eleven of the modes for editing virtual projects in Samplitude 2496. The icons corresponding to each mode can be found in the **Mouse Mode** toolbar (Fig. 5.124).

Fig. 5.124. The **Mouse Mode** toolbar

The VIP Mouse Modes are the following (from left to right in Fig. 5.124).

❏ **Universal Mode**
❏ **Range Mode**
❏ **Object and Curve Mode**
❏ **Draw Volume Mode**
❏ **Draw Panorama**
❏ **Object Mode**
❏ **Curve move and grab mode**
❏ **Mouse Mode Samplitude 4.0**
❏ **Scrubbing Mouse Mode**
❏ **Cut Mouse Mode**
❏ **Zoom Mouse Mode**

Chapter 5: The Samplitude 2496 Application as a High-Quality Virtual Studio   425

The *Universal* Mode

The **Universal Mode** combines two other modes, namely, the **Range Mode** and the **Object Mode**. It has the following features:

- In the universal mode, *every* track of a VIP project is divided into two halves, horizontally
- The area of the **Range Mode** is above the demarcation line, and that of the **Object Mode** is below it
- When the mouse pointer crosses the demarcation line dividing a track, it changes its shape
- In the universal mode, you can edit the pan and volume automation curves just like in the **Object and Curve Mode**
- A right click on any graphical object of the program opens the pop-up menu

The *Range* Mode

The **Range Mode** is used to work with ranges. It allows you to select ranges and save them using the **Range** menu. The features of this mode are the following:

- You can move a range in the **Range Mode**, having grabbed it with the mouse pointer while holding the <Shift> key pressed.

    NOTE You must first press and hold the <Shift> key, then left-click within the range and, holding the left mouse button, drag the range along the track of the VIP project. (Working with ranges is discussed in the section "*Playback Modes*").

- A right click on any graphical object of the program opens the pop-up menu.
- A left click positions the multitrack cursor.

    NOTE You can thus change the cursor position without interrupting playback.

- It is possible to temporarily leave the **Range Mode** for other modes. This is done using the following hotkeys: the <.> key switches to the **Object Mode**, and the <-> key switches to the **Curve Mode**.

    NOTE When you release the hotkey, the program switches back to the **Range Mode**.

The *Object and Curve* Mode

The **Object and Curve Mode** is a combination mode. Here you can perform the following operations:

- Select an object with a left click

> **NOTE** Recall that a selected object shows five handles, which are used to edit it graphically.

- ☐ Select a group of objects
- ☐ Copy an object (or group of objects)
- ☐ Open the **Object Editor**
- ☐ Edit an object by dragging its handles
- ☐ Edit the pan and volume automation curves
- ☐ Open a pop-up menu with a right click

You can select a group in two ways.

- ☐ The first method is quick. You must:
  1. Press and hold the <Shift> key.
  2. Click the first and last object in the group.

> **NOTE** All the objects located on the track between these two endmost ones will also be selected.

This method can be used to select a group of objects located on different tracks (in Fig. 5.125, the first and last object in the group are indicated with arrows).

- ☐ The second method to select a group of objects uses the following procedure:
  1. Press and hold the <Ctrl> key.
  2. Click each object in the group sequentially.

In this mode, you can drag both an individual object and an entire group.

To copy an object or a group of objects, first press and hold the <Ctrl> key, and then drag the object to the new place with the left mouse button pressed.

The **Object Editor** is opened with a double click on an object.

To edit the pan and volume automation curves, proceed as follows:

1. Click the **V** and/or **P** buttons on the selected track of a VIP project.
2. Create new editing points on the volume automation curve (yellow) or the pan automation curve (blue). These appear after double-clicking on the automation curve.

> **NOTE** A double click on a point deletes it.

3. Select the points you're going to work with. To select a point, click it. To select a *group of points*, use either of the following methods:
   - The first method is to press and hold the <Ctrl> key and then click every point in the group, one at a time.

Chapter 5: The Samplitude 2496 Application as a High-Quality Virtual Studio 427

- The other method is a quick one. First, press and hold the <Shift> key. Then click the first and last point in the group. All the points located on the same track as these two endmost ones and between them will also be selected.

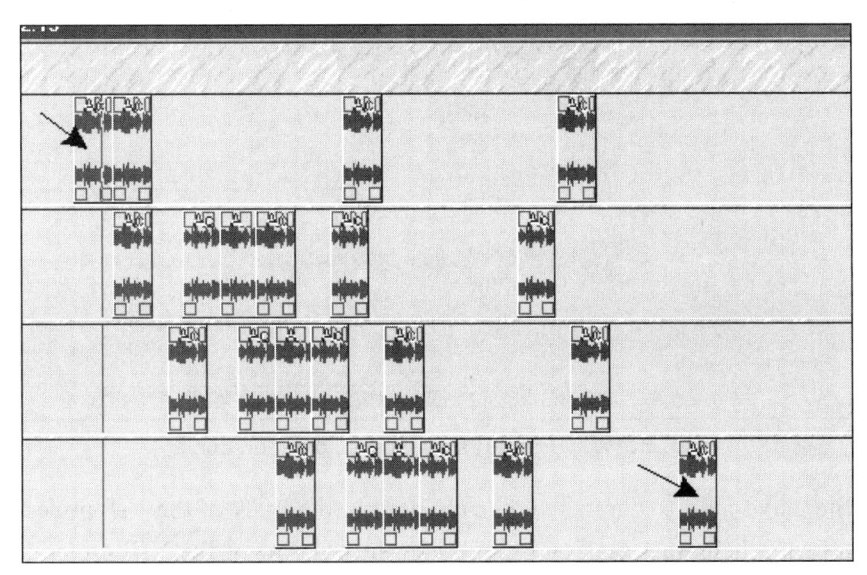

Fig. 5.125. Selecting a group of objects diagonally

A point (or group of points) on the automation curve can be dragged with the mouse. This is the idea of editing automation curves graphically.

> **NOTE** Editing automation curves in the **Universal Mode** is done in the same manner.

The *Draw Volume* Mode

The **Draw Volume Mode** is the mode in which volume automation curves can be drawn directly.

In this mode, the mouse pointer looks like a pencil. To draw an automation curve, set the mouse pointer at the desired position, press the left mouse button, and draw the necessary line without releasing the mouse button.

> **NOTE** The current position of the mouse pointer (the pencil) is displayed in dB in a special field indicated by the arrow in Fig. 5.126.

If you attempt to draw a curve doesn't turn out well, you can try again (the previous curve will disappear), or undo the attempt with the <Ctrl>+<Z> shortcut.

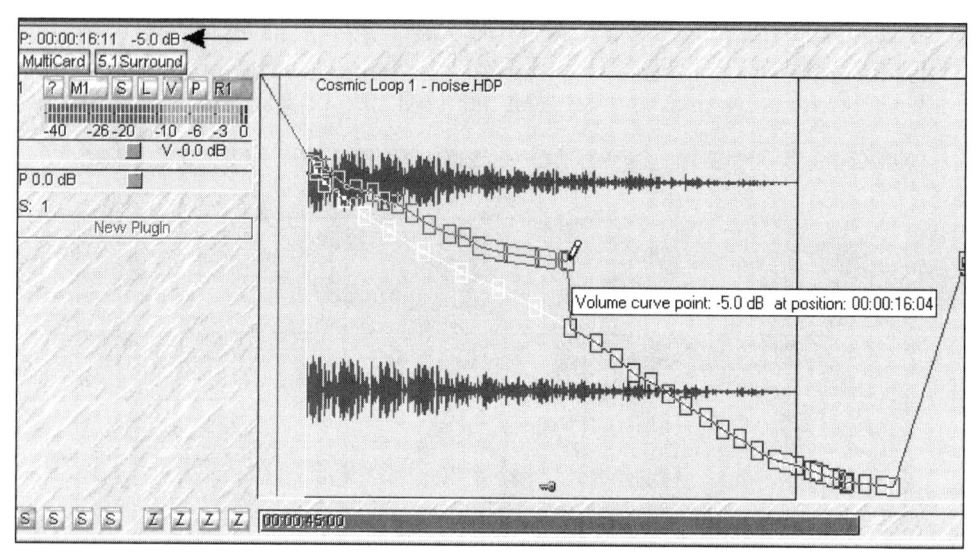

Fig. 5.126. Drawing a volume automation curve

To draw the curve more accurately, you can zoom in the track of the VIP project.

The zoom level where one track takes up the entire window of the VIP project vertically will be most suitable.

The pop-up menu is opened with a right click in this mode, just as in the others.

The *Draw Panorama* Mode

The **Draw Panorama Mode** is used to draw panorama automation curves. It is similar to the **Draw Volume Mode**.

The *Object* Mode

The **Object Mode** is used for "pure" (manual) editing of the objects.

It is actually similar to the **Universal Mode** and **Object and Curve Mode** as regards the editing technique.

The *Curve Move and Grab* Mode

The **Curve move and grab mode** is used to move automation curves. In this mode, you can *simultaneously* move all the points of an automation curve within a track of a VIP project. To do this, proceed as follows:

1. Grab the needed points by drawing a box around them (Fig. 5.127).

Chapter 5: The Samplitude 2496 Application as a High-Quality Virtual Studio 429

NOTE The box is created in the usual manner. While holding down the left mouse button, move the mouse pointer diagonally. All the points in the box will be selected.

2. Drag the selected points in the desired direction.

NOTE If there are automation points close to the grabbed area (to the left or to the right), you'll be able to move the grabbed portion only within the limits set by the points that are outside the grabbed area.

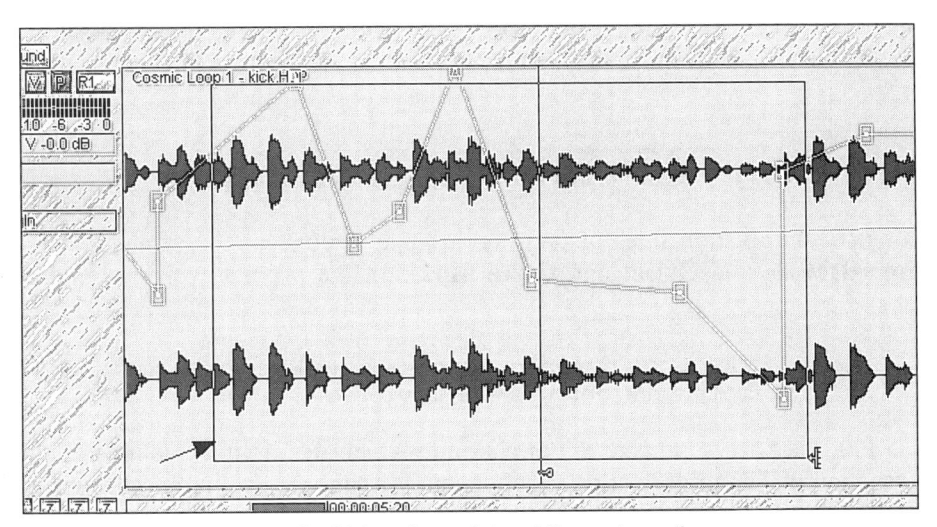

Fig. 5.127. Grabbing the points of the automation curves

Automation curves are edited in this mode in the same manner as in the **Object and Curve Mode** and the **Universal Mode**.

The *Mouse Mode Samplitude 4.0* Mode

This mode is actually the editing mode of earlier versions of the Samplitude application.

The *Scrubbing Mouse* Mode

The **Scrubbing Mouse Mode** is a mode for quick "previewing" (listening). It allows you to:

- Position the multitrack cursor. To do this, click with the left mouse button and hold it until playback starts from the new point.
- Change the speed and direction of the playback. To change the direction, hold the left mouse button and move the mouse pointer to the left or to the right (to the left for reverse playback).

The playback speed depends on the distance between the mouse pointer and the multitrack cursor (Fig. 5.128). The latter always "wants" to meet up with the mouse pointer. If you stop the mouse pointer, the multitrack cursor will reach it, stop at that point, and begin to move back and forth.

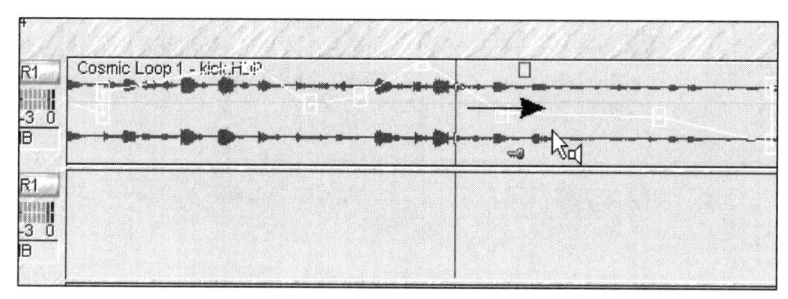

Fig. 5.128. Playback in the **Scrubbing Mouse Mode**

❐ Editing the automation lines of pan and volume is done in the same way as in the **Universal Mode** and **Object and Curve Mode**. In the process, you can monitor the results of editing by ear.

NOTE Notice how convenient this mode is: it allows you to control the pan and volume at a certain point *during playback*.

In Fig. 5.129, the arrows indicate the direction in which the group of volume automation points has moved. The result can be simultaneously listened to in the **Scrubbing** mode.

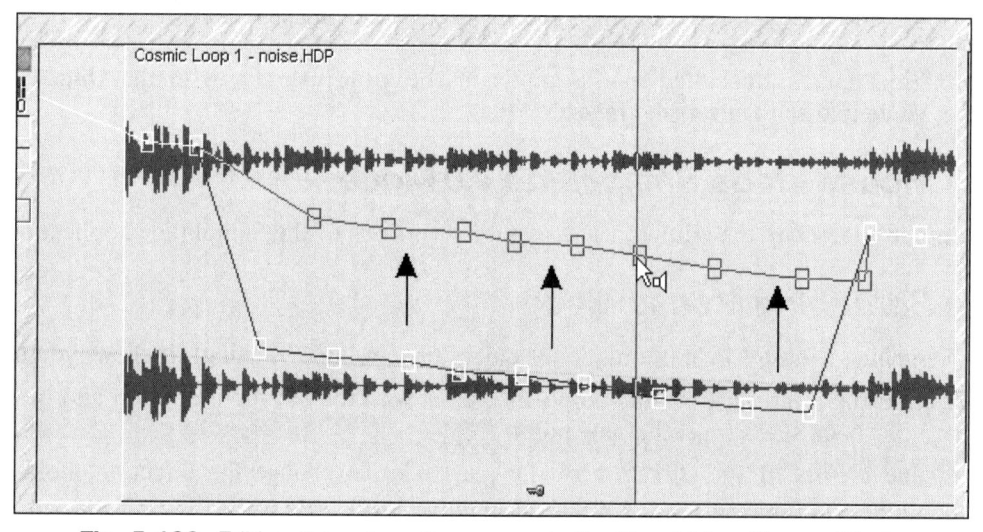

Fig. 5.129. Editing the automation curves in the **Scrubbing Mouse Mode**

Chapter 5: The Samplitude 2496 Application as a High-Quality Virtual Studio 431

The **Scrubbing** mode makes it possible to change the boundaries of a range during playback. For this purpose, proceed as follows:

1. Select the desired range in the **Range Mode**.
2. Enter the **Scrubbing Mouse Mode**.
3. Set the mouse pointer within the range close to the boundary that you want to move.
4. Start the scrubbing playback towards the chosen boundary.

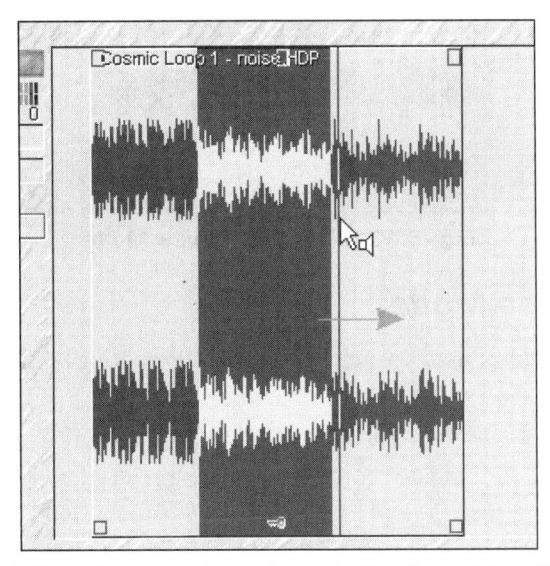

Fig. 5.130. Editing the range boundaries in the **Scrubbing Mouse Mode**

NOTE After the multitrack cursor crosses the range boundary, the boundary will automatically follow the cursor (Fig. 5.130). This function is very convenient, for example, when creating a loop, since it allows you to select the loop accurately.

As in the other modes, the object editor and the pop-up menu are available in the **Scrubbing Mouse Mode**.

The *Cut Mouse Mode*

The **Cut Mouse Mode** is used to cut objects. In this mode, the mouse pointer looks like a pair of scissors (Fig. 5.131), and cutting is done by clicking at the pointer position. The pop-up menu is available in this mode as well.

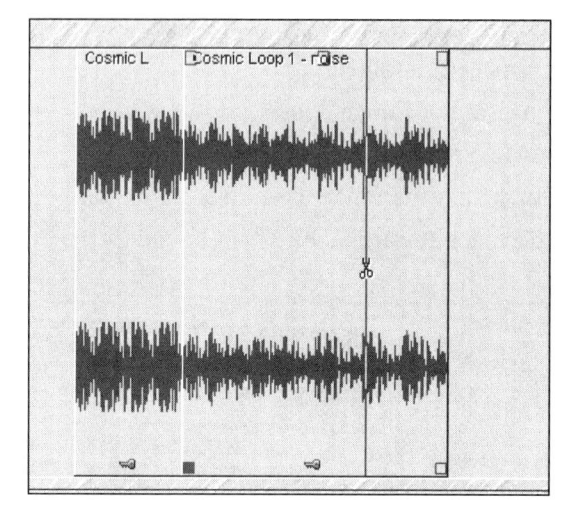

Fig. 5.131. The **Cut Mouse Mode**

The *Zoom Mouse Mode*

The **Zoom Mouse Mode** is used to quickly change the zoom level vertically or horizontally.

In this mode, the mouse pointer looks like a magnifying glass (Fig. 5.132).

To zoom horizontally, the mouse pointer must be set at the point where the chosen fragment is located.

Each click with the left mouse button zooms the picture in horizontally, and each right click zooms the picture out.

Left or right clicks with the <Shift> key pressed zoom in or out vertically.

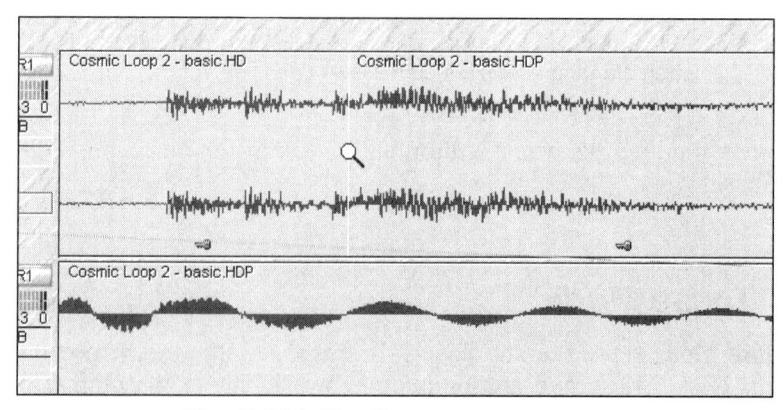

Fig. 5.132. The **Zoom Mouse Mode**

Moving, Copying, and Splitting Objects

Moving Objects

To move an object (or a selected group of objects), just drag it with the mouse. The new positions of the objects are shown as outlines in the multitrack track (Fig. 5.133).

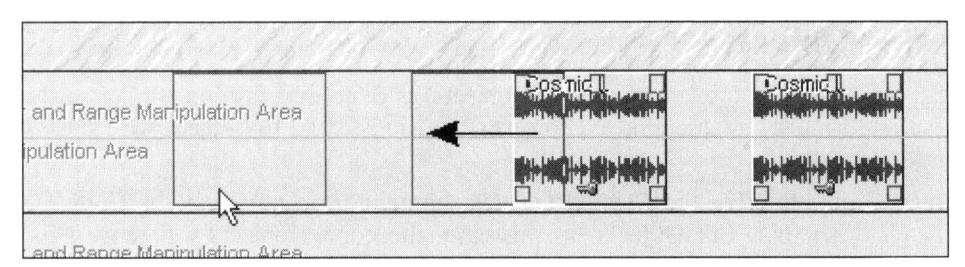

Fig. 5.133. Moving objects

Objects can be dragged from one VIP project to another (Fig. 5.134).

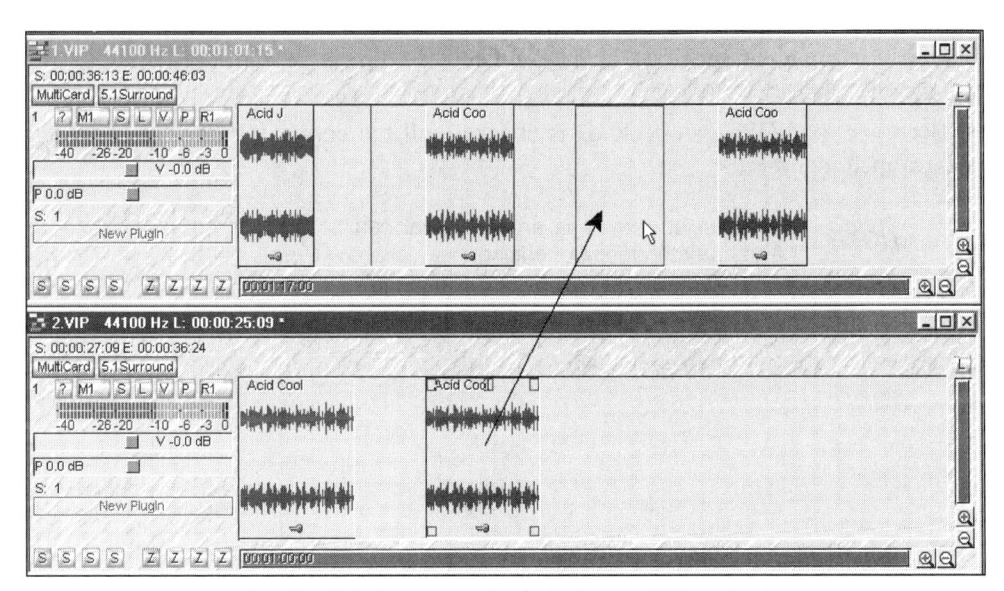

Fig. 5.134. Moving objects between VIP projects

In addition to the suggested method (dragging with the mouse), you can employ another one: using the **Cut Objects** and **Insert Objects** commands of the **Cutting Objects** submenu of the **Object** menu.

In this case, when moving an object (or a selected group of objects), a new virtual project is created, which serves as a clipboard — **VirtClip**. It will temporary hold objects deleted with the **Cut Objects** operation. All the objects in the **VirtClip** project keep their relative positions in the tracks.

The **Insert Objects** operation copies the objects from the **VirtClip** to the specified position in the current or new virtual project. This position is that of the mouse pointer.

Copying Objects

Copying an object (or a selected group of objects) is done in a fashion similar to the one used with moving — by dragging it; however, you must drag the object with the <Ctrl> key pressed.

If you copy objects using the **Cutting Objects** submenu, you must use the **Copy Objects** command rather than **Cut Objects**. In this case, the copied objects will remain in their places.

Samplitude 2496 provides the user with an operation for multiple copying.

This operation is done with the **Duplicate objects multiple** command of the **Cutting Objects** submenu.

The number of copies is specified in the **Number of Objects** field in the **Multiple Object Copy** window (Fig. 5.135).

If the **Group created Objects** checkbox is checked, all the copies (along with the original) will be grouped together.

NOTE A *group* of objects is an entity that can be considered as a single object from the standpoint of editing.

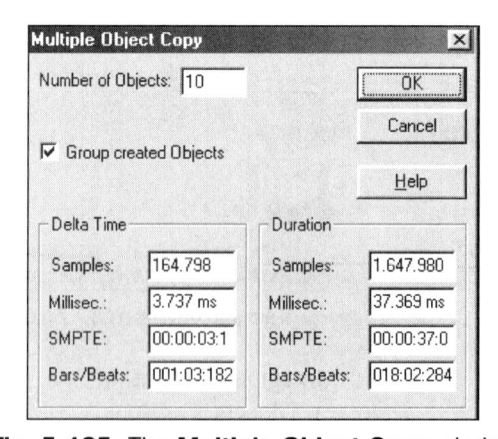

Fig. 5.135. The **Multiple Object Copy** window

Chapter 5: The Samplitude 2496 Application as a High-Quality Virtual Studio

A group can contain any number of objects. To create a group, proceed as follows:

1. Select the objects.
2. Execute the **Group Objects** command of the **Object** menu.

> **NOTE** A group can be ungrouped using the **Ungroup Objects** command of the **Object** menu.

In the **Delta Time** section, the length of the object is presented using four different units of measurement.

The fields of the **Duration** section reflect the duration of the whole group.

> **NOTE** The value in the **Duration** section is equal to the product of the value in the **Delta Time** section and the number of copies specified in the **Number of Objects** field.

By default, the copies are positioned just one after another, without overlapping or pauses. By changing the values in the **Delta Time** and **Duration** sections, you can overlap copies or insert pauses between them.

The values of the **Samples**, **Millisec.**, **SMPTE**, and **Bars/Beats** fields in both sections can be changed by entering new numbers via the keyboard.

Splitting Objects

Splitting objects is done using the **Split Objects** command (the <T> hot key) of the **Object** menu. The objects are split at the position of the multitrack cursor.

If you select a range and apply the **Split Objects** operation, the selected area will have two cutting lines on the boundaries. In other words, it will become a separate object.

The **Trim Object** command (<Ctrl>+<T>) of the **Object** menu trims an object to the boundaries of the selected area.

Splitting objects can also be done in the **Cut Mouse Mode**.

> **NOTE** When splitting an object, its parts inherit the properties of the whole; that is, all the settings made in the object editor are kept.

A Virtual Loop Object

One of the ways of replicating an object is to create a *virtual loop object*.

A virtual loop object is an object of a special type that contains a theoretically infinite number of replicas. This number is determined by the boundaries of the object (Fig. 5.136).

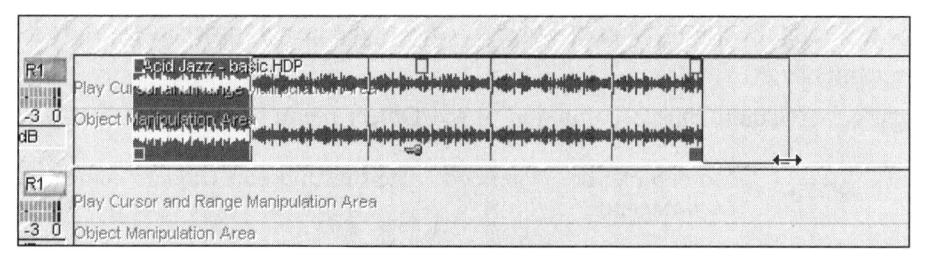

Fig. 5.136. Changing the boundaries of a virtual loop object

A loop object can be created from any regular object. To do this:
1. Click the chosen object to select it.
2. Within the object, select a range, which will then be multiplied.

> **NOTE** The selected range mustn't go beyond the object.

3. To convert to the loop object, do the **Build Loop Object** command of the **Effects** menu.

Like any other object, a loop object can be subject to all the editing operations, such as moving, copying, editing, etc.

Using the Markers

Markers are designed to speed up any multitrack program and make working with it easier. They are very convenient when editing a project, making a "live" recording, mixing, etc.

In Samplitude 2496, you can create a marker through the marker pop-up menu. This menu is opened with a right click on the *marker area* located *just above* the tracks of a VIP project (indicated by the arrow in Fig. 5.137).

> **NOTE** It must be noted that the markers set in a VIP project don't coincide with the markers set in an HD (or RAM) Wave project. However, they are set according to the same algorithm.

Let's look at this pop-up menu.

- The **Other** command of the **Store Marker** submenu allows you to enter the name of a marker via the keyboard.
- The **Auto Number** command automatically assigns a number to each new marker.

> **NOTE** The marker is set at the position of the multitrack cursor.

Markers can also be created with the shortcuts from <Shift>+<1> to <Shift>+<0>.

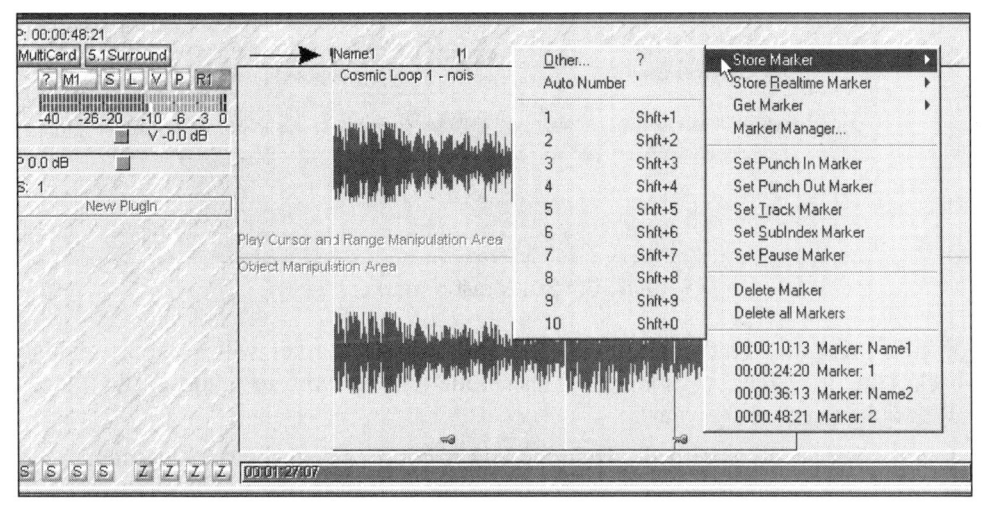

Chapter 5: The Samplitude 2496 Application as a High-Quality Virtual Studio

Fig. 5.137. The pop-up menu for setting markers

- The commands from **1** to **10** of the **Store Realtime Marker** submenu allow you to create up to ten markers *in real time*, that is, during playback or recording in the **Punch** mode.

> **NOTE** The marker is set at the current position of the multitrack cursor.

You can move the multitrack cursor from one marker to another in several ways:
- By selecting the marker names from the list presented in the pop-up menu (Fig. 5.137)
- Using the **Marker Manager** dialog box opened by the command of the same name in the pop-up menu

To distinguish the markers, give them numeric or alphabetic names, or mixed ones.

> **NOTE** As practice shows, it is better to give the markers self-explanatory names. This is especially true when you postpone editing, since it will be difficult to remember later what Marker 1 or Marker 9 means.

You can also move the markers. To do this:

1. Position the mouse pointer on the marker.

> **NOTE** The mouse pointer will change its appearance, as shown in Fig. 5.138.

2. Holding the left mouse key pressed, move the marker horizontally, to the right or to the left.

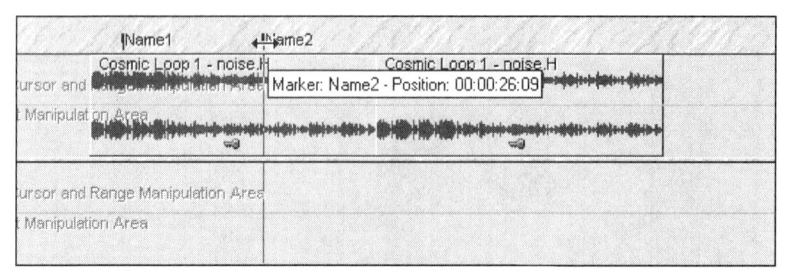

Fig. 5.138. Moving markers

If you first press and hold the <Ctrl> key, moving the marker will be accompanied by playback (this is called scrubbing). This mode allows you to choose the place for a marker quite precisely (by ear).

Deleting markers is done with the **Delete Marker** command of the pop-up menu.

Creating an AUDIO CD in Samplitude 2496

Mixing and Mastering in Samplitude 2496

Mixing

Samplitude 2496 is a rather advanced software product, in which all the stages of creating an audio project with the computer are thoroughly thought out — from recording and editing, to mixing, mastering, and burning the CD directly from the virtual project.

> **NOTE** Mixing in Samplitude 2496 is fundamentally different from mixing in SAWPro and Cool Edit Pro. For one thing, mixing in Samplitude 2496 begins at the stage of sound processing in the object editor.

Indeed, Samplitude 2496 presents users with many features for mixing:

- For those who prefer hardware mixers, a software simulator — **Samplitude Mixer** — is provided
- For fans of musical object-oriented programming, the object editor is provided
- For those who prefer to view pan and volume changes, graphical editing tools are provided

You don't have to use the virtual mixer, since there are pan and volume controls in the VIP project window.

Each user may create his or her own flow chart to work with virtual features of this application.

Chapter 5: The Samplitude 2496 Application as a High-Quality Virtual Studio 439

You should be aware that the process of mixing is greatly influenced by the style of the piece of music and by the performance of the computer.

With this is mind, we're only going to present some general advice.

- All the main stages of processing the objects must be completed before final mixing.
- If surround panning is enabled on the track, you shouldn't use panning in the object editor.
- When you need to change the volume for a portion of an object, you may select this portion, do the **Split Objects** operation (or press the <T> hotkey), and change the volume by dragging the **5** handle (Fig. 5.59).
- If, while mixing a project, you wish to introduce changes typical for "live" sound producing, it will be convenient to employ recording automation in real time. For this purpose, click the **Auto** button on the mixer panel. All the introduced pan and volume changes will be recorded in the form of automation curves.
- Automation curves can be recorded both sequentially, track after track, and simultaneously. When you work with multiple tracks at once, it is convenient to group the necessary mixer components (see "*Some Additional Features of the Samplitude Mixer*" in the section "*Connecting DirectX Plug-Ins to a Track of the Multitrack*").
- If surround panning is on, a surround panning curve (**Surround Handle**) will be created in addition to the volume and pan automation curves (**Volume Handle** and **Panorama Handle**, respectively).
- To delete bad versions of automation curves, you can use the **Edit** menu:
  - **Undo** (or the <Ctrl>+<Z> shortcut)
  - **Delete Volume Handle**
  - **Delete Panorama Handle**
  - **Delete Surround Handle**

  NOTE You must first grab automation points in the **Curve move and grab mode**.

- It is best to record automation curves in real time and subsequently edit them graphically in the **Draw Panorama Mode** and the **Draw Volume Mode**.
- Objects can be linked to automation curves so that the curves will be copied or moved when the corresponding objects are copied or moved. For this purpose, you must check the **Link Curves to Objects** option in the **Preference|Object Mode** menu.
- Mixing can be done in two ways:
  - To a separate HD Wave project with the 32-bit format, using the **Tools|Track Bouncing** menu, having previously checked the **Save in 32Bit (Float) format** and **Only a Wave Project** options.

- As "live" mixing in real time. In this case, you need to check the **Mix in File** checkbox in the virtual mixer.

> **NOTE** In the latter case, mixing is done into the 32-bit HD Wave project while the virtual project is being played back. Notice that during "live" mixing it is possible to introduce changes in addition to the previously recorded automation curves.

☐ If the **Auxiliary Master** section is used in the virtual mixer, the **Exclude Master Effects from Bouncing** checkbox must be unchecked.

Mastering

The developers of Samplitude 2496 provided a separate master block in the virtual mixer, especially for top-quality mastering (Fig. 5.139).

☐ The **Dehiss./Stereo Enh.** (Dehisser/Stereo Enhancer) section contains controls for two effects:

- Those of the **Dehisser** effect combined with the FFT filter
- Those of the **Stereo Enhancer** effect (see "*Built-in Virtual Effects of Samplitude 2496*")

The first of these was developed specifically for mastering purposes. It uses the FFT algorithm, and so it is combined with the FFT filter.

The **Dehisser** effect is designed to eliminate low-level "white" noise from the signal. This kind of noise usually appears when recording on some sound cards.

A right click on the **Dehiss.** control opens the **Dehisser/FFT-Filter Mixmaster** effect window (Fig. 5.140).

To set up the **Dehisser** effect, you may use the following procedure:

1. Set the **Reduction** slider to the maximum (30 dB).

2. When adjusting the **Absorption** slider, find a compromise between the noticeable signal distortions and noise reduction.

3. Listen to the noise, having previously checked the **Inverse Deh.** checkbox. This should be done to inspect whether the **Absorption** parameter has its best possible value.

> **NOTE** The **Inverse Deh.** checkbox allows you to listen to the noise only. If you can hear the useful signal, it is necessary to reduce the **Absorption** parameter.

The **FFT-Filter** effect is a simplified version of the **FFT Analyzer/Filter** effect.

☐ The **Range** radio button group allows you to select the scale of the frequency response curve of the filter in the effect display for the high and low frequencies separately, for a more accurate drawing of this curve.

Chapter 5: The Samplitude 2496 Application as a High-Quality Virtual Studio   441

- Using the **Vol.** slider, you can adjust the volume changes caused by the FFT filter.
- In the **Master Equalizer** section, you will find the parametric equalizer effect (Fig. 5.108).
- In the **Compressor/Limiter** section, the **Multiband Dynamics** (Fig. 5.115) and **Compressor/Expander/Noise Gate/Limiter** (Fig. 5.114) effects are located.

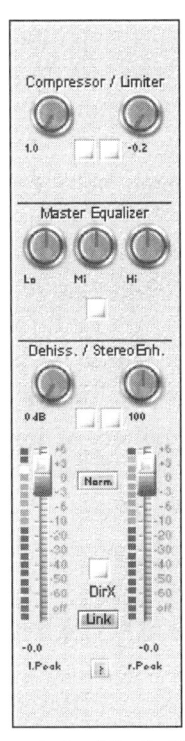

Fig. 5.139. The master block of the virtual mixer

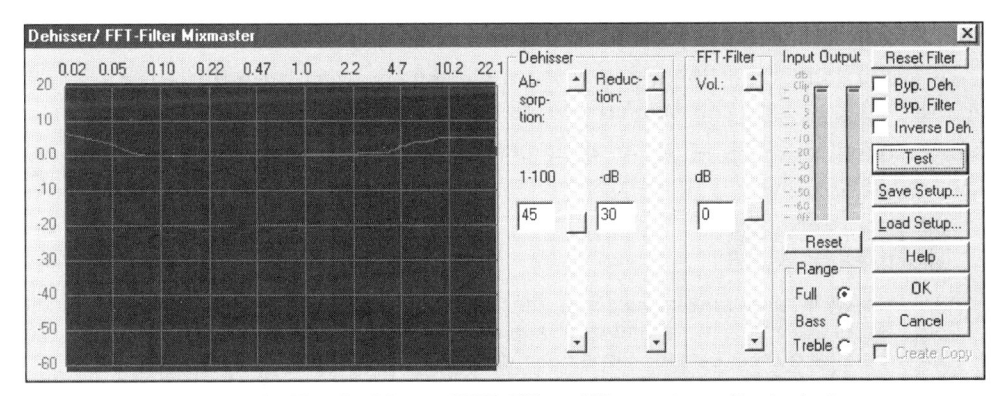

Fig. 5.140. The **Dehisser/FFT-Filter Mixmaster** effect window

Mastering begins by creating a special-purpose, one-track virtual project, **1 Track (CD TOC)** (using the **Track Number** radio button section in the **Setup for new VIP** dialog box).

It is necessary to import a previously mixed 32-bit HD Wave project to this VIP project. All subsequent processing is done with the effects of the master block of the virtual mixer.

The presets of the **Multiband Dynamics** effect will probably be useful for novice users. Depending on the style of the musical composition, you can choose among the **Disco Loudness**, **Techno X-Citer**, and **Max Loudness** presets.

For a preliminary setup of the **Multiband Dynamics** effect, it is better to use the **Master Gain +3 dB** and **Master Gain +6 dB** presets.

You should set the **Compressor/Expander/Noise Gate/Limiter** effect to the **Limiter** mode with a -0.2 dB threshold. (This can be done in the **Multiband Dynamics** window by checking the **Limiter On** checkbox and clicking the **Edit** button.)

During playback, you must click the **Norm** button located between the volume slider in the master block (Fig. 5.139). This is necessary for virtual normalization of the project.

To add some "air" to the sound, you can mix low-level reverberation into the main signal by using a DirectX plug-in of the **Auxiliary Master Section**.

We recommend that you use the **TrueVerb** virtual module from Waves as a reverber (Fig. 5.141).

The **Direct** and **Room** buttons of the **TrueVerb** reverber must be set to the **Out** state.

The **Aux1** slider (Fig. 5.141) specifies the level of the signal sent to the reverber (-11 dB in our case).

The **Aux(1)** slider of the master block specifies the level of the signal received from the reverber (-4.8 dB in our example).

You should use the **Cathedral** preset as a starting point in the **TrueVerb** setup. Also, set the **Direct** and **Room** buttons to the **Out** state.

The input reverber level mustn't exceed -24 dB (in our example). Otherwise, an ordinary reverberation effect will take place, rather than just adding some "air".

You can estimate the contribution of the reverber by ear if you turn this effect on and off using the **DirX** button in the **Auxiliary Master Section**.

Another tool to "enliven" the sound is the virtual *exciter*, based on the **Samplitude Mixer** and some DirectX plug-ins from Waves.

The Exciter

An *exciter* is a sound processing device belonging to the class of psychoacoustic processors that make the sound clear and clean. The sound processed by an exciter comes "alive" and acquires "breath". An exciter can both be used when processing tracks and in final mastering. In our example, one of the variants of exciter emulation is described. This is sometimes called "an exciting compressor".

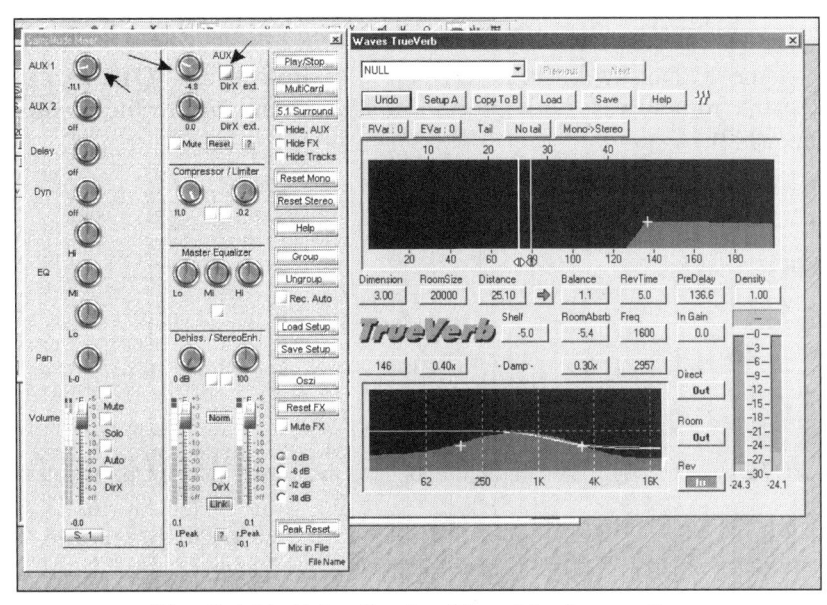

Chapter 5: The Samplitude 2496 Application as a High-Quality Virtual Studio 443

Fig. 5.141. Using the **Auxiliary Master** section

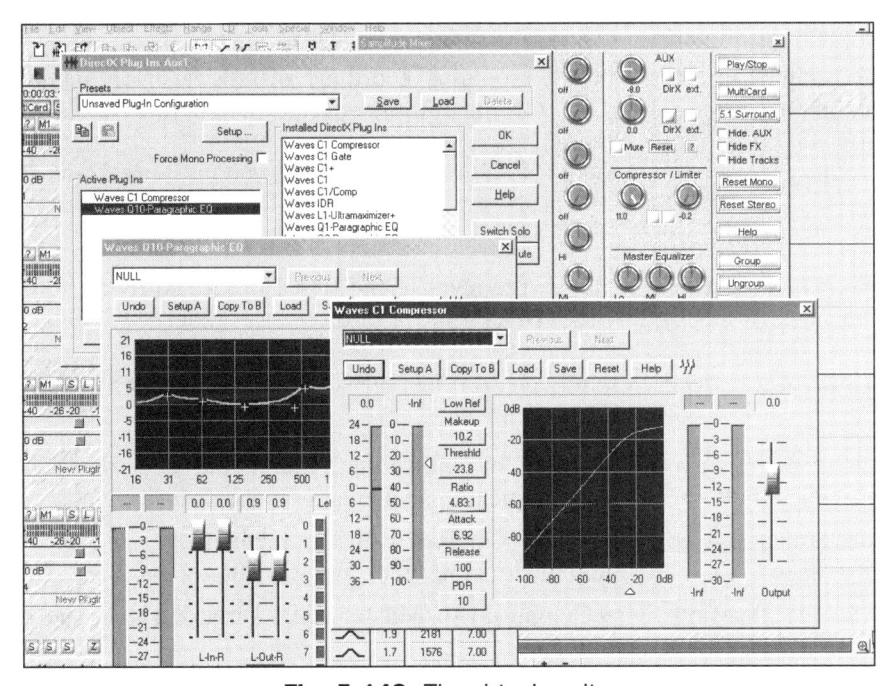

Fig. 5.142. The virtual exciter

Let's consider the virtual exciter in more detail.

To assemble the exciter, we'll need the **C1 Compressor** and **Q10-Paragraphic EQ** DirectX plug-ins from Waves. Both effects should be connected to the **Auxiliary Master** section (Fig. 5.142).

To setup the **C1 Compressor** effect, use the following values:

- **Makeup** — 10.2
- **Threshold** — −23.8
- **Ratio** — 4.83:1
- **Attack** — 6.92
- **Release** — 100

NOTE The suggested configuration isn't the only one for all the situations.

The frequency response curve of the **Q10-Paragraphic EQ** parametric equalizer is set depending on the style of the musical composition:

- In the "classical" exciter, just increase the high-frequency level
- For dance music, you may want to highlight the high and low frequencies
- To highlight vocal parts, increase the middle-frequency level

Using the exciter to process tracks containing recordings of musical instruments requires special techniques when setting up both the compressor and the parametric equalizer.

NOTE To process a track with the virtual exciter, you must use **Track Bouncing** with the **Exclude Master Effects from Bouncing** checkbox unchecked and the **Save in 32Bit (Float) format** checkbox checked.

In the example shown in Fig. 5.142, the level of the signal processed by the compressor and the equalizer is adjusted by the **AUX1** control of the master block.

NOTE The **AUX Send** channel slider specifies the level of the signal sent to the compressor and equalizer effects.

The virtual exciter is a powerful tool for "enlivening" the sound. It is also a means of overcoming the "multimedia" sound typical for personal computers.

The virtual exciter can be successfully combined with the method discussed above, where some "air" is added using the **TrueVerb** virtual reverber. For this purpose, proceed as follows:

1. Connect the **TrueVerb** DirectX plug-in to **Master AUX DirectX (2)** in the **Auxiliary Master Section**.
2. Using the **AUX1** and **AUX2** controls, adjust the exciter level and the "air" level.

Chapter 5: The Samplitude 2496 Application as a High-Quality Virtual Studio

The next mastering stage depends on the availability of a CD recorder that is compatible with Samplitude 2496 in your system. The list of compatible CD recorders can be found at **http://www.sekd.de** and **http://www.sekd.com**, which are the official sites of the Samplitude 2496's developer.

Let's consider a situation where a user has a CD recorder that is incompatible with Samplitude 2496.

In the professional sound recording world, the term "mastering" means preparing the material for AUDIO CD manufacturing (in addition to a certain kind of sound processing).

In a home studio, you can confine yourself to sound processing; that is, the goal of home computer mastering is no more than obtaining a 16-bit sound file with the WAV extension and a 44,000 Hz sample rate.

When album mastering is done, the main criterion of quality is the uniform sound of all the compositions in the album. Otherwise, a listener will feel discomfort, since he or she will have to adjust the volume level and the equalizer parameters again and again on his or her stereo system.

Thus we must perform mastering of a group of sound files in Samplitude 2496 and burn an AUDIO CD with an application compatible with the available CD recorder.

To perform mastering of a group of sound files in Samplitude 2496, proceed as follows:

1. Create a special-purpose, one-track virtual project, **1 Track (CD TOC)**. The type of this project is selected in the **Setup for new VIP** window.
2. Import the already mixed 32-bit HDP project into the VIP project created in Step 1.
3. Set the sound processing parameters for mastering. In doing so, follow the advice given in this chapter.
4. During the project's playback, click the **Norm** button on the master block of the virtual mixer to normalize the signal.
5. Set the multitrack cursor at the beginning of the project.
6. Execute the **Set Track** command of the **CD** menu. This will set the "CD Track Marker 1" index marker at the beginning of the project.

> *NOTE*   You can use the **Auto Track Markers** button (see below).

7. Use the **Make CD** command of the **CD** menu to open the **Make CD** dialog box (Fig. 5.143).
8. In the **Make CD** dialog box, set the **Mode** switch to the **Generate a complete new file** position, and click the **Burn CD** button.
9. The **Choose name for HD-project** dialog box will appear. Here you must name the final file and click the **OK** button.

10. Samplitude 2496 will carry out special **Track Bouncing** and create an audio file with the "44,000 Hz 16 Bit" format.
11. When the **No CDR Drive found!** message appears, click the **OK** button.
12. Respond to the **Writing or simulating CDR finished!** message in the same way — click the **OK** button.

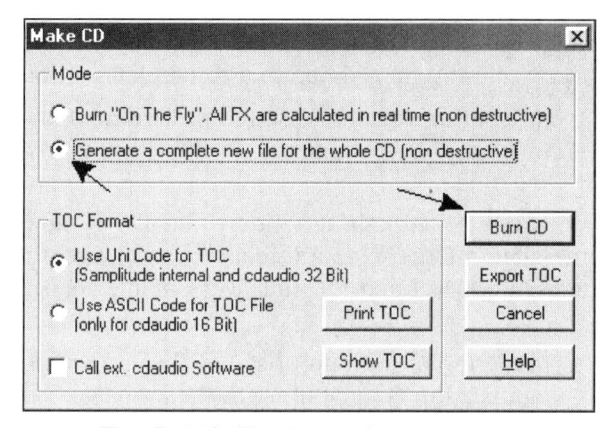

Fig. 5.143. The **Make CD** dialog box

As a result of this procedure, a WAV file with the "44,000 Hz, 16 bits" format will be created. It will be then used by a special application to burn a CD.

When mastering an album, you have to repeat this procedure individually for each composition.

If the sample rate of the mixed file was 48,000 Hz, Samplitude 2496 will resample it down to 44,000 Hz using a high-quality algorithm.

Burning an AUDIO CD in Samplitude 2496

Let's now consider the case of a CD recorder that is compatible with Samplitude 2496.

1. Just as in the previous case, create a special-purpose, one-track virtual project, **1 Track (CD TOC)**. However, now you should import *all* the previously mixed HD Wave projects (Fig. 5.144) in the sequence that they will be in in the future AUDIO CD.

> **NOTE** When importing HD Wave projects, pauses between the objects are inserted automatically.
>
> Objects can be overlapped to obtain a **Crossfade**.
>
> Using object handles, you can control the **Fade In** and **Fade Out** curves of each object.

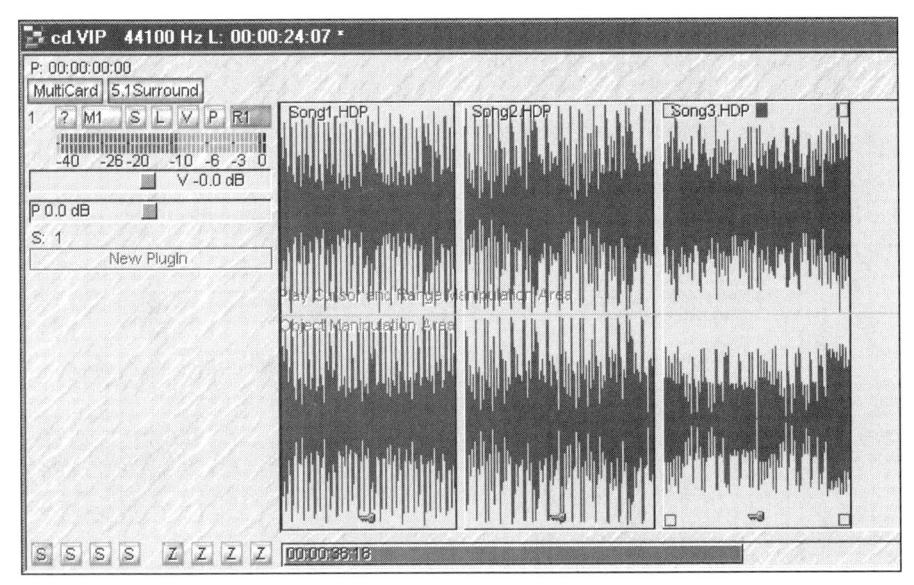

Chapter 5: The Samplitude 2496 Application as a High-Quality Virtual Studio 447

Fig. 5.144. Creating an AUDIO CD project

2. To create an AUDIO CD, you must set an *index marker* at the beginning of every object. To do this, just click the **Auto Track Markers** button in the toolbar used to create CDs (this is the button with the **AUTO** label, Fig. 5.145).
3. Click the button with the CD image, or use the **Make CD** command of the **CD** menu.
4. In the **Make CD** dialog box (Fig. 5.143), select one of the two possible values in the **Mode** section:
   - **Burn "On the Fly". All FX are calculated in real time (non destructive)** — the project is processed while burning the CD.

   > **TIP** The **Burn "On the Fly"...** mode places heavy demands on the computer. This is why we don't recommend that you use it, since you risk damaging the dummy CD. Also, failures are likely, and even the system may even "freeze up".

   - **Generate a complete new file for the whole CD (non destructive)** — an HD Wave file representing the CD will first be created on the hard disk.

   > **NOTE** The **Generate a complete new file...** mode is free from the shortcomings of the previous mode, but it requires up to 700 MB of free space on the disk.

Fig. 5.145. The **Auto Track Markers** button in the **CD Toolbar**

5. After you click the **Burn CD** button, you'll have to name the HD Wave project containing the image of the future AUDIO CD. Then click the **OK** button.

> **NOTE** You may leave the name suggested by default, that is, the name of the **CD VIP** project.

After the long-run **Track Bouncing** process completes, the **Recording options** dialog box will appear (Fig. 5.146), where you must select the **Recording speed**.

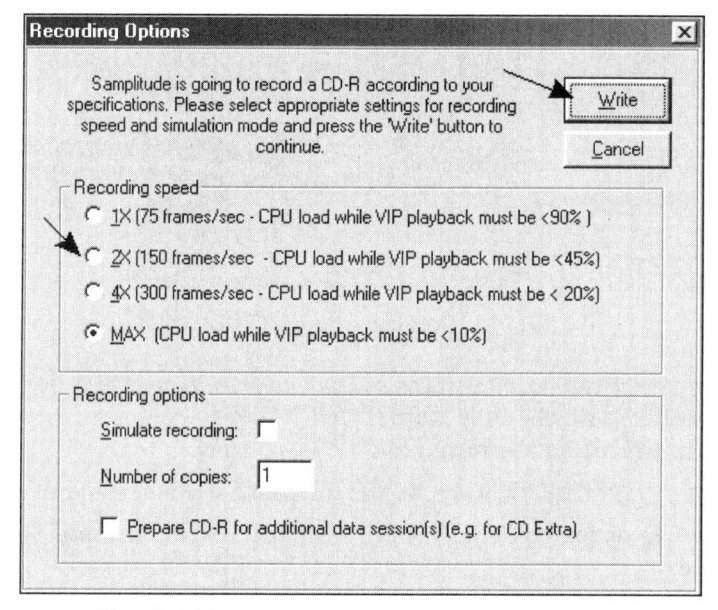

Fig. 5.146. The **Recording options** dialog box

Based on our experience, we recommend that you *always* use the **2X(...)** button to burn AUDIO CDs.

Burning will start after you click the **Write** button.

The burning progress is indicated in a special window (Fig. 5.147).

To conclude this chapter covering Samplitude 2496, we'd like to mention the trend towards erasing the boundaries between certain stages of creating a musical project.

Not so long ago, one could draw clear boundaries between arrangement, recording, sound processing, and mixing. Today, however, this is almost impossible. Modern computer technologies allow you to combine all stages of creating a musical project into one process. Due to this fact, a computer musician becomes an "all-round craftsman", since he or she performs not only the composer's job, but also the arranger's and sound producer's as well.

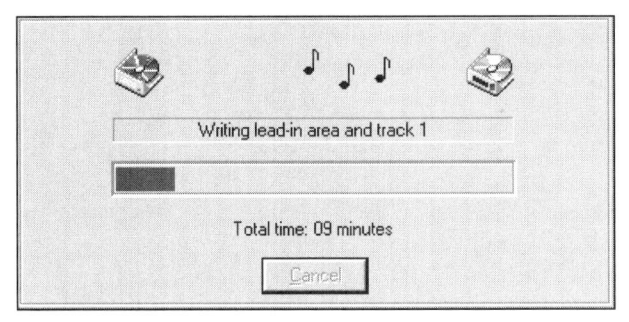

Chapter 5: The Samplitude 2496 Application as a High-Quality Virtual Studio

Fig. 5.147. The burning progress bar

Such a combining of jobs can be explained by the fact that sound processing is closely connected with modern computer arrangement. In Samplitude 2496, when a musical project is created, these stages supplement each other in a natural way.

From the above reasoning, it can be said with assurance that Samplitude 2496 is a great step forward in the area of computer musical technologies.

Chapter 6

THE CUBASE VST 24 APPLICATION AND CREATING "LIVE" MIDI SOUND

You of course know that every piece of music is written down using notes that symbolize sounds of certain length and pitch and that are put into a given sequence. This is, so to speak, the formal shell of a musical composition, whereas its soul is the musical context. The musical context is the idea behind the musical message that is encoded with the notes. When combined together, the notes and the context make up a complete entity called MUSIC.

As a rule, playing the notes correctly seems both difficult and important to those who are learning to play a musical instrument. However, it is the second component of performing — interpreting a piece of music, i.e., revealing its musical context — that is actually the most important in music.

Metaphorically, the notes and the musical context are as dependent upon one another as letters of the alphabet and the idea behind an orator's speech.

Psychologists hold that, in addition to the information transferred by words, so-called nonverbal information (i.e., intonation, stresses, pauses) is extremely important. This is especially noticeable when emotions and interpersonal relations are involved.

Music is an ancient art. With music, people have expressed their emotions and feelings for ages. This is why the information component of a piece of music is always subordinate to something more important (while remaining also very important). Namely, it is subordinate to the essence of the music, that is, its context.

Experts in technical music devices have always tried to answer the question, "How can musical information be passed from the musician's subconscious to the listener's subconscious without any loss?" There are many present ideas on how a recording can most exactly and completely reflect all the nuances of an acoustic performance without losing the most important component when going through the numerous technical stages, that is, the means of expression that were used to create the musical context.

The same task — being able to understand and convey the essence of a piece of music — is the one set at all stages of musical education. Of course, it is treated differently in elementary musical school than it is when teaching those at higher skill levels. In the beginning, it is enough for a student to play notes and reflect the dynamic nuances specified by the composer. At more advanced levels, the musician is required to comprehend a musical composition, to let it into his or her soul, and to suggest to the listeners his or her own interpretation. As composers say, "music is made up of impressions, thoughts, and feelings expressed by sounds".

Today almost every computer is able to play the notes of a piece of music entered into its memory.

At first this fact caused astonishment. (Look, the computer is playing music!) However, the astonishment has gone, and it became clear that computer sounds are far from music. Moreover, they aren't music AT ALL, since they lack something very important. It's kind of like a wax figure — it might look human, but it's not.

While playing notes, a computer plays back what was recorded. It never makes mistakes. However, this correctness and evenness is the main reason why computer music is soulless.

A real musician CAN'T perform music exactly according to the notes. He or she always interprets notes and creates his or her own musical context. A less talented musician does this in a more or less standard manner, whereas a maestro performs brilliantly. However, the performance in neither case is mechanical, since it reflects the individuality of the performer.

So what should we do to "teach" the computer how to detect and demonstrate the musical context?

Modern technologies for musical computer programs provide for one approach to this problem.

Computers are obedient students. They "learn" almost at once, immediately after the necessary program is loaded. Their "talents" are measured by the speed and quality of their algorithms.

However, you should be aware that, first of all, a computer is just a machine. At present, it cannot create a musical context as a human performer does, but the first steps are being made. For example, a computer today can significantly "enliven" a piece of music using special algorithms. It can already imitate a human master's rhythm, melodic phrases, and harmonic sequences.

Currently, "teaching" the computer how to perform music is progressing in various directions. One includes developing more advanced algorithms for reading scores. Another direction is to try to share the performer's experience with the computer by using autoformalization methods. And perhaps the most promising direction in "enlivening" a computer's performance is the attempt to teach the computer to imitate a human in imparting the nuances of a piece of music.

The leading manufacturers of software are constantly doing research in the area of computer performance. There are already some software products on the market that use algorithms to analyze the contents of a piece of music.

For example, NTONYX StyleMorpher 2.4 (**http://www.ntonyx.com**) allows you to transform harmony, rhythm, and musical measure, as well as to create musical phrases from original material recorded in the format of a MIDI file. It also uses an algorithm of intellectual quantization (quantization will be discussed later in this chapter), depending on the contents of a piece of music.

Cubase VST 24 (the application discussed in this chapter) embodies the results of longstanding research conducted by the Steinberg company (**http://www.steinberg.net**) in the area of "enlivening" computer performance.

The application provides various tools to solve this task, so-called Groove Quantize in particular. This feature allows the user to move the positions of the notes and to add stresses so that they correspond to a certain template taken from a "live" performance (for example, an audio recording). Any record or MIDI file (including your own performance) can be used as a template if it has the appropriate style, rhythm, and musical measure.

The application also includes a library of standard templates. Moreover, using another tool — the Styletrax plug-in — it is possible to create a virtual "group" of musicians and improvise with them in real time, using the MIDI keyboard.

When describing Cubase VST 24, we're going to focus mostly on the techniques that allow you to "enliven" sound and eliminate the "computer" sound. Thus, unfortunately, we will not be able to cover certain other features of this large and powerful program.

The MIDI Interface

A language is a system of symbols used to transfer information. MIDI is the abbreviation for Musical Instruments Digital Interface. Figuratively speaking, MIDI is a language used by musical instruments for information exchange.

MIDI was designed especially for musical synthesizers to "understand" each other. Therefore, it is possible to conduct an orchestra of MIDI instruments using the keyboard of a single synthesizer.

The MIDI interface is both like and unlike traditional musical notation. The similarity is that in both cases, musical sounds are written down using a certain system of symbols.

On the other hand, the MIDI system that is used to encode musical sounds is much more diversified than traditional musical notation (the latter hasn't changed for several centuries). Unlike traditional notation, the musical language of MIDI instruments includes many "technical" commands.

It should be mentioned that these complex MIDI commands were not designed simply to describe all the parameters of playing music with traditional acoustic instruments. Their goal is also to reflect the completely new possibilities presented by electronic musical instruments.

Traditional musical notation defines the pitch and the length of a note, how to press the key (legato, staccato, etc.), the dynamic nuances of the fragment containing the note, and the general characteristics of a piece of music.

All the other artistic features intended by the composer are "between the lines". This is why the task of the performer always includes the ability to read and understand the nuances and to reflect them during performance, adding his or her interpretation of the piece.

The predecessors of modern MIDI synthesizers were the simplest musical machines, such as music boxes, street organs, and mechanical pianos. All of them featured something like musical commands that had been coded beforehand and then transferred to the instrument via a mechanical medium (such as a pinned roller or a punched card).

It should be mentioned that MIDI is a serial interface. This means that all the commands (i.e., MIDI messages) are transferred and processed in a sequence rather than all at once.

An example of a list of MIDI commands is shown in Fig. 6.1.

One can say that the sequence of MIDI commands shown here differs from traditional musical notation as significantly as a machine language differs from the Windows graphical interface. However, this is still a computer language, and you shouldn't be afraid of it.

Those who want to create music with their computers don't need to understand MIDI in depth. A general understanding is usually sufficient. Indeed, a great many Windows users haven't the foggiest idea about programming. However, they are able to easily work with computers, thanks to the graphic user interface that was designed exactly for this purpose: so that computers could be used by as many people as possible, including those without a technological disposition.

Start-Pos.	Length	Val.1	Val.2	Val.3	Status	Chn
0005.01.000	=====	0	127	===	BankSelMSB	2
0005.01.000	=====	32	0	===	BankSelLSB	2
0005.01.000	=====	8	===	===	Program Ch	2
0005.01.000	=====	7	127	===	MainVolume	2
0005.01.000	=====	91	98	===	Effect1Dep	2
0005.01.192	96	D#4	93	64	Note	2
0005.01.288	=====	84	114	===	Pitch Bend	2
0005.02.000	=====	42	125	===	Pitch Bend	2
0005.02.000	96	A#3	95	64	Note	2
0005.02.096	=====	42	117	===	Pitch Bend	2
0005.02.192	96	B3	93	64	Note	2
0005.02.288	=====	127	111	===	Pitch Bend	2
0005.03.000	=====	127	103	===	Pitch Bend	2
0005.03.000	288	A3	98	64	Note	2
0005.03.192	=====	84	98	===	Pitch Bend	2
0005.04.000	=====	42	93	===	Pitch Bend	2
0005.04.000	576	C#4	127	64	Note	2
0005.04.288	=====	85	82	===	Pitch Bend	2
0006.01.096	=====	42	77	===	Pitch Bend	2
0006.01.192	=====	85	74	===	Pitch Bend	2
0006.01.192	864	A3	82	64	Note	2
0006.01.288	=====	127	71	===	Pitch Bend	2
0006.02.096	=====	42	69	===	Pitch Bend	2
0006.02.192	=====	0	64	===	Pitch Bend	2
0006.02.288	=====	127	55	===	Pitch Bend	2
0006.03.000	=====	127	47	===	Pitch Bend	2
0006.03.096	=====	85	42	===	Pitch Bend	2
0006.03.192	96	A2	127	64	Note	2

Fig. 6.1. A list of MIDI messages

At present, many people in the humanitarian professions use computers in their work. Among them are artists, writers, architects, and musicians. Those working with sounds have convenient program tools available to them that can provide for fruitful contact between a human being and a computer. One of these tools is Cubase VST 24, which also uses a simple and convenient graphic interface.

A MIDI Device

An example of a device that accepts MIDI messages is the synthesizer of the sound card of your computer. Additionally, an external MIDI device can be connected to the computer, such as a synthesizer or a MIDI keyboard.

Connection of external MIDI devices is quite easy — just use a special connecting cable that has a connector for the sound card and two standard five-pin connectors: MIDI IN and MIDI OUT.

The names of the connectors show that one MIDI device sends MIDI commands, and the other receives them.

Using MIDI, you can transfer commands in both directions: from the computer to the external synthesizer, and from the external synthesizer (or the MIDI keyboard) to the synthesizer of the computer's sound card.

MIDI commands are always transferred sequentially (one after another). Therefore, even when a chord (several sounds emitted simultaneously) is needed, it will be transferred as a series of commands, each representing a separate sound. The listener, however, won't notice the delay, since the transfer rate is relatively high.

In Fig. 6.1, the list of MIDI messages (the **Status** column) contains some **Note** messages. These are commands for the synthesizer that mean "play the note" or "press the key".

Sixteen MIDI channels are used to transfer MIDI messages.

What are the MIDI channels needed for? Every modern synthesizer is a multitimbre musical instrument, containing at least one bank of timbres (for example, GM-General MIDI). MIDI channels are used for concurrent and independent control of different timbres. For example, the first MIDI channel of a MIDI synthesizer controls the violin, while the second one controls the double bass.

As a rule, modern sound cards have two or three MIDI ports, which increases the number of MIDI channels to 32 or 48, respectively.

However, for a user to be able to play 48 musical instruments at once, a MIDI sequencer is necessary.

MIDI sequencers are devices for recording and playing back MIDI messages.

These sequencers somewhat resemble multichannel tape recorders. However, unlike tape recorders, MIDI sequencers memorize and play back only command sequences for synthesizers.

A programmatically implemented MIDI sequencer is a part of the Cubase VST 24 application.

Sound Tracks and MIDI Channels

MIDI sequencers allow you to record music in tracks in the form of MIDI messages. Tracks are designed for the user's convenience. They clearly represent information about the recorded musical parts.

You should be aware that MIDI channels are not the same as the virtual tracks of a MIDI sequencer. You shouldn't mix these concepts or identify one with the other.

Unlike with channels, it is possible to create as many tracks as the musician needs. There can be many more tracks than channels, each track being assigned to a certain MIDI channel or MIDI port.

When editing a MIDI project, it is possible to assign a track to a different MIDI channel and/or MIDI port.

For example, if two tracks are assigned to one MIDI channel, the corresponding MIDI instrument will execute commands coming from both tracks.

The Cubase VST 24 Interface

The Main Arrangement Window

Every time Cubase VST 24 starts, the startup song file (def.all) is loaded. It is located in the same folder as the application itself.

The song contains only one arrangement window, named def.arr by default. The maximum number of arrangements contained in a song is 16.

> **NOTE** The file extensions have a meaning: ALL means "all", ARR means "arrangement".

The file types of Cubase VST 24 are discussed in more detail in the "*File Formats of the Program*" section later in this chapter.

The **Arrange** window (Fig. 6.2) is the main window of the Cubase VST 24 application. The starting arrangement window (def.arr) contains two multitracks: AUDIO and MIDI.

The arrangement window is divided into two sections. The right section contains clips, whereas the left one is used to control tracks.

We've already encountered the term "clip" in the programs described earlier in this book. For the sake of consistency, we'll use the same word here, even though a clip is called a "part" in Cubase VST 24. Let's look at the left section of the **Arrange** window first, that is, at the section controlling tracks (Fig. 6.2).

Chapter 6: The Cubase VST 24 Application and Creating "Live" MIDI Sound 459

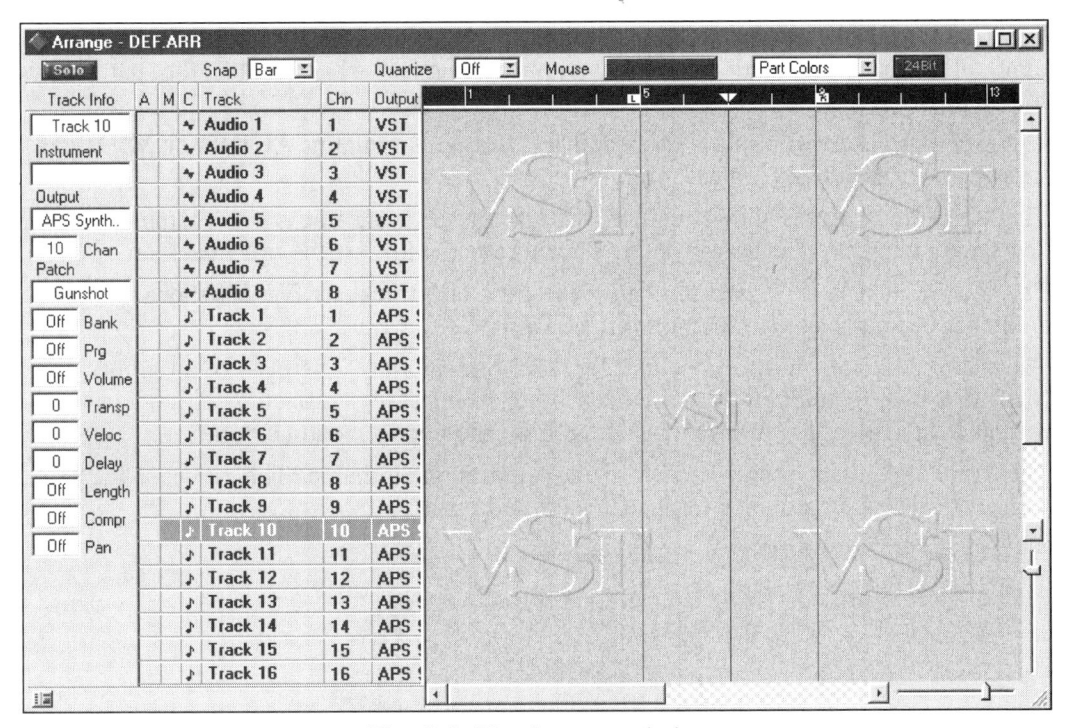

Fig. 6.2. The **Arrange** window

Fig. 6.3. Muting a track (**Mute**)

The **Inspector** panel is found under the **Track Info** column header (in the leftmost column). This panel is used for virtual (non-destructive) changing of the parameters of a track or clip.

The **A** column (**Active**) displays track activity. If a track contains AUDIO or MIDI messages, the corresponding indicator blinks.

The **M** column (**Mute**) allows the user to turn one or more tracks off. To mute a track, you should click its **M** field (Fig. 6.3). Clicking again will turn the track back on.

The **C** column (**Class**) is used to change the class of a track. As Fig. 6.4 shows, there are a number of track classes, ranging from MIDI Track to Chord Track.

The track class icons in the **C** field differ from one another. The class of an empty track (that is, a track containing no clips) can be changed easily. Just click its icon in the **C** field and then select the desired track class from the popup menu (Fig. 6.4).

The **Track** column is used to select a track and enter its name. The name of the track will be automatically given to all the clips created on it.

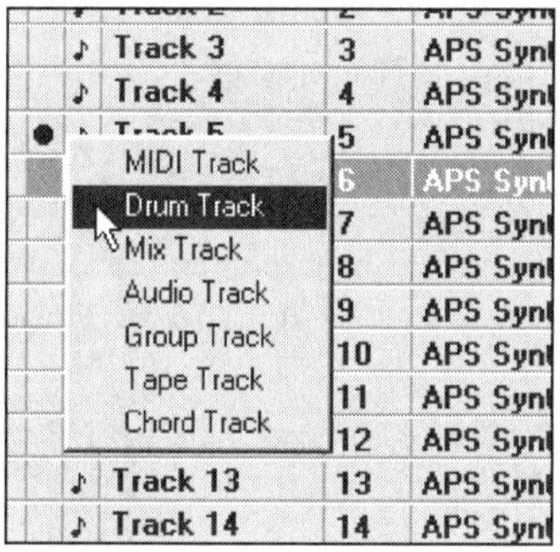

Fig. 6.4. Changing the track class

To enter the name, proceed as follows:

1. Double-click the **Track** field of the chosen track.
2. Key in the name from the keyboard.
3. Press the <Enter> key (Fig. 6.5).

A track is selected by clicking its **Track** field.

The tracks in the list can be dragged up or down.

The **Chn** column (**Channel**) is used to associate a MIDI or AUDIO channel with the selected track.

In Cubase VST 24, there are channels both for AUDIO and MIDI tracks. You can associate a channel with the track using the keyboard. The procedure is similar to entering the track name.

Chapter 6: The Cubase VST 24 Application and Creating "Live" MIDI Sound

Fig. 6.5. Changing the name of a track

Decrementing the channel number (decreasing it by 1) is done by left-clicking the **Chn** field. You can increment it (increase it by 1) by right-clicking the same field. To decrease/increase the channel number quickly, click and hold down the corresponding mouse button. The **Any** value (meaning any channel number) comes before the number 1.

The **Output** column allows you to assign a MIDI port to the MIDI track.

Fig. 6.6 shows an example of selecting from amongst three MIDI ports. Two of them — APS Synth A and APS Synth B — refer to the internal synthesizer of the sound card, whereas the APS MIDI Out 0 port is designed for connecting an external MIDI device.

MROS

MROS (MIDI Real-time Operating System) is the internal real-time operating system of Cubase VST 24. Its purpose is to provide connection with plugged-in MIDI modules. (Using MROS is discussed in the "*Using Plug-ins*" section later in this chapter).

In addition to recording electronic or traditional acoustic musical instruments, the musician with a computer can also use a wide range of virtual instruments.

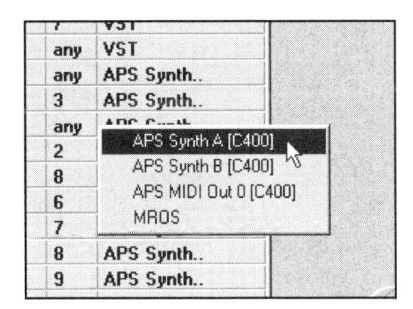

Fig. 6.6. Selecting a MIDI port

Cubase VST 24 makes it possible to use a variety of such virtual VST instruments, namely, virtual VST synthesizers. They are installed in exactly the same way as DirectX plug-ins.

Virtual synthesizers are "connected" to virtual MIDI ports rather than to physical ones. Each instrument has its corresponding port.

To enable a VST instrument, proceed as follows:

1. Open the **Audio** menu.
2. Select **VST instruments**.
3. In the **VST instruments** window, click the **No VST instr** field.
4. Select the desired VST instrument from the list of the installed VST instruments.
5. Click the **Power** button in the **VST instruments** window.
6. Close the **VST instruments** window.

After the necessary VST instruments are enabled, you can proceed with the next operation, that is, assigning tracks to them. Any of the enabled VST instruments can be played back on the selected track.

Fig. 6.7 shows an example of choosing a VST instrument. The selected track (here, Track 1) can be assigned to any of the four VST instruments (Electron, GakStoarD, Neon, or PPG Wave).

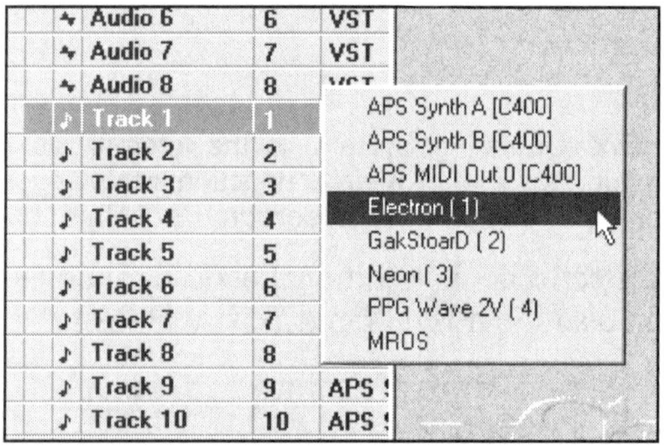

Fig. 6.7. Selecting a VST instrument

You can drag the vertical boundary between the two sections of the **Arrange** window, thus expanding or narrowing the visible parts of the sections.

For example, if you move the boundary to the right, you will see the **Instrument** column of the track control section (Fig. 6.8).

This column is used to set the name of the instrument that corresponds to a certain MIDI channel and MIDI port. Having set the name, you won't have to perform the tedious operations of assigning the MIDI port and channel. Just select the instrument from the list.

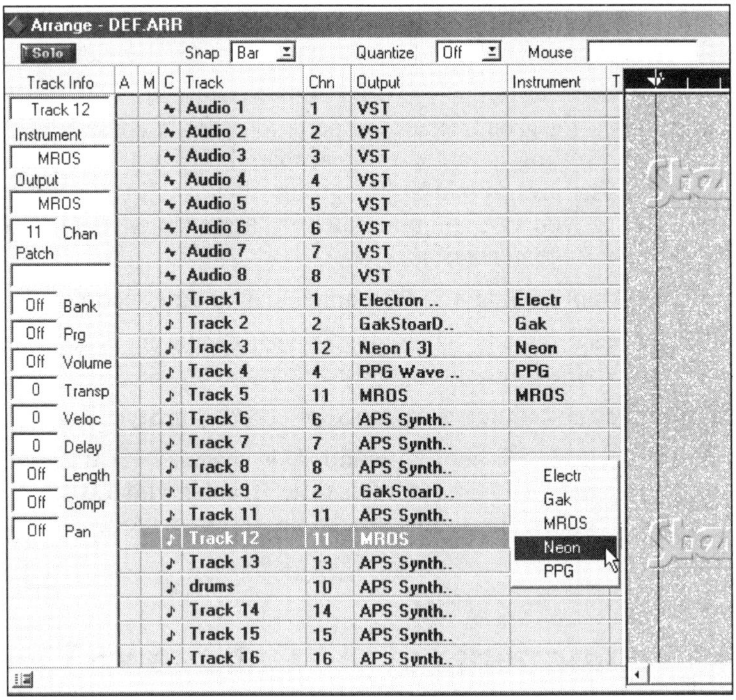

Chapter 6: The Cubase VST 24 Application and Creating "Live" MIDI Sound 463

Fig. 6.8. Assigning an instrument

Types of Tracks

There are 11 track classes in Cubase VST 24. These are: Audio, MIDI, Chord, Drum, Mix, Audio Mix, Group, Tape, Style, and Master.

Two types of tracks can be seen at startup after the def.all song is loaded. These are Audio and MIDI. The Audio track is marked with the "sine" icon in the **C** column, and the MIDI track is marked with the "note" icon.

Now let's consider the other track classes.

❐ Drum Track is a special track for programming the percussion section. Double clicking the clip of this track calls the **Drum Edit** editor.

Using **Drum Edit**, you can also edit the clips of a MIDI track. However, if you do this, you won't be able to assign drums to different MIDI channels and MIDI ports in the same editor.

❐ Mix Track is a separate track of a MIDI mixer. In Cubase VST 24, MIDI mixers are similar to control panels of Cakewalk (in the **Panel** window), which allow you to control studio equipment.

- ❐ Audio Mix is a track of the virtual VST mixer where all changes of the mixer controls and the VST plug-ins are recorded (this is similar to the automation curves of Samplitude 2496).
- ❐ Group Track is a track for grouping several parts together. Cubase VST 24 presents an additional service for editing complex musical material that allows you to group several tracks together. The groups laid on the group track as clips form a complex composition. Using groups, you can combine different arrangements, since the groups are the same for all the arrangements of a song.
- ❐ Tape Track is a track controlling a multichannel analog tape recorder.
- ❐ Style Track is a track available when the **Styletrax** plug-in is loaded. Using Style Track turns Cubase VST 24 into a programmatic arranger.
- ❐ Chord Track is a track containing a sequence of chords for Style Track.
- ❐ Master Track is a track for editing the tempo. It is accessed via the **Edit|Mastertrack** menu, whose **Mastertrack** submenu contains the **Graphic** and **List** items. These provide two modes for editing the tempo track: the graphic mode and the list editing mode.

The Basic Components of the Cubase VST 24 Interface

The **Part** (i.e., clip) is the main element of the arrangement window, where we also find **Events**.

Events in Cubase VST 24

In Cubase VST 24, events are all types of messages, including MIDI messages, AUDIO messages, and internal messages of the application.

The clips are found in the right hand section (**Part Display**) of the **Arrange** window.

The content of a clip depends on the class of the track on which it is created.

Clips can be saved in files with the PRT extension and reused in other arrangements. To save a clip, proceed as follows:

1. Click the desired clip to select it (to select multiple clips, hold down the <Shift> key while clicking each of them).
2. Select **Save As** from the **File** menu.
3. In the **Save File As** dialog box, select **Parts (*.prt)** from the **File Type** text box.
4. Click the **Save** button (Fig. 6.9).

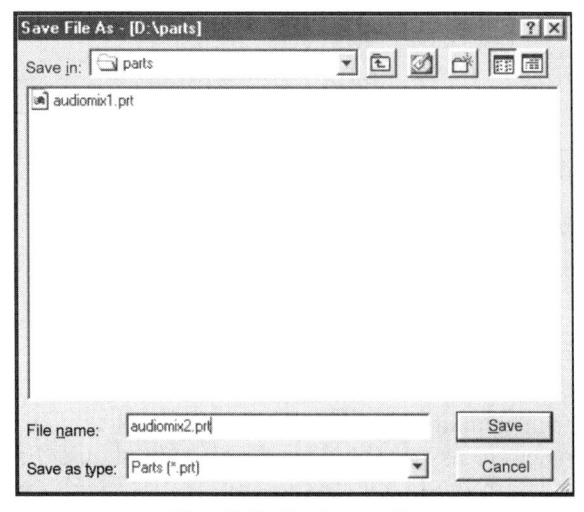

Chapter 6: The Cubase VST 24 Application and Creating "Live" MIDI Sound   465

Fig. 6.9. Saving a clip

Loading a clip into the arrangement window is done using the **Open** item from the **File** menu. When the clip is loaded, a corresponding track is created automatically. The beginning of the clip will match the position of the left locator (**L**). Let's look at this in more detail.

Setting Locators. There are two multipurpose **Locators** in Cubase VST 24. One of them is denoted by **L** (left), and the other is denoted by **R** (right). In fact, the locators (Fig. 6.10) serve as universal markers in the application, since they are used for many purposes.

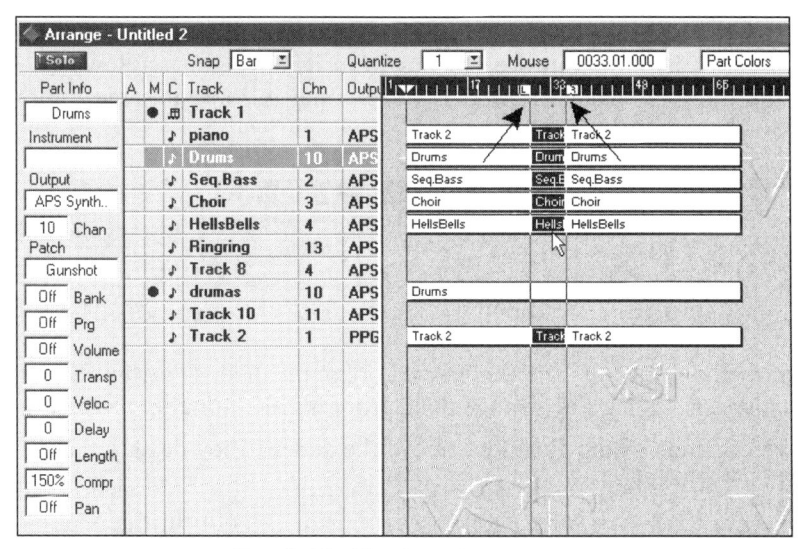

Fig. 6.10. The **L** and **R** locators

Here are just two of them:

- The locators can serve as markers for the **Punch** record mode, and also as markers for **Loop** playback.
- The locators can serve as delimiters of a working area, etc. (the area between the left and the right locators is called the *project editing working area*).

There are various ways of setting the locators, depending on their usage.

- To set the locators, click the desired location in the **Ruler** with the correct mouse button:
  - The left button for the left locator
  - The right button for the right locator
- When editing an arrangement, it is often necessary to set the locators on the boundaries of a clip as precisely as possible. To do so, you should first select the clip by clicking it once. Then use the following shortcut: <Ctrl>+<Alt>+<P>.
- You can fix frequently used locator positions by assigning them to function keys from <F2> to <F11>. To do so, after having set the locators to the desired positions, press <Shift>+<F*n*> (where *n* is the number of a function key from <F2> to <F11>).

The **Transport** Bar is the deck of Cubase VST 24 (Fig. 6.11). The transport bar is the main tool for controlling recording and playback. It is opened and closed with the <F12> function key.

The <Ctrl>+<Shift>+<Alt>+<F12> shortcut opens the transport bar in the center of the screen. You can drag it over the screen by grabbing either of its blue vertical bands on the sides.

This transport bar is quite similar to those already described in this book. This is why we believe that most of its functions are obvious from its appearance. However, since being able to use the transport panel is critical, we're going to look at some important points more closely.

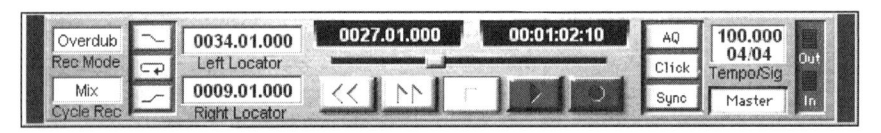

Fig. 6.11. The **Transport** Bar, the deck of Cubase VST 24

In the center of the transport bar, there is a horizontal slider (**Position Slider**). Using it, you can quickly move along the arrangement, from its beginning up to the last clip.

There are two counters (**Song Position**) above the slider. They display the current cursor position in different ways:

- The left counter (**Meter format**) reflects the cursor position in the Measure:Beat:Tick format

Chapter 6: The Cubase VST 24 Application and Creating "Live" MIDI Sound 467

❒ The right counter (**Time format**) reflects the cursor position in time units, that is, Hours:Minutes:Seconds:Frames

By changing the readings of the counters, you change the cursor position.

To enter the coordinates of the cursor position via the keyboard, double-click the counter and then key in the desired values.

After that, the cursor will move to the specified point. Such a method can be applied to any numeric field in the transport bar.

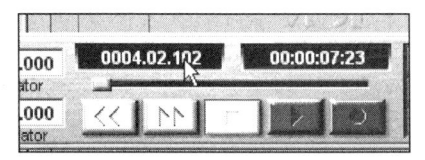

Fig. 6.12. Changing the cursor position using the **Song Position** counter

The current cursor position can be changed in increments. To do this, you should:

1. In either counter, place the mouse pointer on the part of the count that corresponds to the size of the increment you'd like to use. (For example, in Fig. 6.12, the mouse pointer is over the tick area, so the value will be incremented/decremented by ticks.)
2. Press and hold down the left or right mouse button.

NOTE The left mouse button moves the cursor towards the beginning of the song, and the right mouse button moves it towards the end. One click corresponds to one increment/decrement.

You can also move the cursor by setting an offset (Fig. 6.13): first double-click the counter with the left mouse button, then type in the value of the offset along with a plus or minus sign. The sign corresponds to the direction ("+" or "−").

Fig. 6.13. Entering the offset with the keyboard

The **Left Locator** and **Right Locator** fields (Fig. 6.11) display the positions of the locators. The **Tempo/Sig** field indicates the tempo and signature of the arrangement.

The **Master** button toggles the mode of the master track. When the mode is on, the tempo is determined by the master track, and the **Tempo/Sig** field shows the current tempo value.

The **In** and **Out** indicators reflect the activity of the input and output streams of MIDI messages, respectively.

The buttons controlling recording and playback back don't require special comments (Fig. 6.12, from left to right):

- **Rewind**
- **Fast Forward**
- **Stop**
- **Play**
- **Record**

If you click either the **Rewind** or **Fast Forward** button while holding the <Shift> key down, it will speed up the process.

Clicking the **Stop** button stops playback. Another click on this button will move the cursor to the position of the left locator.

If the cursor is at the position of the left locator or stands to the left of it, clicking the **Stop** button moves the cursor to the beginning of the song. Therefore, double-clicking the **Stop** button always moves the cursor to the beginning of the song.

You can position the cursor at any point of the song by double-clicking the ruler at that point (Fig. 6.10).

The **AQ** button (Automatic Quantization) turns on the automatic quantization recording mode.

> **NOTE** *Quantization* is a function that allows the user to "align" the rhythm by moving notes from a live recording to more precise positions.
>
> Rhythmic deviations can be of two types: those created intentionally (for example, swing), or those that emerge as a result of incorrect performance.
>
> Since the feeling of a "live" performance disappears after quantization, you should use this function with special care, and only when it is necessary to eliminate rhythmic blunders. After using quantization, the sound should be "revitalized". Quantization is discussed in more detail in the section *"Quantization in Cubase VST 24"* later in this chapter.

Let's return to the transport bar. The **Click** button turns on the metronome, and the **Sync** button turns on the external equipment synchronization mode.

In the left hand side of the transport bar, the following buttons are found:

- **Rec Mode** toggles between the **Overdub** and **Replace** modes.
- **Cycle Rec** toggles between the three modes of cycle recording: **Mix**, **Punch**, and **Normal**.

To the right of these buttons, you see three buttons with icons (from top to bottom):

- **Punch In** turns on the **Punch In** record mode

Chapter 6: The Cubase VST 24 Application and Creating "Live" MIDI Sound

- **Cycle on/off** turns on/off the looped play (record) mode
- **Punch Out** turns on the **Punch Out** record mode

The Hotkeys of the *Transport* Bar

The **Transport** bar provides a number of hotkeys that make the user's job easier. Here are some of them:

- <1> and <2> on the numeric keypad move the cursor to the position of the left or right locator.
- <9> on the numeric keypad moves the cursor to the position of the last start.
- <Enter> on the numeric keypad turns on the playback mode.
- <Ins> on the numeric keypad duplicates the **Stop** button.
- <*> on the numeric keypad duplicates the **Record** button.
- The key combinations from <Shift>+<3> to <Shift>+<8> on the numeric keypad serve to store cursor positions in memory (up to six). To move the cursor to one of the memorized positions later on, just press the corresponding key (that is, <3> to <8> on the numeric keypad).

Changing the Scale of the Picture

The displayed picture can be zoomed vertically or horizontally. For this purpose, two sliders are provided that are found near the lower right corner of the arrangement window. They are indicated by arrows in Fig. 6.14.

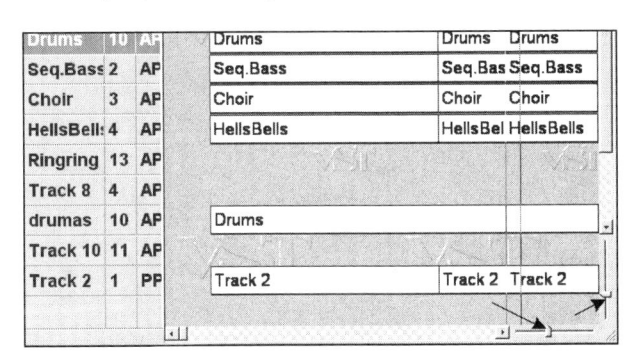

Fig. 6.14. The sliders used to zoom

You can also zoom using the following hotkeys:

- Horizontally: <G> to zoom out, <H> to zoom in
- Vertically: <Shift>+<G> to zoom out, <Shift>+<H> to zoom in

Additional Settings in the Arrange Window

Let's continue describing the **Arrange** window and look at its additional settings.

The **Solo** button turns on the solo mode on the selected track.

The **Snap** field sets the precision with which the cursor moves (Fig. 6.15).

> **NOTE** If 1/16 is selected, the cursor will move by sixteenth (semiquaver) notes; if 1/8 then by eighth (quaver) notes; 1/4 means moving by quarter (crotchet) notes; 1/2 means half (minum) notes; "Bar" corresponds to movement by measures (bars); and "Off" means free movement (to an arbitrary point).

It should be noted that the Bar mode, which is set by default, protects the arrangement against incorrect non-destructive editing operations.

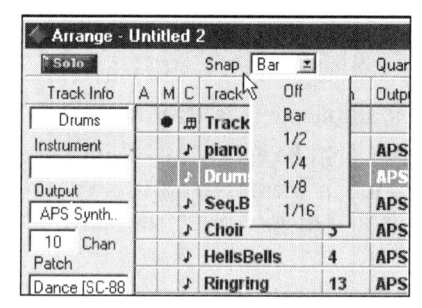

Fig. 6.15. Setting the **Snap** field

Using the **Quantize** field (Fig. 6.16), you can automatically adjust the positions of rhythmically incorrect notes. This field in the **Arrange** window is related to the Automatic Quantization recording mode, as well as to other types of quantization (see "*Quantization in Cubase VST 24*" later in this chapter).

Fig. 6.16. Setting the **Quantize** field

The **Mouse** field displays the current position of the mouse pointer. Clicking this field toggles between two display formats, Meter format (Measure:Beat:Tick) and Time format (Hours:Minutes:Seconds:Frames).

The **Part Colors** field sets the colors of the selected clip.

The 24-bit audio recording mode is switched on using the **24Bit** button. This button duplicates the **24 Bit Recording** mode in the **Audio System Setup** window (see "*Setting Up the Application to Work with Audio*" later in this chapter).

The File Formats of Cubase VST 24

Cubase VST 24 can work with many file formats. In this chapter, we're going to look at the most important of them. These are Song, Arrangement, Part, Drum Map, Setup, and Grooves.

Song

Cubase VST 24 automatically loads a song file (def.all) at every startup. A *song* is a file with the ALL extension, in which most of the settings are saved.

Thus, a song file can contain:

- All the arrangement windows created (maximum 16)
- Groups of the arrangement windows
- All the program settings (setup)
- Audio Pool
- Drum Map
- Groove Quantize
- The settings of the **Preferences** submenu of the **File** menu

As you can see from this list, virtually all settings can be saved in a song file. This is why you should save musical projects in the song format (with the ALL extension).

Arrangement

An *arrangement* is a set of files with the ARR extension. These files are related to the **Arrange** window, and they make up the song. Arrangement files contain:

- The contents of the **Arrange** window
- Groups of clips created in the **Arrange** window
- The tempo settings specified in the **Transport** bar
- The status of the **Master** button in the **Transport** bar
- The status of the **Solo** button

ARR files can be copied to other songs without the arrangement window settings being changed.

Part

A *part* is a file with the PRT extension. Its purpose is to store a clip or a group of clips. When a group of clips is saved, their relative positions don't change. The clips of a group track cannot be saved in a Part file.

When a PRT file is loaded, the beginning of the clip (or the beginning of the first clip in the group) is set to the position of the left locator (**L**).

Every time a PRT file is loaded, new tracks are created in the arrangement window.

PRT files makes it possible to use the same clips in different arrangement windows.

Drum Map

Drum Map files have the DRM extension. They contain a sound map of the percussion. In this map, every sound of a drum is associated with a certain key of the MIDI keyboard.

Drum Editor allows the user to assign names to the keys of the MIDI instruments, to change their positions in the list, and so on. The resulting configuration is then saved in a DRM file.

> *NOTE* For example, if the SB Live sound card is installed in your computer, and you have some SoundFont drum banks installed, you will be able to use mixed drum maps in your arrangements. The configuration of any map can be saved in a DRM file.

Cubase VST 24 comes with a large library of synthesizer drum maps developed by various manufacturers.

Setup

Setup files have the SET extension. They contain all the settings of a song except the arrangement.

The SET files allow you to save and load song settings independently of the arrangement. This might be useful, for example, when changing the synchronization parameters, or when Cubase VST 24 is temporarily switched to Slave mode.

Grooves

Grooves are files with the GRV extension. They can contain up to 16 rhythmic grooves. Using them makes musical parts more versatile and "life-like".

In this section, we looked only at the main file formats available via the **File** menu. The other formats used in Cubase VST 24 will be described later in the course of this chapter.

Chapter 6: The Cubase VST 24 Application and Creating "Live" MIDI Sound   473

Cubase VST 24 Editors

Key Edit

The **Key Edit** editor (or **Key Editor**) is used to edit MIDI messages in keyboard mode. It can be opened either by double clicking the selected clip in the arrangement window or by first selecting a clip and then selecting the **Edit** item from the **Edit** menu (<Ctrl>+<E>).

There is a virtual piano keyboard in the left hand part of the editor window. In **Key Edit**, MIDI messages are represented as note events of these keys (Fig. 6.17).

> **NOTE** This type of representation of MIDI messages is similar to the one used in the **Piano Roll** window in Cakewalk Pro Audio.

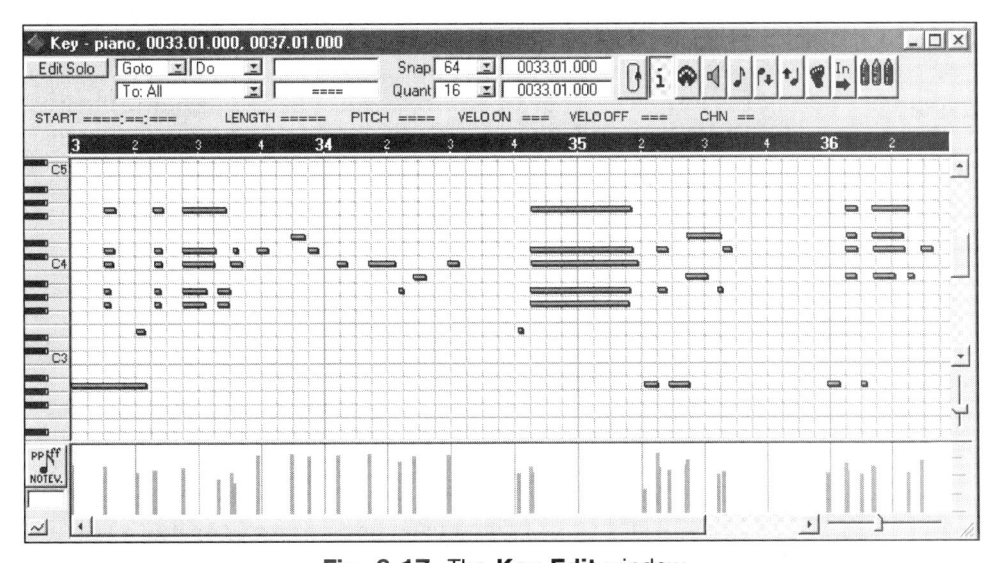

Fig. 6.17. The **Key Edit** window

The note events of the keys correspond to sounds of certain pitch and length — the horizontal level indicating the pitch, and the length of the print reflecting the sound length.

> **NOTE** The longer the note event, the longer the sound. The beginning of the note event indicates the beginning of the sound, and the end of it indicates the end of the sound.

Using the scrollbar on the right side of the window, you can move along the entire virtual MIDI keyboard.

Note numeration corresponds to the standard 128-key MIDI keyboard. A note can be heard by clicking the corresponding key.

The Musical Keyboard

It should be said that the size and range of a real piano keyboard differ from those of the virtual piano. A common acoustic piano has only 88 keys (7 complete octaves and 2 short ones at the beginning and the end). The MIDI standard contains 128 notes (10 complete octaves and 1 short octave).

The names of the octaves also differ in a common piano and in Cubase VST 24. In a piano these are: subcontra octave, contra octave, great octave, small octave, the one-line, the two-line, the three-line, the four-line, and the five-line octaves. In the MIDI standard, octaves are numbered from the negative second up to the eighth. The most popular octave — the one-line octave in a piano — corresponds to the third octave in the MIDI standard.

The position of the mouse pointer is indicated by a letter and a number in the **Mouse Box** field. The letter corresponds to the note name, and the number is the octave number. For example, C3 is the *C* of the third MIDI octave.

Let's continue to examine **Key Edit**. The window of this editor is split horizontally into two sections. The upper section is used to edit the "keyprints", and the lower one lets you graphically edit MIDI controllers. The line that splits the two sections of the editor window can be dragged with the mouse.

MIDI Controllers

MIDI controllers are a group of special MIDI messages that control the parameters of the sound emitted by a MIDI instrument.

The MIDI controller section (called the controller display) can be hidden by clicking the <~> button in the lower left corner of the editor window.

The **Toolbox** panel of the **Key Edit** editor can be opened by right clicking in either window section. The toolbox will stay on the screen until you release the right mouse button.

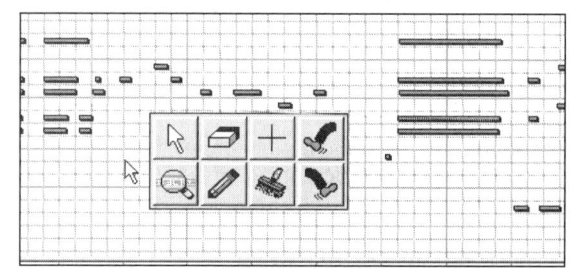

Fig. 6.18. The toolbox of the **Key Edit** editor

Chapter 6: The Cubase VST 24 Application and Creating "Live" MIDI Sound 475

The toolbox contains eight tools: **Arrow**, **Eraser**, **Line**, **Kickers**, **Magnifying Glass**, **Pencil**, **Paint Brush**.

To change the current tool, you should press the right mouse button, and while holding it down, move the mouse pointer to the button of the desired tool. After that, release the button.

Let's look at each tool in turn.

Arrow. The arrow looks just like the mouse pointer.

> **NOTE** In this chapter, we only cover those operations which are performed that use *only* **Arrow** (unless another tool is specified).

Using **Arrow**, you can perform the following operations:

- Select MIDI messages from a section. To select a single MIDI message, you click it, and to select a group of MIDI messages, you click every message in the group while holding down the <Shift> key. A group of MIDI messages can be also selected using a box (Fig. 6.19). To do so, press the left mouse button, and while holding it down, move the mouse pointer diagonally to draw a box.

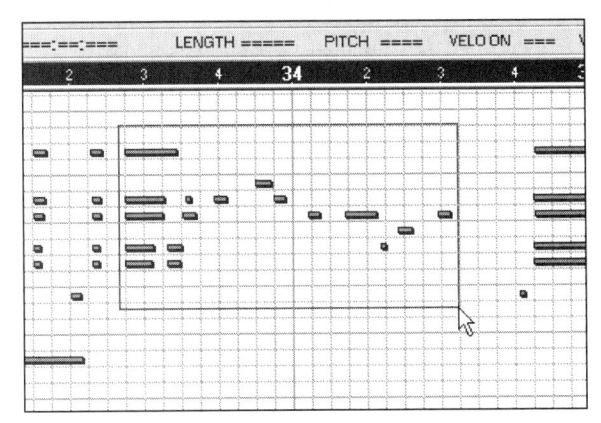

Fig. 6.19. Selecting a group of MIDI messages

- Move and copy MIDI messages (by dragging them with the mouse, and by dragging them while holding the <Alt> key pressed, respectively).
- Change the pitch of a note.

In order not to accidentally move a note to the left or to the right while changing its pitch, stick to the following procedure: in the "keyprints" section, click and hold the left mouse button on the note (the **Transpose 0** message will appear in the **Mouse Box** field, as shown in Fig. 6.20). Then press the <Shift> key and, while holding it down, move the note to the desired pitch.

The Transpose Value

Let's now concentrate on the Transpose value. When a note is transposed (that is, moved), the number of semitones it is transposed by is displayed in the **Mouse Box**. For example, **Transpose+2** means raising the note pitch by two semitones (one tone), whereas **Transpose-2** means lowering it by one tone (Fig. 6.20).

Eraser is a tool used to erase MIDI messages. To delete a single note, just click it. To delete a group of notes, drag the **Eraser** tool over the whole group while holding the left mouse button pressed.

Deleting MIDI messages from the controller display is done in a similar fashion.

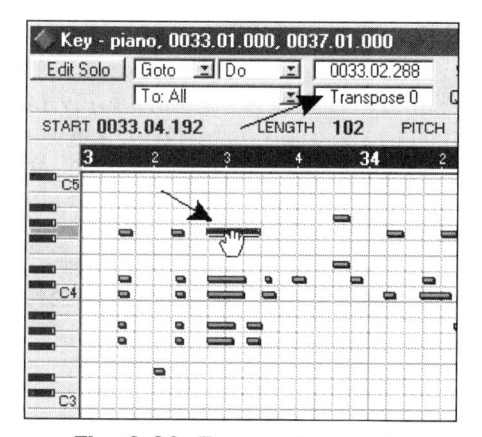

Fig. 6.20. Transposing a note

Line is a tool that allows you to draw lines indicating changes you want to make to parameters in both sections. For example, you can specify a linear law of change for the parameter of the MIDI controller in the controller display (Fig. 6.21).

To draw a line, proceed as follows:

1. Place the cross over the starting point.
2. Press and hold down the left mouse button.
3. Drag the cross in the desired direction to the desired end point.

A line will be drawn between the two points. As soon as the left mouse button is released, the parameters of the MIDI controller will align along the drawn line.

If you want to create a new line in an empty controller display, you need to draw it while holding down the <Alt> key.

In the "keyprints" section, you can use **Line** to change both the length of a single note and the lengths of multiple notes simultaneously (Fig. 6.22).

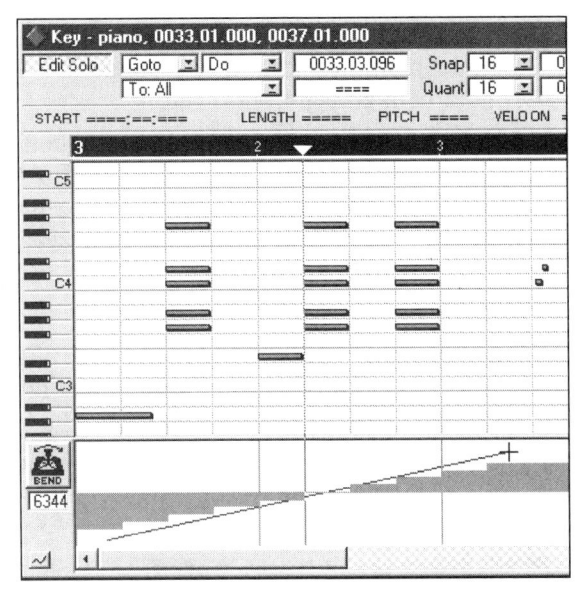

Chapter 6: The Cubase VST 24 Application and Creating "Live" MIDI Sound 477

Fig. 6.21. Using the **Line** tool

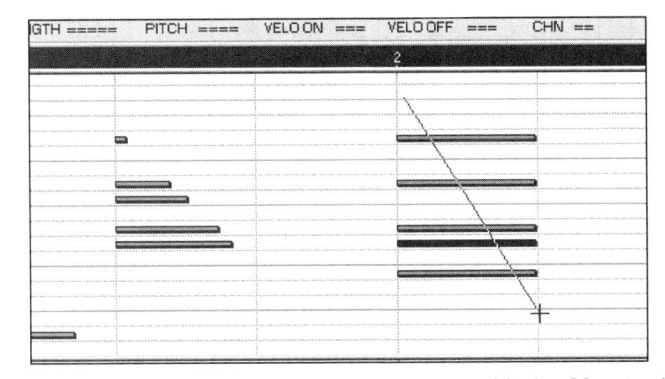

Fig. 6.22. Changing the lengths of notes with the **Line** tool

Kickers. Using these tools, you can move a note by fixed step (the two tools differ only in the direction of movement).

The size of the step is specified in the **Snap** field. To move a note by one step, just click it.

Magnifying Glass allows you to listen to a note or a group of notes. To listen to a single note, move the tool to it and click it with the left mouse button. To listen to a group, drag the tool over the entire group while holding down the left mouse button.

Pencil is used both to create MIDI messages (for example, to draw notes) and to change them.

A note is created with a single click at the desired position (in the "keyprints" section). The length of the note is defined by the value of the **Quantize** field in the editor window (4 corresponds to a quarter note, 8 to an eighth note, etc.).

To create a new series of MIDI messages, draw a curve while holding down the <Alt> key. The smoothness of the curve in the controller display is defined by the value in the **Snap** field in the editor window: the smaller the **Snap**, the smoother the curve, and the greater the number of MIDI messages. However, you should bear in mind that if the curve is smooth, the MIDI channel might become overloaded.

Using the pencil, you can graphically edit MIDI messages in the controller display.

The length of a note can be changed (decreased or increased). To do this, move the **Pencil** tool horizontally from the beginning to the end of the note in the desired direction (Fig. 6.23).

It is recommended that you press and hold down the <Alt> key during this procedure, lest you create an "extra" note.

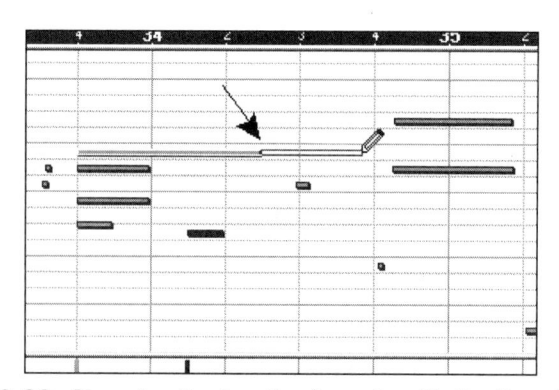

Fig. 6.23. Changing the length of a note with the **Pencil** tool

Paint Brush is used to draw a repeated note of the same length. The length is specified in the **Quantize** field, and the distance between the notes is set in the **Snap** field (Fig. 6.24).

The procedure is quite simple. To draw a required series, move the brush while holding down the left mouse button. If you need to draw horizontally and vertically at the same time, you should also hold the <Alt> key pressed.

The **Paint Brush** tool is useful when creating rhythmic sequences based on a repeated sound of constant pitch (for example, an organ-point).

Let's look at some more features of the **Key Edit** editor. Using it, you can:

❐ Listen to the part being edited separately from the other arrangement tracks (the **Edit Solo** button, Fig. 6.21)

Chapter 6: The Cubase VST 24 Application and Creating "Live" MIDI Sound 479

- Move the cursor by clicking the ruler
- Use transport controls similar to those in the arrange window

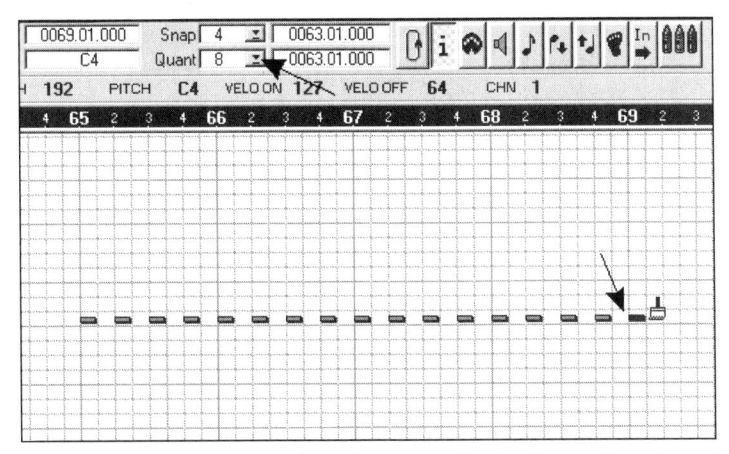

Fig. 6.24. Drawing a series of notes with the **Paint Brush** tool

To edit loops, the editor provides a very convenient feature called a *local loop*.

When it is used, the sound of the arrangement (the **Arrange** window) is accompanied by the loop in the **Key Edit** window. Thus it is possible not only to listen to the looped piece along with any part of the whole arrangement, but also to edit the piece in real-time mode during playback (if necessary).

Let's consider an example illustrating this feature. Suppose we need to create or edit a musical loop of a part so that it better agrees with the other parts of the arrangement. To achieve this, proceed as follows:

1. Place **Locators** in the arrangement window so that the working area between them is greater than the piece being edited.
2. Open the **Key Editor** (by double-clicking the clip).
3. In the opened window, select the **Arrow** tool.
4. Place the arrow on the ruler at the beginning of the loop, and then drag it (with the left mouse button pressed) to the end of the piece being edited. After the mouse button is released, the selected loop will be indicated in blue on the ruler (Fig. 6.25).

If the **Cycle on/off** button is pressed, two loops will be played back simultaneously: the one in the arrangement window (between the **L** and **R** locators) and the other in the editor window (the selected local **Loop**).

You can save or cancel the results of editing. To do this, press the <Esc> key and answer the question **Do you want to keep the edits?** in the dialog box that appears. You have a choice between **Keep** and **No**.

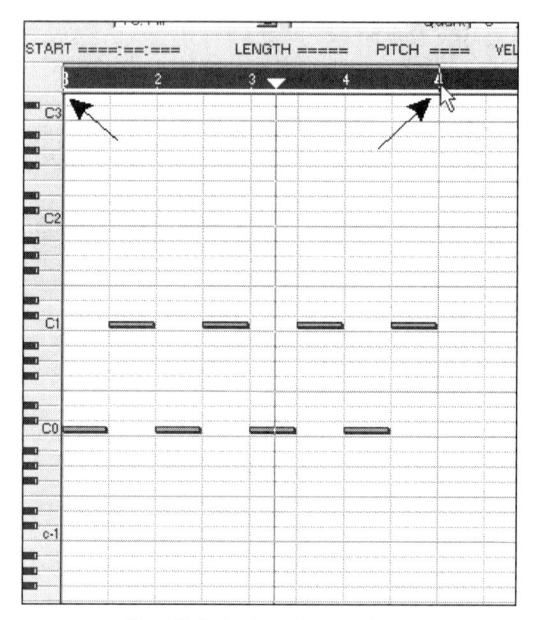

Fig. 6.25. Creating a loop

Drum Edit

Drum Edit is a percussion editor (Fig. 6.26). It is opened via the **Drum** item in the **Edit** menu (<Ctrl>+<D>) or — to edit Drum Track clips — by double-clicking the clip.

The **Drum Edit** window consists of three sections. The left hand section, **Drum Sound**, contains a percussion list. To see all its settings, drag the right side of the section with the mouse and increase its visible part. The upper right section contains notes, and the lower right one — the controller display — is used to graphically edit the controllers. This section can be hidden or shown using the <~> button in the lower left corner of the window.

Drum Edit makes it possible to graphically edit the velocity *individually* for *each* drum. This is why the velocity for only one drum is represented in the controller display — the velocity of the drum selected in the **Drum Sound List** (Fig. 6.26).

The graphic interface of the percussion editor is similar to that of **Key Edit**, but there are some differences. Let's examine some of the peculiarities of **Drum Edit**.

In the left hand part of the window, you see a section containing a percussion list. Each line in the notes section corresponds to a single drum part. Notes are created using the **Drumstick** tool and are shown as diamonds of the same size that exactly correspond to drum beats.

The drumstick transforms into a pencil (used to change the parameters of the controllers) as soon as the mouse pointer moves down to the lower section, to the controller display.

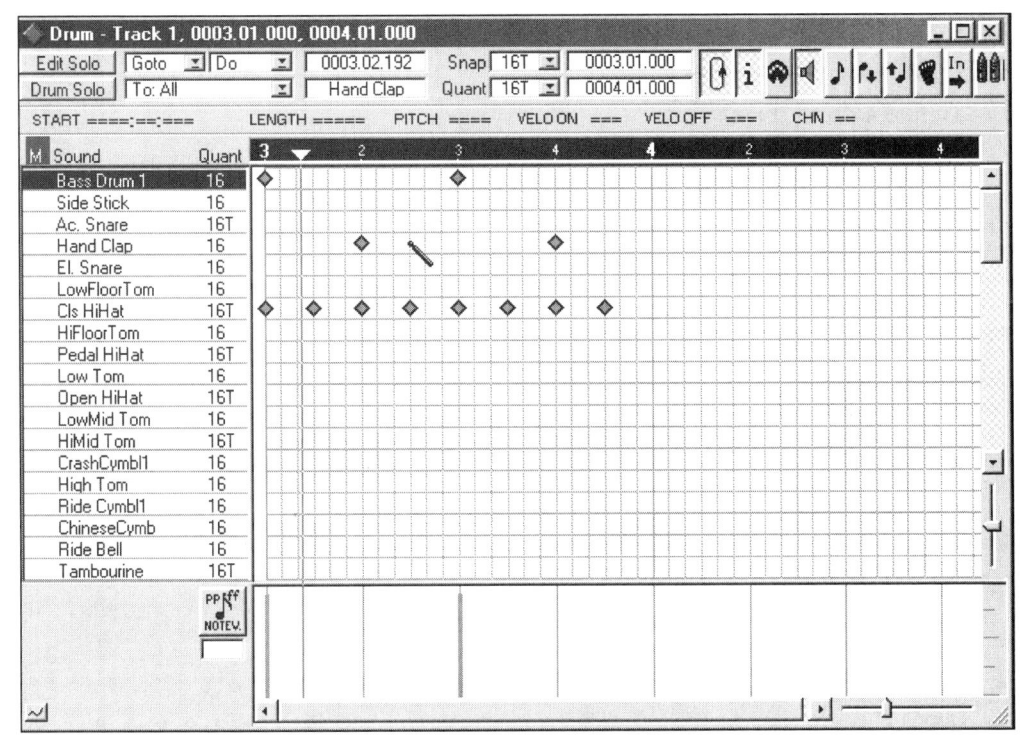

Chapter 6: The Cubase VST 24 Application and Creating "Live" MIDI Sound 481

Fig. 6.26. The **Drum Edit** window

The editor features the **Drum Solo** button, which allows the user to listen to each drum individually, that is, in the solo mode.

Switching on the **Mute** mode (clicking in the **M** column next to the name of a drum) makes it possible to temporarily turn off one or more drums.

In addition to overall quantization, **Drum Edit** provides separate quantization for each drum. It is switched on/off in the **Quant** column, and it is called *priority quantization*.

Priority Quantization

Priority quantization means placing the notes at certain rhythmic positions corresponding to the quantization parameter (the step of the grid). If you select **Off** in the **Quant** column, you'll be able to position notes wherever you like.

The drum editor provides the musician with a wide range of possibilities. For example, you can make your own drum set with a complex configuration, using several synthesizers or sound cards.

To achieve this, perform the following steps:

1. In the arrangement window:
   - Create a drum track.
   - In the **Chn** column of the track, choose **any**. This setting will allow you to assign any drum to any MIDI port and MIDI channel in the **Drum Edit** window.
2. In the **Drum Edit** window, enter the name of each MIDI instrument into the fields of the **Instrument** column according to the drum map.

The names of MIDI instruments are entered via the keyboard. In the example in Fig. 6.27, these are Drum1, Drum2, and Drum3 (by the number of the MIDI channel).

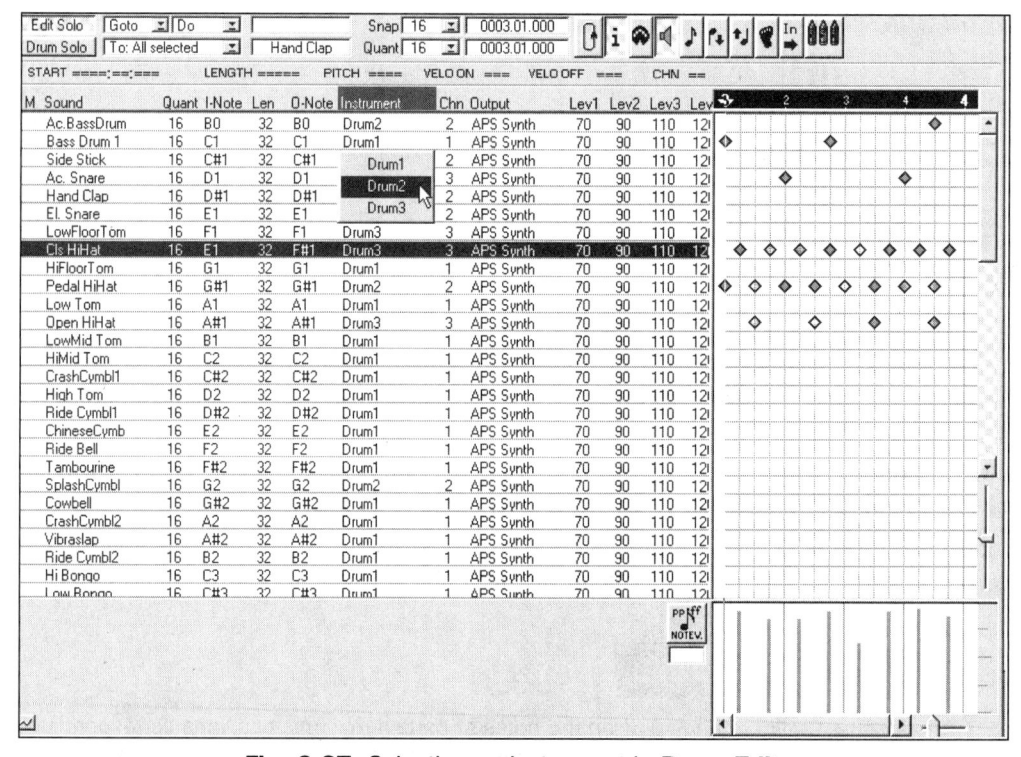

Fig. 6.27. Selecting an instrument in **Drum Edit**

Thus, all the percussion instruments in the **Sound** column can be easily distributed over all the used MIDI channels by just selecting an instrument in the **Instrument** column (Fig. 6.27).

Chapter 6: The Cubase VST 24 Application and Creating "Live" MIDI Sound

Sound vs. Instrument

Let's look at the two terms more closely. They have much in common, but the meaning of "sound" is more narrow. In the user's manual, it is described in the following way: sound (timbre, part, program, patch). To make it simpler, we can say that "sound" means the sound (timbre) emitted by a synthesizer. What we hear can be called a sound, a timbre, a program, a stringed or percussion instrument, a voice, or even a patch (the **Patch** field in the **Inspector** panel in a MIDI track). On the other hand, "instrument" is a concept combining three parameters: the sound proper, a MIDI channel, and a MIDI port.

Let's continue examining the **Drum Edit** window. It can be said that the Drum Track in combination with the **Drum Edit** editor make up a special multitrack (a MIDI multitrack) for percussion.

The **I-Note** and **O-Note** columns (the Input note and the Output note, respectively) allow you to match the standard drum map with a non-standard one of a particular synthesizer.

For sounds not found in the standard GM (General MIDI) set, new percussion instruments are created with new names. For this drum map to be used in the future, it is recommended that you save it in a file with the DRM extension.

Notice that the size of the **Sound** list mustn't exceed 64 drums.

In the **Len** column, the lengths of notes are set, the notes being created with the drumstick.

Entering the Length of a Note

The length of a note is entered in the same fashion as the values in the **Snap** and **Quantize** fields: 4 corresponds to a quarter note, 32 corresponds to a thirty-second note, etc. As a rule, this operation is performed individually for each drum.

If you need to assign the same length to all the notes in the **Len** column, you should enter this parameter while holding the <Alt> key pressed. (Thus, to set the lengths for all the drums to 1/16, you would have to hold down the <Alt> key and specify 16 in any row of the **Len** column.)

Sometimes it is necessary to increase the note length for a certain drum; otherwise its sound might be distorted during playback.

Score Edit

Score Edit is a score editor. It is quite sophisticated, and so a separate file (Score.pdf) is devoted to it in the Cubase VST 24 documentation.

The **Score Edit** editor (Fig. 6.28) is primarily designed for musicians of the traditional (note) school. It allows you to create and print scores.

Users' attitudes towards this editor vary. Often, professional musicians consider it inconvenient; however, others seem to like it.

> **NOTE** First of all, if you enter the **Score** editor (to get there, go to the same place where the other editors are found) and run Cubase, you will definitely notice that the song position cursor is somewhat "nervous", we would say. Perhaps this is a matter of taste. However, also notice that you are able to clearly distinguish the positions of notes in the **Edit**, **List**, and **Drum** editors. They plainly show whether a note is ahead or behind a beat and by how much (so-called outstripping or delay).
>
> Now note the picture below. You may recognize the length of the note, but you'll certainly fail to estimate its delay. In our opinion, the **Score** editor doesn't always represent the real state of things. However, we've met people who cannot do without it.

We're not going to discuss the advantages and disadvantages of **Score Edit**, since it would be beyond the scope of this book. We're just going to concentrate on certain points.

❐ To open the **Score Edit** editor, select a clip and select **Score** from the **Edit** menu. An "empty" clip is created with the **Create Part** item (<Ctrl>+<P>) in the **Structure** menu, or with a double click in the span between the locators in the clips section of the arrangement window. The length of the clip is determined by the distance between the locators. After the "empty" clip is created, you can open **Score Edit** and start to enter notes.

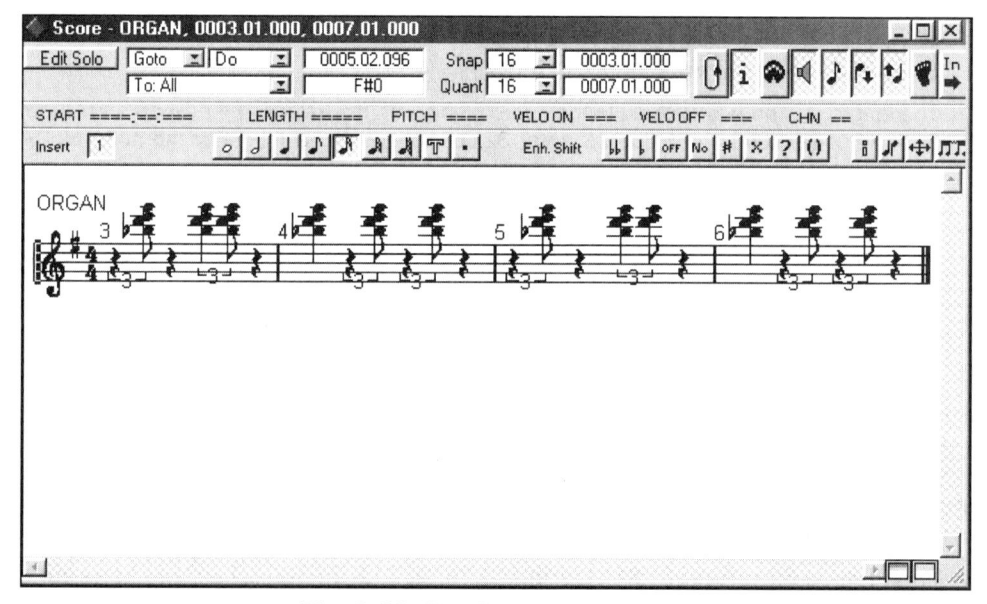

Fig. 6.28. The **Score Edit** window

Chapter 6: The Cubase VST 24 Application and Creating "Live" MIDI Sound 485

- To switch on the **Page Mode**, select the **Page Mode** item from the **Score** menu in the main window. In this mode, you can prepare your score for printing.
- To return to edit mode, select the **Edit Mode** item from the **Score** menu.
- The **MIDI Meaning** window (Fig. 6.29) is a table where musical symbols are matched to two MIDI message parameters. In the **Velocity** and **Length** columns, the corresponding values are set as percentages.
- The **Active** checkbox must be checked. When it is, the dynamic note symbols are converted into MIDI messages. This allows the computer to "read" the score more correctly.

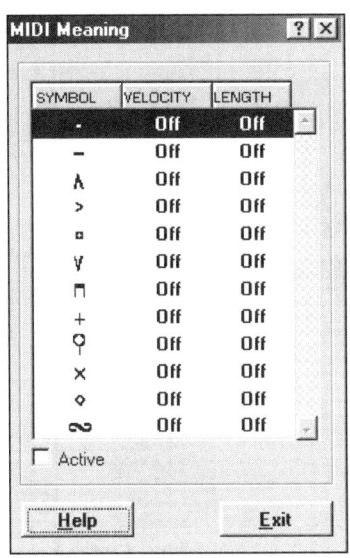

Fig. 6.29. The **MIDI Meaning** window

List Edit

List Edit is an editor for the list of MIDI messages. All the MIDI messages come in the same sequence as they are sent to the MIDI instrument.

The editors examined earlier in this chapter — **Key Edit**, **Drum Edit**, and **Score Edit** — are program modules that translate from the machine language (that is, the MIDI interface) into a language the user can understand.

To open **List Edit**, you must select the clip and then select the **List** item in the **Edit** menu. Alternatively, you can use the <Ctrl>+<G> shortcut. In either case, the window shown in Fig. 6.30 will open.

The **List Edit** window is divided into two sections. The left section is the list of MIDI messages, and the right one displays their graphic representation. Let's look at the window more closely.

❐ The MIDI messages in the list follow from the top down.

❐ The **Start-Pos.** column contains information about the start position of a MIDI message.

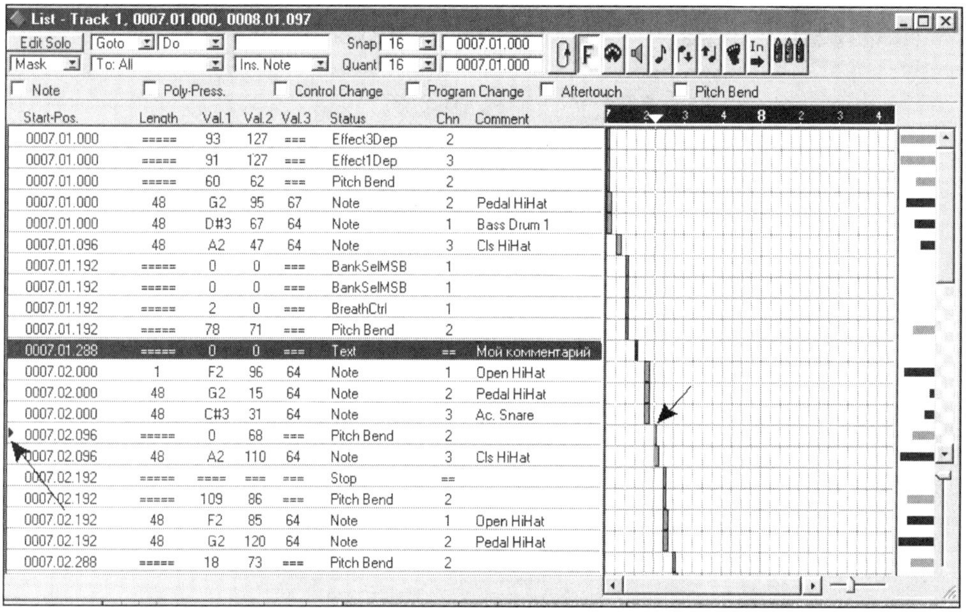

Fig. 6.30. The **List Edit** window

By default, these data are presented in Meter format (Measure:Beat:Tick). However, you can change to Time format (Hours:Minutes:Seconds:Frames) if you wish. Simply click the **Mouse** field found to the right of the **Do** field (Fig. 6.30).

❐ The **Length** column contains the lengths of the notes. This information is measured in ticks and relates only to MIDI messages with the **Note** status.

In Cubase VST 24, each whole note consists of 1536 ticks (a half-note, a quarter note, and an eighth note contain, respectively, 768, 384, and 192 ticks, and so on). The minimum time length of a note is one tick, which is 1/1536 of a whole note.

❐ The **Val.1**, **Val.2**, and **Val.3** columns contain various data, depending on the status of the MIDI message (shown in the **Status** column).

❐ The **Chn** column shows the number of the MIDI channel used to transfer the MIDI message.

Chapter 6: The Cubase VST 24 Application and Creating "Live" MIDI Sound 487

- The **Comment** column contains additional information, for example, the name of a drum instrument (a sound) for **Note** messages of the Drum Track.
- The row in the MIDI list marked with a triangle corresponds to the current cursor position in the graphical section (in Fig. 6.30, this correspondence is indicated by the arrows).
- The MIDI messages themselves (the events) are represented in the graphical section as horizontal bands. Bands of different lengths are MIDI messages with the Note status, the lengths of the bands corresponding to the lengths of the notes. Short bands are all other types of MIDI messages.

The *List Edit* toolbox. The editor of the MIDI message list has the same toolbox as the **Key Edit** editor. For example, using the **Pencil** tool, you can create MIDI messages in the graphical section, change the lengths of notes, and edit the **Velocity** parameter in the right-hand vertical section in the graphical section.

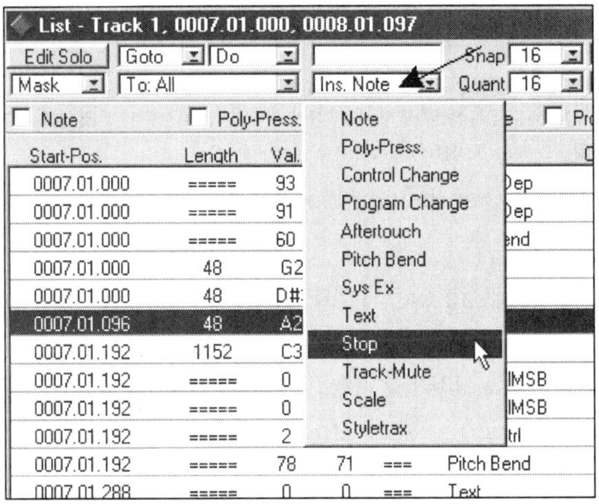

Fig. 6.31. Selecting the type of MIDI message

To create a new MIDI message, proceed as follows:

1. Select the type of the new MIDI message in the **Insert** pop-up menu (opened by clicking the field marked with an arrow in Fig. 6.31).
2. Using the **Pencil** tool, click the point in the graphical section where the new message is to be inserted (Fig. 6.32). After that, a new row with the just-created MIDI message will appear in the list.

It is very easy to delete a MIDI message. Either erase it with the **Eraser** tool in the graphical section, or select the MIDI message in the list by clicking it, and then press the <Del> key.

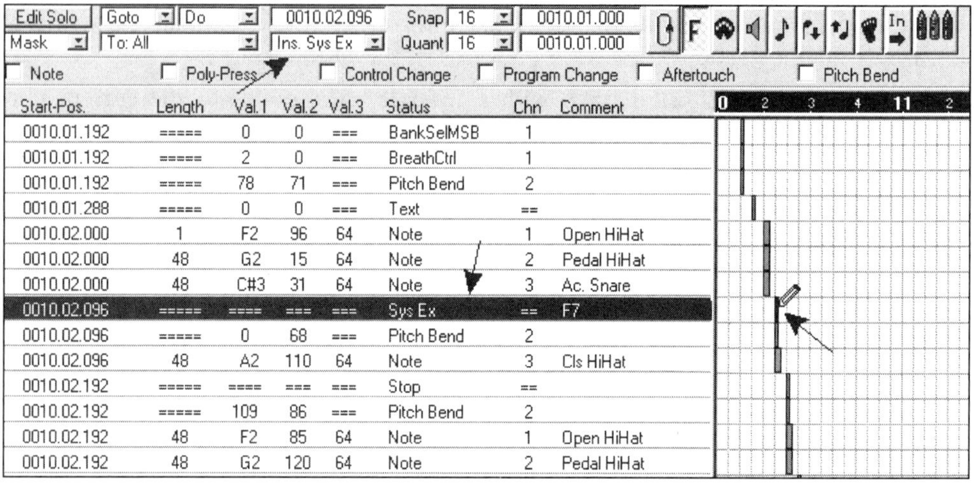

Fig. 6.32. Creating a new MIDI message

Types of MIDI messages. Technically, representing music in the form of a series of commands is a complex task. This is why there are many types of commands (i.e., MIDI messages). We're going to list some of them:

❒ **Note** is a message saying that the note begins.

Parameters:

- **Val.1** — the note's pitch in the MIDI standard.

- **Val.2** (Note On Velocity) — the velocity of emitting the note out (pressing the key), the range of valid values being from 0 to 127.

- **Val.3** (Note Off Velocity) — the velocity of fading the note (releasing the key), the value range being from 0 to 127. It should be noted that in professional synthesizers, the Velocity parameter controls not only the volume of the emitted note, but its timbre as well.

- **Length** — the note length in ticks.

Changing the Values of Parameters

You can change the values of parameters using one of two methods.

The first method: quickly skimming the possible values, select the necessary one. To do so, press the right or left mouse button and hold it down. (Pressing the right mouse button increases the value, while pressing the left one decreases it.)

The second method: enter the new value with the keyboard. First, though, you need to double-click the parameter (thus making the field active), and then you can enter the value.

Chapter 6: The Cubase VST 24 Application and Creating "Live" MIDI Sound

- **Poly-Press (Polyphonic Key Pressure** or **Key Aftertouch)** is a message about the pressure on an individual key (pressure is the force applied to the key after it has been pressed). This message is supported by many synthesizers, but the sound effects may vary.

    Parameters:
    - **Val.1** — the number of the note (the key)
    - **Val.2** — the force of the pressure (ranging from 0 to 127)

- **Control Change** means changing the type and value of the MIDI controller.

    Parameters:
    - **Val.1** — the type of the MIDI controller (0 to 127)
    - **Val.2** — the value of the MIDI controller (0 to 127)

- **Program Change** means changing the program (timbre) of the synthesizer.
    - The only parameter: **Val.1** — the number of the program (1 to 128)

- **Aftertouch** is a message about the average pressure on all the keys.
    - The only parameter: **Val.1** — the force of pressure (0 to 127)

- **Pitch Bend** is a message that means changing the pitch.

    Parameters:
    - **Val.1** — the precise value (0 to 127)
    - **Val.2** — the rough value (0 to 127)

- **Sys Ex** (System Exclusive) is an exclusive system message. It is used to transfer auxiliary information that depends on a specific MIDI device. For example, this message can contain the settings for the whole MIDI synthesizer, such as settings for reverberation and chorus effects, the parameters of synthesis, etc.

    The length of a **Sys Ex** message isn't limited; only the starting and ending markers are defined (F0 and F7, respectively). The device ID is also defined: for example, a Yamaha synthesizer is denoted by 43, a Korg synthesizer is denoted by 42, etc.

    Entering **Sys Ex** codes in **List Edit** can be performed using one of two methods:

- For the first method, you need to create a **Sys Ex** message with the **Pencil**, and then enter the message into the **Comment** field using the keyboard.

- The second, more convenient method is to use the **SysEx Editor** plug-in.

    To do this, you must:
    - Open the **Module Setup** window (Fig. 6.33) by selecting the **Setup** item in the **Module** menu
    - Double-click the **No** field in the **Active** column (in the **SysEx Editor** row)

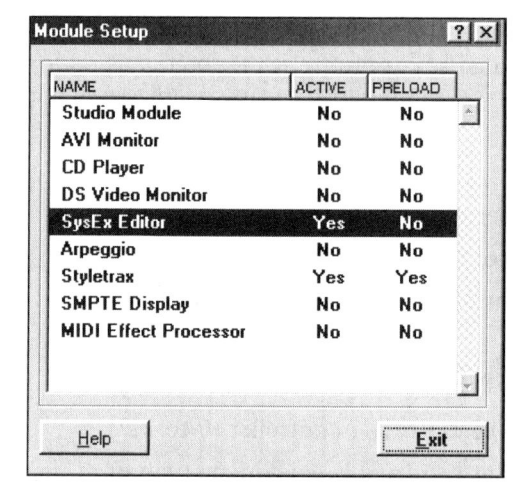

Fig. 6.33. The **Module Setup** window

The **SysEx Editor** plug-in will become active when **No** changes to **Yes**. After that, you need just click the **Comment** field of the Sys Ex message in order to call the **SysEx Editor** plug-in.

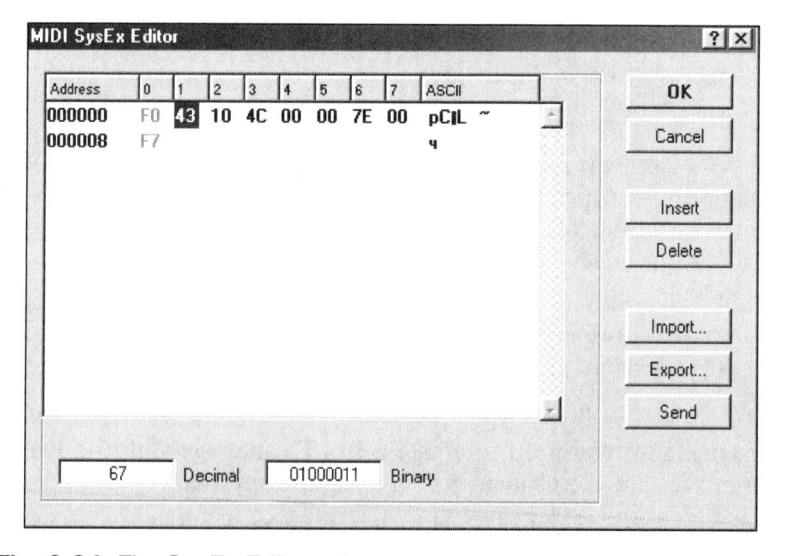

Fig. 6.34. The **SysEx Editor** window for editing MIDI system messages

In Fig. 6.34, you see an example of a **Sys Ex** message for a Yamaha synthesizer. The message can be immediately sent to the synthesizer with the **Send** button, for example, to debug the message code.

Using the **Export** button, it is possible to save the created **SysEx** message in a file with the SYX extension to be able to use it at a later time. The SYX file is loaded into **MIDI SysEx Editor** using the **Import** button.

> *Placing SysEx Messages into the List of MIDI Messages*
>
> Notice that long **SysEx** messages must be placed at the very beginning of the list of MIDI messages. Otherwise, synthesizer failures may occur during transmission of the messages.

Special Messages in Cubase VST 24

Special messages are internal messages of Cubase VST 24. They have no relation to the MIDI interface. We're going to list the most commonly used special messages.

- **Text** — a text comment that can be entered via the keyboard into the **Comment** field (Fig. 6.30).
- **Stop** — a command that stops playback. During playback, the cursor will stop exactly at the MIDI message.
- **Track-Mute** — a command that turns the track off.

  Parameters:
  - **Val.1** — the number of the track (the **Comment** field contains the name of the track)
  - **Val.2** — takes two values: **1** — Mute, **0** — Unmute

- **Scale** — a command that sets the type of scale (tonality, mode).

  Parameters:
  - **Val.1** — the type of scale (major, minor, blues), the name of which is given in the **comment** field
  - **Val.2** — setting the keynote from **C** to **B** by semitones (from 0 to 11)

- **Styletrax** — a command that controls playback of a style track.

  Parameters:
  - **Val.1** — selecting the style of the style track (from 0 to 15)
  - **Val.2** — selecting the variation of the style (from 0 to 127)

"Live" MIDI Recording with Cubase VST 24

Recording Modes

When the programmers at Steinberg were developing Cubase VST 24, they tried to meet as many probable demands of the users as possible. In many respects, they succeeded. For example, very convenient recording modes were created for live performing.

While developing these modes, the programmers took into account that a person recording music with the help of a computer has to combine two somewhat conflicting processes: creative work and fixing the results. In other words, a computer musician has to work with the program, while also being on a "creative quest".

This is why we can say that one of the most important advantages of Cubase VST 24 is the *Cycle Record* mode, which minimizes the number of control operations.

In this chapter, we're going to look at the recording modes for MIDI messages. By musical instruments (sources of MIDI messages), we mean the MIDI synthesizer and the MIDI keyboard.

The *Overdub* Mode

There are buttons on the **Transport** bar designed for switching between modes (Fig. 6.35).

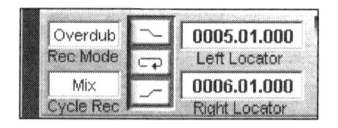

Fig. 6.35. The **Overdub** mode

Every click on the **Rec-Mode** button toggles between the **Overdub** and **Replace** recording modes.

In the **Overdub** mode, you can record new material *over* existing clips, the new MIDI messages being added to the existing ones.

To overdub, proceed as follows:

1. Set the **L** locator at the beginning of the chosen clip.
2. Select the track containing the clip (click the **Track** field).
3. Click the **Record** button (or press the <*> key on the numeric keypad).

In Cubase VST 24, recording always begins at the position of the left locator. However, it begins with a little delay (a few measures) rather than immediately. The delay is set by

Chapter 6: The Cubase VST 24 Application and Creating "Live" MIDI Sound

the user in the **Bars** field (the number of measures) in the **Metronome** window (Fig. 6.36), which is opened by double-clicking the **Click** button in the transport bar.

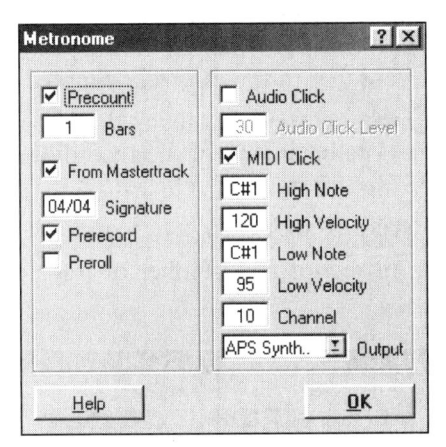

Fig. 6.36. The **Metronome** window

Prior to performing the fragment being recorded, Cubase VST 24 sets the tempo with metronome clicks. The number of clicks is determined by the signature (the **Tempo/Sig** field in the **Transport** bar) and the number of introductory measures (the **Bars** field). For the metronome clicks to be heard, the **Click** button must be in the pressed state.

If you need an introduction before the beginning of the recording, you should check the **Precount** checkbox. Otherwise, recording will begin *at the same time as* the click on the **Record** button.

To begin recording on a weak beat of the measure, you must check the **Prerecord** checkbox.

> **NOTE** Recording will be done while the metronome clicks, and the clip will get longer towards the beginning (to the left of the **L** locator).

The **Preroll** checkbox turns on the mode in which playback begins earlier than the **L** locator specifies. Outpacing is determined by the number of measures specified in the **Bars** field. Recording is switched on when the cursor gets to the position of the **L** locator.

During recording in the **Overdub** mode, the previous recording is heard.

The *Replace* Mode

In the **Replace** mode, the previous recording is deleted, and a new one takes its place. In this mode, the previous recording isn't heard.

The *Punch* Mode

We'd like to remind you that in the **Punch** mode, recording is done in a certain segment of the track without interrupting the playback. There are two ways to record in **Punch** mode in Cubase VST 24. The first is **On the fly**, that is, at any place in the track. The other method is to perform recording in the interval delimited by the **L** and **R** locators.

To record in the **On the fly** mode, you need to click the **Record (Punch In)** button without interrupting the playback. The beginning of the recording will match the cursor position at the moment when the **Record** button is clicked.

To stop recording, click the **Record (Punch Out)** button once again. The playback will go on.

In such a way, it is possible to record any number of fragments without stopping playback (Fig. 6.37).

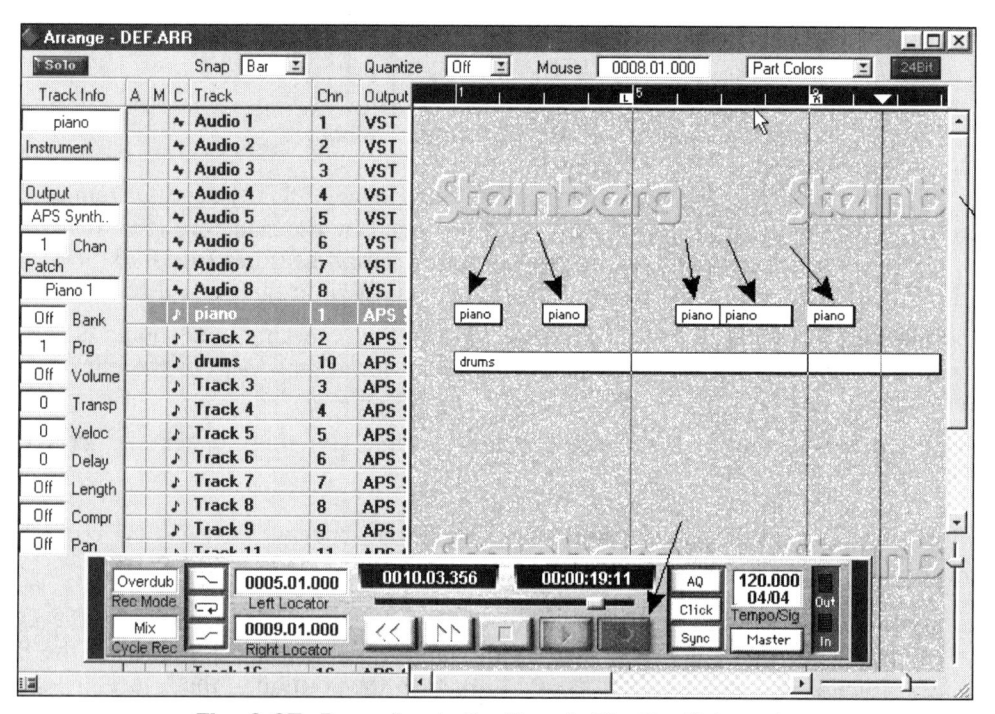

Fig. 6.37. Recording in the **Punch** (**On the fly**) mode

Recording in the **Punch** mode can be done using the **Punch In/Out** buttons (Fig. 6.38).

To record in this mode, proceed as follows:

1. Mark the interval to be recorded with the **L** and **R** locators.
2. Click the **Punch In** and **Punch Out** buttons.

Chapter 6: The Cubase VST 24 Application and Creating "Live" MIDI Sound 495

3. Set the cursor position a little earlier than the position of the **L** locator.
4. Click the **Play** button.

Recording will automatically turn on when the cursor reaches the position of the **L** locator. It will turn off as soon as the cursor reaches the **R** locator.

The **Punch** record mode is used in combination with the **Overdub** or **Replace** mode.

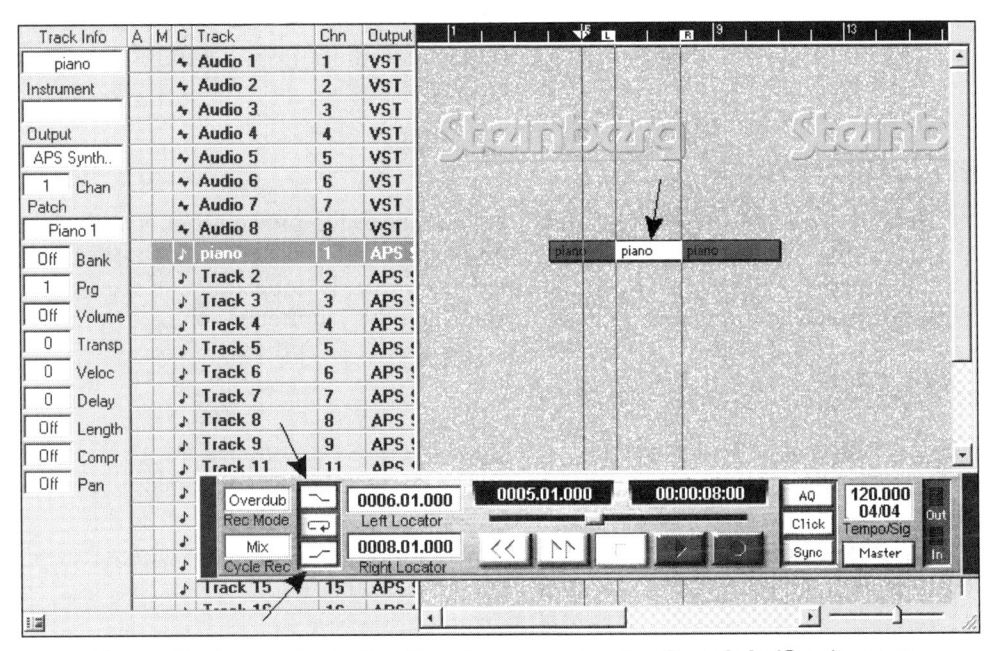

Fig. 6.38. Recording in the **Punch** mode using the **Punch In/Out** buttons

Cycle Record

Cycle Record means recording during continuous (looped) playback. This can be done in three modes — **Mix**, **Punch**, and **Normal** — between the **L** and **R** locators while the **Cycle** button in the **Transport** bar is in the pressed state. You toggle between the modes with the **Cycle Rec** button.

Let's look at the Cycle Record modes more closely.

The *Mix* Mode

In the **Mix** mode, a new record is mixed with the previous ones, all the records being heard simultaneously. Such a method is useful, for example, when recording parts that are technically difficult to perform in a single pass.

The *Punch* Mode

The **Punch** mode allows the user to replace a poorly performed fragment. The mode is somewhat unique in that it erases all the previous recordings. The area between the position where you pressed the first note in this mode up to the position of the **R** locator (that is, up to the end of the fragment) is erased.

The previous recordings are erased in any case, even if only one note has been played!

Thus it is wise to use the **Punch** mode to correct recordings from a certain place to the end of the fragment.

The *Normal* Mode

In the **Normal** mode, each cycle recording totally replaces the previous one if a single note has played during the cycle (at any place of the fragment). During recording in the **Normal** mode, the previous versions aren't played back. If recording is stopped before the end of the cycle, the previous version will be retained, rather than this "shortened" one.

The *Cycle Functions* Menu

The **Cycle Functions** menu is valid for all three cycle record modes: **Mix**, **Punch**, and **Normal**. Using the items in this menu (Fig. 6.39), you can edit a cycle recording on the fly, without stopping it.

To open the **Cycle Functions** menu, you must click the **Cycle Rec** label (without stopping the cycle recording process).

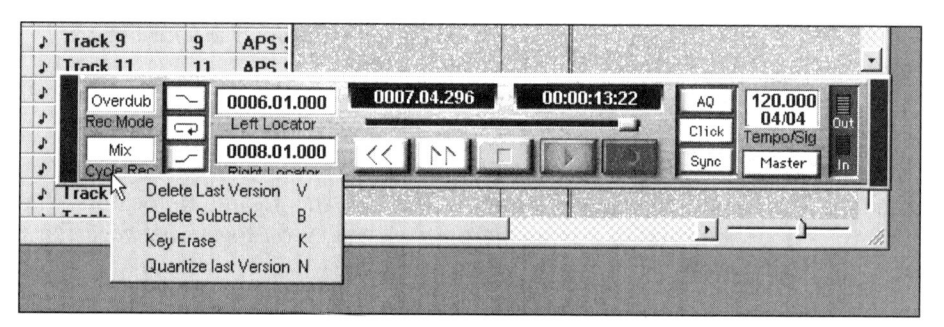

Fig. 6.39. The **Cycle Functions** menu

Here are the items of the **Cycle Functions** menu:

- **Delete Last Version** (<V>) erases the last recording in the cycle, all the previous recordings being retained. This command acts sequentially. In other words, it erases one recording at a time (from the last to the first).

- **Delete SubTrack** (\<B\>) erases all the recordings in the cycle. After you issue this command, you can start recording from the beginning.
- **Key Erase** (\<K\>) erases all notes with the same pitch. It is quite an interesting command, since it allows you to delete all the unwanted notes from the entire fragment. For example, if you wish to erase all the *C* notes of the four-line octave, you should hold down the corresponding key on the MIDI keyboard, and then press the \<K\> key on the computer keyboard or select the **Key Erase** option.
- **Quantize last Version** (\<N\>) quantizes the last recording in the cycle. The quantization parameter is set in the **Quantize** field in the **Arrange** window.

Replace Mode vs. Overdub Mode

If cycle recording is performed over a previously recorded clip, this clip will be entirely replaced by the new recording in the **Replace** mode. However, in the **Overdub** mode, the new recording will be laid down on the original clip.

Switching between Tracks in the Cycle Record Mode

In the Cycle Record mode, you can switch from one track to another. Such switching can be done without interrupting the recording process.

Using this mode, you can perform all the parts of a piece, and they'll be played on the MIDI instrument sequentially — "live", and in real-time mode.

To create a new track, you must double-click on an empty **Track** field.

In the example in Fig. 6.40, four clips were created in continuous Cycle Record mode (this can be seen in the **A** column which shows active tracks). The clip in the tenth track (selected) is "at work" at the moment.

NOTE Notice that in the selected track, the field in the **A** column (indicating whether the track is active or not) is divided into two parts (Fig. 6.40). The upper part reflects the activity of the material being played back from the track, whereas the lower one reflects the activity of the recording channel.

The **Mix** mode is the most convenient one for cycle recording and track switching, since in this mode you can listen to the last (just recorded) version.

If a version appears to be poorly done, it can be immediately deleted with the **Delete Last Version** (\<V\>) command from the **Cycle Functions** menu.

On the other hand, if the version is good, you may proceed to record the next part. To do this, just click the **Track** field of any free track. After that, the clip that was just recorded (with the successful version) will become visible. This means that cycle recording for this track is over, and the result has been fixed.

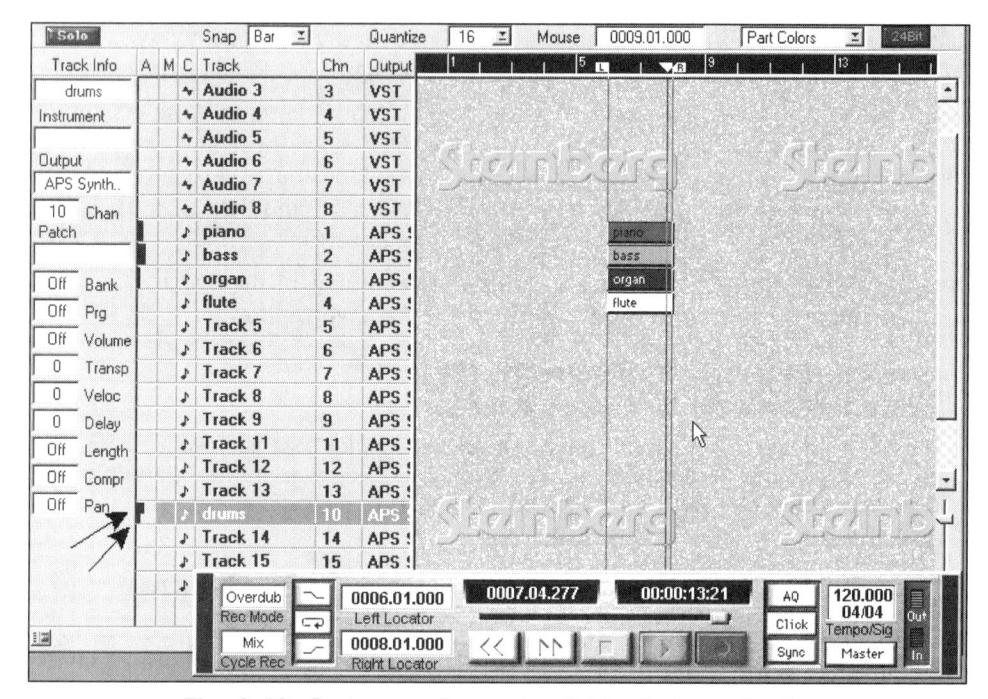

Fig. 6.40. Cycle recording and switching between tracks

You can keep recording in this mode as long as your musical imagination allows you to.

To stop the process in the **Mix** mode, click the **Stop** button in the **Transport** bar. The last recording will then be fixed in the clip.

All clips created using the Cycle Record mode and switching between tracks can be used in various parts of the arrangement. For example, they can be used as building material or as looped pieces for the next recording stages.

Cycle recording and switching between tracks allows the user to quickly create a live MIDI sound for a musical project, since all the parts are performed in real time, and the performer is best protected against mistakes.

How to Record Technically Difficult Parts

Perhaps one of the ways to record technically difficult parts is to slow down the tempo while recording. Unlike step-by-step programming with the **Score Edit** or **Key Edit** editors, this method allows you to obtain a more life-like performance.

Cycle recording while switching between tracks has another advantage. It allows the user to record difficult percussion parts performed on the MIDI keyboard by splitting them into easier parts.

Chapter 6: The Cubase VST 24 Application and Creating "Live" MIDI Sound   499

This method of recording percussion parts is very productive if you need to obtain a "live" sound for the percussion section. However, this requires a good sense of rhythm, as well as certain skills.

MIDI Editing in Cubase VST 24

The Toolbox in the Arrange Window

To perform operations with clips (parts), a special toolbox is provided in the arrangement window (Fig. 6.41). To show this toolbox, you need to right-click on the clips section while keeping the right mouse button pressed. As soon as you release the button, the toolbox will disappear.

To change a tool, you must move the mouse pointer to the desired tool without releasing the right mouse button.

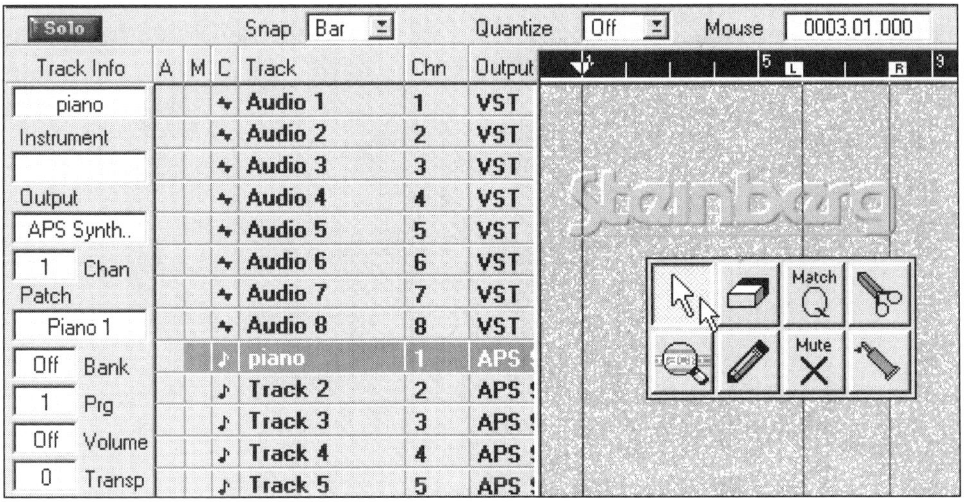

Fig. 6.41. The toolbox in the **Arrange** window

Let's look at the tools in the box more closely (from left to right, upper row first).

❒ The **Arrow** tool is a universal multifunction tool. Using it, you can:
  - Create a track by double-clicking an empty **Track** field (or by selecting the **Create Track** item from the **Structure** menu.
  - Create a clip by double-clicking the selected track in the clips section between the locators (or by selecting the **Create Part** item from the **Structure** menu). In this case, the length of the clip is determined by the distance between the locators.

- Select a clip by clicking it with the left mouse button.
- Unselect a clip by clicking an empty field in the clips section.
- Select multiple clips as follows: while holding down the <Shift> key, click each clip you want to select, one by one.
- Select multiple clips with a box as follows: click at the chosen position and, while holding the left mouse button pressed, drag the mouse pointer down and to the right, so that a box appears (Fig. 6.42).
- Move a clip by dragging it (with the left mouse button pressed) to a new position. To move a group of clips, you must first select the group and then drag any clip in the selected group. Before you release the button, the future position of the clip (or group of clips) will be shown as a rectangle (Fig. 6.43).
- Copy a clip or a group of clips in the same way that you move them, but with the <Alt> key pressed.
- Rename a clip as follows: while holding the <Alt> key pressed, double-click the clip, enter the new name via the keyboard, and press the <Enter> key.
- Create a ghost copy of a clip or a group of clips in the same way that you move them, but with the <Ctrl> key pressed.

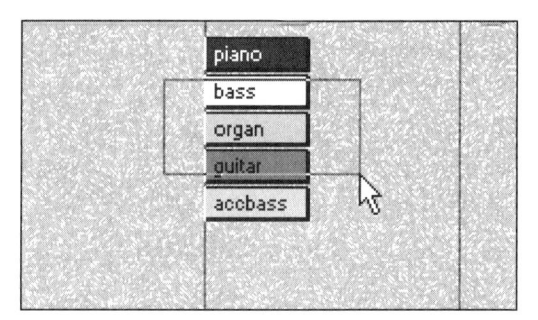

Fig. 6.42. Selecting a group of clips

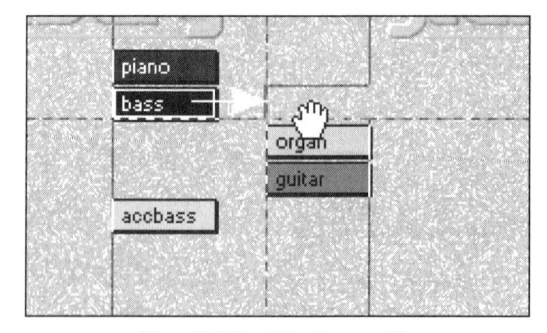

Fig. 6.43. Moving a clip

Chapter 6: The Cubase VST 24 Application and Creating "Live" MIDI Sound

Ghost Copy

A ghost copy of a clip (Fig. 6.44) is a reference to the original clip that contains information as to where the original clip should be played back.

When creating multiple copies of a clip — for example, of a loop fragment — it is better to create ghosts.

Ghosts can be edited in the same manner as original clips. To do this, you should give the correct answer to the question asked when exiting the editor (**Convert Ghost to Normal Part?**) If you answer **Yes**, the ghost will be converted to a normal clip (part), the original clip and all its copies remaining unchanged. If you answer **No**, all the changes will be applied both to the original clip and all its ghosts.

Using ghosts makes editing much easier for two reasons. First, the results of editing one clip are automatically applied to all the other ones. Second, converting a ghost to a normal clip after editing makes it easy to diversify a repeated clip at various places in the arrangement.

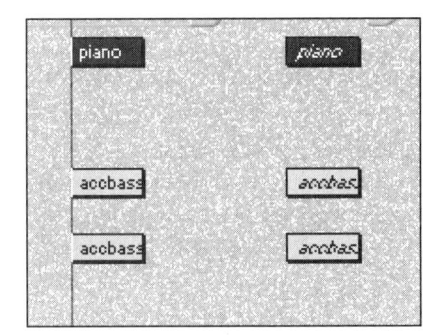

Fig. 6.44. Ghosts of a clip

Ghosts can be created with the **Repeat** command in the **Structure** menu (<Ctrl>+<K>) as shown in Fig. 6.45.

Fig. 6.45. Creating clip copies in the **Repeat selected parts** window

The number of necessary copies is to be specified in the **Number of Copies** field of the **Repeat selected parts** window. To create ghosts, check the **Ghost Copies** checkbox.

In addition to these functions, the **Arrow** tool allows the user to merge clips. Clips are merged by simply placing one over another (Fig. 6.46). If you do it in this manner, it will be easy to separate them.

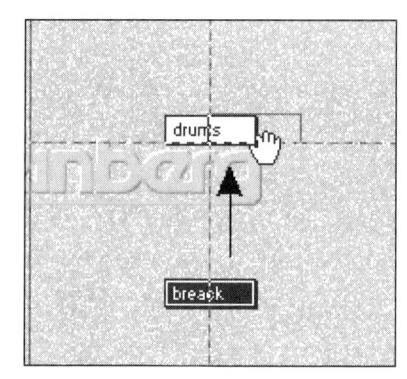

Fig. 6.46. Merging clips

If you overlap clips while holding down the <Ctrl> and <Alt> keys, you'll be able to disjoin the overlapping pieces by just undoing the last operation (select **Edit|Undo**).

❐ The **Eraser** tool is designed for deleting clips. Deleting a single clip is done by clicking it, and deleting a group is done by clicking the group while holding the <Alt> key pressed. Not only the clicked clip will be deleted, but also those to the right of it in the track.

❐ The **Match Q** tool ("Q" stands for "Quantize") is used when it is necessary to quantize a clip based on another one. **Match Q** is one of the main tools used to enliven a "lifeless" computer performance. It will be discussed in detail in the section called "*Quantization in Cubase VST 24*" later in this chapter.

❐ The **Scissors** tool is designed to cut clips. A clip is cut with a single left click.

The interval of movement of the scissors (like that of the cursor in the arrangement window) is specified by a value in the **Snap** field. If the value is equal to one measure (**Bar**), it will be possible to use the scissors only at measure boundaries. If you set the value in **Snap** to 1/4, you will be able to cut the clip only at quarter notes, and so on.

It is definitely not a good idea to switch off the **Snap** field, since any mistakes may impair the synchronization of the clips in the arrangement window.

Using the **Scissors** tool with the <Alt> key pressed allows you to cut a clip into *equal* parts along its entire length. For example, suppose the length of a clip is four measures, and **Snap** is equal to one measure. If you click the scissors at a distance of one measure from the beginning of the clip (with the <Alt> key pressed), this clip will be cut into four equal parts (one measure each), as shown in Fig. 6.47.

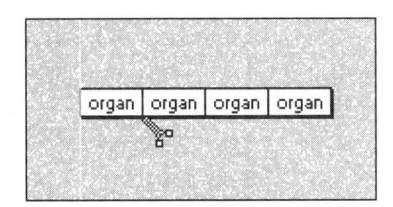

Chapter 6: The Cubase VST 24 Application and Creating "Live" MIDI Sound   503

Fig. 6.47. Using the Scissors tool

❐ The **Magnifying Glass** tool is designed to monitor (listen to) clips.

This instrument's actions are similar to those of the **Scrubbing Mouse Mode** in Samplitude 2496.

Using the **Magnifying Glass** is different for AUDIO clips and MIDI clips.

- To monitor an AUDIO clip, simply set the magnifying glass at the desired position and press the left mouse button.

  Playback will continue until you release the left mouse button.

- To monitor a MIDI clip, you need to move the magnifying glass along the clip while holding the left mouse button pressed. In doing so, you can change the speed and direction of movement. The speed determines the tempo of the playback, and the direction determines whether the playback goes forward or backward.

❐ The **Pencil** tool is used to create clips and change their lengths.

- Creating a clip is done in two steps. First, click with the pencil in the clips section (in an empty space next to the chosen track). Then, while holding the left mouse button pressed, drag the pencil rightward to the desired point.

- A group of clips is created in the same manner as a single clip, but with the <Alt> key pressed. To create a group of clips with ghost copies, the <Ctrl> key must be held pressed.

To change the length of a clip, you must drag the pencil from the end of the clip in the desired direction — left or right — as shown in Fig. 6.48. If this shortens the clip, all the data in the deleted fragment are lost.

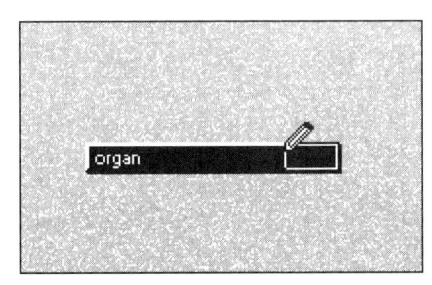

Fig. 6.48. Changing the length of a clip using the **Pencil** tool

- ❑ The **Mute** tool allows you to mute individual clips. To switch off the sound of a clip, you must click it with this tool selected. The next click will switch the sound on. A muted clip changes its color to gray.
- ❑ The **Glue Tube** is designed to glue clips. The gluing of clips is very useful, since it allows the user to free up some computer memory, just as when using ghost copies.
  - Gluing two clips is very easy. Just click one clip with the **Glue Tube** tool. For each click, the clip that is to the right of the current clip will be glued to it (Fig. 6.49).
  - To glue a group of clips found on one track, you must press the <Alt> key and, while holding it pressed, click with the glue tube on the first clip of the group.

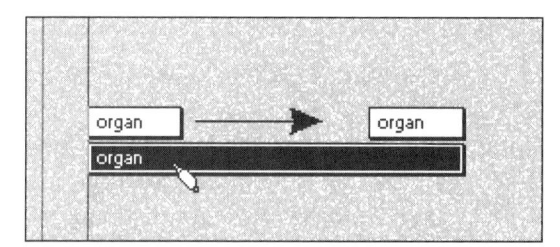

Fig. 6.49. Gluing two clips with the **Glue Tube** tool

The *Undo* Command

In Cubase VST 24, you are only allowed to undo one operation (the last). This is done with the **Undo** command in the **Edit** menu, or with the <Ctrl>+<Z> shortcut.

Undoing only one operation is a somewhat "exotic" feature of Cubase VST 24, and it is a real disadvantage. However, it is compensated to some extent by the ability to edit non-destructively (discussed in the next section).

After undoing, the **Undo** item changes its name to **Redo**. In turn, the **Redo** command undoes the undo. In other words, it allows you to return to the previous variant.

The *Inspector* Panel

The **Inspector** panel is designed for changing the properties (parameters) of clips. The appearance of this panel depends on the type of track. In this section, we're going to examine the **Inspector** panel for MIDI tracks.

In Cubase VST 24, this panel is similar to the object editor in Samplitude 2496.

The **Inspector** panel is opened with a special button located in the lower left corner of the arrangement window (Fig. 6.50).

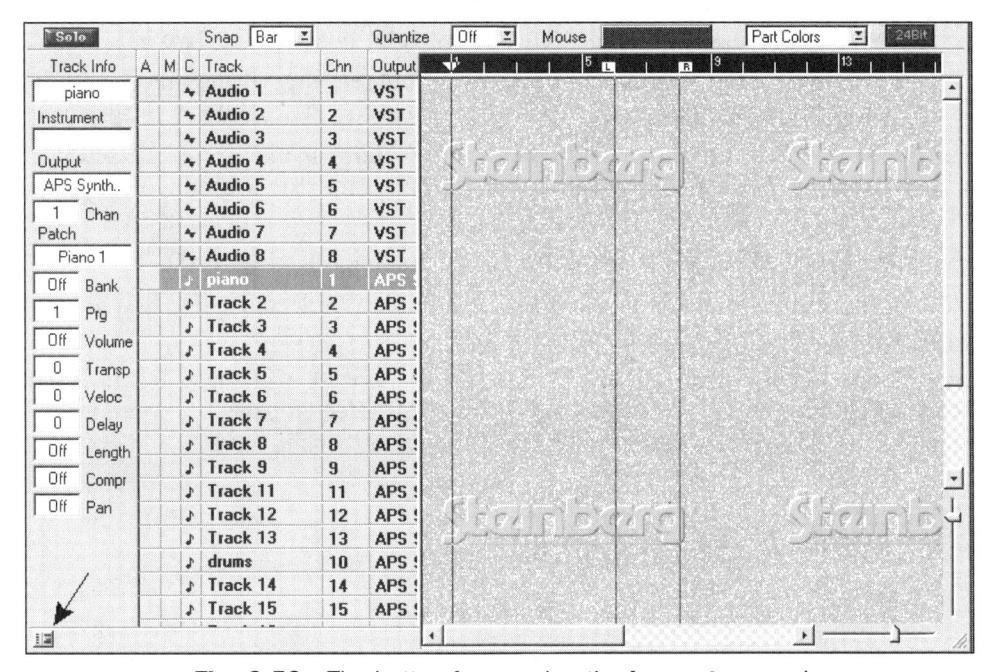

Chapter 6: The Cubase VST 24 Application and Creating "Live" MIDI Sound 505

Fig. 6.50. The button for opening the **Inspector** panel

Non-destructive and destructive MIDI editing. To get a better understanding of the purpose of the **Inspector** panel, we need to introduce such concepts as *non-destructive* and *destructive MIDI editing*.

Non-destructive editing (editing that doesn't destroy the original) is identical both for MIDI and AUDIO. Destructive editing (that does destroy the original) changes AUDIO material for good. However, these changes are not as "dangerous" for MIDI, since the changes in MIDI can in most cases be adjusted manually.

It is non-destructive editing that is done using the **Inspector** panel, since all the parameters of this panel are virtual and easy to change.

If you look at the list of MIDI messages in **Edit List**, you won't notice any commands corresponding to the parameters set in the **Inspector** panel. Of course, Cubase VST 24 does actually generate the appropriate MIDI messages, but they are, so to speak, "behind the scenes". This is why, for example, a note transpose performed with the **Inspector** panel isn't reflected in **Key Edit**.

However, there are cases where settings done in the **Inspector** panel must be destructively fixed in the list of MIDI messages. This may be necessary when a MIDI project is transported to another program, such as when it is exported from Cubase VST 24 to a standard MIDI file (with the MID extension), in order to then be imported into Samplitude 2496.

There are two ways to make the settings in the **Inspector** panel destructive:

❐ Reset the **Leave MIDI File Track Data as is** option, the settings in the **Inspector** panel then being fixed in order to export the project to a MIDI file.

❐ Use the **Freeze Play Parameter** option in the **Functions** menu. Here, the settings will be fixed for the selected clip, a group of selected clips, or a group of clips in the selected track.

Let's look at some features of the **Inspector** panel more closely (Fig. 6.51).

The title of the **Inspector** panel depends on the number of selected clips. It is **Track Info** if no clip is selected, and **Part Info** if at least one clip is selected.

When a group of clips is selected, and at least one parameter is changed in the **Inspector** panel, the program asks the question **Copy value to all selected parts?** If you answer **Yes**, the value of the parameter will be copied to all the selected clips (parts).

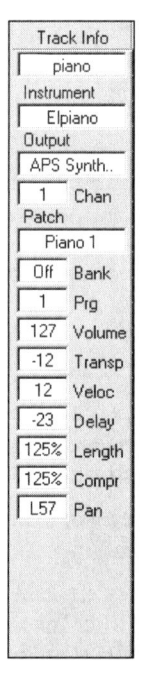

Fig. 6.51. The **Inspector** panel for a MIDI track

The four upper fields — **Track Info**, **Instrument**, **Output**, and **Chan** — correspond to the columns of the arrangement window. You can enter the name of the selected clip in the **Part Info** field.

The **Patch** field is used to select the timbre (program, patch). The value entered into this field is called "sound (timbre, part, program, patch)" in the documentation for Cubase VST 24.

Chapter 6: The Cubase VST 24 Application and Creating "Live" MIDI Sound

The **Bank** field is used to select a timbre bank.

The "GM/GS/XG Editor" mixer. When using a Roland or Yamaha MIDI synthesizer, you can use a virtual mixer — GM/GS/XG Editor — instead of the **Inspector** panel (Fig. 6.52). This mixer is opened with the **GM/GS/XG Editor** command of the **Edit** menu.

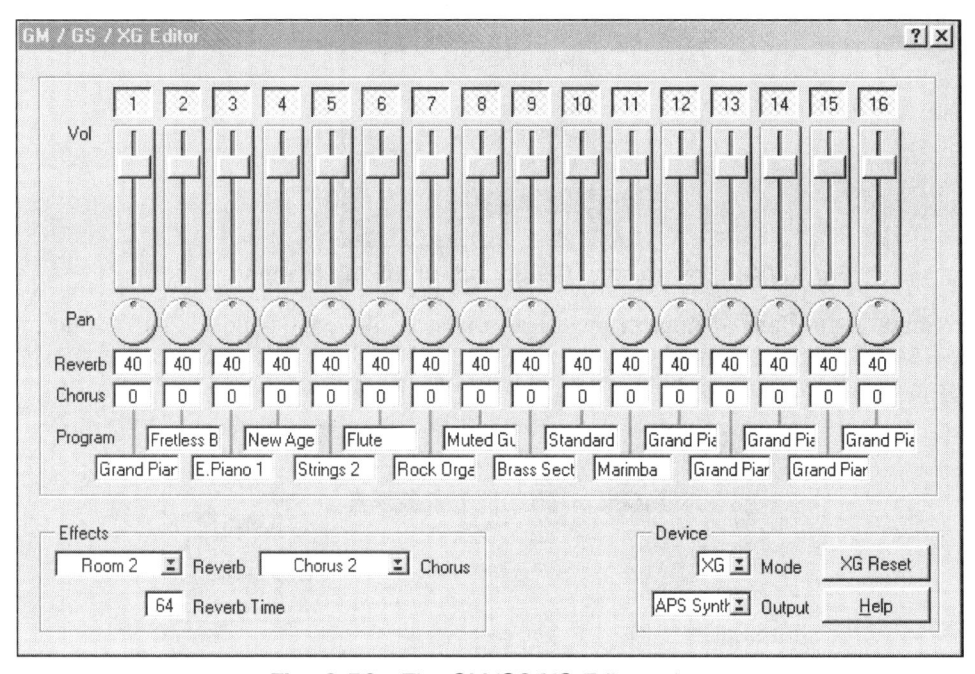

Fig. 6.52. The GM/GS/XG Editor mixer

Let's examine some features of this mixer.

You can select a timbre in the **Program** section, and you can set MIDI specifications in the **Mode** field (the **Device** section). In the GM/GS/XG Editor mixer, you can select one of the three MIDI specifications: GM (General MIDI), GS (General Standard), or XG (Extented General).

The *SoundFont Bank Manager* window. For sound cards supporting SoundFont (such as the SB Live sound card) a feature is provided in Cubase VST 24 that allows you to load individual banks of instruments using the **SoundFont Bank Manager** window.

To open this window, you need to click the **Bank** field in the **Inspector** panel and select **Manage** from the pop-up menu (Fig. 6.53). In the example shown in Fig. 6.53, the GM GS MT standard bank is loaded.

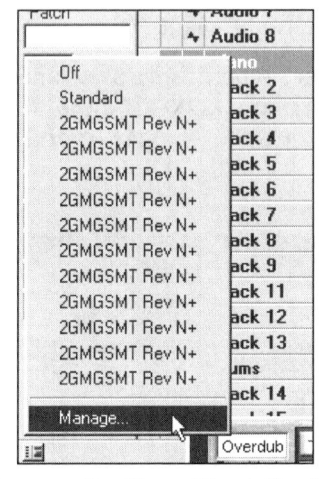

Fig. 6.53. How to open the **SoundFont Bank Manager** window

The **SoundFont Bank Manager** window consists of two panels that contain lists (Fig. 6.54). The lists are **Banks**, a list of the loaded banks, and **Patches**, a list of patches (i.e., timbres) contained in the bank selected in the **Banks** list.

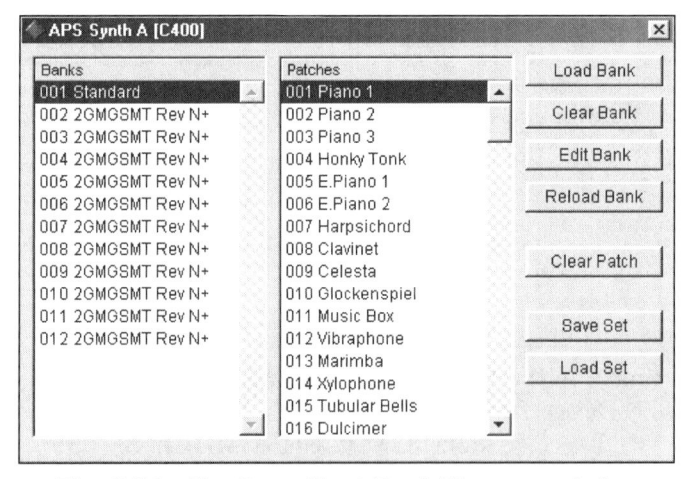

Fig. 6.54. The **SoundFont Bank Manager** window

To view the patches (timbres) of a bank, just select the bank from the **Banks** list by clicking it.

On the right side of the **SoundFont Bank Manager** window, you see a column of buttons. Let's look at them in detail.

❐ **Load Bank**. When you click this button, the **Load SoundFont Bank** window will open (Fig. 6.55). There you can select a sound font bank file with the SF2 extension.

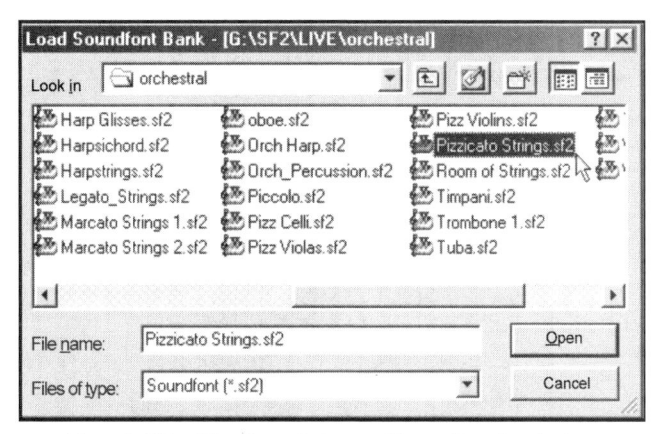

Chapter 6: The Cubase VST 24 Application and Creating "Live" MIDI Sound 509

Fig. 6.55. The **Load SoundFont Bank** window

- **Clear Bank**. To clear (delete) a bank, you must first select it in the **Banks** list, and then click this button.
- **Edit Bank** allows you to edit the selected bank using an external program.

Editing a SoundFont bank

Editing a bank without exiting Cubase VST 24 is a very convenient feature, since you may need to perform "basic" editing on a sound, that is, inside a **SoundFont** bank. This may be useful, for example, when you are working with an arrangement. It is impossible in principle to perform such editing using MIDI messages.

The external program that allows you to edit sounds in a **SoundFont** bank is Vienna SoundFont Studio, developed by Creative Technology Limited. This program must be installed in your computer beforehand. A bank edited with this program must be saved on the hard disk with the **Save** command of the **File** menu. After that, you must reload the bank with the **Reload Bank** button in the **SoundFont Bank Manager** window.

- **Reload Bank** reloads a bank.
- **Clear Patch** deletes the selected patch from the **Patches** list.
- **Save Set** saves the **SoundFont Set** (that is, the list of loaded banks) in a file with the SFC extension. Using **SoundFont Set**, you can later restore the original configuration of the loaded banks corresponding to your MIDI project.
- **Load Set** loads the **SoundFont Set**. Using this button, you can load banks that were previously saved as a **SoundFont Set** list in a file with the SFS extension.

Searching for sf2 Files

Warning! The program doesn't perform an automatic search for SF2 files. This is why files that were deleted, renamed, or moved won't be loaded.

Bank selection. To select a bank after it has been loaded, you must first close the **SoundFont Bank Manager** window and then click the **Bank** field in the **Inspector** panel (Fig. 6.56).

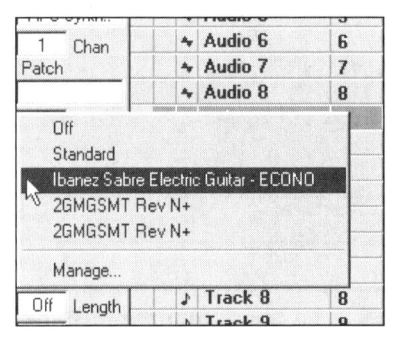

Fig. 6.56. Bank selection

Timbre selection. To select a timbre, you must click the **Patch** field. After that, a list of the timbres comprising the bank will appear (Fig. 6.57). After you select a certain timbre, its name will appear in the **Patch** field.

Let's go on examining the **Inspector** panel for a MIDI track (Fig. 6.51).

❒ The **Prg** (Program) field is designed to switch between the timbres (programs) in the bank. In the example shown in Fig. 6.57, the bank consists of sixteen timbres (programs). The user can switch between them in the **Prg** field just as if switching TV channels (from 1 to 16).

Changing the Patch (Timbre) and the Bank

You can change the patch and the bank for any clip (including ghost copies). This is done in the appropriate fields of the **Inspector** panel. After changing the patch or the bank, the timbre will be automatically switched during playback (when the arrangement cursor crosses the start boundary of the clip).

❒ The **Volume** field is used to set the volume level of a track or a selected clip. The valid range is from 0 to 127.

❒ The **Transp** (Transpose) field is used to virtually change the pitch of a track or a selected clip. The valid range in semitones is from −127 to +127. You can quickly enter the transpose value with the keyboard, using the <Shift>+<O> shortcut.

❒ The **Veloc** (Velocity) field is used to correct dynamics. The value entered into this field is added to all the velocity values of a track or a selected clip. The valid range is from −127 to +127. You can quickly enter the velocity value with the keyboard, using the <Shift>+<V> shortcut.

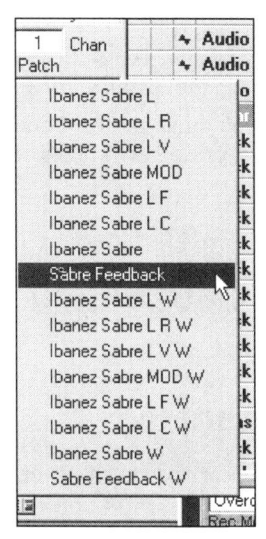

Chapter 6: The Cubase VST 24 Application and Creating "Live" MIDI Sound 511

Fig. 6.57. Timbre selection

Delay and Outpacing Values

The delay value is measured in ticks, the valid range being from −256 to 256. You might remember that the length of a quarter note is 384 ticks. A negative delay value means outpacing, whereas a positive value indicates a delay proper. For example, negative delays can be used to compensate for the response of a "slow" MIDI synthesizer.

- The **Delay** field is used to specify the delay for a MIDI message of a track or a selected clip relative to other clips. You may also use the <Shift>+<D> shortcut.
- The **Length** field is used to virtually change the lengths of notes. To increase the length of a note, click with the right mouse button, and to decrease it, click with the left one. The valid range of values is from 25% (1/4 length) to 200% (notes with double length).
- The **Compr** (compression) field is used to compress the dynamic range. Here, the **Compr** field is used in combination with the **Veloc** field, since the value in the **Compr** field is multiplied by the velocity values of the notes. For example, if the compression value is 50%, all the velocity values will be reduced by half. On the other hand, if compression is 200%, the notes' velocity will be doubled.

Compressing the Dynamic Range

Suppose you are editing a clip that consists just of two notes. The velocity value of one note is 100, and the velocity of the other is 40. If the compression value is 50%, the velocities of the notes will be halved. So their new values will be 50 and 20, respectively. If you then set the **Veloc** field to 70, the new values will be 50+70=120 for the first note and 20+70=90 for the second. In other words, the resulting velocity value will be 120 and 90, instead of 100 and 40. Thus we have compressed the dynamic range.

To extend the dynamic range, you must set the **Compr** field to a value greater than 100%, and the **Veloc** field to negative values. The valid range for the **Compr** field is from 25 to 200%.

- The **Pan** field is used to create MIDI messages for the pan (MIDI controller 10). The valid values are from L1 to L64 (for the left channel), from R1 to R64 (for the right channel), 0 for the center, and Off, which means that control from the **Inspector** panel is switched off.

Editing the Arrangement

The process of creating music always consists of several stages. First, the composer creates the main musical themes, the fragments of the future piece of music. In doing this, many versions of the same musical element can appear. Then, the composer "combines" the created material into a piece of music, writes missing fragments, and links them together.

Composers in the "pre-computer" era had to do this either in their mind or on sheets of paper laid out in the required order (sometimes all over the room).

Today, it is possible to create different versions of individual fragments and try out the whole composition at the arrangement editing stage. This is easy and convenient, and you can listen to all of the changes in real time.

Before, a composer had to imagine the sound of every instrument both individually and in a group. To achieve this, he or she had to develop an inner sense for music, for example, by listening to a symphonic orchestra while reading the score.

Now, the computer can play music of any level of complexity, simulating any instruments. It doesn't even need time to study the score.

Of course, the opportunity of using the computer to model a musical composition doesn't let a real musician off the hook — he or she still has to develop an inner sense for music. The computer is just a tool. It doesn't replace the composer, but rather complements him or her, thus speeding up the process of creating music significantly.

Let's examine the possibilities that Cubase VST 24 provides for creating variations on musical parts and for combining them.

In this application, a musical project has a three-level structure.

- The upper level, Tracks
- The middle level, Parts (the clips on the tracks)
- The lower level, Events (that include all the musical information)

Chapter 6: The Cubase VST 24 Application and Creating "Live" MIDI Sound 513

As we said before, there can be up to sixteen arrangements in a single song project.

The Group Track. Clips can be grouped together. Grouping allows you to make several arrangements simultaneously, and to edit your project at the upper level. You can use up to sixty-four groups in a single song. A special track of the Group Track class is designed for groups. The groups located in this track are virtually transposed using the **Inspector** panel.

When required, a group can be unpacked back into the tracks and clips it consists of. To do this, you must first select the clip in the group track, and then select the **Unpack Group** item in the **Structure** menu.

Creating a Group. Let's consider an example of how groups are created and used in related AUDIO and MIDI arrangements.

Suppose we need to record an AUDIO arrangement after we have created a MIDI one.

If we plan to create many tracks for AUDIO and to save lots of versions, it is better to open the AUDIO component of the project in a separate arrangement window.

To create a group and convert a MIDI project to AUDIO, proceed as follows:

1. Select the clips in the MIDI arrangement window (the **Select All** command in the **Edit|Select** menu, or the <Ctrl>+<A> shortcut).

2. Build a group out of the selected clips (the **Build Group** command in the **Structure** menu, or the <Ctrl>+<U> shortcut).

3. In the opened **Build Group** window, give a name to the newly created group and click the **New** button.

The group has now been created.

Let's look at the buttons in the **Build Group** window (Fig. 6.58): **New** creates a new group, **Replace** replaces the previous contents of the group, and **Add to** adds new information to the group.

Now we need to create a new (empty) arrangement (the **New Arrangement** command in the **File** menu, or the <Ctrl>+<N> shortcut). In this new arrangement window, we should create a group track. To do this:

1. Create a MIDI track (double-click the **Track** field)

2. Change the class of the track to Group Track (click the **C** field).

After the group track is created, drag the name of the group from the group list (common to all arrangements) to the clips' section (Fig. 6.59).

At this stage, you can create AUDIO tracks and record in the new arrangement window. Notice that the MIDI material in the group takes up much less space than before (Figs. 6.60 and 6.58).

514 Live Music on Your PC

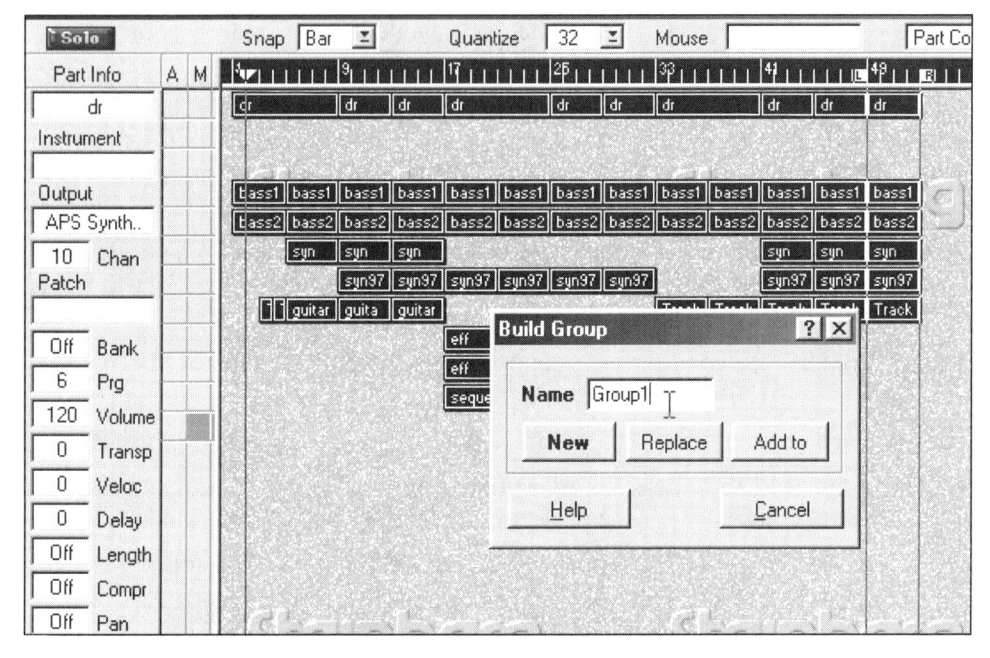

Fig. 6.58. Building a group out of selected clips

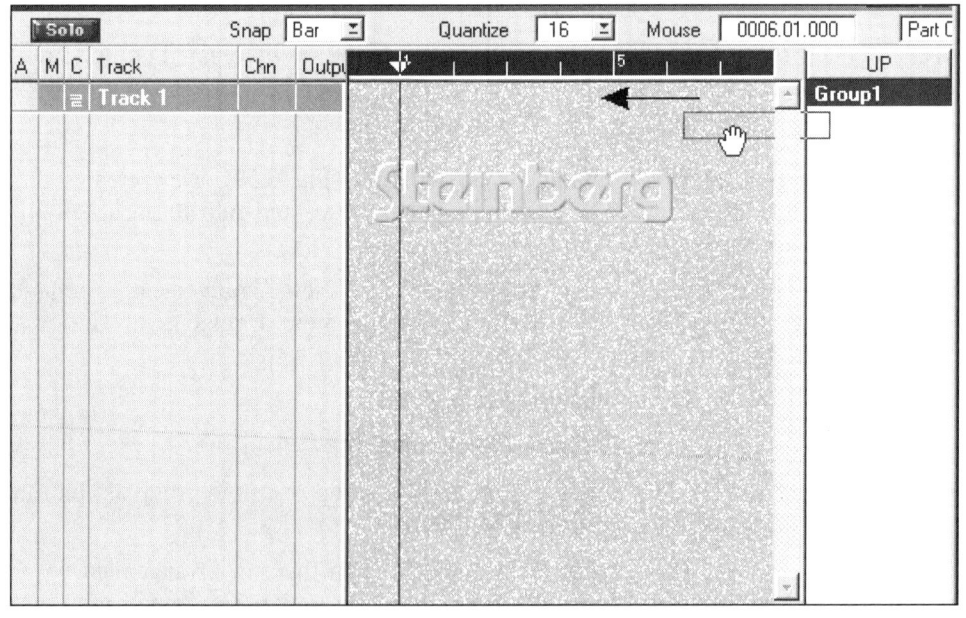

Fig. 6.59. Dragging the group to a new track

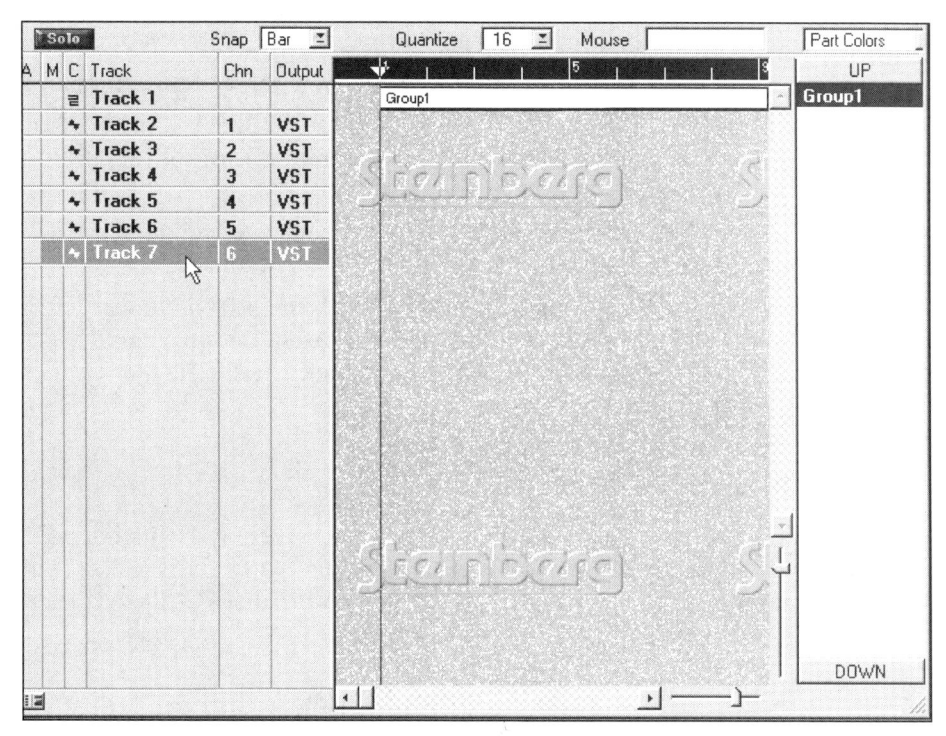

Chapter 6: The Cubase VST 24 Application and Creating "Live" MIDI Sound 515

Fig. 6.60. Preparing an arrangement for an AUDIO recording

The suggested procedure is useful when converting a project from MIDI to AUDIO. To do this, you must first click the **Solo** button in the MIDI arrangement window. While the button remains pressed, select all the tracks in the MIDI window one by one, and re-record them individually to the AUDIO arrangement window.

Unpacking a Group. If you wish, you may unpack a group back into the tracks and clips it consists of. To do this, proceed as follows:

1. Select the clip in the group track.
2. Select the **Unpack Group** item from the **Structure** menu.

The Peculiarities of Working with Groups. Let's look at some more peculiarities of working with groups.

❐ If you mute a clip contained in the group (with the **Mute** tool), it won't be heard in the group either.

❐ If you mute a track with a clip from the group, this will also have an effect on the overall sound of the group.

❐ If a clip from the group is moved within one track, it won't have any effect on its playback in the group.

- To delete a group from the list, simply drag it beyond the list, upwards or downwards.
- If a group track is located in another arrangement, you must set the tempo of this arrangement equal to that of the original arrangement.
- The position of the cursor and the locators are synchronized for all the arrangement windows.
- You can switch between the arrangement windows without interrupting playback using the **Windows|Arrangements** menu (or the <Ctrl>+<Tab> shortcut).
- You can hide the arrangement window. To do so, click the x in the upper left corner of the arrangement window, and then click the **Set Aside** button after the program asks **Do you want to save this arrangement?** You can access the hidden arrangement using the **Windows|Arrangements** menu.

The *Transpose/Velocity* Module

This is another tool used to create variations that should probably be mentioned when speaking about creating different versions of arrangement parts. It is called with the command of the same name in the **Functions** menu or with the <Ctrl>+<H> shortcut (Fig. 6.61).

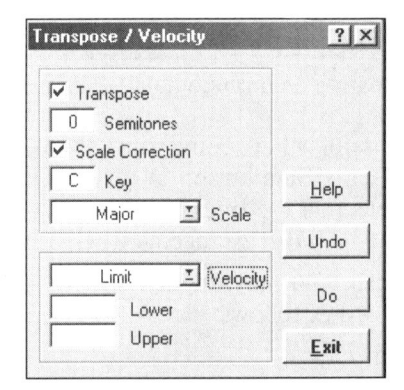

Fig. 6.61. The **Transpose/Velocity** window

The **Transpose/Velocity** window consists of two sections. The upper section is for transposition, and the lower one is for changing the Velocity parameter.

If only the **Transpose** checkbox is selected, the module performs simple transposition by the number of semitones specified in the **Semitones** field.

To switch off changes to the Velocity parameter, select **None** in the **Velocity** drop-down list.

The **Scale Correction** function of this module is of prime interest for us.

Chapter 6: The Cubase VST 24 Application and Creating "Live" MIDI Sound

Mode, Key, and Keynote

In order that readers unfamiliar with the basics of music theory understand the following material, we now have to discuss some musical concepts. We'll try to make this information as simple and clear to everyone as possible.

Imagine a simple melody (such as "Twinkle, Twinkle, Little Star") without the last note. Even a person who doesn't know this melody will feel that it has been interrupted untimely. Moreover, he or she will likely be able to guess the very note that ends the melody.

This is due to the fact that the modern musical system presents us with a special set of sounds that are in a certain relation to each other. Some of the sounds are stable (the melody, so to speak, is based on them). The unstable sounds are attracted to the stable ones. In most cases, the next to last sound is attracted to the last, which is the most stable. This is why we can feel how a melody should end.

The system specifying the relations between stable and unstable sounds is called a modal system.

There are many kinds of modal systems. Even if you don't know their names, you can distinguish by ear between melodies performed in different modes: between an Oriental melody and a European one, or between a merry melody and a sad one.

A mode can consist of a various number of notes (degrees), and the distance between them can also vary (a tone, a semitone). However, the sequence of degrees in each mode is strictly determined and cannot change. The attraction between stable and unstable sounds is also constant.

To understand the algorithm of mode quantization (scale correction), it is important to be aware that the computer treats mode as a set of rules and rigorously follows them. If you play an "incorrect" note (that is, one beyond the mode), your computer will correct (quantize) it. In other words, it will replace the note with the nearest one that is in the mode specified.

The most common modes are *major* and *minor*. We can easily distinguish the difference if the same melody is played in the major and the minor mode. In the first case, the melody sounds happy, in the second case it is sad. (By the way, such "switching" is done easily using Scale Correction.)

A mode can be built from any note. If a mode is "secured" to a certain note, the mode is called *a key* (or *tonality*). The first degree of a key is called the *keynote* (*tonic*). The keynote is the most stable sound of the key.

The name of a key comes from the keynote from which the mode is built, and the name of the mode. For example, the key of *C major* is the major mode built from the *C* note, whereas the key of *A minor* is the minor mode built from the *A* note.

The sequence of the sounds of a mode from the key-note to the key-note of the next octave is called a *scale*.

Quantization

Quantization means that notes recorded during a "live" performance are automatically moved to more precise positions. These positions are determined either from the standpoint of the rhythm or from that of the pitch (scale correction). During scale correction, notes that don't match the degrees of the mode for one reason or other are moved to the correct degrees.

Having gained this new knowledge, you can continue to examine the **Transpose/Velocity** window. And so now we know that changing the mode and the keynote in Cubase VST 24 is called Scale Correction.

If you click the **Scale** drop-down list, you'll see a list of the modes offered by the module (Fig. 6.62). Here, "Major" means major, "Harm. Minor" means harmonic minor, and so on, up to "No Scale", meaning all notes are allowed. The keynote (tonic) is set in the **Key** field.

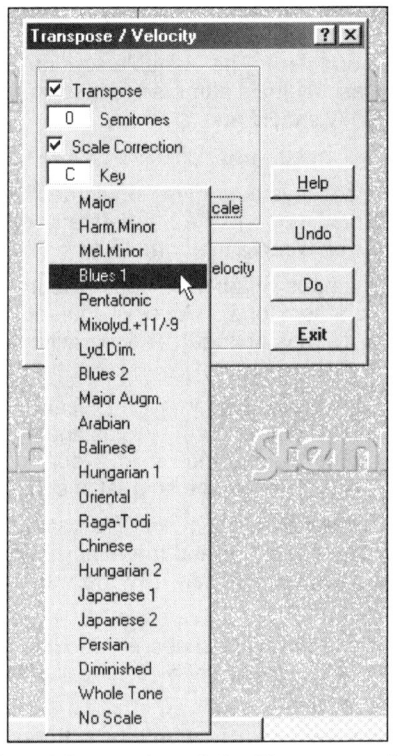

Fig. 6.62. The list of the modes of the **Transpose/Velocity** module

To change the mode and keynote, proceed as follows:

1. Select the desired clip or group of clips in the arrangement window.
2. Specify the keynote in the **Key** field.
3. Select the mode from the **Scale** drop-down list.
4. Click the **Do** button.

After that, all the notes of all the selected clips will move to new positions according to the selected mode and keynote. In other words, Scale Correction will be performed.

Warning: Only One Undo!

When using **Scale Correction**, you must be aware of the fact that this operation allows only one undo. Therefore, if you change the material repeatedly, you won't be able to return to the original version.

To undo quantization, click the **Undo** button, and its label will then change to **Redo**. The next click on this button will redo the quantization.

You can apply scale correction not only to whole clips, but to their fragments as well. To cut a clip into fragments and glue these fragments together, use the **Scissors** and **Glue Tube** tools. These new fragments can be used to make up the final version of the composition.

Scale Correction and "Traditional" Harmony

Here is another theoretical digression. Scale correction is a powerful and rather complex tool of Cubase VST 24. Of course, if you like, you may use it by intuitively "groping" your way around. Perhaps you'll have some interesting results. But in our opinion, only those who understand the basic laws of musical harmony are able to appreciate all the advantages of this function.

It is well known that the basis for a good musical composition is in the combination of diversity, sense of proportion, and taste. An interesting composition combines not only various rhythmical patterns, diverse melodies, rich facture, and justified instrumentation, but also harmonic development (dynamics) as well.

Every composer has his or her own harmonic language. However, there are common features, and understanding them can be very useful, particularly for novice computer composers.

So, using the **Scale Correction** function, you are able to move musical fragments to other keys. It should be mentioned that changing the key can be done in various time intervals — from several chords to relatively large musical fragments. In the theory of musical harmony, these changes are called *elongation*, or *modulation*. Both terms mean a temporal shift from the main key to other keys. The difference between the two terms is as follows: during modulation to a new key, a new keynote is established (the musical composition is established by its ending), whereas this doesn't happen during elongation.

Modulation is most often used to move to certain keys, for example, to the key of the triad located on the fifth or third degree of the mode or to relative keys. (For triads, see the "*Using Plug-ins*" section later in this chapter.) *Relative keys* are pairs of keys — major and minor — with the same key signatures, such as *C major* and *A minor* (without any key signatures), *F major* and *D minor* (one flat), etc. The keynotes of relative keys are always spaced at a certain distance: three semitones below a major key's keynote is the keynote of its parallel minor key (*C major* and *A minor*).

When changing keys, you should remember that a sharp shift is rarely pleasing to the ear. This is why "manual adjustment" of transitions may be needed (that is, changing some notes or chords with the appropriate editors).

By changing the key or mode of individual fragments with the help of **Scale Correction**, you can create variations on the recorded theme.

To move a clip fragment to another key, cut the clip at the boundaries, select the desired fragment, and then apply the **Scale Correction** function to it.

To conclude, we'd like to encourage you and wish you good luck when working with your "magic wand" — the **Scale Correction** function.

Let's now turn back to the **Transpose/Velocity** module. In the **Velocity** section of the window, you can compress or expand the dynamic range. Here are the available commands and parameters:

- **None** — no action is taken
- **Compress/Expand** — compression or expansion is performed
  - Ratio — the compression/expansion ratio as a percentage. If it is greater than 100%, the dynamic range is expanded; otherwise it is compressed.
  - Center — the central value of Velocity that is the reference point for compression/expansion. This means that if Ratio is greater than 100%, the Velocity values that are greater than center will be increased, while those less than the central value will be decreased.
- **Add/Subtract** — simple addition or subtraction of a constant value specified in the Amount field
- **Limit** — limits the Velocity values within a certain range, whose upper and lower boundaries are set in the **Upper** and **Lower** fields, respectively

Editing Percussion Parts

Many modern synthesizers designed to create computer music contain standard sets of percussion sounds. These sets are included in SoundFont banks.

These standard sets are quite convenient, and the features built into them are enough to solve most musical tasks.

However, there are situations where it is necessary to combine sounds contained in different standard sound sets. In such cases, you have to "assemble" the percussion section by yourself.

Creating a percussion part. In Cubase VST 24, a special Drum Track is provided for this purpose. Let's look at the procedure of creating a percussion part for the popular Sound Blaster Live sound card with the help of the **Drum Edit** editor. The procedure can be split into three stages.

Stage 1

1. In the arrangement window, create four MIDI tracks and assign them to four MIDI channels — from 1 to 4 (Fig. 6.63).
2. Using **SoundFont Bank Manager**, load the four standard banks of percussion instruments: Kit1, Kit2, Kit3, Kit4.
3. Using the **Bank** field of the **Inspector** panel, select the bank for each track, for example Kit1 for the first track, Kit2 for the second, etc.

   In our example, Kit1 to Kit4 contain one program (timbre) each. This is why the first program ("1") is set in the **Prg** field of the **Inspector** panel, and the name of the program appears in the **Patch** field. (In our example, the name of the program coincides with the name of the bank.)
4. Now enter the names of the percussion instrument sets from the keyboard into the **Instrument** column. For the sake of convenience, give them the same names as the banks: Kit1, Kit2, Kit3, Kit4.
5. Create the fifth track (Fig. 6.63), change its class to Drum Track (in the **C** column), and set the **any** value in the **Chn** column.

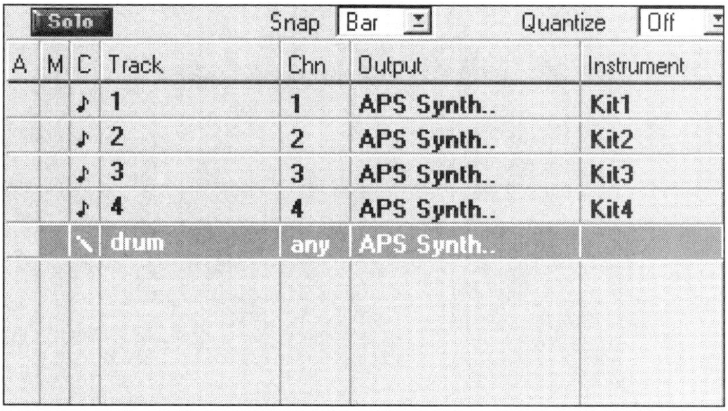

Fig. 6.63. Creating a combined percussion section

6. After that, position the **L** and **R** locators so that they enclose one musical measure.
7. Create a clip by double-clicking between the locators at the Drum Track level, and double-click the clip to open the **Drum Edit** editor.
8. Grab the vertical border between the two sections of the **Drum Edit** window and drag it as far to the right as possible.
9. In the function panel located in the upper part of the editor window, click the button with the speaker icon on it to switch on the listening mode (Fig. 6.64).

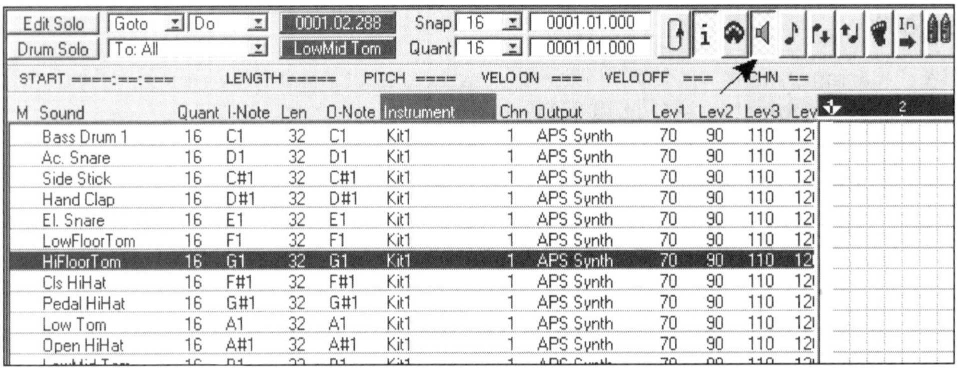

M	Sound	Quant	I-Note	Len	O-Note	Instrument	Chn	Output	Lev1	Lev2	Lev3	Lev
	Bass Drum 1	16	C1	32	C1	Kit1	1	APS Synth	70	90	110	12
	Ac. Snare	16	D1	32	D1	Kit1	1	APS Synth	70	90	110	12
	Side Stick	16	C#1	32	C#1	Kit1	1	APS Synth	70	90	110	12
	Hand Clap	16	D#1	32	D#1	Kit1	1	APS Synth	70	90	110	12
	El. Snare	16	E1	32	E1	Kit1	1	APS Synth	70	90	110	12
	LowFloorTom	16	F1	32	F1	Kit1	1	APS Synth	70	90	110	12
	HiFloorTom	16	G1	32	G1	Kit1	1	APS Synth	70	90	110	12
	Cls HiHat	16	F#1	32	F#1	Kit1	1	APS Synth	70	90	110	12
	Pedal HiHat	16	G#1	32	G#1	Kit1	1	APS Synth	70	90	110	12
	Low Tom	16	A1	32	A1	Kit1	1	APS Synth	70	90	110	12
	Open HiHat	16	A#1	32	A#1	Kit1	1	APS Synth	70	90	110	12

Fig. 6.64. Switching on the listening mode

10. Now you can listen to an instrument in the list after clicking the name of the instrument in the **Sound** column.
11. When in the listening mode, a percussion instrument is selected from the four sets (from Kit1 to Kit4), which in turn are selected in the **Instrument** column (Fig. 6.65).

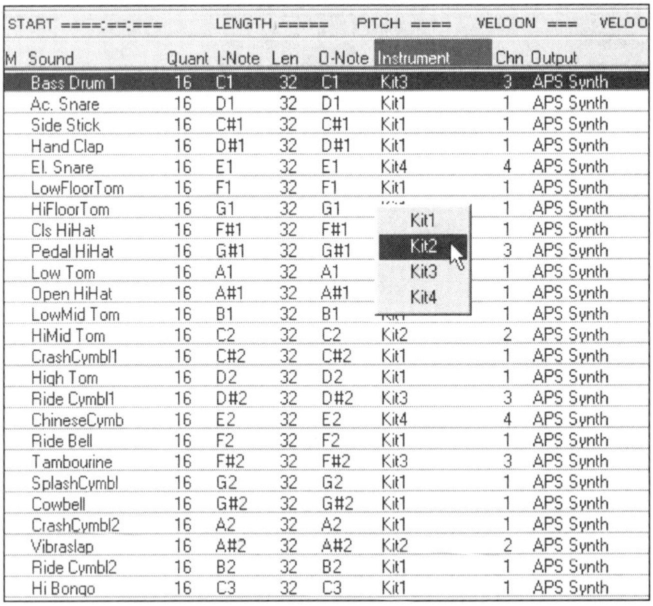

M	Sound	Quant	I-Note	Len	O-Note	Instrument	Chn	Output
	Bass Drum 1	16	C1	32	C1	Kit3	3	APS Synth
	Ac. Snare	16	D1	32	D1	Kit1	1	APS Synth
	Side Stick	16	C#1	32	C#1	Kit1	1	APS Synth
	Hand Clap	16	D#1	32	D#1	Kit1	1	APS Synth
	El. Snare	16	E1	32	E1	Kit4	4	APS Synth
	LowFloorTom	16	F1	32	F1	Kit1	1	APS Synth
	HiFloorTom	16	G1	32	G1		1	APS Synth
	Cls HiHat	16	F#1	32	F#1		1	APS Synth
	Pedal HiHat	16	G#1	32	G#1		3	APS Synth
	Low Tom	16	A1	32	A1		1	APS Synth
	Open HiHat	16	A#1	32	A#1		1	APS Synth
	LowMid Tom	16	B1	32	B1		1	APS Synth
	HiMid Tom	16	C2	32	C2	Kit2	2	APS Synth
	CrashCymbl1	16	C#2	32	C#2	Kit1	1	APS Synth
	High Tom	16	D2	32	D2	Kit1	1	APS Synth
	Ride Cymbl1	16	D#2	32	D#2	Kit3	3	APS Synth
	ChineseCymb	16	E2	32	E2	Kit4	4	APS Synth
	Ride Bell	16	F2	32	F2	Kit1	1	APS Synth
	Tambourine	16	F#2	32	F#2	Kit3	3	APS Synth
	SplashCymbl	16	G2	32	G2	Kit1	1	APS Synth
	Cowbell	16	G#2	32	G#2	Kit1	1	APS Synth
	CrashCymbl2	16	A2	32	A2	Kit1	1	APS Synth
	Vibraslap	16	A#2	32	A#2	Kit2	2	APS Synth
	Ride Cymbl2	16	B2	32	B2	Kit1	1	APS Synth
	Hi Bongo	16	C3	32	C3	Kit1	1	APS Synth

Fig. 6.65. Selecting a percussion set

Thus you can "assemble" the first version of your percussion section. Later, you are sure to introduce some changes when editing the project.

It is better to drag together the percussion instruments used. The "assembled" version of the percussion section can be saved in a separate Drum Map file with the DRM extension. This is done with the **File|Save as** command.

Stage 2

1. Drag the border between the sections of the window to the left so that the **Event display** can be seen (this is a section for percussion notes). Then create a local loop in the same fashion as we did in **Key Edit**. For those not having much experience with the application, we recommend that you set the length of the loop equal to one musical measure.
2. Now turn on the playback.
3. Then select the **Drum Stick** tool and enter the notes (events).

An example is shown in Fig. 6.66.

❐ A single click with the drumstick enters a note, whereas the next click on this note erases it

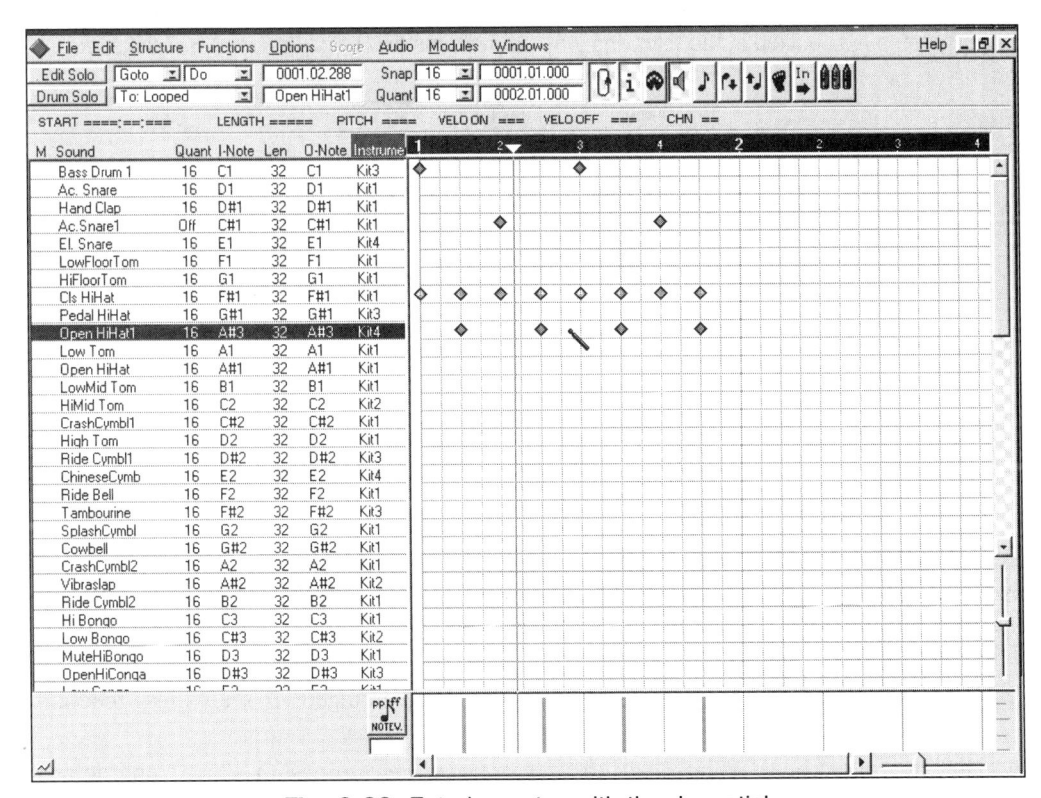

Fig. 6.66. Entering notes with the drumstick

❐ The precision of the notes is determined for each individual row by the value in the **Quant** (Quantize) column

❐ You should remember that each row represents the track of a single instrument

In turn, the **Snap** field specifies the precision level of moving a note to the left or right with the **Arrow** and **Kickers** tools.

However, a percussion part created in such a manner sounds mechanical, that is, lifeless. It is "too correct", since each note is exactly in place. In fact, a human performer never puts beats absolutely evenly. Moreover, every performer has his or her own individual rhythmic deviations.

How can we enliven rhythmic parts and give them a more natural feel? There are several ways of going about the problem.

One method is to shift certain notes with the **Kickers** tool in the special precise **Snap** mode by 2 to 7 ticks (Fig. 6.67).

NOTE We'd like to remind you that every click on a note with the **Kickers** tool shifts the note by one step, equal to the value set in the **Snap** field. The step is specified in the following way: 2pp means two ticks, 7pp means 7 ticks, etc.

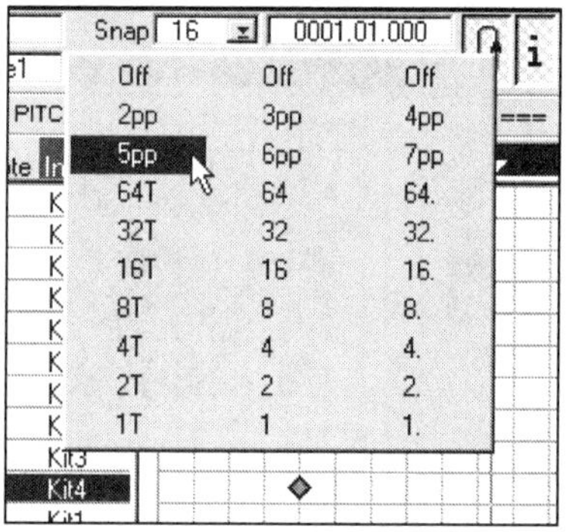

Fig. 6.67. The precise **Snap** modes

Let's consider an example of how the **Snap** mode works.

Turn off the Open Hi Hat 1 instrument by clicking the **M** (Mute) column. Then try to move every other note of the Cls Hi Hat instrument 3 ticks backwards (that is, leftwards) using the **Kickers** tool (Fig. 6.66). After that, hold back the Ac. Snare1 instrument by 4 ticks, and move the second note of the Bass Drum 1 instrument by 4 ticks.

The computer's performance of the percussion part has changed. It seems less mechanical now.

However, not only the starting position of the notes determines the "live" character of a performance, but also the way of emitting the sounds.

Chapter 6: The Cubase VST 24 Application and Creating "Live" MIDI Sound

NOTE Note that the starting position of the selected note is always reflected in the **Start** field of the information bar located under the function bar (Fig. 6.68).

Fig. 6.68. The starting position of a note reflected in the **Start** field

In our example, the problem of emitting sounds is somewhat simplified, since we have confined ourselves to editing the velocity of pressing the keys of a MIDI instrument (or hitting a drum).

In the current stage, we need a MIDI keyboard or a MIDI synthesizer, since the **Key Edit** and **Drum Edit** editors provide the ability of "live" step-by-step recording of the velocity of pressing a key of a MIDI keyboard for every note.

It's very easy to tune **Drum Edit** to receive MIDI messages from the keyboard: just click the **MIDI** and **Velocity On** buttons on the function bar (Fig. 6.69).

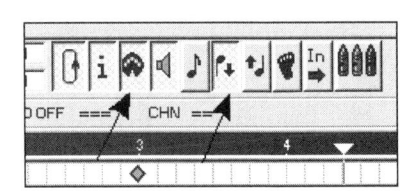

Fig. 6.69. The buttons that switch on the mode for recording the Velocity parameter via the MIDI keyboard.

Next, apply "live" recording to the part of the Open Hi Hat 1 instrument:

1. Turn the instrument on, or in other words, release the **Mute** button.
2. Select the correct row by clicking the name of the percussion instrument.
3. Select the first note in the part by clicking it with the **Arrow** tool.
4. Press a key of the MIDI keyboard four times, with a different force each time.

The rhythm doesn't matter now, since recording is step-by-step. Every time you press a key of the MIDI keyboard, it moves the selection from the current note to the next one. This is why you must press the key as many times as there are notes in the row.

Recording will be performed on the selected row.

> **NOTE** You should choose the key to press on the MIDI keyboard beforehand. Its timbre must correspond to the drum being edited, since it is this sound that will be used in the "performance".

As a result of this procedure, a new graphical representation of Velocity will appear in the MIDI controllers section (the lower one).

After that, you need to select another percussion instrument and repeat the described procedure.

After such "live" step-by-step recording, the notes will differ in their Velocity parameter, and, what is more important, they will match the performing style (Fig. 6.70).

Recall that displaying and editing the Velocity parameter in **Drum Edit** is done for every individual row that corresponds to a percussion instrument. To view Velocity or edit this parameter graphically, just select the corresponding row.

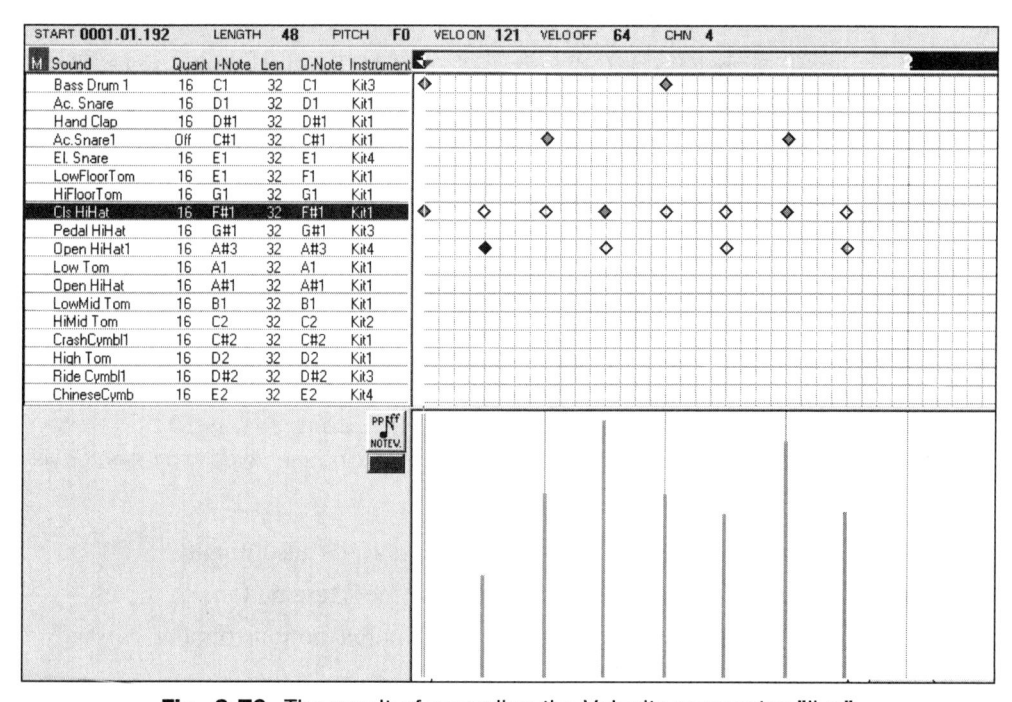

Fig. 6.70. The result of recording the Velocity parameter "live"

It should be mentioned that recording with this method requires certain skills. An inexperienced user probably won't get good results the first time.

However, this method is better than graphically editing haphazardly with the **Pencil** tool or with the **Random Velo** function of the **Functions|Logical** menu, which changes the

Chapter 6: The Cubase VST 24 Application and Creating "Live" MIDI Sound

Velocity values randomly. This method is better because the Velocity values reflect the performer's feelings and style, at least partly.

"Live" recording for the Velocity parameter can be done without interrupting the loop playback. In this case, the recorded values are heard immediately, thus increasing the "fidelity" of the performance. You can also first record the Velocity values and then shift the "enlivened" notes by some number of ticks.

In the described example, the technique was demonstrated on a small fragment one measure long. Obviously, this isn't enough to enliven the whole rhythmic part.

Depending on your musical task, you can write a long and rhythmically complex percussion part, or create many various patterns. In doing so, you should bear in mind that an interesting piece of music doesn't contain mechanically copied fragments.

Even in an extreme case, if you repeat one measure many times and apply "live" Velocity recording to each copy, the overall sound won't be perceived as "wood-pecking", since a human basically cannot exactly repeat even pressing a key (when recording Velocity).

Stage 3

The next stage of editing the percussion part is performed in the arrange window. Here you work at the clip level:

1. Select the clips in the Drum Track and position the locators on the boundaries of the clips using the <Ctrl>+<Alt>+<P> shortcut
2. Select the **Remix** command in the **Structure** menu and mute the Drum Track (Fig. 6.71).

In the Drum Track, every row containing notes will be converted to a separate MIDI track. The **Remix** command must only be performed between the locators.

The **Inspector** panel lets you adjust the volume, compression, and pan.

You can introduce variety if you experiment with delays of individual clips (the Delay parameter), cut the clips and selectively mute the smaller parts, and so on.

> ### A Method of "Enlivening" MIDI Sound
>
> There is a method used to make MIDI sound more "life-like". Copy the clip vertically to an adjacent track (with the same instrument). Then apply Velocity compression while decreasing the values. In other words, set the **Compr** field to 0.25%, the **Veloc** field of the **Inspector** panel to a value from 16 to 30, and the **Delay** field to a value from 2 to 4 ticks.

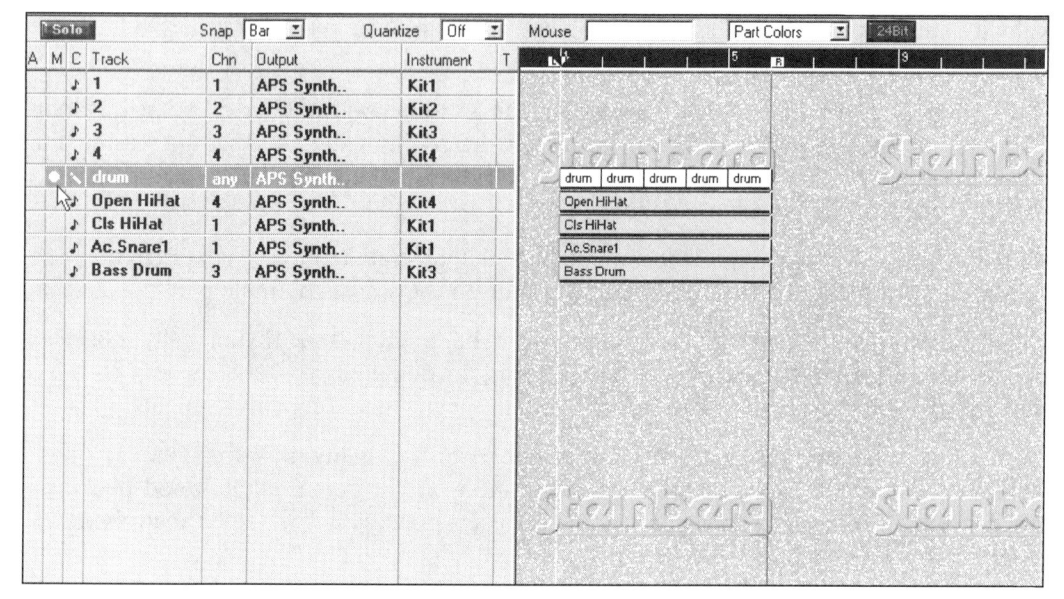

Fig. 6.71. The **Remix** command for the Drum Track

Graphically Editing MIDI Messages

Graphically editing MIDI messages in the **Key Edit** or **Drum Edit** editors is done in the **Controller Display** section found under the **Event Display** section (Figs. 6.72 and 6.73).

The **Controller Display** section can be hidden or unhidden by repeatedly pressing the <Ctrl>+<Alt>+<C> shortcut or by clicking the <~> button (indicated by the arrows in Figs. 6.72 and 6.73). The boundary between the two sections can be dragged up or down with the mouse.

Editing MIDI Messages. Since editing MIDI messages is identical in both editors, we're going to demonstrate it with **Key Edit**.

Prior to editing, you must select the type of MIDI message from the pop-up menu that contains the type names.

This menu is opened by left-clicking the **Data type** button (with the note icon on it, Fig. 6.73) found at the left end of the boundary between the **Controller Display** and the **Event Display** sections. You should bear in mind that the pop-up menu will appear only after a certain delay (Fig. 6.74).

The type of MIDI message is selected with a left click. After that, the icon on the **Data type** button will change in accordance with the type of the MIDI message.

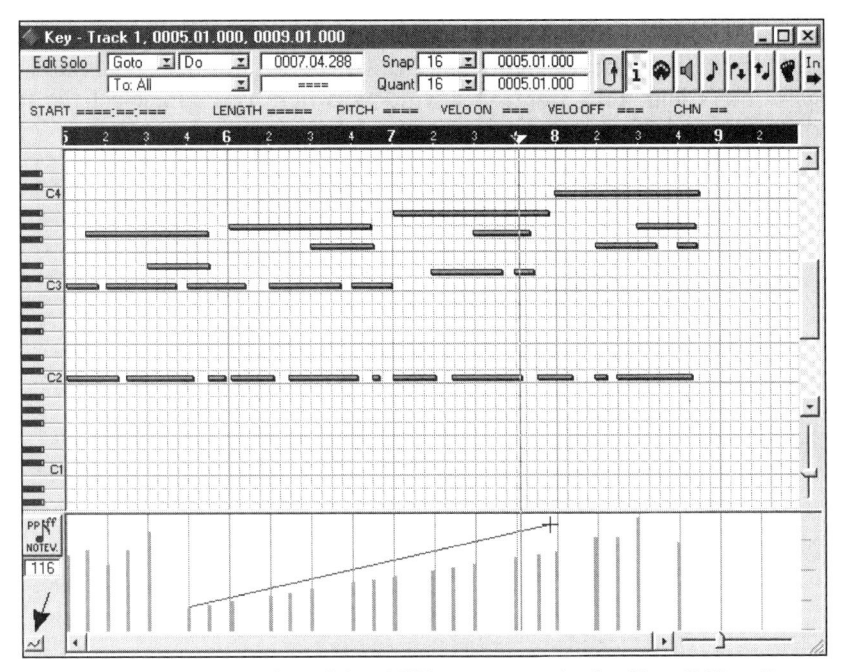

Chapter 6: The Cubase VST 24 Application and Creating "Live" MIDI Sound 529

Fig. 6.72. Graphically editing MIDI messages in the **Key Edit** editor

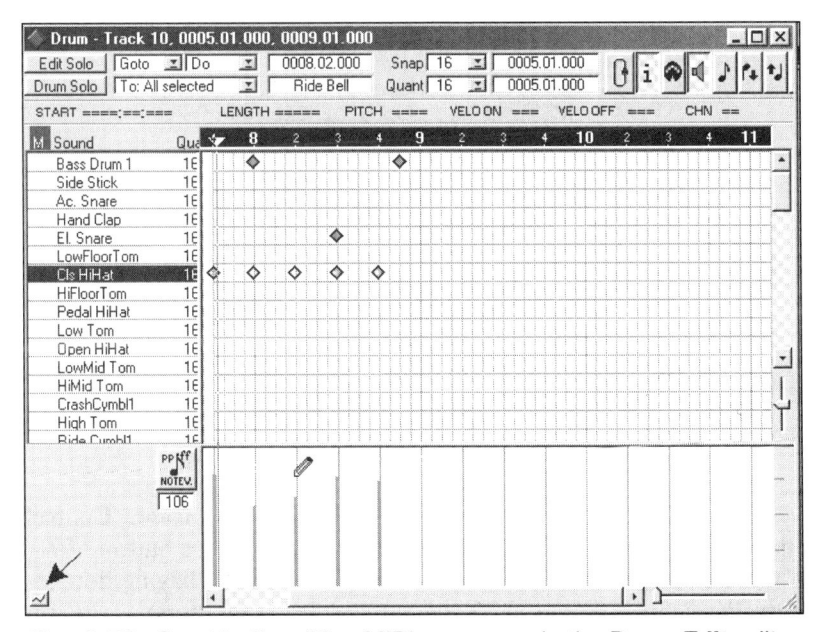

Fig. 6.73. Graphically editing MIDI messages in the **Drum Edit** editor

The pop-up menu contains the standard MIDI messages. To edit messages specific to a certain MIDI device, use the **Unknown Ctrl** (unknown controller) command. Selecting this item opens the **Continuous Controller** window, where you can select the type of the MIDI controller (Fig. 6.75).

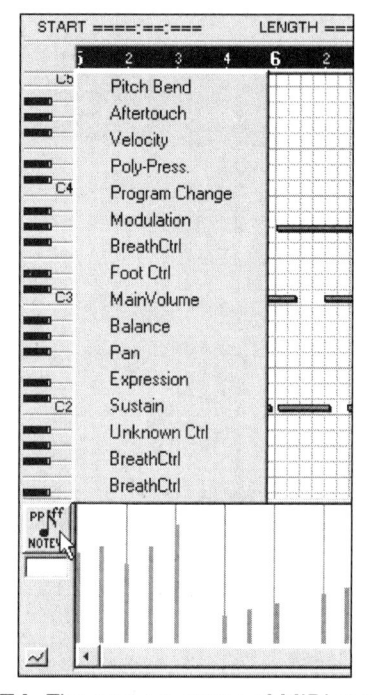

Fig. 6.74. The pop-up menu of MIDI messages

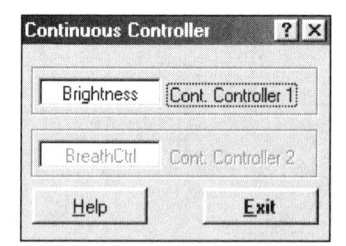

Fig. 6.75. The **Continuous Controller** window

- A list of the MIDI controllers can be obtained in the **Cont. Controller 1** field. For this purpose, you must hold down the left or right mouse button after clicking, or enter the number of the MIDI controller via the keyboard, having double-clicked the **Cont. Controller 1** field. In Fig. 6.75, we entered 74 (Brightness) as the number of the MIDI controller.

Chapter 6: The Cubase VST 24 Application and Creating "Live" MIDI Sound 531

❐ If you want certain MIDI controllers to be in the pop-up menu permanently, you must right-click the **Data type** button.

After that, the **Continuous Controller** window will open, with both the **Cont. Controller 1** and **Cont. Controller 2** fields available. There you'll be able to set two MIDI controller types. The next time you open the pop-up menu, the selected MIDI controllers will be present (Fig. 6.76).

In the example shown in Fig. 6.76, the pop-up menu contains such MIDI controllers as Harmonic Content (71) and Brightness (74). We aren't going to concentrate on this topic any more, since a detailed examination of the features of specific MIDI controllers is beyond the scope of this book.

Changing the Pitch. Let's demonstrate changing the pitch using an example of drawing a Pitch Bend (a diagram of the changes to a MIDI message).

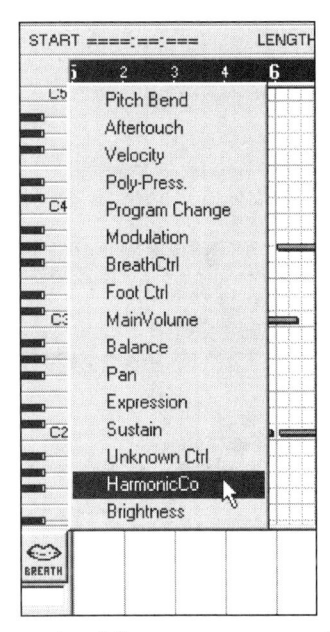

Fig. 6.76. An example of the pop-up menu of MIDI controllers

A linear diagram is drawn with the **Line** tool (Fig. 6.21), whereas a complex one should be drawn with the **Pencil** tool (Fig. 6.77). We'd like to remind you that in **Drum Edit**, the **Drum Stick** tool turns into **Pencil** in the Controller Display.

The position of the drawing tool is reflected in the field located under the **Data Type** button (Fig. 6.77). This position is displayed in units of measurement of the MIDI message parameter.

532 Live Music on Your PC

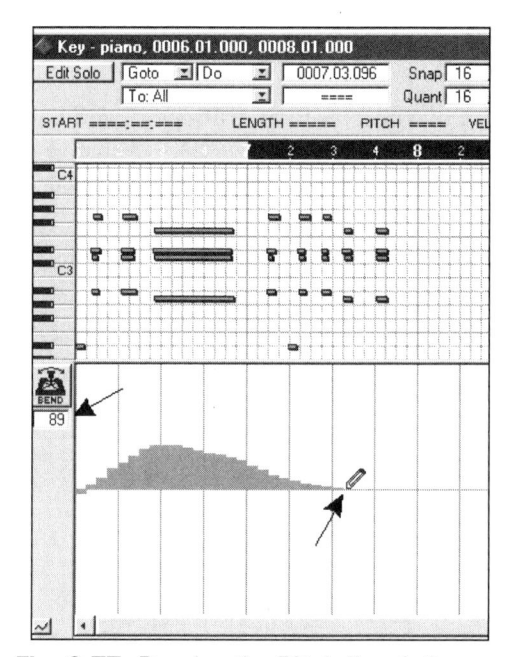

Fig. 6.77. Drawing the **Pitch Bend** diagram

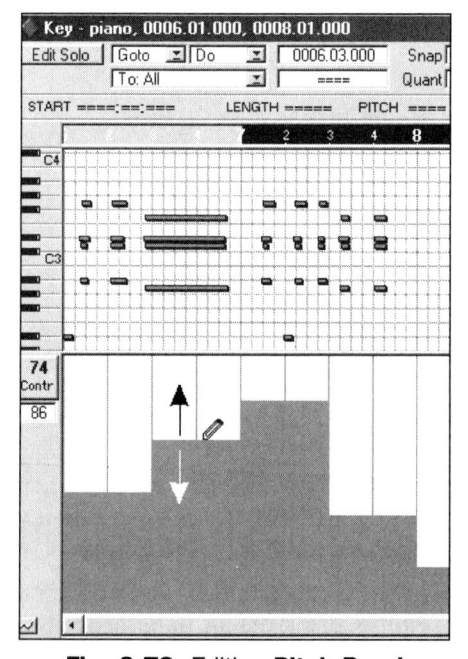

Fig. 6.78. Editing **Pitch Bend**

Chapter 6: The Cubase VST 24 Application and Creating "Live" MIDI Sound 533

The diagram's level of aliasing is specified in the **Snap** field.

To create a new diagram, draw it keeping the <Alt> key pressed. Otherwise, only editing of the existing diagram is possible.

Every bar of the diagram can be dragged up or down with the **Pencil** tool (Fig. 6.78). Unsuccessful attempts to create the diagram can be discarded using the **Eraser** tool.

If the diagram falls beyond the clip being edited, the application will ask, **Keep appended Events?** If you answer **Yes**, the clip will get longer. The same question appears if notes that fall beyond the clip were created in the editor.

Continuous MIDI messages can be deleted with a special command — **Delete Cont. Data** from the **Functions** menu. To do this, you must first select the clip from which you plan to delete a message.

The **Delete Cont. Data** command deletes the following types of MIDI messages: Controllers, Pitch Bend, Channel Pressure, and Poly Pressure.

If the MIDI interface is overloaded with continuous MIDI messages, this fact manifests itself in errors, missing notes, etc. In such a case, you can use the **Reduce Cont. Data** command from the **Functions** menu.

Another Technique for "Enlivening" MIDI

Here is another technique used to "enliven" MIDI. It includes applying MIDI messages of the Pitch Bend type to cymbals and Hi Hat parts assigned to different channels. This technique simulates a human performer who occasionally varies the parameters of drumstick hits (the point of the hit, the attack angle, etc). The ear perceives this as minor changes in the pitch of the cymbals and Hi Hat. Using Pitch Bend MIDI messages (with very small deviations in pitch) simulates this component of a live performance.

Step-by-Step Recording

In Cubase VST 24, the mode of step-by-step recording from the MIDI keyboard (MIDI instrument) is done in the **Key Edit**, **Score Edit**, **List Edit**, and **Drum Edit** editors, the procedure being the same in each of them.

Let's demonstrate this with the example of the **Key Edit** editor.

- To switch the editor to the step-by-step recording mode, click the button with the footprint icon on it (Fig. 6.79)
- After that, move the cursor to the desired position and play notes on the MIDI keyboard
- Playing each note moves the cursor by one step

- The length of the recorded notes is determined by the **Quantize** value, and the length of the rest is determined by the **Snap** value
- Recording can be done in several passes, with new notes being superimposed on the previous ones

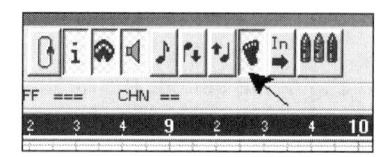

Fig. 6.79. Entering the step-by-step recording mode

The button with the **In** label on it (found to the right of the step-by-step recording button, Fig. 6.79) switches on the insertion mode.

In this mode, the previous recording is shifted to the right. In other words, if a note is played on the MIDI instrument, all the previously recorded notes (that are located to the right of the cursor position) are shifted one note rightward.

The insertion mode also works when drawing notes with the **Pencil** tool. To listen to the notes being created, click the button with the speaker icon on it (Fig. 6.79).

The step-by-step recording mode is convenient when entering technically complex parts from a MIDI instrument. For example, these could be complex solo parts or sequences of chords that are difficult to play quickly. To conclude, we'd like to say that parts recorded step-by-step are basically more "live" than those created with the **Pencil** tool, since "live" values of the Velocity parameter are fixed during step-by-step recording.

Using Plug-ins

To expand the functions of Cubase VST 24, plug-ins are used. Plugging in is done via the **Setup** command in the **Modules** menu.

To install a plug-in, open the **Module Setup** window (Fig. 6.33) and right-click in the **Active** column to change **No** to **Yes**. When you want the plug-in to load automatically at application startup, set **Yes** in the **Preload** column.

In this chapter, we're going to look only at some of the plug-ins, since a full description of the features of Cubase VST 24 is beyond the scope of this book.

The Studio Module Plug-in

This plug-in is designed to read and sustain the setup of a certain MIDI device, usually a professional one.

Chapter 6: The Cubase VST 24 Application and Creating "Live" MIDI Sound 535

Cubase VST 24 uses the concept of MIDI device drivers. The driver library shipped with Cubase VST 24 is continuously updated. Moreover, you can develop your own driver with the Dmaker application (which can be downloaded from **ftp://ftp.steinberg.net**).

A MIDI device driver is a file with the DEV extension. Such files are located in the **StudioModuleDrivers** folder, and sorted by the name of the device manufacturer.

Let's demonstrate the general principles of using the **Studio Module** with an example of the Roland Groovebox MC-505 musical instrument.

First, we have to load the driver for this device.

After the **Studio Module** plug-in is activated, the **Studio Module** submenu appears in the **Modules** menu. In this submenu, select the **Setup** item to open the **Studio Setup** window (Fig. 6.80).

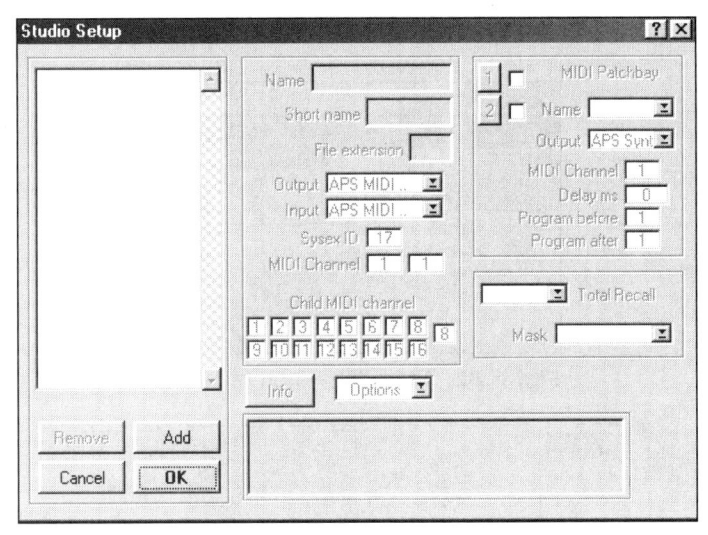

Fig. 6.80. The **Studio Setup** window

Since no driver is loaded yet, the window is inactive. To load the driver, you must click the **Add** button and select the desired file with the DEV extension in the opened window (in Fig. 6.81, this is MC-505.DEV).

After the driver is loaded, click the Roland MC-505 item in the device list and set the I/O of **Studio Module** in the **Input** and **Output** fields. The latter must be set to the output MIDI port of the sound card, and the former must be set to its input MIDI port.

Now activate **Patch Manager** in the **Studio Module** menu, and select, say, the **Patches** item (Fig. 6.82).

In the **Instrument** field of each MIDI track, select the new **Roland MC-505** instrument (Fig. 6.83).

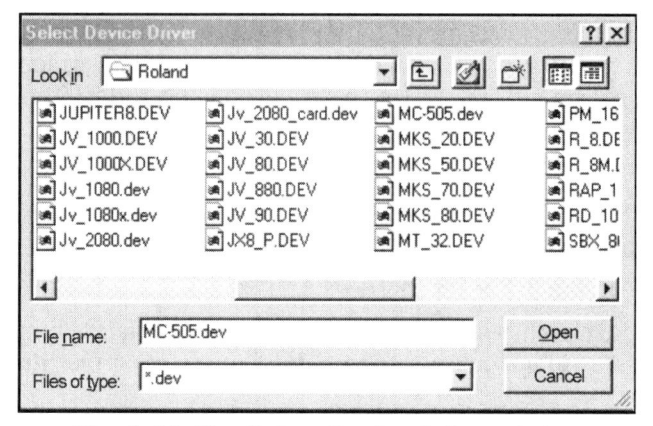

Fig. 6.81. The **Select Device Driver** window

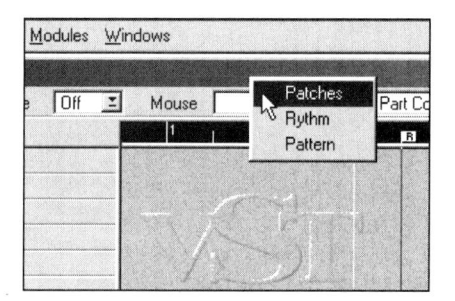

Fig. 6.82. Activating Patch Manager

Fig. 6.83. Selecting the **Roland MC-505** instrument

After that, a click on the **Patch** field of the **Inspector** panel will give you access to the timbres (patches) of **Roland MC-505** (Fig. 6.84).

Chapter 6: The Cubase VST 24 Application and Creating "Live" MIDI Sound 537

Fig. 6.84. The **Patches** window of the **Roland MC-505** synthesizer

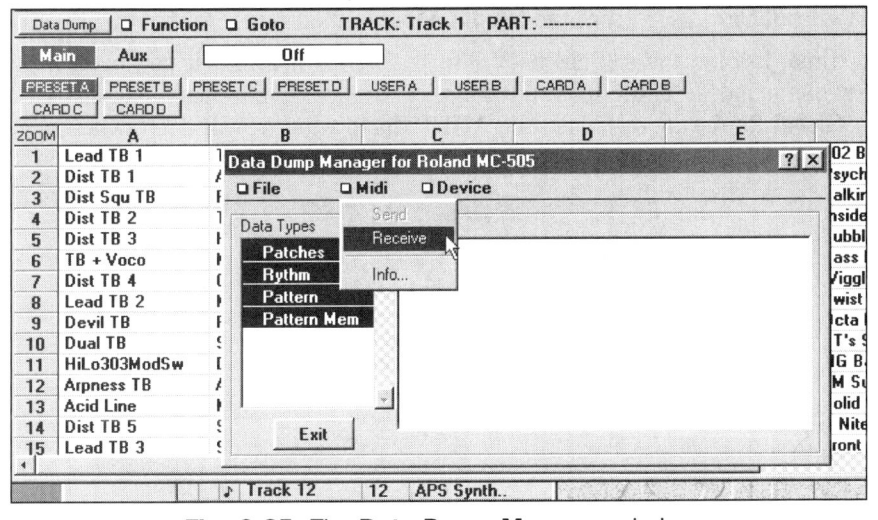

Fig. 6.85. The **Data Dump Manager** window

In the **Patches** window, you can load dumps of internal settings of the synthesizer that usually present data of the System Exclusive type. To achieve this, you must click the **Data Dump** button (in the upper left corner), and the **Data Dump Manager** window will appear (Fig. 6.85). In this window, click the **MIDI** button and select the **Receive** item. Then follow the instructions in the **MIDI Dump** window (Fig. 6.86). These instructions concern the settings of a specific MIDI device, so they must be fulfilled on the device itself.

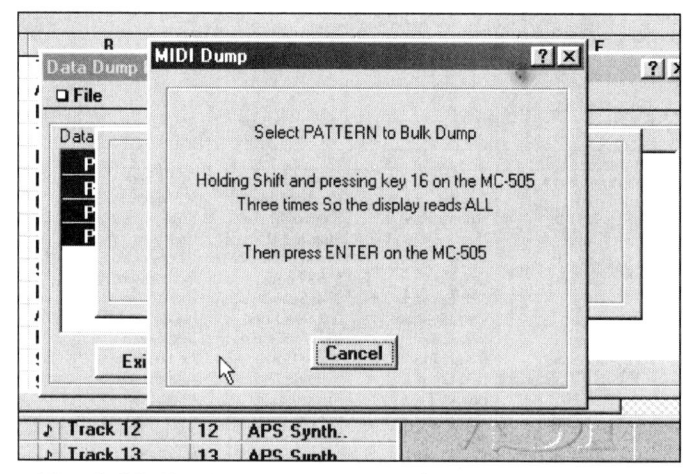

Fig. 6.86. The **MIDI Dump** window when receiving data

The settings must be saved for later use in a file with the MEM extension. To do this, select the **Global Save** item from the **Studio Module** menu.

At a later time, loading the settings back into the MIDI instrument can be done using the **Total Send** command. In doing so, you must select the MEM file containing the settings from the **Open Global Bank** window. Then the **MIDI Dump** window will open, where you will see instructions on how to set the external MIDI device to receive data (Fig. 6.87).

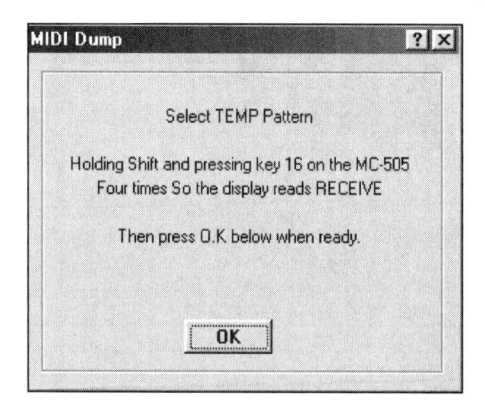

Fig. 6.87. The **MIDI Dump** window when sending data

The MIDI Processor Plug-in

This plug-in is a MIDI analog of a sound effect processor. Using it, you are able to achieve such effects as echo, chorus, and pitch shifting with MIDI, and make MIDI sound more "life-like".

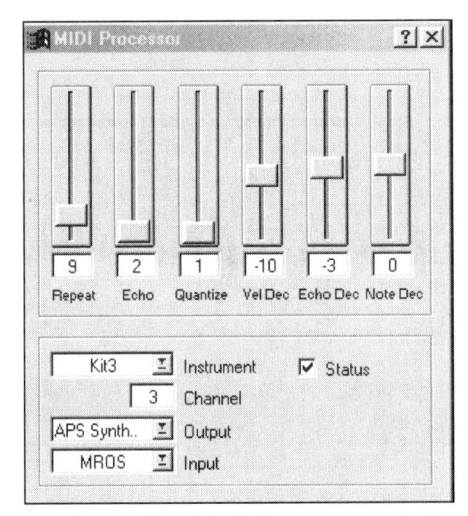

Chapter 6: The Cubase VST 24 Application and Creating "Live" MIDI Sound

Fig. 6.88. The **MIDI Processor** window

Using the MIDI Processor plug-in, it is possible to process various MIDI messages.

- To process messages received from an external MIDI instrument, you must set an input MIDI port of the sound card in the **Input** field.
- When processing messages coming directly from the MIDI Track or Drum Track, you must use the internal virtual MIDI interface called MROS (MIDI Real-time Operating System), designed for internal virtual MIDI interrelation between plug-ins. So set **MROS** in the **Input** field (Fig. 6.88). You must also set **MROS** in the **Output** field of the track being processed.

For the MIDI Processor plug-in to process MIDI messages, check the **Status** checkbox.

The output MIDI port is selected in the **Output** field just like it is selected in the **Output** column in the arrangement window. For example, when VST instruments are used, it is possible to select the virtual MIDI port of a VST instrument in the **Output** column.

If any instruments are specified in the **Instrument** column of the arrangement window, it is possible to select instruments directly in the list in the **Instrument** field of the MIDI Processor plug-in. Setting a MIDI port and a MIDI channel will be done automatically, depending on the instrument selected. You should recall that **Instrument** = **Patch** + + MIDI channel + MIDI port.

Fig. 6.88 illustrates an example of using the MIDI Processor plug-in to process the percussion tracks from the musical example considered earlier in the "*Editing Percussion Parts*" section (Fig. 6.71). This is an area wide open to experimentation. For example, the output of the tracks can be connected to MROS, and the output of the MIDI Processor plug-in can be connected to instruments from Kit1 to Kit4. The number of possible variants is relatively large.

If you use Drum Track, you can connect any selected percussion instrument to MROS (Fig. 6.89).

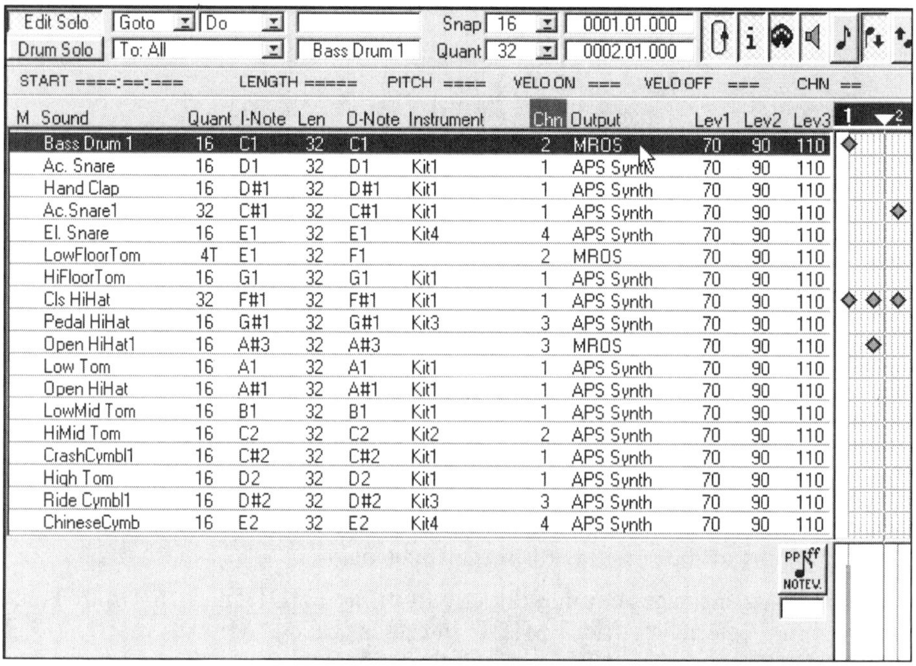

Fig. 6.89. Using MROS for a track of the Drum Track type

To record a MIDI message from the output of the MIDI Processor plug-in to another track, you must use MROS (that is, select MROS in the **Output** field of MIDI Processor). Besides which, you must open the **MIDI Setup** dialog box (in the **Options|Midi Setup** menu), click the **Inputs Enable** field, and select MROS from the list (Fig. 6.90). The selected item will remain checked.

After these operations, you may select any unused track and start recording.

If you want to obtain a "life-like" recording with the MIDI Processor plug-in, you'll have to specify an input MIDI port of the sound card in the **Input** field and set MROS in the **Output** field.

After that, MIDI messages will be recorded to the MIDI track from the source (such as the MIDI keyboard). The messages that have been processed by MROS in the MIDI Processor plug-in will also be recorded. If a duplication effect manifests (the notes are doubled), you can switch off the selected MIDI port of the sound card (the **Inputs Enable** field in the **MIDI Setup** window). Then the MIDI messages will come only to the MIDI Processor.

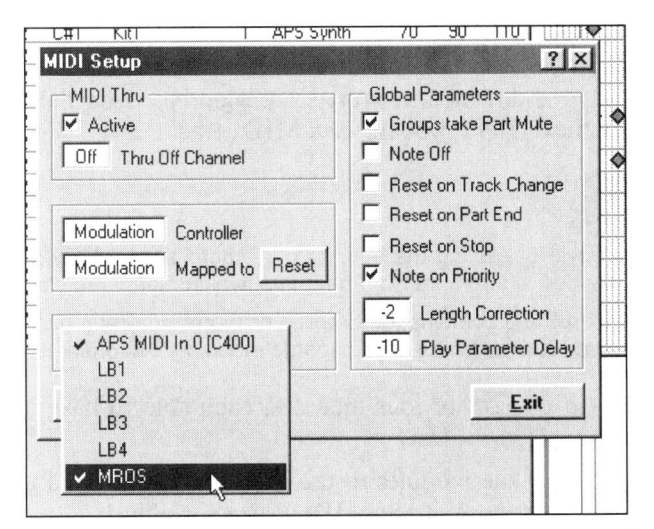

Chapter 6: The Cubase VST 24 Application and Creating "Live" MIDI Sound 541

Fig. 6.90. Switching on the mode of recording from MROS

Let's take a closer look at controlling the MIDI Processor plug-in. To control the plug-in, six sliders are provided:

- Repeat — the number of echo repeats, the valid values being from 1 to 64.
- Echo — the time delay between the echo repeats measured in special units; one unit is equal to 8 ticks.
- Quantize — quantization of repeated notes; this parameter is measured in special units.
- Vel Dec — imitation of an echo decline. This parameter is a number that is added to or subtracted from the Velocity value of each repeat (depending on whether its value is positive or negative). In other words, if you set VelDec to −5, the Velocity value will be decreased by 5 at every repetition. The range of valid values is from −64 to 64.
- Echo Dec — imitation of changing the time delay of echo. This allows you to achieve a more natural MIDI sound. The value of the parameter is specified in ticks, and it is added to or subtracted from the value set with the Echo parameter (depending on whether its value is positive or negative).
- Note Dec — a special effect to obtain arpeggio: every echo repetition is transposed by the number of semitones specified in this field. The range of valid values is from −64 to 64.

(For arpeggio, see "*The Arpeggiator Plug-In*" section below).

You can change the values of the parameters not only by moving the sliders, but also by entering numbers via the keyboard. To do this, double-click the field located under the desired slider.

The Arpeggiator Plug-in

The Arpeggiator plug-in is designed to imitate arpeggio based on the sequence of chords sent to its input from the MIDI keyboard or a MIDI track.

> ### Arpeggio
>
> *Arpeggio* is the style of playing the sounds of a chord sequentially rather than simultaneously (the word is derived from Italian *arpeggiare,* which means "to play the harp").
>
> An *accord* (or chord) is a combination of three or more musical tones with different pitches that sound at once (derives from Italian *accordo* meaning "I coordinate").

The Arpeggiator plug-in consists of four modules, each able to have its own settings. All the modules are synchronized.

The methods of connecting the modules to the MROS interface and to input and output MIDI ports are the same as those of the MIDI Processor plug-in.

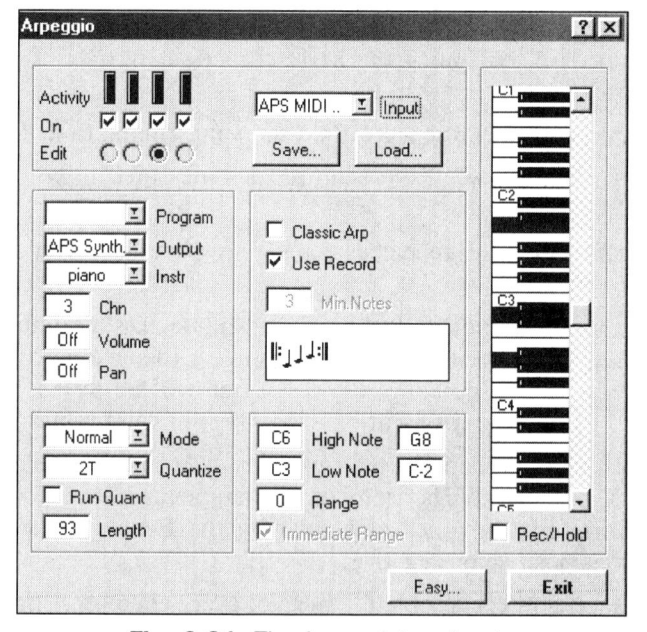

Fig. 6.91. The Arpeggiator plug-in

In the Arpeggiator plug-in, the volume and pan values can be set individually for each module in the **Volume** and **Pan** fields (Fig. 6.91).

The settings of the plug-in can be saved to and loaded from a file with the ARP extension using the **Save** and **Load** buttons.

Chapter 6: The Cubase VST 24 Application and Creating "Live" MIDI Sound 543

Let's now look at the Arpeggiator plug-in in more detail.

The upper section of the window contains the **Activity** display. Using it, you can control the activity of the modules. Just below the display you see the **On** checkboxes that allow you to switch each individual module on/off.

The **Edit** radio buttons switch between the windows with the settings of the modules.

Only one module is available for setup at a time. Since the setup parameters are identical, the modules share the same window. This is why only the values of the parameters change when switching between the module windows.

When the **Classic Arp** checkbox is selected, the **Min Notes** field becomes available. There you can specify the minimum number of notes that determines whether a chord is to be performed as arpeggio. For example, if the field reads 3, arpeggio will be heard only when three or more notes are played on the MIDI keyboard.

If the **Use Record** checkbox is checked, arpeggio is created based on a chord stored in the plug-in's memory. To record a chord via the keyboard, select the **Rec/Hold** checkbox, play the chord on the MIDI keyboard, and then uncheck the checkbox and continue playing.

To change the chord, repeat the procedure, that is, check the **Rec/Hold** checkbox again, play the new chord, and uncheck the **Rec/Hold** checkbox.

Chords to be recorded in the memory of the Arpeggiator plug-in can also be "played" with the mouse: just click the keys of the virtual keyboard in the right section of the window one by one. Clicking again on the same key deletes the note from memory.

There is a display of the arpeggio structure below the **Min Notes** field (Fig. 6.92).

The Arpeggio Structure and the Repeat Mark

The Arpeggio structure is the sequence in which the chord is played, that is, the number of notes and their pitch relation. Cubase VST 24 offers several templates of arpeggio structures, and provides the user with the ability to create his or her own arpeggio structures.

For creation of an arpeggio structure, we are provided with a display where the arpeggio is shown. In Fig. 6.92, you can see that the arpeggio will consist of 7 notes, with their relative pitches also displayed.

The symbols enclosing the note sequence are the repeat marks. They denote that the notes between them will be repeated.

When the **Classic Arp** checkbox is checked, the display is unavailable and its settings are void. If both **Classic Arp** and **Use Record** are unchecked, the plug-in will create an arpeggio based on the notes played on the MIDI keyboard, and taking into account the **Min Notes** parameter.

Fig. 6.92. The display of the arpeggio structure

The structure of an arpeggio can be modified: you can add or delete notes and change their pitches. All this is done in the display of the arpeggio structure, using the mouse. A note is added with a right-click on the right repeat mark, and a note is deleted by holding down the left mouse button on the last note.

It is impossible to delete a single note from inside a group. If you try this, all the subsequent notes will also be deleted.

To raise the pitch of a note, right-click it. If you press and don't release the right mouse button, the pitch will rise gradually.

To lower a note, left-click it. If you press and don't release the left mouse button, the pitch will go down to the point of deletion from the arpeggio structure.

The **Mode** field specifies the type of arpeggio:

- **Normal (up/down)** — the chord is arpeggiated normally up/down
- **Invert** — inverted arpeggio
- **Up Only** — arpeggio is done only up the chord
- **Down Only** — arpeggio is done only down the chord
- **Random** — the arpeggio sounds are played in random order

Arpeggios of the Invert, Up Only, and Down Only types work only in the **Classic Arp** mode.

The **Quantize** field specifies the speed of playing arpeggio in relation to the note length. The lowest speed is achieved when the length is 1. (a whole note with a dot after it), the highest speed corresponds to a value of 32T (a thirty-second triplet note). The **Run Quant** checkbox is used to synchronize the notes of the Arpeggiator plug-in with the other notes of the arrangement in the playback mode.

The **Length** field sets the length of the notes of the Arpeggiator plug-in in ticks. Recall that the length of a quarter note is 384 ticks.

The **High/Low Note** fields specify the maximum range in which arpeggio can be played (the **Range** field must be set to zero).

The **Range** field shows the number of notes making up the arpeggio range. The range is set relative to the lowest note played on the MIDI keyboard. For example, if the **Range** field reads 24, the range is two octaves wide.

You can obtain interesting results when confining the range to an octave or even a fifth (7 semitones). In such a case, the arpeggio is "compressed" within a narrow range, and, with certain settings, it sounds unusual, not particularly resembling classic arpeggio.

The **Immediate Range** checkbox allows you to switch on the mode in which, if the chords on the MIDI keyboard change quickly, arpeggio will immediately shift to the nearest note from the range specified in the **Range** field. In this mode, the Arpeggiator plug-in is forced to monitor the harmonic sequence of chords. This is why no dissonance is heard when the chords change quickly.

Recording arpeggio to a MIDI track. Let's consider how arpeggio can be recorded to a MIDI track. First of all, you'll need to connect all the modules used to the MROS interface. If a MIDI track serves as the source of MIDI messages, the corresponding module inputs and the output of this track must also be connected to MROS.

You must set the **any** value in the **Chn** field of the track to which you are going to record. This is necessary in order to record messages from all the MIDI channels used in the Arpeggiator plug-in.

The **Run Quant** checkbox must be checked for all the modules in order to provide synchronization with the other tracks (especially during a "live" performance on the MIDI keyboard). Remember that recording is done on the selected track, so a track with **any** in the **Chn** field must be selected before recording starts.

After recording, you may apply the **Remix** command (from the **Structure** menu) to the newly created clip. This will let you separate MIDI messages of different MIDI channels to different tracks.

To conclude, we'd like to state that the Arpeggiator plug-in takes into account the velocity of pressing a key on the MIDI keyboard. Because of this, the arpeggio sequences are "enlivened" by the dynamics of the musician's performance.

While setting up the Arpeggiator plug-in, a "hanging note" effect may arise. If so, use the **Reset Devices** command of the **Options** menu.

The Styletrax Plug-in

The Styletrax plug-in (Fig. 6.33) is a virtual device for automatic accompaniment. Using this plug-in, you'll be able to create music of different styles in real time.

The Styletrax plug-in can also perform real-time scale correction. A specialized arrangement file (ARR) is used as a style. You may use both ready-to-use styles delivered with Cubase VST 24 and arrangements you have created on your own.

Let's examine the features of this plug-in more closely.

For the plug-in to work, you need to create a track of the Style Track class.

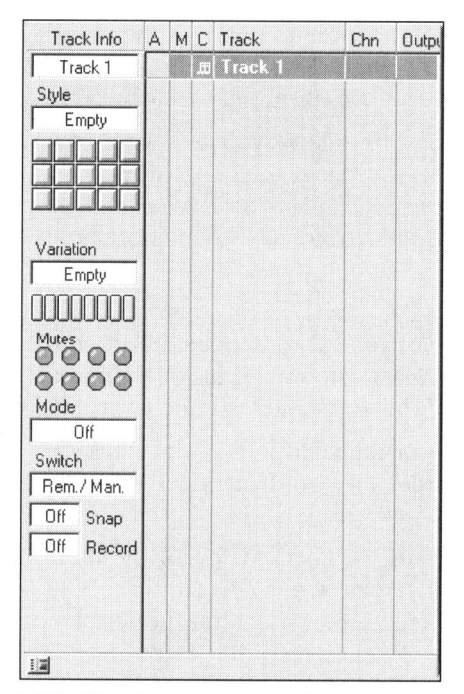

Fig. 6.93. The **Inspector** panel for a Style Track

This track displays its own **Inspector** panel (Fig. 6.93), which lets the user control the Styletrax plug-in in real time. Let's look at it in more detail.

❐ There are fifteen buttons below the **Style** field. Their number reflects the maximum number of styles that can be loaded. In Fig. 6.93, the **Style** field reads **Empty**, since no style is loaded yet. To load a style, click any of the buttons and select the desired arrangement file (with the ARR extension) in the **Load Style** dialog box. After the style is loaded, the **Inspector** panel will change as shown in Fig. 6.94: the name of the style (the arrangement file) will appear in the **Style** field. A click on another unused button allows you to load another style, and so on.

❐ The color of the button tells whether the style is active.
- Red means that a style has been loaded and is in an active state, that is, the Styletrax plug-in is going to process it
- Blue means that a style has been loaded, but it is inactive, and the Styletrax plug-in isn't processing it
- Gray means nothing is loaded to the button (it is empty)

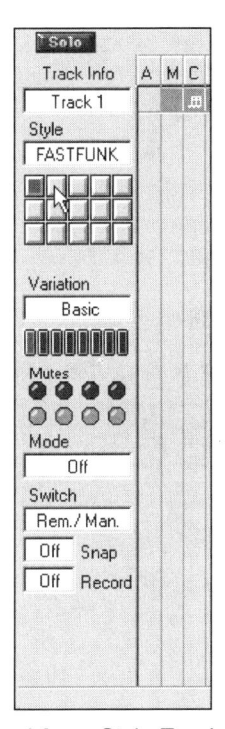

Chapter 6: The Cubase VST 24 Application and Creating "Live" MIDI Sound

Fig. 6.94. The **Inspector** panel for a Style Track after a style has been loaded

To activate a style, click the corresponding button. It will change its color to red.

❒ The **Variation** field contains the name of the current variation of the style. A click on this field opens the list of variations, where you can select the needed one.

❒ The row of eight buttons located below the **Variation** field serves the same purpose. As with the style buttons,

- Red indicates the current (active) variation
- Blue means that there is a variation matching this button but it is inactive
- Gray means that no variation corresponds to the button

If a style has more than eight variations, the buttons disappear, and an additional field (**Vari.**) emerges where you can enter the variation number directly, via the keyboard.

❒ Below that, eight **Mutes** buttons are located, which are designed to turn off the style track selectively. A red color indicates that the track is muted. If the button is gray, it means the track isn't used in the style arrangement. That there are eight buttons isn't by chance. Eight is the maximum number of tracks that can be contained in a style arrangement.

For music to be heard on the output of Styletrax, you must switch the plug-in on. To do this, set any mode in the **Mode** field (by default, the Styletrax plug-in is in the **Off** mode), and click **Play** on the **Transport** bar.

We're going to describe the **Mode**, **Switch**, **Snap**, and **Record** fields later, after we examine the principles of the Styletrax plug-in.

Let's look first at the process of arranging a style. Fig. 6.95 demonstrates an example of a style arrangement delivered with Cubase VST 24.

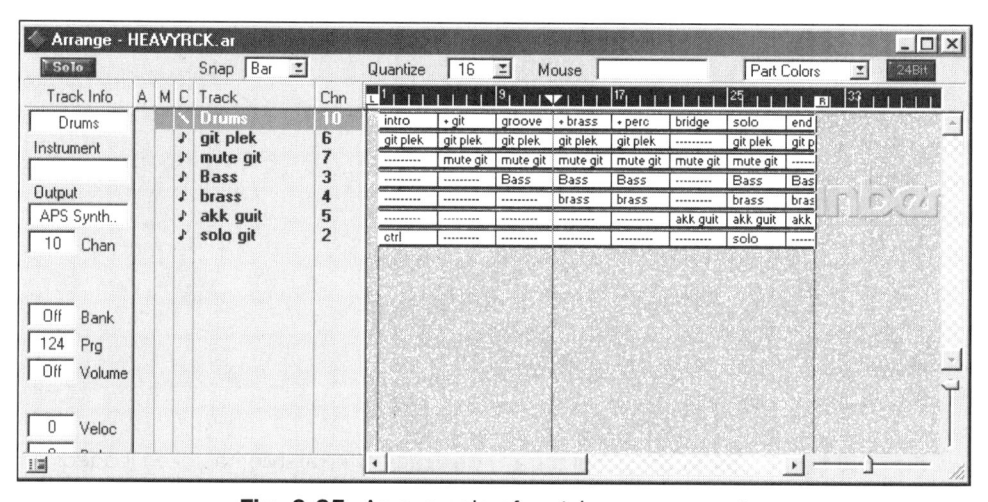

Fig. 6.95. An example of a style arrangement

A style arrangement differs from a common arrangement in the following points:

❐ The maximum number of tracks mustn't exceed eight.

❐ For the Styletrax plug-in to "accept" the tracks, they must be numbered from 1 to 8. This is why it is better to create them in an empty arrangement, immediately after executing the **New Arrangement** command of the **File** menu.

❐ There mustn't be any pauses between the blocks, and the clips must be of the same length. Each vertical block consisting of clips of equal length is a variation of the style. If a track in the block isn't used, an empty clip must be created at this place.

❐ In Fig. 6.95, empty clips are marked with dashed lines.

❐ The name of the clip in the first track serves as the name of the variation. The **Chn** fields of the style tracks mustn't contain the **any** value. It is always better to use the Drum Track style for a percussion track.

❐ A block may be of any length less than 64 measures (bars).

❐ The developers of Cubase VST 24 don't recommend changing chords during the style arrangement, that is, they try to dissuade users from creating sequences of chords.

Chapter 6: The Cubase VST 24 Application and Creating "Live" MIDI Sound 549

NOTE We hold another viewpoint: chord changing during the style arrangement is a fertile field for experimentation, and much is determined by the creative task and the style of the composition.

- The developers of Cubase VST 24 recommend that users perform quantization of style arrangements, in order to avoid duplicate notes. It is better to perform such quantization using special methods — Groove quantize and Match quantize — which will be discussed later.
- Virtually editing the style arrangement with the **Inspector** panel must be done only to a track; such editing mustn't be done to clips.
- Transpose and delay must be done destructively, using such editors as **Drum Edit** and **Key Edit**.
- The result will be best if the clips have a common musical context and style.

The tempo of the arrangement automatically becomes the tempo of the Style Track. If a Master Track is used, its settings will determine the tempo of the Style Track.

Now we can turn to the settings of the Styletrax plug-in itself.

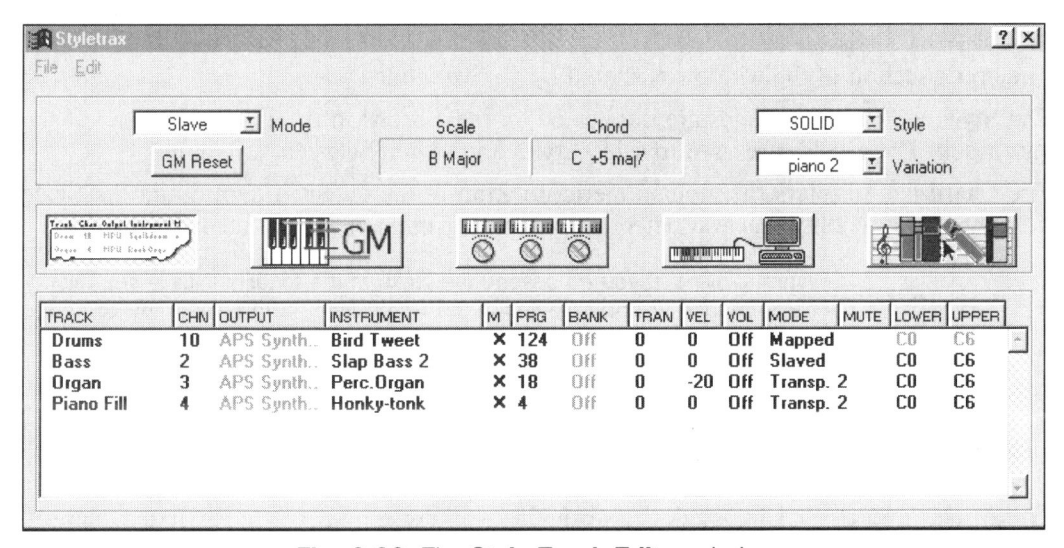

Fig. 6.96. The **Style Track Editor** window

Changing the parameters of the Styletrax plug-in is done with the **Style Track Editor** (Fig. 6.96). To open this editor, you must select a Style Track and select the **Edit** item from the **Edit** menu (<Ctrl>+<E>).

The principles of the Styletrax plug-in are based on detecting sequences of chords with subsequent scale correction of the style arrangement.

The Styletrax plug-in accepts chords coming from the MIDI keyboard in the real time, or from a special track of the Chord Track type.

A style arrangement can initially contain a sequence of chords. During scale correction, these chords will be transformed into another sequence matching the new scale.

The work of Styletrax is determined by various settings, and results obtained with different settings can differ significantly.

So let's examine the structure of the Styletrax plug-in.

A style can be loaded or saved directly in the **Style Track Editor** with the **Load Style** and **Save Style** commands of the **File** menu, respectively.

The **Update Style** command is used to save the results of style editing. All the style settings are also saved.

The style settings can be saved separately from the style itself, by using the **Save Setup/Load Setup** commands. The settings are saved in a file with the XET extension.

The **Style Track Editor** has five editing modes: **Tracklist**, **GM Map**, **Settings**, **Remote**, and **Styles**. You can toggle between these modes either with the commands of the **Edit** menu or with the five big buttons located in the middle section of the editor window (Fig. 6.96).

The upper section of the window is shared by all five modes.

The **Style** and **Variation** fields are duplicated by the buttons in the **Inspector** panel of the style track. These fields are used to select styles and switch between variations.

The **Chord** field displays the alphanumeric notation of the detected chord, and the **Scale** field shows the tonality that was detected by the plug-in based on the received chord.

NOTE When playing, if you go beyond the limits of the tonality initially set, this tonality change will be reflected in the **Scale** field. In this case, the computer will take into account the scale specified in the **Scale Preference** field.

It must be noted here that scale and tonality detection is a difficult task, even for professional musicians. Because of this, you needn't strictly adhere to the tonality detection performed by your computer. The **Scale Preference** field is available in the **Settings** mode of the editor.

The **Mode** field is used to toggle between the working modes of the Styletrax plug-in. It should be mentioned that this plug-in is quite difficult to master. However, the game is worth the candle, since using Styletrax opens new fields for experimentation and helps to inspire new musical ideas.

Let's now look at the working modes of the Styletrax plug-in. As stated earlier, they are selected in the **Mode** drop-down list in the **Style Track Editor** window, and this is duplicated in the **Mode** field of the **Inspector** panel. The following modes are available:

❐ **Off** — the Styletrax plug-in is off.

- **Slave** — detection of the chords coming from the Chord Track.
- **Listening** — detection and interpretation of the chords done by the program, so to speak, "by ear", while they are being played on the MIDI keyboard, with the chord inversion being taken into account. The Styletrax plug-in detects the chords by the lowest note played on the MIDI keyboard.

A Chord and Its Inversion

Let's tackle some more theory, and discuss what a chord and its inversion are.

As we already know, a *chord* is a combination of three or more musical tones of different pitches that are emitted simultaneously. Even if the notes are played in different octaves, they still make up a chord. (An *octave* is the interval between two sounds where the frequency of the lower sound is half as high as that of the higher sound. The interval between two neighboring *D* notes can serve as an example.) The most common chords are triads (3 notes separated by thirds) and seventh chords (4 notes). The extreme sounds of a seventh chord comprise the seventh interval, which gave the name to the chord.

If the sequence of sounds in a triad or a seventh chord changes so that the central or upper notes appear to be the lowermost, this is called inversion. Thus, the inversions of the *C-E-G* chord will be *E-G-C* and *G-C-E*.

All the inversions of triads and seventh chords have corresponding names and notations.

- In the **Easy** working mode, the Styletrax plug-in makes decisions on selecting a certain chord based on a single note played on the MIDI keyboard. The tonality in this mode is specified in the **Easy Mode Scale** and **Easy Mode Key** fields (available in the **Settings** mode of the **Style Track Editor**). This working mode can be recommended for novice musicians who aren't particularly strong in music theory. The chords in each scale are made up in agreement with certain laws. As we said earlier, the distance between the degrees is constant for every scale. According to the mentioned laws, the sounds of a chord can be positioned only at the degrees of the scale. (To put it simply, for example: since all the degrees of a scale in *C major* tonality are located on the white keys of the keyboard, there mustn't be any chords containing black keys while playing in this tonality.)
- The **Roland**, **Yamaha**, and **Casio** working modes switch the Styletrax plug-in to the chord detection systems that correspond to the synthesizers from these manufacturers. This feature is useful for musicians who are accustomed to a certain system of auto-accompaniment.

Now we're going to look at the working modes of the **Style Track Editor**.

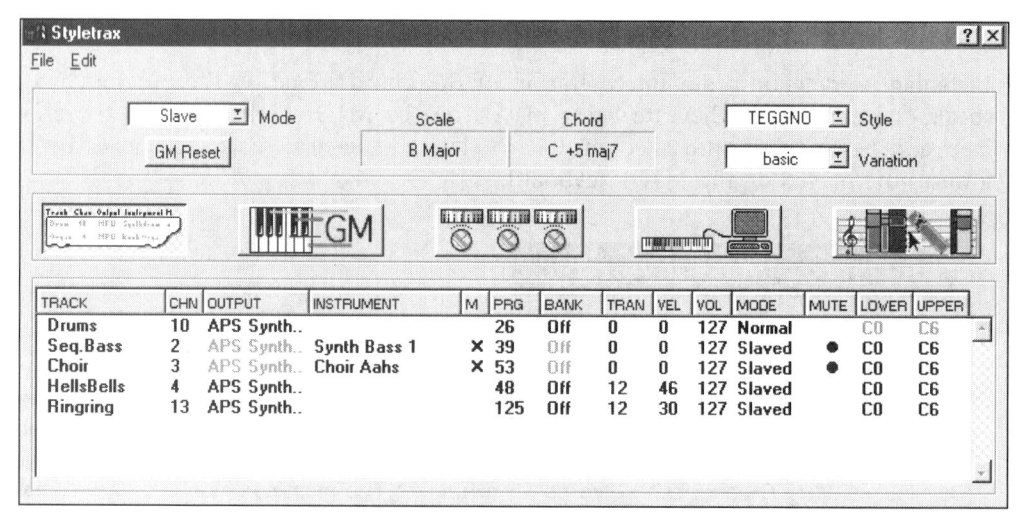

Fig. 6.97. The **Tracklist** editing window

- **Tracklist** — the mode for editing the style tracks. After selecting this mode, the **Tracklist** window will open (Fig. 6.97), which displays the list of style tracks along with fourteen columns containing the editing parameters for each track. The layout of the **Tracklist** window is similar to the layout of the track section in the arrangement window. Here are the columns of the **Tracklist** window and their contents:

- **Track** contains a list of the names of the style tracks.

- **Chn** contains a list of the numbers of the MIDI channels used in the style. These numbers are changeable.

- **Output** is the column where it is possible to select the output MIDI port for every track if there is no x in the **M (Mapping)** column.

- **Instrument** is the column where you can create an instrument (like in the arrangement window).

- **M (Mapping)** turns on the timbre selection mode corresponding to the General MIDI standard. This mode lets the user select the timbre directly in the **Instrument** field of the track for which the Mapping mode is on. When this mode is on, you see an x in the **M** column. The program allows the user to create his or her own GM map. A special mode of the editor is provided for this purpose, and it will be discussed later.

- **Prg** and **Bank** are designed to set up the numbers of the program and the bank directly. When the **Mapping** mode is on, the **Bank** field is disabled.

- **Tran** means track transpose. It is done in the same way as in the **Inspector** panel of the MIDI track.

Chapter 6: The Cubase VST 24 Application and Creating "Live" MIDI Sound

- **Vel** (Velocity) and **Vol** (Volume) serve to change the velocity and volume values (in the same way as in the **Inspector** pane of the MIDI track).
- **Mute** turns the track off (this is duplicated by the buttons in the **Inspector** panel of the MIDI track).
- **Lower** and **Upper** specify the range where the notes can be played. Notes falling out of the range are automatically transposed so that they appear within the range.
- **Mode** specifies the working modes that determine how the track responds to chord changing on the MIDI keyboard or on the Chord Track.
- Here are these modes:
    - ⇨ **Normal** — no note modifications, the track is played back as in the original style arrangement. This can be recommended for percussion parts where note transposition isn't possible.
    - ⇨ **Mapped** — no note modifications, the track is played back through the Drum Map. This mode must be used with Drum Tracks.
    - ⇨ **Slaved** — note transposition depending on the pitch of the detected chord and the tonality. In other words, this is scale correction that corresponds to the pitch of the detected chord.
    - ⇨ **Modal** — scale correction according to the tonality and the detected chord, but without transposition. This mode is most suited for parts containing melody (including arpeggio and so on).
    - ⇨ **Transpose 1** — monitoring the pitch of the detected chord and transposing (without scale correction). In this mode, when the tonality changes, dissonant note combinations may appear.
    - ⇨ **Transpose 2** — note transposition depending on the pitch of the detected chord and the tonality. Unlike in the **Slave** mode, melodies in this mode are heard in a narrow pitch range (not all over the entire keyboard). This is recommended, for example, for bass parts.
- ❐ **GM Map** — the mode for editing the GM Map (Fig. 6.98). The GM Map is used when one or more style tracks are marked with an x in the **M** column in the **Tracklist** mode.

If the style track is used with a General MIDI synthesizer, there is no need to make changes to the GM Map. However, when specific sound patterns are required, it may be more convenient to edit the GM Map and put an x in the **M** field than to set the bank and program numbers manually in the **Tracklist** mode.

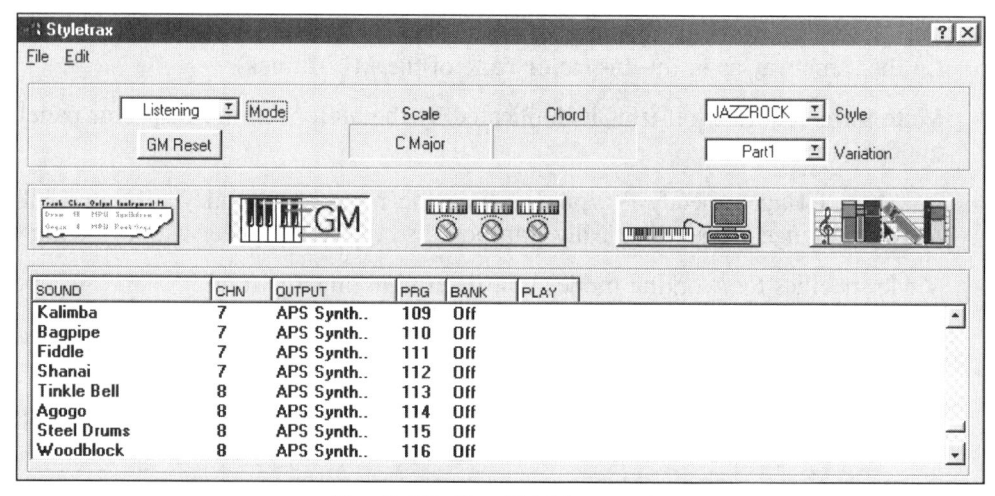

Fig. 6.98. The GM Map mode

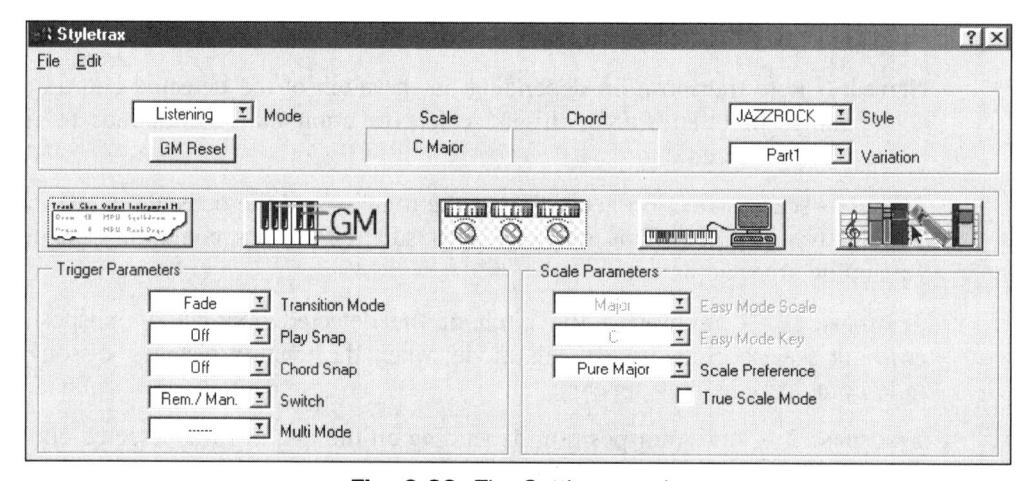

Fig. 6.99. The Settings mode

- **Settings** — the working mode for editing plug-in settings (Fig. 6.99). In this mode, the parameters of two sections can be edited. These are the **Trigger Parameters** and **Scale Parameters** sections. The fields of the **Trigger Parameters** section are:
  - **Transition Mode** — switching between the **Fade** and **Start** modes that control variation changing. In the **Start** mode, a new variation always begins at the beginning in response to a variation changing command. If this happens in the middle of a variation, an unwanted effect may appear that is perceived by ear as a mistake. To avoid this effect, it is necessary to set the **Bar** or **Part** value in the

Chapter 6: The Cubase VST 24 Application and Creating "Live" MIDI Sound

Play Snap field. In the **Fade** mode, variation changing is always done smoothly, and the effect above doesn't manifest.

- **Play Snap** — the mode that fixes transitions between the variations.

  If the **Bar** value is set, variation changing is done only at the beginning of the next measure; if the **Part** value is set, variation changing is done when a style track is "looping", i.e., being repeated. The meaning of the **Off** value is obvious. When the variations that comprise the style are of different lengths, it is better to set the **Bar** value in the **Play Snap** field and the **Start** value in the **Transition Mode** field. The **Play Snap** and **Switch** fields are duplicated in the **Inspector** panel of the style track.

- **Chord Snap** — the mode that fixes chord changes.

  The possible values are: **Part** — chord changing is possible only at the next beat (the next quarter note); **Bar** — chord changing is possible only at the beginning of the next measure; **Off** — the mode is off.

- **Switch** — selecting how to switch between variations. The following options are available:

  ⇨ **Rem./Man.** — remote switching with the MIDI keyboard. For this, special keys on the MIDI keyboard must be reserved.

  ⇨ **Ext.Ctrl** — remote control using the MIDI controller.

  ⇨ **Random** — random switching between variations by the Styletrax plug-in itself.

  ⇨ **Random-Mix** — random switching and mixing: the clips of various variations change their positions at random.

  ⇨ **Vel.Switch** — switching between the variations depending on the value of the Velocity parameter. This is a rather interesting feature, because the Styletrax plug-in behaves as if it takes into account the manner of a human performer playing on the MIDI keyboard. If you create a style of multiple variations that contains only percussion instruments, selecting the **Vel.Switch** feature will create the illusion of playing with a "live" virtual performer. This allows you to use the Styletrax plug-in, say, as a training device for free improvisation.

Well, now we'll look at the fields of the **Scale Parameters** section.

- **Easy Mode Scale** and **Easy Mode Key** are designed to set tonality. They are available only in **Easy Mode**.

  As stated earlier, in this mode, the Styletrax plug-in detects chords by a single note (played on the MIDI keyboard).

  However, to do this, it needs to "know" the tonality that is specified in the **Easy Mode Scale** and **Easy Mode Key** fields.

- **Scale Preference** allows you to select the scale used for scale correction.

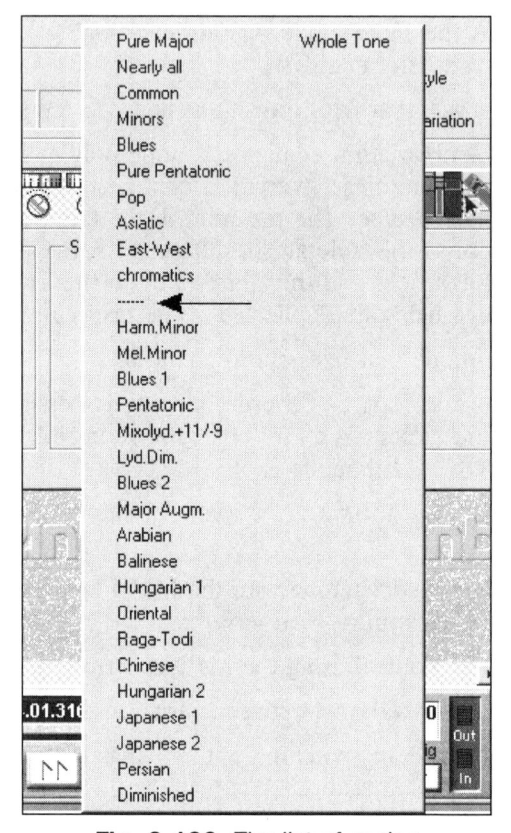

Fig. 6.100. The list of scales

The list of scales. A list of all the scales available in the application is opened with a click on the **Scale Preference** field (Fig. 6.100).

As you can see in Fig. 6.100, this list is divided into two parts by a dashed line. Below the line are listed standard scales, and multiscale *macros* are shown above the line.

The standard scales include the harmonic and melodic minors, blues, a pentatonic (a scale of five degrees), a mixolydian scale (a major scale with a lowered seventh degree, a raised eleventh degree, and a lowered ninth degree), an Arabian scale, two Hungarian and two Japanese scales, an Oriental scale, and others.

If you choose a multiscale macro, the Styletrax plug-in will select (*in real time*) the scale you will be playing at that moment. If you change the scale during playback, the plug-in will detect this and keep scale correction in line with the new scale. For example, the Asiatic macro provides automatic switching between the Oriental, Japanese, and Persian scales. In practice, you should use the trial-and-error method to find the macro that best fits the musical idea of your project.

Chapter 6: The Cubase VST 24 Application and Creating "Live" MIDI Sound 557

The **True Scale Mode** checkbox allows you to eliminate dissonant sounds when a style loaded into the plug-in contains long notes. This feature is needed so that dissonance won't emerge when the current chord changes, but so that its long notes are still heard. This feature immediately takes away notes that don't fit the scale and creates new ones with the "right" pitches.

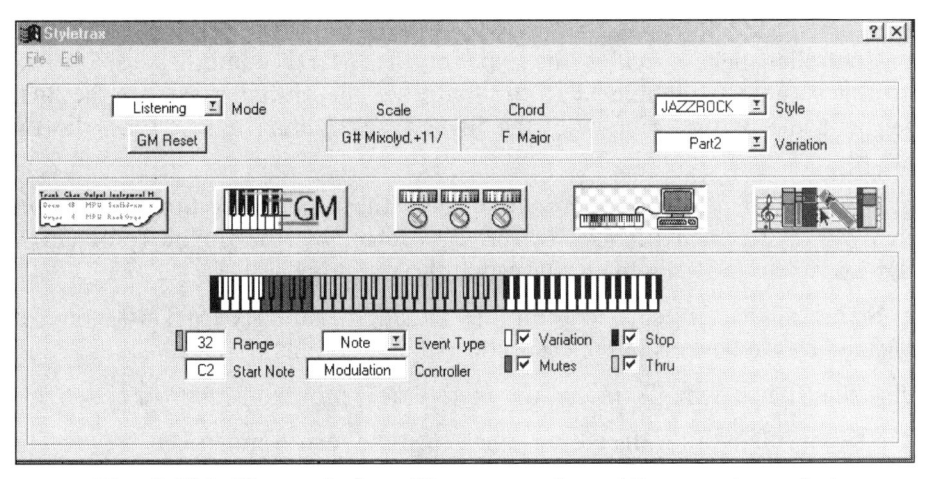

Fig. 6.101. The mode for editing parameters of the remote control

❐ The **Remote** mode (Fig. 6.101) allows you to edit the parameters of remote control with the MIDI keyboard. In this mode, the picture of the MIDI keyboard is divided into several sections. They are colored according to the various groups of keys of the MIDI keyboard.

- The only black key (the leftmost one) is used to stop playback of the Style Track. It is active when the **Stop** checkbox is checked.
- The yellow keys serve to switch between the variations. They are active only when the **Variation** checkbox is checked.
- Using the red keys, you can selectively mute the style tracks. The keys are active when the **Mutes** checkbox is checked.
- The blue keys are designed to detect the chords.
- When the **Thru** checkbox is unchecked, the keys turn green, and this part of the MIDI keyboard becomes inactive.
- Melodies are played with the white keys. They have no additional function.

Let's continue looking at the **Remote** mode window (Fig. 6.101).

The **Range** field allows you to change the range of the blue (or green) keys, and the **Start Note** field lets you specify the shift of all the ranges except the white key range. These operations are needed to set the MIDI keyboard to work with the Styletrax plug-in in order to complete a certain task. For example, if the variations are switched automatically in the **Random-Mix** mode, using the yellow keys makes little sense.

In this case, you may uncheck the **Variation** checkbox and expand the blue key range.

The **Controller** field specifies the type of the MIDI controller used to control switching between variations. For this purpose, the **Switch** field (in the **Inspector** panel or in the **Setting** window of the **Style Track Editor**) must display the **Ext.Ctrl** mode.

The **Event Type** field allows you to change the type of control MIDI messages from **Note** to **Program Change**. In this case, changing the timbre (program) of the MIDI instrument will automatically switch the variations.

❐ The **Styles** mode serves to control the variations and styles. This mode is fully duplicated by the buttons in the **Inspector** panel of the Style Track.

Recording the Style Track. To record the Style Track, proceed as follows:

1. In the **Record** field of the **Inspector** panel, turn the record mode **On**.
2. Select the style track.
3. Click the **Record** button in the **Transport** bar.
4. Stop recording with the **Stop** button in the **Transport** bar.

After recording stops, new tracks will be created in the arrangement window, and their names will be identical to those of the original style tracks.

You need to switch off the Style Track (the **Off** mode in the **Mode** field) during playback; otherwise, the duplicate-note effect will emerge.

If a style track is recorded to an existing arrangement in the **Punch** mode, you must set the **Replace** mode in the **Transport** bar. Otherwise, the clips created while recording the style track will be laid over the previously created clips.

The clips created while recording the style track can be edited using the general editing tools of Cubase VST 24.

To record your own performance on the MIDI keyboard along with the Style Track, you have to turn on the record mode (the **Record** field in the **Inspector** panel of the Style Track), create a separate track, select it, and start recording.

Recording the Chord Track. The Style Track can be controlled not only with the MIDI keyboard, but with a special Chord Track as well. To do this, it is necessary to set the **Slave** mode in the **Mode** field in the **Inspector** panel of the Style Track.

Chapter 6: The Cubase VST 24 Application and Creating "Live" MIDI Sound 559

Track Position Priorities

You should keep in mind that here the Chord Track must be placed above the Style Track in the arrangement window. It is also desirable that it be the uppermost, having the first number. The reason for this lies in how Cubase VST 24 sets its priorities. The application requires that the controlling tracks must be above the controlled ones.

There are two ways to record chords to a Chord Track: using **Score Edit**, and while performing "live" on the MIDI keyboard.

Let's consider the second method. To make a "live" recording to a Chord Track:

1. Create a track of the Chord Track class near the style track (in the same arrangement window).
2. Select the Chord Track and start recording as usual (click the **Record** button in the **Transport** bar). The style track must have the **Off** value in the **Record** field and the **Listening** value in the **Mode** field.

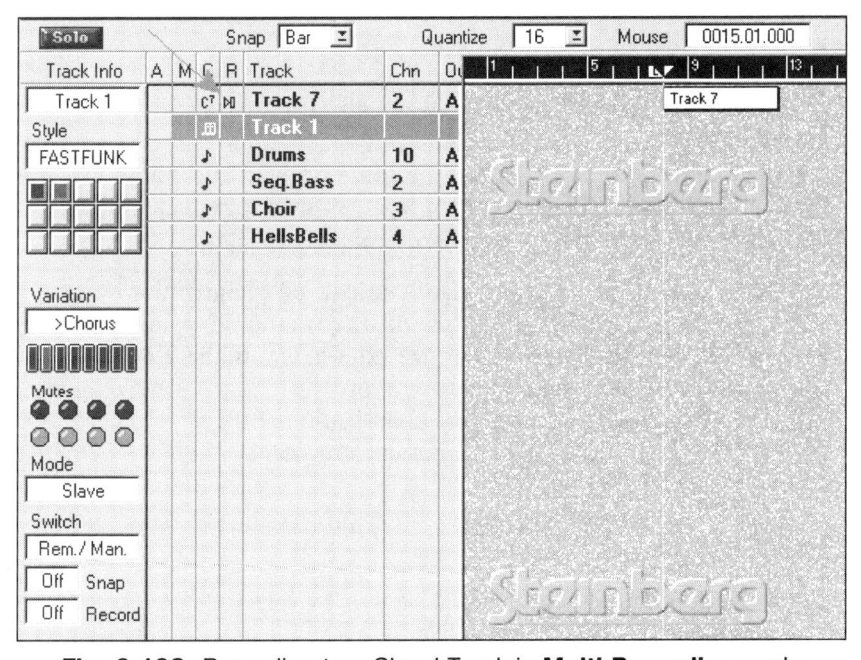

Fig. 6.102. Recording to a Chord Track in **Multi Recording** mode

The **Stop** and **Mutes** commands aren't reflected in the Chord Track.

You can also record to the Chord Track a sequence of switching between the variations and the loaded styles. This is done using the **Inspector** panel of the style track. For this, you need to activate the **Multi Recording** mode and set it to the **Merge Mode** value. Proceed as follows:

1. Check **Active** and **Merge** in the **Options|Multirecord** menu.
2. Click the **R** column for the Chord Track so that the "record" icon appears (Fig. 6.102).
3. Select the style track and start recording. During the process, you may switch both variations and styles; all the switching will be reflected in the Chord Track.

Quantization in Cubase VST 24

We'd like to remind you of some terms. *Quantization* means automatically moving the notes to more precise positions. Furthermore, *scale correction* means moving the notes that for some reason don't match the scale degrees to the correct degrees.

Cubase VST 24 provides many variants of these types of quantization. This is why the user always can "adjust" musical material by introducing selective changes which don't distort the "live" sound.

The quantization discussed in this section is called rhythmic quantization. It changes only the time position of the note, leaving its pitch untouched.

Rhythmic quantization in Cubase VST 24 is implemented in various ways. Moreover, some implementations have almost nothing in common with the traditional understanding of rhythm that is taught at the elementary levels of musical education.

Let's begin our discussion with the options of the **Functions** menu.

- The **Over Quantize** option is a standard variant of quantization where notes are moved to the nearest precise positions of the rhythmic grid. The precision of quantization is determined by the Quantize parameter in the **Key Edit**, **Drum Edit**, **List Edit**, and **Score Edit** editors, or in the arrangement window. Let's consider an example of this type of quantization. In Fig. 6.103, you can see the **Key Edit** window with the original musical fragment (that is, before the **Over Quantize** procedure).

    Set the **Quant** (Quantize) parameter to 8. This means the grid step is equal to an eighth note (quantization to eighth notes).

    Perform quantization by pressing the <Q> key or by selecting the **Over Quantize** item from the **Functions** menu. The notes will move to the nearest precise values according to the grid step (1/8), as shown in Fig. 6.104.

    Cancel quantization by pressing the <U> key or with the **Undo Quantize** command of the **Functions** menu. Then change the quantize parameter to 4, making the grid step equal to a quarter note (1/4). Perform quantization once more (the result is shown in Fig. 6.105).

Chapter 6: The Cubase VST 24 Application and Creating "Live" MIDI Sound 561

Compare Figs. 6.104 and 6.105. In the latter case (quantization to quarter notes), the notes of the second triad have moved to the position of the third beat. In our example, it appears that a more rough quantization (to longer notes) is more appropriate. Therefore, you should try a different quantize parameter for each specific case.

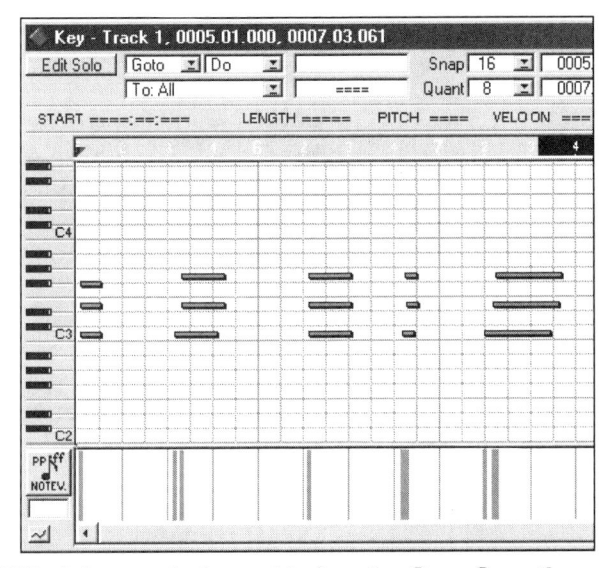

Fig. 6.103. A fragment of a part before the **Over Quantize** procedure

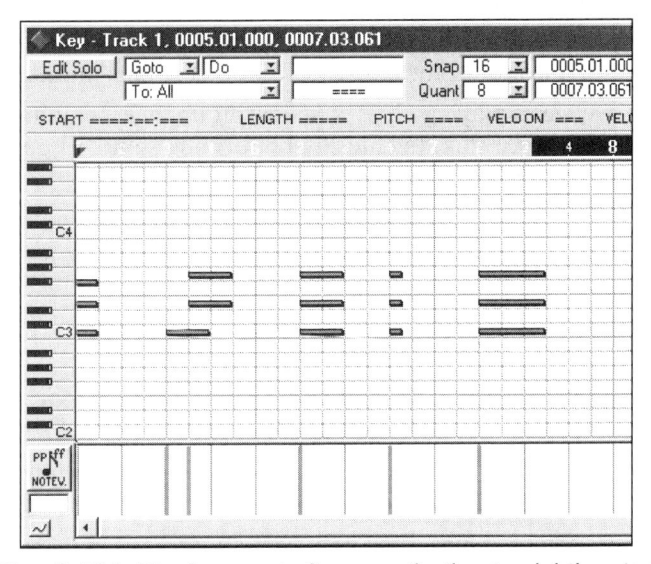

Fig. 6.104. The fragment after quantization to eighth notes

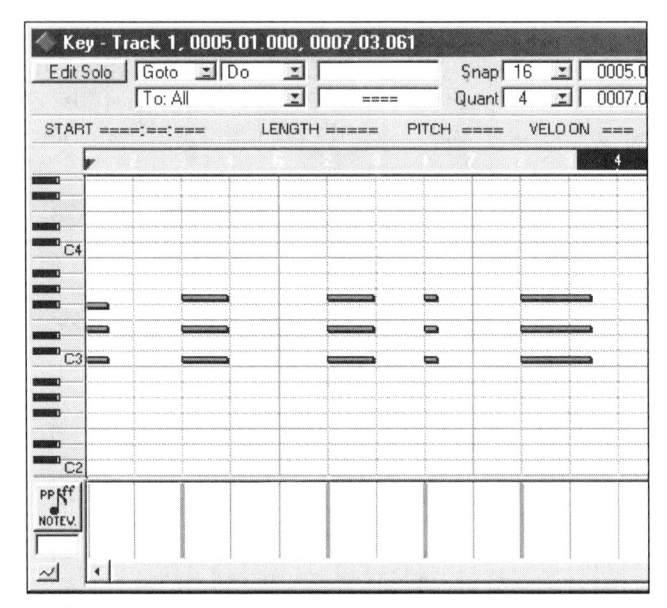

Fig. 6.105. The fragment after quantization to quarter notes

❒ The **Iterative Quantize** option indicates quantization with a gradual nearing to precise note positions.

How can this type of quantization be used? Well, standard quantization "kills" all the nuances of a "live" performance. It is the procedure that is usually responsible for lifeless computer performing. Certain rhythmic deviations, stresses, and slight tempo changes are typical both for a maestro and a beginner musician.

However, when we hear playing that contains pronounced rhythmical mistakes, we have a strong desire to stop this "torture" by performing standard quantization, even at the cost of making the music "lifeless".

The developers of Cubase VST 24 suggested a trade-off, namely, the Iterative Quantize procedure. It allows you to do a fine quantization by gradually moving the notes to their ideal positions.

To perform one quantization step, press the <E> key or select the **Iterative Quantize** item from the **Functions** menu.

The parameters of **Iterative Quantize** are set in the **Setup Grooves** window, opened using the item of the same name in the **Functions** menu (Fig. 6.106).

Let's consider the **Iterative Q** section of the **Setup Grooves** window. Here, you see two fields: **Strength %** and **Don't Quantize**.

- In the **Strength %** field, you set the quantization step as a percentage. For a smooth approximation, choose values from 10% to 30%.

- In the **Don't Quantize** field, a value is set (in ticks) that specifies the minimum distance between the note and its ideal position. In other words, the note cannot move any closer to the ideal position than this distance. For example, if the **Don't Quantize** field reads 4, the process of moving the notes will stop 4 ticks before the notes reach the nearest vertical line of the grid. In other words, the notes don't move to anywhere within a distance of 4 ticks from the ideal positions.

When editing parts, it is better to apply the **Iterative Quantize** procedure to selected groups of notes where rhythmic mistakes are noticeable, rather than to all the notes at once. Quantization can be applied to the selected notes, provided no less than two notes are selected.

The **Iterative Quantize** procedure can also be used to solve other tasks, for example, to achieve a rhythmic effect that can be compared to a sort of "computer swing". For this purpose, individual groups of notes are shifted in a process called *shuffling*.

Fig. 6.106. The **Setup Grooves** window for setting up the parameters of iterative quantization

Let's consider an example of shuffling.

1. Use a simple rhythmic pattern (Fig. 6.107) and switch on the cycle playback mode.
2. Select a group of notes of the Cls Hi Hat instrument.
3. Set the **Quantize** parameter to 16T (sixteenth triplets).

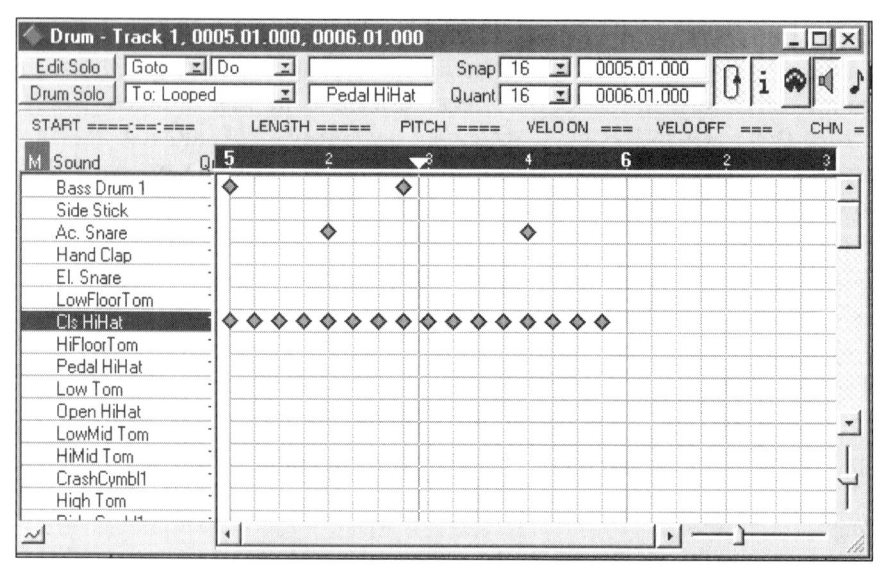

Fig. 6.107. The original percussion part

Triplet Quantization: Traditional and New Sage

Now we're going to explain this new term, that is, the triplet. We already know that the main note lengths are "straight". This means that every whole note is divided into two half notes (minims), each of which is divided into two quarter notes (crotchets), each of which is divided into two eighth notes (quavers), etc. However, there are lengths divided into other numbers of parts (three, five, seven). In particular, a triplet is a note (whole, half, quarter, etc.) divided into three rather than two parts. In traditional music notation, a triplet is denoted by the number 3 written under the notes combined in a triplet group. The triplet is performed as three equal hits per one beat.

We also have something called triplet quantization, whose main purpose is to correct mistakes made while performing triplets.

In our example, we suggest that you use triplet quantization in a somewhat non-standard way: Let's apply it to even lengths, for example to sixteenth notes (semiquavers). In this case, the sixteenth notes quantized by triplets are "attracted" by the nearest triplet snap lines, and we obtain a rather peculiar rhythm change. You should keep in mind that the rhythm changes in an unpredictable manner if it is entered via the MIDI keyboard rather than "drawn" (as in our example). This is due to the fact that live performing naturally contains certain rhythmic deviations.

Notice that the number of grid nodes between the quarter-notes is different in Figs. 6.107 and 6.108. This is because the note lengths are divided into a different number of parts: four in the former case and three in the latter.

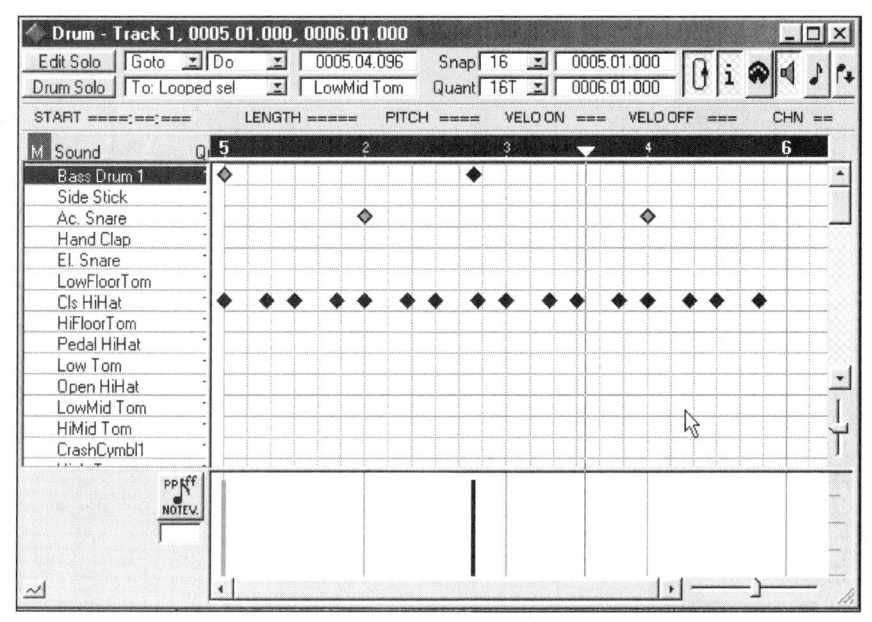

Chapter 6: The Cubase VST 24 Application and Creating "Live" MIDI Sound

Fig. 6.108. The percussion part after the **Iterative Quantize** procedure was applied

Now start the step-by-step iteration quantization without interrupting the loop playback. At each step, some notes will shift towards others (Fig. 6.108), thus creating the "computer swing" effect. The shift size must be determined experimentally.

If you use the standard **Over Quantize** procedure instead of the iterative one, the even rhythmic pattern of the sixteenth notes of the **Cls HiHat** instrument will be transformed into a dotted rhythm, without any swing.

Dotted Rhythm

We're now going to explain what dotted rhythm is. It is somewhat similar to Morse code, since it presents us with both long and short sounds.

A dotted (or syncopated) rhythm is obtained when, among two neighboring notes of the same length, one is made longer, and the other is made shorter (in traditional notation, augmentation of the length of a note by half is denoted by a dot put next to the note).

For example, two quarter notes is the same as four eighth notes (each quarter note is two quavers). If we give two quarter notes syncopated rhythm, we'll get a quarter note with a dot and an eighth note. In other words, the first note (the crotchet with the dot) will last for three eighth notes, and the second note (the eighth note) will last only for one eighth note.

The swing effect can be enhanced by decreasing the **Velocity** value of the shuffled notes (Fig. 6.109).

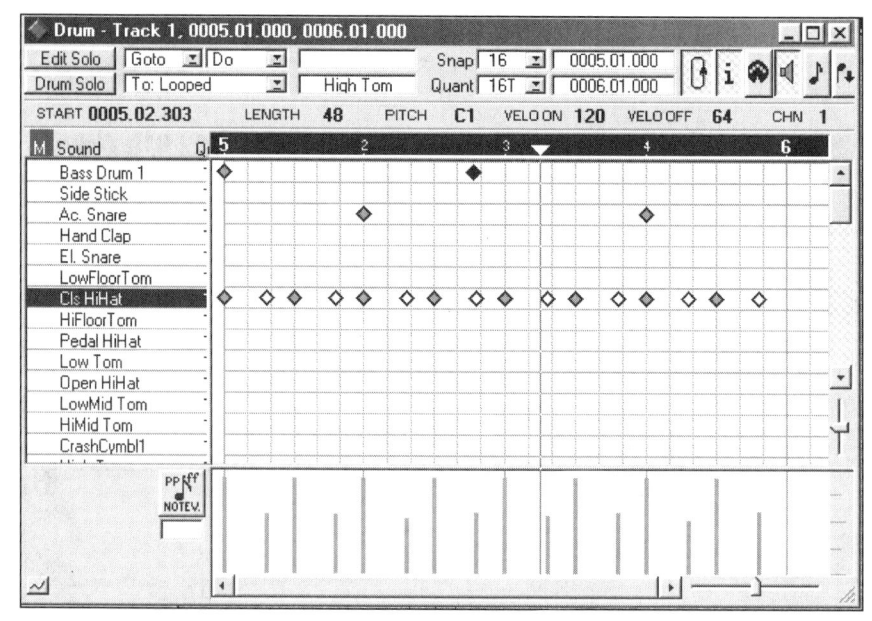

Fig. 6.109. Enhancing the swing effect by editing the **Velocity** parameter

Let's now continue the discussion of the commands of the **Functions** menu.

❐ The **Analitic Quantize** option was intended by the developers of Cubase VST 24 for quantization of complex parts. Having analyzed the contents of a part, the application itself decides which notes must be corrected (quantized). Conceptually, this procedure should maintain the style of a "live" performance. However, in our viewpoint, it is worth using only for experiments with musical material.

❐ The **Freeze Quantize** option fixes the results of quantization. All the quantization procedures (except for the steps of **Iterative Quantize**) are applied to the original material. When you need to perform two quantization procedures in a row, you must freeze the intermediate result with the **Freeze Quantize** command.

❐ The **Match Quantize** procedure isn't represented by a separate command in the menu. It is built into the toolbox of the **Arrange** window (the **Match Q** tool). The procedure can be done in the arrangement window only.

Using the **Match Q(Quantize)** tool is quite easy. You simply drag the model clip onto the clip being quantized (Fig. 6.110) and answer the question asked by the application. The possible answers are:

- **No** — notes are moved, but their Velocity values don't change in the clip being quantized
- **Copy** — the velocity values of the notes of the clip being quantized are set equal to those of the model clip

Chapter 6: The Cubase VST 24 Application and Creating "Live" MIDI Sound

- **Merge** — the velocity values of the clip being quantized and of the model clip are combined with a certain averaging. However, if the velocity values of the clip being quantized are large, they remain unchanged.

The **Match Quantize** procedure is performed with the same **Quantize** parameter as in the arrangement window. If the **Quantize** parameter in the arrangement window is set to **Off**, the notes won't move, and only the Velocity values will be copied. Let's consider an example. For a model, we'll take a "live" part that consists of quarter notes. Using this match, we'll quantize a part consisting of sixteenth notes.

To do this, it is necessary to set the **Quantize** field to 16 (sixteenth notes). After that, the sixteenth notes of the clip being quantized that are close to the quarter notes of the model clip will be moved, and the sixteenth notes that are far from the model's quarter notes will stay in their positions.

Suppose we set the **Quantize** field to 4. Then the sixteenth notes that are between the quarter note positions will be moved to the nearest quarter notes. In other words, the time intervals between the closest notes will have the length of a quarter note. The arrows in Fig. 6.111 show the correspondence between the model clip's notes and the notes of the clip being quantized. The lower notes are the quarter notes of the model, whereas the upper ones are the match-quantized sixteenth notes of the processed clip. As you can see from the figure, two clips are being edited in the **Key Edit** window simultaneously. This is why the brightness of the notes is different. (To edit two clips in the editor window, you must select both clips before you open the editor.) During quantization, the notes located on the clip's boundaries cannot move beyond the clip.

❏ The values of the **Quantize** parameter must be found experimentally when the two parts (the model clip and the clip being quantized) are rhythmically complex — that is, contain notes of various length.

The **Match Quantize** procedure can be performed not only between MIDI clips, but between clips of different types as well (for example, between an AUDIO clip and a MIDI clip). This procedure is used, for example, to adjust the rhythm of MIDI parts to imported sound fragments of Drum Loops. Suppose some Drum Loop fragments are imported to audiotracks, and their tempo is put into agreement with the tempo of the MIDI parts. The **Match Quantize** procedure is done in just the same way as when MIDI clips are matched. In other words, it is done by dragging the AUDIO clip onto the MIDI clip with the **Match Q** tool. The only difference is that, in this case, the application asks another question, and the **Get Match Points** window opens (Fig. 6.112).

❏ **Match Points (M-Points)**. Let's now discuss what Match Points (M-Points) are. In Cubase VST 24, a special algorithm is used to analyze the audio material and determine the rhythmic structure of the composition. According to this algorithm, the application detects the rhythm of the material and remembers all the stresses (strong and relatively strong beats). These stresses make up the basis of the rhythmic structure, and they are called match points (M-Points).

The sequence of such points is the rhythmic pattern. It can be applied to other material, which will then take on the same "pulse" as the pattern.

Jumping a bit ahead of ourselves, we can say that this rhythmic pattern is called a groove.

The M-Points by themselves are not a pure note sequence, but they can be easily transformed into a sequence.

Look at the **Get Match Points** window more closely. It consists of the following fields:

- **Sensitivity** — the general sensitivity of the algorithm for analyzing audio samples. The larger this parameter is, the more M-Points are created.
- **Attack** — the sensitivity to the attacks of the signal analyzed. As practice shows, this parameter should be found experimentally for every specific case.
- **Max. Number of Events per Sec.** — the maximum number of M-Points per second.

This limits the number of the created points. The algorithm for obtaining M-Points is the main method of capturing a "life-like" rhythmic structure of audio clips. This is why you should be very careful when setting the parameters in the **Get Match Points** window. For example, the default settings may appear to be inappropriate. Thus it would be better to visually control the number and positions of M-Points. You'll learn how to do this later in this chapter.

To analyze the rhythm, start the process with the **Process** button and, when asked, answer how the Velocity parameter should be changed. The valid options are the same as in the case of **Match Quantize** for MIDI clips, namely, **No**, **Copy**, and **Merge**. The procedure of adjusting the rhythm can also be performed in the opposite direction, that is, you can use a MIDI clip as a model. In this case, the application will ask, "**Dynamic Time Correction?**" and you must give a positive answer. After that, the **Get Match Points** window will appear, where you must click the **Process** button. When the playback speed is increased on a tape recorder, the pitch gets higher (a person's voice, for example, becomes "doll-like"). However, nothing of this sort happens during rhythm adjustment in Cubase VST 24. This is thanks to a special Time Stretching algorithm that stretches or compresses a clip without changing the tone pitch. We already came across this algorithm when discussing the Samplitude 2496 application.

For this algorithm to be used correctly (in respect to the rhythmic structure of the model, i.e., the MIDI clip), the program needs first to analyze the audio clip and obtain M-Points of its rhythmic structure, and then move these points according

Chapter 6: The Cubase VST 24 Application and Creating "Live" MIDI Sound 569

to the model. Only after that is the Time Stretching procedure performed. This is why the **Get Match Points** window appears before its execution.

Match Quantize can also be used for scale correction. To do this, a clip of the Chord Track must be used as a model. In doing this, the sequence of chords can be recorded using the Style Track (this method was discussed in the section "*Using Plug-Ins*" earlier in this chapter) or can be entered in the **Score Edit** editor. The **Match Quantize** procedure is done by dragging the clip of the Chord Track onto the MIDI clip. In the process, the application asks, "**Use Chords?**" If you click **Yes**, scale correction will be performed in compliance with the sequence of the clip's chords.

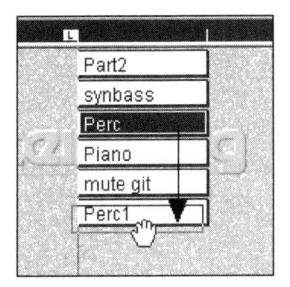

Fig. 6.110. Performing the **Match Quantize** procedure

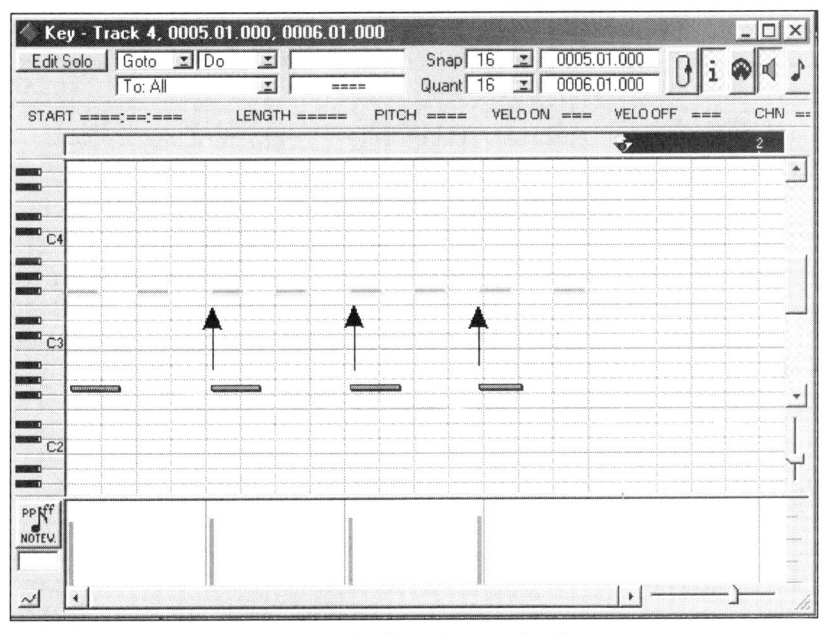

Fig. 6.111. Match quantization

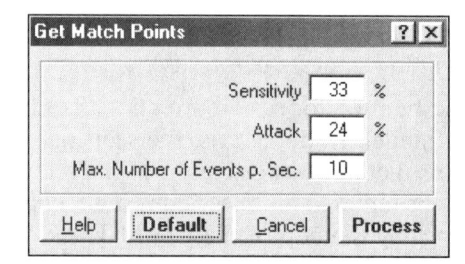

Fig. 6.112. The **Get Match Points** window

☐ The **Groove Quantize** option in the **Functions** menu resembles the match quantization discussed above. The difference is that here the model is saved (in the **Groove Map** form) for later use.

Groove quantization can be used, for example, to make music more life-like after its rhythm has been "precisely and soullessly" changed by the **Over Quantize** procedure. Using **Groove Quantize**, you can also "enliven" rhythmic parts that were laid out exactly according to the grid in the **Key Edit** and **Drum Edit** editors.

The Groove Library. The def.all song file contains the groove library of Cubase VST 24. To select a groove, call the **Groove Quantize** command from the **Functions** menu and select the desired groove (the active groove is checked).

When a groove is selected, quantization is applied to the clips selected in the arrangement window or to the notes selected in the **Key Edit** and **Drum Edit** editors. (If no notes are selected, all the notes are quantized.) If a track is selected in the arrangement window, all the clips in this track will be quantized.

Groove quantization can be performed using the <J> hotkey. In the process, the active (checked) groove will be used.

The results of groove quantization may differ depending on the value of the Quantize parameter. This may be both in the arrangement window and in the **Key Edit** and **Drum Edit** editors. The difference between the results is determined both by the rhythmic pattern of the specific groove and the structure of the part being quantized. Besides which, the user can switch off changing the Velocity parameter. For this purpose, you must select the **Setup Grooves** item in the **Functions** menu and uncheck the **Use Velocity** checkbox.

Creating a Groove

In Cubase VST 24, there is a feature that allows you to create a groove based on an audio clip. For simplicity's sake, we won't go into the process of recording or importing an audio clip (this will be discussed in the next section). Let's just suppose the audio clip is located on the audio track, and that it is one measure (bar) long.

Chapter 6: The Cubase VST 24 Application and Creating "Live" MIDI Sound

To create a groove, open the audio clip in the **Audio Editor** by double-clicking the clip and then clicking Audio Event (the "sound wave" icon) shown in Fig. 6.113.

The Segment and the Audio Event

We'd like to explain what an audio event is. But first we need to introduce the concept of a segment. A *segment* is a reference to a fragment of a sound file that contains information about the boundaries of the fragment. (A segment in Cubase VST 24 is equivalent to a *region* in SAWPro.) An *audio event* is a segment with its additional settings.

Since an audio event is a reference to a fragment of a sound file, it always contains a representation of the sound wave.

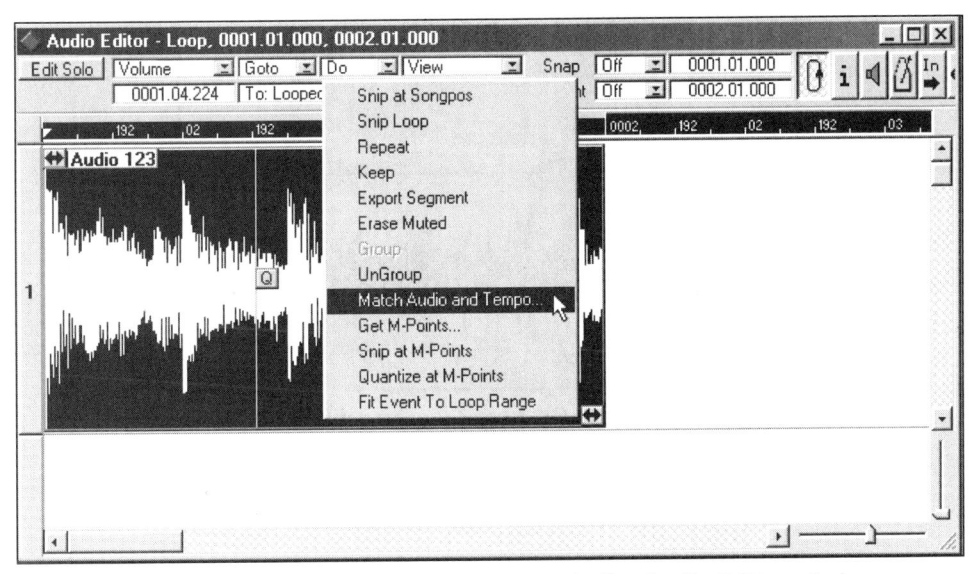

Fig. 6.113. Preparing to create a groove in the **Audio Editor** window

Let's go on creating the groove. Select the **Match Audio and Tempo** item from the **Do** drop-down list. The **Graphic Mastertrack** window will open, in which you must select the **Get Match Points** item from the **Audio** drop-down list (Fig. 6.114).

In the **Get Match Points** dialog box (Fig. 6.112), set the best values for the parameters for obtaining M-Points. At the end of the procedure, the precision of the analysis can be estimated visually (Fig. 6.115).

If the audio clip represents a percussion part, the position of the M-Points must correspond to the attacks (the points where the loudest sounds begin). These are easily viewed as amplitude peaks in the image of the sound wave. To convert the obtained M-Points to a groove, select the **M-Points to Groove** item from the **Audio** list (Fig. 6.114). After that, the newly created groove with the name of the used audio file will appear in the **Groove Quantize** submenu (Fig. 6.116).

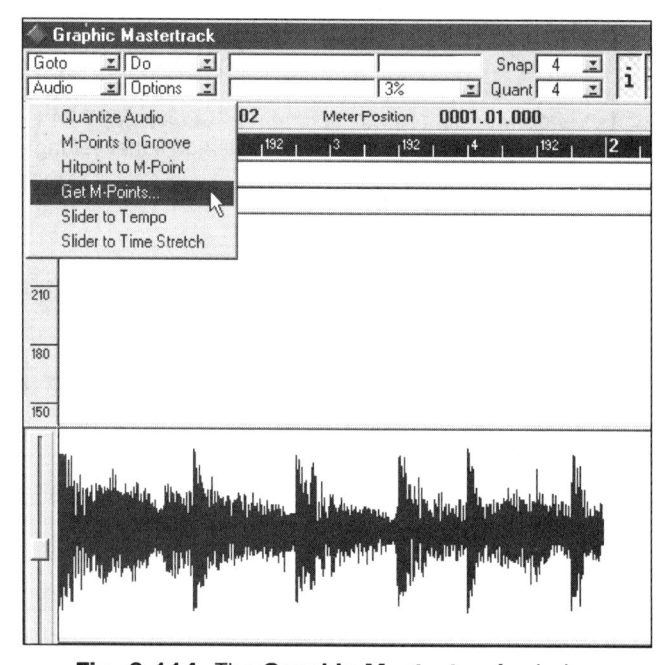

Fig. 6.114. The **Graphic Mastertrack** window

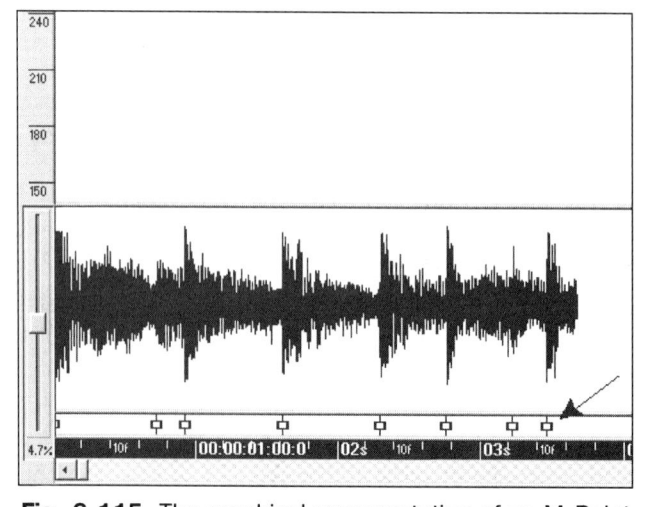

Fig. 6.115. The graphical representation of an M-Point

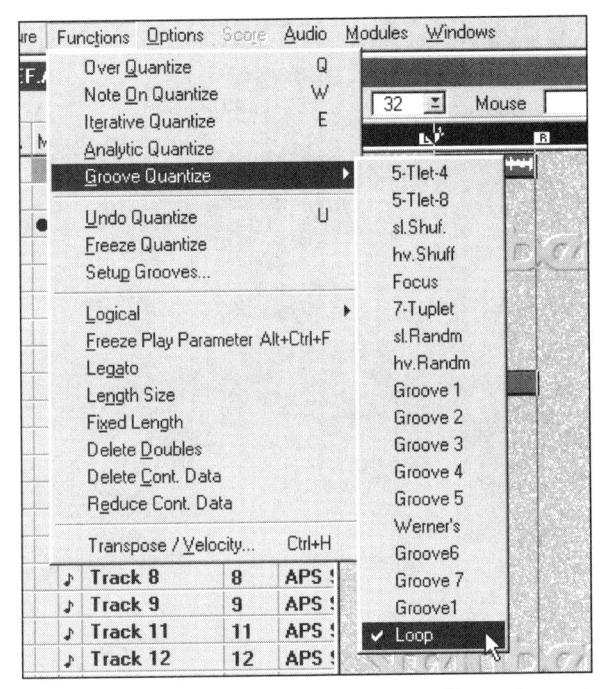

Chapter 6: The Cubase VST 24 Application and Creating "Live" MIDI Sound

Fig. 6.116. The new groove in the **Groove Quantize** submenu

Grooves can be saved in files with the GRV extension for use in other songs.

Working with Audio in Cubase VST 24

Setting up Cubase VST 24 to Work with Audio

Since this chapter is devoted mainly to techniques of working with MIDI, we're only going to look at a few points of working with Audio. A more detailed discussion of all the features of Cubase VST 24 would be quite long, and it is worth a separate book.

Again, we'd like to repeat the "golden" rule: prior to working with the application and recording Audio, you must clearly understand where the program settings are and how they can be changed.

In Cubase VST 24, the program settings are found in the **Audio System Setup** window (Fig. 6.117) available in the **Audio|System** menu.

574 Live Music on Your PC

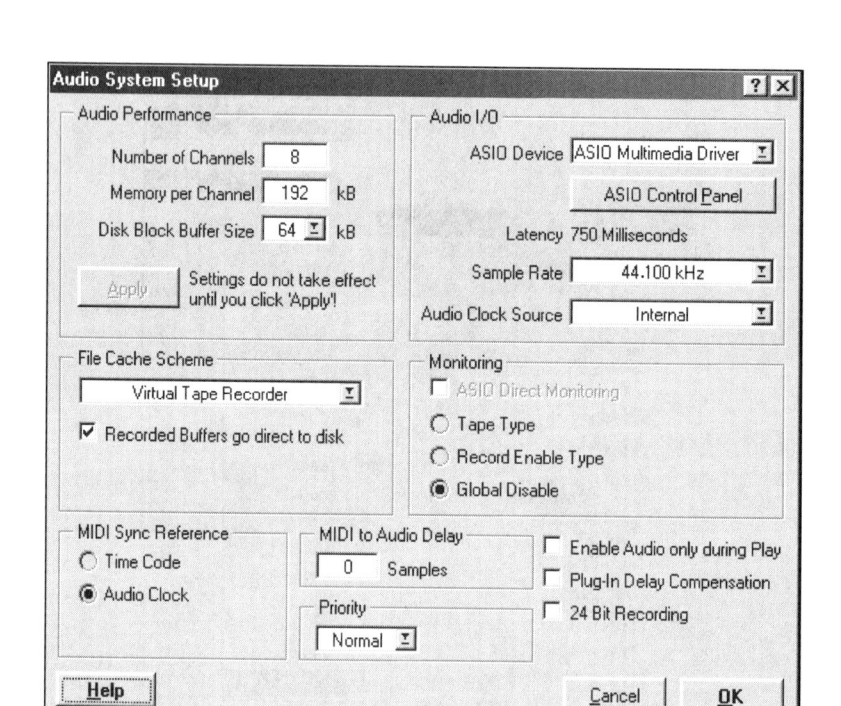

Fig. 6.117. The **Audio System Setup** window

Let's look at the Audio settings more closely:

❐ The **Audio Performance** section. All the settings in this section take effect only after you click the **Apply** button.

- The **Number of Channels** can be set to a value from 4 to 96 in Cubase VST 24.

  In Cubase VST 24, a system of virtual audio channels is implemented. The number of audio tracks is actually unlimited, each being able to use any of the available channels (like MIDI tracks and MIDI channels). The optimum number of audio channels should be learned from experiment. It is determined first of all by the size of the computer memory.

- The **Memory per Channels** parameter is the size of the computer memory allocated by the application to each audio channel. The larger this value, the less the probability of failures during the playback. The maximum valid value is 1024 KB. The total size of the computer memory allocated by the application is equal to the product of the number of channels and the value of the **Memory per Channels** parameter. It is easy to calculate the memory size necessary for 96 audio channels at a maximum value of the **Memory per Channels**. Depending on the memory size available in your computer, you have to decide whether to set the maximum values or compromise and decrease the **Memory per Channels** value.

Chapter 6: The Cubase VST 24 Application and Creating "Live" MIDI Sound

If the application detects that the product of the two parameters is too high, it will issue a warning (**Not enough memory for the Audio Engine**) after you click the **Apply** button.

- **Disk Block Buffer Size** is the size of the buffer used by the program to work with the hard drive.

  For this parameter, the same trend is valid: the larger the buffer, the less the probability of error. The minimum valid value is 32 KB, and the maximum is 256 KB. The minimum value of the **Memory per Channels** parameters depends on the buffer size. When the buffer increases, the lower limit for this parameter increases as well, and this implies increasing the size of the allocated memory.

❏ The **File Cache Scheme** section. Here, you can select one of three types of cache, depending on the sizes of the sound files:

- **Virtual Tape Recorder** is a cache used for long sound files that are seldom repeated on the audio track
- **Audio Sequencer** is a cache used for short but numerous sound files, for example, loop files
- **Tape Recorder/Audio Sequencer** is a cache used when there are sound files with various lengths, both long and short

The **Recorded Buffers go direct to disk** checkbox toggles the mode of direct (synchronous) writing of the buffers to the hard disk. When this is unchecked, the buffers are written to the hard disk from the Windows system cache. If you encounter any failures during recording, you should choose this option.

❏ The **MIDI Sync Reference** section contains two radio buttons: **Time Code** and **Audio Clock**.

You must select the **Time Code** radio button for external synchronization when Cubase VST 24 is used as a slave device. A loss of synchronization with Audio may occur in this case, but on the other hand, this mode provides the best synchronization of MIDI tracks with the master device.

The mode switched on by the **Audio Clock** radio button is used in all cases where external synchronization isn't provided. In this mode, synchronization between Audio and MIDI is best.

The mode can also be used with external synchronization, but in such a case, a good synchronization will be implemented only between the Audio and MIDI tracks of Cubase VST 24. As for the external master device, there may be some unsynchronization.

❏ The **MIDI to Audio Delay** section is used to compensate for the delay of MIDI playback with respect to Audio (if such a delay is present).

❐ The **Priority** section is used to change priorities in the processes that take place in Cubase VST 24.

- The **Low** mode. In this mode, the highest priority is given to MIDI processes. This mode must be used when Audio isn't used (or when it used rarely). If virtual real-time effects are employed, using this mode can lead to errors.
- The **Normal** mode. In this mode, MIDI and Audio processes have approximately equal priority. If there are errors in the Audio processes in the **Low** mode, you should switch to the **Normal** mode.
- The **High** mode. In this mode, Audio has a higher priority than MIDI. This mode should be used when you work with Audio. As a rule, there aren't any MIDI errors in this mode.
- The **Highest** mode. Here the Audio processes are given the highest priority. This mode is best suited for virtual real-time effects.

❐ The **Audio I/O** section is designed to set up the program in accordance with a certain sound card. The application interacts with the sound hardware via the ASIO driver (Audio Stream Input/Output).

Many inexpensive sound cards use the ASIO Multimedia Driver that is installed by default during the installation of Cubase VST 24.

For professional and semiprofessional sound cards, specialized ASIO drivers are available on the market. If a sound card has a specialized ASIO driver, you should install it, since it will help you to make the most of your sound card. You'll be able to use external hardware effects, for example.

The **ASIO Device** drop-down list is used for ASIO driver selection, and the **ASIO Control Panel** button opens a panel for additional settings that must be supported by the ASIO driver. These settings depend on the type of hardware. If the ASIO Multimedia Driver is used, a standard control panel is opened for those sound cards that don't have a special driver.

The **Latency** field shows the time of the application's response to manual mixing and the delays of the monitoring signal.

When the ASIO Multimedia Driver is used, the response time is 750 milliseconds (Fig. 6.117) at a sample rate of 44.100 kHz. This means that if we change the volume of any channel — say, the first — we'll hear this change 750 milliseconds (0.75 seconds) later. Because of this, you'll need to use another driver for mixing, namely, ASIO DirectX Driver, which has a response time of 204 milliseconds (at the same sample rate).

Unfortunately, it is impossible to use the ASIO DirectX Driver for recording, since it doesn't support the sound card input. So, for sound cards that aren't supported by specialized ASIO drivers (whose response time is even less), you can employ the fol-

Chapter 6: The Cubase VST 24 Application and Creating "Live" MIDI Sound   577

lowing method. To record, use the ASIO Multimedia Driver, and to process and mix, use the ASIO DirectX Driver.

- **Sample Rate.** To obtain a high-quality recording, you must set the sample rate to no less than 44.100 kHz. (If your hardware allows, you should set an even higher value.) For the Sound Blaster Live sound card, set it to 48.000 kHz, which is the maximum possible value for this sound card.
- The **Audio Clock Source** is used with advanced hardware that supports external synchronization.

❐ The **Monitoring** section allows the user to toggle between three modes of internal monitoring.

- The **Tape Type** mode. In this mode, you can listen to the signal at the track input. To do this, click either the **IN X L** or **IN X R** button (which means **Input Selector**). The buttons are found in the **Inspector** panel of the Audio track, or in the **VST Channel Mixer** panel. Here, X is the number of the active input of the sound card. For the standard multimedia sound card, these buttons will be **IN 1 L** or **IN 1 R**.

    The monitoring signal is delayed for the time interval specified in the **Latency** field. This is why it isn't very convenient to use monitoring with the ASIO Multimedia Driver, whose latency time is 0.75 sec. When using specialized ASIO drivers, the delay time is significantly less. The monitoring signal can be listened to in the stop and record modes. In the playback mode, the signal from the recorded track arrives to the output, and the monitoring signal is switched off.

- The **Record Enable Type** mode. Unlike in the **Tape Type** mode, the monitoring signal can be listened to during playback in this mode.
- The **Global Disable** mode turns off internal monitoring. It is recommended that you disable internal monitoring for most sound cards not supported by specialized ASIO drivers, and monitor without any delays via the external mixer or the mixer of the sound card.

❐ The **Enable Audio only during Play** checkbox enables the transferring of a continuous stream of audio blocks only during playback. When it is unchecked, Cubase VST 24 sends a continuous stream of audio blocks as soon as connection with the audio hardware is established.

❐ The **Plug-in Delay Compensation** checkbox serves to compensate for the delays of VST plug-ins. It is recommended that you check this checkbox, since some virtual effects of VST plug-ins can delay the processed signal. In such an event, undesirable side effects can occur during simultaneous playback of several tracks.

❐ The **24Bit Recording** checkbox turns on the mode of the same name (it is duplicated by the **24Bit** button in the arrangement window). In this mode, 24-bit sound files are created in 24-bit Packed Int format (Type 1 (24 bit)). Both 24-bit and 16-bit files can be simultaneously used in the arrangement window.

Making inputs active is the next stage of preparing Cubase VST 24 for audio recording. Select the **Inputs** item from the **Audio** menu. The **VST Inputs** window will open, in which you must click the button in the **Active** column. When the input is active, the button "glows" green (Fig. 6.118).

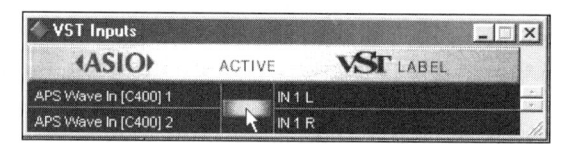

Fig. 6.118. The **VST Inputs** window

It should be mentioned that if Cubase VST 24 does sound processing and mixing, the inputs must be inactive (disabled) in order to free up the processor.

Fig. 6.118 shows an example of the configuration of inputs with the standard ASIO Multimedia Driver. If a specialized ASIO driver designed for a specific sound card is installed, the configuration of inputs will change according to the hardware characteristics of the sound card (Fig. 6.119).

Fig. 6.119. The **VST Inputs** window with many inputs

The settings assigned in the stage of preparing Cubase VST 24 for recording can be saved in the def.all song file located in the **Cubase Audio VST** folder.

Audio Clip Recording

In this section, we'll describe two ways of recording: the normal recording mode and the **Punch** method.

Chapter 6: The Cubase VST 24 Application and Creating "Live" MIDI Sound

For the normal mode of audio clip recording, proceed as follows:

1. Create a track of the Audio class.
2. Activate the **Inspector** panel of the Audio track (click the button in the lower left corner of the arrangement window).
3. Enter the name of the track into the **Track Info** field of the **Inspector** panel. (This isn't mandatory, but it is recommended in order to facilitate further work.)
4. Select the audio channel number in the **Chan** (Channel) field of the **Inspector** panel. In doing so, you must choose odd numbers for stereo recording, and you may choose any numbers for mono recording. (Cubase VST 24 reserves two audio channels for the stereo signal, the stereo track being marked by an asterisk in the **Chn** field.)
5. If you intend to record in stereo, turn off the **Mono** mode by clicking the **Mono** field (Fig. 6.120).

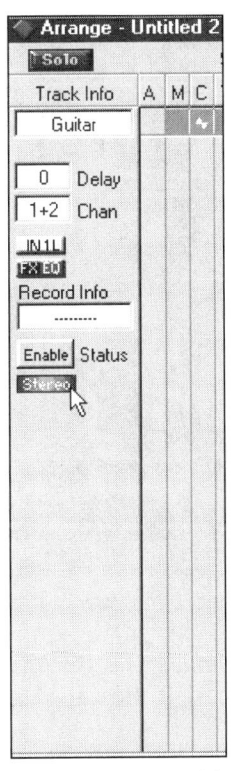

Fig. 6.120. The **Inspector** panel for an audio track

6. Click the **Enable** button. The **Select Folder for Audio** window will open, where you must select (or create) the desired folder and click the **Select** button.

Cubase VST 24 saves audio data in sound files with the WAV extension. You should create a separate folder for them, or better yet, keep the files of each musical project (ALL, GRV, WAV, etc.) in separate folders. The folder for audio is selected once, and the **Select Folder for Audio** window won't appear when you click the **Record** button again.

To set the recording level, you can use an external mixer or the sound card mixer. To control the recording level visually, you must first open the virtual mixer of Cubase VST 24 by selecting the **Monitor** item from the **Audio** menu.

In the **VST Channel Mixer** virtual mixer window, you must click the **In** button located on the recording level indicator of the desired channel (Fig. 6.121). However, if monitoring is on, you must click the **IN 1 L (IN 1 R)** button instead.

If the track is in the stereo mode (Fig. 6.121), clicking the **IN 1 L/IN 1 R** button of either channel will automatically affect the corresponding button of the channel.

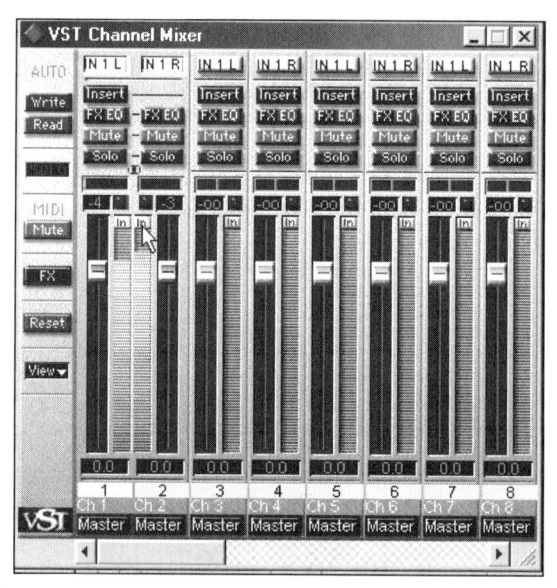

Fig. 6.121. Controlling the recording level in the **VST Channel Mixer** window

Now you can start recording by clicking the **Record** button on the **Transport** bar. Recording begins at the position of the left locator (**L**), and doesn't differ from MIDI recording.

After you stop recording with the **Stop** button, an audio clip will appear on the Audio track.

If the **Precount** checkbox is checked in the **Metronome** window (see Fig. 6.36), recording will start after the precount (just like with MIDI recording).

Deleting an Audio Clip

If you select the **Undo** command from the **Edit** menu after recording an audio clip, only the audio clip will be deleted from the arrangement window, the sound file being retained on the hard disk. When you need to delete an audio clip along with the sound file, you must select the clip and press the <Ctrl>+<Backspace> shortcut.

The **Punch** mode is identical to the mode of the same name used in MIDI recording:

1. Set the locators at the boundaries of the fragment to be recorded.
2. Click the **Punch In** and **Punch Out** buttons on the **Transport** bar.
3. Place the cursor to the left of the left locator and click the **Play** button.

Recording will automatically begin when the cursor reaches the left locator, and stop when the cursor reaches the right locator.

Playback won't stop until you click the **Stop** button.

If you activate only the **Punch Out** button, recording will take place in the following fashion: after you click the **Record** button, recording will begin from the position of the left locator and stop automatically when the cursor reaches the right locator.

Cycle Audio Recording

Cycle recording in Cubase VST 24 is very simple. To record a take in the cycle record mode, proceed as follows:

1. Confine a working area in the arrangement window with the locators.
2. Click the **Cycle** button on the **Transport** bar.
3. Start recording from the **Stop** mode.

In each loop, when the cursor passes through the area inside the locators, a new take will be recorded. After cycle recording stops, a new audio clip containing the recorded material will be created.

To access any of the recorded versions, open the corresponding audio clip in the **Audio Editor** window (Fig. 6.122) by double-clicking the clip.

All the recorded takes are available in the **Audio Editor** window as audio events. However, only one of them can be listened to during playback.

If you see just one version in the editor window, uncheck the **By Output** option in the **View** menu.

To ease picking a version out of the recorded ones, you may selectively mute the unneeded versions. This is done with the **Mute** tool found in the toolbox (Fig. 6.122).

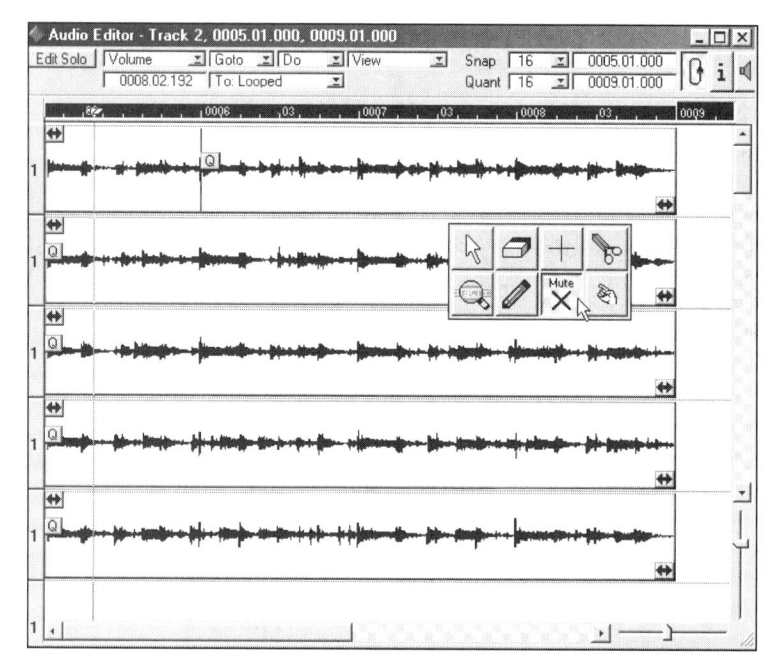

Fig. 6.122. Editing the takes in the **Audio Editor** window

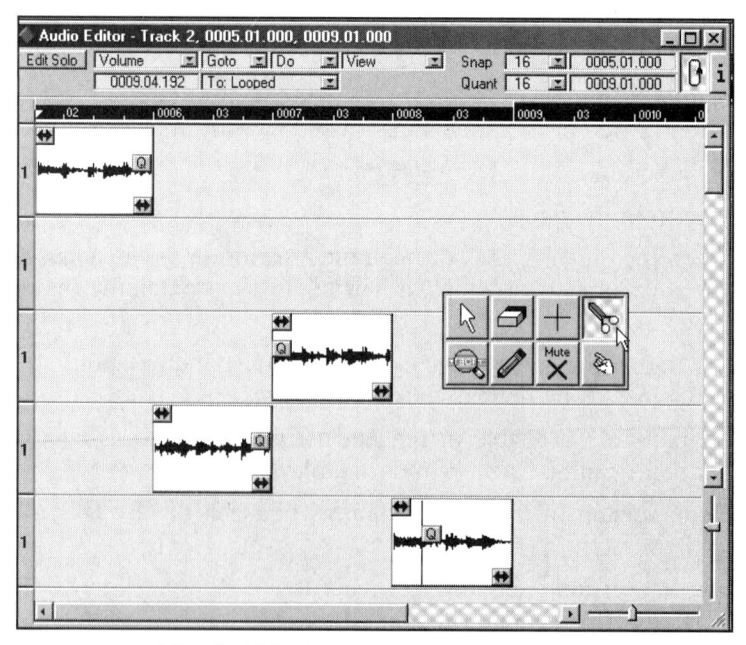

Fig. 6.123. Building an "perfect" take

The toolbox of the **Audio Editor** is opened in the standard manner: click and hold the right mouse button.

Bad takes are deleted with the **Eraser** tool. The "perfect" take can be easily obtained from successful fragments of various versions with the **Scissors** tool used for cutting (Fig. 6.123).

Editing Audio Events in Audio Editor

We've also come across such notions as a segment and an audio event. Recall that a *segment* is a reference to a sound file, whereas an *audio event* is a segment and its additional settings (this is equivalent to the notion of *object* in Samplitude 2496).

Segments and audio events are used in Cubase VST 24 to edit audio material non-destructively, since they allow you to use references to files rather than the original audio files themselves.

Despite some similarity to Samplitude 2496, it should be mentioned that non-destructive editing in Cubase VST 24 is more sophisticated. This is due to the fact that the tracks are separated from the audio channels.

In SAWPro and Samplitude 2496, the concepts of a "channel" and a "track" are identical. Thus, after connecting a virtual effect to a track, we aren't able to use the effect for another track.

Unlike these programs, Cubase VST 24 lets the user connect any track to any channel. In other words, a single virtual sound processing channel can be used by multiple tracks.

This scheme is somewhat complex. For example, if one channel is shared by several tracks, they each try to intercept it (there is a sort of competition among the tracks). Non-destructive editing of audio clips can also be done in the arrangement window, using the toolbox (in the same fashion as when MIDI editing).

The **Audio Editor** allows you to perform operations on audio material with greater accuracy.

You can open the **Audio Editor** either with a double click on the audio clip or after having selected one or more audio clips with the **Edit** command of the **Edit** menu. You can also use the <Ctrl>+<E> shortcut.

The interface of the **Audio Editor** is similar to the interfaces of the other editors in Cubase VST 24. Thus it is not difficult to master.

Fig. 6.124 shows an audio event that resembles an object of Samplitude 2496. Like the object of Samplitude 2496, the audio event has operators to move the boundaries (indicated by the arrows in Fig. 6.124). Let's now examine the techniques used in work with audio events.

To move the boundaries of an audio event, place the **Arrow** tool onto the operator and drag it to the left or right (Fig. 6.125). In the process, the arrow will temporarily turn into the **Pencil**.

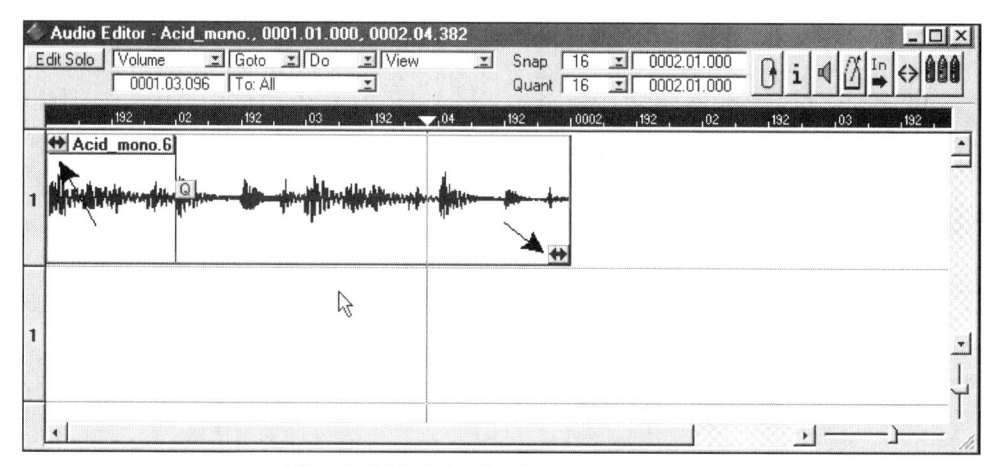

Fig. 6.124. The **Audio Editor** window

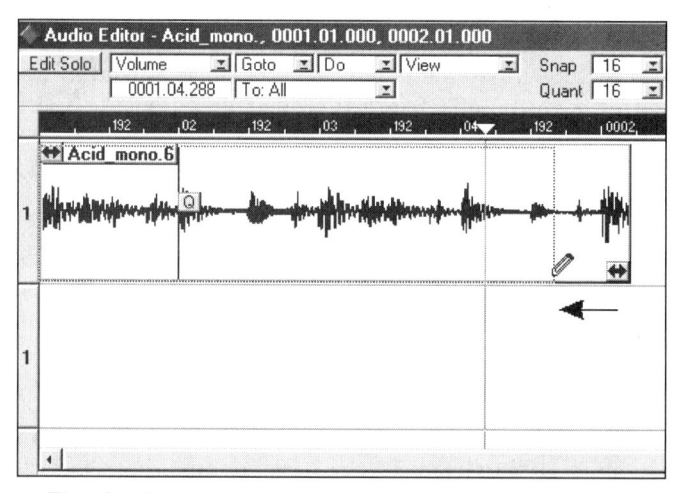

Fig. 6.125. Moving the boundaries of an audio event

Using the **Pencil** tool, you can import a sound file directly into the **Audio Editor** window. To do this, click with the **Pencil** tool at the desired position and select the WAV file from the list in the **Select an Audio File** window. The starting position of the created audio event will be at the very place you clicked.

Audio events can be dragged with the **Arrow** tool. While dragging, the position of an audio event will be determined by the position of the Q-Point (quantization point), as shown in Fig. 6.126.

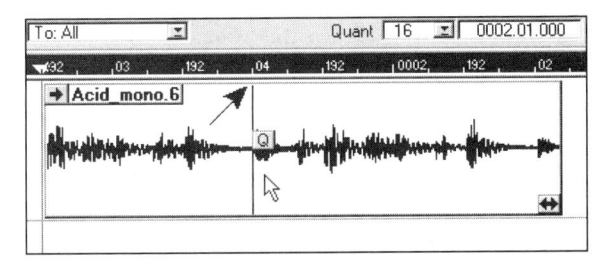

Fig. 6.126. Using the Q-Point

The precision of positioning an audio event depends on the value of the **Snap** parameter. The Q-Point is set to a precise position on the time axis. It can be freely dragged around the audio event. For example, you can put it at a strong beat of a musical audio fragment, etc.

To copy an audio event, you must drag it while holding down the <Alt> or <Ctrl> key. The result will be an ordinary or a ghost copy of the audio event, respectively.

Coordinating Audio and MIDI Tempos

You can easily coordinate Audio and MIDI tempos with one another in the **Audio Editor** window. Suppose you need to coordinate the tempo of an imported loop one measure long with the tempo of a MIDI. Do the following:

1. Place the audio event so that its starting boundary coincides with the beginning of a musical measure.
2. Create a local loop in the same way you did in **Key Edit** (see "*The Basic Components of the Cubase VST 24 Interface*" earlier in this chapter). The boundaries of the local loop must coincide with the boundaries of the musical measure (Fig. 6.127).

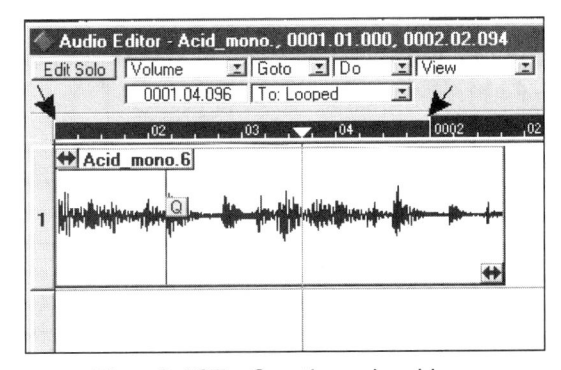

Fig. 6.127. Creating a local loop

3. After that, select the audio event with a single click, and select the **Fit Event to Loop Range** item in the **Do** drop-down list.
4. When the message **Fit Audio to Loop by adjusting** appears, select either of the two methods:
   - **Tempo** — the MIDI tempo is fitted to the Audio tempo
   - **Audio** — the Audio tempo is fitted to the MIDI tempo

> **WARNING** This operation employs a destructive algorithm — Time Stretching — which can lead to sound distortion!

Cubase VST 24 allows the user to transform an audio clip so that the tempo of its playback will follow that of a MIDI's.

As an example, let's look at a loop whose tempo is coordinated with a MIDI tempo.

The audio event transformation will take three stages:

1. Select the **Get M-Points** item in the **Do** drop-down list to obtain M-Points.
2. Perform the **Snip at M-Points** command to cut the audio event at these M-Points (Fig. 6.128).

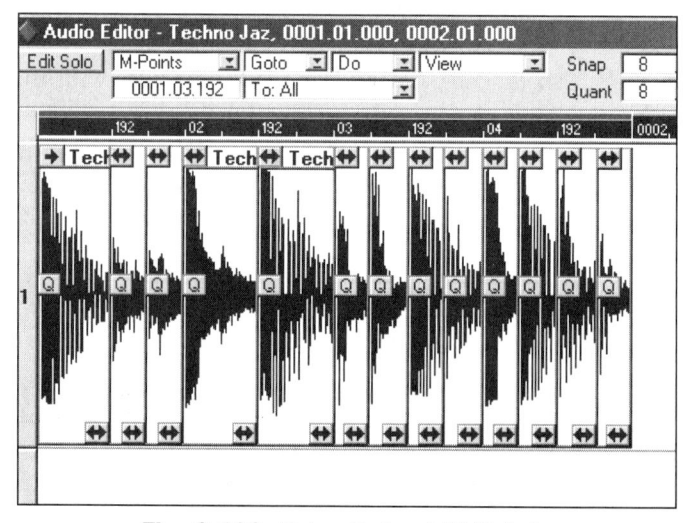

Fig. 6.128. Using **Snip at M-Points**

3. Select the **Group** item in the **Do** drop-down list to group together the audio events.

The tempo of the resulting audio clip will exactly follow changes of the MIDI tempo.

The VST Pool Window

Like SAWPro, Cubase VST 24 provides a database of sound file segments (regions) used in a musical project. It is accessed either through the **VST Pool** window (select **Audio|Pool**) or with the <Ctrl>+<F> shortcut.

The **VST Pool** window displays all the audio files recorded in and imported into Cubase VST 24.

You can import audio files using either the **File|Import Audio** menu in the **VST Pool** window or the **File|Import Audio File** menu in the arrangement window.

Fig. 6.129 shows how segments are distributed after the **Snip at M-Points** command has been performed (based on the last example). The list item marked with a triangle in the upper left corner of the window is the audio file itself, while the list items marked with a "loudspeaker" icon are the segments of this audio file.

For convenience, the segments are graphically represented as clips in sound wave form. Each click on the triangle hides or shows the list of the segments.

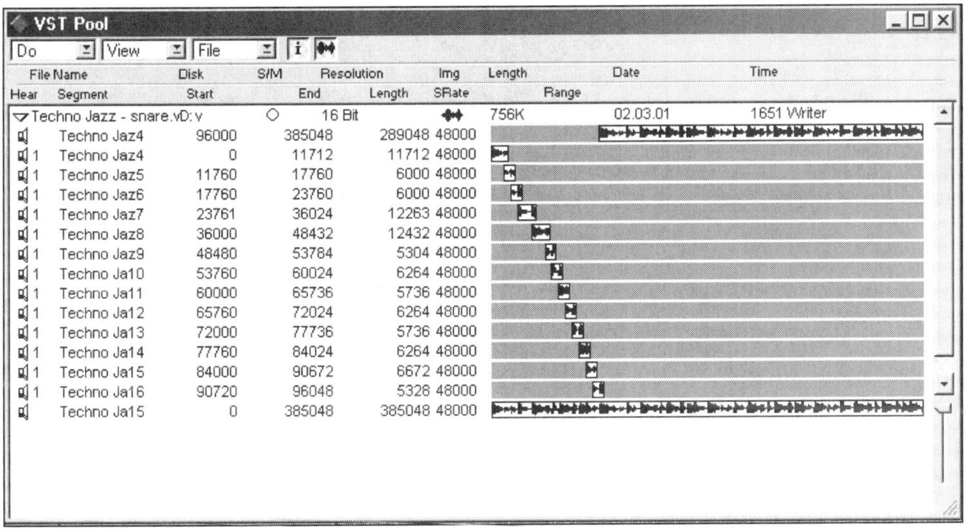

Fig. 6.129. The **VST Pool** window

Recorded files or files imported into Cubase VST 24 are the main items of the list. They are marked with triangles. Each main item contains its own internal list of segments belonging to this audio file. In other words, the list represents a hierarchy.

The segments can be listened to by left-clicking the "loudspeaker" icon of the desired segment and keeping the mouse button pressed.

Using the **VST Pool** window, it is very convenient to assemble Audio from the available segments. Just drag the segment (grabbing its name in the **Segment** column) from the **VST Pool** window to the **Arrange** or **Audio Editor** window (Fig. 6.130).

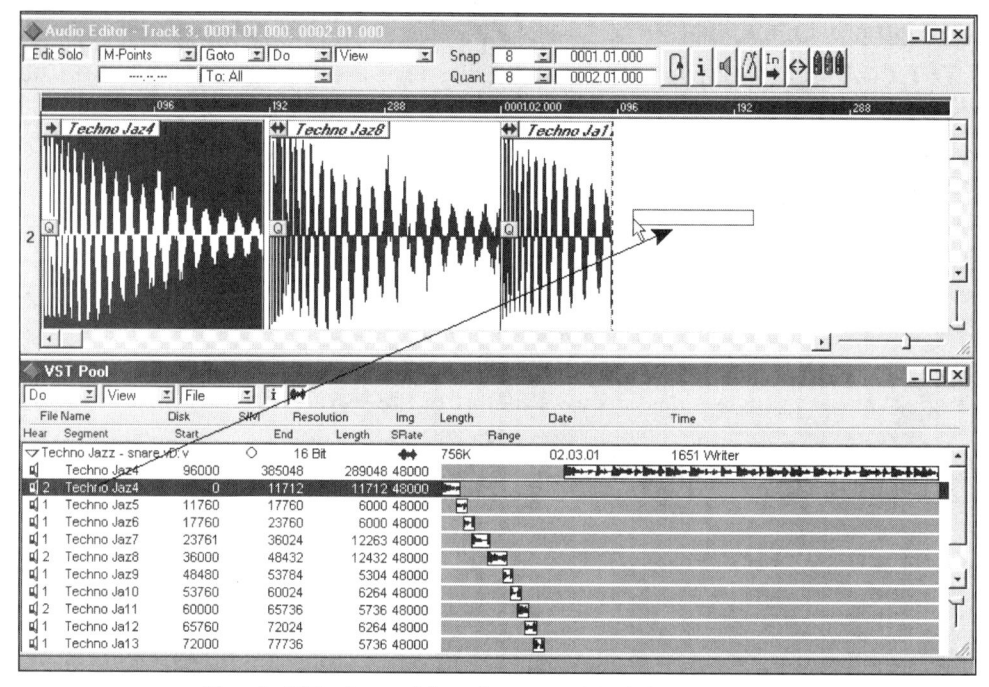

Fig. 6.130. Assembling the material of the segments

The **VST Pool** window makes it possible to perform some other useful operations with audio files and segments. You can:

❒ Delete audio files not used in the song in order to free up the disk (**File|Delete Unused File**), and delete segments from the list (**Do|Purge Segments**).

❒ Destructively delete unused segments from the original sound files, using **Do|Erase Unused**. (There is a similar operation in Samplitude 2496, namely, **Remote unused Samples** in the **Tools** menu.)

Before performing the destructive deletion, you must select the audio file in the list in the **VST Pool** window (since the operation is done for one audio file at a time). One condition is imposed: the audio file must be used in the song, and at least one of its segments must be unused.

To delete the unused segments of all audio files at once, you must previously select the files in the list in the **VST Pool** window (by clicking each audio file while holding the <Shift> key pressed).

Chapter 6: The Cubase VST 24 Application and Creating "Live" MIDI Sound

- Create an archive. This operation copies all the audio files contained in the VST Pool list along with the song file (ALL) to a folder defined by the user. The procedure is performed using the **File|Prepare Archive** menu.
- Create copies of the sound files used in the song in a new folder (defined by the user), and destructively delete the unused segments from these copies. This is done using the **File|Prepare Master** menu.

Sound Processing in Cubase VST 24

Cubase VST 24 belongs to the class of virtual studio programs, and therefore mixing and sound processing are performed in it virtually.

This application has its own internal standard for virtual VST effects. Besides which, it allows you to use DirectX plug-in effects.

A distinctive feature of using VST effects in Cubase VST 24 is the possibility of recording and subsequently playing back the changes to effect settings in real time. While Samplitude 2496 allowed us to record only automation curves of volume and panning in real time, in Cubase VST 24, we can record automation curves of the parameters of a virtual effect in a separate Audio Mix track.

So let's discuss the sound processing features of Cubase VST 24.

Fig. 6.131. The **Inspector** panel for an audio track

The **Inspector** panel for an audio track provides quick access to the **VST Channel Settings** panel that contains a dynamic processor — VST Dynamics — and a parametric equalizer.

To open this panel, use the double **FX EQ** button (Fig. 6.131). A click on **FX** opens the section of the **VST Channel Settings** that contains the dynamic processor (Fig. 6.132), and a click on **EQ** opens the section with the parametric equalizer (Fig. 6.133).

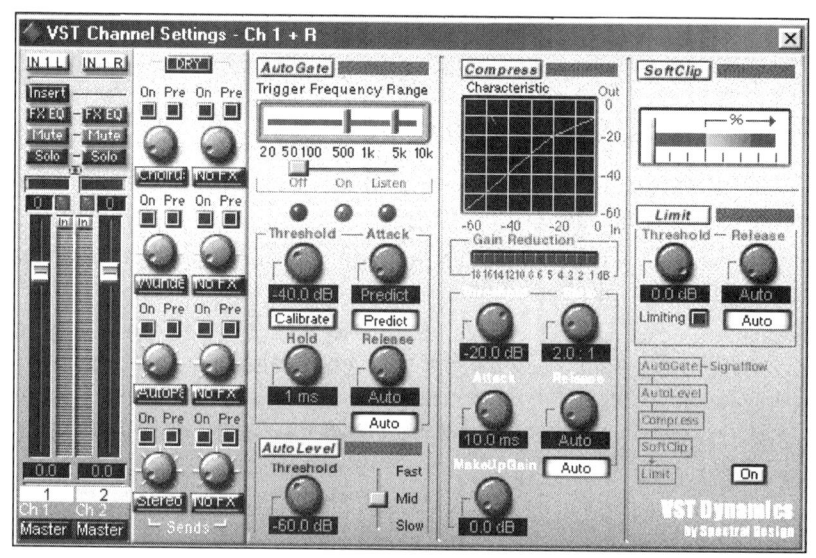

Fig. 6.132. The **VST Dynamics** dynamic processor

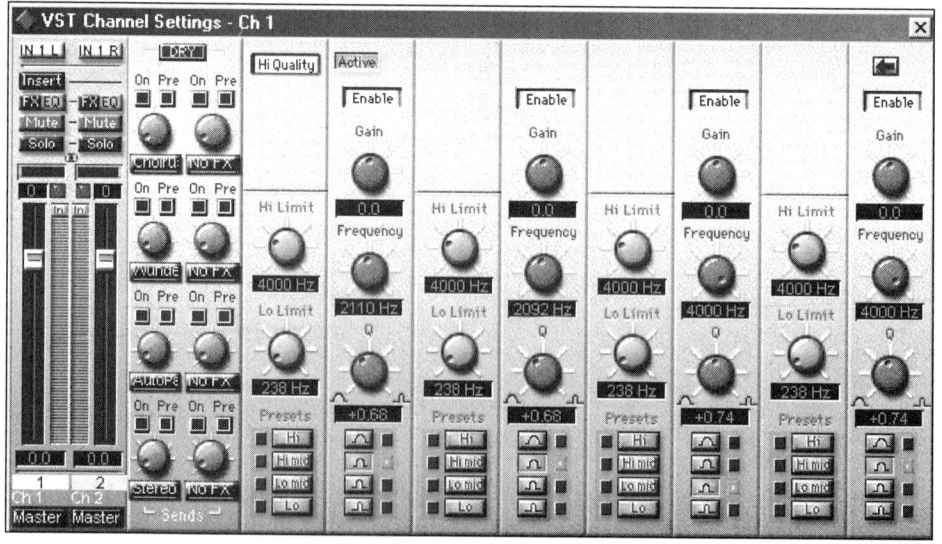

Fig. 6.133. The parametric equalizer in the **Channel Settings — Ch1** window

Chapter 6: The Cubase VST 24 Application and Creating "Live" MIDI Sound 591

Undoubtedly, one convenience of the application's interface is that the dynamic processor and the parametric equalizer are combined with the virtual mixer section. This allows you to quickly adjust many parameters of the channel in just one window.

The **FX EQ** double button can be also found in the virtual mixer section. It is used to switch quickly between the sections of the **VST Channel Settings** panel.

The virtual mixer section consists of:

- The record/playback level indicators
- The volume and pan controls
- The **Solo**, **Mute**, and **Input Selector** buttons (shown as **IN 1 L** and **IN 1 R** in Fig. 6.133)

To switch between active inputs, click **Input Selector** while holding down the <Ctrl> key.

Inserting virtual effects. To insert VST and DirectX virtual effects into a channel, you must click the **Insert** button in the virtual mixer section. The **VST Inserts** panel will appear (Fig. 6.134).

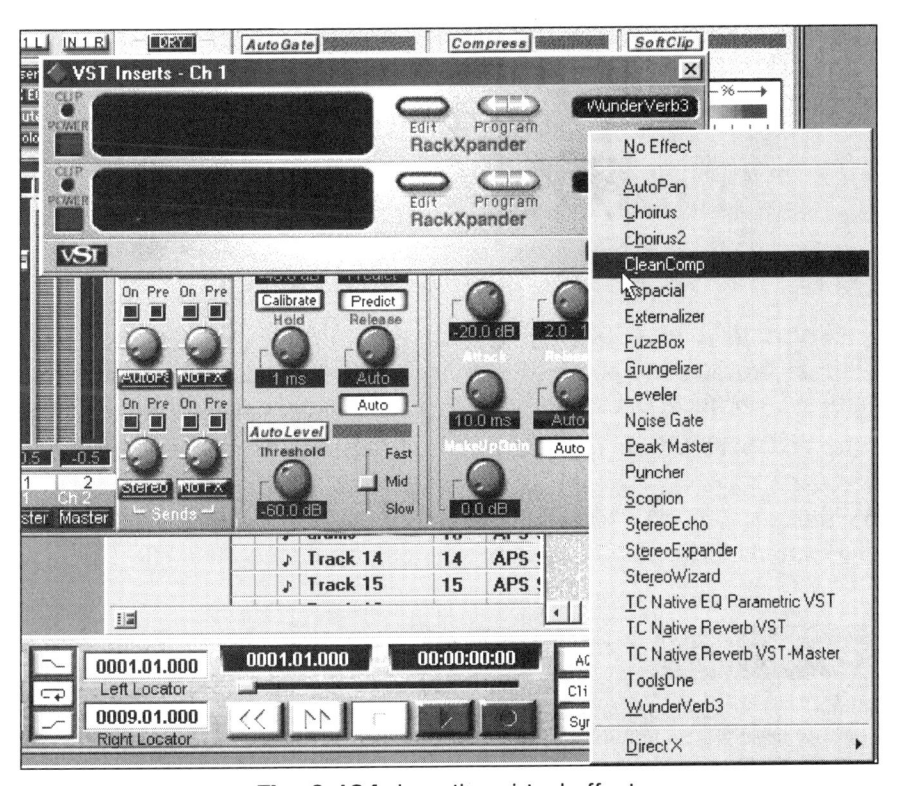

Fig. 6.134. Inserting virtual effects

If no effect has been inserted, the **VST Inserts** panel contains one field, **No Effect**. To insert effects, click this field, and the list of virtual VST effects will appear. At the bottom of the list, you'll see the **DirectX** submenu item, which allows you to insert DirectX effects (Fig. 6.134).

Inserting each successive effect is done in the same manner, since the **No Effect** field doesn't disappear.

An inserted effect remains inactive until the **Power** button is clicked. The internal parameters of any effect are available via the **Edit** button.

To unload a virtual effect, select the **No Effect** item from the list of effects (Fig. 6.134).

The exterior of the panel depends on the type of effect inserted.

Fig. 6.135 illustrates various types of the effect panel (from top to bottom):

❐ Standard — all the settings are done directly on the panel

❐ RackXpander — the settings are available via the **Edit** button

❐ No Effect — no effect has been inserted

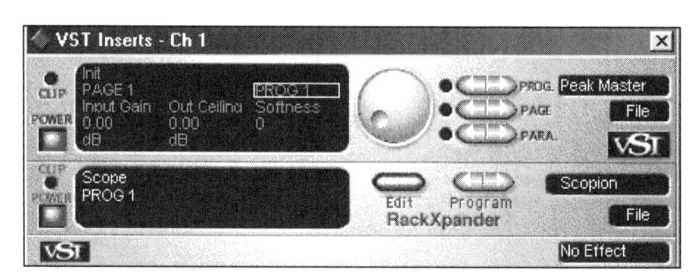

Fig. 6.135. Various types of the effect panel

Inserting the VST Send Effects. In addition to the virtual effects connected to a channel, Cubase VST 24 provides the possibility of using virtual effects called VST Send Effects (in Samplitude 2496, the AUX section of the virtual mixer is used for similar purposes).

To open the **VST Send Effects** panel, select the **Effects** item in the **Audio** menu.

The **VST Send Effects** (Fig. 6.136) and **VST Inserts** panels have almost identical interfaces. The differences are: the **Effects Master** control (that controls the signal level at the effect input) and the possibility of directing the output of the virtual effect to the external effect processor.

Bus System

Cubase VST 24 uses a bus system for maximally effective usage of the sound cards supported by special ASIO drivers. The bus system allows the user to organize the best routing for audio streams. By default, the output of every section of the virtual mixer is connected to the Master bus.

Chapter 6: The Cubase VST 24 Application and Creating "Live" MIDI Sound 593

The outputs of the VST Send Effects can be connected to the Master bus, but they also can be connected to the external effect processor. Unfortunately, the discussion of this interesting topic is beyond the scope of this book.

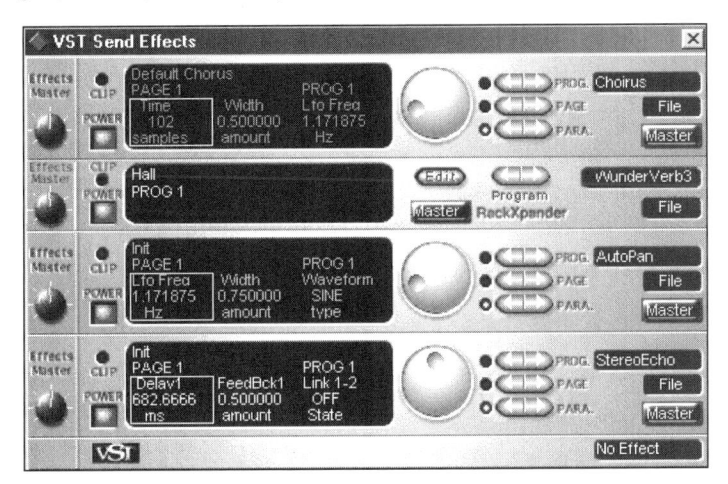

Fig. 6.136. The **VST Send Effects** panel

In the simplest case, the outputs of the effects on the **VST Send Effects** panel are connected to the Master bus.

To send a signal from a channel to the VST Send Effects, a special routing section is provided on the **VST Channel Settings** panel (Fig. 6.137).

Fig. 6.137. The routing section

The routing section contains eight controls of the output signal level. In other words, one channel can send the signal to eight effects.

There are routing buttons under the controls. A click on any routing button opens a list where you can select a signal route. The VST Send Effects are found at the beginning of the route list.

To send the signal by the specified route, click the **On** button (Fig. 6.137).

The **Pre** (Prefader) button toggles between two modes. When it is pressed, the sent signal is received after volume control (this is called "post fader"). When the button is in the released state, the sent signal is received before volume control ("pre fader").

The **Dry** button locks the sent signal on all the routes.

Inserting Master Effects

A separate panel, **VST Master Effects**, is provided in Cubase VST 24 for general signal processing.

The number of master effects is limited to four. These effects are those intended for mastering (like the effects of the master block of the virtual mixer in Cubase VST 24). To open the **VST Master Effects** panel, select the **Master Effects** item in the **Audio** menu.

Using Automation

To control recording and playback of the automation curves, the **VST Channel Mixer** panel is provided. It is opened with the **Monitor** item in the **Audio** menu.

After clicking the **Write** button in the **Auto** section in the **VST Channel Mixer** panel (Fig. 6.138), a special audio mix track of the Mix Track class is created. This is an automation track.

Later, during playback, it will be possible to perform "live" mixing, and all the changes will be frozen in the positions of the controls. For the written changes to become active automatically, the automation track must be read. For this purpose, you must switch off the writing mode and switch on the reading mode. In other words, you must click the **Write** button (thus releasing it) and click **Read**.

Leaving the **VST Channel Mixer** window will automatically switch off the **Write** function.

Automation can be written down step-by-step. After clicking the **Write** button, set the cursor to the specified position, and change the position of the control. Then set the cursor to the next position, again change the position of the control, and so on.

Cubase VST 24 allows the user to read and write automation simultaneously. To switch this mode on, click both the **Read** and **Write** buttons. It will be possible to write changes for one channel and simultaneously listen to the automation for another.

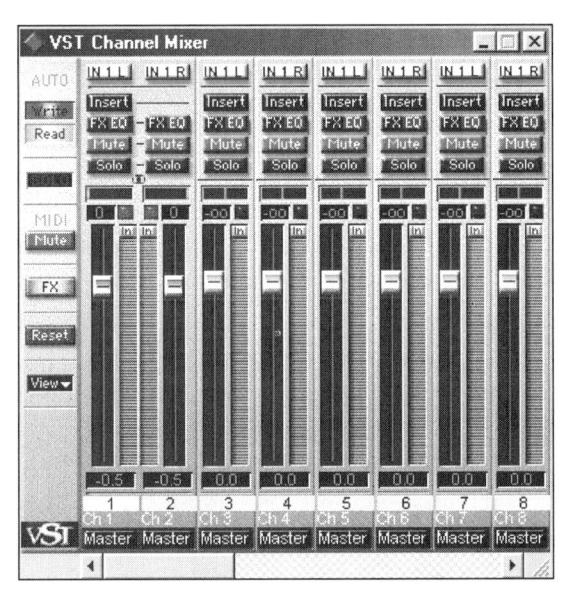

Chapter 6: The Cubase VST 24 Application and Creating "Live" MIDI Sound

Fig. 6.138. The **Write** and **Read** buttons in the **VST Channel Mixer** panel

In Cubase VST 24, the following settings can be automated:
- Volume
- Pan
- Mute
- Solo
- EQ On switch (switching the parametric equalizer on/off)
- Settings for 4 EQ modules
- 8 x Effect Send Active switches (switching on/off the signal sent along the route, eight **On** buttons)
- 8 x Effect Send levels (eight sliders)
- 8 x Effect Send PRE Switches (eight **Pre/Post Fader** buttons)
- Effect DRY switch (blocking the signal sent)
- 4 x Insert Effect Program selection (audio channel 1 to 32 only)
- 4 x Insert Effect parameters (the first 15 parameters for each effect — audio channel 1 to 32 only)
- Master volume Left and Right (the volume level on the **VST Channel Mixer** panel)
- 8 x Send Effect "Master" level (the signal levels of the eight virtual effects on the **VST Send Effects** panel)

- 8 × Send Effect Program selection (on the **VST Send Effects** panel)
- 8 × Send Effect parameters (the first 16 parameters for each effect on the **VST Send Effects** panel)
- 4 × Master Effect Program selection
- 4 × Master Effect parameters (the first 8 parameters for each effect)

When writing the automation, it is convenient to create a separate automation clip (Audiomix Part) for each audio channel. To do this, proceed as follows:

1. Write an automation clip for the first channel in the usual manner.
2. Create a new track of the Mix Track class and move the clip just written onto the track. (The names of the track and the clip should correspond to the number of the channel.)
3. Open the **VST Channel Mixer** window and click the **Write** button. A new automation clip will be created. Write a new automation clip for the next channel.
4. Go to step 2.

Each automation clip for each channel will be put on a separate track (Fig. 6.139).

Fig. 6.139. Separating the automation tracks for each channel

To create the final audio file or perform intermediate mixing, Cubase VST 24 provides the **Export Audio** function. It can be called in two ways: either with the **Export Audio File** command of the **File** menu, or with the **Create File** button on the **VST Master Effects** panel. The second method is preferable from the standpoint of controlling the output level (Fig. 6.140).

The **VST Master Effects** panel is opened with the **Master** command of the **Audio** menu.

After the **Create File** button is clicked, the **Export Audio** dialog box (Fig. 6.141) will open, where you must set the necessary parameters:

- In the **Resolution** section, set the resolution of the audio file, 16 bits or 24 bits (24-bit resolution ensures better-quality processing results).
- In the **Sample Rate** section, specify the sample rate. If intermediate mixing is being performed, the sample rate must be the same for all the audio files of the song. To obtain audio CD quality, set the sample rate to 44,100 Hz or higher.

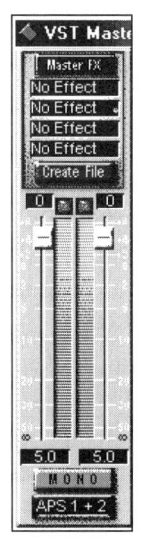

Chapter 6: The Cubase VST 24 Application and Creating "Live" MIDI Sound 597

Fig. 6.140. The **VST Master Effects** panel

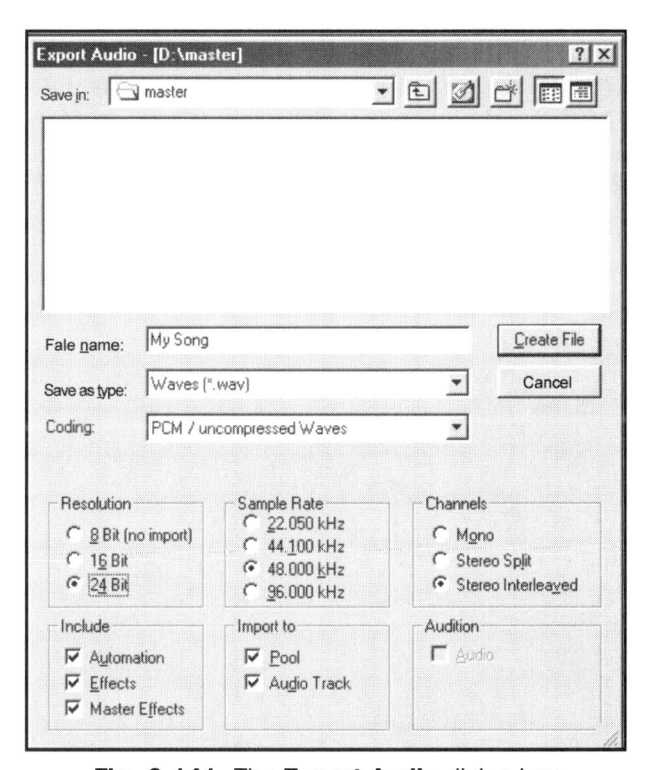

Fig. 6.141. The **Export Audio** dialog box

- ❏ In the **Channels** section, you can change the signal (if necessary) to mono or stereo (**Stereo Interleaved**), or split the stereo channels into two mono audio files.
- ❏ The **Import to** section is used for intermediate mixing. If the **Pool** and **Audio Track** options are both checked, the audio file will be imported to the song, and a separate audio track will be created.
- ❏ The **Include** section contains the following mixing parameters.
    - **Automation.** When creating a sound file, the changes in parameters written on the automation track will be taken into account. In this case, the **Read** button on the **VST Channel Mixer** must be pressed.
    - **Effects.** When this parameter is unchecked, the sound isn't processed with the effects of the **VST Send Effects** panel.
    - **Master Effects.** When this parameter is unchecked, the sound isn't processed with the effects of the **VST Master Effects** panel.

The process of creating of an audio file will start after clicking the **Create File** button in the **Export Audio** window.

When exporting a sound file, you must take into account the positions of the **L** and **R** locators. Exporting is performed only from the area enclosed by the locators. The muted tracks are ignored.

At the end of this chapter, we'd like to say that Cubase VST 24 is an application that is definitely worth the attention of those musicians who are interested in creating "live" music with their computers.

Chapter 7

USING CUBASE VST 24 IN COMBINATION WITH SAMPLITUDE 2496

Chapter 7: Using Cubase VST 24 in Combination with Samplitude 2496

In our opinion, certain peculiarities of working with AUDIO in Cubase VST 24 prevent you from creating a project from start to finish in one application. What is the reason for this?

In its earlier releases, Cubase VST 24 was merely a programmable MIDI sequencer. The possibility of working with AUDIO appeared in it later. Obviously, due to this, recent versions of the application have inherited certain rudimentary features.

Among these, for instance, is the fact that there is only one undo level.

> **NOTE** We are convinced that with only one Undo level, comfortable work with AUDIO is almost impossible.

Undoubtedly, Cubase VST 24 has significant advantages, but only when special ASIO drivers are installed.

However, since most inexpensive sound cards aren't supported by specialized ASIO drivers, the advantages of expensive sound cards aren't available to many amateur computer musicians.

In connection with the aforementioned features of Cubase VST 24, the need may arise to create a musical project in two applications simultaneously.

The best application to use in combination with Cubase VST 24 is Samplitude 2496.

The last statement is to a great extent based on the possibility of processing AUDIO and saving the intermediate result in the 32-bit floating-point format with the help of Samplitude 2496.

> **NOTE** A more detailed discussion of how to process sound in this format is reserved for *Chapter 8*.

Besides, we also think that the interface of Samplitude 2496 is the best suited for non-destructive editing.

Let's consider two ways of using these two programs in combination:

- By exporting a MIDI file from Cubase VST 24 and then importing it to Samplitude 2496
- By synchronizing both applications via a virtual MIDI cable

Exporting a Song from Cubase VST 24 to a MIDI File

There are two ways to export a song to a MIDI file.

- According to the first one, you need to execute the **Export MIDI File** command of the **File** menu. In doing so, you must take into account the state of the **Leave MIDI**

File Track Data as is checkbox. When it is unchecked, the virtual settings of the **Inspector** pane are transferred to the MIDI file.

❐ The second method is to employ the **Freeze Play Parameters** command of the **Functions** menu before exporting a MIDI file. Prior to this, you must select all the arrangement clips with the <Ctrl>+<A> shortcut or the **Select All** command of the **Edit|Select** menu.

Unlike in the first method, the **Leave MIDI File Track Data as is** checkbox must be checked in order to correctly export the project to the MIDI file. This is necessary, because otherwise the new settings of the **Inspector** pane, frozen by the **Freeze Play Parameters** command, may distort the information being exported.

When exporting, you should keep in mind that:

❐ The muted tracks aren't exported

❐ The tempo of a standard MIDI file is the tempo specified for the **Mastertrack** track in Cubase VST 24 (in the **Edit|Mastertrack** menu).

Importing a MIDI File to Samplitude 2496

Importing a MIDI file into a virtual project in Samplitude 2496 is quite easy. Just proceed as follows:

1. Select a short fragment on the track of the virtual project.
2. Execute the **Midi (*.MID)** command of the **File|Open Project** menu.
3. Select the original file with the MID extension from the **Load MIDI File** dialog box.

The **Import MIDI File** dialog box will be displayed (Fig. 7.1).

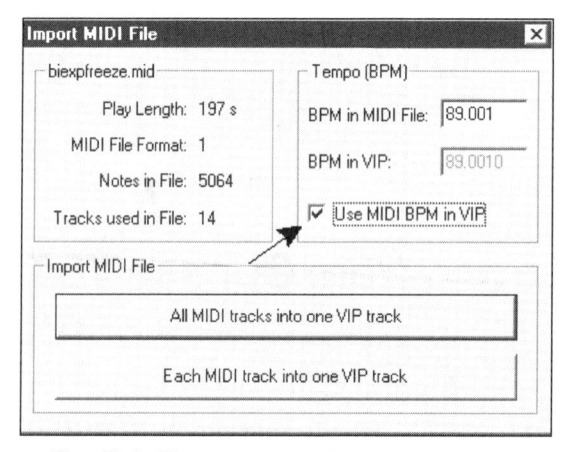

Fig. 7.1. The **Import MIDI File** dialog box

Chapter 7: Using Cubase VST 24 in Combination with Samplitude 2496

Here you can check the **Use MIDI BPM in VIP** checkbox if the tempo of the VIP project must match the tempo of the MIDI file.

If you click the **All MIDI tracks into one VIP track** button, one MIDI object will appear on a single track of the VIP project.

If the **Each MIDI track into one VIP track** button is clicked, several MIDI objects will be created on adjacent tracks of the VIP project in accordance with the number of the tracks in the original MIDI file. This isn't always convenient, since it wastes the space of the multitrack.

To convert a MIDI project into AUDIO, just copy the MIDI tracks to AUDIO tracks. For this, the developers of Samplitude 2496 have provided a very useful tool — **MIDI Object Editor** (Fig. 7.2).

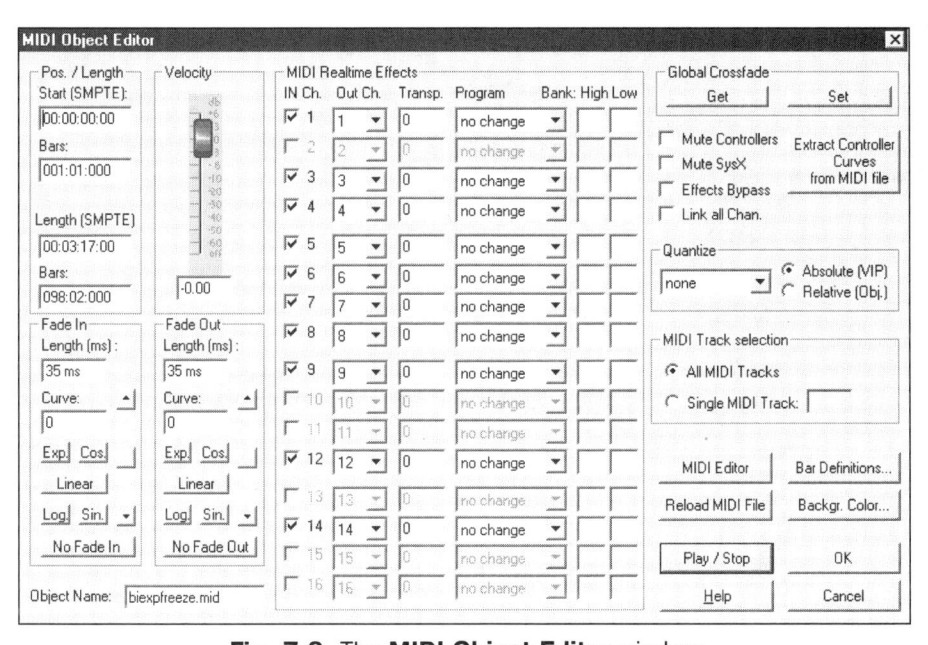

Fig. 7.2. The **MIDI Object Editor** window

This editor can be opened via the context menu or by double clicking the MIDI object in the lower half of the VIP project track.

In essence, **MIDI Object Editor** is analogous to the **Inspector** pane of Cubase VST 24.

In its middle section — **MIDI Realtime Effects** — the number of the MIDI channel and the instrument (sound) can be changed. You canb virtually transpose as well.

In the right-hand **MIDI Track selection** section, you can switch to the **Single MIDI Track** mode and set the number of the track you are planning to move to AUDIO.

Fig. 7.3. The **MIDI controller curves settings** window

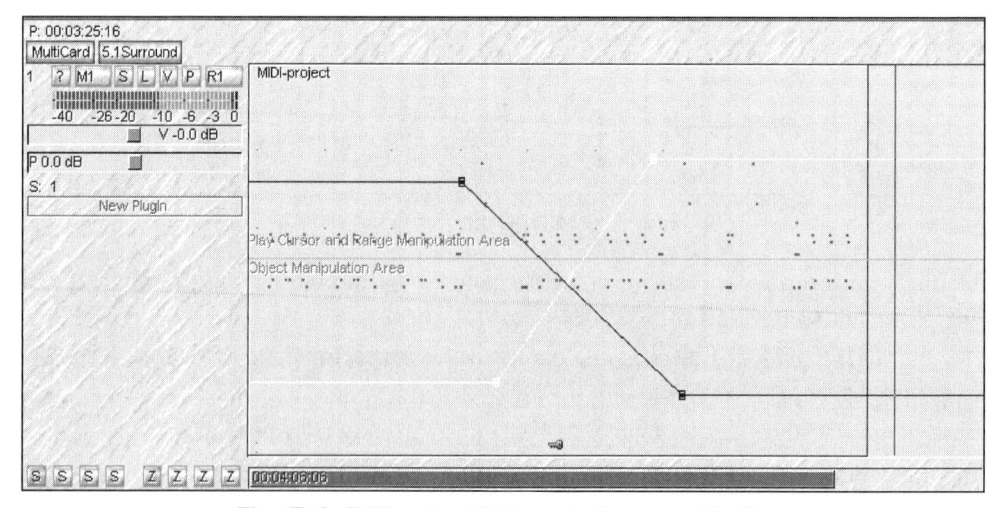

Fig. 7.4. Editing the MIDI controllers graphically

Chapter 7: Using Cubase VST 24 in Combination with Samplitude 2496   605

NOTE   This operation is equivalent to the **Solo** function. It is required for moving individual MIDI tracks to AUDIO.

In addition to the described features, Samplitude 2496 supports virtual editing for MIDI controllers. To enter this mode, right-click the **[?]** button of the track with the MIDI object.

The **MIDI controller curves settings** window will open (Fig. 7.3), in which you can select MIDI controllers and match them with MIDI channels.

Graphically editing the MIDI controllers is done in the same fashion as automation curves (Fig. 7.4).

Synchronization of Cubase VST 24 and Samplitude 2496

The method of exporting a MIDI file from Cubase VST 24 can be used for simple MIDI projects. For example, this is appropriate in cases where **MixTrack** tracks aren't used.

Also, when recording AUDIO, it is often necessary to correct the MIDI project (or create new parts).

Due to these reasons, the synchronization of the two applications becomes an important condition of using them together.

To synchronize these applications, special virtual tools have been designed, so-called virtual MIDI drivers for connecting multiple MIDI programs. One of these is Hubi's Loop Back device Version 2.5. It can be downloaded from the Internet (**http://people.freenet.de/sblive2/hubismlbk26a.zip**).

After the Hubi's Loop Back device driver is installed, four virtual MIDI ports are created, through which you can connect musical applications using the MIDI interface.

When two applications are synchronized, one of them must be a master, and the other a slave.

The master generates synchronizing signals, and the slave obeys them.

We're going to use Samplitude 2496 as master and Cubase VST 24 as slave.

Let's consider two different synchronization methods:

❐ MIDI synchronization. In this mode:
- The master sets the tempo for the slave
- MIDI time intervals are used (MIDI Clock)

❐ MTC synchronization. This is a sequence of MIDI commands that converts SMPTE code.

606   Live Music on Your PC

> **NOTE**   *MTC* stands for MIDI Time Code.
>
> *SMPTE* stands for the Society of Motion Picture and Television Engineers. This organization has adopted a time code standard for synchronization of picture and sound in the movies and on TV. For synchronization with a MIDI sequencer, the SMPTE code is converted to the MTC (MIDI Time Code). Samplitude 2496 generates MTC directly.

❐ To setup Samplitude 2496 as a master device, open the **Synchronization** window using the **File|Properties|Synchronization** menu (the <G> key). The window is shown in Fig. 7.5.

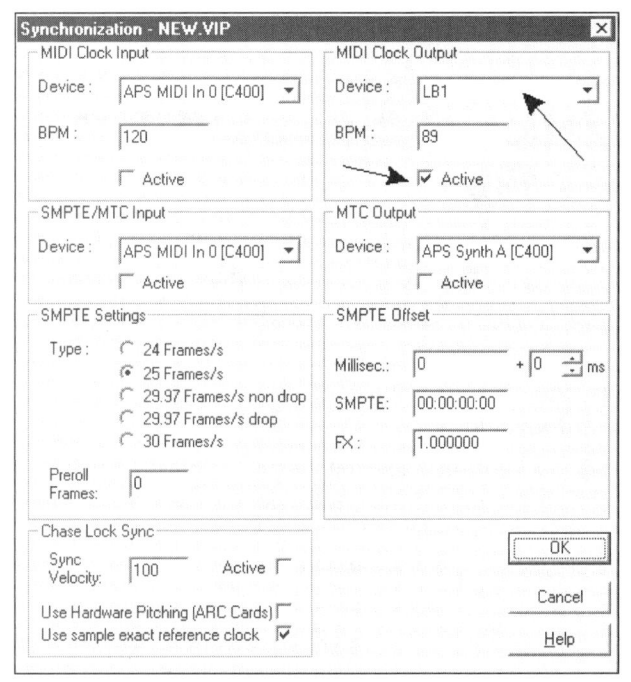

Fig. 7.5. Setting MIDI synchronization in Samplitude 2496

When you use MIDI synchronization, you must:

1. Select a virtual MIDI port (in our example, **LB1**) from the **Device** drop-down list in the **MIDI Clock Output** section.
2. Set the tempo in the **BPM** field.
3. Check the **Active** checkbox.

If MTC synchronization is used, select a virtual MIDI port from the **Device** drop-down list in the **MTC Output** section (in our example, **LB1**), and also check the **Active** checkbox.

Chapter 7: Using Cubase VST 24 in Combination with Samplitude 2496

To setup Cubase VST 24 as a slave device, proceed as follows:

1. Double-click the **Sync** button on the **Transport** bar.
2. Set the parameters in the **Sync Source** section of the **Synchronization** window as shown in Fig. 7.6.
3. Select a virtual MIDI port in the **From Input** drop-down list (in our example, **LB1**).
4. Check the **Detect Frame Change** checkbox in the **Sync Options** section if MTC synchronization has been chosen (indicated by the arrow in Fig. 7.6).

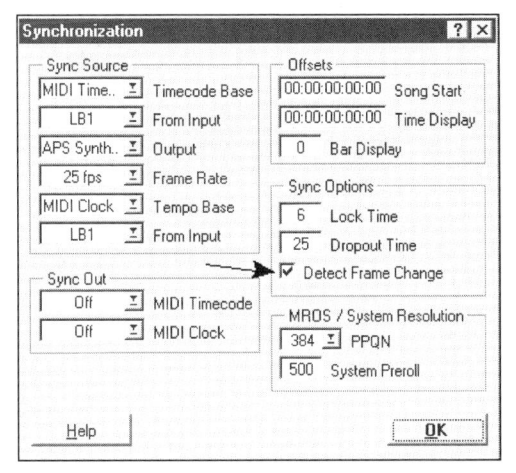

Fig. 7.6. Setting Cubase VST 24 to be a slave

NOTE According to the SMPTE standard, the rate of the synchronization signal is measured in frames per second.

The **Sync** button on the **Transport** bar of Cubase VST 24 must be in the pressed state. You may also wish to switch off AUDIO in the MIDI synchronization mode. To do this, check the **Disable Audio** item in the **Audio** menu.

NOTE When MTC synchronization is used, set the **Time Code** option in the **MIDI Sync Reference** section of the **Audio System Setup** window (the **Audio|System** menu) in Cubase VST 24.

Chapter 8

Mastering
in the WaveLab 3.0
Application

Chapter 8: Mastering in the WaveLab 3.0 Application

In the previous chapters, we intentionally gave no consideration to the essence of the digital signal. This was done to make it easier to understand the material.

However, the topic of high-quality digital sound is so important that we decided to devote a separate chapter to it.

We have many times heard computer musicians (even those who own 24-bit sound cards) holding an absolutely wrong point of view: "If the AUDIO CD format contains just 16 bits, there is no reason to *employ digital processing or save intermediate results* using a higher resolution."

Strangely enough, some "professionals" also show a basic misunderstanding of this problem. We were greatly surprised when a mixing engineer who had professional 24-bit digital sound processing studio equipment at his disposal was convinced that it made no sense to process sound with a resolution higher than 16 bits.

This is why we're going to discuss the nature of digital sound before we introduce the WaveLab 3.0 application.

Quantization Noise

The basics of digital sound processing were outlined in extremely simplified form in *Chapter 3*.

Here, the material will be somewhat more complex, but we'll try to put it as clearly as possible.

Some Major Points of Analog-to-Digital Sound Conversion

The general algorithm for analog-to-digital conversion is the following:

1. The analog signal is supplied to a low frequency filter. This filter limits the signal bandwidth.

   NOTE A signal continuous in time is called an *analog* signal. For example, a signal that comes from a microphone is analog.

2. Next, *samples* are taken from the signal. These are the values of the signal amplitude taken at certain time intervals. Such an operation is called *sampling*.
3. The values of the samples are measured with a certain accuracy. They then are replaced by approximate values within each sampling interval. This step is called *quantization*.
4. Each approximate amplitude value is *encoded* by a number (or code word).

The device used for the described conversion is called an *analog-to-digital converter* (ADC).

> **The Sample Theorem**
>
> Analog-to-digital conversion is subject to inherent limitations that are stated in the *sample theorem* by Nyquist.
>
> A signal with a bandwidth from 0 to F_{max} (a low frequency signal) can be fully represented by quantized samples if the sample rate (F_s) is at least twice as high as F_{max}.
>
> When this requirement isn't satisfied, the sampling spectra are overlapped (this is called aliasing), and the original analog signal cannot be restored. Since the upper limit of the sound range is 20 kHz, the sample rate must be higher than 40 kHz.

According to Tim Kintzel, CD technologies are subject to certain limitations. In particular, a sample rate of 44.1 kHz has been chosen to maintain compatibility with older audio systems that worked with audiocassettes, rather than to obtain the best sound quality (indeed, professional systems normally use a sample rate of 48 kHz).

Increasing the sampling frequency significantly lowers the intermoduation distortions due to aliasing. It also increases the fidelity of analog signal restoration. Statistically authentic restoration of the original analog signal takes places at sample rates no less than 5 F.

Due to these reasons, the new Audio DVD format for CDs has a sample rate of 96 kHz.

> **NOTE** Owners of Sound Blaster Live sound cards can appreciate sound quality at a sample rate of 96 kHz, since this sound card allows you to play back WAV files at this rate.

Another point to watch out for as a source of distortions is the quantizing step. The corresponding special type of distortion is called *quantization noise*.

Let's demonstrate this phenomenon with the Cool Edit Pro sound editor.

> **WARNING** The **Dither Transform Results** checkbox in the **Data** tab in the **Settings** window must be unchecked.

Let's generate a sine-form signal with a level of 0 dB.

1. Select the **Generate|Tones** menu and, in the **New Waveform** window, set the **Sample Rate** to 48,000 Hz, the **Resolution** to 16 bits, and select **Mono** from among the **Channels** radio buttons.
2. Set a value of 0 dB in the **dB Volume** section of the **Generate Tones** window (Fig. 8.1).
3. In the **Base Frequency** field, set 1,000 Hz.

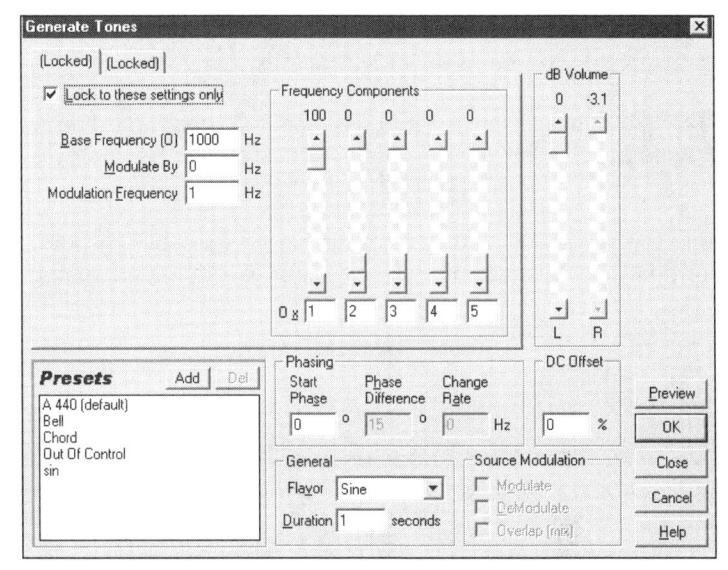

Fig. 8.1. Generating a 16-bit sine with a base frequency of 1000 Hz

4. In the **General** section, select **Sine** in the **Flavor** drop-down list, and set the **Duration** field to 1 second.

5. In the **Frequency Components** section, set the leftmost slider to the 100 level, and set the others to zero.

6. Now everything is ready for generating the sine. So click **OK**.

After that, decrease the signal level by 80 dB. To do this, use the **Amplify** effect in the **Transform|Amplitude** menu and zoom in along the vertical axis (Fig. 8.2).

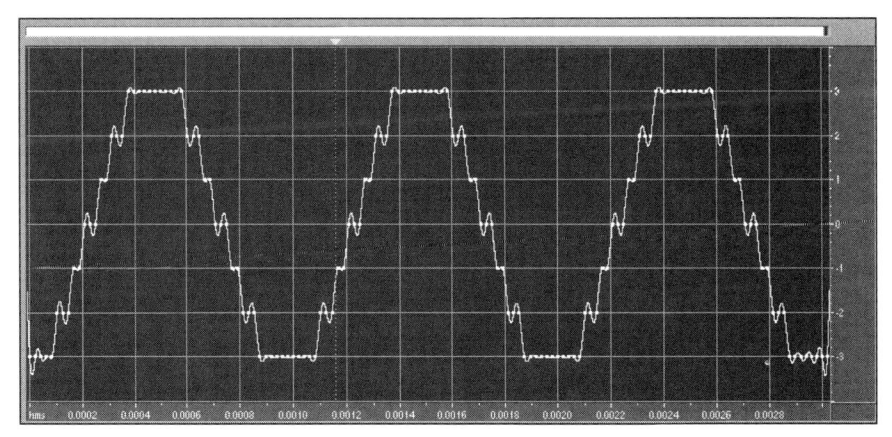

Fig. 8.2. The sine waveform at a level of −80 dB

In Fig. 8.2, you can see the quantization distortions caused by a small number of quantization levels or a low resolution being specified for this signal level.

WARNING: It is *absolutely* obvious that if we increase the sine level back to 0 dB, the distortions won't disappear. In other words, when the level is decreased, the loss of information is *irreversible*.

Let's now examine the spectrum of the distorted signal. For this purpose, we're going to call the spectrum analyzer with the **Frequency Analysis** command of the **Analyze** menu (<Alt>+<Z>).

In Fig. 8.3, you can see spurious (that is, parasitic) spectral components (the arrow indicates a frequency of 1,000 Hz).

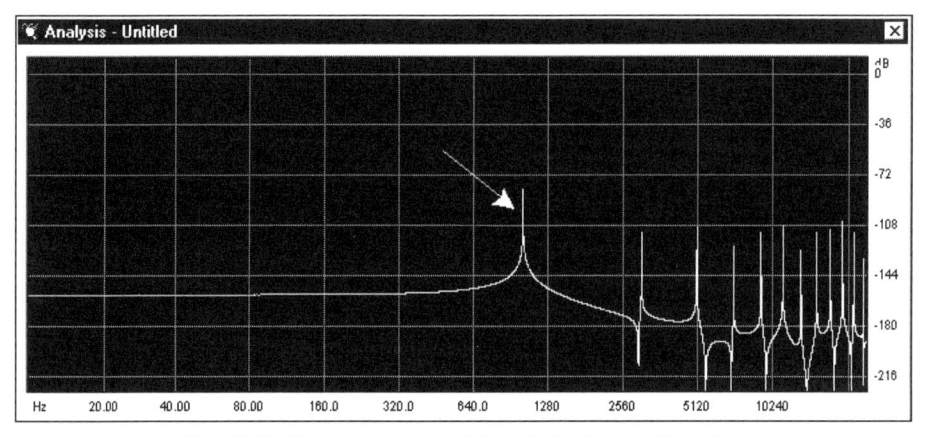

Fig. 8.3. The spectrum of the distortion of the sine

Quantization errors are perceived by ear as "tainted" sound. The fact of the matter is that the errors are equivalent to non-linear distortions whose spectrum consists mostly of non-harmonic components. In the case of low-frequency signals, or when the number of quantization levels is small, the spectrum of distortions consists mostly of discrete upper-level harmonics of the signal and of combinations of signal frequencies and sampling frequencies.

It is common practice to estimate the dynamic range of a digital signal with the formula $(6N + 1.7)$ dB for harmonic signals, where N is the number of bits.

This system is non-linear in principle, and non-linear distortions increase as the signal level decreases. They constitute more than 2% for the −60 dB signal, and they reach 10% for a level of −80 dB with 16-bit resolution.

The calculated range implies a model of analog-to-digital conversion of "white" noise. This means that the white noise is supplied to the ADC input, and this noise plus the quantization noise are obtained at the output.

Chapter 8: Mastering in the WaveLab 3.0 Application

Music is represented by a complex signal whose characteristics are far from white noise. This is why the conversion error, which depends on the amplitude and frequency of the signal being converted, manifests itself as "tainted" sound and non-linear and intermodulational distortions.

So the actual dynamic range appears to be much narrower than the one we calculated. For example, with a signal at −48 dB, we have 8-bit quantization (256 levels).

To diminish quantization errors, *dithering* is used. According to Tim Kintzel, this conversion allows you to turn noticeable quantization errors into less noticeable high-frequency noise.

The essence of dithering is in the low-level mixing of the signal with a special noise (a pseudo-random digital signal). Thanks to this, the errors are dithered. Using the low-level noise brings the process of analog-to-digital conversion into agreement with the model. One can say that, at the lower level, it is mainly noise that is converted.

This is the reason why the quantization noise becomes independent from the signal and has a smooth spectrum. Of course, the quantization errors are then diminished as well.

If we use some of the peculiarities of human hearing to our advantage, we will be able to create the illusion of increasing the signal/noise ratio. This is achieved by creating a quantization noise spectrum that is the inverse of the curve of human sound perception. This processing is called *noise shaping*. Noise shaping makes it possible to perceive signals that have a level lower than the low-order bit of the sample (see CD-ROM included).

Let's repeat our experiment by decreasing the amplitude of the sine signal by 80 dB. However, this time we'll first check the **Dither Transform Results** checkbox in the **Data** tab in the **Settings** window.

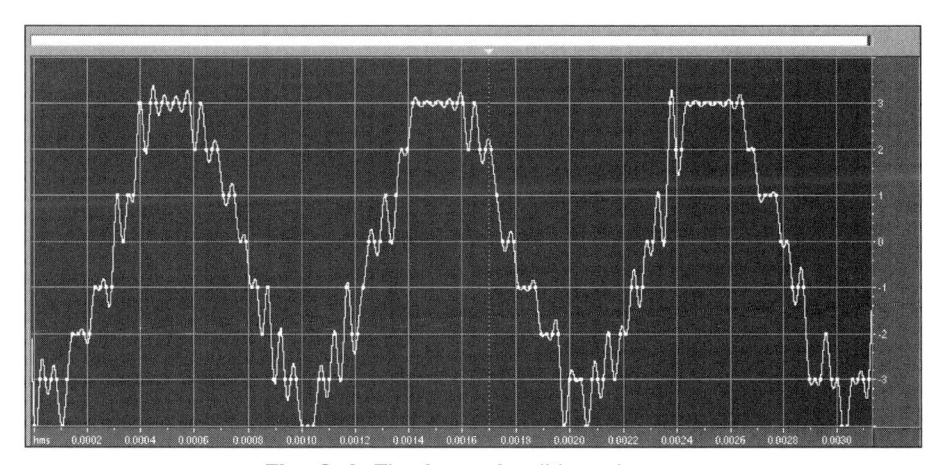

Fig. 8.4. The form of a dithered wave

As you can see in Fig. 8.4, the 1,000 Hz signal is mixed with the high-frequency noise.

Perform a spectral analysis.

You'll see (Fig. 8.5) that the spurious spectral components obtained in the previous example (Fig. 8.3) are replaced with the noise; in other words, they are dithered. Does this mean we should just be satisfied with 16-bit resolution? Well, we don't want to jump to conclusions.

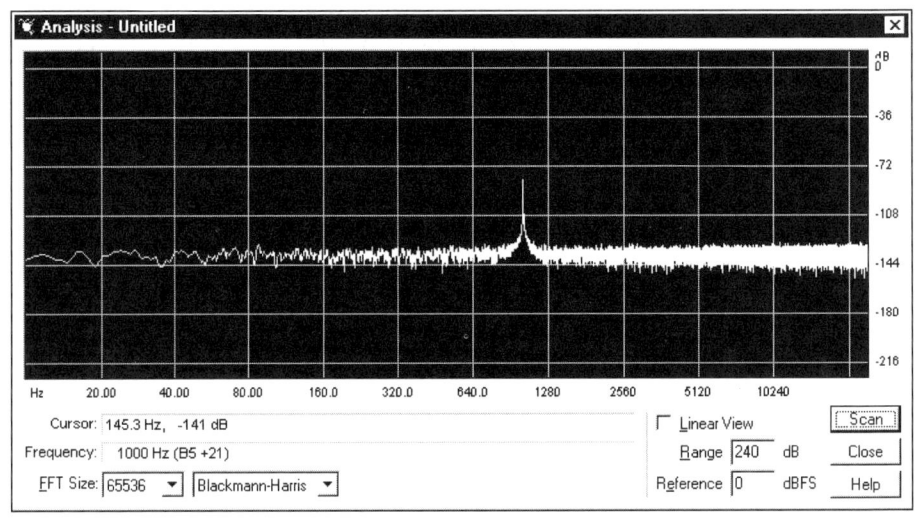

Fig. 8.5. The signal spectrum with dithering applied

When creating music with the computer, the signal is processed repeatedly. Not only must we perform analog-to-digital conversion with the maximum level, but we also have to avoid a loss in quality during processing.

For example, if we apply the reverberation effect to a 16-bit signal with the −80 dB level, we'll get the same quantization noise.

Low-level signals are always present in a real acoustic environment. A human's ear uses the information contained in low-level signals to create a sound image. Because of this, any elimination of low-level signals leads to the disappearance of the acoustic space and transparency.

If we draw an analogy to vision, we can say that, like good vision, low-level signals allow a person to perceive the world in all its diversity and to detect its details.

One of the main tools for "enlivening" the sound and creating acoustic space is a reverber.

Consider a typical case where a signal processed by a 16-bit ADC is being processed by a virtual reverber.

As a result of such processing, new information is created. In particular, a reverberation "tail" (decaying sound) appears, which is dissolved in the quantization noise as early as at

Chapter 8: Mastering in the WaveLab 3.0 Application

the −80 dB level. Can we treat this transformation as a correct and valuable one? Of course we can't. So, high-quality processing requires a much wider dynamic range than the one offered by AUDIO CD.

Actually, professional sound processing is performed with resolutions higher than 16 bits.

Decreasing the signal amplitude by 80 dB was done in Cool Edit Pro in the following way:

1. First, the 16-bit signal was converted to the internal 32-bit floating-point format.
2. Then, high-precision decreasing of the amplitude was performed.
3. After that, a reverse conversion back to 16 bits was performed, with a loss of information.

The last stage depended on the state of the **Dither Transform Results** checkbox.

When the checkbox was checked, conversion to 16-bit format was done with dithering.

Again according to Tim Kintzel, to diminish quantization errors, sound signal samples must be represented by floating-point numbers. This increases the accuracy of the smaller values, and solves the problem of distortion of weak signals.

Personally, we'd like to add that floating-point numbers help cope with distortions *when processing signals*, which is more important for us, since sound cards include integer ADCs.

Let's perform a simple experiment that shows us why we should appreciate the advantage of sample representation in floating-point format.

1. Switch off dithering (uncheck the **Dither Transform Results** checkbox).
2. Generate a 16-bit sine signal with a frequency of 1,000 Hz and a level of 0 dB, as in the previous examples.

> **NOTE** We could generate a 32-bit floating-point signal from the get go, but here we want to simulate 16-bit processing with subsequent conversion to 32-bit resolution.

3. Convert the generated signal to 32-bit floating-point format by using the **Edit|Convert Sample Type** menu. In the **Resolution** section of the **Convert Sample Type** window, change the value to 32 bits.
4. Decrease the signal level by 80 dB. After zooming in along the vertical axis, you'll see a clear, undistorted sine (Fig. 8.6).
5. Decrease the signal level by 120 dB more. To do this, you must enter −120 into the **Amplification** field in the **Amplify** window via the keyboard. After that, increase the signal level by 200 dB. You'll again see a clear, undistorted sine with a level of 0 dB.
6. Increase the signal level by 50 dB. After zooming out along the vertical axis, you'll once again see a clear, undistorted sine (Fig. 8.7).

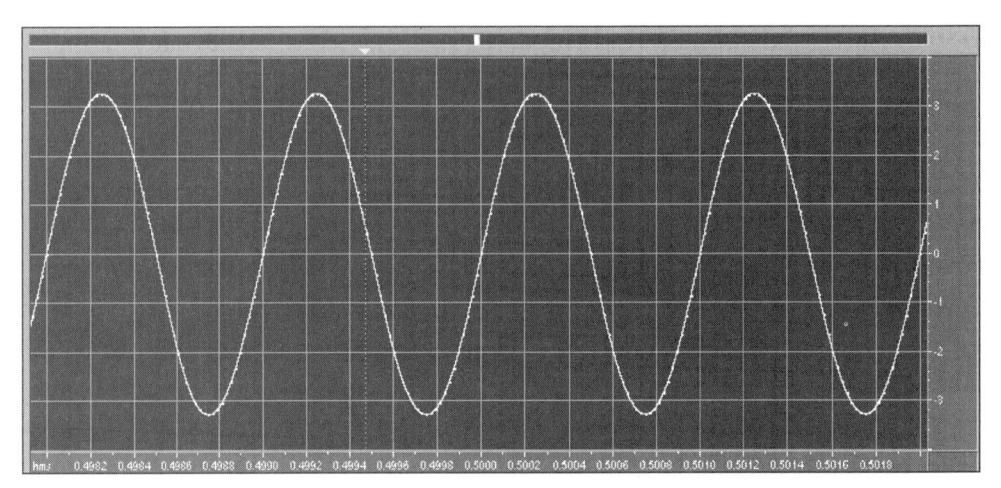

Fig. 8.6. The waveform of the sine at a level of −80 dB in 32-bit floating-point format

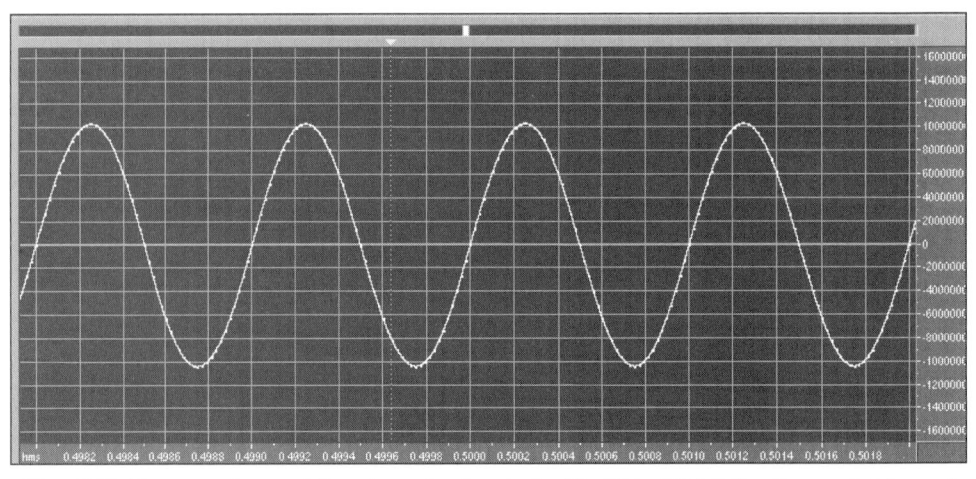

Fig. 8.7. The waveform of the sine at a level of −50 dB in 32-bit floating-point format

If you convert this signal to integer format, amplitude values above 0 dB will be cut off. This is how using floating-point numbers ensures protection against overloading. Well, we've now seen how wide the dynamic range of the 32-bit floating-point digital signal actually is, especially relative to the "quality" of AUDIO CD.

It is in this format that sound processing calculations are performed in Cool Edit Pro and Samplitude 2496. This is why these applications provide for high-quality sound processing; however, this is only true if the *intermediate results (of destructive editing or intermediate mixing) are saved in this very format.*

Chapter 8: Mastering in the WaveLab 3.0 Application

If rounding to 16 bits is done in any stage of processing, it will be *impossible* to restore the information.

Now we're going to discuss another important point — mixing. If we have a 16-bit representation of a signal, we must try to digitize it at the 0 dB level, since decreasing the level by each 6 dB (by half) means a loss of one bit (that is, the −6 dB level signal has a 16-bit resolution).

However, when mixing two signals with original levels of 0 dB, it is necessary to decrease the level of each one by 6 dB, otherwise the total signal will be limited. When mixing four 0 dB level signals, their levels must be decreased by 12 dB, etc.

In a real-life situation, the level of a signal is determined by creative work, and so they cannot be equal. In practice, then, the process of mixing can include signals with resolutions of both 15 and 12 bits, and so on.

> **NOTE** It is for this purpose that multitrack applications automatically convert signals to higher resolutions before mixing them. For example, the internal resolution of a multitrack in SAWPro is 24 bits, and in Samplitude 2496 it is 32 bits (floating-point). However, during destructive editing or intermediate mixing, the quality of tracks with levels lowered to the 16-bit format is sure to decrease.

To maintain the dynamic range, it is necessary to mix signals after converting them to the 32-bit floating-point format. *Besides which, the final sound file obtained through mixing must also have a 32-bit floating-point format.* This is why Samplitude 2496 provides mixing in just this manner with the help of a virtual mixer (**Mix in File**). During the subsequent mastering, the dynamic range is compressed to get AUDIO CD "quality".

> **NOTE** The new Audio DVD digital format uses 24-bit resolution. So you can now save your musical projects as WAV files with a high resolution — for better times, so to speak.

Let's perform yet another experiment illustrating the importance of converting a 16-bit signal to 32-bit floating-point format for subsequent sound processing.

1. Generate a fragment of a sine 15 seconds long in the 16-bit format at a level of 0 dB.
2. Create the envelope curve with the **Envelope** effect (the **Transform|Amplitude|Envelope** menu), as shown in Fig. 8.8.
3. Apply the reverberation effect (the **Transform|Delay Effects|Full Reverb** menu; the **Great Hall** preset value).
4. Use compression to evaluate the reverberation decay visually and by ear (Fig. 8.9).

As a result, the waveform of the signal will look as shown in Fig. 8.10 (if dithering was on). The arrow in Fig. 8.10 indicates the moment when the decaying reverberation signal was "drowned" in the dithering noise. Fig. 8.11 shows the waveform of the signal obtained using the same procedure, but with dithering being off.

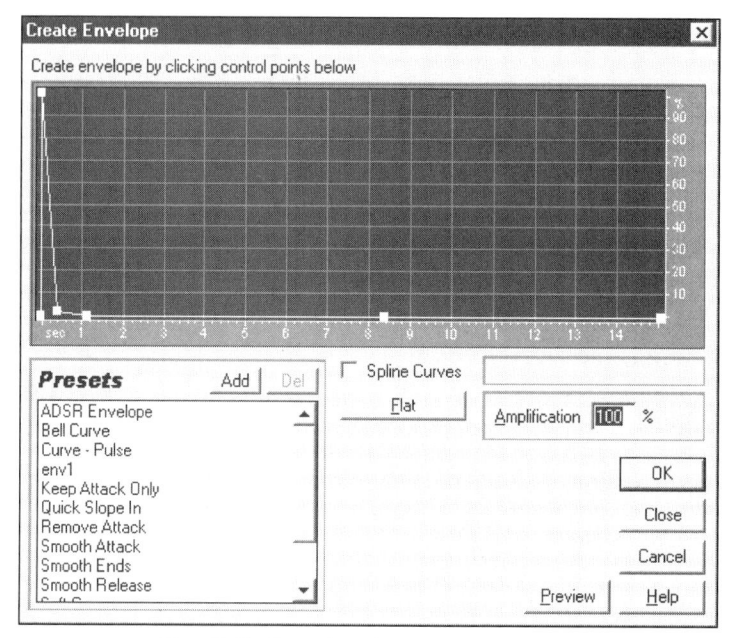

Fig. 8.8. Creating the envelope curve

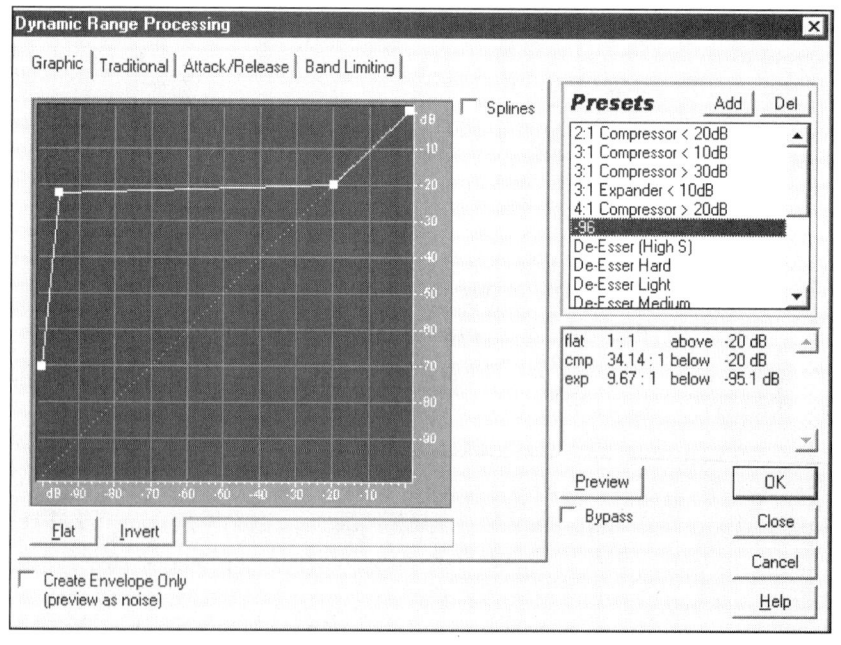

Fig. 8.9. Signal compression

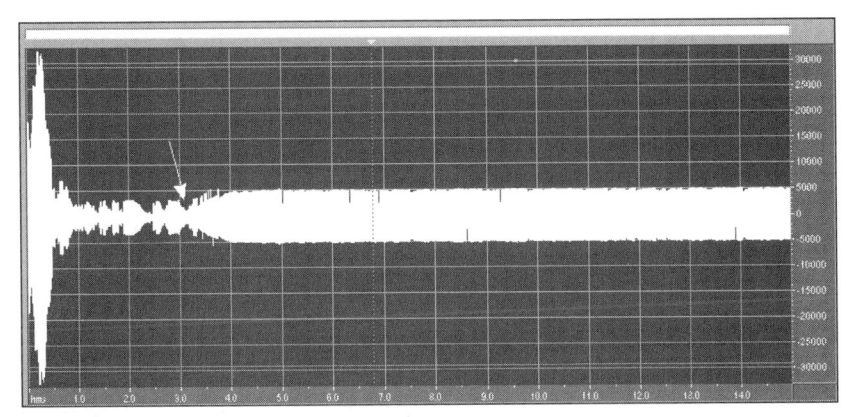

Chapter 8: Mastering in the WaveLab 3.0 Application 621

Fig. 8.10. Reverberation decay in 16-bit format when dithering is on

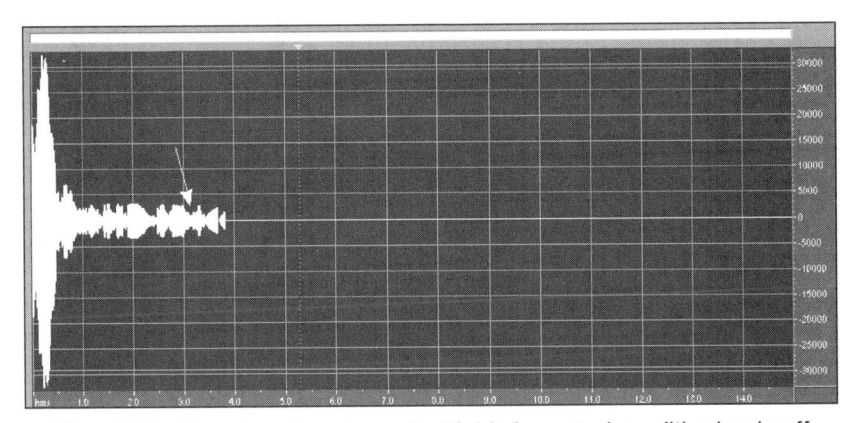

Fig. 8.11. Reverberation decay in 16-bit format when dithering is off

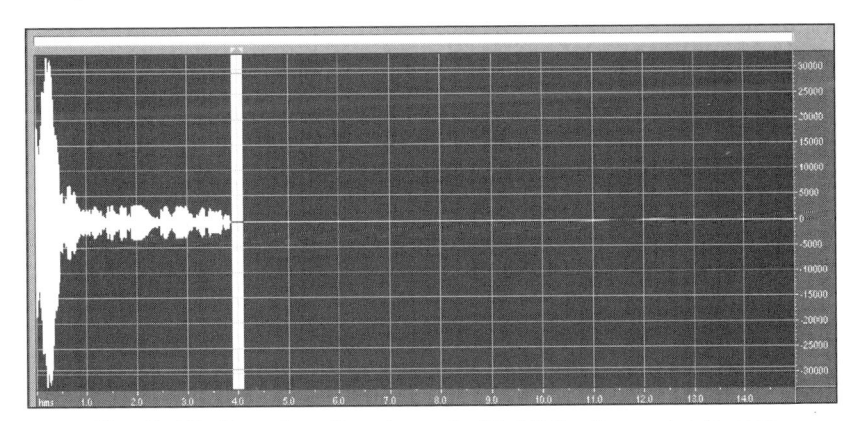

Fig. 8.12. Reverberation decay in 32-bit floating-point format

The arrow in Fig. 8.11 indicates the beginning of the area of strong distortions caused by quantization errors. As we can see from the waveform analysis, the reverberation signal breaks due to the low resolution of the 16-bit representation.

Perform the same procedure, but this time, convert the signal to 32-bit floating-point format immediately after generating the sine.

Reverberation decay happens without distortions. If you zoom into the selected portion (Fig. 8.12), you'll be able to see that the decaying signal has a clear sine form (Fig. 8.13).

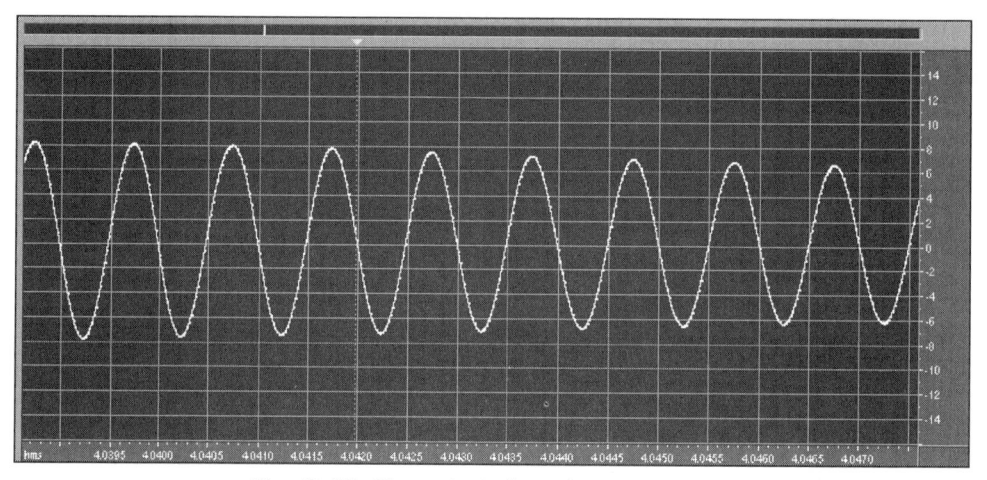

Fig. 8.13. The selected portion, zoomed in

Some "Hidden" Features of SAWPro

When using Cool Edit Pro or Samplitude 2496, maintaining the quality of the intermediate results of signal processing isn't difficult. This is because the interfaces of these applications provide special commands for conversion to 32-bit format. However, to achieve the same goal in SAWPro, we will have to use a command to convert to 24-bit format, since this application doesn't support floating-point numbers.

Let's perform some experiments with destructive signal processing in SAWPro.

1. Generate a 16-bit sound file with Cool Edit Pro and import it into SAWPro.
2. Select the clip and, in the **OFFSET** mode, set the **Fader** slider to −79 dB.
3. Perform destructive editing (see *Chapter 3*).
4. Examine the waveform in the **SoundFile View** window (Fig. 8.14).

We notice typical quantization errors for the 16-bit resolution in SAWPro. If we switch dithering on, the picture will be different (Fig. 8.15).

Chapter 8: Mastering in the WaveLab 3.0 Application   623

The developers of SAWPro provided us with the possibility of simultaneously putting sound files having various resolutions and sample rates onto a multitrack. In other words, it is possible to *simultaneously* play back sound files with formats of 16, 20, and 24 bits.

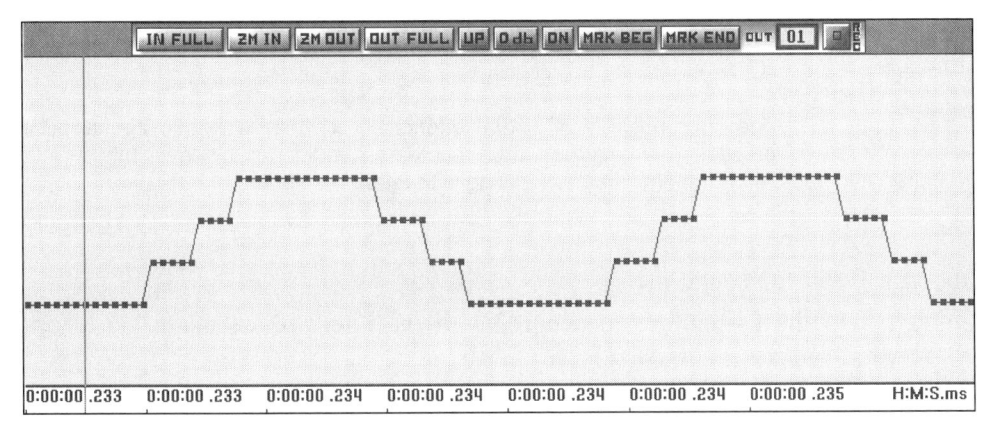

Fig. 8.14. Quantization errors in the **SoundFile View** window

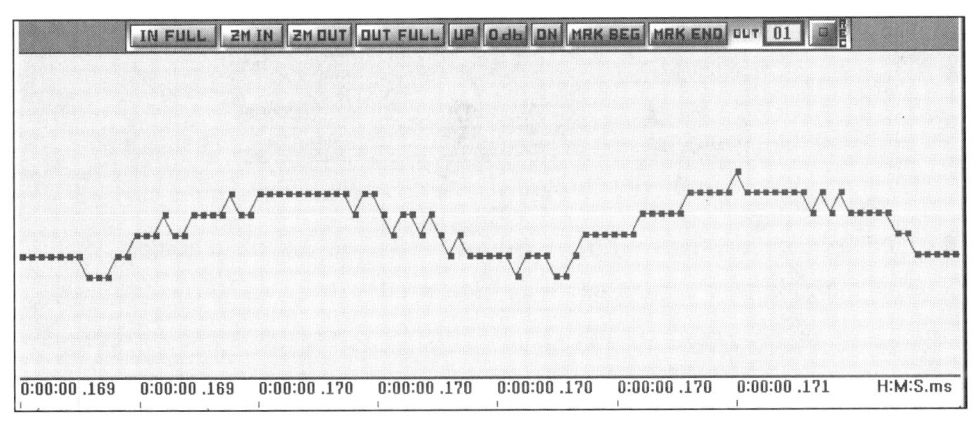

Fig. 8.15. Quantization errors with dithering applied

Furthermore, the resolution of your project can be set in accordance with the potentialities of your sound card.

If the 16 bit value is set (the **Res** button in the **Multitrack View** window), 20- and 24-bit files will be played back with 16-bit resolution.

Nevertheless, the 16- and 20-bit signals are converted to 24-bit in SAWPro in order to increase the accuracy of processing. (Problems of mixing and processing 16-bit signals were discussed earlier.)

However, when editing non-destructively, the intermediate result (24 bits) is rounded to the resolution of the original sound file. This means that a 16-bit sound file is first converted to 24-bit format, is processed, and then is rounded back to 16 bits.

Therefore, to maintain maximum accuracy of the intermediate results during *destructive processing*, it is necessary to convert 16-bit sound files to 24-bit ones *immediately* after recording.

> **NOTE** The superposition of virtual effects — such as an equalizer, a dynamic processor, a reverber, etc. — creates additional low-level bits which are taken into account at the final stage of mixing with 24-bit resolution.

Let's do some research.

1. Import a 16-bit test sound file.
2. Convert it to the 24-bit format, according to the intermediate mastering algorithm described in *Chapter 3* (Fig. 8.16).

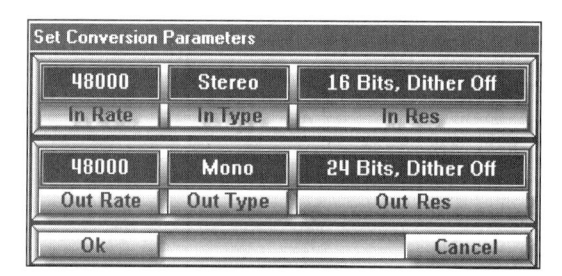

Fig. 8.16. Converting a file to 24-bit format

3. Destructively decrease the level by 79 dB for this file, as described earlier.
4. Examine the waveform in the **SoundFile View** window (Fig. 8.17).

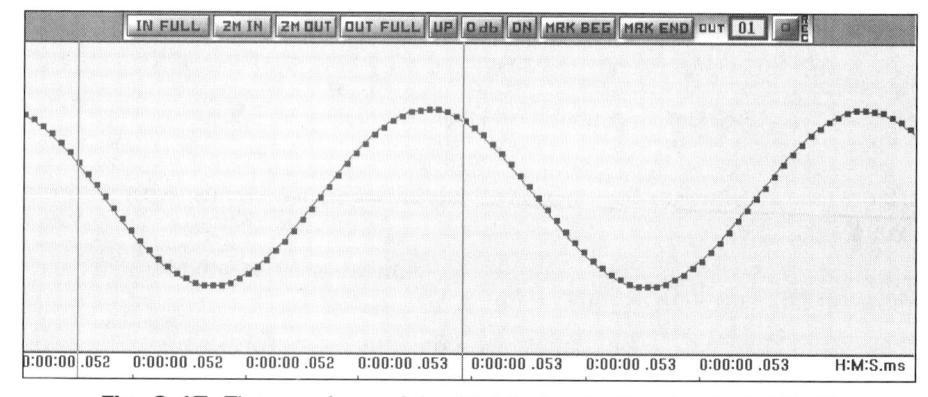

Fig. 8.17. The waveform of the 24-bit signal with a level of −79 dB

Chapter 8: Mastering in the WaveLab 3.0 Application

Thus, the results of destructive editing will be automatically saved in 24-bit format. However, you must watch the parameters in the **Set Conversion Parameters** window (Fig. 8.16) when performing intermediate and final mixing.

When AUDIO CD mastering is performed in SAWPro, the resolution should be lowered to 16 bits (with dithering) *only in the final stage*. If you intend to use WaveLab for mastering, final mixing must be done to a 24-bit file.

The Master Section in WaveLab

The WaveLab 3.0 application is a multitrack 32-bit audio editor with the possibility of plugging in DirectX and VST virtual effects.

This program was developed at Steinberg (**http://www.steinberg.net**). In our book, this wonderful editor will be examined only from the standpoint of its usage for mastering.

First of all, we'd like to mention that it is impossible to perform *professional* mastering at home without having the necessary special equipment.

We're going to discuss home mastering of acceptable quality here.

Our point here is that the technologies of creating a musical project in a professional studio and creating one at home are quite different.

A computer musician has to develop his or her own flow charts, whereas in professional studios, the techniques were long ago perfected, down to the very smallest detail.

The process of creating a high-quality digital sound at home is somewhat similar to assembling an amateur radio. (There are people who like to spend their time and money constructing their own radio sets, rather than buying ready-made ones. Sometimes they manage to achieve a very high quality product.)

Judging from some publications on the Internet, the task of achieving a high-quality digital sound at home is quite "hot".

By "home mastering" we mean the release of a musical project in domestic conditions. When creating an album, the result can be, say, a number of WAV files in 16-, 24-, or 32-bit format, or an AUDIO CD.

When mastering an album, the most important thing is to make the listener as comfortable as possible. You must spare him or her the necessity of adjusting the volume or the equalizer when going to the next composition.

Besides which, the waveforms and the pauses between the compositions mustn't contain any noise.

In this chapter, we're going to concentrate on the most difficult stages of mastering, namely, equalizing (changing the frequency-response curve) and compressing. Some techniques of spectrally enriching the sound are also discussed.

Preliminary Program Setup

WaveLab creates temporary files in its work. These files must have the maximum possible resolution. Setting this parameter is done via the **Options|Preferences** menu. Select the **Create 32 Bit (Float) temporary files** option from the lower list in the **File** tab in the **Preferences** window. Also, check the **Save preferences on exit** checkbox in the **General** tab.

There is a separate *mastering section* in WaveLab (**Master Section**, Fig. 8.18) for processing the signal using virtual effects, which can be enabled in six slots.

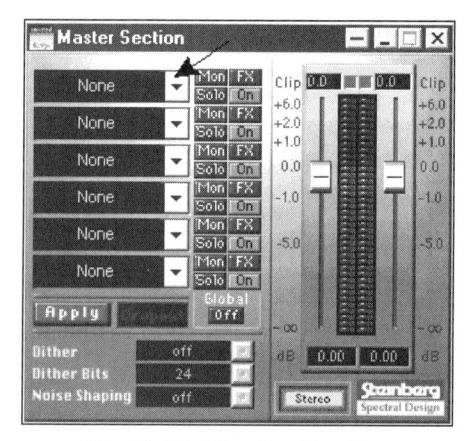

Fig. 8.18. Master Section

It is very easy to enable an effect — just click the button with the triangle next to the chosen slot (indicated by the arrow in Fig. 8.18).

A list of available effects will appear (Fig. 8.19).

To disable an effect, select the **None** item.

The internal structure of the Master Section according to the program documentation is illustrated in Fig. 8.20.

The signal from a sound file comes to the first slot, then to the second, etc. In other words, the virtual effect enabled in the first slot will be the first to process the signal.

The signal from the sixth slot is supplied to the **Master faders** of the left and the right channels, then to the dithering processor, and then to the output block, where the signal is reflected by the output level indicators.

Each slot has its own set of buttons: **Mon**, **Solo**, **FX**, and **On** (Fig. 8.18).

❏ **Mon** (Monitoring) is designed to connect the level indicator to the output of the effect. This button is used for monitoring the signal level at the output of the effect.

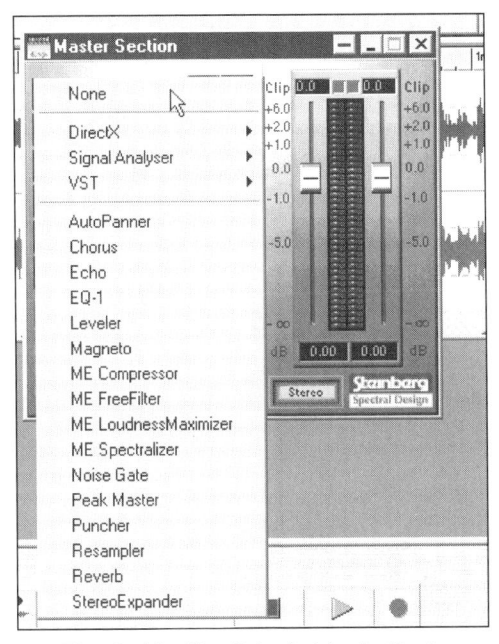

Chapter 8: Mastering in the WaveLab 3.0 Application

Fig. 8.19. The list of virtual effects

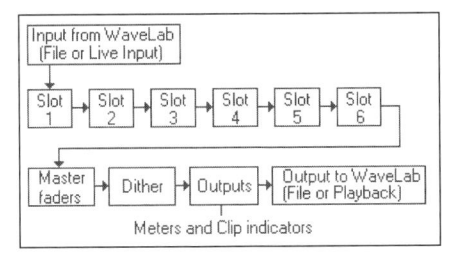

Fig. 8.20. The internal structure of the Master Section

> **NOTE** When setting up the parameters of the effects at the mastering stage, monitoring is necessary for each effect.

- **Solo** is used to listen to the effect assigned to a specific slot. The signal bypasses the effects enabled in the other slots. You can only use the Solo mode with one effect at a time.
- **On** turns the effect enabled in this slot on and off.

> **NOTE** When this button "glows" yellow, this means the effect is active.

- **FX** is designed to open the control panel (the window) of the virtual effect.

> **NOTE** When this button "glows" green, the control panel is on the display. Another click on the **FX** button will close the window.

The **Global Off** button located below the other buttons is used to switch off all the effects enabled in the slots. However, the dithering processor and the output controls remain active.

The dithering processor performs the dithering and noise shaping algorithms discussed earlier.

- In the **Dither Bits** field (Fig. 8.18), the dithering resolution is specified. The range of valid values is from 8 to 24.
- In the **Dither** field, the type of dithering is given:
  - **off** — no dithering
  - **Type 1** — a universal method
  - **Type 2** — high frequencies are boosted
- In the **Noise Shaping** field, the noise spectrum can be shaped. The valid values are: **off**, **Type 1**, **Type 2**, and **Type 3**.
  - The **Type 3** value corresponds to the maximum shift of the noise spectrum to high frequencies
  - The **off** value means that the noise shaping algorithm isn't used

The WaveLab user's manual strongly recommends the user to rely on his or her own ear when setting the dithering parameters.

However, there are special dithering algorithms designed especially for AUDIO CD mastering. For example, you can use **Apogee UV 22** in WaveLab 3.0 as a VST plug-in (Fig. 8.21). When doing so, the dithering processor in the Master Section must be switched off.

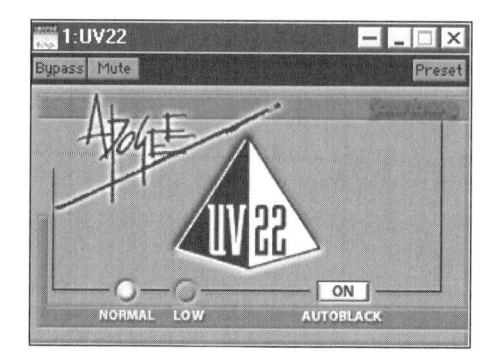

Fig. 8.21. The **Apogee UV 22** VST plug-in

Chapter 8: Mastering in the WaveLab 3.0 Application

The **Apogee UV 22** VST plug-in has just few settings:

- **NORMAL** — a universal mode that can be used in most cases
- **LOW** — a low-level dithering noise mode
- **AUTOBLACK** — an additional function to lower the dithering noise in fragments with a low volume

The **Apogee UV 22** algorithm must be used only when the resolution is set to 16 bits.

Let's go back to the Master Section.

The **Stereo** button allows you to toggle the **Mono** mode to check the compatibility of the stereo waveform with the mono mode.

And lastly, the most important button is **Apply**.

When you click it, the **Process preferences for** dialog box will open (Fig. 8.22).

If the **Whole file** radio button is selected in the **Range** section, the file will be processed as a whole.

In the **Result** section, you can make your choice between the **Process in place** and the **Create new file** options:

- **Process in place** — the original sound file is processed
- **Create new file** — a new sound file is created in the editor window

If the **Create new file** radio button is selected, the **Create specific file** checkbox becomes available. With it, you can create a sound file in a certain format and specify its location on the hard disk (Fig. 8.23).

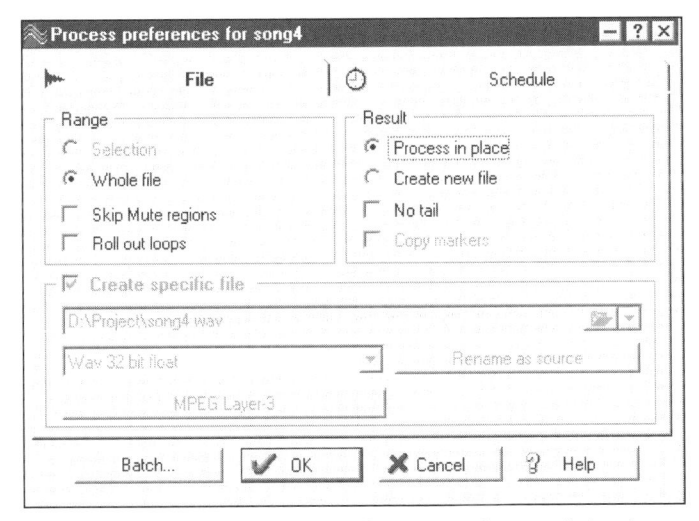

Fig. 8.22. The **Process preferences for ...** dialog box

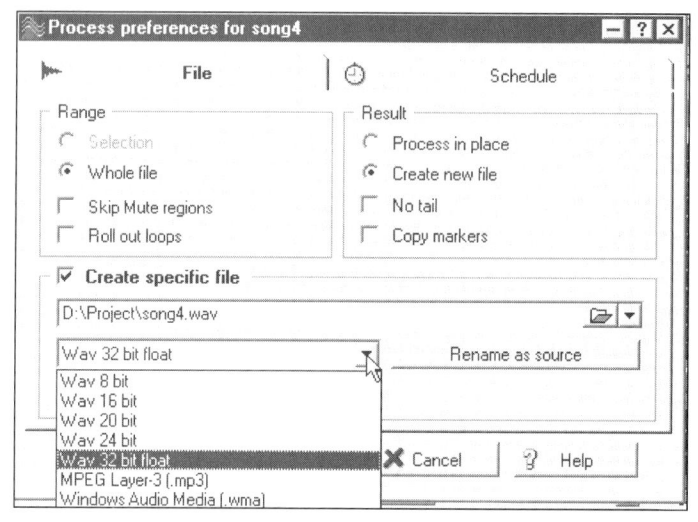

Fig. 8.23. Selecting the format of an audio file

WaveLab provides for very convenient **Batch Processing**.

If you click the **Batch** button in the **Process preferences for ...** dialog box, the **Batch Processing** dialog box will open (Fig. 8.24).

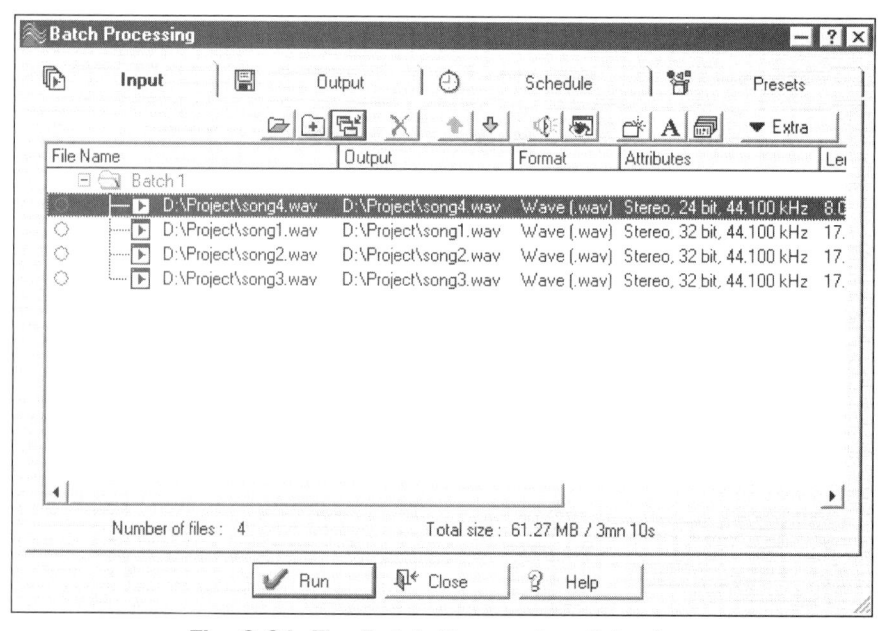

Fig. 8.24. The **Batch Processing** dialog box

Chapter 8: Mastering in the WaveLab 3.0 Application

Batch processing makes it possible to automate the process, that is, to apply the general settings of the Master Section to a *group* of sound files.

Fig. 8.24 shows the **Input** tab of the **Batch Processing** dialog box. To add files for batch processing, click the button with the open folder icon on it.

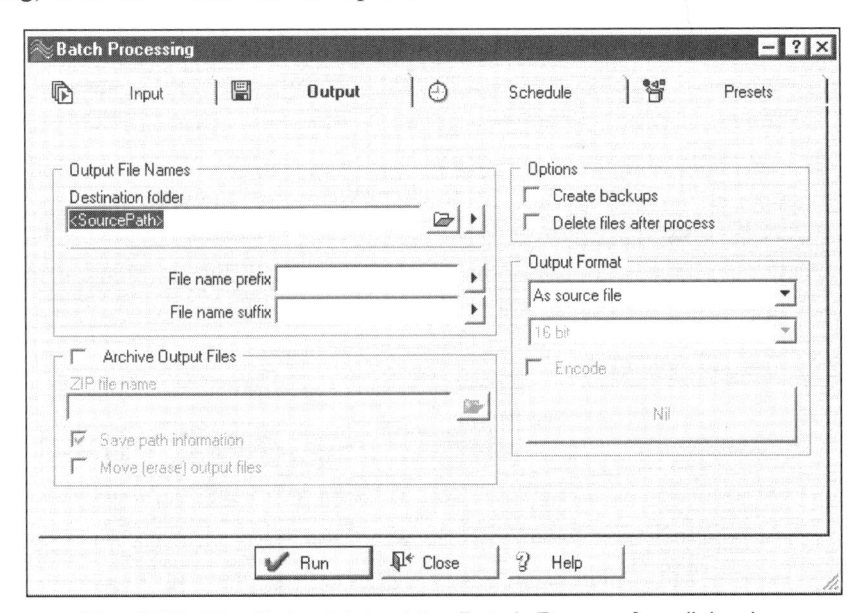

Fig. 8.25. The **Output** tab of the **Batch Processing** dialog box

> **NOTE** Since there are pop-up help messages in WaveLab, it isn't difficult to understand the meaning of the buttons.

Before you click the **Run** button, you must open the **Output** tab and inspect the parameters of the results of batch processing (Fig. 8.25).

In the **Output Format** section, you can select the **As source file** option. Then the result of processing will be saved in the same format as the original file.

In the **Output File Names** section, you'll see the **Destination folder** field, where you can select the **<Source Path>** item. If you do, the original files will be replaced with the processed files.

The Virtual Effects Necessary for Mastering

When processing sound at the mastering stage, WaveLab uses various virtual effects plugged into the slots in the Master Section. Below we'll discuss the most successful (from our point of view) plug-ins.

The *ME FreeFilter* Intelligent Equalizer

One of the most important stages of mastering is equalizing, that is, making the frequency-response curves equal for all the compositions in the album.

To perform this operation and get a high-quality result, professional equipment and certain skills are required.

To ease equalizing, Steinberg has developed a special plug-in, **ME FreeFilter**, which allows you to automate the process to some extent.

ME FreeFilter can be compared to the **FFT Analyzer/Filter** effect of Samplitude 2496 (see *Chapter 5*), since **ME FreeFilter** combines a spectrum analyzer and an FFT filter. However, unlike **FFT Analyzer/Filter**, **ME FreeFilter** is "intelligent" and can learn.

The **ME FreeFilter** effect is contained in a plug-in package that is intended for mastering, called **Steinberg Mastering Edition (ME)**.

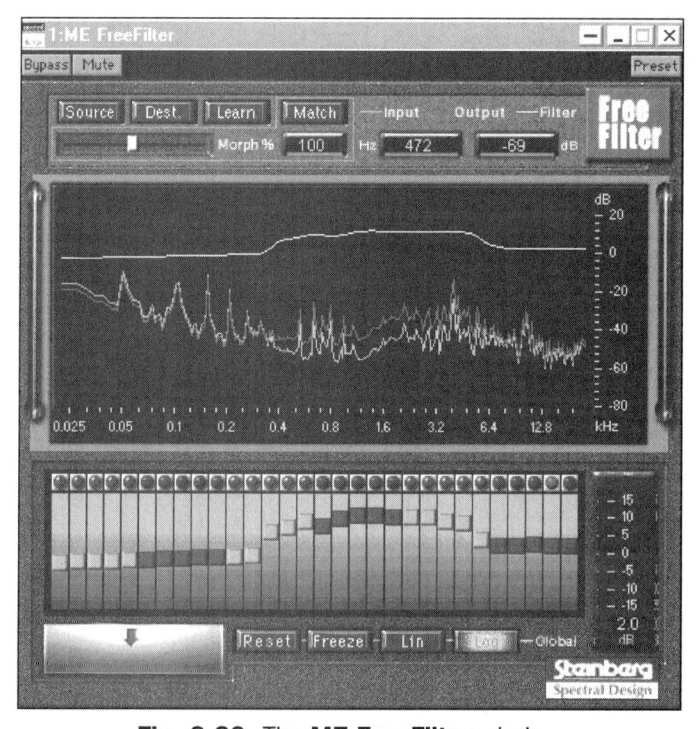

Fig. 8.26. The **ME FreeFilter** window

In Fig. 8.26, you can see the window of the **ME FreeFilter** effect, whose elements are discussed below.

Chapter 8: Mastering in the WaveLab 3.0 Application

❏ **Frequency monitor**, located in the middle of the **ME FreeFilter** window, is used to display the frequency-response curve of the equalizer and the spectra of the input and output signals:
- The spectrum of the input signal is shown in green
- The spectrum of the output signal is shown in red
- The frequency-response curve of the equalizer is shown in yellow

Unlike the **FFT Analyzer/Filter** of Samplitude 2496, here you cannot change the scales of the level (dB) and frequency (kHz) axes. To determine the precise value of the signal level and frequency, place the mouse pointer at the desired point, and its coordinates (dB, kHz) will be displayed in the two fields above the frequency monitor.

❏ The equalizer contains thirty sliders, each of them able to change the level of its frequency band from −15 to +15 dB.

❏ The **ME FreeFilter** effect can work in two modes — linear and logarithmic.
- The linear mode is switched on using the **Lin** button in the **Global** section

    NOTE In this mode, the frequency range is divided into 30 bands of the same width, and the frequency monitor display changes accordingly.

- The logarithmic mode is switched on with the **Log** button

    NOTE In this mode, the width of every band is one-third of the corresponding octave.

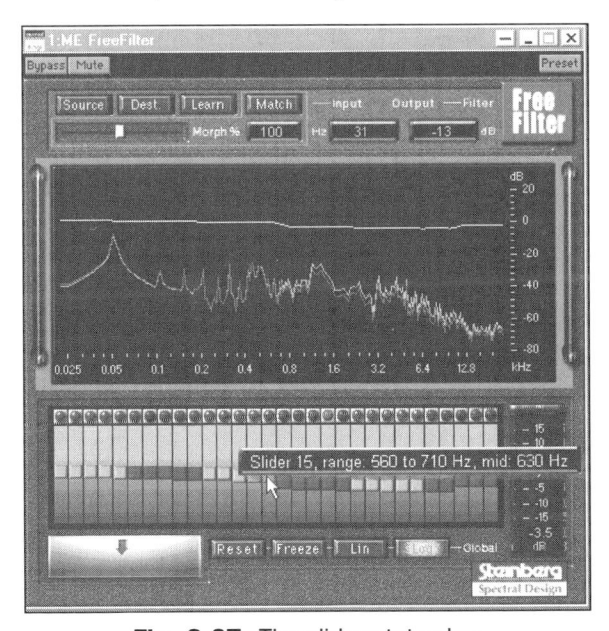

Fig. 8.27. The slider status bar

A right click on any of the sliders causes a status bar to appear with information about the number of the **slider**, the **range** of the frequency band, and its middle (**mid**) value (Fig. 8.27).

❐ A toolbox containing three tools is hidden behind the button with an arrow. To access the tools, you must click this button (Fig. 8.28).

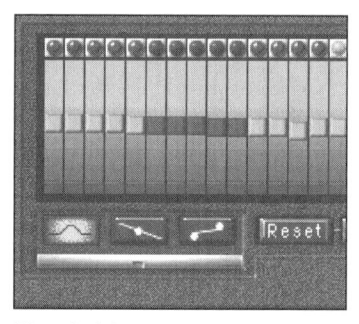

Fig. 8.28. The hidden toolbox

The Toolbox of the ME FreeFilter Effect

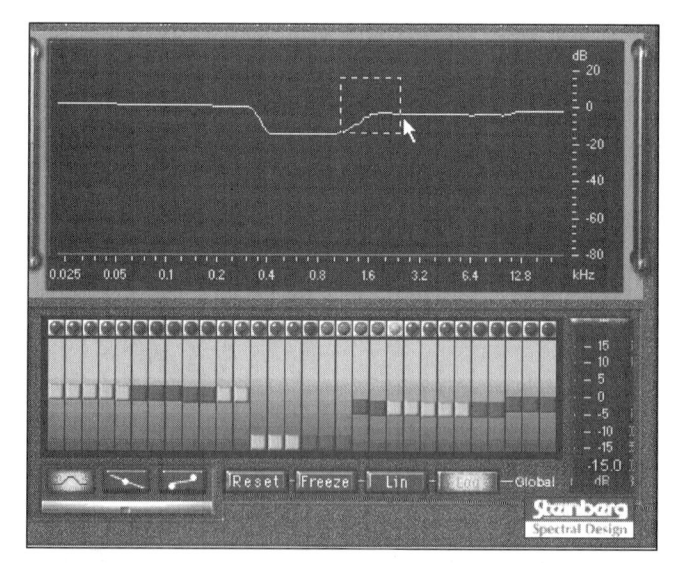

Fig. 8.29. Selecting a part of the frequency-response curve

Let's examine the functions of the toolbox buttons, from left to right.

❐ The button that allows you to group equalizer sliders together. To create a group, you must select a part of the frequency-response curve with a box, as shown in Fig. 8.29.

Chapter 8: Mastering in the WaveLab 3.0 Application 635

(To do this, drag the mouse pointer to the right or to the left with the left mouse button pressed.)

After selecting, the sliders of the equalizer within the selected range become bound together. To move the group, just move any one of its sliders.

Binding the sliders is a very convenient feature when changing the level of the band within the selected range without changing the frequency-response curve of this range. For example, to lower the overall level at the output of the effect, you should select the whole frequency range of the curve and move any of the sliders downwards. The height of the box reflects the depth of controlling the frequency response. To cancel the selection, just click any place on the frequency monitor.

☐ The "rubber band" tool (Fig. 8.30) is used to create linear frequency responses with a certain slope of the curve with reference to the central point.

The central point can be moved along the curve. To change the slope of the curve, you must grab either of its ends with the mouse and drag it up or down. As a result, all the sliders will align accordingly (Fig. 8.30).

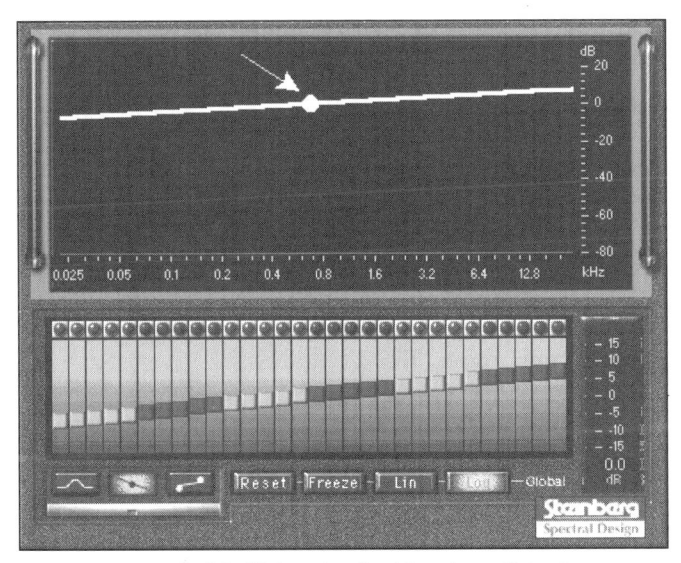

Fig. 8.30. Using the "rubber band" tool

☐ The other tool was humorously called "Bone" by its creators due to its appearance. It allows you to create complex amplitude frequency response curves of the equalizer (Fig. 8.31).

When shaping these curves, you just drag the markers at the ends of the "bone" to the desired positions.

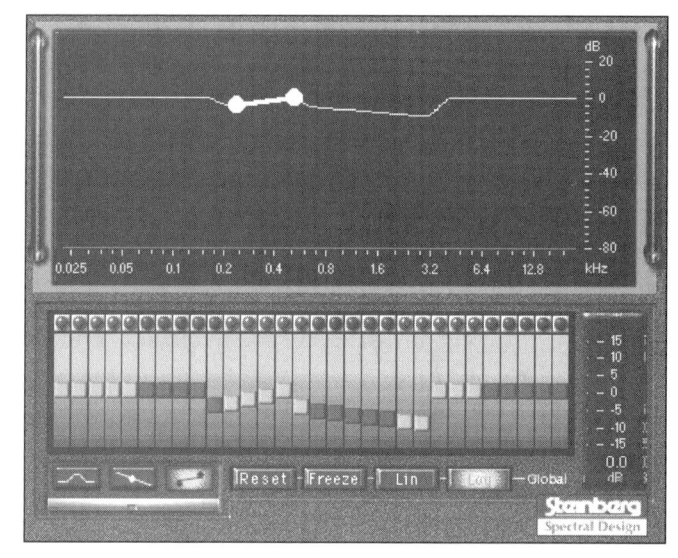

Fig. 8.31. Using the "bone" tool

The Learning Section of the ME FreeFilter Effect

To successfully solve the task of equalizing with the **ME FreeFilter** effect, you should definitely use its learning section, located in the upper left part of the window (Fig. 8.27).

The learning section is used in the following way:

1. Load two files into WaveLab — the original file and the one to be processed.
2. Perform an analysis of the original file. To do this:
   - Click the **Source** button to play back the original file
   - When the playback stops, the **Source learned** message will appear in the frequency monitor display
3. Perform an analysis of the processed file:
   - Click the **Dest** button to play back the processed file
   - When the playback stops, the **Source and Destination learned** message will appear in the frequency monitor display
4. Click the **Match** button. The generated frequency-response curve will appear in the frequency monitor display. This curve adjusts the frequency response of the processed sound file in accordance with that of the original file (Fig. 8.32). In other words, the frequency response is fitted to the source.

Chapter 8: Mastering in the WaveLab 3.0 Application 637

> **NOTE** When you click the **Source** or **Dest** button, the **Learn** button is pressed automatically. This means that the **FreeFilter** effect is in the learning mode. A click on the **Learn** button toggles the learning process on and off.

The **Morph** slider changes the depth of the frequency-response curve adjustment. The valid range is from 0 to 200%.

If you need to repeat the steps of analyzing and generating the frequency-response curve of the equalizer, you must click the **Reset** button to delete the previous results from memory.

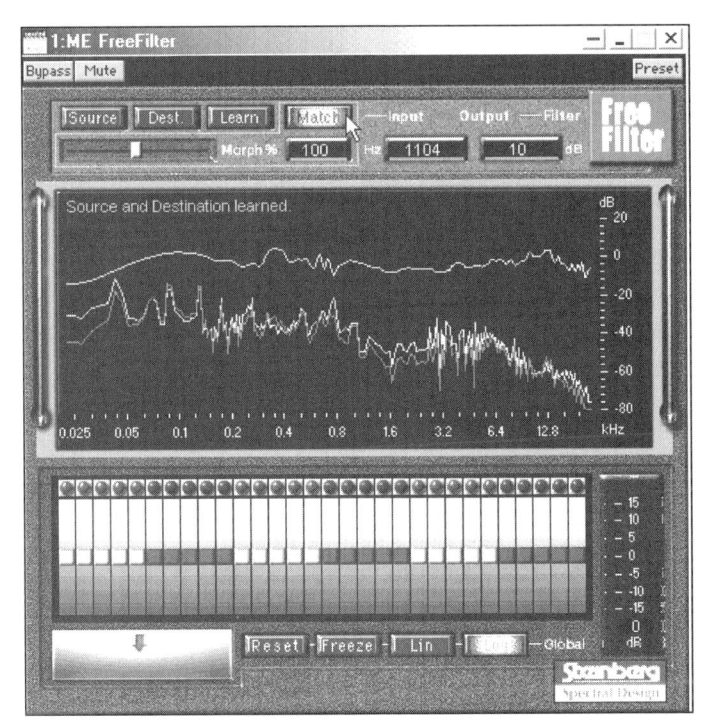

Fig. 8.32. The generated frequency-response curve

> **NOTE** As a source, you may use, for example, a CD with a recording in a musical style similar to the style of your project. To obtain a high-quality equalization, you should choose a CD that is as close to the processed sound file as possible. Digital copying of an AUDIO CD can be performed directly in the WaveLab editor with the **File|Open|Import Audio CD tracks** command.

When working with the **ME FreeFilter** effect, it is important to keep in mind a number of points.

❐ The sample rates of the original and the processed file must be equal.

❐ You mustn't change the working mode of the equalizer in the middle of a stage of analysis and amplitude-frequency response curve generation.

> **NOTE** If the analysis was performed, say, in linear mode, switching to logarithmic mode will distort the results of the analysis.

❐ The accuracy of the analysis depends on the time spent on it, which should be decided experimentally.

❐ It is always better to click the **Reset** button before each new analysis stage to ensure that the effect's memory is erased.

The analyzed material of the source can be saved with the **Preset** button. Later, if the preset is called, you need analyze *only* the processed sound file.

> **NOTE** This feature is very convenient when you want to equalize multiple sound files according to one source. This would be enough to equalize the frequency-response curves of all the compositions in an album.

The generated frequency-response curves of the equalizer can also be saved as presets.

When analyzing the spectrum curves of the input and output signals, you may click the **Freeze** button. When you do this, the moving picture in the frequency monitor display will stop.

For sound sources, you can use the presets supplied with the application (Fig. 8.33).

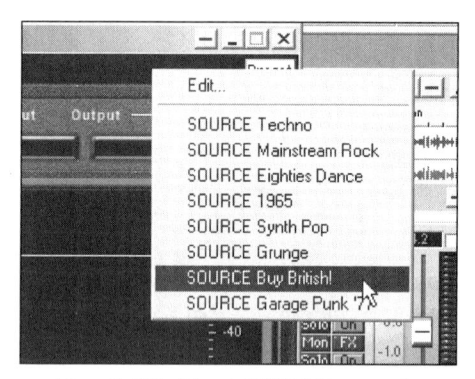

Fig. 8.33. The **SOURCE** presets

Among the presets, WaveLab contains eight samples of various musical styles.

Also, a signal supplied from any device connected to the input of the sound card can be used as a source. To do this, you must:

1. Turn on the **Live Input** mode using the **View|Windows|Live Input** menu.
2. Turn on the playback mode.

Perform an analysis of the sound source with the **ME FreeFilter** effect in the usual manner.

As a rule, an automatically generated frequency-response curve is insufficient for equalization. You also need to experiment with the **Morph** slider and adjust the curve manually. In this process, it is most convenient to group the equalizer sliders together, in order to change the level of individual fragments of the generated curve without destroying its shape.

Improving the Equalizing Quality

Recall that statistically authentic restoration of the original analog signal takes place at sample rates no less than 5 F.

If we use Cool Edit Pro to generate a sine with a frequency of 15 kHz and a sample rate of 44.1 kHz, we'll clearly see that one period of the signal is represented by at most three samples. At a sample rate of 88.2 kHz, the period of a signal with a frequency of 15 kHz is represented by six samples, and so on.

Therefore, for high-quality sound processing in the sound range with the equalizer (which is mastering), you must:

❐ Increase the sample rate (this process is called *upsampling*)

❐ Process the sound at the increased rate

The result of equalizing at the increased sample rate sounds more clear, being less "screechy".

> **NOTE** Some DirectX plug-ins, such as the **Q-Metric** parametric equalizer from Steinberg, use a doubled internal sample rate.

By how much should we increase the sample rate? Most likely, it should be increased to 88.2 kHz, that is, double the sample rate of a CD. The reason for this is that increasing the sample rate by an integer factor is easily achieved, and avoids a loss in sound quality.

> **NOTE** In contrast, the task of converting 48 kHz to 44.1 kHz without losing quality is very difficult. One of its solutions involves upsampling to some rate that is a multiple for both rates, then filtering, and then downsampling to 44.1 kHz. Since the ratio 48/44.1 is equal to 160/147, we need to multiply 48 by 147 (the multiple rate will be 7056 kHz), and then divide the result by 160 (and get 44.1). Because of this, using the 96 kHz sample rate (2 x 48 kHz) makes little sense.

Upsampling in WaveLab is done using the **Process|Convert Sample Rate** command. Just select the new sample rate in the **Sample Rate** section in the **Audio Attributes** dialog box (Fig. 8.34).

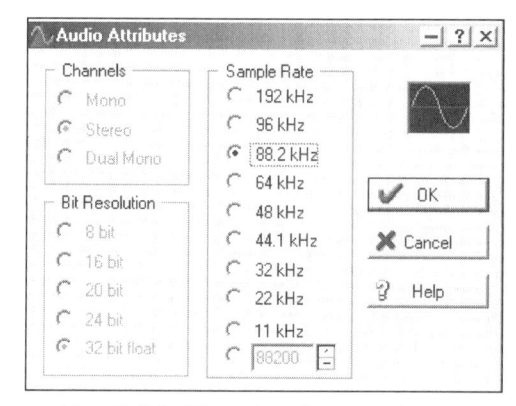

Fig. 8.34. Changing the sample rate

Unfortunately, the **ME FreeFilter** effect doesn't support sample rates greater than 48 kHz.

Nevertheless, there is a way out. The fact is that the frequency-response curve generated with the **ME FreeFilter** effect can be manually, point-by-point, transferred to another effect that supports higher sample rates — for example, the **FFT Filter** effect of Cool Edit Pro. This process isn't as difficult as it may seem. Once you have some experience, it will take no more than 10 minutes.

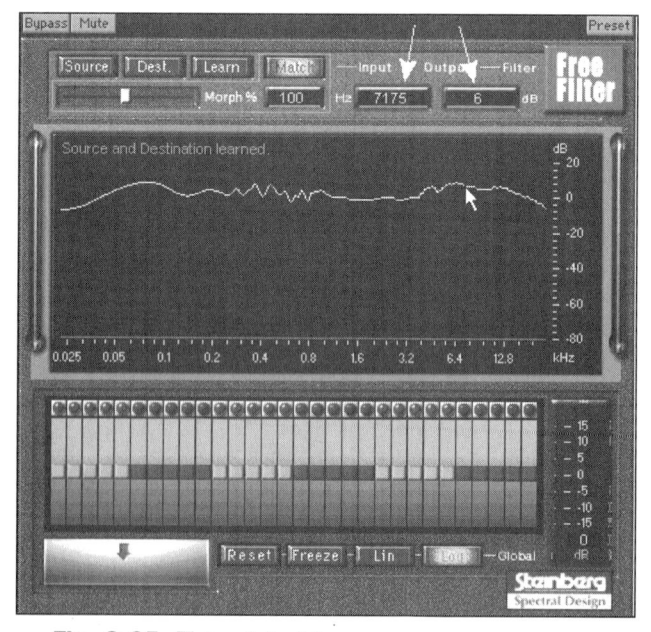

Fig. 8.35. The original frequency-response curve

Chapter 8: Mastering in the WaveLab 3.0 Application

By sequentially moving the mouse pointer to the inflection points of the curve, you can quickly read the frequency and level values in the indication fields (Fig. 8.35).

NOTE It is recommended that you use the logarithm modes of the **ME FreeFilter** and **FFT Filter** effects. The **Log Scale** checkbox in the **FFT Filter** effect must be checked for this.

The read values should be entered through the keyboard into the **FFT Filter** window in the Cool Edit Pro editor by double-clicking the corresponding point in the curve display.

After the click, the **Edit Point** dialog box will open (Fig. 8.36), where you can enter the values into the **Frequency** and **Amplification** fields.

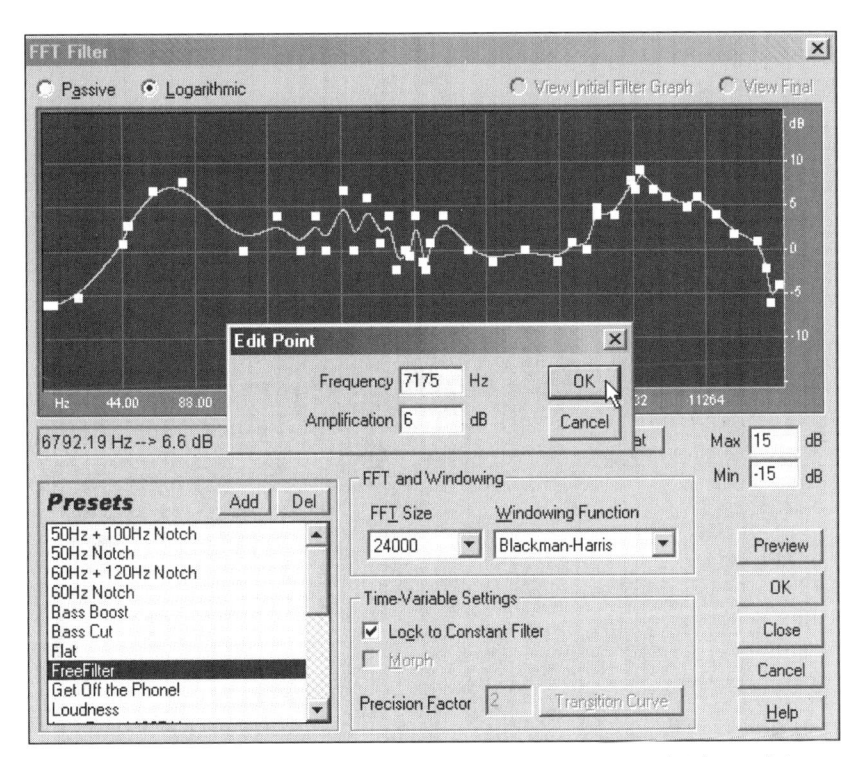

Fig. 8.36. Entering the frequency-response curve point-by-point

The described method can be also used at conventional sample rates (44.1 kHz and 48 kHz), since the **ME FreeFilter** equalizer provides a quality of sound processing that is significantly less than the **FFT Filter** effect of Cool Edit Pro.

However, you can still use its analytical features, since the generated frequency-response curve is highly accurate.

The Waves C4 Multiband Parametric Processor

In 2000, Waves Ltd. (**http://www.waves.com**) released a DirectX plug-in package known as Waves Digital Audio Processor, version 3.0.

In addition to the new versions of popular virtual effects such as **Q10**, **S1**, **C1gate**, **C1comp**, **MaxxBass**, **DeEsser**, and **TrueVerb**, many new effects were included in the package, for example, the **Waves C4** multiband parametric processor.

The **Waves C4** parametric processor that performs 48-bit processing is unrivaled among the products of other companies.

This processor can be thought of as a multiband compressor with parametric controls, or as a dynamic four-band equalizer.

Both viewpoints are true, but, judging by the interface, it appears to be more of an equalizer with a dynamic curve (Fig. 8.37).

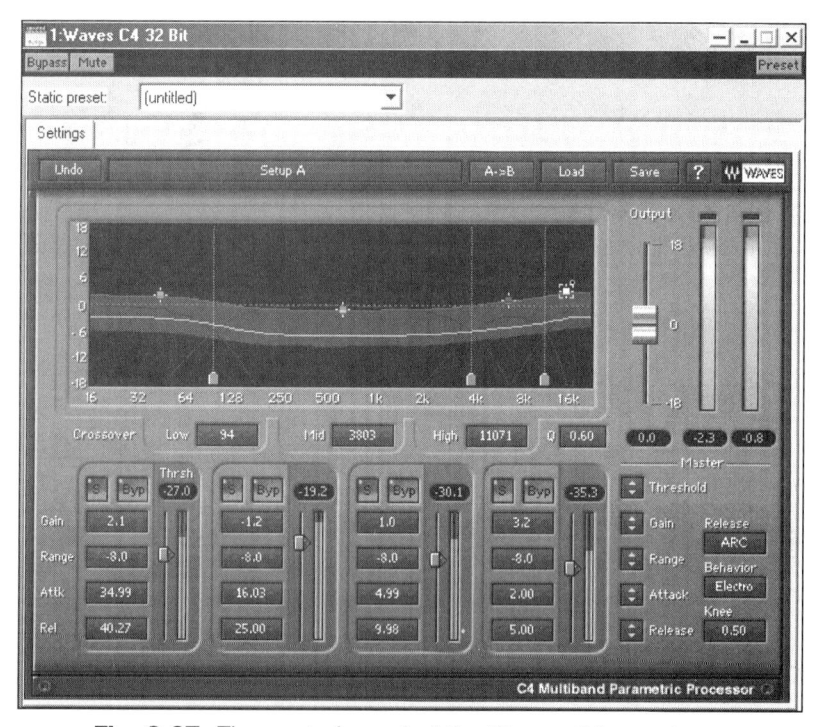

Fig. 8.37. The control panel of the **Waves C4** processor

The **Waves C4** processor has a unique display, with a curve that reflects the real changes in the signal level. Combining the dynamic curve with the other control functions gave it a very convenient and intuitive interface.

Chapter 8: Mastering in the WaveLab 3.0 Application

Waves C4 is a multifunctional device that has many more features than a standard multiband compressor. It can be a compressor, an expander, a de-esser (that is, an "s"-sound suppressor), a limiter, and an equalizer, all at the same time. Using **Waves C4**, you can create clean and transparent sound and work with small details of the sound picture.

Waves C4 can be thought of as a combination of four Waves C1 modules (which were present in older versions).

The frequency range of the signal is divided into four *crossover* bands (the **Crossover** section).

Each band has a separate set of controls. Besides that, general adjustment is performed in the **Master** section.

Let's examine the controls of one frequency band (Fig. 8.38).

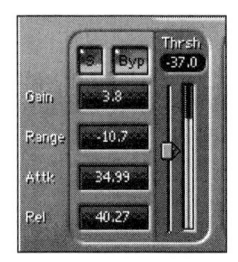

Fig. 8.38. The control panel of an individual band

- **Gain** sets the signal level in the selected band (it is similar to the **Output Gain** parameter of the **Dynamics Processing** effect in Cool Edit Pro).

- **Range** sets the range within which the signal can change. If a negative value is specified, the compressor is enabled; otherwise it is an expander. When **Range** equals 0, dynamic processing is off.

  The **Range** parameter performs the simultaneous regulation of two parameters of a classic compressor:
  - The compression/expansion **Ratio**
  - The maximum **Gain**

- **Attk** and **Rel** (Attack and Release) are the parameters typical for a conventional dynamic processor. **Attk** is the attack time of the processor, and **Rel** is the release time. The release value is adapted according to the ARC (Auto Release Control) algorithm developed by Waves for the **Renaissance Compressor** effect.

- **Threshold** functionally corresponds to the threshold of action of a conventional compressor. The indicator found next to the **Threshold** slider reflects the real signal level in the given frequency band. Thus it is very convenient to set **Threshold**.

- **S** (Solo) is the button that switches the Solo mode on.

❐ **Byp** (Bypass) is the button that switches the Bypass mode on. When it is clicked, processing in the corresponding frequency band won't be performed.

The **Master** section allows you to make global changes to the parameters of all four of the bands. For example, changing the **Range** parameter adjusts the **Range** parameters of all the frequency bands.

❐ The **Release** field is designed to toggle between two modes:
- **Manual** is the mode for manual adjustment of the processor release time. In this mode, the release time in each frequency band is equal to the **Release** parameter.
- **ARC** (Auto Release Control) is the mode where the release time in each frequency band is computed for each sample individually, in order to minimize distortions.

NOTE The **ARC** mode is ideal for the **Waves C4** effect, and is recommended for use in most cases. The value of the **Release** parameter, set in each frequency band, becomes a reference point for computing the actual release time.

In this mode, you can achieve the maximum value of the root-mean-square (RMS) level with minimal distortions.

❐ The **Behavior** field is designed to toggle between two models of compressor behavior.
- **Opto** is a classical model of a compressor with optocoupler feedback. This variant is preferred for deep compression.
- **Electro** is a compressor model developed by Waves. It is the inverse of the **Opto** model.

NOTE The **Electro** model provides for minimum distortions at moderate compression. It is recommended that you use it to obtain the maximum value of the root-mean-square (RMS) level with minimal distortions.

❐ **Knee** sets up a working mode of the program at the knee points of all the frequency bands. The range of modes is from **Soft** to **Hard**.

NOTE The **Hard** mode is most suitable for compression of percussion instruments. When mastering, you should try and find the value of the **Knee** parameter experimentally.

To begin with, you can use either the **Multi Opto Mastering** or **Multi Electro Mastering** preset.

The boundary frequencies for the bands can be changed in the **Crossover** section (Fig. 8.39).

To do this, just double-click either the **Low**, or **Mid**, or **High** field, and enter the desired value from the keyboard.

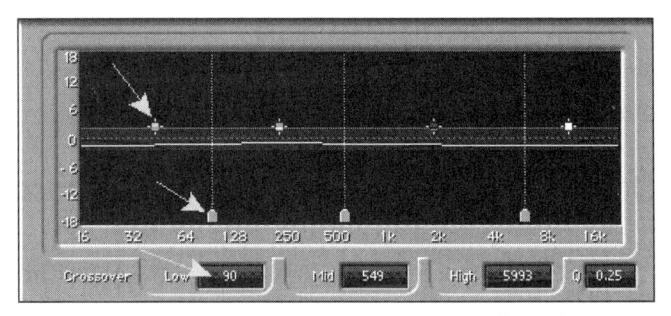

Fig. 8.39. The display of the **Waves C4** effect

There are also three special crossover points, shown with vertical lines on the display, which are provided for the same purpose. They can be dragged with the mouse. The **Q** field is designed to change the steepness of the slopes of the band filters. The valid range is from 0.10 to 0.75.

- The 0.10 value corresponds to a steepness of 6 dB per octave
- 0.60 — 12 dB per octave
- 0.70 — 18 dB per octave
- 0.75 — 24 dB per octave

NOTE For more intensive processing (that is, processing with a lower ratio of the peak level to the RMS level), you must use a larger steepness for the filters. To obtain the "gentle sound" that is a result of softer processing, you should decrease the **Q** parameter to anywhere from 0.10 to 0.30.

There are also additional controls called *band center markers*. By dragging one of them, you can change three parameters simultaneously.

- Moving a marker horizontally moves the center of the frequency band (thus changing the boundary frequencies for the bands)
- Moving a marker vertically changes the **Gain** parameter
- Moving a marker vertically with the <Alt> key pressed changes the **Range** parameter

The **Waves C4** parametric processor employs the concepts of **Threshold** and **Range** instead of traditional control using the **Ratio** parameter (which is the compression/expansion ratio).

Whereas in a classical processor setting an operation threshold to a low level leads to attenuation of the high-level signal, in the **Waves C4** parametric processor the situation is different. First, the maximum possible range within which you can change the signal level is set in the **Range** field, and then the **Threshold** slider is used to determine the level that will be the reference for signal changing.

When the range is negative, the level moves downward; when the range value is positive, the level moves upward.

Let's illustrate the threshold/range concept with some examples.

High-Level Compression (the Downward Compressor)

Fig. 8.40 shows an example of high-level compression implemented using the popular dynamic processor **Waves C1** with the following parameters: **Threshold** = −35 dB, **Ratio** = 1.5:1.

> **NOTE** This kind of compression is called "high-level" because only signals with levels higher than −35 dB are processed.

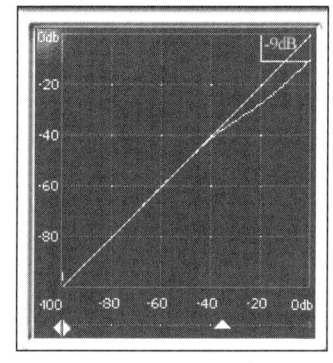

Fig. 8.40. High-level compression

The equivalent settings of the **Waves C4** processor will be the following:

- **Range** = −9 dB (approximately)
- **Gain** = 0 dB

Thus, to compress the high-level signals with the **Waves C4** processor, you should set **Threshold** to a value between −24 dB and 0 dB, and **Range** to a value between −3 and −9.

High-Level Expansion (the Upward Expander)

An example of high-level expansion implemented using the **Waves C1** dynamic processor with **Threshold** = −35 dB and **Ratio** = 0.75:1 is shown in Fig. 8.41.

To perform equivalent processing with **Waves C4**, you must set the **Range** value to +10 dB.

Setting **Range** to a value from +2 to +5 (decompressing) can be used to restore the dynamics of a signal distorted by previous overcompression (for example, by compressing multitracks).

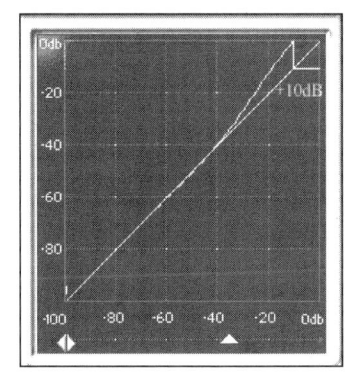

Chapter 8: Mastering in the WaveLab 3.0 Application

Fig. 8.41. High-level expansion

In this case, when the signal level exceeds the **Threshold** value, its dynamics will be expanded upwards.

In other words, if **Range** is equal to +5 dB, the maximum expansion of the dynamic range will be 5 dB.

Low-Level Compression (the Upward Compressor)

An example of low-level compression with the **Waves C1** effect is shown in Fig. 8.42.

High-level signals remain intact, and low-level signals undergo upward compression.

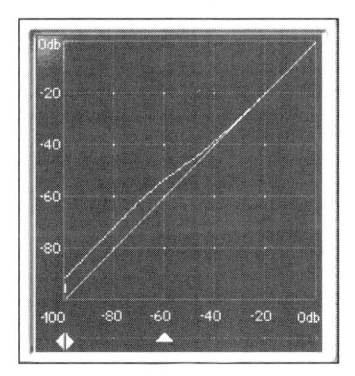

Fig. 8.42. Low-level compression

To perform low-level compression with the **Waves C4** processor, you may set, for example, the range approximately equal to −5 dB, the threshold to a value from −40 dB to −60 dB, and the gain to +5 dB (which is the opposite of the range value).

> **NOTE** The value of the **Gain** parameter must compensate that of the **Range** parameter.

Low-level compression can make the sound clearer and softer; it seems to "breathe". The reverberation tails and the fine details are perceived better, and the sound becomes warmer and more "alive".

One of the main advantages of low-level compression is the absence of distortions of high-level peak signals, which is most important for AUDIO CD mastering, where low-level signals usually suffer from quantization noise.

Low-Level Expansion, Noise Gate (the Downward Expander)

In Fig. 8.43, you see an example of low-level expansion implemented with the **Waves C1** dynamic processor.

To obtain the same result with the **Waves C4** processor, you may set, for example, the range approximately to +5 dB, the gain for compensation to −5 dB, and the threshold to −60 dB.

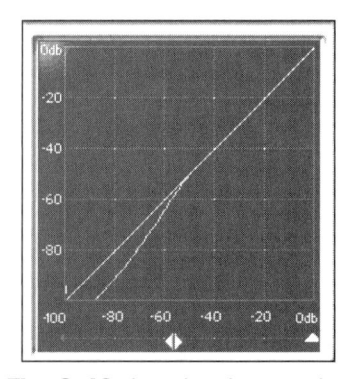

Fig. 8.43. Low-level expansion

With this setup, you can use the **Waves C4** processor as a multiband **Noise Gate** (a downward expander). Of course, the **Gain**, **Range**, and **Threshold** parameters are set separately for each frequency band.

> **NOTE** Again, the value of the **Gain** parameter must compensate that of the **Range** parameter.

It is recommended that you begin your work with the **Waves C4** processor by setting the global parameters in the **Master** section. Then adjust each frequency band separately.

The built-in presets of the effect can serve as starting points.

The Hyperprism Harmonic Exciter

In *Chapter 5*, we discussed a software simulation of an exciter assembled from DirectX plug-ins from Waves. In this chapter, we're going to introduce a separate DirectX effect from Arboretum Systems, Inc. (**http://www.arboretum.com**), called **Hyperprism Harmonic Exciter**. It is included in the Hyperprism DirectX plug-in package, version 2.5.

Recall that an *exciter* is a phycho-acoustic processor that spectrally enriches the sound.

Exciters are devices whose work cannot be appreciated before they are switched on.

As an illustration, imagine an acoustic system covered by a thick blanket and emitting some music. After a while, the blanket is removed, and the sound changes. This change is similar to the work of the exciter.

The sound processed by an exciter becomes clean and clear; it is, so to speak, unveiled. It would be very difficult to describe the work of an exciter with a certain set of parameters, since the exciter is relevant to sound perception by humans, the process studied by phychoacoustics.

You can use an exciter both to process individual parts (say, a guitar or vocal) or to perform final mastering. Since your ear is the main criterion for setting the exciter, we're going to confine ourselves to the examination of the control panel of the **Hyperprism Harmonic Exciter** (Fig. 8.44) and give some general advice.

❐ You can toggle between two modes of harmonic generation in the **Harmonic Type** drop-down list:

- The **Odd and Even (Warm)** mode uses odd and even harmonics to obtain a warm sound
- The **Odd (Bright)** mode uses odd harmonics to obtain a bright sound

❐ The **Quality Level** can be **Good**, **Better**, or **Best**.

> *NOTE* Switching to a higher quality level increases the internal sample rate, and thus requires more system resources.

❐ The **Harmonics** slider sets the number of harmonics generated. The usual range, from 0 to 100%, can be expanded to 200% if necessary. To do this, double-click in the right-hand field nearest to the slider, and enter 200 via the keyboard.

❐ The **Dynamics** slider adjusts the dynamics of the harmonics generating algorithm. The valid range is from 0 to 100%. Increasing the parameter value leads to spectral enrichment of only the high-level signals. When the parameter is decreased, harmonics are generated both for high and low level signals, thus achieving overall spectral enrichment.

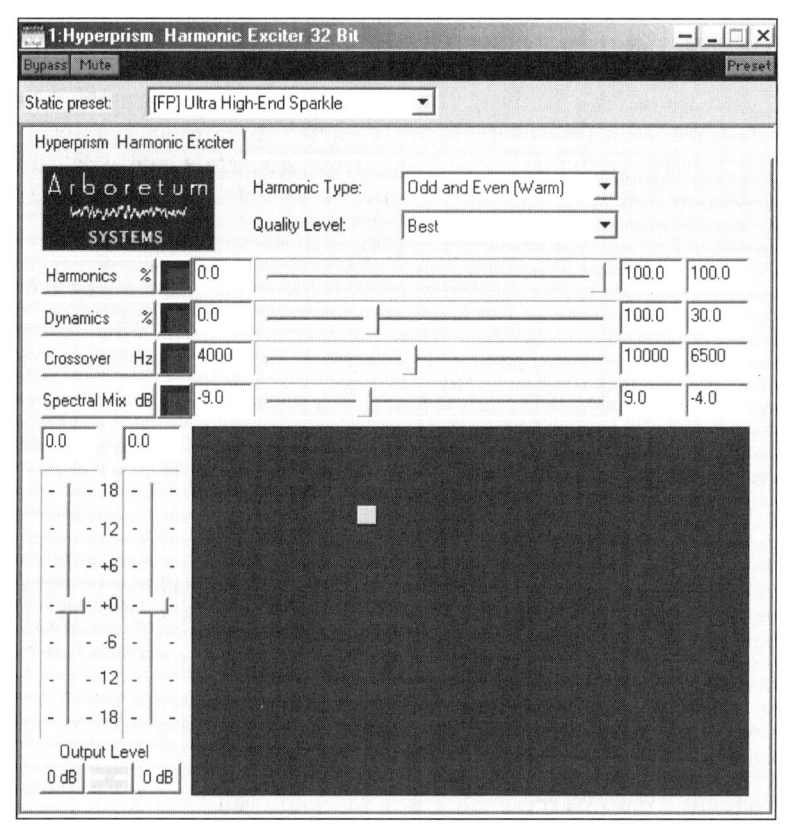

Fig. 8.44. The control panel of the **Hyperprism Harmonic Exciter** effect

- The **Crossover** slider specifies the frequency range in which spectral enrichment is to be done. For example, if a frequency of 6,000 Hz is set, harmonics are generated only for frequencies higher than 6,000 Hz. The range of adjustment is from 500 to 10,000 Hz. To set the boundaries of the range, enter the frequency values via the keyboard into the fields located to the left and right of the slider.
- The **Spectral Mix** slider is responsible for the signal level of frequencies higher than what is specified with **Crossover**. The working range is from −24 dB to 12 dB.
- The purpose of the **Output Level** sliders is obvious.
- The **0 dB** buttons force the output level sliders to the zero positions. The button with the yellow broken line icon located between the **0 dB** buttons binds the output level sliders together.

An additional service of the DirectX plug-ins package from Arboretum Systems, Inc. is **Blue Window**, shown in Fig. 8.45. The horizontal or vertical movement of the box in the blue window can be attached to certain sliders. To do this, click the blue square button found to the left of each slider, or the button with the parameter name on it.

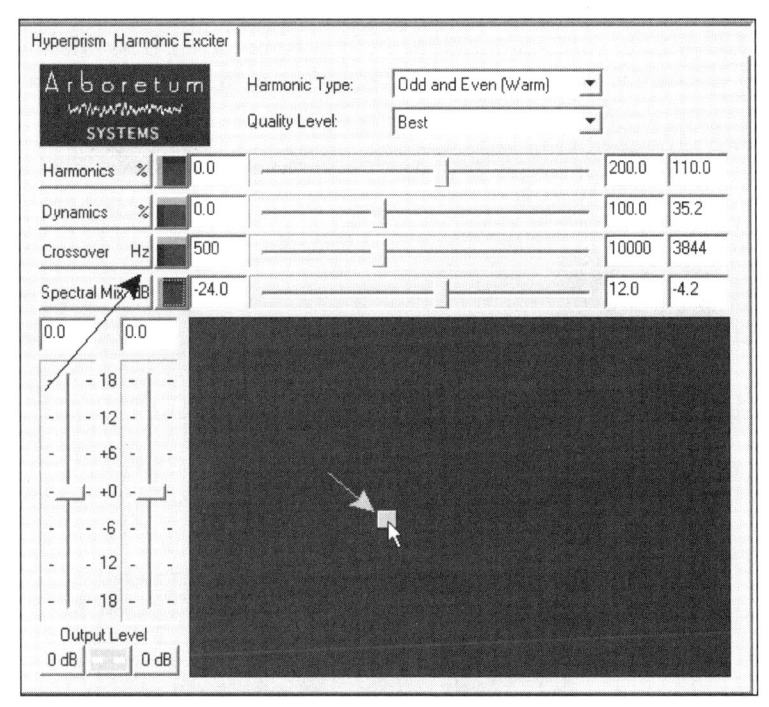

Fig. 8.45. Blue Window

Every click changes the state of connection between the slider and the blue window according to the following cycle:

❏ No connection

❏ Connection with the horizontal movement

❏ Connection with the vertical movement

And so, four parameters can be changed at once by moving the box in the blue window.

The Hyperprism Bass Maximizer Effect

The working principles of the **Hyperprism Bass Maximizer** effect are based on the specifics of human hearing, like those of the **Harmonic Exciter**.

NOTE The **Hyperprism Bass Maximizer** effect is also included in the DirectX plug-in package from Arboretum Systems, Inc.

A similar effect, **MaxxBass**, is included in the DirectX plug-in package from Waves.

The psychoacoustic phenomenon used in this effect is based on the fact that a human ear can subconsciously restore the main low-frequency tone from its harmonics.

In other words, even if an acoustic system doesn't actually emit the low tone, an illusion of it is created, thanks to spectral enrichment. The **Hyperprism Bass Maximizer** DirectX plug-in makes it possible to improve the perception of the bass by using such a phenomenon.

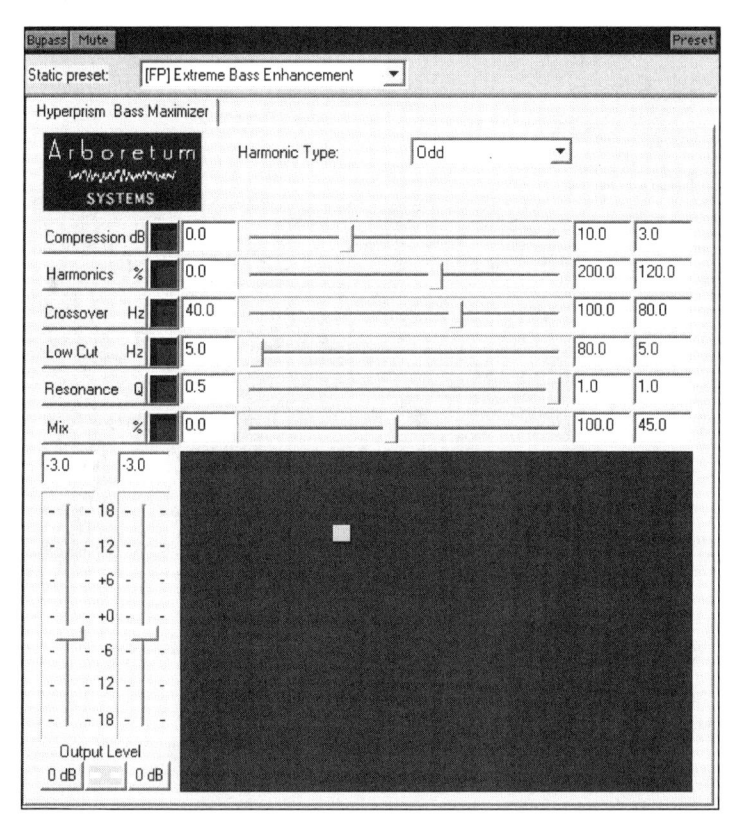

Fig. 8.46. The control panel of the **Hyperprism Bass Maximizer** effect

Let's examine the control panel of the **Hyperprism Bass Maximizer** effect (Fig. 8.46).

- In the **Harmonic Type** drop-down list, you can choose either of the types for harmonics to be generated:
  - **Odd**
  - **Odd and Even**
- The **Compression** slider adjusts the level of compression added to the bass frequencies. The range of values is from 0 to 20 dB.

- The **Harmonics** slider specifies the number of generated harmonics in the 0-to-200% range.
- The **Crossover** slider sets the frequency below which compression and harmonics generation are performed. For example, if a frequency of 80 Hz is set, all frequencies below 80 Hz will have harmonics and undergo compression. The range of valid values is from 40 to 400 Hz.
- The **Low Cut** slider specifies the cutoff frequency of the high-frequency filter. In fact, **Low Cut** is a filter suppressing low-frequency subharmonics in order to prevent overload. The working range is from 5 to 200 Hz.
- The **Resonance** slider is designed to control the quality of the **Low Cut** filter. The valid range is from 0.5 to 5.0. Increasing this parameter results in additional amplification of the signal at the cutoff frequency of the **Low Cut** filter.
- The **Mix** slider is used to set the relationship between the frequency components that lie above and below the frequency specified by **Crossover**. The range of values is from 0 to 100%.

When using the **Bass Maximizer** effect, it is recommended that you begin with the following settings:

1. Set the **Crossover** value between 50 and 100 Hz.
2. Set the **Low Cut** value below 20 Hz.
3. Set the **Resonance** value no greater than 1.0.
4. Using the **Harmonics** slider, gradually increase the number of harmonics up to the desired level.
5. If you need to increase the bass density, you may add some compression with the **Compression** slider.
6. Using the **Mix** slider, set the final balance between the frequency components.

To obtain a "pumping bass" effect, you might try to set the **Low Cut** value to approximately 40 Hz and increase the **Resonance** value to 3.0.

The Waves L1—Ultramaximizer+ Effect

It is well known that the maximum level of the digital signal is determined by the highest peak of amplitude.

Using normalization sets the peak level to 0 dB, but the RMS level can appear to be much lower in this case. Many amplitude peaks have a short duration and can be decreased by several decibels without noticeable distortion of the sound.

Obviously, by limiting the amplitude peaks, you can obtain a higher RMS level than with common normalization.

Especially for this purpose, Waves has developed the **Waves L1—Ultramaximizer+** DirectX plug-in included in the Waves Digital Audio Processors version 3.0 package. This plug-in combines a peak limiter and a dithering processor at the same time.

L1—Ultramaximizer+ uses the "look ahead" algorithm, so it is protected against "over-control" and doesn't create noticeable distortions.

L1—Ultramaximizer+ performs the final processing of the signal. This is why it must be the last in the chain of effects used for mastering. Fig. 8.47 shows the control panel of the **Waves L1—Ultramaximizer+** effect.

The peak limiter is found in the left part of the panel.

- The **Threshold** slider is combined with the input level indicator.
    - To change the action threshold, drag the two **Threshold** triangles upwards or downwards.
    - If the signal level goes above the set threshold, the **Atten** indicator (attenuation meter) will reflect the degree of signal limitation.

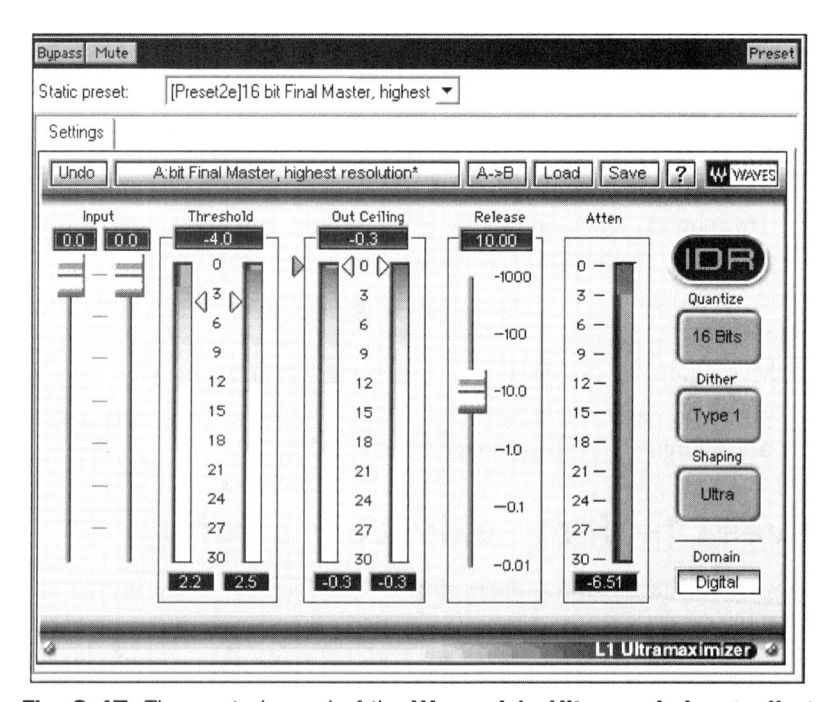

Fig. 8.47. The control panel of the **Waves L1—Ultramaximizer+** effect

- The **Out Ceiling** slider specifies the upper limit for the processed signal level. No sample of the output signal can be higher than the level set with this slider. For visual

Chapter 8: Mastering in the WaveLab 3.0 Application

control of the processed signal level, the **Out Ceiling** slider is combined with the output level indicator.

❐ The **Release** slider specifies the release time of the peak limiter. When setting this parameter, you must be guided by the minimal distortion criteria:

- The lower the limiting threshold, the higher the release time must be set
- For moderate limitations (4 to 6 dB), the release time should be set to 10 msec or more

Thus, when looking for the best value for the **Release** parameter, you can start with a small value of 1 msec, and then gradually increase the release time until a clean and clear sound appears.

The dithering processor is placed in the **IDR** (Increase Dynamic Range) section.

> **NOTE** IDR technology was developed by Michael Gerzon, a world-famous expert in psychoacoustics. It is the result of long-term research in the area of digital technologies for increasing the resolution.

❐ The **Quantize** button specifies the final resolution of the output signal.

> **NOTE** The **Quantize** parameter has no relation to the resolution of the input signal. When mastering a CD, this parameter must be 16 bits.

❐ The **Dither** button sets the type of dithering algorithm:

- **None** — no dithering
- **Type 1** — minimum distortions at a greater noise level
- **Type 2** — minimum noise, the distortion level being higher than for **Type 1**

❐ The **Shaping** button sets the algorithm of noise shaping:

- **None** — no noise shaping
- **Moderate** is recommended for the **Type 2** dithering algorithm
- **Normal** is recommended for the **Type 1** and **Type 2** dithering algorithms
- **Ultra** is preferred for the **Type 1** dithering algorithm

> **NOTE** Actually, there are no strict rules or limitations on using any combination of dithering and noise shaping.

The dithering processor of the master section of WaveLab must be switched off when using **L1—Ultramaximizer+**.

❐ The **Domain** toggle button specifies the domain of the final audio medium. This button has two states: **Digital** and **Analog**. When mastering a CD, you should set **Out Ceiling** to −0.3 dB and choose the **Digital** domain.

When learning the **L1—Ultramaximizer+** effect, it is better to begin with built-in presets, such as **16 bit Final Master, highest resolution**.

A Chain of Plug-ins for Mastering

There is a widely-held opinion that mastering a CD is an art, rather than just the process of using some expensive equipment. The most important mastering tools are the musician's ear and the configuration of his or her acoustic system.

With this in mind, we aren't going to limit the reader's creative initiative. We will simply offer you one possible way of sound processing as a starting point.

You can make up chains of the aforementioned DirectX plug-ins for the purpose of AUDIO CD mastering.

The maximum number of effects that can be plugged in simultaneously is limited to the number of slots in the master section of WaveLab, and by the performance of your computer.

For a first approximation, you can use the following chain of DirectX plug-ins: **Waves C4**, **Hyperprism Bass Maximizer** (or **Waves MaxxBass**), **Hyperprism Harmonic Exciter** (when necessary), **Waves S1—StereoImager+** (for stereo correction), and **L1—Ultramaximizer+**.

The sequence of effects must begin with the **Waves C4** parametric processor and end with the **L1—Ultramaximizer+** peak limiter. Between these two, additional processing stages may be placed (or not).

With the suggested DirectX plug-in configuration, the final processing of the sound file (in 32-bit floating-point format) is done after the equalizing stage discussed earlier.

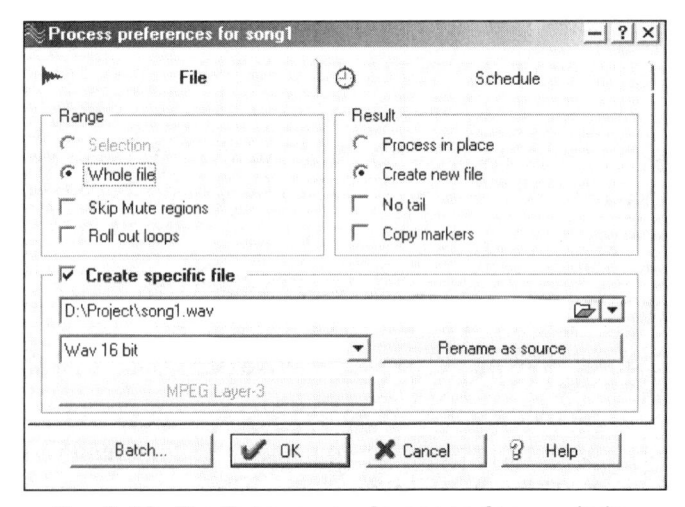

Fig. 8.48. The **Process preferences for ...** window

Since the described chain requires significant resources, on less powerful computers it is necessary to break the process into stages and save intermediate results in 32-bit floating-point format.

The final sound file must have a 44 kHz sample rate and a 16-bit resolution. This is why, if processing was done at the 88.2 kHz sample rate, the rate must be lowered to 44.1 kHz before using **L1—Ultramaximizer+**. After clicking the **Apply** button, you must select the **Create new file** radio button in the **Result** section of the **Process preferences** dialog box. Also, check the **Create specific file** checkbox. In the bottom section of the dialog box, specify the location of the final sound file and set its resolution to 16 bits (Fig. 8.48).

Writing the AUDIO CD

WaveLab makes it possible to burn (write to) a CD. Here we roughly discuss this process.

Creating an AUDIO CD should start with creating a CD project (CD program). For this purpose, open a new window with the **CD Program** command of the **File|New** menu. In this window, the project of the future AUDIO CD will be created (Fig. 8.49).

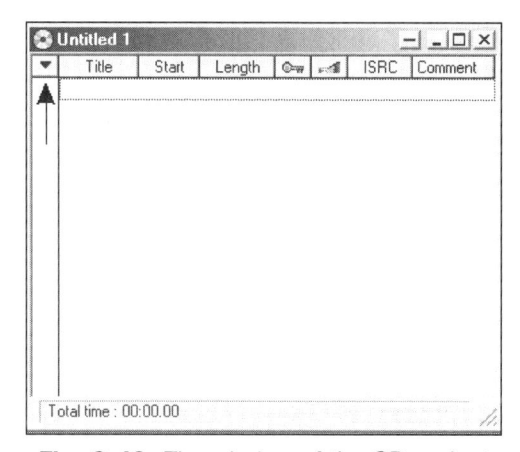

Fig. 8.49. The window of the CD project

In Fig. 8.49, the arrow points to a button with the triangle icon. This button is used to access the menu of the CD project.

> **NOTE** You can use the CD menu that appears in the editor window.

To import a WAV sound file, select the **Add Track(s)** option in the menu (or press the <Insert> key).

The file to read is selected in the **Select file(s) to add to the CD** dialog box.

After you click the **Open** button, another dialog box will appear. It contains a message that the file doesn't have CD-track markers, and that they will be set at the file boundaries by default.

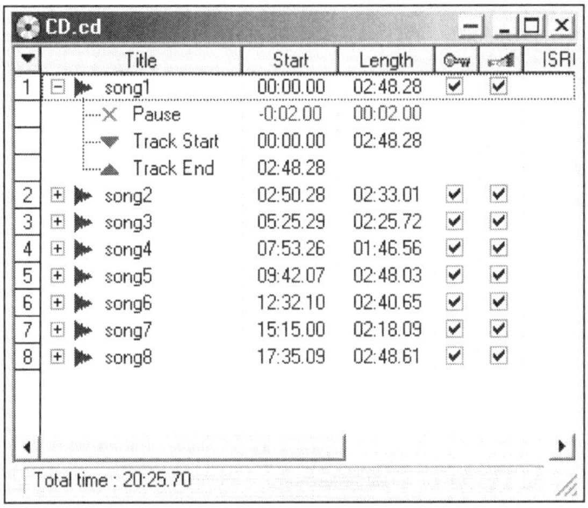

Fig. 8.50. Editing a CD project

In the project editing window, you can quickly change the positions of the markers and the length of the pause between the tracks.

To do this, click the "+" sign in the **Title** column (Fig. 8.50). A tree structure will open that contains the pause symbol and the starting and ending markers.

To change the length of the pause, double-click in the **Start** or **Length** column of the **Pause** line.

The length of the pause can be controlled in real time by double-clicking the **Pause** icon. The playback of the track will start with the pause.

To estimate the correctness of the positions of the markers by ear, double-click the **Track Start** or **Track End** marker. The track playback will begin:

❐ At the 0% position for the **Track Start** marker

or

❐ At the 98% position for the **Track End** marker

To correct the position of a marker, double-click in the **Start** column of the line containing the marker. The sound file editing window will open (Fig. 8.51), where you'll have to drag the marker to a new position.

Having finished editing the CD, you can start to write to it. A special option — **Write CD** — is provided for this purpose in the CD project menu.

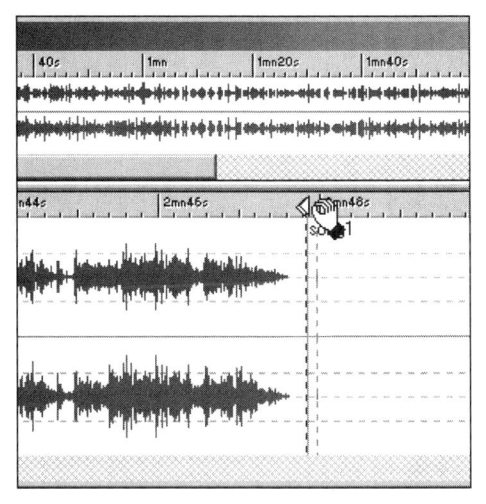

Fig. 8.51. Correcting the marker position

In the **Write CD** dialog box (Fig. 8.52), specify the number of copies and the writing speed.

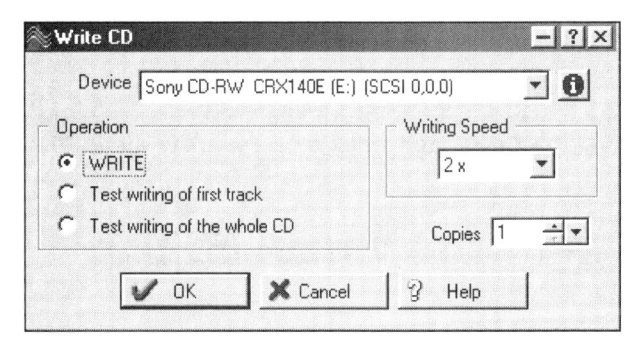

Fig. 8.52. The **Write CD** dialog box

To check the potential of your hardware, click the **i** (Information) button.

The **CD Recorder** window will open (Fig. 8.53) and provide you with the requested information.

In the **CD Program** window, you can prepare your sound files for burning in another specialized application.

To do this, the **Save each track as a separate audio file** command must be used. It opens a window with the same name (Fig. 8.54).

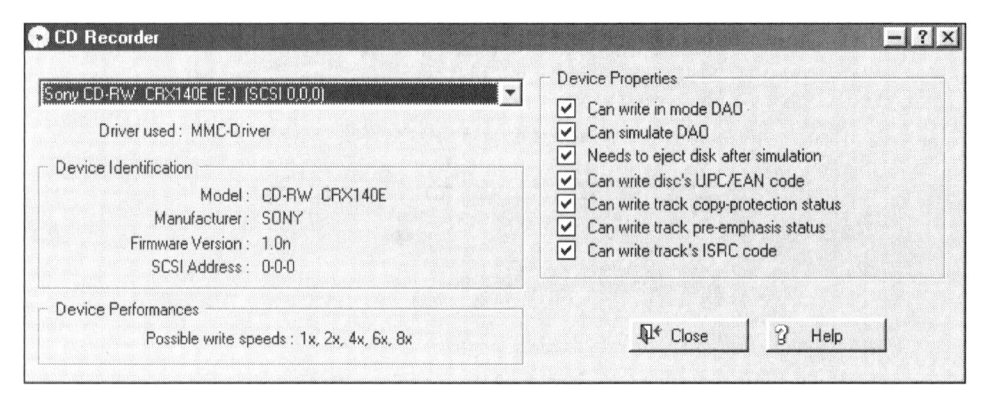

Fig. 8.53. The **CD Recorder** window

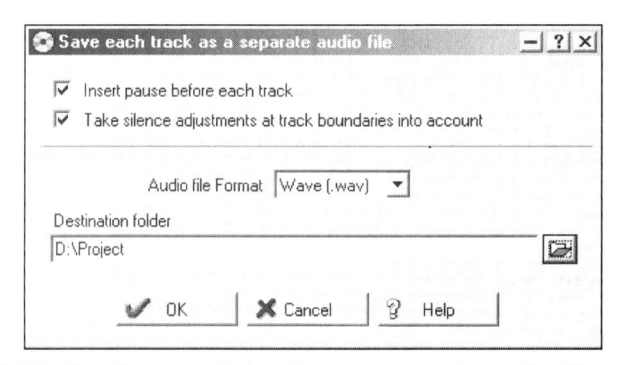

Fig. 8.54. The **Save each track as a separate audio file** window

The Audio Montage Virtual Editing Environment

For AUDIO CD mastering purposes, WaveLab offers the user a virtual editing environment called Audio Montage. It is somewhat similar to the VIP virtual project of Samplitude 2496.

The Audio Montage editing environment allows the user to perform complete AUDIO CD mastering, including writing. First of all, execute the **Audio Montage** command from the **File|New** menu.

Then load the sound files by right-clicking the virtual track of the window that opens (Fig. 8.55).

This will ensure that all the sound files of the future CD will be placed one after another (like in a VIP project in Samplitude 2496).

Chapter 8: Mastering in the WaveLab 3.0 Application 661

The next step is to call **CD Wizard**:
1. Click the **CD** button (indicated by the arrow in Fig. 8.56).
2. Click the button with the "Wizard's wand" icon.
3. Immediately click the **Apply** button.

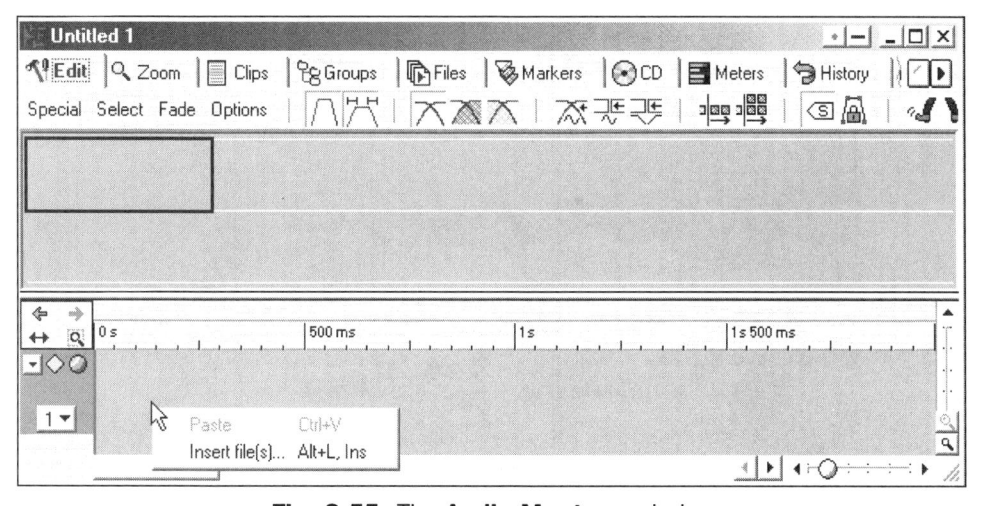

Fig. 8.55. The **Audio Montage** window

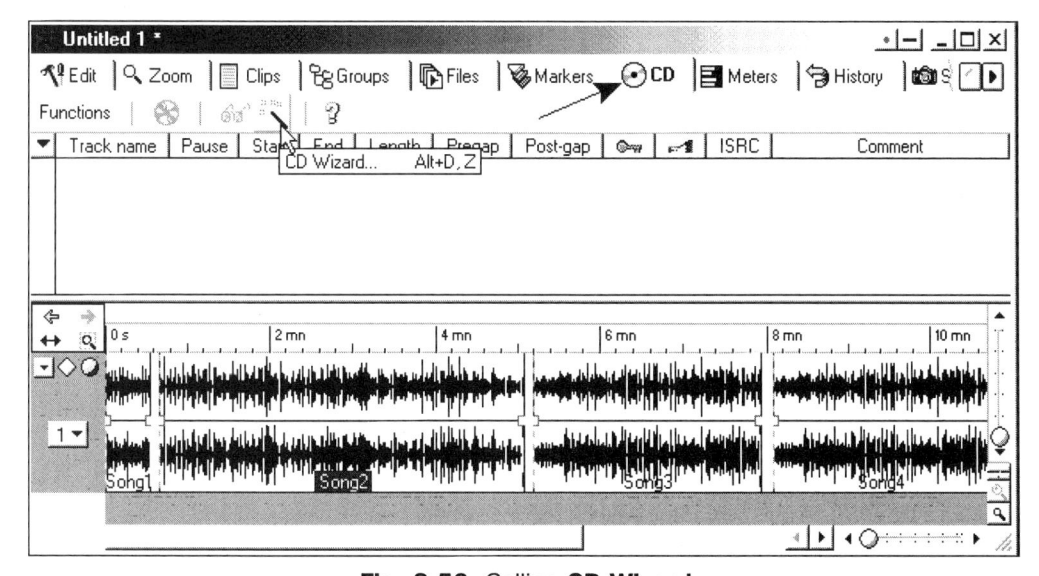

Fig. 8.56. Calling **CD Wizard**

TIP In the **CD Wizard** window, you should agree with the default settings.

The CD-track markers will be automatically set at the boundaries of the clips, and equal pauses will be set between the clips.

The clips in the Audio Montage environment are similar to the objects of Samplitude 2496. This is why their editing is completely virtual (that is, non-destructive).

TIP To change the volume gradually (to fade out), just drag the marker to the desired distance from the boundary of the clip (Fig. 8.57).

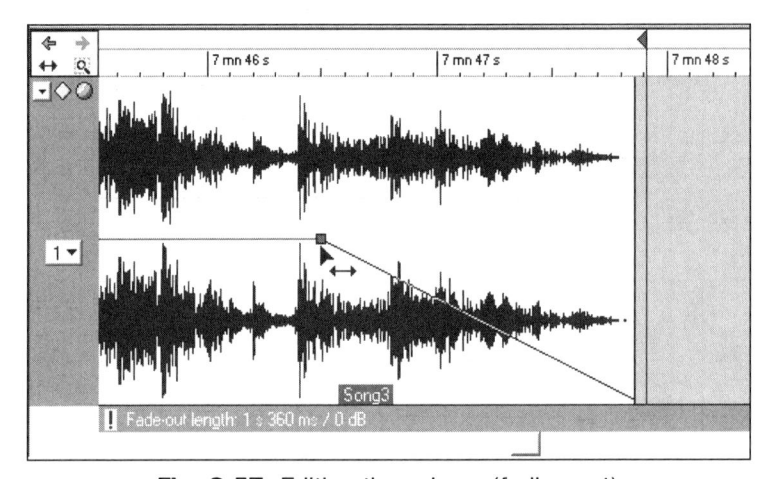

Fig. 8.57. Editing the volume (fading out)

Well, now everything's ready for writing:

1. Click the button with the CD icon located to the left of the button with the wand icon. Alternatively, you can select the **Write CD** command from the **Functions** menu.
2. The **Write CD** window will appear (Fig. 8.52). Here you can choose the number of copies and the writing speed.

Sound processing is also convenient in the Audio Montage environment.

To control the signal level and spectrum, the Audio Montage environment provides a separate level indicator — **Monitor peak/volume**, combined with a phase meter. There is also the **Monitor spectrum** spectrum analyzer (Figs. 8.58 and 8.59). These indicators are connected to the output of the master section, so sound processing by virtual effects is also taken into account.

To open these indicators, click the **Meters** button (indicated by the arrow in Fig. 8.58).

The level meter and the spectrum analyzer correspond to the **Level** and **Spectrum** tabs.

The level meter allows you to visually estimate the relationship between the peak and RMS levels of the signal (the blue bar reflects the RMS level).

Chapter 8: Mastering in the WaveLab 3.0 Application

Processing the sound with the effects of the master section can be applied both to the whole audio montage and to a separate clip. The selection is made after clicking the **Apply** button in the master section.

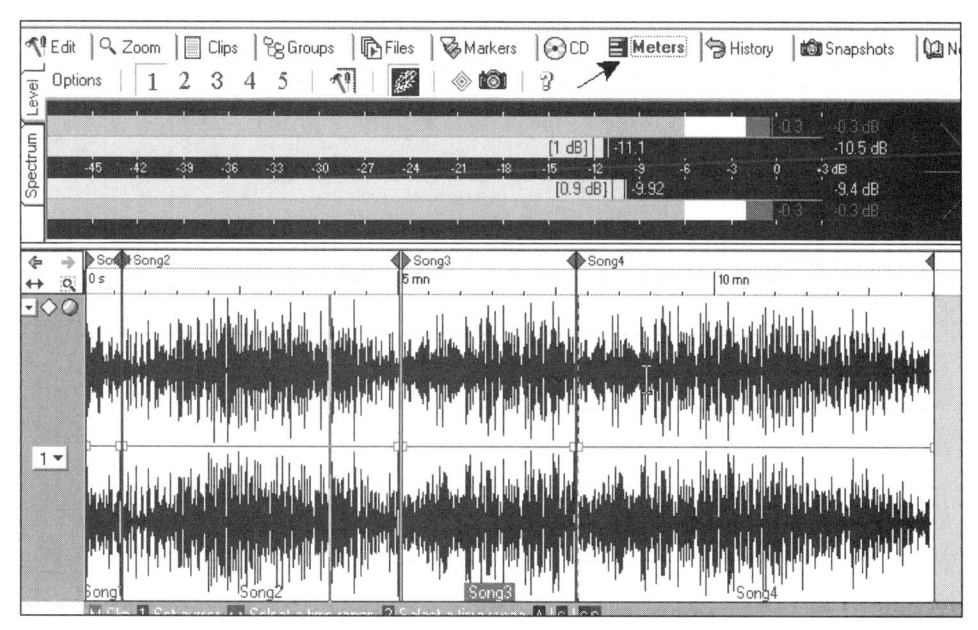

Fig. 8.58. The output level indicator

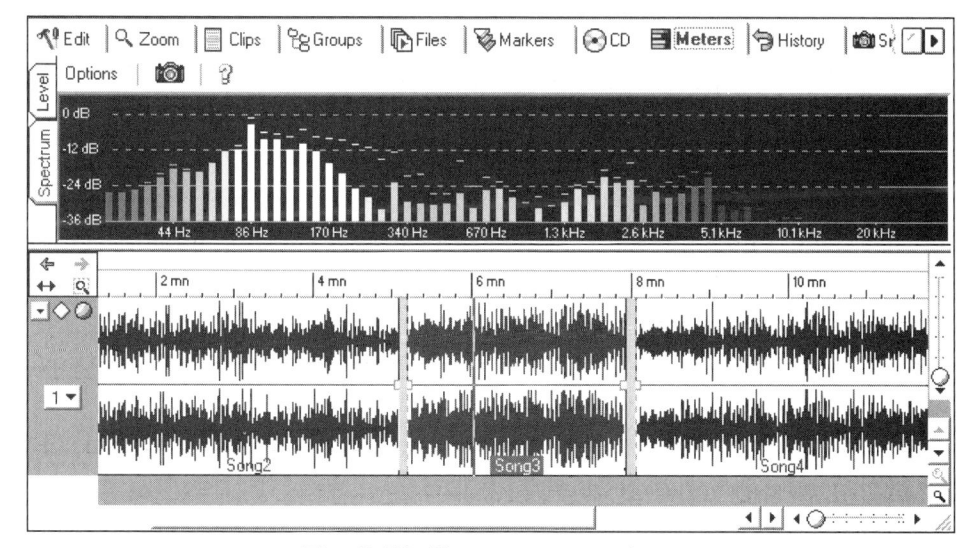

Fig. 8.59. The spectrum analyzer

To apply processing to the whole audio montage, select the **Whole montage** radio button in the **Range** section and check the **Create CD program** checkbox (both in the **Process preferences for ...** window), as shown in Fig. 8.60.

NOTE The CD project can be created only after **CD Wizard** finishes its work.

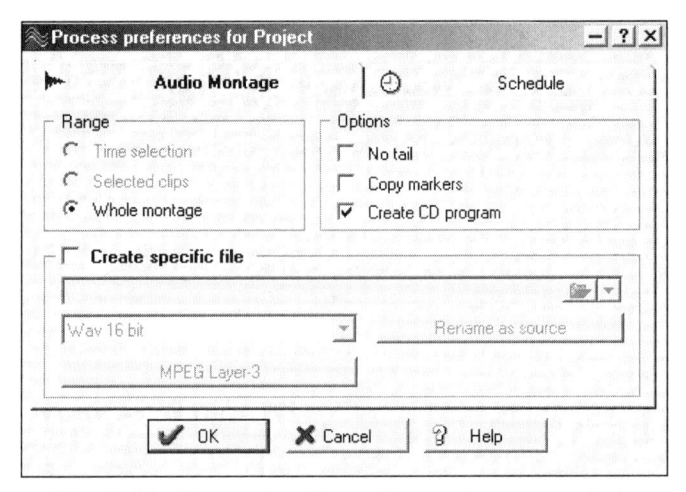

Fig. 8.60. Processing the audio montage as a whole

After you click the **OK** button, a new audio file will be created (an "image" of the AUDIO CD) along with the CD project.

Then you should proceed with writing as described in the *Writing the AUDIO CD* section.

This method is recommended when the project is "overloaded" with virtual effects, since writing a CD imposes heavy demands on the computer resources.

To apply processing to a certain clip, you must:

1. Select the clip by clicking it in its bottom part (its background will turn yellow).
2. Click the **Apply** button and select the **Selected clips** radio button in the **Range** section of the **Process preferences for ...** window.

A new sound file will be created that must be saved.

Then you need to replace the old clip in the audio montage with the new one. To do this:

1. Right-click the selected clip so that the pop-up menu appears.
2. In the menu, select the **Substitute for existing wave** item in the **Source** submenu.
3. In the dialog box, open the previously saved audio file.

With this method, you can independently process each track of the AUDIO CD being created.

Chapter 9

"Tube" Mastering in the T-RackS Application

Chapter 9: "Tube" Mastering in the T-RackS Application

To "enliven" sound at the final processing stage, a mixed digital phonogram is sometimes converted to an analog signal, then processed with one or more tube amplifiers (or equalizers), and lastly converted back to its digital form.

The idea of such a procedure comes from the psychoacoustic phenomenon created by a tube amplifier. Specifically, the low-order harmonics hide the high-order ones. The influence of a tube amplifier upon the sound can be explained by the spectral enrichment of a signal with low-order harmonics (mostly even ones), which is perceived as a so-called "tube" sound.

NOTE Exciters (psycho-acoustic processors) are based on similar principles.

Thus, the effect of "tube" processing is related to psycho-acoustics and is used to change the *subjective* perception of the sound.

It is for this purpose that T-RackS (Mastering software analog by design) was created. This is a software simulator of "tube" mastering developed by IK Multimedia Production (**http://www.t-racks.com**).

The Interface of T-RackS (Version 1.1)

Let's examine the modular structure of this device. (The program even looks like a device, since its interface is "old-fashioned", as you can see in Fig. 9.1.)

Sound processing in T-RackS is done with three modules (or "panels"):

- Six-band parametric equalizer (**EQUALIZER**)
- Classical "tube" compressor (**TUBE-COMP**)
- Multiband mastering limiter (**MULTIBAND-LIMITER**)

The order of connecting the **EQUALIZER** and **TUBE-COMP** panels can be selected with the **PATCH** switches. However, **MULTIBAND-LIMITER** is always the last in the chain of modules.

NOTE The red indicators (**PATCH**) show the actual position of the module. For example, in Fig. 9.1, the parametric equalizer is first, and the tube compressor is second.

T-RackS provides the user with contextual help. To access it, click the button with the question mark located in the button row at the bottom of the window.

When the help mode is on, you need just position the mouse pointer at a control on the panel to call help (Fig. 9.2). The help messages that appear in the upper right corner of the window make it easy to learn the application.

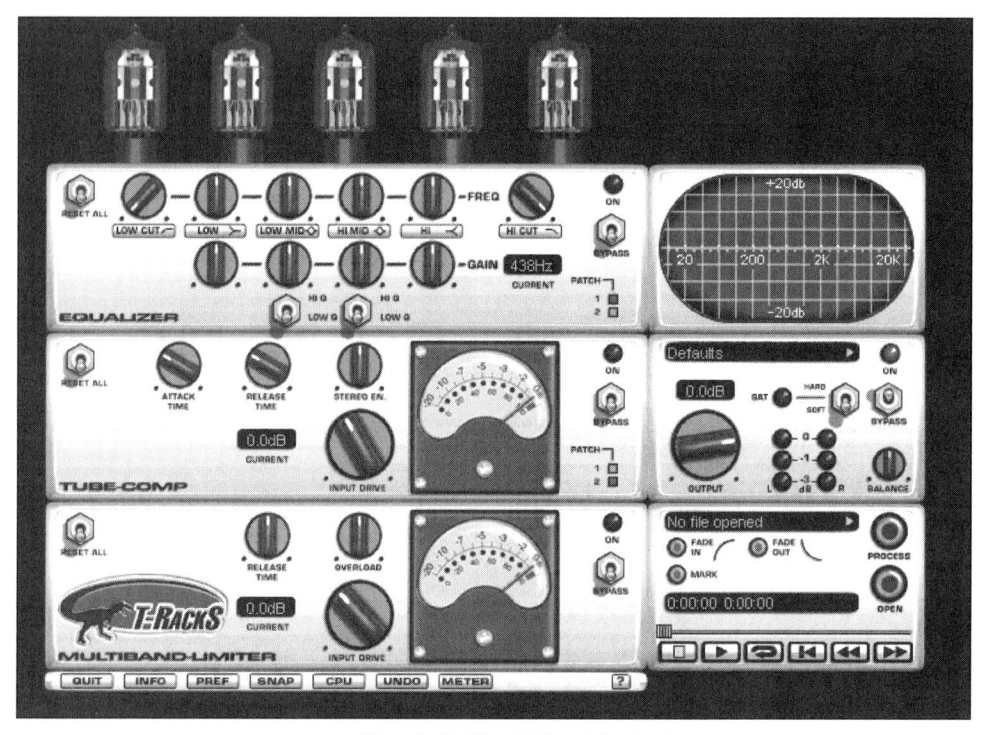

Fig. 9.1. The T-RackS window

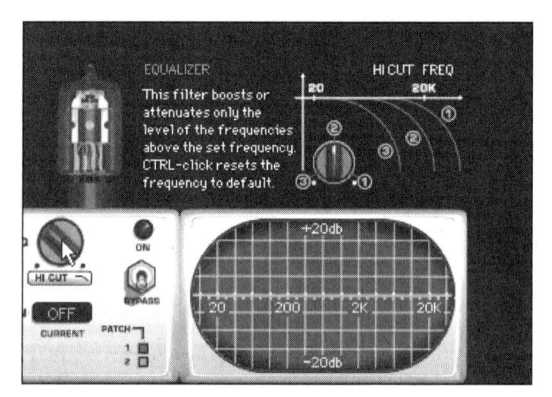

Fig. 9.2. Contextual help

Let's look at the button row more closely:

❐ **QUIT** quits the T-RackS application
❐ **INFO** opens the "About..." information window

Chapter 9: "Tube" Mastering in the T-RackS Application

- **PREF** opens the preferences window (Fig. 9.3), where the following controls are located:
  - The **Dithering** section switches the dithering algorithm on or off
  - The **Audio buffer length** section is self-explanatory

    NOTE The absence of playback failures shows that the buffer length has been chosen correctly.

  - The **Interface material** section changes the appearance of the front panel
  - The **Real time processing** section switches on the on-the-fly processing mode

    NOTE In the **Real time processing** mode, you can change the settings of the modules during processing.

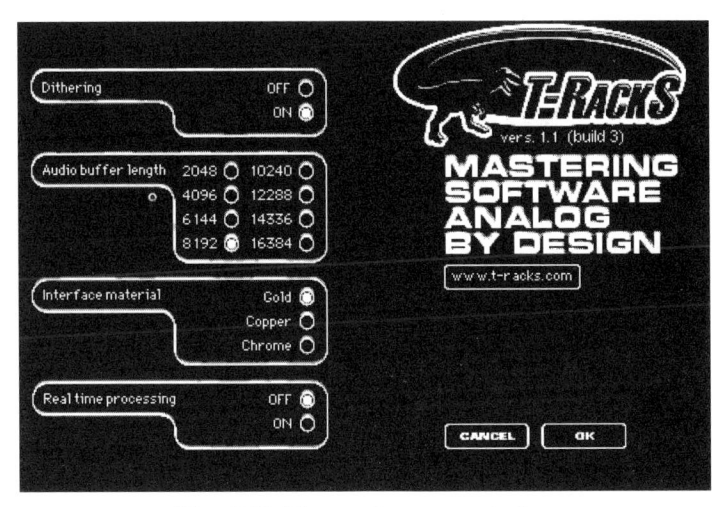

Fig. 9.3. The preferences window

- **SNAP** opens the **Snap** (Snapshots) panel, which lets you "snap" up to eight independent module settings and then call them at a later time
- **CPU** shows the indicator of the CPU load
- **UNDO** undoes the last operation
- **METER** shows the peak indicator for output level

T-RackS (version 1.1) supports only 16-bit audio files. This means you have to load WAV files with 16-bit resolution and a 44,100 Hz sample rate when you wish to master a CD.

To load a sound file, proceed as follows:

1. Click the **Open** button.
2. In the **Open T-RackS Audio File** dialog box, select the desired file (Fig. 9.4).

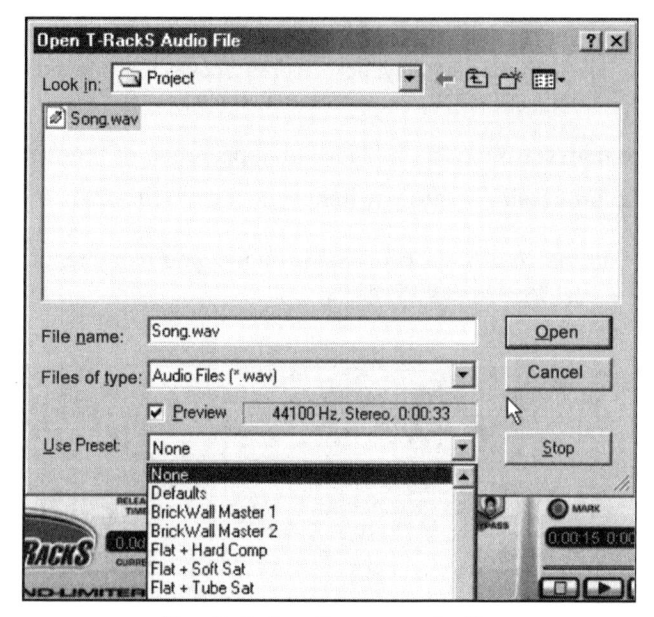

Fig. 9.4. Loading an audio file

You can listen to the processed version of the audio file (in accordance with the selected preset):

1. Check the **Preview** checkbox.
2. Select a preset from the **Use Preset** drop-down list (Fig. 9.4).

Final processing is begun with the **Process** button located on the transport bar.

NOTE A new sound file will be created. Its name will be made up of the original file name with the word master appended (in parentheses). For example, if the original file is Song.wav, the new one will be Song(master).wav.

Processing will start after you click the **Save** button in the **Process T-RackS Audio File** dialog box (or in the **Realtime Process T-RackS Audio File** dialog box, depending on the mode).

Playback is controlled via the transport panel.

The **Loop** mode (loop playback) and the possibility of using markers is an additional service.

Chapter 9: "Tube" Mastering in the T-RackS Application

To switch on the **Loop** mode, click the button with the looped arrow icon on the transport bar (Fig. 9.5).

The boundaries of the loop playback are set with the loop markers (one is indicated by the mouse pointer in Fig. 9.5), which can be dragged along the ruler located above the buttons of the transport bar.

The slider on this ruler lets you quickly move along the audio file. The position of the slider reflects the current playback position.

When you click the **MARK** button, the current position of the slider will be memorized, the triangle marker indicating the position (Fig. 9.6).

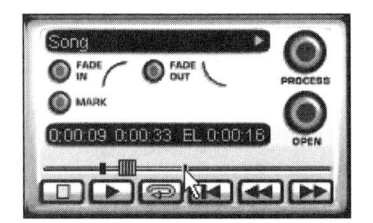

Fig. 9.5. Using the **Loop** mode

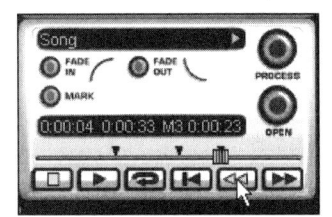

Fig. 9.6. Using the markers

Quick movement between the markers is done with the rewind/fast-forward buttons (with the double arrow icons).

The markers can be dragged to new positions with the mouse.

To select a marker, click it with the left mouse button.

The number and position of the selected marker are displayed in the information field above the ruler.

T-RackS allows the user to set automatic volume control at the beginning and end of the file. This is done with the **FADE IN** and **FADE OUT** buttons in the transport section.

After clicking either of these buttons, the corresponding control panels will appear (Fig. 9.7).

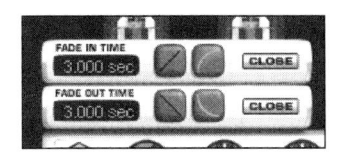

Fig. 9.7. The **FADE IN** and **FADE OUT** panels

To activate this feature, click any button with the fade curve icon. Then set the time length in the **FADE IN TIME** and **FADE OUT TIME** fields.

Let's discuss the processing modules in greater detail.

The TUBE-COMP Module

In T-RackS, 32-bit floating-point processing is implemented to simulate analog processes. The developers of the application strove to obtain the most accurate mathematical model of the processes that take place in real analog devices. When solving this task, they examined the best specimens of analog technology.

TUBE-COMP is a mathematical model of a tube compressor with a very soft knee.

This compressor doesn't provide us with the usual **Threshold** and **Ratio** parameters, and compression begins at very low signal levels. Due to this fact, compression is gentle, which is just what we need for sound mastering. Sound processed by the **TUBE-COMP** module becomes "warm".

The control panel of the **TUBE-COMP** module is shown in Fig. 9.8. Its controls are described below.

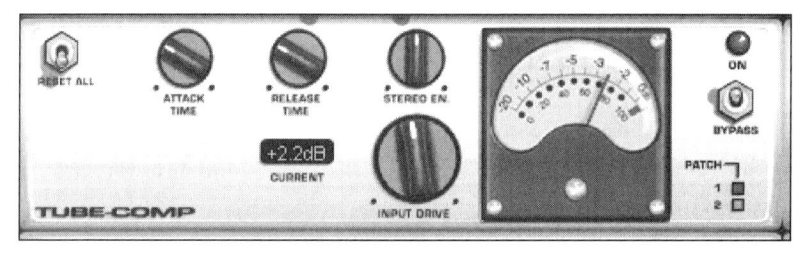

Fig. 9.8. The **TUBE-COMP** panel

❐ The **RESET ALL** switch resets the module parameters to the default values.

> *NOTE* If you want to reset only one control, click it while holding down the <Ctrl> key.

❐ The **BYPASS** switch toggles between the active and passive (bypassed) modes of the **TUBE-COMP** module.

> *NOTE* In the active mode, the **ON** indicator "glows" red.

❐ The pointer indicator reflects the compression level in dB.

❐ The **ATTACK TIME** indicator changes the attack time of the compressor within the range from 12 to 82 msec. When the attack time increases, the steep-slope signals aren't changed by the compressor.

> *NOTE* The actual value of the parameter is displayed in the **CURRENT** field when the mouse pointer is on the control.

Chapter 9: "Tube" Mastering in the T-RackS Application   673

- The **RELEASE TIME** control changes the release time of the compressor within the range from 30 msec to 1.4 sec. The less the release time, the higher the average volume level.
- The **STEREO EN** (Stereo Enhancement) control changes the width of the stereo base.
- The **INPUT DRIVE** control specifies the compression level from −15 dB to +15 dB.

    NOTE   The control takes it name from the fact that the compression level is determined by the input signal level.

- The **PATCH** switch sets the order of connecting the equalizer and the compressor.

    NOTE   In Fig. 9.8, the compressor is first, since the first indicator is red.

The *EQUALIZER* Module

The **EQUALIZER** module is designed specially for mastering, and it contains six controlled bands (Fig. 9.9).

    NOTE   The bands correspond to controls and buttons that can switch these controls on or off. Their names are **LOW CUT**, **LOW**, **LOW MID**, **HI MID**, **HI**, and **HI CUT**.

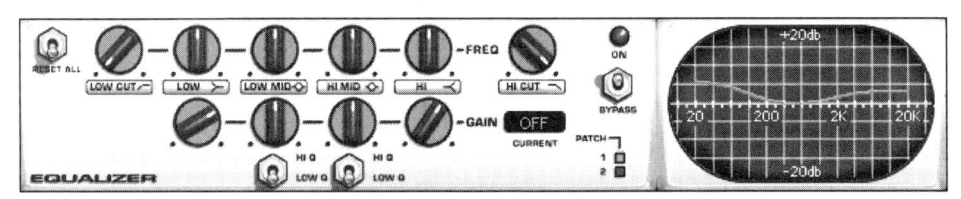

Fig. 9.9. The **EQUALIZER** control panel

Let's now examine the **EQUALIZER** module in detail.

- **LOW CUT** is a high frequency filter with the cutoff frequency adjusted within the range from 16 Hz to 5.3 kHz.
- **LOW** contains two low-frequency controls located one above the other. The upper control (in the **FREQ** row) specifies the knee frequency in Hz, and the lower one (**GAIN**) sets the rise/fall of the frequency-response curve in dB. The valid ranges are 30 Hz to 195 Hz for frequency, and −15 dB to +15 dB for level.
- **LOW MID** are the controls of the band filter. The range of values for the middle frequency is from 33 Hz to 5.6 kHz. Below the controls you see the **HI Q/LOW Q** switch. It changes the sharpness of the frequency-response curve.

- **HI MID** are the controls of the second band filter, similar to the first one. The range for the middle frequency is 200 Hz to 18.1 kHz.
- **HI** contains the high-frequency controls. The values of the knee frequency lie within a range from 750 Hz to 8.5 kHz.
- **HI CUT** is a low frequency filter with the cutoff frequency adjusted within a range from 200 Hz to 19.2 kHz.

The frequency-response curve of the parametric filter is drawn in a special display (Fig. 9.9).

The **PATCH** switch is identical to the one on the **TUBE-COMP** module.

The MULTIBAND-LIMITER Module

The **MULTIBAND-LIMITER** module is a top-quality three-band limiter (Fig. 9.10). Here are its controls:

- **RELEASE TIME** sets the release time of the signal level after limiting the peaks. The range of values is from 80 msec to 1.5 sec.
- **INPUT DRIVE** specifies the degree of limiting the signal. The **MULTIBAND-LIMITER** module has a precise threshold of 0 dB. Increasing the input signal level with the **INPUT DRIVE** control leads to further limitation. The pointer indicator shows the average value of limiting for all the frequency bands. The range of adjustment for the **INPUT DRIVE** parameter is from −9 dB to +16 dB.
- **OVERLOAD** changes the way of limiting the peaks. When the value of the **OVERLOAD** parameter is decreased, the peaks will be limited by dynamic compression. When the value is decreased, analog limiting will be simulated. The parameter is adjusted from −5.3 dB to +5.3 dB.

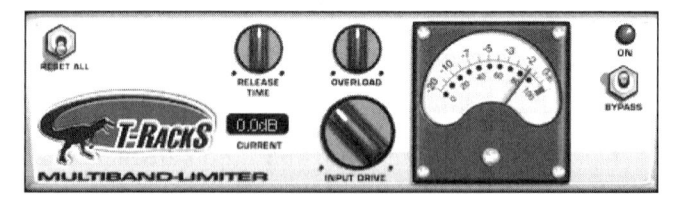

Fig. 9.10. The **MULTIBAND-LIMITER** control panel

The OUTPUT STAGE Module

The **OUTPUT STAGE** module is designed to perform final corrective actions.

The **OUTPUT STAGE** module includes:

- The **OUTPUT** level control

Chapter 9: "Tube" Mastering in the T-RackS Application

- The **BALANCE** control for stereo balance
- The peak level indicator and the **HARD/SOFT** switch for the peak limiting mode

> **NOTE** The **SOFT** mode corresponds to analog limiting, whereas the **HARD** mode means digital limiting.

Competent mastering often achieves a signal level of 0 dB. In such a case, the red indicator glows (0 dB), while the **SAT** (Saturation) indicator glows only when peaks are limited. In addition, the signal can be overloaded with the **OUTPUT** control.

However, if you need to obtain a "clean" master copy (that is, one without peak limiting) all you need to do is watch the **SAT** indicator.

BYPASS allows you to bypass the module and compare the sound before and after processing.

In the indicator field at the top of the panel (reading **Song 1** in Fig. 9.11), you can save and load presets. To do this, click the arrow in the right side of the field. Presets are saved in files with the TRP extension.

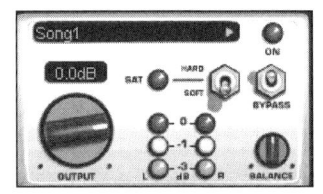

Fig. 9.11. The **OUTPUT STAGE** control panel

Appendix

CD Description

Appendix: CD Description

The companion CD supplied with this book contains files with settings for several programs that we consider, as well as examples illustrating a creative usage of these programs. All files related to specific programs reside in the folders with the names of those programs. Besides this, each folder also contains the ReadMe.txt files with detailed instructions on using the folder's contents.

The SAWPro folder contains the following files:

- Sawpro.clr — a variation of the color palette of the SAWPro program. To use this file, simply copy it to the folder where you have installed the SAWPro software, for example, C:\SAWPro.
- Sawpro.prf — settings of SAWPro screens (see the beginning sections of *Chapter 3*) for 800,600 screen resolution. To use this file, copy it to the folder where the SAWPro software is installed, overwriting the existing Sawpro.prf file. Don't forget to create a backup copy of the initial Sawpro.prf file.
- Besides these files, the SAWPro contains the following nested folders:
  1. 1024 × 768 — the folder containing the SAWPro.prf file intended for a 1024 × 768 screen resolution.
  2. DirectX_Presets — the folder containing preset files for DirectX plug-ins. These files have the DXP filename extension. The structure of the DirectX_Presets subfolder is the same as the structure of the SAWPro working directory of the same name on your hard disk (see *Chapter 3*). The list of all required plug-ins (and the names of their respective manufacturers) can be found in the ReadMe.txt file that resides in the SAWPro folder on the CD.
  3. Project — the folder containing a demo project (tutorial) intended to help you to master the mixing and sound processing procedures in SAWPro. To work with the demo project, copy this folder to the root directory of drive C: (the path to the project directory must be C:\Project\ Fish_and_drum.edl) and remove the Read Only attribute from the files. After this, open the Fish_and_drum.edl file using the SAWPro application. The result of the mixing performed by one of the authors of this book (Medvedev) is saved in the Fish_and_Drum.wav file found in the Audio subfolder.

The Cool Edit folder contains the following files:

- coolcust.ini — custom settings for hotkeys. To use this file, copy it to the Windows folder, replacing the existing coolcust.ini file. Before doing so, it is recommended that you create a backup copy of this INI file.
- Effects.scp and NoiseShaping.scp — files containing script collections. The Effects.scp file contains scripts that implement sound processing algorithms illustrating Cool Edit Pro's capabilities. The Revers_rev1, ..., Revers_rev3 scripts are intended for processing sound files with a sampling frequency of 44,100 Hz, based on the reverse reverberation algorithm. The Fly Up, Touchdown, and Wind scripts generate noise samples with special effects (Sound Design). The NoiseShaping.scp file demonstrates the differences between dithering algorithms with and without noise shaping (*Chapter 8*). To view the difference, convert a 32-bit sound file with a level of 120 dB to 16-bit format using one of the following two algorithms:
  - Using the Dithering script
  - Using the NoiseShaping script

- The Noise Shaping.tif file contains the results of spectral analysis (performed using Cool Edit Pro) of the 16-bit file after applying the noise shaping algorithm.
- The NoiseShaping.wav and NoiseShaping(norm).wav files contain the results that demonstrate the noise shaping algorithm.

The Samplitude folder contains the following files:

- combi_master.mix and TrueVerb.mix — these files contain configuration data for the Samplitude 2496 virtual mixer (see *Chapter 5*). To use these configuration files, load them using the **Load Setup** virtual mixer command. The mixer configuration contains DirectX plug-ins from Waves (version 2.5).
- The Hotkey.ssc file contains custom hotkey settings for Samplitude. To use these settings, open the **Edit Keyboard Shortcuts** window (**File|Preferences|Edit Keyboard Shortcuts**), load the Hotkey.ssc file using the **Load Shortcuts** command, and then click **OK**.

Besides these files, the Samplitude folder also contains the following nested folders:

- Impulse — this folder contains the impulses duplicated in WAV and RAP files. Impulses are intended for the Room Simulator effect of the Samplitude 2496 program (*Chapter 5*). Impulses with the name **Special** are used for creating sound effects.
- FX-Preset — this folder contains preset files for DirectX plug-ins (with the PLG filename extension). To use these files, copy the entire contents of the FX-Preset folder to the folder with the same name found in the installation folder of the Samplitude 2496 program (for example, C:\Sam2496\FX-Preset). The list of all required plug-ins and their respective manufacturers is provided in the ReadMe.txt file residing in the Samplitude folder on the CD.

The Cubase folder contains a nested folder named Styles. The Styles folder contains style files for the Styletrax module of the Cubase VST program (*Chapter 6*). These styles were created by Evgeny Medvedev in cooperation with jazz performer Dimitry Nazarychev (St. Petersburg). When creating these styles, the authors used "live" MIDI music (*Chapter 6*).

The styles can be used for improvisation with the Styletrax module, as a tutorial, or for constructing new compositions. Files with names containing (3x) characters enclosed in parentheses are intended for Cubase VST version 3.x; other files are intended for Cubase VST version 5.

The Audio folder contains audio tracks (WAV format) that illustrate the use of the technologies discussed in this book. All these audio tracks (WAV format) were created using virtual sound technologies and without using external sound processors.

The ReadMe.doc file located in the Audio folder contains detailed information on the performers and authors of all compositions, along with the information about the programs and musical instruments used.

Tracking, mixing, sound processing, and mastering for all compositions was performed by Evgeny Medvedev on the PC, using the technologies and programs described in this book. (The only exception is the "The dark side of pink dream" composition, which Medevedev only mastered.)

Authors: Evgeny Medvedev and Vera Trusova (musiclive@ratrunner.com, mt_authors@emptymail.com, pclivemusic@hotmail.com)

INDEX

3

32-bit floating-point format, 316, 619

A

Absorption, 419
Accord, 542
Acoustic mirror, 208, 413
Additional low-level bits, 624
Aliasing, 612
Amplitude, 188
  peak limiter, 99
Amplitude response of the compressor, 407
Analitic quantize, 566
Analog:
  domain, 655
  signal, 611
Analog-to-digital converter, 612
Apogee UV 22, 628
ARC, 643, 644

Arpeggio, 542
  structure, 543
ASIO, 601
Attaching to the musical measure, 258
Attachment to the bar grid, 245
Attack time, 196
Audio:
  device, 313
  DVD, 612
  event, 571
  file, 299
  mix, 464
  montage, 660
  objects, 303
Auto:
  crossfade mode, 309
  mode, 366
  release control, 643, 644
  track markers, 447
Autoblack, 629
Automation, 149
  curves, 426
AutoPan, 203
Auxiliary master section, 369, 444

B

Background premastering, 271
Band center markers, 645
Batch processing, 267, 269, 630
Beat, 112
Behavior, 644
Blue window, 650
BPM (beat per minute), 233, 310
Burn CD, 445

C

Calculating time factor, 421
CD:
    program, 657
    recorder, 139, 659
    TOC, 442
    track marker, 445, 658
    wizard, 661
Changing;
    scale, 77
    zoom, 263
Chord, 542
    track, 464
Chorus, 203
Click/Pop/Crackle Eliminator, 224
Clip, 46, 61, 245, 263, 303
    context menu, 252
    restoration, 227
Compressing, 625
    ratio, 407

Compressor, 117
Compressor/noise gate, 119
Compressor/Limiter/Expander/Gate effect, 407
Compressor/Maximizer, 408
Configuration file, 237
Connecting a DirectX plug-in, 357
Converting sample type, 240, 617
Convolution, 417
Copying:
    object, 434
    region, 61
    selected clip, 67
Creating:
    32-bit floating temporary files, 626
    copy checkbox, 388
    new clip, 61
    region, 48, 82
    sequence, 71
CrossFade, 148, 351
Crossover, 643, 650
    points, 645
Cue list, 272
Cycle:
    playback, 479
    record, 495

D

Db-audioware, 159
DC bias adjust, 190, 202

De-esser, 197, 643
Dehisser, 419
Dehisser/FFT-Filter Mixmaster, 440
Delay, 203, 206
   section, 369
Destructive, 60
   editing, 127, 186, 242, 387, 505
   editing the wave project, 391
   editing the objects, 387
Digital domain, 655
Direct relation, 374
Direct/Match editing mode, 404
Direction pan mode, 423
DirectX, 40, 186
   linker, 41, 115, 120
   plug-ins, 355, 357, 361, 369, 393, 639, 651
   plug-ins track, 361, 367
DirX button, 367
Distortion, 408
Dither:
   depth, 277
   transform results, 239, 617
Dithering, 140, 615, 622, 628, 655, 669
   algorithm, 239
   processor, 654
Dotted rhythm, 565
Downsampling, 639
Downward:
   compressor, 646
   expander, 648
Drum:
   edit, 480
   track, 463

Dynamic:
   four-band equalizer, 642
   processing, 195
   range, 512, 617
   section, 368

E

Echo, 117, 207
Echo/Delay/Reverb, 416
Echo/Delay/Reverb Effect, 369
Editing keyboard shortcuts, 286
EDL, 304
Effects patch builder, 36, 40, 154
Electro, 644
Encode, 611
Envelope, 198, 408
   editing, 264
Equalizer, 667, 673
   section, 368
Equalizing, 625, 632
Exciter, 442, 649, 667
External program, 392

F

Fade, 148, 191, 254, 341, 344, 662, 671
Fader, 37, 144
Favorites, 234
FFT, 398
   filter, 640
   size, 228, 230, 231

File formats, 237
Finite impulse response filter, 399
Flanger, 209, 210
Floating-point numbers, 617
Freezing play parameter, 602
Frequency monitor, 633
Frequency response curve, 635
Full:
　duplex, 53
　view, 81

G

Gain, 195, 643
processor, 196
Gentle:
compression, 672
sound, 645
Ghost copy, 501
Global crossfade, 350
Graphic:
　editing the volume and the panorama, 264
　equalizer, 116
Grid, 113, 308
Groove quantize, 570
Group, 373, 374
　of objects, 434
　of points, 426
　track, 464

H

Handles, 341

Hard:
　limiter, 200
　limiting, 277
Harmonics, 221, 405, 649
HD wave project, 299
High-level:
　compression, 646
　expansion, 646
Hiss reduction, 228, 418
Hot track, 36, 152
Hotkeys, 76, 77
Hyperprism:
　bass maximizer, 651
　harmonic exciter, 649

I

Identification file, 299
IDR, 655
Import:
　audio CD tracks, 637
　MIDI file, 310
　sample, 298
Impulse, 208
　noises, 224
　response, 413, 414
Increasing dynamic range, 655
Index marker, 447
Infinite impulse response filter, 399
Input:
　attenuation, 375
　drive, 673, 674
Instrument, 483

Index

Intermediate:
    mixing, 385
    premastering, 257, 274
    reduction, 132
    results, 618
Inverse dehissing, 420
Iterative quantize, 562

K

Key editor, 473
Keyboard, 474
Knee, 644

L

Limiter, 99, 117, 408
    100 mode, 409
Link, 367
List of takes, 254
Live input mode, 638
Local loop, 479
Locators, 465
Look ahead, 654
    time, 197
Loop, 82
    duplicate, 254, 261
    markers, 671
    playback, 670
Low-level:
    compression, 647, 648
    expansion, 648
    signals, 616

M

Main screen, 25
Making CD, 445
Marker, 436
    view window, 89
Master:
    block, 366
    equalizer, 441
    faders, 626
    section, 626
    track, 464
Mastering, 94, 139, 140, 157, 277, 440, 625, 656
Match quantize, 566
Maximum peak level, 191
ME FreeFilter, 632
Measure, 112
Meter bridge, 140
MIDI, 94, 455
    clock, 606
    control change, 489
    controller curve settings, 605
    controllers, 474
    device, 457
    file, 302
    message, 458
    object editor, 603
    objects, 303
    real-time effects, 603
    synchronization, 605
    time code, 606
    note, 488

Index

poly-press, 489
system exclusive, 489
Mixing, 94, 438
   down to track, 257
   gauge, 271
   in file, 374
   track, 463
Mixer, 364
Mode, 517
Modulation, 519
Monitor:
   peak/volume, 662
   spectrum, 662
Monitoring, 626
Moving:
   clip, 71
   selected clip, 67
   object, 433
M-points, 567
MROS, 540
MTC synchronization, 605
Multiband:
   compressor, 642
   dynamic processing, 410
   dynamics effect, 409
   limiter, 667, 674
   mode, 423
Multitrack, 26, 33, 300
   cursor, 36
   view window, 246
Musical context, 453

N

Narrow-band compression, 198
New multitrack project, 283, 306
Noise:
   floor, 230
   gate, 117, 409
   profile, 231
   reduction threshold, 230
   reduction, 231, 418
   sample, 418
   shaping, 140, 628, 655
   suppression algorithm, 418
Non-destructive:
   editing operations, 262
   editing, 60, 289, 505
   processing, 341
   sound processing, 317
Normalization, 117, 191, 201, 346, 395

O

Object, 281, 303, 341
   editor, 346
   handles, 343
   normalizaion, 346
Offset, 147
Over DC, 190
Opto, 644
Out:
   ceiling, 654
   stage, 674

track, 33
Overdub, 492

P

Pan/Expand, 202
Parametric:
   EQ, 352
   equalizer, 222
   processor, 642
Peak:
   level, 191
   limiter, 157, 200, 654
Phase Correlator, 424
Phasing, 210
Phychoacoustic processor, 649
Pitch bender, 233
Play control window, 97
Play toolbar, 329
Playback, 74
   while recording, 317, 320
Plug-in, 40, 631
Pop-up menu, 315
Position bar, 333
Post fader, 140, 154
Precision factor, 230
Premastering, 276
Preset, 191
   section, 398
Prevent clipping, 402
Preview, 393
Process/MixDown, 128, 157

Project, 91
Pumping bass, 653
Punch, 107, 494
Punch In, 253, 258
Punch In Loop, 325
Punch In Mode, 323

Q

Q10-paragraphic EQ, 444
Quality, 223
Quantization, 468, 560, 611
   distortions, 614
   noise, 611, 612
Quick filter, 224

R

RAM wave project, 290, 297
Range, 330, 643
   mode, 321
Ratio, 407
   level adjustment, 54
   panel, 45, 57
   parameter dialog box, 316
   record control window, 97
   remote transport, 45
Recordable compact disk, 139
Recording, 54
   and playing back, 311
   takes, 320
Reduction, 132, 155, 420
Region, 48, 355

Regions view window, 85
Release, 643
　time, 196
Remote:
　transport, 58
　transport panel, 74
Remove unused samples, 322
Removing a clip, 70
Replace, 493
Resampling /Time Stretching /Pitch Shifting, 420
Resolution, 402, 617
Reverse:
　audio, 116
　phase, 116
Rhythmic quantization, 560
RMS, 197
　level, 653, 662
Room simulator, 413

S

Sample, 198
　rate, 308, 317
　rate and bit resolution, 101
Samplers, 198
Samples, 611
Sampling, 611
Samplitude 2496, 127
Samplitude Mixer, 364, 372, 377
Saturation, 675
Save in 32-bit (floating) format, 385, 439, 444
Saving an object, 357
Saw Native, 41, 116
SAWPro, 21, 622
Scale correction, 516, 517
Score edit, 483
Script, 267
Scrubbing, 430
Segment, 571
Select mode, 66
Selective filter, 222
Semitones, 233
Sequence view window, 88
Session, 246, 301
Settings of Samplitude 2496, 292
Setup for new VIP dialog box, 307
Seventh chord, 551
Shortcut keys, 263
Shuffling, 563
Signal envelope, 198
Slave, 605
Slider, 649, 650
Slope, 38, 148
Slot, 626
SMPTE, 606
Snap, 113
　to objects, 308, 322
　to ruler, 245
Snapping, 258
　to the musical meter and tempo, 110
Snapshots, 669
Sonitus plug-ins ultrafunk, 211
Sound, 483
　field, 379

Index

field character, 378, 381
file import, 47
files, 30
font, 304
Spectral decay rate, 230
Split range, 338
Splitting objects, 435
Standard scales, 556
Step-by-step recording, 533
Stereo:
   enhancer, 422
   vibrato, 203
Style track, 464
Subharmonics, 405
Submix, 422
Substitute for existing wave, 664
Surround panning, 378
   module, 377, 379
Sweep, 148
System menu, 290

T

Take, 104
   history, 254, 260
   manager, 326
Tape track, 464
Tempo mode, 111
Test, 393
Threshold, 407, 643
Time:
   line, 46, 111
   mode, 112

TOC file, 304
Tonality, 517
Toolbars, 62, 284
Track, 33, 458
   bouncing, 383
   context menu, 256
   info, 313
   info panel, 249
   properties, 256, 311
   speed settings, 295
T-RackS, 667
Transport pane, 286
Transpose value, 476
Triad, 551
Trim objects, 322, 435
Triplet, 564
   quantization, 564
Truncate operation, 70
Tube-comp, 667, 672

U

Undo, 92, 290
   depth, 392
   history, 92, 390
   options, 289
Ungroup, 374
Universal mode, 321, 341, 424
Upsampling, 639
Upward:
   compressor, 647
   expander, 646

V

Very soft knee, 672
VIP, 284
　display mode, 339
　mouse mode, 424
　multitrack, 305
VirtClip, 434
Virtual:
　loop object, 435
　mixer, 144
　project, 281, 284, 297, 300
　tape recorder, 52
Vocal compressor, 194
Volume, 188
VST, 40
　linker, 41, 115, 120
　plug-ins, 363
VST-DX Wrapper Lite, 363

W

Wave:
　project, 297
　properties, 252
Waveform block, 245
WaveLab, 625
Waves, 119
　C1 Compressor, 444
　C4, 642
　Digital Audio Processors, 642
　L1 − Ultramaximizer+, 654
Wide stereo field, 192
Widening the stereo base, 192
Writing CD, 658

Z

Zoom, 263, 334, 432